PRAISE FOR *AFTERMATH*

"A searing, first-hand account of the consequences of America's 'war on terrorism' by one of the most respected voices on the Middle East. Honest, fearless, devastating. No one but Nir Rosen could have written this book."
—Reza Aslan, author of *No god but God* and *Beyond Fundamentalism*

"A brilliantly told story of post invasion Iraq—and the Middle East's descent into a sectarian hell mess we'll all pay for generations to come. There's no one out there more courageous or better equipped to tell it than Nir Rosen. And when Rosen speaks, I listen."
—Robert Baer, author of *See No Evil*

"Nir Rosen has been reporting from Iraq for years the way it should be reported—from the inside out. He spends his time in Iraq not at American news conferences in the secure Green Zone, but in the villages and cities of the battered nation, interviewing the victims of Saddam Hussein as well as the victims of our seven-year-old war. His dispatches, and this book, reflect the madness of the mission."
—Seymour Hersh

"Nir Rosen is always provocative—he makes you see another side of an issue. In *Aftermath,* Rosen, at great personal risk, captured how Iraqis, Lebanese and Afghans from across society view U.S. actions in their nations. You may disagree and you will probably be angry, but if you wish to understand these conflicts and their impacts into the future, you need to read this book."
—Colonel Thomas X. Hammes, United States Marine Corps (Ret.), author, *The Sling and the Stone: On War in the 21st Century*

"For Americans, the story of U.S. military involvement in the Islamic world centers on 'us' not 'them,' with Afghans and Iraqis cast as victims or bystanders. In this brilliantly reported and deeply humane book, Nir Rosen demolishes this self-serving picture, depicting the relationship between the occupied and the occupiers in all its nuanced complexity."
—Andrew J. Bacevich, author of *Washington Rules: America's Path to Permanent War*

"If you think you understand the war in Iraq, or just think you should try to, read this book. This is a deep dive through the last seven years of America's foray into the Middle East. No one will agree with everything here, but anyone interested in what we are doing in Iraq and Afghanistan will benefit from reading it."

—Thomas E. Ricks, author of *Fiasco* and *The Gamble*

"The world would be a more dangerous place without Nir Rosen's *Aftermath*. His bracing recounting of the invasion of Iraq and subsequent insurgency, and blunt dissection of the myths surrounding the surge are an essential antidote to the complacency that has set in as America exits Iraq—and which could lead to similar debacles in the future."

—Parag Khanna, author of *The Second World: How Emerging Powers Are Redefining Global Competition in the Twenty-first Century*

"*Aftermath* is a masterwork, the product of a life devoted to a relentless pursuit of the knowledge and understanding of strange men who walk in nearly unimaginable paths across the far places of the world. I first met Nir Rosen when we sat together on a panel discussion on the 'Newshour.' I wondered then how this quiet young man could have acquired so much expertise so early in life. By the time of our next meeting years later I had learned of his incredible persistence and willingness to go and sit among those whom most of us would fear to meet at all. Over the years I have come to expect to hear from him or of him in his wanderings in places so perilous that one would expect that only soldiers would venture there. Nir Rosen's marvelous book is the record of the disaster that ignorance, often willful ignorance produced in Iraq, continues to produce in Afghanistan and is likely to produce in places like Yemen and Somalia. Read *Aftermath* and hope not to repeat this history."

—Colonel Walter Patrick "Pat" Lang, United States Army (Ret.), former executive at the Defense Intelligence Agency

"It is a painful experience to read Nir Rosen's highly informed account of the destruction of Iraq and the spread of the plague of sectarian violence incited by the invasion to Lebanon and beyond. The image this meticulously detailed rendition brings to mind is of a brutal ignoramus wielding a sledgehammer to smash a complex structure he does not understand, with unpredictable but predictably awful consequences. Amazingly, Rosen finds rays of hope in the ruins. No less compelling, and distressing, is his vivid account of his experiences in Taliban-controlled territory. An indispensable contribution to the understanding of great contemporary tragedies."

—Noam Chomsky

AFTERMATH

Also by Nir Rosen

In the Belly of the Green Bird:
The Triumph of the Martyrs in Iraq

AFTERMATH

Following the Bloodshed of
America's Wars in the Muslim World

NIR ROSEN

NATION
BOOKS
New York
www.nationbooks.org

Published by Nation Books, A Member of the Perseus Books Group
116 East 16th Street, 8th Floor
New York, NY 10003

Nation Books is a co-publishing venture of the Nation Institute
and the Perseus Books Group.

Books published by Nation Books are available at special discounts for bulk purchases in the
United States by corporations, institutions, and other organizations. For more information,
please contact the Special Markets Department at the Perseus Books Group, 2300 Chestnut
Street, Suite 200, Philadelphia, PA 19103, or call (800) 810-4145, ext. 5000,
or e-mail special.markets@perseusbooks.com.

Designed by Jeff Williams

Library of Congress Cataloging-in-Publication Data
Rosen, Nir, 1977–
Aftermath : following the bloodshed of America's wars
in the muslim world / Nir Rosen.
p. cm.
Includes bibliographical references and index.
ISBN 978-1-56858-401-0 (alk. paper)
1. Iraq War, 2003—Social aspects. 2. Iraq War, 2003—Influence. 3. Iraq—Social conditions—
21st century. 4. Iraq—Politics and government—2003– 5. Iraq—Strategic aspects.
6. Middle East—Strategic aspects. 7. Islam and politics—Middle East. I. Title.
DS79.767.S63R67 2010
956.7044'31—dc22
2010023467
10 9 8 7 6 5 4 3 2 1

To my mother and father for making me who I am,
To Tiffany, my love, my challenge,
To Dakota, may you defy the world
the way you defy me.

OUR COUNTRY IS A GRAVEYARD

Gentlemen, you have transformed
our country into a graveyard
You have planted bullets in our heads,
and organized massacres
Gentlemen, nothing passes like that
without account
All what you have done
to our people is
registered in notebooks

—*Mahmoud Darwish*

Translation: As`ad Abu Khalil

CONTENTS

Maps   x

PART ONE: THE LEBANONIZATION OF IRAQ

1 Occupation   3
2 Road to Civil War   27
3 Slaughterhouse   75

PART TWO: THE IRAQIFICATION OF THE MIDDLE EAST

4 Among the Jihadis   123
5 Exiles   151
6 The Battle of Nahr al-Barid:
  Iraq Comes to Lebanon   181

PART THREE: THE SURGE

7 "Iraqi Solutions for Iraqi Problems"   221
8 The Battle Over Amriya   289
9 The Eclipse of the Mahdi Army   337

PART FOUR: AFTERMATH

10 Lebanon: Toward Zero Hour   379
11 A Guest of the Taliban   439
   Epilogue: The New Iraq?   521

Acknowledgments   559
A Note on Sources   561
Index   563

Research support for this book was provided by

THE PUFFIN FOUNDATION INVESTIGATIVE FUND
AT THE NATION INSTITUTE

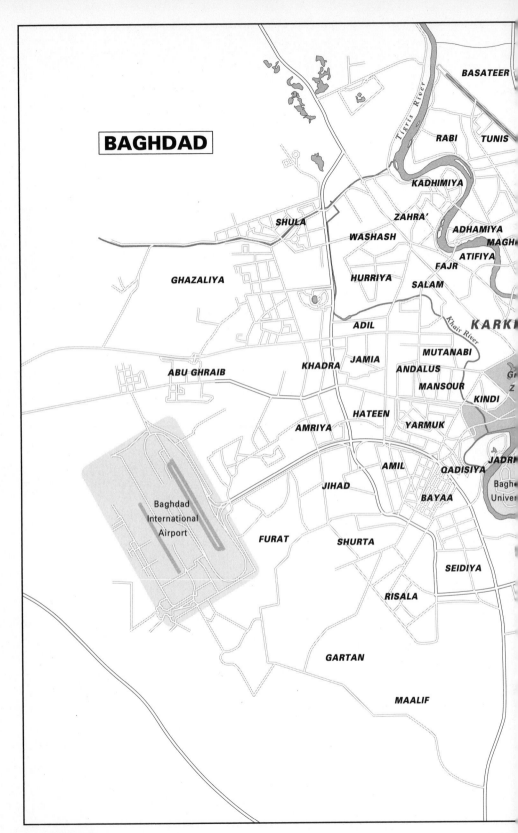

Baghdad

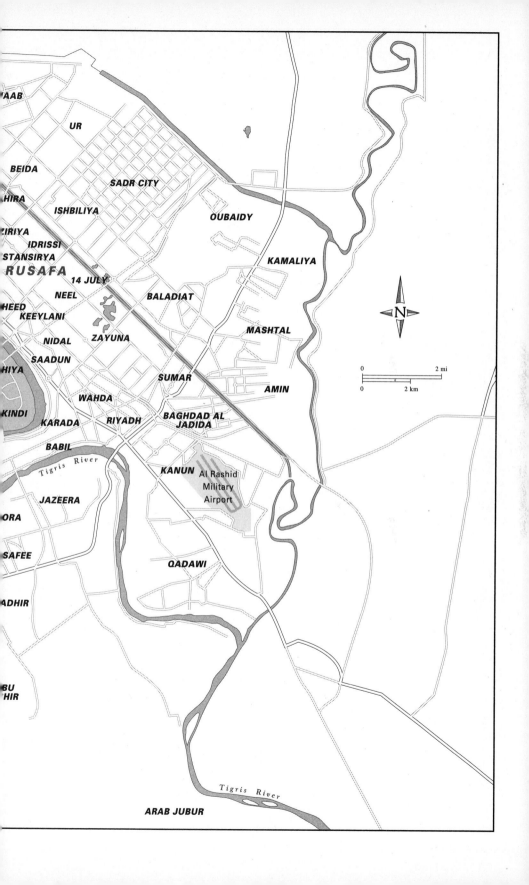

Iraq

LEBANON

SYRIA

Nahr al Barid

Tripoli○ ■

Bedawi

Mediterranean

Sea

LEBANON

○ Arsal

Beqaa Valley

BEIRUT ⊛

Majd al○
Anjar

Masnaa

Qaraun ○

Sidon ○

*Ayn al
Hilweh*

SYRIA

N

| 0 | 10 mi |
| 0 | 10 km |

ISRAEL

Lebanon

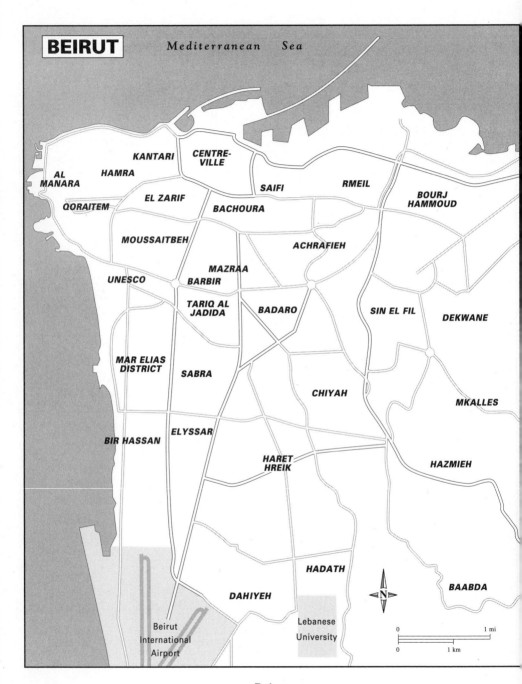

Beirut

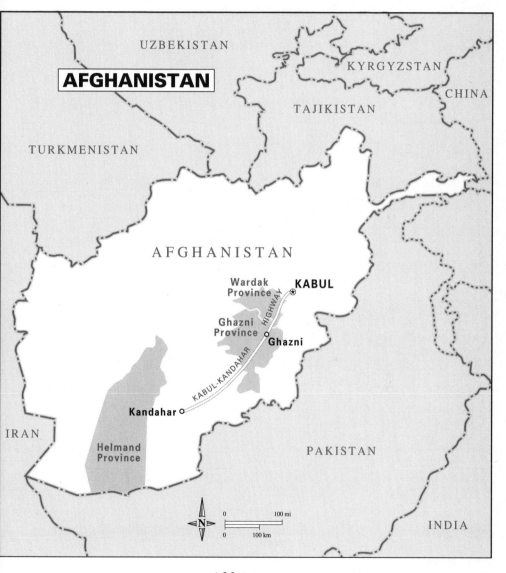

Afghanistan

Part One

◆◆◆◆◆◆◆◆◆

THE LEBANONIZATION OF IRAQ

CHAPTER ONE

Occupation

ABDEL SATTAR AL-MUSAWI'S DECOMPOSED REMAINS LAY ON THE ground above his grave. His older brothers sat beside them, holding them, crying. Although he had been arrested in 1998 and killed in 2001, they had just learned of his death three days earlier, and now they had come to claim his body. "His crime was loving freedom," said his friend Abdel Karim, who had come to find his own brother too.

It was April 2003, and I was beginning my career as a journalist. I had been in Iraq for only a few weeks, and I thought nothing good would come of the war: it was predicated on lies, and would subvert democracy and law at home as well as abroad. I was skeptical that a foreign occupation would be welcomed by Iraqis, and I knew that the American civilian and military leaders were ill prepared to understand a different culture, especially a Muslim one, and especially after the trauma of September 11. But I had come to Iraq wanting to give a voice to Iraqis, and this meant restraining my views and listening. As Iraqis rubbed their eyes and awoke to the new reality in a mix of shock, depression, and euphoria, I was as confused as they were; nothing seemed black-and-white.

With the collapse of Saddam Hussein's regime, the circumstances surrounding the disappearance of thousands of political prisoners were finally being revealed to their families. Iraqis could find files on their loved ones and discover what had become of their fate. More often than not, the news was not good.

Several dozen members of the Musawi family had come to claim four of their brethren from the Karkh cemetery. The cemetery, in Haswa, just outside Baghdad, entombed political prisoners, many of whom had been murdered at the nearby Abu Ghraib prison. All four murdered members of the Musawi family were cousins: Abdel Sattar al-Musawi, born in 1966, hailed from the Dora neighborhood of Baghdad and was married with two children; Salah Hadi al-Musawi, born in 1974, was from Baghdad's Thawra neighborhood; Salah Hasan al-Musawi, born in 1971, was also from Thawra, as was Saad Qasim al-Musawi, born in 1967, who was married with six children. The body of family friend Qasim Ahmad al-Maliki was here too. He was Abdel Sattar's age, from Thawra as well, married, with no children. All had been killed in 2001. "They were killed for no reason," a friend of the Musawis explained. "There was no justice, no court, no defense."

The Musawis had traveled by bus and in a pickup truck. They carried with them flimsy wooden coffins made of boards and a black flag of mourning. At seven in the morning, they were the first family in the cemetery that day. The *dafan,* or grave digger, Muhamad Muslim Muhamad, was a small man in sweatpants with a buttoned shirt tucked in. He assisted with an obsequious eagerness, and I suspected that he was compensating for an unconfessed complicity in the crimes he helped bury.

Karkh was the size of a football field, surrounded by a brick wall fringed with eucalyptus trees. The ground was a sandy gray, with mounds to mark the shallow graves. Some of the mounds had holes burrowed into them where animals had fed on the corpses. On a stick in each mound was a card with a number on it. The Musawi family had the plot numbers for their dead, and Muhamad led them to the first one, casually strutting over other graves. It belonged to Abdel Sattar. When the family found the grave, the previously silent men collapsed in loud sobs. They kneeled on the ground and clung to one another, quieting down only when the grave digger began to undo his work. They watched in an apprehensive and lachrymose silence. Perhaps they still hoped that the grave would be empty? The digging slowed as the earth being removed turned to a wet, dark red, as if stained with blood. Muhamad abandoned his shovel and used his hands. Abdel Sattar's exhumed body was the color of the earth, thin and dry. Amid calls for "my brother!" his body was placed on a plastic sheet and wrapped in a *kiffin,* or white cloth. It was then placed in the wooden coffin to await the trip to Najaf, south of Baghdad, where it would be buried in the City of Peace—the biggest cemetery in the world outside China, and the preferred burial site for all Shiites.

As Abdel Sattar's brothers and a handful of others remained by his coffin, the rest of the family moved on to another cousin's grave. The body emerged in separate pieces, and the bones were placed together in a pile around the skull. By nine in the morning six other families had arrived to reclaim their loved ones, and their wailing cries could be heard from all corners of the cemetery. I couldn't help but cry too. Abdel Sattar's former employer was also present. "He was a lovely boy," he said. I asked if this had happened to many people he knew. He gestured behind him to the hundreds of graves and said, "See for yourself."

I felt ashamed to be intruding on the Musawis' private pain, and I sobbed with them. One month into my career as a journalist, I was not yet able to watch other people's pain without participating in it.

Hussein al-Musawi told me he had served time in the Saddam City security prison with his four murdered cousins. He was jailed for seventy days beginning in July 2001 because the regime had learned that in 1991, after the failed uprising against Saddam following his defeat by the Americans, a relative of the family attempted to defect to Iran. The relative had visited Abdel Sattar before escaping, and this was the cause of the Musawi family's suffering: eleven men were arrested. In prison Hussein's interrogators had tortured him with electricity. They had tied his hands behind his back and hung him from them, dislocating his shoulders. And they had beaten him with cables and metal rods until he was drenched in his own blood. At the cemetery he told me he would still be able to recognize the faces of the security officers who had done this to them. "If I saw them I would seek revenge," Hussein said. "I would eat them."

Before leaving the cemetery, several men of the Musawi family voiced their resentment toward the Arab press. "They were a part of these crimes," one said. "They covered it up. They always said Saddam was a hero, and they took his money."

Baghdad—City of Decay

The Musawis had not known whether their lost sons were dead or alive until three days before they dug up the bodies. They received the information from a remarkable organization called the Association of Free Prisoners. Located in the confiscated riverside villa of a former security official in the Kadhimiya neighborhood of Baghdad, the Association formed right after the war ended. Muhamad Jamal Abdel Amir, a twenty-eight-year-old volunteer, explained that the Association was created by four former prisoners. It was an entirely Iraqi project; the founders had not coordinated their activities with anyone foreign or received any outside help. After the war, when Iraqis began looting the headquarters of the security organizations that had terrorized them for so long, many handed over the files they found to the Association.

On the external walls of the Association hung sheets of paper with alphabetical listings of prisoners' names. Hundreds of desperate people ran their fingers down the lists taped to the walls, hoping to learn their relatives' fate. Inside, past the two boys with machine guns who guarded the Association, workers bustled back and forth, their faces blocked by the immense piles of documents they carried to different rooms in order to organize them by subject. They planned to enter all the information into a database, but for now the dozens of rooms were full of thousands of files going back to the 1960s. The files were stacked on top of one another, stored in sacks or kept in their original file cabinets. They were marked "Dawa" (for a banned Islamist party) or "Communist," or had other labels that indicated independent political activity—all designating the subjects as victims of ruthless repression.

New files continued to come in by the thousands from all over Iraq. One revealed that a soldier accused of joining the Dawa Party in 1981 and criticizing the regime had been sentenced to five years in prison for his crimes. Another file documented the mass execution of sixteen people. Saad Muhamad, a volunteer at the Association responsible for gathering information, explained he was imprisoned for four years for criticizing Saddam. He showed me a Procrustean British-made traction couch that had been found in the general security headquarters. It was used during interrogations to stretch victims until their bodies broke and tore. He also showed me a meat grinder used for humans.

I found my own trove of records one day as I was walking through Baghdad's streets. In the poor neighborhood of Betawin, I stumbled across an abandoned police station housing the Saadun General Security Directory Office on its second floor. It was clear that a systematic attempt had been made to destroy the documents on the second floor, presumably by the minor intelligence officials who had worked there. I found two overturned document shredders and thin strings of paper strewn all over the floor, along with broken glass and ashes, the only remnants of the bureaucratic records of various horrors. Most file cabinets and their contents had been thrown into a few rooms that were torched; all that remained in the drawers were ashes. A young Christian boy brought sacks for me to load files into. Those that were salvageable documented the mundane daily operations of a dictatorship's local security station over the previous years, right up to March 2003, the final days before the war. The files recorded: the 2001 duties of security officers, changes of residence of ordinary Iraqi citizens, information from a snitch about a stolen antique sword, lists of people belonging to enemy or sectarian organizations, lists of people who criticized Saddam, lists of people under surveillance, reports on people observing religious ceremonies, information on participants in the 1991 Shiite uprising, weekly orders to spread proregime rumors and combat antiregime rumors, lists of executed political prisoners and the reasons for their execution, information on bank employees in Baghdad, lists of spies in mosques and churches, names of applicants to study in the Islamic university, reports on people who had tried to leave Iraq illegally, orders to spread rumors that Iraq could defeat the U.S. and would attack Israel and liberate Palestine, a list of people accused of belonging to a group seeking to avenge the murder of Shiite leader Muhammad Sadiq al-Sadr, and a report about a man accused of breaking a picture of Saddam, among others.

One dense folder particularly caught my attention. It contained numerous security service memos concerning the arrest of Abed Ali Safai Ahmad, who had been accused of insulting Saddam and the Baath Party. According to the files Ahmad was a taxi driver, born in 1975, who lived in the Shiite slums then known as Saddam City. He was a veteran of the war against Iran, and one of his brothers had been killed in that war.

On July 4, 2002, the leadership of the Abtal al-Tahrir (Heroes of Liberation) section of the Al Aqsa group office of the Baath Party ordered the arrest of Ahmad for his "assault on the person of the master and leader the President may Allah bless and protect him." Basically, he stood accused of assaulting Saddam, and it had been decreed that he undergo detention for "a reasonable period."

Basher Aziz al-Tamimi, Ahmad's neighbor, also a taxi driver living in Saddam City, testified against him. A staunch Baath Party member from the Al Aqsa branch, Tamimi alleged that he encountered a very drunk Ahmad on the night of July 3. According to Tamimi, Ahmad suggested they sell a privately owned car, but Tamimi reminded him that such a sale would be illegal. Tamimi then testified that Ahmad cursed Saddam Hussein, saying, "Saddam's sister's pussy over this law!" (In Arabic, as in any other language, referring to the vagina of a man's female relatives is a terrible insult.) Tamimi asked Ahmad why he was attacking the president when he knew that Tamimi was a member of the Baath Party. Ahmad is quoted as replying: "Your sister's pussy and the Baath Party's sister's pussy!" A fistfight ensued. Tamimi presently reported the case to his Baathist supervisor, Saad Khalaf: "He requested I file a written report, and then we went to Shahab because he is responsible for the branch security." The men organized a group to go to Ahmad's house and confront him. Apparently, when they arrived Ahmad hit Tamimi and threatened, "I will shave your mustache and the Baath Party's mustache." (In Iraq a mustache is often considered a symbol of manhood and honor, and threatening to shave a man's mustache—like referring to the genitals of a female relative—is a terrible insult. A man can also take an oath, swearing by his mustache, and if he or his sister, for example, has been humiliated, he can shave his mustache and refuse to grow it until his honor has been restored.)

Other witnesses testified in support of Ahmad's accusers. In his defense Ahmad claimed, "I did not assault the person of the master and the leader president, Allah bless him and keep him." Ahmad insisted he had witnesses who supported his side of the story. He admitted that he had assaulted Tamimi on the night the party committee came to arrest him: "I was in a bad temper and I hit him, and as he does not have a mustache I said to him, I shave yours and the party's mustache, and I did not mean to direct the assault on the party in my words. . . . I was under the influence of alcohol and was drunk and in a bad temper for I had a brother who was martyred in the great battle of Qadisiat Saddam. His name was Abad al-Radha, and he died in 1986. . . . I seek forgiveness, and this is my testimony." Ahmad claimed that Tamimi owed him ten thousand dinars and that when he asked for it back they got into an argument. Ahmad was jailed but released in an amnesty granted two months later.

Another file I found documented the arrest of a woman accused of being a witch. I tracked down the accused witch, Aliya Jasem, who lived in the village of Huseiniya, north of Baghdad. Amid sewage and waste-filled unpaved roads where half-naked toddlers played, I finally found Aliya's modest house. Her husband, Sadiq Naji Muhamad, was a tailor in Baghdad. They had four children. Sadiq had been a prisoner of war in Iran for nine years. He told me that Shiite prisoners were singled out for special punishment by the Iranian guards, who viewed them as traitors fighting for Sunnis. He was held in the Hashmetiya prison in Tehran, where he saw many fellow prisoners killed or tortured.

As an unrelated male, I could not meet Aliya; I could only catch a glimpse of her silhouette or the end of her dress, hear her voice as she spoke with her husband and hear her moving about in the kitchen. Sadiq related their shared story. Aliya was a fortune teller, psychic, and traditional healer. Many Iraqi Shiites believe that descendants of the Prophet Muhammad can treat the spirit using the Koran. Aliya was one such descendant. She treated spiritual ailments such as depression. If a woman had been expelled from her husband's family's home, Aliya could treat her and she would be taken back. If a dog had attacked a child, she would open and close the Koran three times in the child's face in order to cure it. She cured women who were not wanted as wives by placing special stones in front of the afflicted woman's house, washing her, and reading from the Koran and the sayings of Imam Ali, Muhammad's nephew and a key figure for Shiites. Sadiq proudly related that even though Aliya could not read or write, she could know everything about a person by looking at her face.

When Aliya was a child, her legs were paralyzed. No doctor could treat her, so her family took her to a Shiite shrine near Hilla—where, Sadiq explained, she was able to stand and walk. Since that moment she had possessed special powers. "There are two types of magic," said Sadiq, "the devil's magic, practiced by some sects in Iraq but which is against the Koran, and merciful magic, which can combat the devil's magic and which she practiced."

Aliya was paid for her services, but very little. Traditional healing is very common in Iraq, and since every woman in the neighborhood knew about her (she only treated women), word of her abilities spread. Sadiq maintained that most women in his wife's field were also security agents or collaborators. The security service wanted Aliya to work with them because she had access to every woman in the city and could discover the secrets of each home, such as who was involved in illegal political activity. Aliya refused to be an agent and was subsequently accused of harboring an anti-Saddam political group in her home. In describing this course of events, Sadiq accused the mayor of being a security agent and Baath Party official.

On August 10, 2002, Aliya was arrested by the Iraqi Security Forces. She was found guilty of witchcraft and spent two months in jail. The order to arrest her came from the national security directorate. The documents said she was released because of her husband's request. He wrote a letter to the security service saying that she had only been using special spiritual techniques to cure ailments of the soul. She only had treated women and only had used the Koran. Sadiq asked for another chance, promising that Aliya would never practice healing again. He also mentioned that he had been a POW in Iran and had chosen to return to Iraq, unlike other Shiites who had joined Iranian-sponsored anti-Saddam militias.

Although Aliya was sentenced to six months, she was released after seventy days from the Rashas women's prison (she was transferred from the Al Rusafa prison) in a general amnesty. Aliya had been beaten in the police station, and Sadiq was still bitter. "She is a good wife, and they put her in the same prison with prostitutes," he complained. "She was so traumatized she has ceased performing her magic."

After her release Aliya went to the tomb of Abbas, an important Shiite shrine to one of Ali's sons, and said, "If I am really your relative, prove it by destroying Saddam and all his men within a year." Six months later, his government fell. Sadiq explained that this happened because "God answered the prayers of those who had suffered."

I AM OFTEN ASKED now if it was all worth it. Would it have been better to leave Saddam in power? Are Iraqis better or worse off than they were before the American war? I never know what to say. How do you compare different kinds of terror? Those who were spared Saddam's prisons and executioners may be better off, though they have not been spared the American prisons, or attacks, or the resistance's bombs, or the death squads of the civil war. The Kurds are certainly better off, on their way to independence, benefiting from their relative stability and improved economy. But the rest of Iraq? Under Saddam the violence came from one source: the regime. Now it has been democratically distributed: death can come from anywhere, at all times, no matter who you are. You can be killed for crossing the street, for going to the market, for driving your car, for having the wrong name, for being in your house, for being a Sunni, for being a Shiite, for being a woman. The American military can kill you in an operation; you can be arrested by militias and disappear in Iraq's new secret prisons, now run by Shiites; or you can be kidnapped by the resistance or criminal gangs. Americans cannot simply observe the horror of Iraq and shake their heads with wonder, as if it were Rwanda and they had no role. America is responsible for the chaos that began with the invasion and followed with the botched and brutal occupation. Iraq's people suffered under the American occupation, the civil war, and the new Iraqi government, just as they did under the American-imposed sanctions and bombings before the war and just as they did under the years of Baathist dictatorship.

While the spontaneous burst of repressed fury from one segment of Iraqi society often caused more damage to property than the American bombs, another segment demonstrated solidarity and a volunteer spirit eager to re-store security and normalcy. Common civilians stood all day directing traffic in a country with no traffic lights or rules, where there was absolute liberty to drive anywhere, in any direction, at any speed. These volunteers protected neighborhoods and established order, but it was too late. After the war, looters pillaged the country, stripping everything but the paint from the buildings they preyed upon. Under the gaze of U.S. troops, looters destroyed the physical in-frastructure of the Baathist state, while the U.S. occupation eliminated its bureaucracy.

The atmosphere of lawlessness that pervaded the country in those first few days and weeks never went away. Eventually it allowed for criminals, gangs, and mafias to take over; it replaced the totalitarian state and the fear it had im-posed with complete indifference to the idea of a state. It was a shock from which Iraqis did not recover. In Baghdad the dominant man in any area was called a *shaqi*. He was normally a thug who would sometimes engage in extor-tion and other small crimes; after the war these *shaqis* were recruited into armed groups and even religious militias.

A few weeks after the war against Saddam's regime ended and before the war against the resistance began, I moved into a house in the Mansour district, where I stayed for a month. I was stringing for *Time* magazine, but I clashed with my colleagues, who were focused on the English-speaking elite Iraqis, the American military, and the Shiite clerical establishment, but ignored the Iraqi street, the mosques, the Sadrists. At night, to the sound of gunfire and frogs calling, I would sit by the pool and watch bats swoop down to sip water, as I fought loneliness by making calls on the satellite phone to my future wife. Taha was our somnolent guard. He arrived in the afternoon and left in the morning. He had a chair in the driveway, where he sat with his Kalashnikov leaning lazily against the wall. I bought newspapers for him every day because I sympathized with the solitude and ennui of his job, but mostly so that he would remain awake a little longer. He was a sound sleeper. He sat reading the newspapers, or staring in front of him, his head hanging down wearily, and evinced no perceptible reaction when machine gun fire erupted outside our walls, as it did intermittently all night. I grew accustomed to it, but sometimes, when I was sitting on the lawn eating dinner and a burst went off on our street, I still jumped.

Five minutes from the house was a market that sold looted goods and heavy-caliber machine guns, bazookas, grenade launchers, RPGs, handguns, and ammunition. The grenade launcher was fifty dollars. I was inquiring about prices one day when a large burst was fired from right behind me. I leaped high in the air, checking my body for holes. The sellers were demon-strating their merchandise to interested consumers by firing them into the sky.

Not far from the neighborhood I was living in was the Washash district, its narrow streets awash with sewage. Like much of Baghdad, a greenish brown deluge had descended upon the streets, reaching from one side to another. Residents waded through the putrid liquid, and children ran barefoot through it. Women gathered in a loud gaggle, anxious to voice their complaints. There was no electricity, no gas, the water was dirty, and their children were sick. There was shooting all night, and they were afraid to go out. These families, like 60 percent of Iraqis, relied entirely on the state's food distribution program to survive.

In a field in the Jihad neighborhood of Baghdad, I found every little boy's fantasy. Several dozen abandoned Iraqi tanks lay beside bushes and palm trees. Their treads had been sabotaged by the Americans, but they had plenty of ammunition. Fifty feet away were mud houses, with cows beneath the shade of a tree. A troop of local boys, ages five to twelve, avoided the cluster bombs on the ground and climbed on top of and inside the tanks. They lit some explosive powder. Somebody blew up a tank, and the turret shot a few dozen meters in the air before embedding itself in the ground by a house. I gave an eleven-year-old named Ali a dollar to show me around. He was timid at first, denying ever having played with the tanks, so I asked him to show me the tanks others had played with, and then I asked him which one he had played with, and which one he and his friends had shot, and he admitted more and more. His cousins joined us and said they were scared to take me to the ammunition. I told them they were girls, and they said, "No, we are strong!" and puffed their chests. Then their uncle showed up and ruined our fun. He told me he was scared for the children, but it didn't seem like he was making any attempt to control their behavior.

My driver's children, about five and three years old, played with ammunition their uncle had found in a nearby arms depot that had been abandoned and looted. He showed me live anti-aircraft bullets and a bundle of detonation cords for explosives, which Iraqis were using to cook. Five-year-old Fahad lit one and watched the flame shoot through it while his three-year-old sister held one of the charges in her mouth. In a restaurant where I often had lunch, I took note of an increasingly common sight—a customer walked in with a pistol stuck in his belt behind him.

We assumed with egotistical condescension that Iraqis were "used to" the ubiquitous hardship that has been their unearned fate, as if they were different from us, suffered less than we did, and did not have the same hopes for a prosperous, peaceful life. Iraq has the second-largest oil reserves in the world, and Iraqis were in no way used to the nadir to which life had sunk. Since the Gulf War they had slowly watched their heavily developed, educated, and industrialized society deteriorate and regress to a preindustrial era. Power, water, and security were not just abstractions; they meant life or death.

Imagine bombs raining on your city, the ground shaking, the walls rever-
berating. Imagine your city losing its power, its water, its security, its communications, and its government. Law and order disappear, weapons abound,
machine guns rattle, and bullets fly. Mountains of garbage grow higher on the
streets as goats, donkeys, and children sift through them, dispersing the waste
everywhere. Rivers of sewage cut through neighborhoods and roads, and
people wade through them. The food supply dwindles, dead dogs litter the
streets, their legs frozen in midair with rigor mortis, and a modern city becomes a jungle. Hundreds of thousands of foreign occupiers are ensconced in
the bedrooms and barracks of the former dictator, their leviathan tanks dominating traffic, but the newcomers do not replace the system they destroyed.
Armed gangs roam freely, and dogmatic religious organizations attempt to fill
the power vacuum, though they too have no experience in governance and es-
pouse an intolerant and regressive political ideology.

A UN representative explained to me that after the war Iraq had "gone back
to the stone age." It was a stone age lived in the midst of a modern state.
Sheep were herded through traffic jams, unexploded bombs hid like snakes, diarrhea killed children minutes away from immense hospitals, and tantalizing
glimpses of a different possibility beckoned on satellite television—it was not
an impossible or unfamiliar dream but a return to the future Iraqis had taken
for granted only a decade or two ago.

Baghdad in 2003 was a neglected city, broken like the spirit of its people,
who seemed ashamed that they had not put up more of a fight against the occupiers, as was expected by the rest of the world. Um Qasr in the south took a
week to fall, but the Republican Guard protecting the city barely put up a
fight. They were perceived outside Iraq as the elite, as those who would fight
to the death for their city, but this mythic status had more to do with their
privilege than anything else. The American military was warned that the battle for Baghdad would be the most bitter and desperate. The Republican
Guard felt no loyalty to Baghdad, though. They were terrified of the American
juggernaut, and they could see what had already transpired in the rest of the
country.

The media showed Iraq only during the day, when stores were open and
Americans patrolled. At night, darkness and fear emerged. Most people had no
electricity and resorted to oil lamps and fans made from straw to cope with
the heat—which drove some to sleep on their roofs, under the moonlight.

There were rumors that Americans were paying three dollars for every cluster bomb returned. It did not matter if the rumors were false. If people believed them, they would touch a cluster bomb; and if a bomb was moved, it
would explode. Children played with them, attracted to their shape. A child
threw a stone at one and blew up a nearby house.

·

Iraq had thousands of locations serving as weapons depots that contained unexploded ordnances, abandoned missiles, armored vehicles, and tanks. Even if the Americans had known where to look, there were not enough soldiers to protect all of the sites from looters. Removing them required a delicate expertise, which meant that some locations might take several days to clear. Baghdadis would have to wait years for their city to be free from the dangerous detritus of war that the American and Iraqi militaries had left behind.

On streets throughout Baghdad people tried to hawk their wares, hoping that buyers would be interested in the screws, pipes, sneakers, computers, soccer balls, AK-47s, and grenade launchers they had likely stolen. Every neighborhood had its own weapons bazaar, an unofficial collection of a few dozen men, who displayed heavy weaponry of every variety and eagerly demonstrated their use by firing them repeatedly into the air right next to you. A rocket-propelled grenade launcher could be found for fifty thousand dinars, or fifty dollars. When an American patrol drove by, the men hid their goods under boxes or in the trunks of their cars, and then took them out again as soon as the patrol moved on. The chatter of Kalashnikov shots and exchanges of fire punctured the empty silence of Baghdad nights. Iraqis evinced no perceptible reaction to these new sounds; they were normal, and no thought was given to the unknown circumstances and actors responsible for nearby violence or to its many victims.

The victims usually ended up in Baghdad's Criminal Medicine Department, which squatted on a muddy congested road next to the Ministry of Health. On the morning I visited it in May 2003, a busload of sobbing women sat in the entrance. An old man vomited on a wall to the side, while several other men sat glumly on the floor. An empty coffin made of wooden planks lay abandoned by the entrance, a large blood stain in its center. The sour stench of death wafted out into the halls. Ninety percent of Baghdad's violently killed passed through the Criminal Medicine Department before burial. Ever since Baghdad fell on April 9, Dr. Lazim had been seeing an average of fifteen to twenty-five corpses a day—all murdered, he said, pointing to a large stack of files on a shelf and opening a drawer to show another stack. Before the war he would see about five such cases a month. The state had a monopoly on violence, but victims of the regime were taken elsewhere. He said it was also possible to accommodate oneself to life under Saddam, and to live without arousing the state's ire and incurring its wrath. The new violence was random, and Lazim attributed it to the lack of security.

"Weapons are easy to find, and Iraqis are full of anxiety from three wars and the economic circumstances after 1991," Lazim said. Since it was so easy to obtain a weapon and there were no legal consequences, disputes were often settled violently and with impunity. "I am afraid to argue with any person on the street," he said. "There is no regime, no order." He added, "It is the duty of the international forces to create security." Lazim recently had begun seeing female victims for the first time. One was a teenager found by American soldiers with her throat slit. Two others set a ghoulish precedent—they had both been raped and then murdered.

For those wounded in Baghdad's gun battles, there was little hope of finding help. Yakub al-Jabari, a microbiologist at the National Blood Transfusion Center for Iraq, located in the complex of buildings known as Medical City, summarized the situation when asked if there was a shortage of blood. "There is a shortage of everything," he said, "blood, equipment, staff." He had not received his salary for three months. The labs looked like a dusty basement where a hospital might store its obsolete machines. The staff used food refrigerators to store blood, though frequent blackouts made Jabari's efforts worthless, as everything became contaminated. "If you want to save people's lives, bring us more of these machines—you will go to paradise," he said, opening a dirty refrigerator and pointing inside. "We kill people here, we don't save them." He smiled bitterly. "Many people are dying because of our shortages. We lie when we give people hope, but we can't be honest with them." Iraqis in need of blood must bring their own, which meant bringing a friend or relative to donate. I heard shooting from outside the blood center as I hurriedly asked Jabari about HIV and other concerns the center faced without the ability to screen donors. He told me he knew of only two cases of HIV in the past decade. He believed Saddam had executed them.

Baghdad's hospitals had collapsed at a time when improved health care was needed more than ever. Hospital directors and doctors complained that they had received no assistance from the coalition forces, only promises. They relied on generators, because they got only a few hours of electricity a day. Sometimes they were forced to operate by candlelight. Most hospitals and clinics received contaminated water or none at all. Contamination resulted in outbreaks of typhoid, gastroenteritis, and diarrhea. They had no air-conditioning, medicine, oxygen, or anesthesia. And there was no one to clean the floors, so they remained stained with blood.

Chaos reigned, as staff were overwhelmed. They had no computers and they recycled carbon paper. Ambulance crews had no gas or security escorts, and Americans stopped them at night for violating curfews when they transported patients. Security concerns led staff to leave work early in order to get home safely. When hospitals did receive supplies, staff worried about attracting looters. Hospitals had no cooling systems because of electricity shortages, so medicines and vaccines were routinely destroyed.

A visit to a hospital coincided with a car screeching to a halt in front. A shrieking, black-clad woman was thrown onto a broken wheelchair; relatives had to hold it together as she was wheeled in, blood pouring from her womb.

A midwife had botched her labor. A thick trail of blood led from the hospital driveway to the reception and down the hall to the emergency room.

Iraqis grumbled about their invisible ruler, the proconsul Paul Bremer, who rejected representation for them, declaring Iraqis too immature to decide their own fate. The country had three dictators in three months: Saddam was replaced by the bucolic Gen. Jay Garner and then the urbane Bremer, while others, such as Gen. Tommy Franks and President George W. Bush, issued edicts that affected their lives, and Arnold Schwarzenegger visited but did not greet his Iraqi fans. Even the name of the government changed three times: the Baathist regime became the Office of Reconstruction and Humanitarian Assistance (ORHA), which was replaced by the Office of the Coalition Provisional Authority (OCPA). In his "freedom message to the Iraqi people," Franks, the commander of coalition forces in Iraq, announced that the Americans had "come as liberators, not occupiers," adding that they aimed to "enforce UN resolutions requiring the destruction of weapons of mass destruction." These weapons, of course, had not existed for years.

The foreign troops became an onerous presence as the burden of Saddam was removed. Iraqis had to suffer numerous intrusive checkpoints, roadblocks, and lines for gasoline, and there were raids, killings, arrests, and property damage. They were awakened by the rumbling of tanks through streets. Unaware of the fact that many soldiers chewed tobacco, they asked me why Americans spit so much. Frustrated young soldiers pointed their machine guns at grandmothers and teased Iraqi youths about how easily they could kill them.

In the face of the American juggernaut, Iraqis were lost and confused. They were used to the way ministries got things done. Now they had to march through long paths carved out with barbed wire and stand in the sun with gun barrels facing them. They were searched, patted down, and questioned; their IDs were declared unsuitable; they were told they could not be helped, or sent elsewhere, their protests and supplications falling on deaf ears. Tempers were lost, and Americans screamed in English as Iraqis shouted in Arabic, neither understanding the other. American soldiers did not sympathize with the inconvenience. "We stand in the sun all day," said one soldier, looking at hundreds of men standing or squatting, waiting.

Falluja 2004

A year later I was in Falluja, a small town forty-three miles west of Baghdad on the Euphrates, in the Anbar province. Before the American invasion Falluja was rarely thought of unless Iraqis were stopping to get kabobs on their way to a picnic at Lake Habbaniya, an artificial lake in the middle of the desert with bungalows and a 1960s-style resort built along its rocky banks. True, it had a reputation for being conservative, with tribal mores still important, and its claim to fame was having the highest per capita number of mosques, earning it the nickname City of Mosques. But Falluja was conservative, not radical; it had not been a center of religious extremism or loyalty to the former regime. But it became a case study of how American policy in Iraq promoted sectarianism and armed resistance.

The city, once a Sufi bastion, suffered at the hands of the former regime because of the importance of religion there. Its Sufis began to depart in the 1990s, when Saddam stopped oppressing Salafis. Named after "al-Salaf al-Salih" (the virtuous predecessors), meaning the companions of the Prophet Muhammad and their followers, Salafis seek to purify Islam of innovations introduced over the centuries since Muhammad received his revelations, and they seek to return to a way of life similar to that of the early Muslim community, basing life only on the Koran and the Sunna, the deeds and words of the Prophet. Saddam began to encourage their revival, perhaps to counter a perceived Shiite threat. In the aftermath of the U.S. invasion Falluja also suffered political purges, uprisings, and killings of tribal members who had served the previous regime. It was not a wealthy town, with little signs that it received preferential treatment. It was a trucking and smuggling hub, which would later prove useful to other clandestine networks.

Although it is common to blame the American decision to dissolve the Iraqi army and security agencies in May 2003 for the emergence of the resistance, the truth is that resistance in Falluja and elsewhere in the Anbar province began before this order. No hostile shots were fired at the Americans from Falluja during the invasion, and the city saw little looting. Instead, after the war, local officials and dignitaries took control and tried to establish order. It took two weeks before the Americans even established themselves in Falluja. Key influential foreign fighters later told me that they had tried to organize an armed resistance in Falluja and failed in those early days, because Falluja's people wanted to give the Americans a chance. But the American perception was that Sunni Arabs were loyal to Saddam and thus to be treated with hostility. The Americans took a more aggressive posture in Sunni areas than in Shiite ones.

The Americans set up an imposing presence on the main street in the center of town, using a school as their base, and mounted aggressive patrols. Their presence in other civilian areas, and their practice of observing neighborhoods from rooftops, offended traditionally minded locals. The elites who had taken control of the town following the war were not recognized by the Americans. Little interest was shown in improving the local economy. A demonstration in April calling for the Americans to leave the school ended up with nearly twenty dead civilians, as the Americans met it with extreme force. There was no public American inquiry or attempt to reconcile with the locals. One foreign fighter I spoke to would later name this as a turning point. Similar demonstrations occurred in Shiite areas, but they were met with a different response from the Americans. In Diwaniya, a Shiite city that was also a bastion of the former army, anti-Bremer demonstrations following the disbanding of the army featured pictures of Saddam and Baathist slogans, but the Americans did not respond aggressively.

More demonstrations and more killings followed in Falluja, and the Americans adopted the attitude that "Arabs only understand force." Tanks on the streets, low-flying helicopters, frequent patrols—Fallujans felt like they were under a foreign occupation. Local leaders who sought to avoid violence would eventually change their minds. The American view that there was a monolithic group of Iraqis called Sunni Arabs had always been mistaken, just as it was a mistake to identify a Sunni Triangle. The Baath Party was incorrectly viewed as an exclusively Sunni party, and Saddam's regime was incorrectly viewed as a Sunni regime, since not all Sunnis were loyal to it. Many Sunnis felt they were victims of Saddam, and even Sunni clerics had been executed by the former regime. Some tribes were given privileged status, while others were weakened or marginalized. That there were no obvious Sunni leaders after Saddam was removed was but one sign that his own community had been weakened by his regime. But Sunnis would soon consider themselves the targets of collective punishment. Treated as the enemy, many of them soon became just that, fearing that they were about to be exterminated. These fears would be manipulated by those interested in promoting violence.

THOSE FEARS WERE the political effect of ideas and decisions that were fermenting thousands of miles away from Iraq. Much of what we have come to know about Iraq has come from self-styled "Iraq experts" or "terrorism experts"—celebrity pundits—who catered to the political demands of the occupation and the American administration. Most of these experts could not speak or read Arabic, had not been to Iraq, and had only a superficial experience of the Middle East. They hailed from Washington think tanks like the Brookings Institution, the American Enterprise Institute, the Center for Strategic International Studies, and others. If they visited Iraq (or Afghanistan), they hopped from base to base, with the military as their baby-sitter and escort. They invoked terms that were barely in use before 2003, such as "Sunni Arab." Geographical regions were simplistically layered onto Iraq's ethnic groups, and simplistic labels like the "Kurdish north," "Sunni Triangle," and "Shiite south" were popularized. The importance of class identity—and the revolutionary potential of the poor, who supported Communists in the '50s and the Sadrists in the '90s and later—was ignored, as was the heritage of nonsectarian nationalism.

The Iraqis the Americans installed after the invasion, however, came mostly from the former opposition parties, many of which were formed on a sectarian or ethnic basis. None had a broad base of support. The American approach to Iraq was sectarian, as Iraqis quickly complained. The Americans viewed Sunnis as the bad guys and Shiites as the victims, and the U.S. media followed suit. The Iraqi Governing Council, a symbolic body created in July 2003 as a concession to Iraqi demands for representation, was established on purely sectarian grounds, as Iraqis were quick to note. Members were chosen for being Sunnis, Shiites, Kurds, or Turkmen, rather than for representing Iraqis. Even the Communist Party member was chosen for being a Shiite rather than for being secular or leftist. Barbara Bodine, a veteran Arabist from the State Department and former ambassador to Yemen, was briefly put in charge of Baghdad and then fired when the CPA needed a scapegoat to blame for the descent into chaos. "One of the first mistakes we made was to put Iraq into three neat little packages, homogeneous, monolithic," she told me.

The occupation empowered Shiites and Kurds, specifically the most sectarian and ethnocentric leaders, and punished the Sunni population. It also empowered parties with little grassroots support (with the exception of the Kurdish parties), which meant that their members had to appeal to sectarianism. Sunnis and some Shiites were driven to resist the occupation. At first the resistance was a nationalist one. Foreign Arabs had flocked to Iraq during the war to defend their brethren. Some were radical Sunnis who sought a jihad. Their numbers grew as volunteers flocked to kill Americans and Shiites, often at the behest of Sunni clerics and theologians throughout the Arab world. The most radical among them sought to destroy the American project in Iraq by provoking sectarian warfare, setting off suicide bombs at key religious sites. Although the Iraqi government under Saddam had not been a Sunni regime, as many outside observers have claimed, the new sectarian Sunni parties in Iraq have come to view that era as a "Sunni golden age."

Arabs are often criticized for their "conspiracy theories," and it was common in Iraq to view the Americans as new colonists intent on dividing and conquering Iraq. But the approach implemented by Paul Bremer attempted to do just that. In Bremer's mind the way to occupy Iraq was not to view it as a nation but as a group of minorities, so he pitted the minority that was not benefiting from the system against the minority that was, and expected them to be grateful to him. Bremer ruled Iraq as if it were already undergoing a civil war, helping the Shiites by punishing the Sunnis. He was not managing a country, in his view; he was managing a civil war. As a result, he helped to create one.

The Bush administration believed that Shiites could lead the Arab world to an Islamic reformation that would increase secularism. Bremer claimed that Saddam had "modeled his regime after Adolf Hitler's," and he compared the

Baath Party with the Nazi Party. This was sheer fabrication: there is no proof or mention of this in any of the copious literature about Iraq. (If anything, Saddam's inspiration was the Soviet dictator Joseph Stalin or Michael Corleone from *The Godfather*.) The Iraqi Baath Party was established by a Shiite, and the majority of its members were Shiites. So Bremer created this Nazi analogy and imagined himself de-Nazifying Iraq, saving the Shiites from the evil Sunnis. (Deputy Defense Secretary Paul Wolfowitz also often compared Baathists to Nazis.) Indeed, one of the reasons Bremer performed so horribly in Iraq is that he viewed the country through this distorting lens.

Defense Secretary Donald Rumsfeld was unwilling to commit resources to the stabilization of Iraq. When Larry Di Rita, Rumsfeld's de facto chief of staff, arrived in Kuwait to serve as the political commissar over ORHA, he met with the humanitarian assistance team led by Chris McMullen. McMullen began the briefing by saying, "What we intend to bring to the Iraqi people," but he never got to finish his sentence. Di Rita slammed his fist on the table and shouted, "We are bringing freedom to the Iraqi people! We don't owe them anything more!" Later Di Rita explained that the U.S. military would not be in Iraq for long. Rumsfeld considered Bosnia and Kosovo to be failures, and he considered Afghanistan a potential failure because U.S. troops were still there. The doctrine of the day was "shock and awe" and a hasty U.S. withdrawal.

President Bush had approved of a plan to take over the Iraqi army, but Bremer and Pentagon officials Paul Wolfowitz, Doug Feith, and Walter Slocombe reversed the decision, casually agreeing to fire more than three hundred thousand armed men without a second thought. ORHA officials had not planned on maintaining the Iraqi army indefinitely. Instead they had hoped to put the army to work until they could get it through a demobilization process. The men of the Iraqi army thought that they would be part of the solution. Iraqi generals did not acknowledge defeat, and the Iraqi army did not feel defeated. The CPA's refusal to maintain state industries led to the loss of a further 350,000 jobs. In August 2003 the Americans removed agricultural subsidies, forcing many farmers off their land.

Bremer later claimed that Iraqis hated their army, which was, in fact, the most nationalistic institution in the country and one that predated the Baath Party. In electing not to fight the Americans, the army had expected to be recognized by the occupation; indeed, until Bremer arrived it appeared that many Iraqi soldiers and officers were hoping to cooperate with the Americans. Bremer, however, treated Iraqis as if they harbored ancient grievances, claiming in an article after he retired that "Shiite conscripts were regularly brutalized and abused by their Sunni officers." This was not true: although Sunnis were overrepresented in the officer corps and Shiites sometimes felt there was a glass ceiling, there were Shiite ministers and generals, and at least one-third of the

famous deck of cards of those Iraqis most wanted by the Americans were Shiites. Complex historical factors account for why Sunnis were overrepresented
in majority-Shiite areas. Many attribute this to the legacy of the Ottomans and
the British colonizers, while others theorize that minorities took power in several postcolonial Arab countries—Alawites in Syria, Maronites in Lebanon,
and Sunnis in Iraq. Although there is debate about these matters, nobody has
ever argued on behalf of Bremer's ludicrous view of a Nazi-like regime where
Sunnis were the Germans and Shiites were the Jews. There were many Shiite
officers in the army. The elite Republican Guard and Special Republican Guard
were dominated by Sunni tribes from Anbar and Salahaddin, as were sensitive
security services, but there is a false notion that Shiites had no access to power.
It implies that there was an open political field for Sunnis from which Shiites
were excluded.

Iraq had a legacy of statism. The state controlled the country's oil wealth as
well as production in industries such as agriculture. The government also employed the majority of the Iraqi workforce. Strict regulation governed the
economy, controlling the movement of capital. The American occupiers
found an Iraq where the state had played a tremendous role in the lives of citizens, and they assumed this was a timeless character of the culture that they
would have to repair, but in fact it dated to the sanctions imposed from 1990 to
2003. The sanctions led to a huge increase in the role of the Iraqi government
in the daily lives of the population.

Denis Halliday, the UN assistant secretary general and the humanitarian coordinator of the oil-for-food program in Iraq, resigned in 1998 in protest at the
economic sanctions on Iraq. The oil-for-food program was meant to alleviate
the impact of the sanctions, but Iraq could not pump enough oil to get
enough money to cover its food and medicine needs, and the drop in oil prices
at the time made it even worse. Halliday admitted that Iraqi children were dying directly because of the sanctions. The UN itself estimated that about half a
million children under five died because of the sanctions.

Iraqis had few political or civil rights under Saddam, but they had economic
rights and a decent standard of living. The sanctions took even those. Halliday's successor resigned in 2000 protesting the "tightening of the rope around
the neck of the average Iraqi citizen. . . . I felt that I was being misused for a
United Nations policy that was punitive, that tried to punish a people for not
having gotten rid of their leader."

To prevent the Iraqi people from starving, the Public Distribution System
was established to deliver rations to the population via more than fifty thousand local agents. Rations included soap and basic food needs. For the first
time, the people now depended on the government to eat, giving Saddam
more control over them than ever before, and making dissent more difficult
and dangerous than ever. The middle class, which might have formed the base

of that dissent, was wiped out as savings were made worthless. Many Iraqis were driven from towns back to a rural and agricultural life, and the power of feudal landlords increased.

A stated goal of the American occupation was to transform Iraq into a free-market economy. One of the first measures taken by the American occupation was to impose laws that liberalized capital accounts, currency trading, and investment regulations, and lifted price regulations and most state subsidies. An important principle guiding the occupation was not to invest in any state institution that could be privatized in the future, in anticipation of the liquidation of state assets.

Extreme measures such as these radically changed the lives of Iraqis as they struggled with higher inflation and reduced state subsidies while imported consumption goods flooded the market at lower prices. Consumer spending increased drastically. This was coupled with the growth of new private institutions that sought to replace the role formerly played by the state. National industry and the export sector were severely undermined. The entire structure of the Iraqi state has been shattered and the central state in Iraq has been vitiated, as shown by the clauses in the Constitution that address control over oil. Although similar attempts at "shock therapy" techniques applied to countries in the 1980s and '90s showed poor results, often only damaging countries in Eastern Europe and Latin America, these same techniques were imposed on Iraq in extreme form. The measures taken in Iraq were neither democratic nor successful, but their ramifications will be felt for years.

America's relationship with Iraq did not begin in 2003. The U.S. encouraged and helped Iraq go to war against Iran in 1980. It was a war that devastated both countries. The U.S. and its Gulf allies also helped support Iraq's massive army, which encouraged the adventure in Kuwait and which later, after the Americans disbanded this vast army, led to such a large group of unemployed armed young men in 2003. The American project in Iraq resembled and was sometimes even consciously modeled after other colonial endeavors in the region. The act of occupying a country, dismantling and rebuilding its institutions, economic structures, and even its political identity, is not a new feature in the modern history of the Middle East. But occupied Iraq has rarely been studied as a colonial case. There has been a clear effort to avoid labeling the American project a colonial one. This has led to analysis of Iraq through an ahistorical framework.

Outside observers, including American politicians, have a tendency to assume that the current political divisions, violence, and prejudices in Iraq have "always been there," and the new conflict between Sunnis and Shiites has been conceptualized as "timeless." But Iraqis were merely adapting to the American view of Iraq as a collection of sects and trying to fit into the political system the Americans were building around that idea. These observers disregard the fact that the American presence actively created many of these problems and "read history backward" in an attempt to minimize the American role in Iraq. But Iraq is not Rwanda, where Americans could watch Tutsis and Hutus slaughter each other and claim it was not their problem. The civil war in Iraq began with the American occupation.

The occupation was based on a vision that saw Iraqis as a collection of atomic sects. Even before the invasion, theorizers of the "new Iraq" such as Kanan Makiya sought to de-Arabize the country. They blamed Arabism for the ills of totalitarian Iraq and proposed ideas such as "regional autonomies" and federalism as alternatives to a centralized, top-down, state-sponsored identity. Prescient critics such as Azmi Bishara warned that if Iraqis ceased to be "Arab," then they would simply adopt more primordial forms of identity that would not necessarily be less violent or damaging.

After the war Iraq was treated as a tabula rasa experiment, and the political institutions built by the occupation reflected these views. They were devised to undermine the idea of Iraqi nationalism that Saddam had tried to promote, and to correspond to the vision of Iraq as a trinational state. This further politicized sectarian forms of identity, making them the only avenue of political action in Iraq. Several incompatible views of Iraqi identity were promoted by the occupation and postwar Iraqi politicians: Iraq as a tribal society; Iraq as a liberal, multicultural polity, where a concept of Iraqi citizenship trumps other loyalties (promoted by Ahmad Chalabi, Kanan Makiya, Mithal al-Alousi, and other "liberal" politicians); Iraq as a collection of nations or sects. The last definition was the most potent. Electoral laws and sectarian violence played the largest role in cementing this vision. In addition, the Americans divided Iraq into winners and losers, and they soon made it clear to the Sunnis where they fell into that divide.

In late 2003 an American NGO arranged a meeting in the Green Zone between several representatives of Falluja's major tribes (such as the Albu Eisa, Jumaila, Albu Alwan, and others) and representatives of the Coalition Provisional Authority. "We had a lot of hopes of big and meaningful projects that could show a more attractive future for the people," said one of the organizers. "We were talking with the sheikhs about good projects for the city, and they were really interested in the business centers and the links with the foreign companies. They told us the 'troubled kids' were few and they could arrange with the bigger tribal leaders to control the situation as long as they can have something to show their people. Their other concern was about the Shiite domination. They said they would really appreciate it if the Americans promised to protect the city from the Badr Brigade [the huge Iranian-trained Shiite militia of the Supreme Council for the Islamic Revolution in Iraq, or SCIRI]. They were really concerned about this point. The CPA attended the meeting, but they seemed so uninterested. I can say that their general feeling was, 'You lost, and we don't care about you.' To everyone's disappointment, the main representative of the CPA left fifteen minutes into the meeting. The sheikhs left to Falluja knowing they would have nothing to offer there. One of them was kidnapped and killed a couple of months after the meeting, and the other was attacked and his son was killed. One of them got connected to the armed groups and went on his own."

In the spring and summer of 2004, I met many fighters and leaders of the resistance in Falluja. They believed they were defending their city, the country, and their religion. They clashed frequently with their rivals, the Al Qaeda–inspired jihadists and foreign fighters who had based themselves in the Anbar province and threatened to undermine the power of the more conservative Fallujan leadership. Many Sunnis had no alternatives even as the Al Qaeda men undermined the Anbar establishment and imposed a reign of terror, which not only bloodied communities but destroyed infrastructure, institutions, and businesses there. Their traditional leadership was more pragmatic and wasn't ideologically opposed to an accommodation with the Americans at that time, though they had yet to be chastened by Shiite militias into reducing their expectations.

A FOREIGN MILITARY OCCUPATION is a systematic imposition of violence on an entire population. Of the many crimes committed against the Iraqi people, most have occurred unnoticed by the American people or the media. Americans, led to believe their soldiers and marines would be welcomed as liberators, still have little idea what the occupation is really like from the perspective of Iraqis. Although I am American, born and raised in New York City, I came closer to experiencing what it feels like to be Iraqi than many of my colleagues. I often say that the secret to my success as a journalist in Iraq is my melanin advantage. I inherited my Iranian father's Middle Eastern features, which allowed me to go unnoticed in Iraq, march in demonstrations, sit in mosques, walk through Falluja's worst neighborhoods, sit in taxis and restaurants, and look like every other Iraqi. My ability to blend in also allowed me to relate to the American occupier in a different way, for he looked at me as if I were another "hajji," the "gook" of the war in Iraq.

I first realized my advantage in April 2003, when I was sitting with a group of American soldiers and another soldier walked up and wondered what this hajji (me) had done to get arrested. Later that summer I walked in the direction of an American tank and heard one soldier say about me, "That's the biggest fuckin' Iraqi [pronounced "eye-raki"] I ever saw." Another soldier, who was by the gun, replied, "I don't care how big he is, if he doesn't stop movin' I'm gonna shoot him."

I was lucky enough to have an American passport in my pocket, which I promptly took out and waved, shouting, "Don't shoot! I'm an American!" It was my first encounter with hostile checkpoints but hardly my last, and I grew to fear the unpredictable American military, which could kill me for looking like an Iraqi male of fighting age. Countless other Iraqis were not lucky enough to speak English or carry an American passport, and entire families were killed in their cars when they approached checkpoints. In 2004 the British medical journal *The Lancet* estimated that by September of that year, one hundred thousand Iraqis had died as a result of the American occupation; most of them had died violently, largely from American airstrikes. Although this figure was challenged by many, especially partisan backers of the war, it seemed perfectly plausible to me based on what I had seen during the postwar period in Iraq. What I never understood was why more journalists did not focus on this, choosing instead to look for the "good news" and to go along with the official story. I never understood why more journalists did not write about the daily Abu Ghraibs that were so essential to the occupation.

The occupation pitted Iraqis against one another as old scores were settled and battles for resources and Iraq's identity raged. Sectarian differences that had previously been suppressed are now exaggerated. This book, which begins by looking at the events and trends that led to the outbreak of civil war in Iraq, tells the story of what happened to Iraq as it descended into the nightmare of sectarianism and militia fighting between Sunnis and Shiites in the aftermath of the U.S. invasion. And it tells the story of what happened after "the Events," or "the Sectarianism," as Iraqis called their civil war, much as the conflict in Northern Ireland is called "the Troubles." It is a story of Iraq after dark, so to speak, away from the glare of the Western media and far from U.S. patrols and, most important, away from the elite politics of the Green Zone. I focus on the Iraqi "street," because after the overthrow of Saddam, power was distributed there.

I first came to Iraq when I was twenty-five years old, a former nightclub bouncer with a skill in languages who hoped to remake himself as a journalist. I have been traveling and living in Iraq ever since, and the longer I have stayed the more interested I have become in what Martha Gellhorn described as the "view from the ground," a narrative of Iraq that transcends the clichés of much journalism about the region. As a new Iraq emerges, I hope this book will serve as a reminder of the terrible suffering millions of civilians have endured. This book also attempts to understand how the civil war in Iraq ended and what role Americans played in that. More specifically, it is an attempt to understand the role of the "surge," the term for the increase in American troops that has become a blanket term for a change in the American strategy and military operations in Iraq (and later in Afghanistan). That the Americans began to have more influence on the Iraqi street during the "surge" is reflected in the chapters that cover this period, where they play a larger role in my narrative, and I show that the power dynamic between the Americans and the street was never as simple as one between an occupier and a puppet. For the surge also marked the period coinciding with the cease-fire of the main Shiite militia and the simultaneous cease-fire of most Sunni militias, who changed sides and allied themselves with the Americans. I was a surge skeptic, expecting the worst. I feared that the civil war in Iraq might become a regional war, and I did not immediately see the importance of the new American approach or foresee the role the serendipitous change in Iraqi dynamics would play. The civil war burned itself out faster than I expected, and the Americans went from being an oppressive occupying force, to a neglectful occupier allowing Iraqis to slaughter one another, to a power broker and quasi peacekeeper, and finally, perhaps, to an uneasy strategic ally and partner.

This book is not limited to Iraq, however. This is a book about what the Americans have wrought regionally, how the invasion and its aftereffects have spilled over into neighboring countries. It shows how Iraq underwent a process of Lebanonization and how the Middle East, in many ways, was Iraqified. I attempt to chart where Iraqi refugees fled to and how they lived. I also look at the effect of this Iraqi exodus: the radicalization and destabilization of Iraq's neighbors, the exodus of ideas, weapons, and tactics from Iraq. In particular I focus on Lebanon and the extent to which it was Iraqified, with an Al Qaeda–inspired group leaving Iraq and establishing itself there at the same time as tensions between Lebanon's Sunnis and Shiites led to clashes in its streets. The regional tensions between Sunnis and Shiites stoked by the Bush administration remain a legacy that can lead to future violence. The book ends in Afghanistan, a "virtual" neighbor of Iraq's, where President Barack Obama, who inherited a more broken and unstable Middle East, initiated his own surge and where the American military tried to apply the lessons it thought it had learned in Iraq. COIN—the acronym for the counterinsurgency warfare in vogue after the "surge" in Iraq—is talked about as a war of the future, and its use and efficacy in Iraq and Afghanistan will determine the way America fights those future wars. As I write there is talk in Washington about whether American troops should be used to "solve" Iran, Pakistan, Yemen, or Somalia. Regardless of where, there is a certainty that they will be used again. This book, then, as well as being a personal journey through the violence that has cascaded through the region over the last decade, is a reminder of the human cost of America's wars to remake the Muslim world.

CHAPTER TWO

Road to Civil War

ALTHOUGH MANY SEE THE FEBRUARY 2006 SAMARRA SHRINE BOMBINGS by Al Qaeda in Iraq as the incident that ignited the civil war, ethnic and sectarian militias had been battling each other long before that. Since the invasion the lives of many Iraqis had become restricted to their small neighborhoods, with travel too treacherous to attempt. These neighborhoods became "purified" of minorities; mini-cities made up of a single sect or ethnic group were set up. Those conditions shaped the political consciousness of Iraqis; they became increasingly isolated, with no public spaces for debate or interaction. Even the new media in Iraq was segmented, with each institution targeting specific sections of Iraqi society. As a result, Iraqis stopped watching the same news, following the same issues, or even watching the same TV shows.

New parties emerged in postinvasion Iraq, and old ones resurfaced. Others formed new electoral coalitions. Most of this activity revolved around identity politics. Very few Iraqis voted for nonsectarian parties in any of the postwar elections, and most political groupings saw their main function as the "representation" of sectarian and ethnic groups rather than the proposition of ideas and projects for the future of the state. Identity was politicized and confessionalized, much as it is in Lebanese politics, in a manner unseen since the creation of Iraq.

The debates since the invasion pertained to the design of power-sharing formulas that represented the different communities. To newcomers this may have seemed like the true nature of Iraqi society, which many presented as three self-contained "nations." But this simplified the concept of Iraqi identity and reduced it to a sectarian one. In the American view, the only way through which Shiites observed their surroundings was through their sectarian identity, and they participated in Iraqi politics only through their Shiism.

Sectarianism has always existed in Iraq, just as racism exists in every society. But pre-American invasion sectarianism was very complex. Since the capture of Mesopotamia (then compromising the provinces of Baghdad and Basra) by the Ottoman Turks in 1638, minority Sunnis had been Iraq's ruling group. Following the dissolution of the Ottoman Empire, the British Mandate authority further empowered Sunnis in Iraq while Shiites remained mostly rural and confined to the laboring classes. By the 1950s many Shiites had migrated to urban areas; some filling the vacuum created by the departure of Baghdad's Jewish commercial class, others working in the government. Sunnis and Shiites intermarried, and typically the father's sect would become the dominant one in the family.

Sectarianism existed before the war; it was just muted and not very important politically. But it could always be used as an alternative interpretation of events as well. Abdul Karim Qasim, who led Iraq after the monarchy was overthrown in 1958, increased the numbers of Shiites in the officer corps. Some Shiites believe he was overthrown by Sunni officers in 1963 because of that, since afterward Shiite attendance in the military academy declined. The regime that followed also expropriated some Shiite businesses. But politics in 1950s and '60s Iraq was broadly aligned around ideological, not sectarian, fault lines, inspired by Nasser's secular Arab socialist state in Egypt. The 1968 coup that brought the Baath Party to power, dubbed the "White Revolution," got most of its legitimacy from its promise of stability and an end to the retributions and political violence that had scarred Iraqi society. Saddam, who participated in the coup and rose to the top of the military and government throughout the '70s, officially took power in 1979. For a long time his approach to ruling was not sectarian. Although most neighborhoods in Baghdad had a clear sectarian majority, Saddam tried to prevent the emergence of "pure" areas in the city. The government regulated access to the city, and moving into Baghdad required the government's permission. In the early 1980s, when plans were made to modernize the city, the government planned many neighborhoods to accommodate specific professions (military officers, teachers, professors, engineers, etc.) in order to assure that they were mixed. Most of these areas have now been rendered homogenous because of the violence and mass expulsions. The same applies to the government's plans for social engineering (moving Arabs into the north and Kurds into the south). Internal displacement is a grave obstacle to peace in Iraq today.

During the '70s the Baath Party, though not without sectarian bias, was focused on using its oil wealth for modernizing Iraq and building the Iraqi state. As Saddam accumulated more power it was often at the expense of rival Sunnis. Initially loyalty and competence were sufficient to advance in his regime. Saddam weakened ideological parties like the Communists but backed religious and tribal leaders who supported his regime.

But the Iran-Iraq War increased regional sectarianism. Arab states like Saudi Arabia expected Iraq to be a Sunni bulwark against Shiite Iran. The war created the first real fissures between Sunnis and Shiites in Iraq. Some Shiite

Baathists in the intelligence and security establishment and presidential palace began to feel marginalized and mistrusted, even targeted. Some who defected complained about this to Dawa Party officials in London, but the officials weren't sure if the complaints were valid or just an attempt to penetrate the party. "If the Iran-Iraq War had only lasted one or two years, it wouldn't have had an impact," a Dawa insider and longtime official told me. "But it lasted eight years." And the war was followed by the 1991 intifada, which was not Shiite at first—it grabbed anything around it to give it an identity, and Imam Hussein's "revolution" against oppression resonated in the south. Saddam crushed the intifada, treating it as if it were a Shiite uprising. His brutal suppression was led by a Shiite, Muhammad Hamza al-Zubaidi, but Shiites would feel that a Sunni regime had punished them, and they would harbor these grievances following Saddam's overthrow.

Some Shiite activists in exile circles belonging to Dawa and the Supreme Council began talking about the historical unfairness Iraqi Shiites faced. Abdel Karim al-Uzri was a secular Shiite and the godfather of this idea. He argued that Shiites had been treated unfairly ever since the state of Iraq was established. Uzri and a few others outside the mainstream of Dawa and the Supreme Council began talking about the political bias against Shiites. Dawa and Supreme Council rhetoric was about Islamic revolution, though. People like Sami al-Askari and Muafaq al-Rubaei, who would rise to power in postwar Iraq, were staunchly against talking about Shiite rights. "I was accused of being a foreign agent to undermine them," said the Dawa insider. "It was about Islamists against evil powers of everybody else. It was about Islamic revolution, not Sunnis versus Shiites. At one point the Supreme Council even had Sunnis in its leadership." But even this insider admitted Saddam was not sectarian. "Saddam played one community against another. He executed many Salafis and influential Sunnis. Saddam wasn't a Sunni. He didn't care about Sunnis and Shiites. After the 1991 failed uprising, there was a strategic shift in the Supreme Council. It wasn't about Samarra; it was a strategic plan to destroy Sunni power." After the Gulf War the Iraqi state became much more narrowly based. Shiites were removed from jobs, or kept out of jobs, while power became more and more concentrated in the hands of Sunnis from certain tribes. The regime responded to the threat from the uprising by closing ranks on a tribal and clan basis, mostly people from Tikrit and Mosul. To many Shiites, it felt like the state religion was Sunni Islam, and the public practice of Shiism was prohibited. At Saddam University, one of Baghdad's biggest schools, the senior party official who had taught Baathist ideology just before the war told his students that if he found them visiting Shiite shrines, he would beat them. Naturally, he also condemned the Dawa Party— the party of the largely exiled Shiite intelligentsia—and described it as murderous.

State schools had mandatory religion classes, but only Sunni Islam was taught and the teachers were usually Sunni, at least in Baghdad. The religious endowment, or *waqf,* was an ostensibly ecumenical ministry, but many Shiites perceived it as being Sunni. They worried that collection money donated to Shiite shrines was used to build Sunni mosques. Shiite calls to prayer from mosques were often not allowed. When mosques challenged the government and broadcasted the Shiite call, they were punished. Many Shiite religious books were banned, perhaps because some of them condemned figures revered by Sunnis, so Shiites would exchange these books secretly. Sometimes Shiites found with them would be accused of belonging to the Dawa Party and executed. Between Iraqis, the level of social sectarianism often depended on whether or not they were devout practitioners of their faith.

Saddam's faith campaign of 1993 was meant to bolster his legitimacy. It meant that Baath Party members had to attend classes on Islam. This would influence not only them but their sons as well, who ten years later would take part in the resistance. The generation raised in the 1990s also had much more Islamic education in school. The regime even introduced an Islamic-based mutilation as punishment for military desertion.

Many upscale whites living on Park Avenue in New York view blacks and Hispanics with disdain. Many minorities resent whites. Even in New York City one can hear blacks referred to as "niggers" and Chinese as "chinks." But this racism does not normally translate into violence. It takes more than just resentment or even hatred. It takes fear as well as mobilization and manipulation by politicians and the media. This happened in the Balkans and Rwanda, and this happened in Iraq as well. For sure, the potential was there to be manipulated. In 2003 Shiites referred to other Shiites as *"min jamaatna,"* or "from our group," to let somebody know that a stranger could be trusted. But the American occupation divided Iraqis against one another, pitting the winners against the losers, and persistent Al Qaeda–style attacks against Shiites combined with this manipulation to unleash an awful tempest. The occupation empowered sectarian, ethnic, and tribal parties that had no rivals thanks to Saddam's legacy.

The Americans, much like the exile Shiite and Kurdish parties, identified the former regime and its security forces with Sunni Arabs. Most Iraqis viewed the army as the national army, not Saddam's army or the Baath Party's army, even if they viewed the Republican Guard as having a more sectarian hue. But despite the national embrace of the army, it was Sunnis who suffered the most and felt most vulnerable following its dissolution. Nearly four hundred thousand men lost their jobs following Bremer's decision to disband the army and security forces. Shiites and Sunnis alike protested. The resistance would later benefit both from the chaos resulting from the dissolution of the security forces and from the pool of unemployed and embittered men it created. As

Sunnis saw exile sectarian and ethnic parties taking over, their sense of disenfranchisement only increased—especially when the new government and its security forces became dominated by those same Shiite and Kurdish parties.

Bremer's de-Baathification order led to the sweeping dismissal of Iraq's entire managerial class. De-Baathification was not a neutral judicial process; it was politicized from the beginning. Former American ally Ahmad Chalabi used the process to target opponents. Shiite ex-Baathists were rehabilitated, but Sunnis often were not. In effect, the state was de-Sunnified. The American-selected Iraqi Governing Council (IGC) was dominated by sectarian and ethnic exile parties that had little support within Iraq, and its Sunni members were especially weak. The Sadrists, who had real indigenous support and had not been in exile, were excluded, while Dawa and the Supreme Council for the Islamic Revolution in Iraq, perceived to be Iranian tools, were empowered. Crucially, this was the first time sect and ethnicity had been used as the official principles underlying politics and institutional formation. Although the IGC was weak and had little support, it wrote the interim Constitution. In June 2004 the IGC was replaced by the interim government, led by secular Shiite and former Baathist Ayad Allawi. The exile sectarian and ethnic parties remained dominant. Many Shiites reported that violence against them started with the formation of the "Shiite"-controlled government.

As the resistance adopted a more Sunni identity, the Americans, who already viewed Sunni Arabs as pro-Saddam and pro-Baathist, had their preconceived notions reinforced. The U.S. military's brutal attempts to suppress the resistance also reinforced the Sunni sense of persecution, and there were no prominent Sunni leaders who could act as intermediaries between the resistance and the Americans.

The January 2005 elections were based on proportional representation, with all of Iraq as one electoral district. This weakened local parties with grassroots support but strengthened countrywide ethnic and sectarian blocs. Sunnis boycotted, strengthening the hands of Shiite and Kurdish parties. Sunnis were then locked out of the constitutional drafting committee. They feared that the federalism in the new constitution would deny them access to the country's resources and wealth. In October of that year Kurds and Shiites voted for the Constitution in a referendum, while Sunnis overwhelmingly voted against it.

While it was once taboo to ask about somebody's sect, it now became an essential part of daily interactions, with people asking indirect questions about where somebody was from, what neighborhood, what tribe, until they could figure it out. Many Sunnis, of course, also had a condescending and suspicious view of Shiites, encouraged by Saddam's policies in the 1990s. To them, and to many Sunnis in the region, the new Shiite-dominated order was a shocking historic reversal. Iraqi Sunnis feared revenge, especially as they saw that Shiite-dominated security forces were indeed targeting them en masse. By 2005 mass-casualty attacks on Shiite civilians were widespread. Shiites were restrained in response to these attacks, thanks in large measure to their leadership. Following the January 2005 elections, things began to change. The Supreme Council took over the Interior Ministry, and its men from the Badr militia filled senior positions. That year Sunnis began to be killed during curfew hours, when civilians could not drive. The killers reportedly had official vehicles. Missing Sunnis would be found executed with signs of torture.

Sunni Arabs were the primary victims of the sectarian cleansing in part because they were the weaker party, subject to attacks by the Americans, the new Shiite-dominated security forces, and the Shiite militias. But Sunnis also were more likely to live in Shiite areas than Shiites were to live in Sunni areas. While there were few Shiites in the Anbar province or in the north, there were significant Sunni minorities in the south. Many have been expelled from their homes.

The Iraqi elections of January 2005 enshrined the new, sectarian Iraq. The Shiite government unleashed its vengeful militias on Sunnis, replicating Saddam's mass graves, secret prisons, torture, and executions. Neighborhoods were cleansed of their minorities, and a once-diverse fabric frayed and came apart. Baghdad was slowly emptied of its Sunnis. Iraq fell apart. The violence was systematic and horrific. Rapes, beheadings, and extreme torture were used as strategic weapons. Kidnappings reached levels exceeding those of Colombia, Mexico, or Pakistan. Millions of Iraqis were internally displaced. Millions more became refugees in neighboring countries. Iraq's middle class, business class, intellectuals, doctors—all left the country. It was one of the fastest destructions of a country and its polity in history.

The Rise of the Mosque

With the removal of Saddam's regime, mosques and clerics acquired an inordinate power in Iraq. Though only one of many complex factors influencing life in the Muslim world, the mosque traditionally had an important role in the community, one that encompassed the religious, social, and political. The call to prayer echoed through neighborhoods five times a day, serving to regulate time and the cycle of life. The mosque was a place for men to pray, learn, talk, bond, and mobilize for collective action. The Friday *khutba* (sermon) was often a call to action, in which the imam—the head of the mosque, who led prayer—would lecture his flock about issues that mattered to the community, from religion to international affairs. Particularly in authoritarian states, the *minbar* (pulpit) is a rare source of alternative authority. Likewise, in authoritarian states that restrict freedom of expression, the *khutba* is an important alternative source of information and views. In post-Saddam Iraq the mosque became the most important institution in the state. It served to unite communities, functioning as a provider of welfare and a weapons depot, a source of news and a rallying point. Certain mosques became key locations in neighborhoods or even rallying points for movements and sects; they became the perfect vantage from which to watch how sectarianism became a dominant and destabilizing force in Iraq.

I first visited Baghdad's Adhamiya district on Friday, April 18, 2003, for the triumphal return of Dr. Ahmad Kubeisi, Iraq's most famous living Sunni theologian and a television preacher who had been based in the United Arab Emirates. A staunch Sunni bastion in majority-Shiite eastern Baghdad, Adhamiya was named for its mosque of Al Imam al-Adham, "The Greatest Imam," as the 1,300-year-old mosque and tomb of Abu Hanifa al-Nu'man was called. Abu Hanifa was a ninth-century theologian whose legal judgments are still followed by about half the world's Muslims. The Abu Hanifa Mosque is Iraq's most important Sunni shrine, visited by hundreds of thousands of pilgrims a year. It had been a favorite mosque of the former Iraqi government; before the war Iraqi state television often broadcast Friday prayers from there. In the past, the imam, Sheikh Abdul Ghafar al-Kubaisi, had held up a Kalashnikov during his sermons, exhorting his listeners to protect Saddam and his regime. He was now in hiding.

Adhamiya sits on the east bank of the Tigris River, right across from the important Shiite neighborhood of Kadhimiya. Many of Iraq's Shiites believe that Abu Hanifa was a treacherous student of Imam Kadhim, a key religious leader venerated by Shiites who participated in Kadhim's killing, and some had a tradition of spitting in the direction of the shrine when they passed by it. Others told a story that Abu Hanifa had committed suicide by throwing himself in a barrel of acid. In fact, my friend Sayyid Hassan Naji al-Musawi, a close ally of the Shiite cleric Muqtada al-Sadr in Baghdad and a commander in Sadr's Mahdi Army, once confided to me that Abu Hanifa was an *"ibn zina"* (son of adultery), and that a "dog is buried there." Salafis, whose numbers in Adhamiya had grown in the 1990s, also despised the mosque, which was revered by Sufis, because of the Salafi rejection of all shrines and tombs. After the war, posters of Saddam could still be bought in Adhamiya, and some Shiites called it "Saddamiya." Shiite mosques in the district were frequent targets of Sunni attacks.

Adhamiya was both very old and very rich, and the former regime found many supporters there. Up-and-coming Baathists would often purchase a house in the district once they could afford it. In March 2003, just before the war started, Gen. Mustafa al-Azzawi—who would command the Iraqi forces that fought the invading U.S. Army in Nasiriya, in southeast Iraq—began building a home in Adhamiya. Saddam himself hid there during the Gulf War of 1991. Afterward he appeared on Iraqi television to thank the people of Adhamiya for helping him, and declared it Baghdad's original neighborhood.

On Wednesday, April 8, 2003, Saddam was spotted and filmed at a rally outside the Abu Hanifa Mosque. He wore his military uniform and was flanked by a man resembling his son Qusay. The cheering crowds lifted Saddam up onto a car hood, from where he waved. A voice in the film that was made of the event said, "Conquered people eventually triumph over invaders. Your leadership is not weakened." On April 10 a fierce gun battle occurred in Adhamiya between members of the First Marine Expeditionary Force and what U.S. Central Command called "an Iraqi leadership group trying to get together for a meeting" in the house of a top Baath official. One vehicle was hit by three rocket-propelled grenades and at least one marine was killed in the seven-hour battle.

Adhamiya was the last part of Baghdad to fall. The defenders were mostly foreign fighters who regrouped from the rest of the country and tenaciously held out. Twenty-two prisoners were taken from the mosque, including its sheikh, Watheq al-Obeidi, and his two sons. Some of the prisoners were not Iraqi. Inside, a cemetery for "the martyrs of April 10" would be built. Before the gravestones were ready, the names of at least twenty dead foreign fighters—including Egyptians, Syrians, Lebanese, and Yemenis—were written on paper and put into soda bottles stuck into the ground. Foreign fighters who had survived were hidden in mosques or homes by sympathetic locals; some were even driven to the Syrian or Iranian border. The mosque itself was damaged, its walls pockmarked with deep holes and its minaret nearly cracked in two, with a gaping hole left by a missile launched from an American plane several hours after the April 10 battle. A nearby telephone exchange was destroyed by American bombings, and the buildings across from the mosque were blackened from the attacks. A dozen burned-out cars, including Sheikh Watheq's blue Volkswagen Beetle, blocked traffic. To prevent looting after the battle, Adhamiya's residents formed a committee of armed volunteers. Life began to return to normal, with the tea houses across from the mosque open and the neighborhood's men gathering once more to chat and play dominoes.

A week after the gun battle, as looting was still occurring across Baghdad and the Ministry of Information was emptied and set aflame, loudspeakers atop the U.S. Army's Humvees warned in Arabic that if the looters did not immediately leave, "there will be consequences." Meanwhile, the recently returned Dr. Kubeisi warned the Americans in his sermon of the consequences they would face if they did not leave immediately. For Kubeisi's triumphal return the mosque was covered in banners proclaiming "One Iraq, One People," "No to America," "We Reject Foreign Control," "Sunnis Are Shiites and Shiites Are Sunnis; We Are All One," "All the Believers Are Brothers," "Leave Our Country, We Want Peace," and similar proclamations of national and Islamic unity. Demonstrators chanted "No to America, no to Saddam, our revolution is Islamic!" The angular and white-bearded Kubeisi had been a strident opponent of the war, which he had warned would fail, but shortly after he was proved wrong he made haste from his comfortable life in Dubai for Baghdad, reportedly being flown in from Amman on an official UAE private jet.

The sermon that followed the prayers elaborated the nationalist sentiments on the banners. Baghdad had been occupied by the Mongols, Kubeisi said, referring to the sacking of what was then the capital of the Muslim world in 1258. Now, new Mongols were occupying Baghdad; they were destroying its civilization and creating divisions between Sunnis and Shiites. The Shiites and Sunnis were one, however, and they should remain united and reject foreign control, he said. They had all suffered together as one people under Saddam's rule. Saddam had oppressed all Iraqis and then abandoned them to suffer. There were no Sunnis or Shiites, Kubeisi said. All Iraqis were Muslims, and they had defended their country from the Americans and British as a united people. Kubeisi also thanked the Shiites of Basra for "defending their country against the foreign invaders." He demanded an administration governed only by Iraqis and a council of Shiite and Sunni scholars to oppose any government the Americans tried to establish. "We fear that sectarianism will be exploited by our enemies," he said, referring to the Americans, and urged unity between Sunnis and Shiites. "We will reconstruct our country," he said, rejecting American interference and "a government that will oppress us," calling instead for elections. He mocked the "continuous lies" that the Americans had come to get rid of Saddam's weapons of mass destruction. "Where are these weapons?" he demanded. The Americans were the enemies of mankind, and had come for Iraq's oil, he said. The American occupiers were the masters today, but they should not consider staying in Iraq. "Get out before we expel you," he said, warning of the humiliation they would suffer. The sermon ended with shouts of "God is great!"

The parallel with the fall of Baghdad to the Mongols in 1258 was ominous. It had shocked Muslims in the thirteenth century. Theologians like Taqi al-Din ibn Taimiya (1263–1328) from Aleppo in modern-day Syria blamed Muslims for failing to be sufficiently devout. A wave of conservatism spread throughout the Muslim world, trying to return Islam to its original purity. Often quoted by Osama bin Laden, Ibn Taimiya is the spiritual father of radical Sunnism, in particular the Wahhabi form of Islam dominant in Saudi Arabia and the general Salafi trend dominant in international terror movements like Al Qaeda. Taimiya viewed offensive jihad as a duty of every Muslim and expressed extreme hatred for Shiites, who were treated as apostates. He even blamed Shiites for the Mongol sacking of Baghdad. Ayman al-Zawahiri, the Egyptian fundamentalist who acts as Al Qaeda's ideologue, has also relied on Taimiya's *fatwas*, written as the Mongols devastated Baghdad. The Saudi government has been distributing the works of Taimiya throughout the world since the 1950s.

Across from the Abu Hanifa Mosque I found a shop selling magazines that promoted Taimiya's thoughts. Perhaps more ominous, many Sunnis blamed Shiites for the betrayal that led to the fall of Baghdad. In the thirteenth century the sultan had a Shiite adviser called Ibn al-Alqami, who was said to have sold out his people and helped the Mongols. Abu Musab al-Zarqawi and other Salafi jihadists would later curse Shiites as the "grandsons of Ibn al-Alqami" for their collaboration with the Americans, the new Mongols.

Also in attendance at prayers that day was Sheikh Muayad al-Adhami, whom Kubeisi appointed as the new leader of the mosque. Adhami was angered by the entry of American marines into his mosque the previous week. The marines, who had not removed their shoes and had carried weapons, had violated Iraqi dignity, he said. Kubeisi's close ties with the previous regime in Iraq would allow him to galvanize the Sunni elite and lead the community that had become disenfranchised with the end of the regime. There were few other Sunni personalities as well-known. His previous five years in exile created the false impression that he too had been opposed to Saddam, and he would attempt to use this to forge ties with former opposition figures who had returned. In the early months of the occupation, Kubeisi's followers held joint demonstrations and prayers with anti-occupation Shiites such as the Sadrists. Their constant message was *"maku farq,"* meaning "there is no difference" between Sunnis and Shiites: "We are all Muslims." But in retrospect they were protesting too much; behind the stentorian insistence that they were all united was the fear that they were not and the knowledge of what would happen should this secret become known.

When Supreme Council leader Abdul Aziz al-Hakim became head of the Iraqi Governing Council in late 2003, he began distributing land in Adhamiya to Shiites in order to increase its Shiite population, and he supported the construction of Shiite mosques there. But these mosques were often attacked, and some were blown up while still being constructed. Tensions continued to escalate. After Saddam's capture in December 2003, rumors spread in Adhamiya that it was not their beloved leader after all. Residents emerged to celebrate, carrying pictures of Saddam and wielding Kalashnikovs and even RPGs. They clashed with U.S. troops, and locals maintained that U.S. forces were accompanied by the Supreme Council's Badr Brigade. Others claimed that Iraqi police from Sadr City attacked the Sunni revelers. Residents of Adhamiya accused these forces of raiding the hospital to arrest those they had wounded. It was the first time Sunnis accused Shiite militias or security forces of attacking them.

Adhamiya remained a bastion of support for the resistance. Although most of the resistance in that area was not Salafist, following the destruction of Falluja by the Americans in late 2004, a large number of Zarqawi's Tawhid and Jihad fighters moved into a building called Ras al-Hawash, which was close to the Abu Hanifa Mosque. There were foreign fighters among them, and they enjoyed the hospitality of the neighborhood's families and employed local youths to collect information on their behalf. One test of bravery they gave local youths seeking entry into their group was to challenge them to place the flag of Tawhid and Jihad on the walls of the Abu Hanifa Mosque.

At the same time as I was tracking the fate of the Abu Hanifa Mosque and the neighborhood around it, I was also curious about the neighborhood of Ghazaliya and would visit it often. Built in the 1980s for Baath Party members and Iraqi army officers, it had twelve Sunni mosques but none for Shiites, even though the area was mixed—Saddam had refused to allow Shiite mosques to be built there. Sunni mosques in Iraq rarely attracted the same large crowds as their Shiite counterparts. Sunnis merely went to the closest mosque in their neighborhood, which in this case was the Um Al Qura Mosque. Built by Saddam at the cost of $7.5 million, the mosque was originally named Um al Maarik (Mother of all Battles) but later changed to Um Al Qura (Mother of Villages), a reference to Mecca. The mosque served as a symbol of Saddam's turn to Sunni Islam to legitimize his rule, and commemorated his glorious (albeit failed) battle against the United States and its allies in the Gulf War. A plaque by its door said it was "built by the order of President Saddam Hussein, may God keep him." Its minarets are visible from a great distance, four of which are shaped like Kalashnikovs and four like Scud missiles, and its dome is taller than most in Iraq. The bright white marble mosque is surrounded by a moat shaped like the map of the Arab nations, and has a huge parking lot that has not been full since the heady days of the spring of 2004. Inside it feels more like a Gothic cathedral than any other mosque I have been to. It is silent, with natural light coming in from up high. It is more vertical in its orientation than most, which have a tendency to feel horizontal. Its walls are cream-colored with green and gold decorations. The imam's voice echoes like a Gregorian chant.

On July 18, 2003, a day after the old Baath coup anniversary, more than a thousand men with white skullcaps gathered for the Friday prayer and sermon. Signs were still up displaying the mosque's original name. An adjoining museum contained a Koran allegedly written with Saddam's donated blood. That day, Dr. Harith al-Dhari, head of the Association of Muslim Scholars, warned that the Americans should think of leaving Iraq to spare them and the Iraqis time, blood, and money. "It is the right of occupied people to resist the occupiers . . . the Iraqis will resist," Dhari said. Did the Arabs not have the same right to resist occupation and expel the occupiers that other nations had? The Americans had to leave at once, and the Iraqi people would establish their own government, unite, and live as brothers. Dhari commended the members of the resistance, calling them "an honest opposition" of which Iraqis could be proud. He called on them to continue defending Iraq and resisting the occupation.

Dhari condemned the Interim Governing Council, which, he claimed, had been established by "dishonest parties" and divided Iraq along sectarian lines. It would only cause hostility among the Iraqi people, he said. He was infuriated by the council's declaration of April 9 as a national holiday, a day he described as "the downfall and surrender of Baghdad," which should be commemorated with sorrow and pain. Dhari's anti-Shiism came across obliquely, when he condemned the IGC for allowing one community (the Shiites) to dominate the others, despite statistics to the contrary (meaning he rejected claims that Shiites were the majority population in Iraq). Dhari also condemned exiled opposition leaders who came on the backs of U.S. tanks and called for killing former Baathists. Up to half the country's population were former Baathists, he said, defending them as pious and well intentioned.

As his voice built to a piercing, shrill cry, Dhari screamed out about crimes the Americans were committing: breaking into homes, searching women. "Do you agree with this?" he demanded of the crowd. "No!" they shouted back. Dhari reminded his audience that the Iraqis knew how to resist occupation, recalling the 1920 revolution against the British, when Sunnis and Shiites had fought together. As prayers ended and the men streamed out of the mosque, their bellicose spirit continued with shouts of "No to colonialism!" "No to the occupiers!" The crowd chanted rhyming slogans calling for the extermination of the infidel army, for Baghdad to revolt, and for Paul Bremer to follow the fate of Nuri as-Said, the British-protected prime minister who was killed by mobs in 1958. Leaflets distributed during the demonstration contained a statement calling on Muslims around the world to come to their aid to confront the atheist occupying forces and to re-establish the Islamic caliphate to defeat the American and British aggression.

A few weeks later, on August 11, the Association of Muslim Scholars issued a statement condemning American violation of the mosques, which they said even the Mongols had not done. Iraq's Islamic endowments were now being looted by criminals "from across the border," meaning Shiites from Iran. The statement claimed that seventeen mosques had been robbed with the blessing of American forces. While acknowledging Grand Ayatollah Ali al-Sistani for his statements protecting Sunni mosques, they blamed the Americans for giving Shiites too much power, including control over the ministry of religious endowments. These Shiites did not protest the arrests of thirty clerics or the American violation of holy places.

The Rise of the Sadr Current

The Sadr Current, as its supporters describe it, was a surprise to all outside observers of Iraq and even most middle-and upper-class Iraqis, but there were clues in the 1990s that this was a growing movement. Following the Gulf War, many Iraqis fled to Saudi Arabia or surrendered to the Americans. In the refugee camps where they were housed, fighting erupted between supporters of the Sadr Current and the rival Supreme Council of Hakim. The Hakim family was perceived to represent the elite; it also backed Ayatollah Khomeini's system of clerical rule, known as *wilayat al-faqih*. Although theological differences existed, the bitter rivalry between followers of Hakim and Sadr can best be seen as both a class conflict and a symptom of the resentment of Iraqi nationalist Shiites who stayed in Iraq toward Hakim and his followers, who were in exile in Iran.

The Sadrists are inspired by the example and teachings of Ayatollah Muhammad Baqir al-Sadr, arguably the most important Shiite theologian of the twentieth century, who challenged the quietist and traditional role of the Shiite clerical establishment, known as the *hawza*. He eventually confronted Saddam and was executed by him in 1980. His cousin Ayatollah Muhammad Sadiq al-Sadr inherited his mantle, building an immense following among poor Shiites. Much as the Iraqi Communists once exploited the revolutionary potential of poor Shiites, so too did the Sadrists. The Shiite masses were attracted to these movements not so much for their ideology but for their anger. The *hawza* had historically been dominated by the traditional Shiite view that religious leaders should eschew politics and focus on the spiritual world and on advising their flock. In the 1950s, however, responding to government oppression and encroaching Western secularist trends, a more activist brand of Shiism developed. The activist Shiites sometimes referred to themselves as the outspoken *hawza*, or the revolutionary *hawza*, or active *faala*, and they disparagingly viewed their introverted counterparts as the silent *hawza*.

In many ways the Sadrists are the subalterns of Iraq, part of the recurring phenomenon of Iraqi mass politics. The Sadrists rejected the obscure theological obsession of the establishment because they had little to do with the daily struggles of real people. Although Muhammad Sadiq al-Sadr was killed in 1999 along with his more prominent sons, his surviving son, Muqtada, along with Muhammad's top students, Muhammad al-Yaqoubi and Kadhim al-Haeri, led the movement in the underground phase it assumed until 2003. The Sadrists viewed attendance at Friday prayers, and particularly the Friday sermon, as an act of defiance and revolution, the moment when followers gathered, often pouring in the thousands into the streets, as a powerful collective. The Sadrists were fierce Iraqi nationalists and Arab nationalists, even pro-Palestinian. They were not Persianized, unlike Dawa and the Supreme Council.

Muqtada, the populist upstart who inherited his father's network of mosques and clerics, led the revolutionary class of poor Shiites. Educated and middle-class followers of his father split from him and joined the Fadhila movement, led by Yaqoubi. A dialectic developed between Muqtada and the angry masses: he followed them as much as they followed him. Soon the CIA would order its analysts to stop using the word "firebrand" every time they described him, and to find some variety.

Immediately after the war, Muqtada and his network seized control of the Shiite sections of Baghdad and much of the south, and to occupy hospitals, Baath Party headquarters, and government warehouses, establishing themselves as the state in much of Iraq. Sunnis were the primary victims of the murderous settling of scores that began on April 9, 2003. The killers were usually Kurds or Shiites. Thousands of Arab families were also expelled from areas in the north of Kirkuk and Diyala, which Kurdish militias perceived as part of their territory. After Baghdad fell, angry Shiite mobs in the newly named Sadr City slaughtered radical Sunni foreign fighters, even burning tires around their necks. Many Iraqis wanted revenge. These foreign fedayeen had been given weapons and the authority to control Baghdad's streets before the war. In April 2003 I met with a Shiite young man whose ear was cut by a group of Arab mujahideen because they accused him of being a deserter. Just as frightening for Sunnis was the seizure of their mosques throughout Iraq. Following the 1991 Shiite intifada, Saddam ordered the construction of large Sunni mosques in Shiite-dominated cities throughout the south. These were often named "the Great Saddam Mosque." Immediately after the regime collapsed, these and other Sunni mosques were occupied by Shiites.

"It is the beginning of the separation," one Shiite cleric explained to me with a smile in May 2003. Immediately after the war Sunni clerics complained that at least thirty of their mosques had been taken over by Shiites and issued statements in newspapers demanding their return, but they were never returned. In some cases Shiites were reclaiming places of worship that Saddam had seized and given to Sunnis. This was the case with the Shiite Hassan Mosque in Karbala, which was given to Sunni hardliners in the 1990s.

According to a friend of mine in Najaf, the cleric Sheikh Heidar al-Mimar, "There were no Sunnis in Najaf before the 1991 intifada, but Saddam brought all these Wahhabis to the Shiite provinces in order to control Shiites. These Wahhabis were very bad with us, and all Shiites were afraid of them. Saddam wanted to Sunni-ize Najaf and Karbala." As a result, following the war these Sunni interlopers were immediately targeted by the inchoate Shiite militias.

Shiite pilgrims traditionally donated money to the shrines of the imams they visited. This money added up to millions of dollars every month. Shiites believed Saddam used it in the 1990s to finance his Faith Campaign, which involved promoting Sunni practices in Iraq and even, for the first time, tolerance toward Wahhabis, perhaps because of their deep hatred for Shiites. Shiites resented the alleged theft of their money for Sunni purposes and sought to impose justice after the war. In July 2003 members of Muqtada al-Sadr's Mahdi Army militia even debated seizing the giant Um Al Qura Mosque in Baghdad's Sunni bastion of Ghazaliya. The mosque served as the headquarters for the

Association of Muslim Scholars, the neo-Baathist body that had been formed just after the American invasion to protect Sunni interests and unite Sunni leaders under the command of the Baathists-turned-clerics who would soon control much of the insurgency.

The revolutionary Shiite wave that swept Iraq in the wake of the American invasion overthrew the order that had existed in Iraq until then. Shiites would not let history repeat itself. On April 7 Ayatollah Kadhim al-Haeri, a cleric born in the Iraqi city of Karbala but exiled in the Iranian holy city of Qom since 1973, appointed Muqtada as his deputy and representative in Iraq for all *fatwa* affairs. Haeri urged Iraqis to kill all Baathists to prevent them from taking over again. In the southern city of Kut on April 18, Abdul Aziz al-Hakim, brother of Shiite opposition leader Muhammad Bakr al-Hakim and leader of the Supreme Council's ten thousand–strong Badr Brigade militia, proclaimed that Shiites were the majority in Iraq and hinted that they hoped for an Islamic government. That same day in Baghdad, Sheikh Muhammad al-Fartusi, Muqtada's deputy for Baghdad, warned that Shiites would not accept a democracy that would obstruct their sovereignty. If Shiites did not have a say in the government, he said, it would be worse than under Saddam.

In late April 2003 Shiites staged a massive celebration of their identity and show of force. They descended in the millions upon Karbala for Arbaeen, the day marking the end of the forty-day mourning period for the Prophet Muhammad's slain grandson Hussein. These ceremonies had been severely restricted under Saddam, and it was the first time anybody could remember openly expressing such pride in their identity as Shiites. Sunnis watched with concern and some disdain for rituals they rejected as un-Islamic or primitive. On my way down to Karbala, I was detained by armed Shiite men who feared I was a Wahhabi. I talked and smiled my way out of it. Being an American wasn't so bad in those days. At the time the incident did not seem significant, but in retrospect I realized it was: members of a Shiite militia were protecting their village from Sunni extremists—as early as April 2003. Throughout the ceremonies it was clear that Shiites were terrified of a phantom Wahhabi threat. In centuries past Wahhabis had swept up from Arabia and sacked Shiite shrines. Now Shiites feared Wahhabis would poison the food distributed to pilgrims. Soon many Shiites would view all Sunnis as Wahhabis.

The ceremonies of Arbaeen and the more important holiday that precedes it by a month, Ashura, are not merely individual acts of contrition. They are performed collectively and publicly by Shiites, and these rituals unite and define the Shiite sense of community. For nearly two months of the year Shiites are engaged in these unique rituals and mourning processions. The messages are lashed into their bodies and minds. The virtues of Shiite leaders are contrasted to the alleged immorality of early Sunni leaders, who supposedly stole the mantle of leadership wrongly from Hussein and showed no mercy to his family, even the children. The founders of the Umayyad dynasty, perceived to be usurpers of the throne that should have gone to descendants of the Prophet through his cousin and son-in-law Ali (Hussein's father), are condemned—and by implication so are their followers, Sunni Muslims. That first Arbaeen after the war was marked by Shiites not with the traditional sorrow or mourning that lead to flagellation and crying but with triumphalism. Iraq was now theirs. The Shiites who made their way to Karbala were united in one message: the *hawza*, or Shiite theological seminary and seat of the ayatollahs in Najaf, was their leader. Banners, songs, statements, all demanded that the *hawza* should lead Iraq. These sentiments did nothing to assuage Sunni fears, nor were they consistent with the promises of exiles such as Ahmad Chalabi, who promised that Iraq's Shiites were secular and sought democracy. A few years later Shiite religious parties like the Supreme Council would control the country, and their militias would become the Iraqi police and army, running their own secret prisons, arresting, torturing, and executing Sunnis. Iraq now belonged to the followers of Muhammad Baqir al-Sadr and his relative Muhammad Sadiq al-Sadr—the first and second martyr, respectively. Even Ahmad Chalabi, during the December 2005 elections, waved posters of Sistani in Sadr City after Sistani was criticized on Al Jazeera.

IN MARCH 2004 I witnessed the Ashura bombings that killed nearly 200 Shiite pilgrims in both the holy city of Karbala and Baghdad's Kadhimiya district. These attacks failed to provoke massive retaliation, but the sectarian violence did increase. A few days after the bombings, in Baghdad's Shurta neighborhood, an SUV with masked men shot up a Shiite mosque; several days after that a Sunni cleric was killed in a drive-by shooting while walking to his mosque for the evening prayer. Hundreds attended his funeral, which was guarded by a phalange of very anxious armed men. Surrounded by his bodyguards, Sheikh Ahmad Abdel Ghafur al-Samarai of the Association of Muslim Scholars spoke at the funeral, calling on the youth to protect their religious leaders. It was like calling for the creation of self-defense militias. Following the murder of another Sunni sheikh, Dhamer al-Dhari, Samarai blamed the Americans for paying mercenaries to commit murders and cause sectarian strife. At the same time, he blamed the Americans for favoring the Shiites and discriminating against the Sunnis, and criticized them for not disarming the Kurdish and Shiite militias. Samarai also called for uniting Sunnis to prevent other militias from taking over, and blamed the occupiers and the Zionists for playing with Iraq's factions. No one seemed to be talking about Sunni-Shiite unity anymore.

Two nights after the Ashura bombings, the Qiba Mosque—a Sunni mosque in a Shiite stronghold in Baghdad's Shaab district—was attacked. I had befriended a young man my age called Firas from the neighborhood; he called to tip me off about this, adding that the mosque was for "Wahhabis." I asked the hotel where I was staying for its taxi driver, but I didn't explain why I was going to Shaab. Not a single car was out as we drove for twenty minutes from the city center to the mosque. The streets of Shaab were misty and unlit. The road before the mosque was blocked by a truck and about twenty men holding Kalashnikovs.

They surrounded the taxi, and young men in shabby civilian clothes pointed their barrels in through our windows. They demanded to know who we were and what we wanted. They were very tense. I asked the one on my side who he was, but he ordered me out of the car. The taxi driver explained that I was not an Iraqi. "He's a foreigner!" they shouted to one another, and all the men came to the car. We tried to explain that I was a journalist, but they had never seen an American passport or a press ID before. Why was I here? What did I want? It was clear from the fear in their eyes and the anger in their voices that they wanted to find somebody to kill. They used none of the polite expressions that color even hostile Arabic conversation. They only gave orders, as if we were their prisoners, their voices echoing against the empty city's buildings.

The man with the slurred voice pointed his Kalashnikov at me and ordered me out of the car in a drunken rage. The driver and I protested that I was just a journalist, here to investigate an attack. Not knowing if they were Sunni or Shiite, I recited the names of every Iraqi Sunni and Shiite leader I could think of and said they were all my friends. I won over two men and they began struggling with the drunk man, who still wanted to shoot me. An argument broke out over whether or not they should kill me. The drunk man would not move the barrel down as they tried to push it, and I moved away from its sway- ing range. The others were undecided and nervously eyed me. One man rushed me into the mosque for safety. More armed guards stood inside. I tried to remember how to speak Arabic and felt ashamed that my knees were very weak. It was the first time I had ever been confronted with death. They con- firmed that after the last prayer that night, as the devout were emptying onto the street, a car had driven by and opened fire. "Praise God, nobody was wounded," they said, pointing to the white gashes in the wall where the bul- lets had torn chunks of plaster off. They added that only a few months ago, the same thing had happened. More men holding their Kalashnikovs in a ready-for-fire position came out.

The next morning I returned. Shaab's streets were busy with children play- ing amid garbage and sewage pools. Donkeys pulled carts carrying gas for stoves, and boys banged on the containers to let the neighborhood know they were passing. Before the war many forbidden Shiite books were printed ille- gally in Shaab, and it was known as the "Little Hawza." American soldiers manned a checkpoint along with fresh Iraqi recruits, searching suspicious cars. A house near the mosque was riddled with bullets and burned. It belonged to a Wahhabi Muslim who had been killed in the summer of 2003 by local Shiites.

Sheikh Walid Al-Dulaimi, the leader of the Qiba Mosque, was well liked in the neighborhood for being a friend to the Shiites, and locals said he even had problems with the previous regime because of this. Abu Hasan, the mosque caretaker, was busy fixing the generator, his hands and *dishdasha* robe blackened with grease. He explained that the attackers had opened fire from two cars, an Opel sedan and a Nissan pickup, at 7:30 the previous evening. They were dressed like police, he said, and before they managed to fire an RPG, one of the bystanders had grabbed it from them. "They want to create *fitna* [strife] between Sunnis and Shiites, but it won't happen. I am sixty years old. I have never seen any problems between us. We intermarry and are friends. America is responsible for this." Abu Hasan added that Shiites from the city and from nearby Sadr City had visited the mosque to show solidarity. Sheikh Dhia from the local Shurufi Mosque came along with tribal leaders. "We are a targeted mosque because Sunnis and Shiites both come here and are united," he said. He insisted that fifty-two Sunni visitors had also been killed in the Kadhimiya attacks along with the Shiite victims.

The mosque was first attacked in August of the previous year, he said, and three people had been wounded. After last night's attack the police shot a man in the leg in a case of mistaken identity. Sayyid Nasr of the Sayyid Haidar Husseiniya—a *husseiniya* is a Shiite place of worship and communal gathering— also visited the Qiba Mosque to pay respects with thirty friends and relatives. As the honorific title of "sayyid" revealed, he was a descendant of the Prophet Muhammad, and thus respected. He was also the oldest and best-known sayyid in Shaab. I visited his large home, which was down the street from a wall with posters of Ayatollahs Khomeini and Khamenei. The walls of his study were decorated with posters of Supreme Council leader Muhammad Bakr al-Hakim, who had been slain six months earlier in Najaf, as well as other ayatollahs. Nasr wore a black turban and thick glasses. "Our good leaders will prevent *fitna*," he said. He explained that when he visited the Qiba Mosque, he told the gathered people that "I am Sunni and I am Shiite. We are all Muslims." He was certain that "there will not be any problems between us," and blamed Zarqawi for the attacks.

He explained that the Wahhabi who had been killed the previous summer and whose house had been burned the night before was called Muhamad. On the day of Hakim's murder in August 2003, Muhamad had gone to a nearby square that had a painting of the late Muhammad Sadiq al-Sadr and Ali al-Sistani. "Muhamad spit and threw stones at the paintings, and then shot at them with his Kalashnikov," Nasr said. "He killed one Shiite and wounded another. After that the men from the neighborhood shot him and burned his house. The Americans came to take his body and found many weapons in his house as well as pictures of bin Laden." Muhamad was from the Dulaimi tribe, and in order to make peace the Dulaimis gave monetary compensation to the family of the murdered Shiite. "After this Sunnis and Shiites prayed together in the Qiba Mosque, and tomorrow we will do so again." Nasr also mentioned that fifty-two Sunnis had perished in the Baghdad explosions. When I went to find the leader of the Qiba mosque, he did not unlock his door; instead, he suspiciously peered out, and even after being reassured that I was only a journalist, he did not remove the Kalashnikov strapped around his torso for a moment, afraid of everybody.

The Cleansing of Amriya

In the summer of 2003 I met two young Sunni clerics in the Sunni stronghold of Amriya, who I would come across many times over the next few years. Sheikh Hussein Abu Mustafa, a round dark man with a round black beard and white turban, and Sheikh Walid were old friends. They had graduated together from the Baghdad Islamic Institute. I met them both in Sheikh Walid's Tikriti Mosque, which had been built in 1999 by the head of intelligence. What happened to them over the next few years in many ways symbolized the topsy-turvy experience of many influential anti-occupation Sunnis. They were the first Sunni clerics I had met who seemed to be offering strong support to the Iraqi resistance. "We are very happy with the resistance of the Iraqi people to the American occupation, but we don't support killing civilians and innocent people and taking impulsive actions," they said.

When I revisited Amriya and saw Sheikh Hussein in March 2004, mosque security was higher than ever. Amriya had been home to former Iraq military bases as well as former officers in the army and intelligence services. The sounds of gunfire and explosions reverberated through the neighborhood's walls, ignored by the children playing in the street until a particularly loud explosion sent them scurrying inside. Neighbors spoke of the nightly attacks and raids. Just last night, they said, U.S. soldiers had raided a house, and when the suspect was not found they took his younger brother. Nearby was the house of a former intelligence officer. When the U.S. soldiers came for him, his family said he was not home and he escaped, wisely trading his conspicuous SUV for a smaller, older wreck of a car. And also last night, they said, from this very street—"We saw them," they laughed—a car pulled over and shot three artillery rounds at the nearby base where U.S. soldiers trained the new Iraqi Security Forces. One round landed in a small mosque by the walls of the base, damaging its tower; one went over and past the base; and one landed somewhere inside.

The walls of the Maluki Mosque were covered in pro-Saddam graffiti that had been unsuccessfully crossed out. Neighborhood boys surrounded it at prayer time, wielding Kalashnikovs unconvincingly. As the men strolled in for the Friday prayer, they were searched for concealed weapons. Slowly several hundred of the neighborhood men entered, greeting one another and gossiping in the courtyard and then removing their shoes and entering. As the muezzin finished his call to prayer, Sheikh Hussein carefully stepped between the closely seated worshipers, making his way to the podium and climbing up the steps. He began with blessings and reminded the people who their God and Prophet was, his voice low, slow, and gentle, his arms still; then he picked up the pace, arms waving faster, voice getting higher as he got more excited, until his voice cracked and he was nearly crying, chopping the air in a frenzy; and then he placed both hands out in supplication, his voice exasperated, slowing down as he answered his own questions, only to begin the cycle again, from low raspy rumble to the screaming crescendo that woke up those whose heads had sunk lower and lower into their chest in drowsiness.

Sheikh Hussein began by discussing Ali, whom Sunnis consider the fourth caliph, who succeeded the Prophet Muhammad in leadership of the umma (Muslim nation). Ali is also revered by Shiites as the only caliph who should have followed Muhammad, since he was the Prophet's relative. "Ali was the first feday [fighter willing to sacrifice his life] in Islam," Sheikh Hussein lectured. "He taught the nation how to sacrifice oneself. Be like Ali and sacrifice yourself for Islam. Be like Hassan, who tried to unify the people and who compromised with Muawiya for the sake of unity so the Muslim world would not be weak like our situation now." This was interesting. Hassan was the son of Ali, who expected to succeed his father as caliph but was turned down for Muawiya, a man from a family that rivaled the Prophet's Hashem tribe. At first Hassan disputed Muawiya's claim to leadership, but he ultimately compromised. Shiekh Hussein's reference to this episode could only be directed at Iraq's Shiites, the descendants of those who had wanted Muhammad's family, starting with Ali, to lead Muslims. He was asking them to compromise and let Muawiya's descendants, the Sunnis, maintain power.

"Muhammad prophesied when Hassan was a child," Sheikh Hussein explained, "that 'my grandson will one day reconcile between two sects of Islam.' Be like Hassan so we will be strong." It seemed Sheikh Hussein might avoid mentioning Hassan's more recalcitrant brother, Hussein, who chose to dispute the claim of Muawiya's family after Muawiya and Hassan both died and Yazid, Muawiya's son, was appointed caliph. "We condemn the attacks in Karbala and Baghdad," he declared. "The first goal of the enemies of Islam is to make this country weak. They have a plan to make this country weak by causing a sectarian war so people will be busy fighting each other and they can control it, and our enemy the occupier will remain seated on our chests. So we condemn these attacks that are designed to provoke a sectarian war in this country." Sheikh Hussein also condemned an earlier attack in Baghdad that had killed a young Shiite cleric. Then he continued, with a surprise, "We have to unify and be like Hussein, the martyr of Karbala, because he sacrificed himself for this country where many warriors were born. Hussein came to Iraq to fight a tyrant because he said, 'I will not allow a tyrant to rule,' and he did not want oppression. So he came to teach the people that any Muslim should sacrifice himself to prevent the creation of tyranny, and Hussein defined the path of martyrdom for the people who followed him and told them to follow it." This is something you rarely hear from a Sunni. The divide between Hussein and Yazid split the Muslim world into Sunnis and Shiites and led to centuries of *fitna* between the two communities, with Shiites revering Hussein and hating Yazid and Muawiya, and Sunnis defending them and disparaging Hussein and his followers. "We are sorry, Hussein," the sheikh cried out. "We are ashamed to meet you in the next life, because Baghdad has fallen." By the end of the sermon, Sheikh Hussein had lost his voice and was too exhausted to talk to me.

After prayer was over Sheikh Hussein shook hands with many of his flock, and they embraced and kissed in the way Sunnis of western Iraq do. (Sheikh Hussein is from the Dulaimi tribe, whose stronghold is the western Anbar province.) He then retreated to his house inside the mosque, where he feasted with his guests from the nearby town of Abu Ghraib as his horde of little boys sat in the corners. American helicopters flew low overhead, shaking the room while Sheikh Hussein and his guests discussed the latest killings of sheikhs and attacks on mosques, and grumbled about the Americans.

In late 2003 at least four people were killed and seven injured when a drive-by shooting targeted the Hassanein Mosque in Amriya after the evening prayers. Sheikh Adnan, the cleric, explained that Shiite militiamen had attacked former regime intelligence men who were praying there. Some locals complained that Sunnis were complacent while attacks were perpetrated against them with impunity. Sheikh Adnan warned that this would lead to worse trouble for Shiites and Sunnis. He also complained that when Sunni clerics went to pay their condolences after the killing of Ayatollah Muhammad Bakr al-Hakim of the Supreme Council, they were called "Jewish Wahhabis."

THE MOOD WAS COARSENING in Amriya. Wall advertisements that featured photos of women were painted black to remove the female faces. Amriya is a wealthy neighborhood too; it has many English-speaking citizens, some of whom worked as translators with the American military. Many of them were killed; many others had to flee Amriya for safer neighborhoods. In the months leading up to the first election for a provisional national assembly in January 2005, Amriya's streets were full of leaflets and walls calling for "death for those who disappoint what they had promised God," meaning death for those participating in the election. Some insurgent groups patrolled the streets at night and launched their mortars toward the airport. Hundreds of Shiite families were brutally cleansed from the area; they would find sanctuary in areas under the control of the Sadrists.

Jafar was a Shiite originally from the predominantly Shiite town of Nasiriya in southeast Iraq. His family moved to Baghdad in 1940 but maintained connections with their tribe in the south. Jafar lived in Amriya in a big house with his seventy-year-old mother, two of his brothers, and their wives. Each brother had three or four children. The family was known in Amriya for practicing the Shiite tradition of cooking food and giving it away to poor people on Ashura; they did this even under the former regime, when it was permitted in the last two years of Baath rule.

Mueisar, Jafar's third brother, was a soldier in the Iraqi army and was captured at the beginning of the Iran-Iraq War in 1982. He had been a soldier with the Badr Brigade—who were stationed in Iran as an armed exile group—but he was too physically weak to be a soldier, so he left it in 2001. Mueisar returned home to Amriya after the U.S. invasion, accompanied by his Iranian wife and three children. He was the only member of his Iranian family who spoke Arabic. When he returned to Amriya Mueisar registered his children in the local school so that they could learn Arabic and mix with other Arab children.

A few days after the second battle of Falluja started in late 2004, a new family belonging to the biggest Sunni tribe, the Dulaimi, moved to Amriya to live with their relatives, the Abu Khalel family, who were Jafar's neighbors. Just like many displaced families who fled Falluja, they were too poor to rent a house, so they were hosted by relatives. Because Amriya's houses are often large enough to host large families, many displaced decided to go there. A few days later some Shiite families received threats demanding that they leave their houses. After one Shiite family vacated their house, which stood next to the one Abu Khalel owned, his relatives took it over.

Jafar's family had been trying to sell their house since 2003, because each brother wanted to have his own house near his work. But it was very old, and they did not get the price they wanted. Jafar and his brothers were shocked on September 4, 2005, when they found an envelope in their garage containing a letter with printed script threatening their lives if they did not leave their home within forty-eight hours. The text said: "In the name of God, do not think God is unaware of what the oppressors are doing. To Anwar, Shubbar, Mueisar, and Jafar: We are watching your movements step after step, and we know that you have betrayed God and his messenger, for that we give you forty-eight hours to leave Amriya forever, and you should thank God that you are still alive. And there will be no excuse after this warning."

The writer was not very well versed in the Koran. The letter had no header or signature to reveal its origins, and there was no hint suggesting which jihadi group had issued it. It seemed more like a threat from somebody angry at the family than from someone involved in jihadist activities. Despite this, the family did not want to risk ignoring the letter.

Jafar's family was one of four Shiite families living on a street that had twelve Sunni homes, but his became the third Shiite family on that street to flee Amriya within a month. One of the families had a son working as a translator with the U.S. Army; they fled the area after he was murdered at the gate of his home. The other had a son working in the Iraqi police; they also fled after receiving a threat. Jafar's family took their threat seriously and started calling relatives and seeking help to find another house to live in before the forty-eight-hour deadline ran out. They also rushed to tell all the neighbors that they were leaving in order to send the message to whoever had made the threat.

More refugees from the siege of Falluja settled in western Baghdad neighborhoods such as Ghazaliya, Amriya, and Khadra, as well as in the villages just west of Baghdad such as Abu Ghraib. These were majority-Sunni strongholds where both insurgents and Salafis had a formidable presence. Soon after, more Shiite families in Amriya received threats urging them to leave. Those who ignored the threats had their homes attacked or their men murdered by Sunni militias. Shiites began to take these threats more seriously, and the process of sectarian cleansing began. Homes vacated by Shiites were seized by displaced Sunnis. These operations were conducted by insurgents as well as relatives of the displaced who wanted to house them somewhere. Shiites, in turn, fled to areas controlled by Muqtada al-Sadr's supporters.

"And speed the appearance of the Mahdi, and damn his enemies and make victorious his son Muqtada! Muqtada! Muqtada!"

In Baghdad's Kadhim Mosque, in the northern district of Kadhimiya, in the spring of 2004, the Shiite faithful began the traditional chorus of "Our God prays for Muhammad and Muhammad's family." But they continued with a strange innovation: "And speed the appearance of the Mahdi, and damn his enemies and make victorious his son Muqtada! Muqtada! Muqtada!" This had never been heard before, but Turkmen Shiites were shouting it at demonstrations in front of the Coalition Provisional Authority headquarters and repeating it in their daily prayers. Thousands of Muqtada's followers, including two thousand members of his militia, demonstrated at a February 27 show of force in Kirkuk.

I first met Muqtada al-Sadr in May 2003, when he was just beginning to outrage the Shiite establishment embodied in the *hawza*. Each *marja* (cleric) had his
own office and received a tithe from his followers. Muqtada came out of
nowhere, with no experience or education, but he commanded thousands of
young men almost immediately. He spoke in the name of his revered father and
of the *mustad'afin* (the poor and downtrodden masses), and he spoke in their language, Iraqi dialect and its slang, much as his father had. He alone was known by
his first name, because Iraq's Shiite masses felt a personal bond with him. While
Iranian-born Ayatollah Ali al-Sistani was the most respected religious authority
for Iraq's Shiites, Muqtada represented them, he spoke for them, he led them politically and spiritually. Tens of thousands would die for him. He was the most
important person in Iraq after the war, and his power has only grown. Chubby,
with an unkempt beard, he was awkward and unsure of himself back then, coming across more like an arrogant street punk with a lisp than a religious leader
among Najaf's refined and somewhat snobbish clerical aristocracy.

He rejected all other Shiite clerics and scoffed at America, but it would be
nearly a year before his men would openly fight the occupation. Still, he
warned that the time would come. His men had already taken over much of
Shiite Iraq, providing social services and security and imposing their strict interpretation of Islam on women and more liberal Muslims. His network of
clerics coordinated their sermons, and his *bayanat* (statements) were posted on
mosque walls throughout Iraq.

On June 23, 2003, Muqtada, having just returned from a trip to Iran—where
he had met with government officials and Ayatollah Haeri, his father's official
successor and intellectual heir, and commemorated the death of Ayatollah
Khomeini—visited Baghdad for the first time since his father's death in 1999.
He visited the neighborhoods of Kadhimiya and Shula before arriving in Sadr
City, where tens of thousands greeted him with Iraqi flags as well as flags from
the Bahadal, Msaare, Al Jazair, and Fawawda tribes. Before Muqtada took the
stage, a speaker read the victory verse from the Koran: "If you receive God's
victory and you witness people joining Islam in great numbers, thank your
God and ask him to forgive you, for God is very merciful." People chanted:
"Muqtada, don't worry! We will sacrifice our blood for the *hawza*!" A melody
for a song that had once praised Saddam now carried a song praising Muqtada.
There was a lot of clapping, and a speaker asked the people to make way for
Muqtada, but they would not move, each wanting to get closer to their
revered leader. "I visited this city when my father was alive, and I will visit this
city on this day every year," Muqtada cried. "People should join the *hawza* and
the *marjas* and support them . . . do not believe in rumors, verify them with
the *hawza* first . . . a humanitarian office will be established for Sadr City."
Muqtada spoke of the memory of the martyrs and promised the Iraqi people
that the unemployment problem would soon be solved because companies

would return to Iraq. He spoke for seven minutes, after which the crowds of
adulators would not let him leave.

That month the U.S.-appointed Iraqi Governing Council proposed including Muqtada as a member, but other Shiite members on the council rejected
the idea. Muqtada and his constituency were radicalized by the exclusion, and
he was pushed further into the arms of Haeri, who was living in exile in Iran.
Though Muqtada's politics were inchoate, lacking ideology and seeking only
inclusion and power, Haeri was a rigid Khomeinist, with a clearly defined political program aimed at establishing a theocracy in Iraq, just as Khomeini had
established his in Iran twenty-five years ago when he ousted the monarch.

The next month, on July 20, Muqtada claimed that American soldiers had
surrounded his home and were planning to arrest him. Thousands of protesters descended upon Najaf, heeding their leader's call. Many were bused or
trucked in from Baghdad or Basra. Some even came in ambulances. They confronted American soldiers and marines. Demonstrators chanted, "No Americans after today," echoing the motto of Saddam's storm troopers in the 1991
intifada, who had ransacked southern Iraq warning that there would be "no
Shiites after today." Demonstrators also chanted against America, colonialism,
tyranny, and the devil. Some carried swords and flags. Clerics bellowed condemnations of the Americans, comparing them to Saddam. Their protest in
Najaf opened with a message from Haeri, read aloud to the crowd. Haeri condemned the "American agents" of the Iraqi Governing Council and called on
the clerics to rule Iraq. Meeting outside the shrine of Ali, they walked past Najaf's cemetery in rows and columns, like soldiers. Marching to the American
base in Najaf, Sheikh Aws al-Khafaji spoke out against the Americans and the
IGC, accusing them of spreading corruption and defiling the holy city of Najaf. The leaders of the protest handed a list of demands to an American
colonel, demanding that Americans leave Najaf immediately.

Muqtada continued to test the limits of Americans' tolerance, sometimes
virtually declaring war on them, then retreating and welcoming them as
friends. In March 2004 the Americans closed his newspaper, *Al Hawza*, accusing it of calling for violence, and arrested an influential associate of his. This
further alienated his followers from the American-led project in Iraq and increased his prestige and following among Shiites, whose sect is preoccupied
with martyrdom and resisting oppression.

Following the January 2005 elections, Muqtada's representatives in the National Assembly demanded a timetable for a U.S. withdrawal, a demand also
made by Sunni rejectionists. The initiative had the support of 120 of the 275 Assembly members. Muqtada joined these Sunni rejectionists in condemning the
draft constitution—especially its federalism—warning that it would lead to the
break up of Iraq. Like Sunni Arabs in Iraq, Muqtada opposed federalism for
the Kurds as well as the move by Supreme Council leader Abdul Aziz al-Hakim

to establish autonomous Shiite regions in the south on the model of the northern Kurdish Regional Government. Muqtada's followers demonstrated against
the Constitution, marching with Sunnis in some cases. In the summer of 2005,
militiamen loyal to Muqtada clashed with Supreme Council militiamen in several Iraqi cities, including Baghdad, Nasiriya, Najaf, and Amara. Despite the tensions between Supreme Council and the Sadrists, Muqtada was invited by
Supreme Council and Dawa to join the United Iraqi Alliance, the dominant Shiite list competing in the December 15 elections for the National Assembly. They
needed the numbers he could provide. Muqtada was granted equal status with
the two other parties and potentially more than thirty seats in the Assembly. He
was legitimate now, it seemed, no longer on the outside. Later that year he visited Saudi Arabia on the hajj pilgrimage as an official guest of the Saudi king,
and then he visited Iran, Syria, and Lebanon, practicing his diplomatic skills but
also establishing a close relationship with Syrian leader Bashar al-Assad and with
Lebanese Shiites. Muqtada would be the protector of newly targeted Shiites, and
their avenger.

The articles that the Sunnis were reading in their newspapers, as well as the
statements of prominent Sunni leaders however, made it clear that the alliance
with Muqtada's militant Shiites was a temporary measure to battle a common
foe. One article in *Basair*, (The Mind's Eye), a newspaper published by the Association of Muslim Scholars, condemned the (Shiite) police for killing Sunnis
"for the benefit of groups for whom the police work [the Americans]," and
supported the (Sunni) resistance's attacks on the police. "Iraqis know about
the conspiracy to cause sectarian strife among them," an article began, quoting accusations made by Naseer Chadarchi, a Sunni member of the Iraqi Governing Council, that "thousands of Iranians [Shiites] are sneaking into Iraq."
"They should not get citizenship, as already happened in Amara, where 10,000
Iranians received Iraqi citizenship." The article, voicing typical Sunni paranoia
that all Shiites were in fact illegal Iranians, suggested that "many groups are
sneaking into Iraq to get passports" and hinted at the Sunni fear of a democracy that would result in the Shiite majority determining the shape of the new
country. "This is why some people [meaning Shiites] want direct elections and
a census that will benefit them," the article continued.

Another article expanded on this theme, describing the "dangerous demographic changes in Iraq after the war" and referring again to an imagined influx of Iranians who created a Shiite majority. "Occupation forces will change
the demography of Iraq for their benefit," the article warned, "using the huge
capabilities of the occupation forces, their intelligence and experience in this
field. These new demographic changes are worse than Saddam's because they
[Americans] are using migrations, economic rules and killing to increase the
population of certain sects such as Iranians, Kurds and Turks. We want to say
that the reaction [meaning violent attacks] of Arabs [meaning Sunnis] in the

west and south is a reaction to these changes. Jordan and Saudi Arabia are also part of Iraq, so there are more Arabs [Sunnis] but borders separate them. America is the cause of these changes."

The article attributed the secret plot to "the Jewish and Zionist strategy in the Middle East and the security of Israel in the future." The author warned that "these demographic changes and their direct effects on future elections and the type of government will lead to a civil war to divide Iraq, and we will have a racist government that will oppress most nationalities and minorities." The author explained that "Iranians want to increase the ratio of Persians among the [Arab] Shiites, which will increase the ratio of Shiites in Iraq and Baghdad in hidden and declared ways."

Dora—First Outbreaks of Civil War

Dora, in southern Baghdad, was one of the first areas where the civil war began. Although mixed, it was majority Sunni. The cleansing of Dora's Shiites was mostly carried out by local insurgents who lived in the adjoining rural areas of Arab Jubur and Hor Rajab, but some of it was conducted by crooks who kidnapped members of rich families and demanded money for their release.

Solaf was a thirty-three-year-old carpenter working out of his large house in Dora. He was the youngest of five brothers and one sister from the poor Abu Mohammed family, which had lived in Dora since 1974. Mohammed, the eldest brother, joined the police in mid-2004, and in May 2005 he was told he would be killed if he did not quit. Mohammed moved out of his parents' house and rented a small house in eastern Baghdad's majority-Shiite Shaab district, but because he had no other profession to turn to, he kept his job as a policeman.

It took Solaf's family more than a month to find a good offer on their house. In mid-July 2005 they finally agreed to sell, though there was a delay in signing the contract. Solaf's street was full of children every evening, and he would spend many nights sitting at the gate of his home chatting with friends. On July 28 he was sitting there as usual with one of his Sunni friends when a white Hyundai stopped a few meters away from them. An unmasked gunman emerged wearing civilian clothes and started shooting, killing Solaf and his friend. Solaf's brothers and his relatives gathered the next day and buried his body. On the second day of Solaf's funeral, the family received another letter warning them to leave the city. The family ended the funeral and left Dora forever.

A week after Solaf's murder, his mother phoned several of her old neighbors and bitterly complained about Sunnis and her family's new but much smaller house in the majority-Shiite neighborhood of Shuula. She said she had received a call from the mother of Solaf's Sunni friend. The Sunni man's mother told her that her family had received *jizia* (blood money) of two million Iraqi dinars and an apology from the mujahideen for killing her son, because Solaf had been the only target. Solaf had been targeted because his brother was in the police. The mujahideen who killed him were from the Jubur tribe, which dominated the insurgency in Dora and was the main Sunni tribe in Baghdad. Two Sunni families moved into Solaf's old house; among them was a twenty-four-year-old man named Mustafa, who was a member of the insurgency.

Haji E'nad was a Shiite who owned a shop on the corner just down the road from Solaf's house. At the end of September 2005, three unmasked gunmen raided his shop and killed his son Rashid. They walked away; they did not even use a car. Haji E'nad's family fled Dora the next day. They did not have a funeral, nor did they tell any of the neighbors where they were going. They simply locked the doors and moved out, leaving their property, and nobody in Dora heard from them again. Families were afraid to tell anybody that they had been threatened so as not to further antagonize those who had threatened them.

More followed suit. Abu Ali, a Shiite whose family had been neighbors of Solaf and who also said he had been threatened, sold his property and moved to Hilla province in mid-December 2005. One week later his neighbor Iyad, whose shop was about 100 meters away from Solaf's house, closed it and fled Dora, too. Iyad moved some of his most important property out, left the rest in one room, and locked the house. He phoned some neighbors two days later and asked them to watch the house and report any attack. He explained that he was afraid because he was Shiite and had a brother who had been executed by the former regime for allegedly belonging to the Dawa Party. "Dora is not for Shiites any more, and only Sunnis can live there," Iyad said. "Sunnis are attacking Shiites to force them to leave and sell their houses for cheap prices. I am not going to give my house to Sunnis for free." Although sectarianism was the primary motive, some Sunnis did derive economic benefit from the removal of Dora's Shiites. Soon poor Sunnis could purchase a good house in Dora and live among other Sunnis for much less than what they would normally have paid before.

The Brothers Mulla Murder Gang

Shiites had militias of their own, which were prepared to avenge the deaths in their community and sometimes to profit from the violence too. Maalif is a majority-Shiite neighborhood in Seidiya, which is in southwestern Baghdad. It was established in the late 1980s when the government decided to transfer tribes from villages in the Taji area north of Baghdad so that it could build a factory and a military camp where they had been living. The families preserved their tribal habits and traditions in the city. Maalif was divided among a few large tribes and a collection of other poor people (Sunnis and Shiites) who moved to the city in the 1990s for cheap living, but its population was overwhelmingly Shiite, unlike Seidiya, which is nearly evenly split. Being a poor neighborhood, Maalif tended to see higher rates of violence, criminality, and religiosity among its residents.

In Maalif people from the same tribe often enter the same profession and cause problems for outsiders seeking to compete. The Dilfi tribe had buses for transportation, the Chaab had pickups for transportation, and the Tual were all butchers. Hussein was a butcher from the Tual tribe who had about five butcher shops in Seidiya. His partner, a man called Ahmed al-Mulla, was also from his tribe. Hussein and Ahmed had many contracts with the former regime to provide meat for the army. This had enriched them and sealed their friendship.

After the Americans overthrew Saddam, two of the Mulla brothers returned home from exile in Iran, where they had been soldiers in the Badr Brigade. Ahmed and Hussein became religious and hung portraits of Shiite leaders like Sistani and Khomeini all over their shops' walls. They joined the Badr Brigade and formed an assassination group, transforming one of Hussein's shops in the Elam neighborhood into an office for interrogating former regime loyalists, whom Hussein called Saddamists. Hussein and Ahmed obtained Baath Party records with the names, addresses, and details of members in Seidiya—they even included the types and serial numbers of weapons owned by the men. The records were a gift to Ahmed from Shiite locals who had raided the Baath Party office in their neighborhood and transformed it into a Shiite mosque after the fall of Baghdad. Hussein and Ahmed scanned the records and interviewed about ten former Baath Party members a day. They would knock on their doors and inform the Baathists: "You were a Baath Party member, and you need to come visit us in our office in the Elam Market to clarify a few issues." Then they would leave.

They opened their office in May 2003. It had a desk with two chairs for Ahmed and Hussein as well as a long bench and portraits of Sistani and Khomeini. The Baathist would enter their office, sit on the bench, and sign a statement that he was innocent and not involved in any of the Baath Party crimes. The statement said: "I condemn all the former regime's activities against the Iraqi people and I regret everything I have done with that regime and I promise to never help the Baath Party again." Then they would be asked to hand over their weapons, and Ahmed and Hussein would compare the serial numbers with those on record.

Local Baathists were frightened of this organization and started fleeing Seidiya. Ahmed and Hussein were careful not to let any Baathist retain his weapons. The murder of Baathists in Seidiya intensified one month after the office opened. Hussein and Ahmed sought to obtain a *fatwa* that would give them legitimate cover for their militia, but they failed to find a respected cleric to provide one. Even their dearest friend and neighbor Sheikh Dhafer al-Qeisi,

Sistani's representative for southern Baghdad, refused to acquiesce, although he backed their activities.

Their group was very professional, driving fast Opel cars with many young members who moved quickly. They assassinated more than fifty alleged "Saddamists." Ahmed spoke proudly about his operations in public and often said that he would exceed 100 dead Saddamists by the end of 2005. He was also known to kill Salafis from the Sunni mosque next to the Elam Market. Sunnis in Elam began to fear Ahmed, worrying that they might be targeted next, since most of the former Baathists in his neighborhood were Sunni. In late 2004 Sunnis from the Omar Mosque in Elam formed an assassination squad; their main targets were Ahmed and Hussein.

One evening in March 2005, Kadhim, a member of Ahmed and Hussein's group, was hanging out in a shop with Ahmed when they were attacked. Kadhim died immediately. Ahmed was seriously wounded and remained in the hospital for one month to recover from his injuries. One week after he left the hospital, while he was visiting his shop again, he was assassinated. His sixteen-year-old assistant died with him. After Ahmed's death the group ceased conducting operations, and Hussein received letters in his shops threatening him with death if he did not leave the neighborhood. Hussein was shot in October 2005 with his brother Mohammed while they were driving their truck home one evening. Hussein died immediately but Mohammed remained conscious long enough to make a phone call. He was seriously wounded, but he survived.

The day after Hussein's murder, his eldest brother was locking up his shop when he found another letter: "In the name of God, we did not oppress them but they were oppressing themselves, those who killed the sons of Sunnis and Baathists, they killed the men, made the children orphans, and made the wives widows, they are cursed for what their hands have done. We will beat them like they beat us, and we will kill them everywhere."

Hussein had lived in a big house with his brothers and cousins and was surrounded by fellow tribesmen. His area had a robust Shiite majority and was full of Mahdi Army men, but his family did not feel safe enough to stay in Maalif. They left their houses and shops to return to the south, from where they had come thirty years earlier.

A few months later, on December 25, 2005, thirteen Sunni families were threatened and ordered to leave their homes in Maalif. Two families responded immediately, leaving the next day. The men in other families hid or left the area, leaving only the women. (Militias typically did not target women.) A Sunni woman in Maalif who hid her son at home explained the dilemma that many experienced: "There is a conspiracy to force Sunnis out of Baghdad. We are limited in the cities we can move to. We cannot move to Shula, Hurriya, Dolaie, Shaab, New Baghdad, or Al Amin, because we might face the same threats there. We can only move to Sunni neighborhoods dominated by the resistance, such as Dora and Amriya, but it is not even safe to live there. We cannot write on the walls that we are Sunnis to avoid attacks. And we might be attacked by the army by accident, since we live next to terrorists."

Maalif was a neighborhood in the larger Bayaa district. The Bayaa Mosque, located off of the highway, had belonged to followers of Muhammad Sadiq al-Sadr, Muqtada's father. It was led by Sheikh Muayad al-Khazraji, a former student of Sadr's who had been jailed by Saddam following Sadr's assassination in 1999. On Friday, April 25, 2003, Sheikh Muayad warned his flock that if he learned of any Iraqi woman sleeping with American soldiers, he would inform her tribe and call for her death. As well as worrying about how Iraqi women comported themselves, Sheikh Muayad hid many weapons in his mosque. Eventually the Americans arrested him for this, provoking massive protests by Shiite supporters. But the civil war seemed to extend itself to prison, where Sheikh Muayad's life was constantly threatened by Salafis. Upon his release, Sheikh Muayad paid a visit to another Sadrist cleric, Sheikh Haitham al-Ansari, and told him that his experiences in jail had changed his view of the Americans. "After I was in the jail, I knew who is my enemy and who is not," Sheikh Muayad said. "The Americans are not my enemy. The Americans have interests, and anybody who wants to block Americans from obtaining those interests becomes their enemy, and they destroy him. Stay away from their road and they will not touch you. Our enemies are the Wahhabis. They used to attack us in the jail many times, they wanted to assassinate me more than once, and one of their main goals is to damage Ali's tomb in Najaf."

Sunnis perceived the post-Baathist state as the enemy because state organs, along with the Americans, had been treating Sunnis as the enemy since 2003. Even before the elections of 2005, the government felt pressured to show Shiite masses that something was being done about the daily car bombs slaughtering them in the streets. Iraqi television began showing a highly sectarian program titled *Terror in the Hands of Justice,* on which alleged Sunni insurgents were shown confessing to crimes such as rape and sodomy. On one episode an interrogator accused prominent Sunni tribes such as the Jubur, Janabi, and Dulaimi of being terrorists. The show increased Sunni fears that the Shiite-dominated security forces were targeting them en masse.

When Abu Musab al-Zarqawi—the brutal leader of the jihadist group that morphed into Al Qaeda in Iraq after Zarqawi pledged his allegiance to Osama bin Laden—declared war on Shiites in a speech on September 14, 2005, Iraq's radical Sunni leadership were quick to condemn it. The Association of Muslim Scholars announced that Iraq's Shiites were not responsible for the crimes the government was committing with the Americans' blessings, and that they were innocent of the attacks against Sunnis carried out by the Americans. No religious principle allowed one to seek revenge on an innocent person, they said, and accused Zarqawi of colluding in the Americans' plan to create civil war in Iraq. Meanwhile, five resistance groups, the Army of Muhammad, the Al Qaqa Battalions, the Islamic Army of Iraq, the Army of Mujahideen, and the Salahuddin Brigades, condemned Zarqawi's statements as well, calling them a "fire burning the Iraqi people" and explaining that they only attacked the occupiers and those who assisted them, and did not base their attacks on sectarian or ethnic criteria.

But these Sunni condemnations did not suffice for Muqtada al-Sadr. In late 2005 he sent a letter to various Sunni leaders stating that Zarqawi had labeled all Shiites infidels and that he and all Shiites were being targeted by Zarqawi's deadly attacks. Muqtada demanded that Sunni leaders label Zarqawi an infidel and condemn him. No Sunni leader acceded to his demands. Some explained that it was too dangerous for them to do so, but Muqtada refused to accept their apologies and did not grant their fear of Zarqawi any merit. In addition, the Association for Muslim Scholars didn't just fail to heed Muqtada's call to condemn Al Qaeda; one of its spokesmen, Muhammad Bashar al-Faidih, dismissed the letter with sarcasm. And its leader, Harith al-Dhari, allegedly said, "We are from Al Qaeda and they are from us." This must have been especially galling for Muqtada, because in the early period of the occupation the young Shiite cleric referred to Dhari respectfully as "al Ab al-Mujahid," the Mujahid Father. The Mahdi Army in Karbala had always been different from the one in Baghdad. It was less sectarian, less criminal, focused more on providing services. But even their language started to change after the AMS rejected Muqtada's condemnation of Zarqawi.

This was a key moment for the Sadr movement and for sectarian relations in Iraq. Sadr decided to join the United Iraqi Alliance, the dominant Shiite coalition list in the December 2005 elections. For the first time one could see Mahdi Army soldiers sitting with Sistani followers and discussing politics amicably, whereas in the past it had been difficult even to have them in the same room without arguments occurring. Mahdi Army fighters complained bitterly about their betrayal by the Sunnis.

In March 2005 Sheikh Ahmad Abdel Ghafur al-Samarai, director general of the Sunni Endowment and a former top official in the Association for Muslim Scholars, gave a sermon in the Um Al Qura Mosque calling on Iraqi Sunnis to join the Iraqi military and police as long as they supported their nation and not the occupiers of Iraq. If the "honest and loyal elements" of Iraq, meaning its Sunnis, did not participate, then those who sought to harm the security of the nation, meaning Shiites, would dominate the security forces. Samarai later explained that the "real resistance" understood the importance of such a move because they did not want militias, meaning Shiite and Kurdish militias, ruling Iraq. Sixty-four other high-ranking Sunni clerics from throughout Iraq signed on to Samarai's *fatwa*.

The Balance of Power Shifts

The balance of power shifted that year, and Shiite militias, led by the Mahdi Army, took the offensive. Bayan Jabr Solagh took over as interior minister after the 2005 elections. A Shiite of Turkoman origin, he had been the Supreme Council representative in Damascus in the 1990s. At the Interior Ministry he inherited more than one hundred thousand armed men. Along with Badr Brigade leader Hadi al-Amiri and others, he turned commando units such as the Hawk, Volcano, Wolf, and Two Rivers brigades into death squads. (In late 2005 the American military uncovered secret prisons these death squads were running, which were full of Sunnis. Bayan Jabr was not surprised by the revelations, a minister at the time told me. He didn't question them; he just wanted to minimize the fallout, like Defense Secretary Donald Rumsfeld questioning how cameras got into Abu Ghraib.)

The Multinational Security Transition Command-Iraq, or MNSTCI (pronounced "minstikee"), run by Gen. David Petraeus, was in charge of rebuilding the Iraqi Security Forces. The Americans were focused on building institutions, but they neglected the training of individuals, leading to huge numbers of inexperienced and poorly trained police being pushed out into the provinces without supervision. They were easily co-opted by sectarian forces. In late 2004 MNSTCI was planning on working with the Interior Ministry to create a riot police force. When MNSTCI decided to create the riot police, they ordered batons, plastic shields, and the other appropriate gear, but the security situation was so desperate that the Iraqis decided to turn it into a light infantry battalion under the Interior Ministry's control.

Americans at MNSTCI heard that an Iraqi battalion had established itself in an old Republican Guard palace outside the Green Zone. Several hundred Iraqis served under the nominal command of a self-appointed Iraqi brigadier general, who was a Shiite former Republican Guard and had been imprisoned in Abu Ghraib. Most of his senior officers were ex-prisoners he knew from Abu Ghraib. It didn't hurt that Bayan Jabr was his nephew. Money flowed to the unit. After the elections in January 2005, another battalion was added to it: the Iraqi police commandos.

The Americans wanted to create a "special police" and already had two battalions of those, so there were four battalions of infantry—essentially, a mini army under the Interior Ministry. At the time the Americans had just realized that the Iraqi army had to be pulled off the line and trained again, so for a while the only units fighting were the police commandos. "It was the era of the pop-up unit," one senior American official from MNSTCI told me. "You had a unit in the Iraqi army that was a militia called the Boys of East Baghdad. There were a lot of self-organized units. Right from the outset we were concerned about

Shiite sectarianism, but even the concept of setting up comprehensive basic training [fifteen weeks of training in a centralized depot] was alien."

The Americans had firm control over the Defense Ministry because they destroyed the army and recreated it from scratch, attaching many advisers to it. But they never dismantled or took over the Interior Ministry. The few American intelligence officers at Interior were cooperating with the Iraqis to get information on Sunni armed groups. They couldn't tell the difference between the Supreme Council, the Badr militia, and the Mahdi Army. The Americans hadn't even translated the Iraqi laws into English.

Soon after Petraeus departed, the deputy minister of interior for finance explained to the outgoing commander of the Civilian Police Assistance Training Team (CPATT), General Fils, that none of the weapons they distributed were accounted for because they were distributed directly to the police stations. One of those weapons was traced to a murder in Turkey. Many ended up in the hands of militias or the resistance. I would find them in Lebanon as well.

The way MNSTCI and CPATT were handled led to many of the troubles Iraq would later face, such as weapons in the hands of insurgents, the expansion of Shiite militias into security services, and difficulty assessing Iraqi police capabilities. Petraeus was spared approbation because he left before the impact of these problems became clear and returned when some corrections had already been made.

The road to Kut in the south was the site for many attacks on military and logistical convoys for the Americans and the Iraqi state, as well as ordinary Shiite civilians. To counter this, Interior Ministry forces arrested many men living in homes along the road. The security forces were made up of Shiites; the men they arrested were Sunnis. Operations such as this were a result of the increasingly aggressive and Shiite-dominated Iraqi Security Forces. Some of this was inevitable because Sunnis had avoided joining these new forces but the Interior Ministry had been given to Shiites, and poor young Shiite men were the ones most likely to fill the ranks of these forces. Most poor young Shiite men supported Muqtada, so it followed that the security forces fell under the control of Sadrists and their Mahdi Army.

Iran wanted to weaken the Sunni grip on power in Iraq, and the Badr militia was its spearhead, a former minister close to Iraqi Prime Minister Ibrahim al-Jaafari told me. "Iran had a role," he said. "They forced people to confront what was happening and use resources under their control to organize a fighting force. Iran did that with its direct and indirect agents in Iraq." Parliament member Jamal Jaafir Mohammed Ali, known as Abu Mahdi al-Muhandes, was involved in discussions with the loose network of Shiites who had leadership cells on how to take on Sunnis: "How many people from Badr and the Mahdi Army to get into the police, how to do these extrajudicial killings, how to control mixed neighborhoods, how to target Baath Party operatives, they were networked, not following a central command."

Americans working at the Interior Ministry said it was a mess: one floor was full of Mahdi Army personnel, another was full of Badr. During the civil war, Land Cruiser SUVs from the Interior Ministry struck terror in people. They were nicknamed "Monikas" by Iraqis because of their wide ends, which reminded them of Monica Lewinski. The Mahdi Army used government Monikas, and people suspected that Jaafari gave Monikas to the militias.

The battles in the historic town of Madain—once the site of Seleucia and Ctesiphon, two of the great cities of ancient Mesopotamia—in 2005 were another turning point, where the tit-for-tat killing so familiar to urban Baghdad transformed into an open war between sectarian militias. Although the town had Shiites as well as Christians and members of the rare Sabean sect, which combines elements of Judaism and Christianity, it was a majority-Sunni town. Problems arose when about 150 Shiite families belonging to the southern Abu al-Aita tribe migrated north to the town, encamping in former military bases. These impoverished families were accused of looting, stealing, and wreaking havoc on the roads with their highway robbery. Resistance and insurgent groups that were trying to establish themselves as the local authorities soon clashed with the new Shiites. The insurgent groups also needed the roads unobstructed so that they could conduct their own attacks on coalition and Iraqi Security Forces. Among these insurgents were members of Zarqawi's Tawhid and Jihad groups, who brought with them foreign fighters. When the area fell under their control, unemployed youths swarmed to the insurgents. Salafi fighters started driving around the area in their pickup trucks, ordering all Shiites to leave the city.

But in response the Interior Ministry's Wolf Brigade took over a school and based themselves there, fighting with the insurgents and making mass arrests of Sunnis. The Wolf Brigade was later replaced by the Karar Brigade, a unit that was based in the Wasit province in the Shiite south. Because Madain was part of Baghdad province, locals viewed with suspicion these Interior Ministry forces from a different province. The name Karar refers to Imam Ali, whom the Shiites revere, and it was not chosen coincidentally. The Karar Brigade rounded up hundreds of Sunni men, and for the first time the new Iraqi Security Forces established a reign of terror ominously resembling Saddam's methods. Some of the Sunnis arrested were shown on the popular Shiite show *Terror in the Hands of Justice*. When an elderly Sabean (and therefore non-Muslim) man was shown on that program confessing to raping and killing a young Shiite girl, Shiites attacked the home of his wife, Um Rasha, and threatened to rape her daughters.

South of Baghdad, in Latifiya, similar battles were taking place. Although Latifiya was a quiet city in the year following the American invasion, its reputation took a turn for the worse after the attempted assassination of Ahmad

Chalabi and the kidnapping of French journalists there in 2004. Latifiya was seized by Salafi extremists because it connected Baghdad to Falluja through hidden roads and dirt paths and because it allowed command of a crucial highway. The Mahdi Army, in response, commandeered police vehicles to attack suspected insurgents and Baathists, but these attacks expanded to include Salafis as well and even Sunnis merely suspected of being Salafis. Consequently Shiite families became victims of reprisals. The Albu Amir, or Al Amiri tribe, was one Shiite tribe well represented in Latifiya. Its most famous son was Hadi al-Amiri, leader of the Badr Brigade. A group of Sunni jihadis attacked a Shiite police officer from the tribe, killing him and his family, including his children. (The jihadis justified killing the children with a quote attributed to the Prophet Muhammad, calling for pulling the evil out by the roots. Since the jihadis viewed all Shiites as anti-Islam, they viewed their children as future enemies of Islam.) Members from the Al Amiri tribe responded immediately, attacking Sunnis they suspected were responsible, killing them and defiling their corpses, and burning some of them. The Sunni dead were members of several tribes, which retaliated by launching mortars at random Shiite houses. These battles lasted for more than a week, until the Sunni and Shiite tribes met for a reconciliation at which the Shiites settled the dispute by paying blood money to the Sunnis. Latifiya subsequently fell under the control of the Association of Muslim Scholars. When a Shiite contractor from Baghdad who worked with the Americans was assigned a project in Latifiya, he and his partners met with Association of Muslim Scholars leader Harith al-Dhari. They paid him tens of thousands of dollars to guarantee their security. As a result they were able to complete their contract in the otherwise dangerous region without attack.

In August 2005 rumors of a bomb caused a panic stampede among Shiite pilgrims on the bridge linking Adhamiya and Kadhimiya. Up to one thousand people drowned or were crushed to death. Leading Supreme Council cleric Jalaluddin al-Saghir mourned the dead in his sermon the next Friday, calling them "beloved" and condemning the sort of jihad that targets innocent women and children engaged in worship. He also singled out the defense minister, Saadoun al-Dulaimi, a Sunni, for allegedly letting criminals and Wahhabis infiltrate his ministry. Saghir said that the Interior Ministry—which was in the Shiite hands of the Supreme Council—should have been responsible for providing security for the area. Saghir did praise the people of neighboring majority-Sunni Adhamiya, however, for risking their lives to help save some of the drowning pilgrims. Leading Sunni cleric Ahmad Abdel Ghafur al-Samarai, of the Association of Muslim Scholars, speaking in Ghazaliya's Um Al Qura Mosque, echoed Saghir's praise for the bravery of Adhamiya's Sunnis. But without naming sects, because that would have been bad form, he implicitly condemned the Shiite security forces for their "state terrorism" and execution of Sunnis while complaining that Sunnis were unfairly blamed for the Kadhimiya tragedy. He was followed by another cleric, who condemned the Supreme Council and Dawa for killing innocent people and pushing Iraq to civil war out of fear for their waning support on the Shiite street.

By 2005 sectarian attacks and cleansing were increasing elsewhere in Iraq, too. Eleven Shiites from Najaf who worked as fishermen in Haditha were killed in mid-2005. More and more Shiites heading south to visit shrines were attacked, and passing through Latifiya was a nightmare for Shiite pilgrims. In December 2005 government troops intervened, attacking Sunnis and securing the road, but Shiites continued their exodus out of that troubled area, feeling threatened. The same trends were evident throughout much of Iraq, especially in Baghdad. Former high-ranking military officers, especially pilots, who fought in the eight-year war against Iran, were systematically assassinated. In August 2005 the Interior Ministry's Volcano Brigade arrested several dozen Sunni men from the majority-Shiite Baghdad neighborhood of Hurriya. Days later their tortured bodies were found far away, by the Iranian border. In September 2005 five Shiite schoolteachers and their driver were executed in Malha, a village next to Iskandariya. Their killers wore police uniforms. In October Mahdi Army men fought alongside the Interior Ministry in an attack on a Sunni town where some Shiites were being held.

"Human rights departments" of various political parties produced tendentious and one-sided accounts of their victimization, and Iraqi and Arab satellite media magnified their effects. Sunnis despised the Supreme Council's Badr Brigade because it had been based in Iran, but it was the more homegrown Mahdi Army that was primarily responsible for attacks against Sunnis. A Mahdi Army soldier confided, "We kill more Wahhabis than Badr does, and we throw their bodies in our city, but accusation's finger points to Badr anyway." Although the Interior Ministry was controlled by the Supreme Council, the police were outside the ministry's control. With a small number of police cars, they could operate at night—past curfew, when only official cars were permitted—and enter Sunni neighborhoods with impunity to arrest or kill anyone they wanted. In Baghdad and much of Iraq, the police and the Mahdi Army were one and the same—as were the Iraqi army forces posted throughout the country. Iraqi police stations and army bases were decorated with Muqtada al-Sadr's daunting visage, as were their vehicles. Even in the all-Sunni Anbar province, the Iraqi army was composed of Shiite supporters of Muqtada. In the spring of 2006, when Sunni soldiers from Anbar graduated as new members of the Iraqi army and were told they would serve among Shiites outside their home province, they rioted and tore off their uniforms. The Americans had established police forces in Anbar, composed of local Sunni men selected by their tribes. When I visited these police in the spring of 2006, they had not been paid in months because the Interior Ministry was not sending the money.

The Mahdi Army's sudden prowess was attributed to its recent cooperation with Lebanese Hizballah. Muqtada, who was modeling his army on Hizballah, had sent his senior men to Lebanon to make this possible. Mahdi Army men told me that the Lebanese trainers had come to them as well. To the Mahdi Army, the Association of Muslim Scholars were merely Salafis and Baathists in the attire of normal Sunni clerics; they presumptuously claimed that "they are not representing our Sunni brothers." This gave them carte blanche to kill any Sunni they wanted. The Mahdi Army knew that the Sunni insurgency had coalesced, and Iraqi nationalist groups, including the Association of Muslim Scholars, began supporting Zarqawi's attacks and providing his men with shelter. Zarqawi himself was said to have visited Harith al-Dhari's village of Zawba several times.

In late 2005 I returned to Amriya with my friend Hassan to break the Ramadan fast. We were joined by Sheikh Hussein of the Maluki Mosque. The conversation quickly turned to the deteriorating security situation, particularly for Sunnis. Gangs of Shiite killers, targeting radical Sunni clerics or former Baathists suspected of supporting the resistance, were penetrating Amriya. Sheikh Hussein, a Salafi with clear links to the resistance that dominated Amriya, had nearly been assassinated by Badr militiamen belonging to the Interior Ministry, who had arrived at his home in a police car. He had hidden in his home, and they missed him. He had only recently emerged from hiding. Noticing that his significant girth had increased, I asked him, "How did you hide? You're not small." He smiled and said, "We are all targets today." Sheikh Hussein supported Sunni participation in the upcoming elections and agreed with the Sheikh Samarai's *fatwa* urging them to join the security forces. He expressed concern that the "Arabs," meaning foreign fighters, who wanted to fight until judgment day, would refuse to accept negotiations with the government and an eventual ceasefire.

Escalation

The December 2005 elections were hailed as a milestone for the Bush administration, but they further enshrined sectarianism in Iraq. Ayad Allawi, the former prime minister, was the secular nationalist candidate. He fared even worse in these elections than he had the previous January. Other nonsectarian parties failed even to obtain one seat. Sunni participation proved that the resistance was disciplined and controlled by Iraqis: not only did members of the resistance refrain from attacking Sunni voters; in some cases they protected them, since they too viewed a large Sunni turnout as a key element in their struggle to obtain a larger Sunni role in the new Iraq.

Fighting between Sunni militias and the Mahdi Army escalated, but war was never formally declared. One Mahdi Army soldier explained that "Wahhabis know we are killing them, otherwise they would not attack us back, but they have not declared war on us, because then all the Shiites of Iraq would be against them and they would lose." In private conversations, Sunni insurgents and their leaders were seething about Muqtada and his Mahdi Army, claiming they were fighting to protect Iran and not out of Iraqi nationalism. But in public they hid their hostility to the Mahdi Army and instead accused the Badr Brigade of assassinating Sunnis.

During the battles against coalition forces that began in April 2004, the Mahdi Army began forming into divisions and became more organized and hierarchical. Shaab was the neighborhood in Baghdad with the second-largest number of Mahdi Army fighters. When the fighting subsided, the Mahdi Army maintained its divisions and kept many of its guns and vehicles. Many Shiites were assassinated by Sunnis in Shaab, and Shiites retaliated in a tit-for-tat that foreshadowed what was to come. Although Shiites were the majority in Shaab, their operations targeting Sunnis were not well organized or coordinated, and were not launched by one specific group.

Before the war, Shaab—and in particular its Ur neighborhood—had been dominated by anti-regime Sadrists. In the 1990s an Iranian agent called Abu Haidar al-Kheiqani had formed a secret armed opposition group along with a former Communist called Muayad al-Mundher. The two lived in Ur. They recruited a young friend called Haitham al-Khazraji, who would become known as Haitham al-Ansari. Haitham had a brother who was a low-level security officer in what was then known as Saddam City (later Sadr City). Haitham's brother was known as Ali Mustache because of his big mustache and was in charge of arrests there.

Abu Haidar asked Haitham to join the Sadrists in the *hawza* to act as a spotter and recruiter. Haitham joined and became a cleric, and helped build the Shurufi Mosque in Shaab. (My close friend Firas in Shaab would become Haitham's assistant, driver, and bodyguard.) He issued *fatwas* in support of low-level acts of resistance. He would permit a car to be stolen if it was used against the regime. He would permit a woman to take off her *hijab* and sit in a car with a man who wasn't her husband if it helped an anti-regime operation. One time, a female operative sat in a car with a male operative who pretended to be drunk; they got into a fake accident, ramming into an intelligence officer. In the fight that ensued, the officer was shot to death.

Abu Haidar's group is also said to have killed Haji Falah, the head of intelligence in Saddam City, and it was tied to the attempted assassination of Saddam's son Uday. Haitham was said to be personally secular, but he saw religion as the only means to combat Saddam's regime. In about 1998 the Baathists banned Friday prayers in Shurufi Mosque. A riot broke out, and two people were arrested. Others threw stones at security cars.

In about 1998 Abu Haidar, Muayad, and Haitham were all arrested. Abu Haidar and Muayad were executed. Haitham convinced his interrogator, a Sunni from the Dulaimi tribe, that he was just a friend of the other two; he was released after he agreed to work for Iraqi security. But he fled to Jordan, where he became the caretaker for the Jaafar Al Tayar shrine in Karak, the main Shiite shrine in that country. He also sold trinkets on the street and was the only Shiite cleric in Jordan.

In Jordan Haitham was recruited by Ahmad Chalabi's Iraqi National Congress. Haitham's role for the INC was to recruit Sadrists. He told the INC that he would not engage in military operations for them, but he secretly involved himself in small-scale acts of sabotage, using the money the INC gave him, which in those three years was not more than thirty thousand dollars. He met officials from the American Defense Intelligence Agency, who sent Thoraya satellite phones to his network in Iraq in exchange for intelligence about the Iraqi Security Forces. Right before the war, Iraqi security realized that Haitham was running spies in Iraq and arrested and tortured some of his people. Nonetheless, Haitham had strong ambitions in the run-up to the U.S. invasion. He proposed moving his operations to western Iraq—principally the Anbar province—but CIA officials rejected this plan, because they had authorized that area for their own man, Ayad Allawi. On April 11, 2003, two days after Baghdad fell, Haitham returned to Ur, linking up with survivors of his network and the renascent Sadrist movement.

Haitham didn't respect Muqtada and the old guard, and at first he joined the ranks of Muqtada's rival, Ayatollah Muhammad al-Yaqoubi. But he was quickly disenchanted and soon rejoined Muqtada. All the while he was also collaborating with Chalabi's INC. Haitham was friends with two other low-level Sadrists from Ur, Ali al-Lami and Jawad al-Bolani; he introduced them to Chalabi, giving their careers a huge boost.

After the war Haitham set up the Tawhid (Unity) association in Ur. In its building Bolani and Lami had offices, as did a former anti-Saddam activist from the southern marshes named Karim Mahud al-Muhammadawi, known as Abu Hatem, or the prince of the marshes, who would go on to lead Iraqi Hizballah. The Tawhid association became an important center. Shiite politicians would visit it; even the American military came. People returned stolen goods to Tawhid, and it had a religious school for women.

After I went over several hundred of the many thousands of documents I found in the looted security station in Baghdad (see chapter one), I gave them to my friend Firas, and he, in turn, gave them to the Tawhid. Firas drove

Haitham to his weekly meetings with Chalabi in Mansour. Falah Hassan Shan-shal, who would go on to head the Sadrist bloc of Parliament, would also come to the meetings. Haitham brokered a meeting in a Sadr City mosque between Muhammadawi, Lami, and Bolani. Muhammadawi was seeking local Baghdad representatives and had appointed Bolani and Lami as his local first and second deputies. When Chalabi asked his old friend Haitham to introduce him to local Shiite politicians who could reach into Shiite communities, Haitham introduced him to Lami and Bolani. Together they established an umbrella political group, the Shiite House. The Shiite House became the Shiite Political Council and eventually the Iraqi National Alliance, the main Shiite list in the elections. In late summer 2004, when the Iranians started working with the Sadrists, Haitham was invited to Iran. But the meeting was postponed, and he never made it.

After the war, Sadrists took over a Baath Party office in Ur and turned it into a *husseiniya* (Shiite place of worship). It was originally controlled by Ayatollah Yaqoubi's Fadhila organization. Haitham helped oversee the Mustafa Husseiniya, and when he fell out with Yaqoubi he transferred it to Muqtada's followers. In the summer of 2004, Haitham helped establish a local death squad in the Mustafa Husseiniya. Its men targeted Wahhabis and "terrorists."

When the IGC set up its de-Baathification office, Muhammadawi appointed Lami the managing director of the archives department, which housed all the documents that contained background information on Baath Party suspects. (Bolani and Lami apparently despised each other and parted company.) When Chalabi suffered total defeat in the 2005 elections, he grew closer with Lami and grew to depend on him. Chalabi used Lami's bodyguards because they had a fearsome reputation for their skill, and their special privileges allowed them to arrest anybody they accused of being a former Baathist.

Chalabi and Lami visited Iran together often. Both men were sectarian and felt that Shiites had been deprived of their rights in the past. This time they would make sure Shiites took over. Lami became known as Ali Faisal and would run de-Baathification. He hated Baathists and bore a grudge against Sunnis because of his past as a poor Shiite from the slums of Ur. He had lists of Baathists he wanted to dismiss and was determined to purge the Shiite ex-Baathists who had been rehabilitated by the Supreme Council and were protected by it. Meanwhile, Bolani was working with Muhammadawi but looking for other jobs. For a man who would go on to accrue huge political power at the Interior Ministry, he didn't seem to be picky then. He applied for a job as a flour mill manager, but Chalabi adopted Bolani and took him to Washington in 2004, thus giving him his international profile.

On December 31, 2004, Haitham was killed near his house by a local Shaab terrorist group. Passions were further inflamed with the attempted assassination of Muhammadawi, whose car was shot at as he left the funeral.

Muqtada's deputy Sheikh Safaa al-Tamimi decided to avenge Haitham's assassination and established a special assassination squad under his command. All his men belonged to the Mahdi Army, and all their targets belonged to the Salafi movement. A room inside the Mustafa Husseiniya was used for torturing suspects until they confessed. Confessions were filmed, and some included executions of prisoners who admitted to attacking Shiites or civilians. Only the prisoner was shown in the film, with the interrogator in the background calmly asking questions in a southern Iraqi accent (the same one common in Sadr City). Some films showed groups of prisoners sitting together. One such film showed the group that confessed to the murder of Haitham. These snuff films were kept in Sheikh Safaa's possession and were not reproduced, saved as evidence that only people who deserved it were executed.

Sheikh Safaa's death squad was well armed, with grenades, grenade launchers, and Kalashnikovs. The soldiers of the group were selected by the sheikh for their physical strength or martial prowess. The group was supplied with many vehicles by supporters in Shaab. Having Mahdi Army friends in the Vehicle Registration Department made it easy for the group to replace their license plates. Their assassination campaign led to a massive clearance of Sunnis from Shaab, part of a deliberate strategy to cleanse the area of Mahdi Army enemies following two years of clashes with Salafis.

Sheikh Safaa had final approval of all targets, who would then be tracked for a couple of days before their murder. When his men conducted operations and raids, they usually wore either all black or military uniforms. Sometimes they coordinated their operations with the Iraqi army. The group typically raided a target's house at night, dragging him from bed, taking him to the mosque for interrogation, executing him, and then dumping the body on the outskirts of Sadr City in a place locally known as Al Sadda (The Dam), where there was a sand berm. Before these Shiite revenge attacks, radical Salafis had imposed their rule on much of Shaab, even killing barbers to prevent local citizens from having their beards shaved. In January 2006, one Mahdi Army soldier said, "We cleaned our city from all Wahhabis," adding, "now we can live peacefully in Shaab."

At around the same time, Muqtada's spokesman in Kadhimiya, Hazim al-Araji, condemned "terrorists" (his euphemism for Sunnis), but he also asserted that the American occupiers were allied with these "terrorists" against Shiites.

BRUTAL AS THE American occupation was, it was also incompetent. The Americans never controlled much in Iraq. They could destroy, but they had trouble building. They allowed militias to take over Iraq and allowed the police, who should have been protecting civilians from the predations of militias, to become involved in the conflict as one of the main sectarian militias. And they either ignored it for the sake of expediency, as they did when they dealt with warlords in post-Taliban Afghanistan, or they were simply unaware. But there were exceptions, intelligent and sensitive officers who sensed what was happening and could see the sectarian catastrophe that the American invasion had unleashed.

Phil Carter's experience as a captain in the U.S. Army is a disturbing example of what was happening across Iraq. Carter served in Baquba, in the Diyala province, northeast of Baghdad, between October 2005 and September 2006. As part of a team training and supervising the Iraqi police, he saw firsthand the results of that initial failure to build a professional culture within the Interior Ministry, which had become rife with cronyism and Shiite chauvinism. Thanks in part to the Sunni boycott of the elections, Shiites were overrepresented in Diyala, and the Supreme Council was very powerful. Carter's team advised Diyala's chief of police, Maj. Gen. Ghassan Adnan al-Bawi, who was an official with the Supreme Council's Badr militia, and they operated closely with the governor, who was also a Badr official.

"Al-Bawi was running Badr death-squad ops, even targeting other Shiites they had political beefs with," Carter told me. "Badr death squads were doing targeted killings in houses and businesses. Good Shiite officers were sidelined. If they tried to take an initiative they would get fired or moved or, on a couple of occasions, killed." The chief of the major crimes unit, Colonel Ali, was nicknamed "Cable Ali" by the Americans. "He was running a torture chamber. We found them, and we pushed to get him charged by the Ministry of Interior, and he was eventually arrested. But he was sprung by the police chief. We had gotten him fired a couple of times, but he was always reinstated. The rumor was that he was a CIA guy and a CIA source on intelligence." When Carter first arrived, his predecessors told him that they had made a bargain with their colleagues from Diyala: "'They're thugs, but they're our thugs. They keep order, just don't ask questions.' These guys were running their own little organized crime entity, selling fuel on the black market," Carter observed. "There was graft of police funds, extortion. Sectarianism showed in who they picked for leaders and what neighborhoods they would neglect." Even when they had evidence of misconduct, Carter and his men often felt powerless. "Iraqi detainees were tortured by Iraqi officers with power drills," Carter said. They had cigarette burns and bruises on their backs. Every indicator was that they were picked up on a sweep and had done nothing wrong, just been at the wrong place at the wrong time, and were Sunni. Carter wanted to make an example of one Iraqi army officer, but the Military Transition Team [MTT, pronounced "mitt"] with him was obstructive. They thought he was effective.

In November 2005, Carter's team got 200 reports of police abuse from families visiting detained relatives. Carter took the complaints to Bawi, the police chief. He said he would launch an investigation, promising to look into people who were obviously innocent. But what about guilty people? Carter retorted. They got what they deserved. Bawi said. He cited Guantánamo and Abu Ghraib: "'I only do what you do. You don't understand, Captain Carter. You just got here.'"

Between January and March 2006, just as IED attacks and ambushes were increasing in the wake of the Samarra bombings, the U.S. battalion in charge of Baquba decided to close the base in Baquba and move it to Camp Warhorse, on the edge of the city. "It was the height of strategic folly," Carter complained. "At the moment things are getting worse, we pull back."

This pattern was repeated throughout Iraq as the Americans ceded territory to militias and the civil war intensified. Americans realized too late that their presence was provoking hostility, and removed their soldiers from the streets. But by then the occupation was second to the civil war.

ON FEBRUARY 22, 2006, the Shiite Askari Shrine in Samarra was blown up. In the days that followed, more than 1,300 bodies were found in Baghdad, most of them Sunni. Once these figures were revealed, the Interior Ministry—whose forces were probably responsible for a large number of the killings—asked the Shiite-controlled Ministry of Health to cover them up. Shiites took over dozens of Sunni mosques and renamed them after the Samarra shrine. Shiite militias targeted the Abu Hanifa Mosque in Adhamiya with numerous mortars. Muqtada was said to have announced that "we have the legitimate cover to kill al-Nawasib," a pejorative term for Sunnis.

Sunni-controlled television stations in Iraq—such as Baghdad TV, controlled by the Iraqi Islamic Party—showed only Sunni victims of the retaliatory attacks. Shiite stations such as Al Furat and Al Iraqiya focused on the damaged shrine and Shiite victims. Al Furat was even more aggressive, encouraging Shiites to "stand up for their rights."

Following the attack Sunni militias faced the increased wrath of the Mahdi Army. Throughout Iraq Mahdi Army cadres flooded the streets, marching and chanting in unison. Sunni militias understand that the only militia in Iraq capable of defeating the Supreme Council's Badr was the Mahdi Army, which is why they initially courted Muqtada and his men, who opposed Iranian intervention. This is also why Sunni militias hoped to establish a united front with the Mahdi Army against the Americans.

Two days after the Samarra attack, Sheikh Yasser, a young Shiite sheikh in the Shuhada Al Taf Mosque, was passing by the Sunni Al Sajjad Mosque in the Maalif neighborhood. His car was stopped and searched by armed guards working for the mosque. The sheikh later informed the Mahdi Army, who controlled a mosque elsewhere in the neighborhood. Mahdi Army soldiers surrounded the Sajjad Mosque and searched it for explosives. Sunnis informed the media, and local stations claimed that the Mahdi Army had taken over the mosque. On the following Friday Sunnis asked for U.S. Army protection against possible Mahdi Army attacks during their Friday prayers. The Sajjad Mosque belonged to the extremist Ansar Sunnah group: it had celebrated two funerals for Iraqi Palestinian suicide bombers who were killed in late 2004 during operations against coalition forces, and it occasionally celebrated the graduation of children who memorized the Koran in ceremonies named after Al Qaeda videos such as *Winds of Victory*.

Shortly after the Samarra attacks I spoke to a Shiite friend from Maalif. "The Mahdi Army is cleansing my neighborhood," he said, "and they issued threats to many Sunni families forcing them to leave. They also killed many Sunnis. It started after the death of more than fifty civilians in the neighborhood in one day [mortar attacks from Gartan] and another sequence of explosions including two car bombs and several IEDs. The Sunnis in the neighborhood were about 40 percent, and now they are about 20 percent. Only Sunnis who are not involved in the insurgency or were not from the former regime did not receive threats, and so they did not leave the city. Rent prices for houses went down. Sunnis who have Shiite friends in other neighborhoods started switching their houses. Shiite families move to majority-Shiite neighborhoods, and Sunni families move to majority-Sunni neighborhoods. They exchange houses for free but with trust that they will get their houses back. This leads to changing the demography of every neighborhood."

Every morning in 2006 the streets of Baghdad were littered with dozens of bodies, bruised, torn, mutilated, executed only because they were Sunni or Shiite. Power drills were an especially popular torture device. In the spring of 2006 I spent six weeks in Iraq and went through three different drivers. At various times each had to take a day off because a neighbor or relative had been killed. One morning fourteen bodies were found, all with ID cards in their front pockets, all called Omar. Omar is an exclusively Sunni name. It was a message. In Baghdad those days nobody was more insecure than men called Omar. On another day a group of bodies was found with hands overlapping on their abdomens, right hand above left, the way Sunnis pray. It was a simple message: if you are Sunni, we will kill you. Sunnis and Shiites were obtaining false papers with neutral names. Sunni militias were stopping buses and demanding the *jinsiya*, or ID cards, of all passengers. Those belonging to Shiite tribes were executed.

Following the January 2005 elections the Health and Transportation ministries were given to Sadr loyalists, who immediately started cleansing them of Sunnis and ideologically unsound Shiites. Sadrists instituted a program they called "cleaning the ministry from Saddamists." Although not all Sunnis were targeted, many Sunnis felt that all Sunnis were being labeled Saddamists.

In the Health Ministry pictures of Muqtada and his father were everywhere. Black banners for Shiite traditions were all over the walls, and Shiite traditional music played inside the ministry. Only people who supported the Sadr movement could join the ministry now. Doctors and ministry employees referred to the minister of health as *imami*, or "my imam," as though he were a cleric. What Sunnis were left in the ministry worked only in Sunni areas where Shiites were afraid to visit. The Transportation Ministry was also controlled by clerics. Its walls were adorned with Shiite posters and banners as well as those supporting Muqtada specifically. Sunni engineers and staff were pushed out. As in the Health and Interior ministries, Shiites with no experience filled the ranks, the only qualification being an ideological one. In one case a Sunni chief engineer was fired and replaced with an unqualified Shiite who wore a cleric's turban to work. This has led to a dramatic drop in efficiency, with ministries barely functioning. Kurdish-controlled offices also avoided hiring Sunni Arabs.

Attacks increased throughout the country. In Kirkuk the Ahl Al Bayt Huseiniya was attacked by Sunni militiamen who blocked off the street with cars and killed at least two civilians. In the nearby village of Bashir, they attacked the Shiite Imam Ridha shrine. Officially, Muqtada opposed attacks on Sunnis, but he had unleashed his fighters on Sunnis. Sectarian and ethnic cleansing continued apace, with mixed neighborhoods being purified. In Amriya, dead bodies were being found on the main street at the rate of three a day. People were afraid to approach the bodies, or call for an ambulance or the police, because they would be found dead the following day. In Abu Ghraib, Dora, Amriya, and other mixed neighborhoods, Shiites were being forced to leave. In Maalif Sunnis were being targeted. In its statements the Association of Muslim Scholars referred to the police as "government police," not the Iraqi police, because it viewed them as illegitimate, and it called the Mahdi Army the "black sectarians" because of their uniforms, or the "new sectarians." Iraq was a divided country, even in its media. New channels such as Al Furat, which was controlled by the Supreme Council, and Sharqiya, which was controlled by former Baathist Saad Bazzaz, continued the wars fought on the street, inflaming people's fears and hatreds. If Sunni and Shiite militias could not assassinate political figures, they often targeted the close relatives of judges, governors, ministers, and members of the national assembly.

Shiite families fled Abu Ghraib, Al Taji, and Al Mashahada, moving into Shiite strongholds in Baghdad, such as Shuula, where Muqtada's representatives took care of them. Shiites were still angry. "Destroying all Sunni mosques is still not equivalent to bombing the Askari shrine" was the dominant Shiite attitude in Baghdad. Hundreds of Shiite families from Sunni towns settled in Red Crescent–run refugee camps near Kut. The United States constantly shifted its support back and forth between Sunnis and Shiites, calling on Shiites to rein in their militias, a key Sunni demand, while conducting massive and lethal raids on the Sunni population—alienating everyone in Iraq but the Kurds.

In February 2006 the National Accord Front—the largest Sunni coalition, with forty-four seats in the new Parliament—threatened to begin civil disobedience if attacks and arrests targeting Sunnis were not halted. In areas where Shiites were the minority, they feared the *mulathamin* (masked ones), referring to the Sunni militias who covered their faces with their head scarves. Sunnis, in turn, feared "interior," a reference to the Interior Ministry, or "the black sectarians" of the Mahdi Army.

THE CIVIL WAR IN IRAQ was a victory of the slum over the city, or the periphery over the center. The Kurds, the Shiites, and even the Sunnis of the center were marginalized or killed. For the Sunnis, for example, it was the Anbar Sunni—more rural, more tribal—who briefly rose to prominence in 2007. In Kurdistan, the pesh merga and the Kurds of the mountains have prevailed. Under Saddam there were many pro-regime, Arabic-speaking, Iraqified Kurds living in Baghdad and Mosul. They have been pushed into Kurdistan.

For those who resisted having to choose a sectarian identity, there were few choices except exile. The integrated Iraqis had been Saddam's citizens; they were his middle class, his urban dream, and they lived in the heart of the state. Many were state employees under the direct control of the state. They were of the state's making, and they have died with the state. Millions of Iraqis have left Iraq. More than two million Iraqis had fled before the war, in the 1990s, when the UN-imposed sanctions destroyed Saddam's allies and his urban middle-class technocrats. Millions more have fled their homes since the war began, most of them from the mixed areas of Iraq. Many have been expelled from their urban homes by the sectarian militias who descended from the mountains, the desert, the marshes, the slums.

CHAPTER THREE

Slaughterhouse

ON MARCH 26, 2006, AMERICAN AND IRAQI FORCES RAIDED THE Mustafa Husseiniya, the small but locally well-known Shiite gathering place and place of worship in eastern Baghdad's Ur neighborhood, adjoining the larger Shaab district. Sixteen to eighteen people were killed in the raid. A U.S. military statement issued later that day claimed that "Iraqi Special Operations Forces conducted a twilight raid in the Adhamiyah neighborhood in northeast Baghdad to disrupt a terrorist cell responsible for conducting attacks on Iraqi security and coalition forces and kidnapping Iraqi civilians," adding that "no mosques were entered or damaged," that the operation was conducted at dusk to "ensure no civilians were in the area and to minimize the possibility of collateral damage," and that U.S. forces were only advising the Iraqi soldiers who conducted the raid. Some accounts claimed that American and Iraqi soldiers had been pursuing a suspect who fled to the mosque. They were fired upon and returned fire, killing sixteen "insurgents" and arresting fifteen others. It was also claimed they rescued a hostage. Former Prime Minister Ibrahim al-Jaafari of the Dawa Party angrily complained that the sixteen dead had been inside a mosque. Nuri al-Maliki, who had succeeded Jaafari as prime minister, was interviewed on Iraqi state television. "This was a hostile attack intended to destroy the political process and provoke a civil war," he said. He blamed the American military and American ambassador Zalmay Khalilzad.

I visited the Mustafa Husseiniya the day after the raid. I arranged to meet an old friend Firas from Shaab who was a friend of Sheikh Safaa al-Tamimi of the Mustafa Husseiniya. We drove into Shaab and into a long convoy of Mahdi Army pickup trucks and minibuses waving flags and machine guns. Shaab had deteriorated since my previous trip a few months earlier. After the recent Samarra explosions, three Sunni mosques in Shaab had been burned. The siege there was palpable. There were several hundred Mahdi Army fighters, and among the convoy were also blue-and-white Iraqi police pickup trucks. After we passed a police checkpoint, a white civilian car began to follow us. My driver gestured with his head at the rearview mirror to let me know. Suddenly he made a U-turn and squeezed into traffic going in the opposite direction, losing them. We met Firas on the side of the road far from the *husseiniya*. He would act as if he did not know me when we met at the mosque because it could be dangerous for him if people in Shaab knew he had foreign friends. He was himself a journalist and a close confidant of Sheikh Safaa, and had asked the sheikh to guarantee my safety. He wore a black suit and dark shirt with no tie and leather shoes. He had an informal intelligence-gathering capacity in the neighborhood.

Three years earlier I had shared with Firas the thousands of Baathist security files I found in the abandoned and looted general security office. These files contained the day-to-day operations of Saddam's dictatorship and revealed the names of Baathist collaborators and spies. I felt that they were Iraqi patrimony and that I should hand them over to some Iraqi movement. Firas gave them all to the Tawhid association, and I never got them back. I now know from other friends that my files were used to compile hit lists by Shiite militias in Shaab and that Firas was involved in this. I never asked him directly. He had told Sheikh Safaa about me, and the sheikh was expecting me, but Firas warned me once more to pretend I didn't know him.

It was immediately apparent that the raid had targeted the *husseiniya*, which strictly speaking was not a mosque but had the same function as one and even had a minaret with loud speakers on its top to broadcast the calls to prayer. Moreover, the *husseiniya* was not located in the Adhamiya neighborhood, contrary to the coalition press statement. Adhamiya is a Sunni bastion not far from Shaab, but the two neighborhoods are worlds apart. Could the Americans have confused the most heavily Sunni neighborhood in Baghdad with a Shiite stronghold? Could they have confused Muqtada's Shiite militia with a terrorist cell? Before the war the Mustafa Husseiniya had been a Baath Party office. Like other political movements, Muqtada's had seized many Baath Party buildings following the war. Some former Baath Party buildings even had domes now.

A large sign in front of the Mustafa Husseiniya bore the faces of Muqtada's father and local Mahdi Army martyrs. Black banners hung on the wall with Arabic letters in white, red, green, and yellow. "We express condolences to the Mahdi and the whole Islamic nation for the disaster of the martyrdom of the brother believers and the attacks on them in the Mustafa Husseiniya at the hands of the *takfiris* backed by the occupation forces." Other banners echoed this: "The massacre of the Mustafa Husseiniya was done by the Wahhabis with the help of the Americans." Another said that the massacre had been committed by "the forces of darkness with the help of the forces of occupation."

The large lot before the *husseiniya* was blocked off by concrete traffic barriers. A large black *chadir* (a round tent used for mourning) was erected in it. Big red-and-green flags waved from above it. Rows of plastic chairs were lined up, and several turbaned clerics sat talking. It was customary to enter on the right side and shake the hands of all present, wishing peace upon them one by one until the end. Then the visitor would sit down and ask God to have mercy on the one who would read the Fatiha, the first verse of the Koran. Then everyone would recite the Fatiha seated except for the relatives of the deceased, who would say it standing. Following the recital, the men would all wipe their hands down their faces.

A banner on one of the concrete barriers announced, "The followers of the family of the Prophet Muhammad understand this: the money of the Saudis and the hatred of the Americans and the ugliness and the barbarism of the Wahhabis and the cowardice of the political Shiite leaders equals the slaughter of the Shiites of Ali, the commander of the faithful." Beside the banner was a picture of Ayatollah Sistani and Muhammad Sadiq al-Sadr. In front of the *husseiniya* was a small stand on which a pot of tea was boiling. I was offered a small glass of the very sweet and strong tea popular in Iraq, always poured into glasses that taper inward gracefully. Glasses were then rinsed in a bowl of water and reused. I was carrying a film camera with me but was warned not to film the many armed men who stood outside, slinging Kalashnikovs casually. The young men guarding the mosque welcomed me and gave me a tour of the wreckage. Firas was there too, and he introduced himself to me to maintain the charade.

They pointed to an exploded wall and a pile of rubble that had been the imam's home (imams often live on the premises or in a house attached to the mosque). The men explained that an American Apache helicopter had fired a missile at it and destroyed it. They had collected all the shrapnel to prove it, along with numerous shell casings from American M-16s. Three blackened cars sat inside the courtyard. I was told they belonged to people praying in the mosque and had been parked outside but that the Americans had burned them and then dragged them inside the *husseiniya*. Against one wall was a large picture of Muhammad Sadiq al-Sadr and Sheikh Haitham al-Ansari, Shaab's murdered cleric. I asked one of my guides, the caretaker Abul Hassan, who wore a black *dishdasha* with white trousers beneath it, why the Americans had come. "By God I don't know," he said. "We were surprised by their raid." He attributed it to political pressure on the Sadr movement.

Brownish red blood smeared the courtyard, where bodies had been dragged. "They killed people praying, innocent people," the caretaker said. "One of the people praying was shot here," he pointed, "and dragged all the way here." He pointed to a room, "and one was shot here." He showed me dried pools of blood and pointed to the ceiling, where blood and pieces of flesh had splattered from somebody's head. "They brought four here—one of them was fourteen." He gestured to another room: "There were five martyrs in that room." The men were just as concerned with the posters, which had been cut or torn. Adjacent to the *husseiniya* were several rooms that had been given to the Dawa Party-Iraq organization. This was not Prime Minister Jaafari's party but a rival branch (there are three), which had been exiled in Iran. Inside the offices, blood covered plastic chairs and the floor. Political posters covered the walls featuring the first and second Sadr martyrs. "Here they killed one," my guides told me, pointing to more blood. They showed me the *jinsiya* (ID cards) of the three martyrs from the Dawa office. In one of the Dawa rooms they pointed out a vast pool of blood with white pieces of brain stuck in it. The men pointed to more blood. "Torture, you understand? Torture," one man told me. A book written by Muhamad Sadiq al-Sadr was covered in blood. A poster of Jaafari had black ink scribbled on his face. In the room where ceremonial drums and chains were stored, drums had been torn, pictures torn off.

Sheikh Safaa stood in the courtyard by his destroyed home, pacing back and forth while talking on his mobile phone. When he got off, Firas and several other young men surrounded him to consult as I waited. I recognized another one of them, a young man also wearing a black suit and black shirt with no tie, and black leather shoes. He worked for the state de-Baathification committee but was close to the Sadrists and passed information about Baathists along to the Mahdi Army.

Sheikh Safaa spoke to me inside the prayer room. It had a green carpet and a shiny model of the shrine in Najaf. On its walls were verses from the Koran about Judgment Day and a picture of Muhammad Sadiq al-Sadr and Muqtada. Sheikh Safaa looked extremely young; his stylistically groomed beard was still not fully mature. He was very thin, with a long narrow nose. He wore modern wire-framed glasses and had a white *imama* (turban) balanced on his ears. As we spoke he held his mobile phone and prayer beads in one hand, gesticulating with the other.

He confirmed that the *husseiniya* belonged to the Office of the Martyr Sadr, which had permitted the Dawa Party to use some rooms as an office. "They are old people, and they are even not capable of carrying a weapon," he said. "The American forces denied that they attacked the *husseiniya*. They said they just attacked the Dawa office, but it was a lie. The truth is, they entered both the Dawa office and the Mustafa Husseiniya, and they killed in a very barbaric way . . . and nobody expected the Americans would do that, especially those who saw films about freedom, about America."

The young Sheikh Safaa also thought the raid was meant to send a political message. "After the Samarra bombing," he explained, "the Americans started escalating political pressure against Jaafari and other Shiites to prevent Jaafari from being the prime minister, because he doesn't look after their interests.

They think that Jaafari is the closest man to the Sadr Current, and they don't like the Sadr Current to have a friend in the prime minister's position."

Sheikh Safaa warned that his people were irate. "I have seen the feelings of the people in the last few days," he said. "They were very upset from the presence of the occupation. One of the demands put forth by the Sadr Current was that the occupation forces apologize and compensate the families of the victims. America should not kill and compensate. We don't want your compensation; just stop killing. Why do you kill and then compensate? People from different ages and backgrounds were killed in this mosque. Not everyone was a soldier in the Mahdi Army. There were old people from the Dawa Party and visitors to the Dawa Party and people praying. That's why the people in Shaab City are very angry. So the condition was not to let America go inside Shaab City again. We witnessed an American aggression, and maybe with the hands of Iraqis who work with the occupation forces."

The sheikh had been present for the raid. "We were surprised at six o'clock, which is half an hour before the prayer, by a large number of Humvees and another kind of wheeled armored vehicle," he said. "Their entrance was silent. They surrounded the *husseiniya* from everywhere. They started firing random heavy shots. It didn't have the sound of a Kalashnikov and classic light weapons. The major sound was the dushka and a heavy belt-fed machine gun. They also used bombs and grenades to attack the *husseiniya*." I was impressed by his detailed knowledge of weapons. "They came in a very ugly and barbaric way, and they were very quick," he continued. "People tried to run away and go out of the building. Because I am the imam of the mosque I have a family in my house, so I was busy taking my family outside. I have four children, and they were very scared. Until now the condition of the children is not stable. My mother is still not stable. We took her from the hospital yesterday, because of the heavy sound of the bullets and bombs."

On the evening of the raid, he said, "many infantry soldiers entered the building. They started shooting. A lot of the brothers were injured. They took them to a single place and grouped them together and executed them. One of them had a black band on his forehead because he was a sayyid. He was the one who got the most number of bullets in his body. He lost all of his brain outside his head, and I think you have already seen his brain. They went inside the shrine with a grenade, which injured a lot of people who were praying at that time. The mosque should be a place for people who want to feel safe and secure. When the occupier came to this country, we lost the security, and security is one of the most important favors that God gives to us. It's true that there was a strong oppression on Iraqis from the former regime. America came to Iraq proclaiming its liberation, and freedom and democracy and pluralism, but America proclaimed one thing and we saw something else. We saw freedom, but it is the freedom of tanks and democracy of Hummers, and instead of multiparties we saw multiple killings of people in a variety of ugly ways."

But the Americans did not just kill people at the *husseiniya*; they also tortured the men and looted the area. "One was injured with bullets and killed with knives," Sheikh Safaa said. "More than one body was tortured, his eyes were taken out, and we saw them naked after death. Some of them were very old men. The Americans stole all the light weapons: one pistol and two or three guns. Also they stole money and the two computers. They destroyed everything, broke glass, and the religious school for women. Then they blew up the cars and there was more heavy shooting."

After I left Sheikh Safaa asked Firas if I was "clean"—meaning, was I to be trusted—so that he could be sure of protecting me in the event someone tried to intercept me as I made my way home. His assistant, Abu Hassan, asked Safaa the same thing about me.

That Thursday, March 30, after I visited Humineya, Army Maj. Gen. Rick Lynch, spokesman for Multinational Forces-Iraq, gave his weekly press briefing in the Coalition Press Information Center. He stood before American and Iraqi flags wearing pressed fatigues with two stars on his collars. His face remained without expression or emotion, and he spoke in a clipped, rapid-fire style, not in sentences. As he listed his ideas, which he kept simple and repeated, his hands sliced the air to emphasize points in rhythm with his words.

"Our operations continue across Iraq towards the identified end state," Lynch said. "An Iraq that is at peace with its neighbors and is an ally in the war on terrorism, that has a representative government and respects the human rights of all Iraqis, that has security forces that can maintain domestic order and deny Iraq as a safe haven for terrorists. Now we're making progress there every day." He explained that attacks against the coalition forces were concentrated in three provinces: Baghdad, Anbar, and Salah Al-Din. He didn't say that these areas were where U.S. troops were concentrated and where some of the biggest cities were located. "The enemy," he said, "specifically the terrorists and foreign fighters, specifically Al Qaeda in Iraq, the face of which is Zarqawi, is now specifically targeting Iraqi security force members and Iraqi police. In fact, the number of attacks against Iraqi Security Forces has increased 35 percent in the last four weeks compared with the previous six months." General Lynch told the story of Sunni recruits who joined the army even after some recruits had been killed in a suicide bombing. "If that's not a testimony to the courage and conviction of the Iraqi people, I don't know what is. They're united against Zarqawi. As we've talked about before, counterinsurgency operations average nine years. The people who will win this counterinsurgency battle against Zarqawi and Al Qaeda in Iraq are the Iraqi people. And indica-

tions like that show their courage and their convictions and their commitment
to a democratic future. Amazing story."

He switched slides to a satellite image showing the Mustafa Husseiniya but
calling it "Tgt Complex." Several blocks away was a building the slide described as the Ibrahim Al Khalil Mosque, and even farther away was a building
incorrectly identified as the Al Mustafa Mosque. "Last Sunday," he began,
"Iraqi special operations forces had indications that a kidnapping cell was
working out of this target complex." He pointed to the satellite image. "This
was led, planned, and executed by Iraqi special operations forces, based on detailed intelligence that a kidnapping cell was occupying this complex." He
pointed at the *husseiniya* again. "The operation consisted of about fifty members of Iraqi special operations forces and about twenty-five U.S. advisers. The
U.S. advisers there purely in an advisory role. They did none of the fighting.
There wasn't a shot fired by U.S. service members during conduct of this operation. They surveyed the battlefield in advance, looking for sensitive areas, and
they said, Okay, there are mosques in the area, but the nearest mosque is about
six blocks from the target complex, so the decision was made to do the operation, focused on this kidnapping cell, and try to rescue a hostage, an Iraqi
hostage. Operation planned, led, and executed by Iraqi special operations
forces. They got in the area with their vehicles. They immediately started taking fire, from this complex," he said, pointing again to the map. "Now remember, many buildings in that compound and many rooms in the building. They
took fire right away, they returned fire." Once inside, "they had additional gunfire exchange."

I remembered my visit. There were no signs of any gun battle or any fire
coming from inside the *husseiniya*—no random bullet holes, no Kalashnikov
shells (although they could have been picked up). The entire affair had seemed
very one-sided.

"All told," Lynch continued, "sixteen insurgents were killed, eighteen were
detained. We found over thirty-two weapons, and we found the hostage, the
innocent Iraqi, who just twelve hours before was walking the streets of Baghdad. He was walking the streets of Baghdad en route to a hospital to visit his
brother, who had gunshot wounds. He was kidnapped and beaten in the car
en route to this complex." He pointed to the Mustafa Husseiniya again.
"When he got there, they emptied his pockets. They took out his wallet, and
in the wallet was a picture of his daughter. He asked for one thing. He said,
'Please, before you kill me, allow me to kiss the picture of my daughter. That's
all I ask.' The kidnappers told him, 'Hey, we gotcha, and if we don't get
twenty thousand dollars sometime soon, you're dead.' And they showed him
the bare electrical wires that they were gonna use to torture him, and then kill
him, and they said, 'We're gonna go away and do some drugs, and when we

come back, we're gonna kill you.' He was beaten. He was tortured. He was tortured with an electrical drill. Twelve hours after he was kidnapped, he was rescued by this Iraqi special operations forces rescue unit. He is indeed most grateful. He is most grateful to be alive, and he is most grateful to the Iraqi special operations forces. The closest mosque was six blocks away. When they got close to the compound, they took fire, and they returned fire. When they got inside the rooms, a room in this compound, they realized this could have been a 'husenaya,' a prayer room. They saw a prayer rug. They saw a minaret. They didn't know about that in advance, but from that room, and from that compound, they were taking fire. In that room, and in that compound, the enemy was holding a hostage, and torturing a hostage. And in that room, and in that compound, they were storing weapons, munitions, and IED explosive devices. Very, very effective operation, planned and executed by Iraqi special operations forces."

When asked who the enemy the previous Sunday might have been, Lynch responded that "we had no indication, no specific indication, what group these people came from. This was clearly a kidnapping cell that we'd watched for a period of time. There were indications that it was an active cell, and that's why the operation was planned by the members of the Iraqi special operations forces. Now, I can't tell you which particular unit or if they were from the Mahdi militia. I don't know. . . . Extremists, terrorists, criminals—it's all intertwined. We have reason to believe, and evidence to support, that the terrorists and foreign fighters are indeed using kidnapping as a way to finance their operations. And the story that I told about Sunday night's kidnapping could be told many more times."

The news of the American raid was—for once—greeted with delight by Sunnis, who were used to seeing Shiites celebrating when the Americans hit Sunni targets. But what really happened at the *husseiniya*? There was indeed a Sunni prisoner in the Mustafa Husseiniya, the last suspect in the killing of Haitham al-Ansari (see previous chapter). Half the Mustafa Husseiniya was controlled by the Sadrist *hawza*, with Sheikh Safaa as the spiritual leader. The other half was controlled by a man named Abu Sara, who led a Mahdi Army death squad known as a "special group." Abu Sara was an ex-Baathist and ex-member of Saddam's fedayeen militia. Safaa hated him, my friend Firas told me, because he was against armed men coming to the mosque. When the Americans struck just before the evening prayer, Abu Sara and his men had not yet arrived; they were still on their way to pray. The Americans killed ten people inside and seven outside, but they were innocent. They released the suspected Sunni killer, and he fled to Syria.

The Americans called the raid Operation Valhalla. It was conducted by the U.S. Army's 10th Special Forces Group (Airborne), commanded by Lieut. Col.

Sean Swindell and an Iraqi Special Forces unit they were training. The target was one individual who left shortly before the soldiers arrived, though I was never able to confirm what he was suspected of doing. "We came under fire and at that time had to protect ourselves," an American participant told me. "Iraqi Special Operations forces and U.S. adviser forces, as we got to the area, came under intense fire from all directions, including within the *husseiniya*. We assaulted and searched the targeted area. We stumbled upon the Sunni prisoner by accident during the course of the operation. There was one hostage rescued. He stayed with us for a number of months doing small work because he was extremely scared for his life."

One Iraqi Special Operations soldier was wounded. After the raid a senior sheikh from Ur came to complain about the raid to the Americans, along with three or four young "henchmen" of his. "He was one very bad guy," said the American who took part in the raid. "One henchman asked why we were shooting at certain buildings. We showed him we were taking heavy fire from the *husseiniya*. He said they were not shooting at us but at the helicopters." I asked the American soldier which group they were targeting. "We did not make the distinction. Bad guys were bad guys. The sheikh and his henchmen received the same briefing that was given to the prime minister and agreed with everything we presented. They were impressed with what we knew and acted on."

The Americans insisted that immediately after the battle the dead bodies were removed from the *husseiniya* along with their weapons so that it would appear to be a one-sided attack on men in a mosque. The Americans say they conducted an investigation and that the unit effectively halted operations for a month. Some of the men in the unit had cameras on their helmets, which apparently corroborated their versions in the investigation and contrasted with the version presented by reporters on the scene.

The next day, March 31, I returned to the Mustafa Husseiniya for Friday prayers. The neighborhood was shut down. Roads were blocked with tree trunks, trucks, and motorcycles. Mahdi Army militiamen sat on chairs on the main road asking for IDs and observing the men slowly walking in the sun to the noon prayer. The militiamen, most of whom were in their twenties and thirties, sported carefully groomed beards. Some wore all black; others wore cotton shirts that said "Mahdi Army" and named their unit within the militia. Some wore Iraqi police–issued bulletproof vests, and many carried police-issued Glock pistols and handcuffs at their sides. They were off-duty policemen.

By the time I arrived, thousands of people were seated in the bright sun. They wore sweatpants or *dishdashas*, and many of the older men had head scarves on their heads. Plastic, rubber, and leather slippers and shoes lined the street. As the men assembled, they stopped by wooden boxes to pick up a *torba*, a medallion-shaped piece of earth from Karbala upon which their foreheads would rest when they bowed to the ground. When they found an empty spot on the street, they opened their prayer rug, placing the *torba* at the front edge.

A wooden pulpit was set up across from the Husseiniya. Behind it a large truck was parked. It was covered in a green cloth, and a large painting of Muhammad Sadiq al-Sadr stood on its bed. Mahdi Army men patrolled the street and stood atop the *husseiniya* and on the rooftops of neighboring buildings, pacing back and forth, silhouetted against the bright sky. In the front row sat dignitaries such as Sadrist National Assembly member Fattah al-Sheikh and key clerics from the movement like Abdul Hadi al-Daraji. Hundreds of men brought umbrellas with them to provide some shelter from the sun. Young men in baseball caps with exterminator packs on their backs walked through the crowd spraying people with rose water to cool them off. Loudspeakers on the road facing different directions blasted the call to prayer.

As the call ended, a man stood up to yell a *hossa*. "Damn Wahhabism and Takfirism and Saddamism and Judaism, and pray for Muhammad!" The crowd yelled back, "Our God prays for Muhammad and the family of Muhammad!" They shook their fists, "And speed the Mahdi's return! And damn his enemies!" Sheikh Hussein al-Assadi stood up behind the pulpit, wearing a white turban and white shroud to show he was prepared for martyrdom. "Peace be upon you," he greeted the crowd. "And upon you peace and the mercy of God and his blessings," the crowd murmured back. Some in the crowd filmed the sermon on their mobile phones.

"I ask everybody to sit down except those who are on duty," he said, referring to the militiamen providing security. "Before I begin I want to express my sympathy to Muhammad and all the imams, especially the Mahdi, for the martyrs of the Mustafa Husseiniya." They had been martyred by international Zionism, world imperialism, and the American occupation, his angry voice echoed against the city's walls. "We demand that the Iraqi government expel the Zionist American ambassador from Iraq and do not accept any apology from him. . . . We demand the release of all the prisoners of the outspoken *hawza*," he said, along with the prisoners "who survived the Zionist massacre," as he called the raid. He demanded that an Iraqi court supervised by the clergy try the perpetrators of the Mustafa Husseiniya attack. He demanded that occupation forces be prohibited from entering eastern Baghdad at any time. He rejected any need to investigate the attack. It was as clear as the murder of Hussein, he said. He complained that Shiites were still waiting for the results of the investigations of the Kadhimiya bridge disaster, the Samarra and Karbala explosions, and other massacres Shiites had faced. "We demand the execution of the Wahhabi American *takfiris* who were arrested and confessed in front of all who saw them," he said. He blamed the Americans for killing Sunnis and throwing bodies in the Sadda area near Sadr City to ruin the city's reputation and blame its residents for committing crimes. "The American Zionist forces have declared that they have handed the security file to the Iraqi government," he said, "so what is the reason to violate this and attack the holy mosque of God?" The American and Iraqi governments had negotiated agreements without Parliament's review; he demanded that the Iraqi people be told what they were. He demanded that the Iraqi Security Forces declare whether they "work with the American forces against unarmed Iraqis or for Iraq?"

A man in the crowd shouted a *hossa*. "As we learned from the second Sadr, history will be written with the blood of the pious, not the silence of the fearful!" The crowd shouted, "Our God prays for Muhammad and the family of Muhammad! And speed the Mahdi's return and damn his enemies!"

The sheikh continued. "We ask God to support the outspoken *hawza* of mujahideen and the heroes of the Mahdi Army against the enemies of Islam, and to keep the Friday prayer going and to be a fork in the eye of the enemy America and especially Israel."

People ask why the outspoken *hawza* was silent, he said. "But this is the silence before the storm," he answered, warning the Americans and Zionists that he knew what they wanted to do to Muslims. "We already know very well, and I thank God for that. We already know what is going on in the dirty minds of the monkey infidels. They have a conspiracy against Islam and Muslims."

America "brought war to the Iraqi people and ended the wars with sanctions, it was trying to make Muslims hungry. . . . Today it slaughters our sons, and it has started doing the same things Saddam did, and this is exactly the same way Saddam killed us, and George Bush the Cursed said he came to get rid of Saddam's killings but instead he brought Israel's killings, and they started doing it themselves in the holiest places in Iraq, and it's only because they have hated Islam since the beginning and they hate the prayer because it is the way of communication between the servant and his lord, and they are trying to kill the belief." What was the difference, he asked, between Saddam's massacres of Shiites in mosques and the American raid on the Mustafa Husseiniya?

The spirits of the martyrs demanded that those responsible for the massacre at the Mustafa Husseiniya be exposed. The Zionists were killing and torturing injured Iraq, he said, but members of the government were too busy stealing and enriching themselves and were too afraid to lose their positions to speak the truth, as was the clergy. He asked the crowd of thousands to shout "We will never be oppressed!" and they thundered in response. Only the outspoken *hawza* of the mujahideen represented the voice of the Prophet Muhammad and his family, and they were the voice of Muhammad Sadiq al-Sadr. The jihad being waged by Muqtada's *hawza* was the Mahdi's jihad, and nobody could defeat them. "And today the outspoken *hawza* promises the martyrs that were killed in Iraq by the hands of the Zionist *takfiris* that we will return their aggression with a thousand aggressions. And we will step on the face of the Zionist ambassador if he stays in Iraq, and we will do that with our heroes of the Mahdi Army, and we will break all the legs that carried aggression on the houses of God and shed the blood of our brothers, and if the government is unable to prosecute the criminals in front of all people, then we will apply justice ourselves as much as we can, and the battalions of the Mahdi Army will never be handcuffed in case the government suspends their case, just like all the other suspended cases, like the massacres of Karbala and Kadhimiya and the destruction of the domes of the two imams in Samarra and other shedding of believers' blood. . . . The government should not put their hands in the hands of those who killed us, and we want them to prove their Iraqi identity and Islamic identity, and we want them to release our prisoners, or an eye for an eye and a tooth for a tooth."

As the streets of Ur and Shaab filled with thousands of men indolently strolling home in the heat or heading to minibuses and trucks to depart, across town, in the western neighborhood of Ghazaliya, prayer was also ending, and several hundred Sunni men were leaving the Um Al Qura Mosque, which had once been so central to the resistance. It had once been a symbol of Sunni domination; now it was a symbol of vulnerability and fear. Gruesome posters lined the mosque's walls, depicting slain members of the Association and other murdered Sunnis. "Our martyrs are twinkling stars in the Iraqi sky," said one, while others showing dead bodies demanded "yes to the state of law," "no to organized government terrorism," "no to endless sinning," and lamented what they described as a "massacre of freedom," and "massacre of seven innocent men." I was stunned by the shift in tone.

A few days later, on April 4, 2006, I was back at the Um Al Qura Mosque, waiting in the sun after a friend who moonlighted for the Association of Muslim Scholars told me the bodies of Sunnis slain in sectarian violence were coming from the morgue. In front of the Um Al Qura Mosque, Iraqi National Guardsmen manned their machine guns on a pickup truck. Ghazaliya had long been one of Baghdad's main no-go zones for foreigners, journalists, and even many Iraqis. When American or Iraqi army or police forces were not looking, Sunni militias openly patrolled its streets and stopped cars at checkpoints to look for suspicious outsiders. Shiites living in Ghazaliya had been receiving death threats, if they were lucky, warning them to leave the neighborhood. As I stood in the parking lot with a few Iraqi cameramen working for local and international media, I could hear exchanges of fire in the distance; later I saw American Humvees and Iraqi police in pickup trucks circling the mosque.

Finally we heard the sounds of wailing coming from the mosque's gate. Two trucks accompanied by men on foot made their way to the mosque. The men were crying and beating themselves, stopping to collapse on the ground or raise their arms in desperation, then shouting, "There is no god but Allah!" Their screams competing with one another, they cursed the killers. "Faggots!" "Brothers of whores!" they shouted. "This is a disaster! What did they do?"

"We are almost extinct! They broke our backs!" "The pimps! The bastards! The infidels!" I asked one of the men to tell me what had happened. "They took them in the south from their shops. They took them to an office, and then they took their car. We found them yesterday in the fridge in the morgue. They live in Ghazaliya. Four brothers. And two were father and son!" he began crying again.

An older man wearing tribal clothes and hiding his face with his head scarf shouted, "This is an Iranian wave, arranged by Iran. We are Muslims, and this is our country. Why are they doing this to us? And they are saying, 'We are the Mahdi Army.' Did the Mahdi tell them to do that? One of them is only twelve years old!" He explained that the dead were Sunni shopkeepers. "They took them to Kut, and they executed them. In the Jihad district they killed fifty-seven people. They arrested them and executed them. Everywhere they kill Sunnis." He added that when relatives came to pick up their bodies from the morgue, they too were kidnapped.

The trucks stopped at the mosque's steps. The rugs were removed from on top of them, and the wooden coffins were placed on the ground, their covers pulled to the side, revealing bodies hidden by plastic. "Open the bags so they can see," one man said. "This one is only ten years old," cried a man. "They killed him by strangling. This is a kid. Should he be strangled? Look at him. Open the bag, let them see!" The boy did indeed look about ten, his face swollen and eyes closed, thick stitches lining his chest.

They opened another coffin. "This one was tortured before killing!" one man shouted. "Look at his teeth. They pulled out his teeth! He was helping his father. Why did they do that to him? Is it only because they are Sunnis?" he raised his hands up and shouted, *Allahu akbar!* (God is great!) I looked at the corpse's bruised face: a middle-aged man missing some of his front teeth. "God curse the oppressors!" the mourners shouted, embracing the coffins and corpses. "Even Jews wouldn't do this!" shouted one man. "They say that Saddam Hussein was a tyrant, so how do you explain this?"

Then somebody decided the show was over. The coffins were placed on the trucks and driven away, followed by the Iraqi journalists. Members of the AMS remained outside, discussing a Sunni man who had gone to visit his relatives in the hospital but was kidnapped by six men. "They control the hospitals," said one man, referring to Muqtada's followers. He noticed me filming him and angrily covered the lens with his hand. I was later told that he was head of security for the AMS.

On my way back I drove through the wealthy Mansour district, where I had lived briefly in my first months in Iraq. Two bodies were lying dead on the

main street. It was a normal sight. I later found out they had been Iraqi staff of
the embassy of the United Arab Emirates. That day a Sunni friend from Amriya called me distraught because his Shiite neighbor and friend had been
killed the previous night. It was normal. At least ten bodies were found in Amriya that day. A Sunni man who picked up one of them to bring him to the hospital was also killed, for doing just that. On a different day a friend from
Amriya told me that two cars pulled up in front of a Shiite home and riddled it
with machine-gun fire. On another typical night, Shiites in a Sunni neighborhood saw masked men in their garden. They found a letter ordering them to
leave. The following day they did. One day a friend from Amriya was delayed
meeting me because seven bodies had been found on his street.

The Road to Najaf

Three days later I was on the road to Najaf from Baghdad, a key pilgrimage
route for Iraq's Shiites. It was fraught with the unique new dangers of the country's civil war. I drove down with Shiite pilgrims, aware that the day before a
minibus much like mine carrying Shiites had been sprayed with machine-gun
fire from two cars in the Sunni town of Iskandariya, about twenty-five miles
south of Baghdad. Five of the pilgrims had been killed. My companions were a
young man called Ahmed, his mother, and their friend Iskander, who was the
driver. They hailed from Sadr City, and we were going to see Muqtada speak in
the Kufa Mosque, outside Najaf.

Numerous Iraqi police and Iraqi National Guard checkpoints slowed our
progress. At each stop the policemen would peer through the driver's window
and ask where we were going. "We're a family from Sadr City," Iskander
would say, or sometimes just "from the city," since the men would know what
he meant. "We're going to Najaf." We would be waved along with a smile:
"Go in peace." We drove past brick factories and palm groves, and as we approached Najaf we were stopped more and more often, our minibus searched,
our bodies patted down. Finally all roads were closed off to vehicles. Our
minibus was parked on a sandy lot with hundreds of others. Some had
wooden coffins lashed on top. They were to be buried in the City of Peace, the
vast cemetery for Shiites who seek to lie close to Imam Ali in Najaf. ING men
waved metal detectors over all visitors. The day before, there had been a massive car bomb on this very road. Men waited with pushcarts to carry the feeble, or load as many shrouded women as possible, or carry coffins. Other
coffins were carried on relatives' backs in long processions sometimes led by
clerics. We walked past three minibuses that had been crushed and blackened
by the previous day's explosion and one car that had flipped over. ING men in
blue fatigues surrounded the charred wreckage and beseeched the many pilgrims who stopped to stare in silent wonder, "Please, brothers, move on."

Nearby was the cemetery set aside for the martyrs of the Mahdi Army. Hundreds of tombs of young Mahdi Army fighters had flags waving on them. Pictures of the dead wielding weapons were placed behind glass on the stones. Many streets in Sadr City had been named after Mahdi Army men who had been martyred by the Americans on those streets. My friend Ahmed, himself a Mahdi Army fighter, visited the tombs of his friends after regaling his mother with tales of their derring-do fighting the Americans in Sadr City. Ahmed was related to an important Shiite politician, and his oldest brother led Mahdi Army fighters and planted roadside bombs for American convoys. I was told Ahmed dabbled in this as well.

We continued to the Shrine of Ali, cousin and son-in-law of the Prophet Muhammad. A steady stream of pilgrims went through the stringent security procedures to enter. Coffins were carried into the mosque to circle around Ali's tomb before burial. Iranian pilgrims had their pictures taken in front of the shrine by enterprising Najaf boys with enough Farsi to take advantage of the dazed pilgrims. Pilgrims kissed the wooden doors and entered the vast courtyard where the golden shrine shimmered in the sun. Families sat in the shade and picnicked; others prayed together or strolled around. Outside, boys sold souvenir photos of Shiite leaders such as Ayatollah Khomeini, Ayatollah Sistani, Muqtada al-Sadr and his father.

Kufa, a town just outside Najaf, was dominated by followers of Muqtada. As we approached the Kufa Mosque, all roads were once more blocked off. We were searched by members of the Mahdi Army. Lugubrious *latmiyas* (mournful songs) echoed from the stalls, describing in rhythmic beats the death of Hussein, grandson of the Prophet, and professing loyalty to him. The mosque's thick walls looked fortified. It had been used as a base for the Mahdi Army during the 2004 intifada, when thousands of fighters battled the Americans in Najaf and Kufa. Inside the mosque fighters had lined up to receive food and advanced weapons training. Small groups were instructed in how to use grenades and grenade launchers. Crates full of weapons had been stored in the mosque in those days, as well as in Muqtada's office in Najaf.

It was in Kufa that Muhammad Sadiq al-Sadr made his forty-seven famous sermons, beginning in 1998, when Saddam relaxed restrictions on such activities. Saddam promoted Sadr at first, viewing him as an Iraqi nationalist and as a pliable tool to use against Shiite leaders of Iranian or Pakistani descent, and against Iran. But Sadr, like Thomas à Becket, did not show sufficient loyalty to the ruler. In his last sermons he even criticized Saddam. In 1999 Sadr and two of his sons were shot on the road by unknown assailants. The government accused rival Shiites of the murder and executed the suspects, but Sadr's followers blamed Saddam and rioted. Many were killed in Sadr City, then known as Saddam City. Some Sadrists blamed the Hakim family or Iran for the assassination. After the war Muqtada took over the Kufa Mosque, and it was to this mosque that he retreated in April

2004 when his followers began their intifada, urging them to "make your enemy afraid" and assuring them that he would not abandon them. "Your enemy loves terror and hates peoples, all the Arabs, and censors opinions," he said.

Kufa has a mystical importance to Shiites. Some Iraqi Shiites believe Kufa Mosque is the oldest mosque in the world. Imam Hussein's cousin, Muslim bin Aqil, was buried there after being slain by the same traitors who would later kill Hussein. Many Shiites believe that the Mahdi will return to that mosque, descending down from heaven onto its dome.

In the market outside stands sold souvenir pictures or key chains of Muqtada and his father, as well as books by Shiite thinkers like Muqtada's uncle Muhammad Baqir al-Sadr, the most important Shiite theologian of the twentieth century, who led the Dawa Party and was executed along with his sister Bint al-Huda by Saddam in 1980. (Muhammad Baqir al-Sadr was known as the first martyr, and Muhammad Sadiq al-Sadr was known as the second martyr.) Books by Khomeini were also available. One stand sold films of Muqtada's sermons as well as panegyrics to Muqtada and films depicting his men battling the Americans. A large group of men stood around to watch these films. Other stands sold newspapers associated with Muqtada's movement, such as *Al Hawza* and *Sharikat al-Sadr* (Rays of Sadr).

A crowd assembled to receive Muqtada's latest *bayan*, a piece of paper with his rulings on certain questions. That week's *bayan* was formulated in a typical way: a real or hypothetical question was posed, followed by Muqtada's response.

"*Seyiduna al mufadda*," began the question, meaning, "Our Lord, for whom we sacrifice ourselves." "In the Iraqi streets these days, there is a lot of talk . . . about militias. And as your eminence knows, some politicians classify the army of the Imam al-Mahdi, God speed his appearance, under this title. So do you classify the army under this title just like the case with the brothers in the Badr Organization and the Kurdish *pesh merga*, or do you classify it under another classification, and does your eminence encourage its members to join the government institutions, especially the security and military ones?" The question was signed by a "group of members of the Mahdi Army," and whether they were real or not, it was clearly also an official attempt to distinguish the Mahdi Army from the Badr Organization, which belonged to the Supreme Council for the Islamic Revolution in Iraq, and the *pesh merga*, which belonged to the Kurdistan Democratic Party (KDP) and the Patriotic Union of Kurdistan (PUK).

Muqtada provided several answers. He began by defining a militia as an "armed group which is outside the control of the government and which belongs to political parties." "According to my understanding," he wrote, "by armed groups they mean a group that has been armed by a specific party or specific political entity. But as you know most of the Iraqis armed themselves by themselves after the collapse of the dirty Aflaqists," he wrote, referring to Baathists by their founder, Michel Aflaq. The Mahdi Army was an outlaw only to oppressive governments, he continued; so as long as the government was legitimate, meaning not oppressive and not associated with the people's enemies, then the Mahdi Army was with it "in a single trench." Most importantly, he wrote, "We are not a political party, we are the *hawza ilmiya* which speaks the truth, and we and the Mahdi Army belong to it, and this is an honor for us in this world and the next world. The fourth answer, the sons of this honest sect [Shiites], God make them victorious, consider themselves soldiers of the imam. . . . And that means their actual leader is the imam himself, God speed his return." His fifth answer was that "according to what I know, the registered armed militias under the so-called current government are only nine, and the Mahdi Army is not one of them. In addition, the Mahdi Army is not a party and it is not an organization. There is no salary, no headquarters, there is no special organization, there is no arming, and every weapon is a personal weapon, if they have one." Muqtada added that it was the occupiers, the Saddamists, and the *takfiris* who had provoked these questions. "If they really want to benefit the people," he wrote, "they must fight terrorism and take off its arm, and they should provide security and safety to our patient people. Otherwise they are not protecting Iraqis, and they are not letting the Iraqis protect themselves." Finally, he wrote that the Mahdi Army belonged to the Shiite leadership in the *hawza*, which had refused to dissolve it in the past, "especially after they knew it belongs to the Mahdi," because the Shiite leadership were the deputies of the Mahdi. He was both implying that Ayatollah Sistani supported the Mahdi Army and appointing himself one of the Mahdi's deputies.

Reassured that they could all belong to Muqtada's militia because Muqtada had said so, his followers marched into the mosque, past more security, who asked me to turn on my camera and confirm that it was harmless. Many of the men carried their prayer rugs on their shoulders and set them down on the concrete courtyard. The mosque was being restored, and scaffolding lined some of its walls. It had shiny marble columns and new wooden rafters on its ceiling. Next to each column were grim-faced men wearing dark suit jackets. Beneath the jackets were guns, and they had their arms pressed down both to hide the guns and to reach them quicker. They looked like cruder versions of the Hizballah security men who protected Sayyid Hassan Nasrallah in Lebanon when he spoke in public. In the past they had openly carried Kalashnikovs, but this was considered undignified. More than ten thousand people were in attendance, many of them women, who sat in a separate section. There were more children than I had ever seen at a mosque, for Muqtada was the "cool" cleric, a fighter who defied authority, and he specifically reached out to children, offering them notebooks and stickers for their schoolbooks. As the call to prayer ended, the crowd chanted and sang songs they all knew by heart. For Shiites, praying at a mosque is very much a communal activity. Unlike Sunnis, who go to whatever mosque is nearest to their home, Shiites take buses to attend the Friday prayers at several key mosques, leading to crowds in the tens of thousands and to expressions of communal pride and solidarity.

Muqtada waddled with his head down as he always did, surrounded by his assistants and bodyguards. A murmur and then a frisson went through the crowd spreading out to the back, and people stood up to glimpse him. They had not been expecting him to speak that day, but rather one of his deputies. *"Ali wiyak!"* they thundered, waving their fists, meaning "Ali is with you!" Muqtada was flanked by his two closest friends and advisers. On his left stood the young and very thin Ayatollah Ali al-Baghdadi, originally from Sadr City. On his right stood his more rotund brother-in-law, Riyadh Nuri. Nuri was normally the imam of the Kufa Mosque and had also led Muqtada's Islamic courts, which arrested and tortured people for suspected infractions ranging from homosexuality, selling pornography, and theft to insulting Muqtada. Nuri lived with Muqtada in the same house and had often taken care of Muqtada's mentally handicapped brother, who died in 2004. He also commanded Mahdi Army fighters, whom he would dispatch to arrest people. Nuri raised his hand to quiet the excited crowd as Muqtada began by reading the normal blessings before the sermon. Like his father, Muqtada spoke quietly, without the emotion many clerics invest in their speeches. Not a talented speaker, he almost seemed to mumble in a gruff monotone.

I had been told by his associates that he was not meeting with the media now for security reasons, so the closest I could get to him was sitting before him as he delivered his sermon. "We demand the reconstruction of the shrine in Samarra and protection for it," Muqtada said. "We condemn the malicious hands that exploded the shrines." Muqtada read a verse from the Koran and then switched into Iraqi dialect, as was his style. He kept his eyes down most of the time, reading from his notes and only glancing up occasionally. He spoke of doing the right and preventing the wrong. "This is the time when the right becomes wrong and the wrong becomes right," he said, "when women become corrupt. Occupation became liberation and resistance became terrorism." The occupation had joined the Nawasib, which to Muqtada's followers meant all Sunnis. "Look at both of them," he said, "the occupation and the Nawasib, and look at their values." He called for Muslims to be united. "Which Muslims?" he asked. "The ones who follow the family of the Prophet," meaning Shiites. "In the past God punished people by sending frogs, locusts, lice," Muqtada explained. "Now he punishes them by sending earthquakes, mad cow disease, hurricanes, floods, bird flu, the diseases in Africa, and globalization, armies, politics, solar and lunar eclipses."

Muqtada sat down for a minute, and somebody in the crowd shouted a *hossa*. "For the love of the oppressed, the two martyrs, the Sadrs, pray for Muhammad and the family of Muhammad!" Thousands of people bellowed, "Our God prays for Muhammad and the family of Muhammad." Then they waved their fists and continued, "And speed the Mahdi's return! And damn his enemies!" In the past they had continued with "and make his son succeed. Muqtada! Muqtada! Muqtada!" But this had recently been taken out of the chant, and Muqtada's hundreds of thousands of followers in the country had dutifully followed.

Muqtada stood up once again. "On the anniversary of the Iraqi occupation," he said, "I want to discuss some issues such as a timetable for the withdrawal of the occupation." He expressed his condolences to all the followers of the family of the Prophet for the raid on the Mustafa Husseiniya two weeks earlier. "That attack was not the first done by the occupation forces," he said. "It is part of a series of bad attacks that attack the civilian and the armed, the police and the army. The occupation started attacking everybody: civilians, army, police, even the Iraqi ministers, the minister of interior and the minister of transportation, and some of the Parliament members and others. It started killing civilians in the streets and in public areas. They are killing us randomly. They drag the cars using their tanks. And they torture the prisoners in Abu Ghraib and Um Qasr and other hidden prisons in Iraq. In addition to causing civil strife and civil war, they made our neighbors our enemies, accusing some of them of sending armed people and others with hosting armed people and another with sowing terrorism."

"We did not have a country under Saddam, and now that Saddam is gone, why can we not have a country?" He added that the occupiers could not prove anything they had accused Iraq's neighbors of doing. "Even though we and our neighbors have one religion and we have one fate, the United States succeeded in dividing us and making us enemies. Instead of reconstructing the shrine of the two imams in Samarra, the occupation is building prisons," Muqtada said, then switched to Iraqi dialect to quip, "preparing them for the Iraqi people."

He returned to classical Arabic and continued. "They steal Iraqi resources to torture Iraqis. They arrest a lot of people from any force in Iraq that is against the occupation." Iraqis had gotten used to these attacks, Muqtada said, adding that his father's followers had gone from oppression under "Haddam" (playing on the former dictator's name and replacing it with "the destroyer") to oppression and torture under the occupation. "So be patient, my brothers," he said. "They are trying to plant a civil war. Do not let them drag you into the war. We know that they are going to assassinate our clerics and our leaders to make a sectarian and civil war. We will never be oppressed. So do everything not to apply the American idea called democracy." America said it sought democracy for Iraq, but it had changed its mind, Muqtada claimed. It now wanted to grant power to the terrorists, he said, referring to recent American attempts to include Sunnis in the government. "So the American interference in Iraqi politics is very clear," he said, "because you see the American ambassador appear in all the Iraqi conferences, meeting with Iraqi politicians, which we consider a terrible assault on us. . . . We all know that for every minister there is a foreign adviser assigned by the occupation. This is against the religion. Even the press, when they insult the Prophet Muhammad, they say this is the freedom of the press. And when our press writes something which is a fact but is against America, they say it is calling for terrorism. So this is all proof that the small Satan has gone and the big Satan has come. Everyone knows that we have demanded a timetable for the American withdrawal. They refused our demand because they said scheduling the withdrawal of the occupation is a victory for the terrorists, and that is a bad justification."

Muqtada asked all the nationalist forces in Iraq to help him pressure the occupying forces to schedule their withdrawal. He called for the United Nations, the Arab League, and the Organization of the Islamic Conference to cooperate with him in what he called "the national project for scheduling the withdrawal of the occupation of Iraq." He explained that the withdrawal should begin in Iraq's stable areas, such as the south, some of the middle (the Shiite areas), and the north. He demanded a phased withdrawal, beginning in the cities, "but in a real way." He insisted that security be handed to Iraqis, and that Iraqi airspace be used by military planes only with the permission of the Parliament and the governorates. He wanted the Iraqi Security Forces to be trained without the occupiers and all government members to refrain from associating with the occupiers. "The Iraqi Parliament should be able to schedule the withdrawal of the occupation from Iraq," he said, "but the withdrawal should be scheduled in steps. Every place the Americans leave, Iraqi forces that are fully trained and fully supplied should replace them. The hot areas—and of course they are on fire—they should be controlled by the national battalions composed of the army, the police and national security forces, and other people's forces, and should be supervised by the Iraqi Parliament. And there should be an operations center to design a good plan to make it stable, and the Iraqi leaders should take some of the responsibility in controlling that."

Muqtada withdrew, and the prayer leader led the mosque in prayer. After prayers ended thousands of excited men rushed the windows and fences along the passageway from which Muqtada and his entourage would depart, hoping to see him one last time. "Ali is with you!" they shouted over and over again as he quickly walked by. The crowd slowly made its way out of the mosque as more *hossas* were shouted. "Curse America and Israel, and pray for Muhammad and the family of Muhammad!" shouted one man, and thousands of departing faithful shouted with him. Then they sang a song known to them all. "Oh Mahdi, oh awaited one, return him safely, this is the son of Sadr."

IN BAGHDAD that same day the important Shiite Buratha Mosque was attacked, leaving nearly one hundred dead and more than one hundred wounded. It was the second postwar attack on this mosque (it had a long history of being attacked), and it would not be the last, for another suicide bomber struck in June. Shiite politician Jalaluddin al-Saghir of the Supreme Council for the Islamic Revolution in Iraq was the imam. He angrily placed responsibility on Sunnis, accusing two Sunni newspapers—*Al Basa'ir*, the voice of the Association of Muslim Scholars, and *Al I'tisam*, the voice of Sunni politician Adnan al-Dulaimi—of causing the attacks by falsely accusing the Buratha Mosque of being used as a secret prison for Sunnis and of being the site of mass graves for them.

On the road back to Baghdad my companions could not hide their excitement at having seen Muqtada speak. Ahmed called all his friends on his mobile phone. He repeatedly let me know how lucky I was. It was a quiet ride until we arrived in the southern Baghdad area of Dora. The road was blocked by Iraqi police cars, and we heard gunfights in the distance as we sat in traffic. Dora was a mixed neighborhood, but it was majority-Sunni, and Sunni militias were very strong there. It was once one of Baghdad's nicest neighborhoods, with many expensive homes, but terrorism had brought the prices down, as it had in other unsafe neighborhoods.

IN APRIL 2006 the Mahdi Army attacked a number of high-ranking insurgents, including prominent former Baathists in Baghdad's Adhamiya neighborhood. They captured the suspects and left with them. Irate locals began shooting at members of the Iraqi National Guard (ING), and they accused both the Badr Organization and the Iranian Revolutionary Guards of being involved. In fact, it was a Mahdi Army operation. In the days that followed, Iraqi police fired randomly into Adhamiya. They also shot at generators and cut power cables to punish the residents. Residents could not leave their homes for days in a row. It was more evidence to Sunnis that the state was at war with them.

Following the battles, the Association of Muslim Scholars released a statement accusing the Interior Ministry's Special Forces and the Shiite militias of attacking Adhamiya. "The people of Adhamiya defended their city with honor," the statement said, "and they lost seven martyrs and nineteen injured. We have realized that satellite channels like Hurra and Al Arabiya have changed the truth, and they have shown the Interior commandos and its militias as the helpers who helped the people of Adhamiya from an attack being done by other armed people despite the fact that these forces were the ones who attacked the city. And we saw that the ING leader who is responsible for protecting the city was just watching and doing nothing."

On April 21, 2006, I returned to Adhamiya's Abu Hanifa Mosque—which I had first visited three years earlier, almost to the day—on the Friday following the clashes between local fighters and Iraqi Security Forces. The mosque's security men were so stunned to see a foreigner that they could come up with no objections to my presence. Iraqi National Guardsmen stood watch outside. Following the February 22 Samarra attack, mortars had been fired on Abu Hanifa. It was the most important Sunni symbol that Shiite militias hoped to attack. The clock tower, which had been damaged by American missiles three years earlier, was been repaired. Outside hung banners different from the ones I first saw in April 2003. Now they were white banners for martyrs from the recent clashes. One gave condolences to Sunni politician Saleh al-Mutlaq from the families of Adhamiya for the murder of his kidnapped brother Taha. Another had a photo of a young man called Muhamad Fawad Latufi Annadawi pasted on it. The banner said he had been martyred "in the battle of Adhamiya on the morning of Monday, April 17, 2006. Another banner was for Latif Yawar Alyas, who was also martyred in the battle of Adhamiya. A black banner notified residents of the death of a woman.

Loudspeakers echoed the call to prayer and the reading of the Koran as locals made their way in, their slippers susurrating on the street. They stopped to be patted down by the mosque's militia. The walls inside were intricately detailed, inlaid with geometric carvings, honeycombed in its dome. About five hundred men prayed quietly. Ibrahim al-Naama, an aged cleric wearing a white hat with a red top, took out his glasses, donned them, and stood up. He spoke in a raspy and high-pitched voice. As was custom, he began by discussing Islam. "We want to talk about how the Prophet Muhammad was and how his friends were, so we can be like them in these difficult days." He made reference to the writings of Ibn Taimiya, and thanked God that he was a Muslim and a Sunni. This kind of explicit sectarian pride would have been shocking a year before, but now it was commonplace.

Moving on to the specific matter of "the ugly attack on Adhamiya," he questioned whether the attackers were Muslims and warned that "anyone who kills Muslims on purpose will be in hell forever, and God will prepare a very hard punishment for him." He demanded that the Defense Ministry prevent "other forces," meaning the Interior Ministry, police, and militias, from entering Adhamiya, and that it alone control security. "Do not let other forces interfere in the security issues of Adhamiya," he said.

Iraqis were looking forward to the establishment of the new government, he said, because they hoped it could prevent Iraqi bloodshed. "Therefore any obstacle put in the way of forming the government will increase the bloodshed, and those who are causing it will be responsible before God." He was referring to the obstinacy of Shiite parties that were refusing to accommodate Sunni demands for inclusion and sufficient influence. "Who could have imagined that the blood of Iraqis will be the cheapest blood?" he demanded. "This is how the occupiers want to divide the Iraqi people. This is how they want to plant sectarian division.

This is how the occupiers succeed in their mission." The Americans hated Iraqis' refusal to be defeatist, as did their "tails," he said, referring to the Shiite parties such as Dawa and the Supreme Council with a term Iraqis were sure to recognize (Saddam had often called Israel and Britain the "tails of America").

After the sermon there was more silent prayer, ending with each man turning to his left and to his right while still kneeling, and wishing his neighbors peace as well as the mercy and blessings of God. Men stood up and shook hands, making their way out of the mosque into the blinding sun. Neighbors stopped to greet one another and chat, smiling. A bulletin board by the mosque's door had two papers stuck on it with pictures of middle-aged martyrs, both wearing Iraqi military uniforms. Men paused to read the signs. Past the heavily armed guards, there were no more radical books being sold, only a vegetable stand and a mendicant woman in black rocking back and forth with her baby on her lap as people walked by. I went to eat lunch in Adhamiya's famous kabob and shawarma restaurant. That afternoon I interviewed a doctor in the neighborhood; he paused every so often when the sound of firefights interrupted our conversation. He was most shocked that even the sanctity of the hospital was no more, as militias were entering to capture people.

FOLLOWING THE DECEMBER 2005 elections and the victory of the United Iraqi Alliance, as the main Shiite list was known, U.S. Ambassador Zalmay Khalilzad immediately began working with American favorite Ayad Allawi as well as with the Kurdish leader Massoud Barzani and various Sunni parliamentary leaders to sideline the Shiites and ensure that Prime Minister Jaafari did not remain in office. Jaafari was seen as weak, ineffective, and implicated in Iraq's descent into civil war. Shiites already distrusted Khalilzad because he was a Sunni Muslim who was determined to give Sunnis a greater role in the state. The Shiites got nervous; the Sadrists, who were strong supporters of Jaafari, were galvanized.

Within the Shiite camp the contest was between the Supreme Council's Adil Abdel Mahdi and the Dawa Party's Jaafari. But the Supreme Council was seen as too close to Iran, and there were worries that Abdel Mahdi would not be independent, having to answer to Supreme Council leader Hakim. Khalilzad let it be known that he didn't support Abdel Mahdi.

Khalilzad was a "rogue ambassador," an American intelligence official told me. "He was contravening U.S. policy. He unilaterally blocked Adil. It was U.S. policy to reject Jaafari but not Adil, but [Khalilzad] just personally did not like the Supreme Council, while the White House and Meghan O'Sullivan of the NSC wanted the Supreme Council to be the strategic partner."

The process of forming a government dragged on for four months. Jaafari wouldn't budge. The Iranians backed him. Sistani didn't want to get involved.

The Americans felt as though they were losing the Shiites and hard-liners were taking over. "Hard-core Mahdi Army and Al Qaeda were ascendant, and moderate Shiites were getting weak," a senior American observer told me. "A self-sustaining cycle of violence was developing."

U.S. Secretary of State Condoleezza Rice and British Foreign Secretary Jack Straw went to Baghdad and told Jaafari that he did not have anybody's support and could not form a government, implying that he should give up. But Jaafari was still insisting he had support. The decision to remove him came from within his own political bloc in the government, particularly the Dawa Party.

In 2003 the Dawa Party was very weak. It was a party of Islamist intellectuals with no serious popular base that couldn't challenge Sadr or Hakim. During the Saddam era, many of its leaders were exiled, its local activists executed. The first United Iraqi Alliance, formed in the run-up to the January 2005 election, had been completely shaped by Ayatollah Sistani. But subsequently Hakim, Dawa, and the Supreme Council grew stronger, and in the next elections Sistani had a much smaller role.

Among the governing parties, the modernist, middle-class Dawa was viewed as insignificant. It had never called for clerical rule, unlike the Supreme Council. It gained only ten seats in the first Parliament. The other Shiite parties thought they could control Dawa, especially when they anointed Dawa leader Jaafari as premier in April 2005. But because Dawa now had access to money and the Iraqi security forces, it didn't need its former sponsors. Dawa leaders became arbiters and brokers of power.

Dawa Party insiders described Jaafari to me as indecisive, weak, and guilty of neglect, but not evil. He may have wanted a confrontation with Sunnis, but he did not lead it or organize the formal military response to increased attacks by Sunnis. He lacked the resolve. "Jaafari was incompetent and had no oversight over the Ministry of Interior," an American intelligence official told me. According to another senior Dawa official, "Jaafari was weak, ineffective. He didn't endorse the civil war, he was genuinely nonsectarian. He didn't hate Sunnis, he didn't believe in the exclusive power of Shiites, but he lacked control." There were no books or computers in his office. He read Arabic poetry and drank tea all day long. In meetings with senior American officials, he would quote poetry and talk about how the Iraqi people were like flowers. They dreaded meeting with him. "Iran had a role," one former minister close to Jaafari told me. "They forced people to confront what was happening and use resources under their control to organize a fighting force. Iran did that with its direct and indirect agents in Iraq."

Despite the calls for Jaafari's removal, he would not leave until the *marajiya*, or *hawza* leadership in Najaf, withdrew its support for him. There was an air of desperation among members of the Shiite parties, who felt they were being outmaneuvered by the Americans and their Iraqi rivals. A Dawa insider who was present in senior Dawa leadership circles told me, "In the last days of Jaafari, a number of people convinced the Supreme Council that he would agree to withdraw his candidacy if the premiership stayed with Dawa. His condition was that Adil [Abdel Mahdi of the Supreme Council] would not become prime minister."

Ali al-Adib was the Dawa Party candidate most likely to replace Jaafari. The American and British ambassadors went to see Adib to confirm that they were not opposed to him, and he was, in fact, prime minister for one day. But in a Dawa Party gathering to confirm Adib's nomination, Nuri al-Maliki confronted him with the issue of his father, known as Zandi, who was an Iranian immigrant to Iraq. Maliki asked Adib if he would be able to withstand scrutiny and people saying that Iran was taking over. Not being confrontational, Adib lost heart, and Maliki pounced. This putsch had been organized by Adnan al-Kadhimi, Jaafari's senior adviser, who ran his office and worked in the party's political bureau. Jaafari felt betrayed by Kadhimi and still expected to call the shots within the party and the government. Maliki then turned on Kadhimi. "Maliki is a very vindictive man, and has a dangerous streak," the Dawa insider explained. Kadhimi knew too much. Maliki arrested him on trumped-up charges of theft, and allowed his prearranged escape.

Maliki was a "gruff doer," said his former friend, "a very angry person, angry about his conditions. He had deep hatred of the Americans. He thought they were responsible for keeping Saddam in power. He was full-square against the Americans, avoided opposition conferences. He was the typical Iraqi *dishdasha* type, least affected by foreign non-Iraqi habits. In Syria he was known to be a nonpolished street warrior in the '90s. He had no power compared to Jaafari in those days. Jaafari was the party then, though many people resented it because he lectures people and talks nonsense a lot. Maliki felt aggrieved by the intellectuality of the Dawa Party leadership. The Dawa thought of itself as a vanguard party. Jaafari presented himself as a great theoretician. Maliki wasn't a real leader. He was doing intelligence and jihadi operations in Iraq, out of Damascus: killings of officers at the border, throwing a grenade here, overseeing the militants. Low-level resistance work, so you have to report to Syrian intelligence, and he was resentful of that."

Maliki became premier with the understanding that Jaafari would be the éminence grise, a first among equals. He didn't think much of Maliki. "Jaafari belittled these people," the insider said. "He thought of himself like Lenin, that he had all the makings of a historic leader." This showed when Jaafari ran for Parliament in the 2010 election campaign, especially when he slightly modified a quote of Imam Hussein as he set off to fight Yazid and used it to compare himself to the great Shiite leader. "In April 2006 Maliki came in as prime minister and looked bumbling and foolish," the insider said, "but he is a clever street fighter and surrounded himself with cronies, equally aggrieved people, many from Nasiriya." Maliki has a complex relationship with Iran, the insider explained. "He has some Arab dislike of Iran, he dislikes Iranian arrogance and haughtiness, but he has the Arab Shiite problem: Iran can do without you, but you can't do without them. Maliki has a deep hatred of Syria from his time there. Syrian intelligence thought of these people as disposable blaggards. They abused and humiliated them. You would have to report every day to some jerk and live in great material discomfort. If you're going to be an agent, better to be a Saudi agent."

The United States hardly knew anything about Maliki. The CIA did not have a biography of Maliki prepared when he was chosen to be Prime Minister, but their leadership analysts had many. The White House and National Security Council were surprised when his name came up, but Kurdish President Jalal Talabani, Sunni Vice President Tariq al-Hashimi, and other Iraqis said they could work with him, so American concerns about the unknown Maliki were allayed.

While the Americans didn't select Maliki, they didn't reject him either—which they could have done. "Maliki is cut from a different material than Jaafari," a Dawa insider who worked with him told me. "He is more rural or tribal, not urban. He's from the Hashmiya district outside Karbala. It was a Dawa hotbed. His upbringing was rural, a son of the tribes, *urbi* [with Arab traditions] with certain ethical codes, sacrifice your self-interest for your code. The urbanized are different; self-interest comes first. He is tribal in a general way. He doesn't have ideological or theological issues with Sunnis, just practical ones: if they attack us, we will attack them. Maliki has more political appeal; he is what Iraqis need. Saddam was *urbi* too, so he could mobilize tribal Arabs against Iran. If you ignore ideology and just look at what he did, it's like Saddam, but he is not as smart as Saddam. Saddam had the same social origins. Maliki within the Dawa Party was a very powerful person. He was a hardliner, doubtful of everything foreign, clinging by instinct to people he knows."

At first Maliki was diffident, quiet, nervous. He was concerned about security and the loyalty of his forces. He didn't know anything about the government he was inheriting, nor how its forces were arrayed, nor how the U.S. military worked. It was like Iraq 101. In conversations with the Americans, he made it clear his priorities were getting their help to secure Baghdad and protect the infrastructure. Maliki was suspicious; he saw a Baathist behind every bush. He didn't trust his own army. American Gen. George Casey thought the Iraqi Security Forces were strong and would be loyal to Maliki.

Jaafari's men switched to Maliki once he took over, but he didn't trust them and hired his own people. He set up his office with a close-knit circle of Dawa advisers. It was not a national unity government. The Kurds got suspicious. They thought it was dangerous that nobody saw how decisions were made. The prime minister's office was full of Dawa people nobody knew. It obviously wasn't a national unity government that was forming but rather a patchwork of spoils. Maliki was under pressure from all sides. The U.S. military and Defense Secretary Donald Rumsfeld were pressuring him, and Baghdad was disintegrating. Maliki had to deal with internal United Iraqi Alliance politics and competing Shiite factions. He had been thrust into the worst job in the world.

Maliki was committed to preserving the new Shiite-dominated order and soon threatened to use "maximum force" against the "terrorists." Even if he was committed to the creation of a national unity government and nonsectarian security forces, and even if the Americans tried to reverse the sectarian trend in Iraq, it seemed too late. Muqtada's supporters would not voluntarily relinquish control of the army or police, and having fought the Americans in the past and established their nationalist bona fides, many were eager to rid themselves of the occupiers they felt they no longer needed. Who would replace them? There was no nonsectarian movement, there was no nonsectarian militia, and no social space for those rejecting sectarianism. Even secular Sunnis and Shiites were being pushed into the embrace of sectarian militias because nobody else could protect them. The tens of thousands of cleansed Iraqis, the relatives of those killed by the death squads, the sectarian supporters and militias firmly ensconced in the government and its ministries, the Shiite refusal to relinquish their long-awaited control of Iraq, the Kurdish commitment to secession, the Sunni harboring of Salafi jihadists—all militated against anything but full-scale civil war.

I WAITED AND WATCHED, wondering if Sunnis would be removed from Baghdad slowly; or as the result of a Sarajevo-like incident; or one such as the 1975 Ayn al-Rummanah bus attack in Lebanon, which sparked that country's civil war; or another attack such as the one on the Samarra shrine; or perhaps the assassination of an important Shiite cleric or leader. The Sunnis would be totally cleansed from Baghdad, and Shiites would wage an all-out war against Sunnis. The Kurds, having waited for this opportunity, would be able to secede and tell the world they tried to have good faith and go the federalist route, but those crazy Arabs down south were killing one another, and who would want to belong to a country like that? The Iraqi nation-state would cease to be relevant. Would Sunnis throughout the region tolerate a Shiite Iraq and the killing of Sunnis by Shiites? Iraq's Sunni tribes extended into Syria, Jordan, Saudi Arabia, and elsewhere. Their tribal kinsmen might come to their aid, sending reinforcements of men and matériel across the porous borders. Iraq's civil war would become a regional war.

As the summer heat peaked in Iraq, so too did the violence. North of Baghdad Shiite villagers attacked Sunnis in retaliation for a bombing that killed at least twenty-five Shiites. The Shiite attackers were joined by Iraqi police and

Americans. Following a massive bomb targeting Shiites in Sadr City, several mortars were fired at the Abu Hanifa Mosque. Locals then clashed with Iraqi Security Forces. Sunni parliamentarian Taysir Najah al-Mashhadani from the Islamic Party was kidnapped by alleged Shiite militias as her convoy drove through the Shaab neighborhood, prompting the main Sunni coalition to boycott the government. A reconciliation proposal offered by Maliki was rejected by Shiites like Muqtada for being too soft on Baathists and Sunnis, and it was rejected by Sunnis such as Harith al-Dhari of the Association of Muslim Scholars for not going far enough with its offer of amnesty and inclusion.

Iraqis were breaking the final taboo, asking one another if they were Sunni or Shiite. Sometimes this was done obliquely, the petitioner inquiring about one's name, or one's neighborhood, or one's tribe, to try to figure it out, and sometimes it was explicit. Officially, Iraqis tried to stress that they were non-sectarian. On one television channel a poetry contest featured poets chanting that Iraq was unified, but those sorts of protests typically were a desperate attempt to avoid the fact that Iraq was breaking apart.

By 2005 Sunnis and Shiites were using derogatory terms to refer to one another. To Shiites, Sunnis were "Saddamists" and "Nawasib." "Saddamists" referred to Baathists and former regime loyalists, but many Shiites, especially the poor and uneducated, used it as a blanket term for all Sunnis. Shiite leaders, including Ayatollah Sistani, Ayatollah Yaqoubi, and Muqtada, used the term in their speeches to refer specifically to Salafis. Many Shiites have taken to calling all Sunnis Wahhabis, the strict brand of Islam associated with Saudi Arabia.

Extreme Sunnis believed Shiites were *"rafidha"* or *"turs."* "Rafidha" is technically the opposite of "Nawasib": it means "rejectionists" and referred to those who do not recognize the Islamic caliphs and want a caliphate from the descendant of Imam Ali. It was used initially by Salafis and Wahhabis to pronounce Shiites as outside Islam, and it has become a pejorative term used the way American racists spit out the word "nigger." *"Turs"* is the word for "shield" and refers to human shields used by the enemy infidels. It is permitted to kill these shields according to some interpretations of Islamic jurisprudence. Iraqi Salafis referred to the Iraqi Muslims they killed (such as members of the Iraqi police and army) as *turs* to justify killing people who were nominal Muslims but were shielding the Americans. Salafis and jihadis believed that Shiite religious leaders were supplying shields by encouraging their followers to join the Iraqi police and army.

The Arab world has always been dominated by Sunnis, who make up 85 percent of the world's Muslims. The new Shiite Iraq was aggressive and confident, overturning the Ottoman and colonialist legacies that entrenched Sunnis. It threatened the status quo throughout the Arab world. In Syria, already viewed as dominated by the Shiite-like Alawite minority that is hated by many in the Sunni majority, the Iranians built a mosque commemorating a battle that Imam Ali lost. The unpopular Sunni regimes of Jordan, Egypt, Saudi Arabia, and elsewhere, the so-called moderate Arabs, seeing their power wane, could no longer be anti-American or anti-Israeli, having sold out on those issues and backed the Americans. Instead they were playing the sectarian card to regain the respect they lost from their population and galvanize them against a new threat. Egyptian President Hosni Mubarak accused Shiites of being fifth columnists, loyal to Iran. In Lebanon during the 2006 demonstrations that followed the publication of the Danish cartoons, Sunni clerics condemned Shiites and supported Al Qaeda in Iraq leader Abu Musab al-Zarqawi (one cleric called him "my sheikh, my emir"), perhaps hoping they could appropriate the so-called "sheikh of the slaughterers" as their own to gain more leverage against the powerful Shiite Hizballah. More ominous, in April 2006 Hizballah accused nine men of attempting to assassinate its general secretary, Sayyid Hassan Nasrallah. Hizballah said the culprits had been motivated by a desire to avenge killings of Sunnis in Iraq. In his last statement before his death, Zarqawi specifically condemned Lebanese Hizballah, making arguments that presented a Lebanese Sunni point of view.

After Zarqawi's Death

The death of Zarqawi in an American strike in June 2006 was hailed by the Bush administration as a turning point, but the civil war had its own cruel logic and did not need Zarqawi. Instead, a new Zarqawi emerged. Sunnis began speaking of the "Shiite Zarqawi." In the summer of 2006, rumors began spreading throughout Baghdad of a shadowy Shiite killer known as Abu Dira, a nickname meaning the Armor Bearer. In the Shiite uprisings of 2004, he was said to have held off the Americans in southern Sadr City. He earned his name either by destroying American armored vehicles or after killing an American soldier and stealing his body armor. Some rumors claimed he wore this armor at all times. Hailed by Shiites as a hero who defended them, he was also known by Sunnis as the Rusafa Butcher, a reference to the eastern half of Baghdad, where he was said to live. Another story claimed that a Sunni prison guard under Saddam called Abu Dira was notorious among Shiites for his brutality. The vengeful Shiite known as Abu Dira might have taken his nickname out of irony. All information about him was based on rumors, but he was said to be a man in his thirties called either Salim or Ismail, who lived in Sadr City but was born in the southern Shiite town of Amara. Some said he was a member of the Mahdi Army and commanded hundreds of fighters, but other sources claimed he was a renegade militiaman, out of Muqtada's control. Some said he was a bodyguard in the former regime who had deserted and fled to Iran; others thought he had been a guard who tortured prisoners in one of Saddam's prisons. One website claimed that he controlled the Interior

Ministry's Falcon Brigade, which kidnapped Sunnis from Baghdad's Zafraniya district.

It was said that every time there was a terror attack against Shiites he counted the dead and killed an equal number of Sunnis, although by other accounts he killed a higher ratio of Sunnis when he extracted vengeance. He was said to kill dozens of Sunnis every day in a remote part of Sadr City called Sadda, and he was also said to have threatened to fill the craters left from car bombs in Sadr City with the bodies of Sunnis. Some Sunni sources believed he was obeying the *fatwa* issued by Ayatollah Kadhim al-Haeri in Iran, who was Muqtada's erstwhile backer, urging Shiites to kill Sunnis and former Baathists in particular. One Sunni website claimed he had taken an oath to slaughter a camel and feed the poor people of Sadr City after he had killed Sunni politician Adnan al-Dulaimi. A popular radical Sunni line is, "Our dead are in paradise and your dead are in the hell." Abu Dira changed that, telling Sunnis, "Our dead are in paradise and your dead are in Sadda," Sadda being the dam in eastern Baghdad where Shiite gangs dumped Sunni corpses. Although some Shiites in Baghdad cheered this legend as much as Sunnis feared him, Muqtada and the Mahdi Army denied that he even existed and claimed he had been invented by Sunnis to falsely accuse Shiites of crimes. An American operation in Sadr City in July targeted a funeral for one of Abu Dira's relatives but failed to lead to his arrest.

Muqtada's control over his militia was tenuous. He issued statements such as "We are the enemies of the Saddamists," which were interpreted by his followers as a license to kill all Sunnis. The Mahdi Army was not strictly hierarchical, and Muqtada was unaware of most of its local commanders and activities. The Mahdi Army's cells were loosely organized; many of them were composed of friends who were on local soccer teams. Sayyid Hassan Naji al-Musawi, an important Mahdi Army commander in Sadr City, had been a well-known local soccer star before the war. Different leaders of the Mahdi Army disliked one another. There were jealousies and rivalries. There was nothing stopping a group of Shiite youths from declaring that they were a Mahdi Army unit, collecting weapons, and interpreting Muqtada's statements as they saw fit. Mahdi Army leaders could be imams, sheikhs, or local toughs called *shaqis*. Before the war *shaqis* might have been neighborhood gang leaders, but with the formation of Sunni and Shiite militias and resistance groups, they took the lead. In Baghdad and majority-Shiite towns, most of the police were Mahdi Army as well. The reasons were simple. Most poor Shiite men supported Muqtada and claimed to belong to his militia, and most Iraqi police were poor Shiite men, so they were one and the same. Sunnis came to view the state as their enemy. As early as 2005, I realized that the once-confident and aggressive Sunnis were intimidated and uncertain about their fate. They worried about losing.

Rather than remaking the Middle East, the Iraq War was tearing it apart. Kurdish independence could provoke Turkish intervention. At a minimum it would push the Turks closer to the Iranians and Syrians, who would have the same concerns of Kurdish irredentism. Sunnis throughout the region, who already had so many reasons to hate the United States—Abu Ghraib, Haditha, Palestine, Guantánamo—would now have one more, for the Americans had handed Iraq to the Shiites. As we shall see in the next chapter, Salafi jihadis could pour in to fight the hateful Shiites. Shiites might attempt to push Sunnis out of Iraq, for until they could control the key highways in the Anbar province leading to Syria and Jordan, their economy would be threatened. Arab Sunni countries such as Jordan and Saudi Arabia would support Sunni militias and perhaps intervene directly. Sunni retaliation against Shiites or Alawites in Syria, Lebanon, Saudi Arabia, Bahrain, the United Arab Emirates, Pakistan, and even Afghanistan could provoke sectarian clashes throughout the Muslim world. At some point Iran would intervene, and if it threatened the waters of the Persian Gulf, the entire world's economy could be threatened. It seemed as though we were seeing the death throes, and not the birth pangs, of a new Middle East.

Soon after the war, black and colorful flags appeared on rooftops throughout Iraq. Some Shiites even covered their houses with big sheets of black cloth. Each referred to parts of the story of the martyr Imam Hussein. Under Saddam such public displays of Shiite identity could have been met with punishment. Now more and more areas in Baghdad were full of Shiite symbolism. During the civil war, as more and more territory came safely into Shiite hands, the black flags and pictures of Hussein became ever more pervasive. Shiites were no longer afraid; the city was theirs.

It was soon very clear that sectarian Islamist Shiite militias and parties had won the civil war, empowered as they were by their numerical superiority, their control of the Iraqi Security Forces, and the fact that the Americans were targeting the Sunni population of Iraq. Sunni leaders realized this too.

In late 2006 Sheikh Saad Mushhan Naif al-Hardan strode into a hotel lobby in Amman, Jordan, accompanied by two stern-faced companions. He wore a tailored suit and was more svelte than I remembered him from when I first met him more than two years earlier in his village of Albu Aitha, a collection of family compounds nearly hidden by the thick verdant fauna kept fertile by the wide still waters. One hundred miles west of Baghdad, past Ramadi and Falluja, a left turn off the highway led to dirt roads passing through fecund fields fed by the nearby Euphrates. Sheep and cows drank from the river bank in the shade of towering date palm plantations.

Back then the sheikh had been draped in black and gray robes, his face partially concealed by a white head scarf, crowned with a black rope. His small keen eyes, thick arching brows, and mustache lay still, waiting for an emotion to animate them. He had been joined by his three cousins: a lawyer, a history professor, and a history teacher. Since 1995 the sheikh had led the Sunni Aithawi tribe, the largest subtribe (he claimed) of the Dulaimi tribe, one of Iraq's largest tribes (every sheikh in Iraq, it should be noted, claims his tribe is the largest). Sheikh Saad refused to enumerate his tribe's manpower; it was the tribal equivalent of classified information. The enemy could not know the potential force his tribe could wield. In this case the enemy was the Americans. The Dulaimi tribe, whose lands reached from the Saudi border to the Syrian border and up to the outskirts of Baghdad in Abu Ghraib, was just as recalcitrant in the face of American occupation as it was nearly a century ago, during the 1920 uprising against the British occupation. Sheikh Saad's grandfather Hardan Hamid, head of the Aithawi branch of the Dulaimi tribe, had ridden south to Kut with his five brothers and all the fighting men his tribe could muster to face the invading British army. "The British had more advanced weapons and better tactics," Sheikh Saad said. His relatives were still buried near Kut. Sheikh Hardan had retreated to his tribal lands, fighting all the way. "When the British reached Anbar," he continued, "we told them that the only way Anbar would fall and they could occupy us was if they killed or arrested at least two of our sheikhs." The British took the advice of the Anbar leaders, killing Sheikh Sabar of the Albu Nimer tribe and arresting Sheikh Hardan, who was imprisoned in India for six years. "Then the British occupied the Anbar," Sheikh Saad concluded, adding with pride that it had been the last province to fall to the Americans (though the fact that it did not have a Jordanian or Saudi or Syrian front may have been a factor). "The British occupiers befriended the tribal leaders," he said. "This is the key to winning the people. They understood our traditions, unlike the Americans now. The British did not surround homes and break into them. They consulted sheikhs and respected them, and after they occupied all of Iraq, there was no more resistance." The Americans occupiers, Sheikh Saad maintained, "push people to the ground and step on their heads. They arrest the relatives and wives of wanted men and hold them hostage. They are holding one hundred thousand Iraqis in their prisons. Iraqis have lost their dignity, and for this reason the resistance grows."

Iraqis were incandescent over rumors that their women were being held prisoner by Americans. Sheikh Saad told of three women imprisoned as hostages by the Americans in Khaldiya because their husbands were wanted by the Americans. "I went to speak with the American commander in Falluja, who called the commander in Khaldiya. I told the commander, 'If you don't release these women, you should arrest all the men in Anbar, because there will be an uprising.'" Sheikh Saad said that three hours later the women were released, and added, "The British never arrested women." The sheikh himself was a resistance leader, and his men were fighting the Americans. "For us as the people of Anbar, revenge is an important tradition," he said, "if they kill one of our men we have to kill at least one of their soldiers."

At seven in the morning on July 20, 2003, Sheikh Saad was arrested with eighty-five of his men in an operation that took one hour and included, he claimed, more than 120 vehicles and helicopters. Sheikh Saad scoffed, "like it was a real battle, but they met no resistance from us. They accused me of belonging to an organized group called Nur Muhammad (Light of Muhammad) that is leading the resistance with the support and financing of Saddam and bringing in mujahideen from Syria, and they said 60 percent of the attacks in this area originate in Albu Aitha, so I must know about them, but none of it was true. Their method is to arrest many people and hope to at least find something. Until now they have no accurate information about the resistance" (though it seemed he did). Sheikh Saad was held for twelve days, but the rest of his men were held for a month, and five were still being held in the Abu Ghraib and Um Qasr prisons. "If Americans had not behaved the way they did there would be no resistance," he said. "Their behavior and broken promises increase the resistance."

The sheikh paused to contemplate, looking to the side. "Under the previous regime we all had equality," he said. "We could all study in the university and succeed depending on the degree we achieved. The one exception was the security forces, which went to certain tribes. But I don't want to talk about the previous regime. What's gone is gone. Saddam disliked the Dulaimi tribe, and we had nobody in high positions in his government, because Saddam feared we would overthrow him. The Americans told me that I am the only sheikh in Anbar who did not visit their bases and work with them. They want me to help them against my people? This won't happen. And this is why they make problems for me."

The lawyer leaned forward, his face long and gaunt, unlike his better-fed relatives, and asserted, "Iraq is the cemetery of all its occupiers." He rejected the possibility of a civil war but warned that "they [the Americans] want a civil war. Before the war we didn't use words like "Sunni" or "Shiite." We are one nation and drink from the same two rivers. There won't be a civil war, but there might be problems." The sheikh and his cousins were convinced that "they will never allow elections," and so he smiled proudly, lifting his head. "We are an independent tribe. We don't have relations with other parties or the Iraqi Governing Council."

A lot had changed since those days. There was a civil war, and Sheikh Saad had actually joined the Iraqi government for a while, serving as a minister for provincial affairs. When I met him in late 2006, it was too dangerous for me to attempt such a trip to the Anbar province in a taxi, as I did in 2003. The sheikh and his companions still had thick mustaches, but now they wore the long black leather trench coats that had been popular with intelligence officers in the former regime. Sheikh Saad had brought his wife and children to Amman, where they lived in opulence. "All the leaders of the Anbar are outside of Iraq," he told me. "In the Anbar America is killing and Al Qaeda is killing."

I was stunned to learn that the recalcitrant sheikh had joined the government, and I asked him why. "Our country needs people like us who are well-known, especially in Anbar and its tribes. They wanted me." Although he had received various threats for joining the government, he explained that he did not care. "Any Iraqi who becomes part of the political process is threatened." I wondered if he still supported the resistance. "We all support the *muqawama sharifa*," he said, referring to the "honorable resistance" (a distinction from those groups that attacked civilians), and added, "and I am part of it." When he saw my eyebrows go up at the admission he added, "with words." I asked him if there was still an honorable resistance given the civil war that Sunni and Shiite militias were engaged in. "It still exists," he said. "You don't see how many Americans are killed in the Anbar?" He explained that "the ones who use the name of the resistance but kill innocent people, loot, kidnap, and have contacts outside the border who gave them an agenda and weapons" are not the real resistance.

Sheikh Saad admitted that there was a civil war in Iraq, "but it's not announced or declared yet." America was responsible for this, he told me. "If they want to calm the situation, they can tomorrow" by telling Syria and Iran to stop sending weapons into Iraq. "Why are the Americans fighting in the Anbar but not the militias?" he asked, referring to the Shiite militias. "Why don't they fight Badr and the Mahdi Army?" He answered his own question: "The Americans are part of them." Then he asked, "Why don't they make a balance in the political process between Shiites and Sunnis? They are making Iraq like Iran."

The sheikh was no longer part of the government. "I'm resting now," he said. The minister who had replaced him, Saad al-Hashimi, was loyal to Muqtada, and he had changed the ministry's staff, imposing, Sheikh Saad explained, "the agenda of his party and militia," which in practice meant firing all Sunnis and ideologically disloyal Shiites.

I was shocked when Sheikh Saad admitted that the problems in Iraq were not the fault of the current Shiite-dominated Iraqi government. "The Sunnis left the political process," he said. "This is our fault. Sunni scholars led by Harith al-Dhari forbade political participation." I had never heard an Iraqi Sunni admit such an error. Sheikh Saad added that even though he had realized his mistake, "Harith didn't change his mind."

The men who had accompanied Sheikh Saad were two former generals in Saddam's military intelligence, one of whom had also served as deputy chief of police for the Anbar province during the American occupation. He explained that for this he had survived numerous assassination attempts but had also faced difficulties working with the Americans. The head of his office had been arrested by the Americans and was still in jail, he said, accused of cooperating with the resistance. "The Americans only use force in the Anbar province," he said. "I had many problems with the Americans. We advised them that their behavior is wrong in the Anbar, raiding, putting feet on heads, this is worse than killing." He also blamed the Americans for the sectarianism. "They brought in the militias," he said. "The militias belong to Iran, not Iraq or America. Since the invasion until now they are fighting the Sunnis. There is a new dictatorship now, a religious one." For his trouble, he said, Al Qaeda had blown up his house. "Al Qaeda is not cooperating with the Iraqi resistance," he said. "The real Iraqi resistance considers Al Qaeda an enemy."

IN THOSE DAYS it felt as if the Americans had withdrawn from Baghdad. They were devolving their authority willingly, abandoning their attempt at rebuilding the Iraqi state. It resembled Britain's "colonialism on the cheap." They no longer had the interest or money to micromanage Iraq. Iraq now felt as if it was occupied by Iraqi Security Forces and militias running amok, shooting into the air, shouting out of loudspeakers. Nowhere in Baghdad was safe from the militias. Even hospitals and universities were part of the battlefield. Whereas in the past Muqtada's followers had conducted joint prayers with radical Sunnis to demonstrate their solidarity, by 2006 mosques were no longer sacred. On Friday, December 22, 2006, Mahdi Army militiamen raided the Abdullah Bin Omar Mosque in the Binook area near Shaab. The raid occurred during the important noon prayer, when a large congregation gathers to hear a sermon. Sunnis claimed that fifty Mahdi Army militiamen raided the mosque while the sheikh was giving his sermon; all but four of the prayergoers managed to escape, but the sheikh and the muezzin were taken prisoner. The Shiite version of the story is that the Mahdi Army entered the mosque ten minutes before prayer time. They claim they ordered the Sunni prayergoers not to move and told them they had come only for the sheikh. One of the men praying had brought his pistol with him. He ran behind the pulpit and opened fire. There was an exchange of fire that lasted until the Mahdi Army men ran out of bullets. The Mahdi Army men then captured him, the sheikh, and the muezzin. Their corpses were later found with signs of torture, and it was revealed that the third man who opened fire during the raid was the sheikh's son.

In late 2006 Baghdad's walls and streets were covered with calls for students and professors to stay home. The radical Sunni movement Ansar al-Sunna had declared a "campaign for halting the assassinations of students and academics in Baghdad universities." According to one banner hung in a majority-Sunni part of Baghdad, "In order to protect the lives of our dearest academics and students from the assassinations of Maliki's government and the death squads of Maliki's government, we decided to stop the universities and all academic institutes including the private ones for this academic year 2006–2007." The banner stressed that this applied only to Baghdad. "It is strictly forbidden to attend universities in order to cleanse them from death squads that use the universities as centers to launch their attacks from," the banner said. Such threats, warnings, and announcements are typically distributed to the Iraqi people through leaflets or by hanging banners on walls.

Ansar al-Sunna was the successor to the jihadist group Ansar al-Islam, the Al Qaeda–inspired group that had been based in northern Iraq's autonomous region before the war. The group was remaking itself as the defender of Iraq's Sunnis. While there were signs of clashes between the Sunni resistance and Al Qaeda, the move by Ansar al-Sunna was a sign of how the civil war was uniting the disparate Sunni militias and how Iraq's Sunnis would have to depend on them for protection, sometimes whether they wanted to or not, in the absence of reliable security forces loyal to the state. Some Sunni politicians defended the ban on university attendance. Asma al-Dulaimi, a female Iraqi Parliament member belonging to the Iraqi Accord Front, headed by the Islamic Party's Tariq al-Hashimi, explained that she was sure the army of Ansar al-Sunna knew of threats to students and academics and that its call to halt university attendance was made out of a desire to protect the students. Meisoon al-Damalouji, a Sunni member of Ayad Allawi's Iraqiya Party, condemned Dulaimi's statements as unacceptable. A banner was hung up in Baghdad Mustansiriya University on Palestine Street announcing, "We will not surrender to terrorism, and that is our response." Prime Minister Maliki himself responded to the warnings by threatening to fire all professors who did not show up to work and to expel students who did not attend classes. This move was seen by Sunnis as an attack by the Shiite-dominated government against them, since it was Sunni students and professors who had been warned not to attend.

On December 7 Muhamad Haidar Suleiman, a professor at a sports education college in Mosul, was assassinated, and Harith Abdul Hamid, director of Baghdad University's Psychology Center, was also murdered on his way to work. In early December a girl's high school in Jadida, or New Baghdad, the majority-Christian area of the city, was closed down by order of the school's headmaster after militants left posters on the walls threatening to kill the female students. In Zayuna, a majority-Sunni area, leaflets were scattered in two schools, one of which was called the Tariq bin Ziyad school, cursing Shiites as bastards and threatening them.

In fact, professors and administrators who had belonged to the Baath Party had been targeted ever since the fall of the regime. Student unions were dominated by sectarian and fundamentalist militias, and in Baghdad these militias often belonged to Shiite movements such as the Sadrists, Ayatollah Muhammad al-Yaqoubi's Fadhila, and the Supreme Council. Religious strictures began to be imposed as well. Hundreds of professors were assassinated and hundreds fled. Incredibly, in November the Ministry of Higher Education was attacked by Interior Ministry forces.

University attendance declined drastically because of the violence. Leaflets threatening students and professors at the University of Technology forced the school to shut down. In the Adhamiya and Yarmuk districts, both majority-Sunni areas of Baghdad, leaflets were distributed banning university students from attending their schools. In Abu Ghraib, just west of Baghdad, leaflets threatened students who attended the agriculture college. In the Zafraniya district students of the Technical Institute were threatened by gunmen.

In majority-Sunni western Baghdad, banners signed by Ansar al-Sunna's Department for the Protection of Professors asked students and lecturers to abstain from attending government universities, academic institutes, and private colleges because they were dominated by the government's Shiite militias. Ansar al-Sunna was planning on clearing the universities of the Shiite militias and killing them. As a result they announced that the school year was over.

"To our respected professors and our dear students in the universities and colleges of Baghdad," began one leaflet titled "Final Warning": "In an attempt to protect your lives from the wrongdoings of the Maliki government and its death squads, including the killings, kidnappings, and violations against the scientific talents, and especially the Sunni students, which led to Sunni talents in Baghdad universities becoming a market for the death squads, and to these colleges becoming safe houses for these squads to launch their killings and kidnappings against Sunni students and professors. . . . From these universities the learned and the mujahideen graduated . . . and in these same universities they are being killed today." The group warned it was abolishing the 2006–07 school year for Baghdad university students. The letter was signed by Ansar al-Sunna's "campaign for the aid of the learned and the students in the universities of Baghdad."

As the civil war in Iraq intensified, Sunni militias appeared to be uniting to combat the more powerful Shiite militias as well as the police and army. In mid-October 2006 an alliance was announced between Sunni militias who called themselves Al Mutaibeen. The alliance included the Mujahideen Shura Council, Jeish al-Fatihin, Jund al-Sahaba, Ansar al-Tawhid wa al-Sunna, and some tribal leaders. Its name came from the word "tib" (perfume) and referred to the pre-Islamic custom of putting on perfume. (Before Islam was founded, some notable Meccan leaders agreed to help the needy and defend the weak; they sealed their agreement by putting their hands in perfume.) The members of the Mutaibeen Alliance announced that their goals were to fight the Americans and protect the poor Sunnis from the Shiites.

The Sunni front was not restricted to Iraq. On December 7, thirty-eight Saudi clerics and university professors signed a global *fatwa* calling on all Sunnis in the world to unify their efforts and fight the Shiites to protect the Sunnis of Iraq. This *fatwa* was likely to increase the support Iraq's Sunni militias received from abroad and the number of foreign volunteers attempting to enter Iraq. Sifr al-Hawali, an important Saudi cleric who often took a harder line than the Saudi regime, was one of the signatories. Other prominent Saudi Wahhabi thinkers who signed the letter were Abdul Rahman bin Nasser al-Barrak, Sheikh Nasser bin Suleiman al-Omar, and Sheikh Abdullah al-Tuweijiri. "What has been taken by force can only be got back by force," the letter said. Just two days before, Saudi papers announced that their government had intercepted a cell of fourteen people in the city of Hael who were promoting *takfiri* and jihadist ideology on the Internet and were involved in sending volunteers to fight in Iraq.

The Saudis also hosted Harith al-Dhari, head of the powerful Sunni Association of Muslim Scholars, in an official visit. The Association was closely linked to some Sunni Islamo-nationalist militias, and Dhari had recently defended Al Qaeda in Iraq against criticism. Some veterans of the Afghan jihad viewed the Association as the ideal place to funnel money from wealthy Persian Gulf sponsors. Saudis and other Gulf Arabs were a significant source of funding for Sunni militias in Iraq. Saudi Arabia and Jordan were apprehensive of a Shiite-dominated Iraq, which they viewed as an Iranian proxy. Nawaf Obaid, a close adviser to the Saudi government on security issues, wrote in the *Washington Post* that if the Americans withdrew from Iraq, the Saudis would increase their support for Iraq's Sunnis to undermine Iran's influence. This was viewed less as an analysis and more as a warning by some elements in the Saudi regime.

In November 2006 Jordan's King Abdullah warmly received Harith al-Dhari despite Dhari's public support for Al Qaeda and the fact that the Iraqi government wanted him for inciting sectarianism and supporting terrorists. In January 2007 Dhari was in Saudi Arabia speaking at private gatherings, praising Al Qaeda's Islamic State of Iraq, and raising money for the resistance. He was accompanied by his movement's spokesman, Sheikh Abdul Salam al-Kubeisi, who warned that the fall of Baghdad to the Safavids would lead to the fall of Mecca and Medina. A cleric from Baquba also spoke in support of the resistance.

Meanwhile, by the end of 2006, there were signs that Muqtada al-Sadr, who had been reviled in a sensationalist *Newsweek* cover as the most dangerous man in Iraq, was barely in control of his organization. Muqtada seemed more and more like a mere figurehead for an army with no real leadership or hierarchy. He had gone through many deputies, firing close allies. In a video of an internal debate among his men that was released without his approval, a different Muqtada was seen, one who jealously guarded his power but seemed to have little control over his men. Speaking in poor Arabic, all slang, Muqtada revealed his jealousy and insecurity as well, criticizing a deputy for praising Supreme Council leader Abdul Aziz al-Hakim.

Earlier, in the spring of 2006, Iraqis were as excited about the World Cup as other soccer-crazy countries. They hung flags for their favorite teams. Some who did received visits from Sadrists urging them to remove the flags and hang up Iraqi flags or pictures of clerics. Those who did not were threatened. Even though many of Iraq's top soccer players hailed from Sadr City, that spring Muqtada issued a *fatwa* about soccer, warning that he and his father viewed it as a distraction from worship. It had been created by the West to prevent Muslims from perfecting themselves, he argued. The Israelis and the West kept Muslims distracted with soccer—as with singing and smoking— while they focused on science. The Mahdi Army tried to prevent women from going to the market in Karbala, causing businesses to suffer. Muqtada was desperately attempting to impose moral order on his followers at the same time as they were getting caught up in a maelstrom of violence.

Although politically motivated violence, the occupation, and the resistance all affected and destroyed the lives of civilians, simple, criminally motivated kidnapping also devastated countless Iraqi families. I heard many horror stories—many of them regaled to me by my friend Ali. He told me about his father-in-law, a Sunni, who was once a prominent Palestinian resistance fighter in the 1960s and '70s. "He has a small shop in an area that is controlled by the Shiite militias," Ali said. "About a month ago, there was a roadside bomb just in front of his shop. He survived the explosion, but many people were killed and injured. The police came and took him without asking how a sixty-year-old man could risk his life and put a bomb just in front of his source of living. His family, including myself, now live outside of Iraq, so he had no one in Baghdad with him. His sister-in-law used to call him every day, and at night someone else answered his phone. The man told my aunt that her brother-in-law was in the 'Ministry of Interior' and hung up. She called us, and I contacted everyone I know. I sent my friends to the police station nearest to his shop. They told me they found my father-in-law's car, but the police denied they had him. I am a Shiite, but I had never tried to establish any connections with the militias simply because I despise them. But seeing my family in that condition pushed me to contact some people who know some leaders in the militias. Someone called someone who called someone, and finally they found his trace. He had been taken to a house outside the police station for 'investigation.' Anyway, my contacts were able to set him free the next day, but his head was covered with blood. They beat him on his head with the gun.

"About two months ago, three men remotely related to my wife were kidnapped from their shop in Al Shourja [the economic center of Baghdad]. They had been merchants in the area for more than thirty years. They were taken by the police special force [Maghawir al-Dakhiliya]. Two days after that, someone called their families and asked for ninety thousand dollars ransom. The families were forced to listen to the sounds of torture on the mobile. The families were 'convinced,' and they provided the money for the kidnappers. One of the kidnappers, a policeman, was related to the families by marriage, but it seems he had a grudge against them. The day after they paid the ransom, the kidnapped men's bodies were found in the morgue. They had been tortured to death, and there were marks of electric drills all over their bodies (one of them was eighty years old). When their families went to the morgue, the person in charge there told them he couldn't give them the bodies 'because the bodies belong to the Mahdi Army.' Anyway, they managed to contact some people who had contacts with the militias, and they got the bodies. Their relative, who was one of the kidnappers, confessed he participated in the crime and threatened the families not to say anything. He also looted the shops of the victims two days after they had been killed.

"A Sunni friend of mine was kidnapped near his house in western Baghdad. The kidnappers took him to a place where he saw many people being tortured. They asked him where he was from, and he mentioned the name of his tribe. They said, 'So, you are one of our people, Saddam Hussein's people,' and my friend replied, 'I hope God saves our leader,' and they all replied, 'Amen!' Anyway, the kidnappers apologized to my friend and told him they needed to kidnap people to finance jihad. They called his family on a Friday and told them they would decide his fate after the Friday prayers. A couple of hours later they called the family (who don't even own a house) and asked for fifty thousand dollars.

"His poor family sold everything they had and gathered ten thousand dollars for his ransom. The kidnappers called them and told them the money was not enough and they might sell him to mujahideen in Latifiya for a bigger amount. The family was forced to ask their friends for loans, including me. They were able to provide another ten thousand dollars, and the kidnappers agreed to release him."

Like all Iraqis Ali's friend Rasha also had numerous stories of kidnappings and crime. Perhaps none were as chilling as her young Shiite cousin's tale.

"She was in love with her classmate Ahmed from their time together at the university. They could not get married, however, because Ahmed was young and from a poor family. He was his mother's only son, and his father had died before the war. He is Sunni and lived in Tarmiya, an area north of Baghdad dominated by Sunni militias. Ahmed himself belonged to the resistance. My cousin's family were not rich either, and they could no longer work in Iraq, so they left for Syria. Ahmed borrowed money to buy a car and worked as a taxi driver. In one year he had saved enough to afford to get married. He contacted my cousin in Syria, and she agreed to return to Baghdad to marry him. One night, a few days before their wedding, they were on the phone when he told her, 'I hear someone knocking on the door. I'll be back in a second.' She heard shooting and was so frightened that she hung up the phone and ran to her mother. Her mother redialed Ahmed's number and a man answered the phone. 'He is a traitor,' said the voice. 'He was going to marry a Shiite woman, so we killed him.'"

As more and more Iraqis were disappearing, their desperate relatives were not merely hanging up signs on walls but turning to the Internet. The home page of Iraqi Rabita, a pro-Baathist Sunni website, often posted photos of missing people with the request "Please help us find these people—lost." At first only Sunnis were posting on the site, hoping to locate family members kidnapped by Shiite militias. The site succeeded in finding some of the missing people, but it did not explain how it did so. So Christians and Shiites whose sons had been kidnapped by Sunni militias began posting photos of their relatives on the site, calling for help in locating them. One day in late 2006, the home page had nineteen photos of missing people. Four were Christians, five were Sunnis, and ten were Shiites.

IN LATE 2006 Adnan al-Dulaimi showed his true colors as Iraq's most sectarian politician. Dulaimi had taught at the University of Zarqa in Jordan while he was in exile before the overthrow of Saddam's regime. Zarqa's most famous son is Abu Musab al-Zarqawi. Dulaimi returned to Iraq a week after the fall of Baghdad. He was appointed head of the Sunni Religious Endowment but was removed for what he claimed were political reasons because he was "defending the Sunnis," which could also refer to his staunch sectarianism. He formed the Conference of Iraqi Sunnis to unite Sunnis under what he described as "one umbrella" and to encourage their political participation, and he was appointed religious adviser to President Jalal Talabani.

In late 2006 Dulaimi spoke at a major regional conference in Istanbul, hoping to raise funds for the resistance. He told the audience they should have named the gathering "The Conference for Supporting Sunnis in Iraq" and mocked the organizers' fear of being called sectarian. Iraq is worth nothing without Sunnis, he said, because Sunnis owned it and built it. "Yes, we are sectarian," he said. If they did not awaken, then Iraq would be lost and the Sunnis would be exterminated by the Shiites. He demanded support from Muslims around the world for Iraq's Sunnis. He spoke of the Sunni mosques and neighborhoods that were being destroyed. "Iraq is going to be Shiite, and this will expand to the lands surrounding Iraq. Then you will all regret it, but your regret will be worth nothing because it will be too late. Where is Saudi Arabia? Where is Kuwait? Where is Jordan? Where is Pakistan? And where are the Muslims? Sleep and keep sleeping while Iraq is destroying. You sleep while

Sunni mosques in Iraq are being destroyed. Sleep while Sunni mosques in Iraq are burning. Sleep and keep sleeping, but the fire of Iraq will expand to you. What is happening in Iraq has been planned for over fifty years in order to convert the region into Shiism and create the Persian Empire under a Shiite cover."

In a December 22, 2006, interview with the American-sponsored Radio Sawa, the interviewer pressed Dulaimi on why he avoided criticizing Al Qaeda in Iraq but regularly criticized the Mahdi Army. "Is Al Qaeda a terrorist organization or not?" demanded the interviewer. "I will not and will never answer this question," said Dulaimi, "and if you ask me again I will hang up the phone." The interviewer persisted, and Dulaimi hung up.

The Death of Saddam

The year 2006 culminated with one last insult to the Sunnis of Iraq and the region when Saddam Hussein became the first modern Arab dictator to die violently since Egypt's Anwar Sadat in 1981. Saddam's hanging at the hands of chubby Iraqi men wearing ski masks was likely to be perceived by many as an American execution and as part of a trend of American missteps contributing to sectarian tensions in Iraq and the region. Others viewed it as a lynching by reveling Shiite militiamen. The trial of Saddam was viewed by detractors as an event stage-managed by the Americans. According to Human Rights Watch, the Iraqi judges and lawyers involved in prosecuting Saddam were ill prepared and relied on their American advisers. American minders shut off the microphones and ordered the translators to halt whenever they disapproved of what was being said by the defendants. Saddam was being executed for the massacre in Dujail. It was the least of his crimes, but it had targeted Shiites and the Dawa Party, and they wanted revenge for his crimes against the Kurds—others could even be judged.

For Sunnis the important Muslim holiday of Eid al-Adha began on Saturday, December 30; for Shiites it began on Sunday. According to tradition in Mecca, battles were suspended during the hajj period so that pilgrims could safely march to Mecca. This practice even predated Islam; Muslims had preserved it, calling this period Al Ashur al-Hurm, the months of truce. By hanging Saddam on the Sunni Eid, the Americans and the Iraqi government were in effect saying that only the Shiite Eid had legitimacy. Sunnis were irate that Shiite traditions were given primacy (as was increasingly the case in Iraq) and that Shiites had disrespected the tradition and killed Saddam on this day. Because the Iraqi Constitution prohibits executions from being carried out on Eid, the Iraqi government had to declare that Eid did not begin until Sunday. It was a striking decision, virtually declaring that Iraq was a Shiite state. Eid was the festival of the sacrifice of the sheep. But Saddam quickly became known as "the Martyr of the Sacrifice."

Saddam had been in American custody and was handed over to Iraqis just before his execution. It was therefore hard to dismiss the perception that the Americans could have waited, because in the end it was they who had the final say over such events. Iraqi officials consistently complained that they had no authority and that the Americans controlled the Iraqi police and the army. So it was unusual that Iraqis would suddenly regain sovereignty for this important event. For many Sunnis and Arabs in the region, this appeared to be one president ordering the death of another. It was possibly a message to Sunnis, a warning. The Americans often equated Saddam with the Sunni resistance. By killing Saddam they were killing what they believed was the symbol of the Sunni resistance, expecting its members to realize that their cause was hopeless. But Saddam's death also liberated the Sunni resistance from association with Saddam and the Baathists. They could more plausibly claim that they were fighting for national liberation and not out of support for the former regime, as their American and Iraqi government opponents often claimed. At the same time, the execution created a new symbol for those opposed to the occupation. Saddam was not given a hood, though prisoners normally do not have a choice about wearing one. The execution and the photo of the executed Saddam had the hallmark of the U.S. psy-ops tactics, similar to the deaths of Saddam's sons in 2003. Even the U.S. plane that flew him to his final resting spot indicated U.S. management.

The unofficial video of the execution, filmed on the mobile phone of one of the officials present, further inflamed sectarianism. It was clear from the film that sectarian Shiites were executing Saddam. Men could be heard talking; one of them was called Ali. As the executioners argue over how to best position the rope on his neck, Saddam called out to God, saying, "Ya Allah." Referring to Shiites, one official said, "Those who pray for Muhammad and the family of Muhammad have won!" Others triumphantly responded in the Shiite chant: "Our God prays for Muhammad and the family of Muhammad." Others then added the part chanted by supporters of Muqtada al-Sadr: "And speed his [the Mahdi's] return! And damn his enemies! And make his son victorious! Muqtada! Muqtada! Muqtada!"

Saddam smiled and said something mocking about Muqtada. "Muqtada! It is this . . . " but the rest was blocked by the voices of officials saying, "Ila jahanam" (go to hell). Saddam looked down disdainfully and said, "Is this your manhood?" As the rope was put around Saddam's neck, somebody shouted, "Long live Muhammad Baqir al-Sadr!" (Executed by Saddam in 1980, Sadr was still venerated by all three major Shiite movements in Iraq: the Dawa, the Sadrists, and the Supreme Council.) Others insulted Saddam. "Please all stop," one man pleaded. Saddam then said the Shahada, or testimony, that there is no god but Allah and Muhammad is his prophet. When he tried to say it again the trapdoor opened, and he fell through. One man then shouted, "The tyranny has ended!" Others called out triumphal Shiite chants. Somebody wanted to remove the rope from his neck but was told to wait eight minutes.

The Sunni Islamo-nationalist website Islam Memo claimed that the Safavids burned Saddam's Koran after they killed him, though there was no evidence of this. Similarly, the site made other unsubstantiated claims: that Saddam exchanged insults with the witnesses to his execution and cursed one of them, saying, "God damn you, Persian midget"; that Grand Ayatollah Ali Sistani blessed Saddam's execution; that the Iraqi government refused to provide Saddam with a Sunni cleric to pray for him before the execution; that Saddam said, "Palestine is Arab" and then recited the Shahada before he was executed; that following his death his body was abused. Although the Shiite-dominated official Iraqi media claimed Saddam was terrified before his execution and that he fought with his hangmen, Saddam's onscreen visage was one of aplomb, for he was conscious of the image he was displaying and wanted to go down as the grand historic leader he believed himself to be.

Predictably, there were celebrations in Shiite areas, and the civil war continued. Following the execution three car bombs exploded in Baghdad's Shiite district of Hurriya, killing and injuring dozens. Another one went off in Baghdad's Seidiya district, near its amusement park, killing at least two civilians and two policemen. A roadside bomb exploded near a children's hospital in the majority-Shiite area of Iskan, killing two and injuring several others. In the southern town of Kufa, dominated by supporters of Muqtada, a car bomb exploded near a market, killing and injuring dozens. In the northern town of Tal Afar, a man wearing a suicide belt exploded himself in a market, killing at least five and injuring several others. It was also claimed that Sistani's representative was killed and his office was burned. In the town of Saqlawiya, in Anbar province, there was a big demonstration against Saddam's execution at which marchers carried large portraits of the former leader. Immediately after the execution five mortars were fired in Falluja, targeting the southern checkpoint to that city, known as the Numaniya checkpoint. In Tikrit, site of another large demonstration, Saddam's tribe officially requested that the Iraqi government allow his body to be buried near his parents in Owja, the town where he was born.

I asked a Kurdish Iraqi friend how he felt after seeing the video of Saddam's execution. "It is sad to see someone who knows he is going to die in a minute," he told me, "but I am happy that he died that way and not, as the so-called human rights groups want, to be in a jail where they want to make sure he has access to TV, newspaper, and good health." He agreed with me that the images of Saddam could potentially cause some people to sympathize with him but added, "If anyone who could live the life of an Iraqi for only one day—they would want worse than that to happen to Saddam. Last night, all of a sudden I remembered all the agonies my family went through in their life. We had to leave our home twenty times and walk to the borders and leave everything we had and buy new stuff every few years. He never had the feeling you and I have now for him when he was ordering Ali Hassan Majid and the henchmen to bury people with their kids in the deserts, so why should I now feel sorry for him? But I hope I see one day when the current Saddamlets are hanged too, like Talabani, Ayad Allawi."

One thing was clear: the death of Saddam did not bring closure or peace to Iraq. Sunnis gathered at Saddam's grave, demonstrators showed his iconic image, and revenge was threatened. President George Bush declared his nemesis's death "a milestone." To many in Iraq and the Muslim world, it was a clear message that there would be no mercy for Sunnis in a Shiite-dominated Iraq.

Part Two

❖❖❖❖❖❖❖❖❖

THE IRAQIFICATION
OF THE MIDDLE EAST

CHAPTER FOUR

Among the Jihadis

REMARKABLY, THERE WERE NO ATTEMPTS TO ATTACK THE UNITED States in retaliation for its occupation of Iraq, not by American Muslims or by foreigners. But the jihad in Iraq did lead to a regional blowback, and its neighbor Jordan was the first to suffer.

On February 16, 2006, Mohammad Zaki Amawi, Marwan Othman El-Hindi, and Wassim I. Mazloum were indicted by a U.S. district court in Ohio. The three were accused of conspiring to wage jihad against U.S. forces in Iraq, training in firearms and martial arts, collecting funds to support their mission, studying jihad training manuals on the Internet, meeting to plan how best to assist the Iraqi insurgency, studying how to build IEDs, and threatening the life of President Bush. Amawi flew to Jordan in August 2005 carrying laptops he wanted to donate to the mujahideen in Iraq. The indictment added that Amawi "unsuccessfully attempted to enter Iraq to wage violent Jihad, or 'holy war,' against the United States and coalition forces."

Amawi and El-Hindi were Jordanian-born naturalized citizens of the United States. Mazloum was from Lebanon. It was the first time such charges had been made against U.S. residents, but the charges were very similar to ones in numerous court cases in Jordan since the beginning of the Iraq War. These trials were held in the Marka military court, a squat white building across the road from a military airbase that is planted atop a hill in eastern Amman, the somnolent capital of the Hashemite Kingdom of Jordan. Apart from dealing with wayward soldiers, the court also handles security and terrorism cases. Relatives of prisoners stand on line on the curb outside, most dressed in traditional gowns, deep lines on their unshaven faces, waiting to be searched and allowed in. The winter winds blow hard on Amman's hilltops and muffle the approaching sirens of a police sedan, which is followed by a dark blue van, windowless except for some bars on the back that show only blackness inside. The van is always followed by a pickup truck, with two masked counterterror agents manning a heavy mounted gun on the bed.

On Wednesday, December 28, 2005, the van entered Marka through the main gate and circled around the back of the courthouse. Ten shackled prisoners were taken out and led into a cage in the courtroom. Their lawyers chatted jovially in a smoke-filled waiting room; then made their way past the numerous police officers, security officers, and soldiers bustling back and forth in search of something to do; and headed into the small courtroom, lit with bright fluorescent lights, lined with old wooden benches, and full of blue uniformed Amn al-Am, or General Security, officers.

Muhamad Ibrahim al-Ghawi, twenty-five years old; Faris Sayid Hassan Shoter, thirty-two; Muhamad Jamil al-Titi, twenty-two; Rauf Aballah Abu Mayha, twenty-two; Muhamad Mahmud al-Sharman, twenty-nine; Basil Muhamad al-Ramah, twenty-nine; Monaem Ibrahim Hasan, thirty-one; Raed Ahmed Kaywan, thirty-three; Muhamad Qasim Sulaiman Ramah, thirty-five; and Majdi Khalid Hassan al-Fawar, twenty-one: all stood in the cage, chatting in good spirits, smiling and waving at the few relatives who sat in the back. The cage had a chain-link fence around it, an innovation imposed after one prisoner called Azmi al-Jayusi, a friend of Jordanian terrorist leader Abu Musab al-Zarqawi, threw his shoe at the judge while on trial for attempting to bomb the Jordanian security headquarters. Other prisoners had been known to sing songs in honor of Zarqawi during trial.

All ten prisoners in the cage wore dark blue denim prison suits, wool caps, and slippers. Their beards were shaggy, as was their hair, which curled out of their caps over their ears and the backs of their necks. They were hard to distinguish from one another. Some had a dark stain sunk in above their brows in the center of the forehead. It was a *sima*, a sign of intense piety, acquired by kneeling and bowing forward, placing the forehead on the floor in prayer. Their long beards and hair were a sign of their beliefs. These men were Salafis.

Salafi ideologues dominated Jordan's mosques, and young men filled their ranks. Salafism found a home in Jordan beginning in the 1970s, when a Syrian cleric called Muhamad Nasir al-Din Albani began teaching in Jordan at the invitation of the Muslim Brotherhood. Eventually he settled in the Jordanian city of Zarqa to avoid persecution by the secular Syrian Baathists and began preaching about the need to purify Islam. Hundreds came to hear him speak, and he influenced the ranks and hierarchy of Jordan's clergy. The regime was threatened by the crowds he drew, and he was prohibited from speaking in public. Unable to operate openly, Salafism became an informal underground movement. The late 1970s were a crucial period, as the leftist, secular, and nationalist projects in the Arab world appeared to be failing. Saudi radicals rose up against their regime, temporarily taking the mosque in Mecca; the Soviet Army invaded Afghanistan; and the Iranian Revolution was both a model for political Islamists and a threat to Sunni regimes. By the early 1980s Arab regimes had decided to dispose of their excess radicals by dispatching them to the anti-Soviet jihad in Afghanistan.

Jordan was a ripe environment for political Islam. Since the British invented it in 1924, the kingdom had been ruled by the Hashemites, or Albu Hashem, descendants of the Prophet Muhammad who gained their legitimacy by belonging to Ahl al-Beit, the family of the Prophet. In 1970, when King Hussein fought an uprising of nationalist Palestinians—some of whom promulgated the slogan "The liberation of Jerusalem begins in Amman"—the Muslim Brotherhood, previously disenfranchised, supported King Hussein. The King rewarded them by granting them control over the Ministry of Education, allowing them to inculcate generations of Jordanians. Founded by Egyptian Hassan al-Banna in 1928, it sought to establish a Muslim state through nonviolent cultural revolution.

Radical Islam had received a needed fillip from the Afghan jihad, which began in 1979. But it was following the Gulf War of 1991 that jihadism became an international ideology. The Saudi government's dependence on the American infidels to protect it from Saddam, and the U.S. presence in the holiest Muslim land, coincided with Muslims' increasing resentment of their own governments. Arabs who had fought in the Afghan jihad began returning home and were disillusioned with what they encountered, so they sought to bring the jihad home too. The Israeli peace process was but one more betrayal for them. Also following the Gulf War, the Kuwaitis expelled hundreds of thousands of Palestinians, most of whom settled in Jordan. Returning Jordanian jihadis were repelled by the ostentation that accompanied the arrival of wealthy Palestinians to their poor country. One such jihadi was Abu Musab al-Zarqawi, who would lead the Tawhid and Jihad organization of Iraq, later known as Al Qaeda in Iraq. Other Palestinians brought with them a radical jihadist Salafi ideology. Two of them were Abu Muhammad al-Maqdisi, the most important ideologue for modern jihad and Zarqawi's former mentor, and Abu Anas al-Shami, who went on to become Zarqawi's key cleric and religious adviser in Iraq. Maqdisi's writings influenced the jihadis who carried out the 1995 bombings in Saudi Arabia that targeted Americans as well as the September 11 attackers. Zarqawi, Maqdisi, and Shami were heroes for young Jordanians such as those on trial in Marka.

Bordered by Palestine and Iraq, Jordan was caught between the two most important struggles in the Muslim world, at once both anticolonial wars and jihads. On November 9, 2005, Zarqawi brought the terror back home to Jordan when he dispatched four Iraqi suicide bombers to Amman, three of whom succeeded in detonating their deadly vests in three different hotels, killing sixty and injuring one hundred. It was Zarqawi's third successful attack in Jordan. Each time he had used non-Jordanians to avoid infiltration by Jordan's *mukhabarat* (intelligence service). In 2005 the *mukhabarat* had arrested thirteen terrorist cells, and in 2004 it had arrested eleven, one of which was in direct contact with Zarqawi. It was not a good time to go on trial for terrorism if you were a Salafi.

All of the prisoners held in Marka in 2005 were from Irbid, a northern city by the Syrian border. Six of the ten were originally Palestinians, their parents or grandparents having been expelled from their homes west of the border in 1948 or 1967. One of them paced back and forth in the cage, chanting lines from the Koran. Others joked with their relatives. One leaned forward in conversation with his lawyer, complaining that "the verdict was already decided before the trial. This is just a formality."

The charges against the ten stated that there were five other suspects who had escaped. According to the prosecution, they had met in the Qaqa'a Mosque in the Irbid's Hnina neighborhood, which they visited frequently. The charges mentioned that the men engaged in theological discussions about calling common people, rulers, and scholars infidels. They had agreed it was necessary to fight the Americans in Iraq and planned how they could recruit others, collect money to go to Iraq via Syria, and attack the Americans and the Iraqi Security Forces. In late July 2005 they pooled money to purchase a Kalashnikov and bullets. At different times they snuck into Syria, some of them ferried by a friend who owned a school bus. In Syria one of them met with a Tunisian who took him to an apartment where a Libyan and Saudi were staying. They discussed what operations he could execute and urged him to drive a car bomb, but the charges stated that he refused to become "suicidal." He tired of waiting in Syria and returned to Jordan, where his friends gave him a hard time for turning back. (Another one was invited to become a suicide bomber, but he too refused and returned to Jordan, where he was arrested.) Others later snuck into Syria and discussed joining the ranks of the mujahideen fighters in Iraq. Still others snuck into Syria with a Kalashnikov and four magazines full of bullets. In Syria they argued, and two of them decided to return to Jordan, where they too were arrested.

All the officials in the court had mustaches. Three military judges in olive uniforms sat behind a long wooden bench. Behind them were framed pictures of former King Hussein and current King Abdullah. Two young soldiers with red sashes from their waists to their shoulders stood against the wall. The chief judge sat in the center. As he prepared to read the charges, one of the prisoners shouted, "Say God is great!" The prisoners erupted in unison, yelling fiercely, "God is great! The way of God is jihad!" Perhaps they were imitating one of their role models, Ayman al-Zawahiri, Osama bin Laden's deputy, who made a similar show during his trial in Egypt for the assassination of President Anwar Sadat. The judge waited for them to finish shouting as if he was used to it and read the four charges, which were possession of an automatic weapon with intention to use it in illegal activity, initiation of illegal activities that could harm Jordan's relations with a foreign country, sneaking and helping to sneak from and to Jordan with an automatic weapon, and helping to sneak into Jordan illegally. When the judge got to the part about "a foreign country," he was interrupted by an angry prisoner, who shouted, "Infidel countries, not foreign countries!" The judge looked bored and tapped his pen on the table for silence, asking the prisoner to stop interrupting.

One by one the judge read the prisoners' names, asking if they pleaded guilty or not. He was interrupted by the same prisoner once more, who shouted, "This is a play. When is it going to end? We know that the verdicts have been decided and written in the files!" The judge tapped his pencil impatiently. "I am not guilty, you are guilty!" snapped some of the prisoners. "Jihad is not guilt!" shouted one prisoner. "Is jihad in the way of God guilt? Fighting the Americans and Jews and infidels is now guilt? We are protecting the honor of our sisters in Iraq. Is that guilt? God is our master and you have no master. Your regime is rotten and it stinks. You and your regime and your ranks, you are all guilty!" The judge tapped his pen and told the prisoners to answer without comments. "He who opens alcoholic bars is guilty!" said one prisoner.

The judge lost his temper and angrily told the guards to take the loudest prisoner out of the cage and back to the van, and the prisoner quieted down. Then, as punishment for the prisoners' recalcitrance, the judge ordered their families to leave the court. The military prosecutor, also in uniform and sporting a thick mustache, informed the judge that he had no witnesses, and the trial was postponed for one week. "God is our master and you have no master!" the prisoners shouted in unison. "He is the best master and the best supporter. America is your master and you have the worst master. God is great!"

Following the trial I met with Hussein al-Masri, lawyer for the accused ten. Masri, dressed in an ill-fitting brown jacket with green pants, a red shirt, and a brown tie, told me, "Now the law permits accusing people who only think or talk about terrorism. It is not required to commit the act of terrorism; only thinking or speaking is enough. The prosecution accused the defendants of already going to Syria and meeting and arranging terrorist activities, but they didn't do it."

The following Friday I drove up to Irbid's Hnina neighborhood to the Qaqa'a Mosque, hoping to learn more about what might have motivated the young prisoners in their failed and almost comical attempt to join the jihad in Iraq. As I drove up, my taxi driver recounted how his cousin had suddenly picked up and left for Iraq in March 2003. Many young men from his town, Zarqa, who were not even overtly religious, had poured over the border to fight the Americans. An hour and a half later we drove through Irbid's rolling hills, the elevation making the air cleaner than in Amman. We were a mere thirty kilometers from the Syrian border. Friday is a slow day in the Muslim world, and Irbid's streets were nearly empty. In the Hnina neighborhood, two boys sat on a curb sharing a bag of potato chips. A small group of men and women lined up in front of the Jowharat al-Zein bakery to purchase piles of large flat bread for lunch, which was always a more important occasion on Fridays. Children played in the street, and the few women walking by were not conservatively dressed.

I sat on a step in front of a closed store eating a sandwich with my friends and watching the trickle of men making their way to the Qaqa'a Mosque for the Friday noon prayer and the *khutba* (sermon). Men casually strolled by. *"Assalamu aleikum"* (Peace be upon you), they said as they noticed us, and we responded, *"Wa aleikum salam wa rahmat ullah wa barakat"* (And peace upon you and the mercy of God and his blessings).

The mosque was an inconspicuous white three-story building with a small dome and a loudspeaker. Down the hill from its narrow gated entrance, and around the back, was a small tiled bathroom for ablutions, the ritual washing of the legs, arms, and face required before prayer. Inside was a long sink lined with many faucets and short benches. Upstairs the trickle of men had reached about six hundred; it seemed as if more men were present than the neighborhood could have produced on its own. Their shoes lined the entrance or were stuffed into pigeonholes. They kneeled, or bowed, or stood in silent prayer in rows along white lines painted on the green carpet, in a "fortified wall" the way tradition stipulated. Many small children played by the door; others prayed by their fathers or leaned against the columns. The mosque was unfinished, and unpainted cinder blocks and plaster were visible on the walls. The sun came in from a skylight around the dome. Men wore tracksuits, jeans, and *dishdashas*. I noticed one man wearing a *salwar kameez*, the traditional long shirt and baggy pants worn in Pakistan and Afghanistan but not in the Arab world. It was a statement of support for jihad.

By chance, the mosque's imam was called Sheikh Jihad Mahdi, though the name itself was of no significance (even Christian Arabs are known to call their sons Jihad). Sheikh Jihad wore a simple white *dishdasha* and white cap and sat in the front with a microphone. As he waited for the proper time to begin, he lectured the men in the mosque—and, through the loudspeakers, the entire neighborhood—on how to pray properly, using a strong colloquial accent and slang. As the majority of men completed their prayers in a low murmur, Sheikh Jihad stood up and began with a short prayer, as is the custom. "Thanks be to God, supporter of Islam," he said, "for his victory and his humiliation of infidelity with his power and managing all the matters with his orders and deceiving the infidels with his cleverness, the one who estimates the days going over and over by his justice. Prayer and peace on the one who raises the flag of Islam with his sword." This was no ordinary prayer and was not normally used, but it was the same prayer used by Al Qaeda in Iraq, the movement led by Abu Musab al-Zarqawi, in every message they put out. It was a code, and supporters of the jihad and Al Qaeda would recognize it.

It would soon be time for the hajj, the annual pilgrimage to Mecca and Medina, and throughout the world millions were making their way to Saudi Arabia to fulfill this important pillar of Islam. Sheikh Jihad exhorted his flock to go on the hajj, calling it "the most important act of worship." He warned that if a man did not go on the hajj he was as bad as a Jew. "Remember that we are now building this mosque," he told his listeners. "It is not finished, so give any amount of money to help build this house of God."

Like all sermons, Sheikh Jihad's ended with a prayer. "God support the Muslims and give them victory everywhere," he said, as the crowd responded with an "Amin."

"God support the mujahideen and give them victory everywhere, in Iraq in Palestine."

"Amin."

"God give us the power to break the thorns of the Jews and the Americans and the Crusaders."

"Amin."

"God give us the opportunity to face them."

"Amin."

"Bless us and show us the way to jihad in the path of God."

"Amin."

Sheikh Jihad repeated this last prayer for jihad three times. Interestingly, he omitted the prayer for the leader of the nation (in this case, King Abdullah) that is traditionally invoked by clerics after their sermons.

The sheikh lived beneath his mosque with his family, and I waited on the steps in front of his door as he kissed and greeted well-wishers following his sermon. He invited me to his guest room, which was lined with books on Islam. Green pillows covered the floor, and we sat down to drink tea that he brought in from the house, which was closed off to me lest I glimpse his wife. I could hear his children watching cartoons on television. Colorful plastic flowers, which seemed to be required in Jordanian homes, decorated the room. On one wall in his guest room Sheikh Jihad had hung an immense sword, right out of *Conan the Barbarian*, with a wide sharp blade. On its hilt were two skulls and spikes coming out ominously. It was not a Middle Eastern blade, and I had never heard or seen a cleric with such a décor hanging on his walls. The thirty-five-year-old Sheikh Jihad took his name seriously.

Like many in Irbid, Sheikh Jihad was originally Palestinian; his family's town had been destroyed by the Israelis in 1967. He had been a cleric for ten years, after receiving a degree in Sharia law from a Sudanese correspondence school. "The *khutba* is a standard that measures the direction of people," he said, adding that his sermons had once been much more political, especially at the beginning of the Iraq War. But he had been arrested several times by Jordanian authorities as a result, and was forced to moderate his tone, at least a little. He claimed to have been tortured by them as well. I asked him about the ten young men I had seen in court two days before and who were said to have met to discuss their ideas and plans regularly in his mosque, but he claimed never to have heard of them. He no longer explicitly advocated jihad, in public at least, worrying that the November bombings in three Amman hotels had changed things in Jordan. "People were disgusted by it," he said, explaining that things in Iraq were confusing.

The war in Iraq had changed everything in the Muslim world, creating new confusion and new certainties. In the late 1990s experts on the Muslim world had spoken about the failure of political Islam, even explaining that the September 11 attacks were its last nihilistic act. The planners of the American war in Iraq claimed that the democracy they would install in place of Saddam's dictatorship would create a domino effect, spreading to other authoritarian states in the region, from Saudi Arabia to Syria. Nearly three years later, with religious parties dominating the Iraqi elections, Hamas winning in the Palestinian elections, the Muslim Brotherhood increasing its power in the Egyptian elections, and authoritarian regimes in the region appearing unthreatened by democracy, it was radical Islam that had spread. In fact, it was experiencing a renaissance.

The Story of Hudheifa Azzam

The father of modern jihad was Abdallah Azzam. Azzam was born in 1941 in Jenin, Palestine. Following the 1967 war and the Israeli occupation, Azzam, then a high school teacher, based himself in Jordan and led religious fighters from different Arab countries in cross-border raids against the Israelis from the "sheikhs' camps" supported by the Muslim Brotherhood movement. Azzam led the Qutbi wing of the Jordanian Brotherhood, which was named after Egyptian Sayyid Qutb and made up of those closest to Salafis in their way of thinking. Qutb, who led the Muslim Brotherhood after Hassan al-Banna, was executed by the Egyptian regime in 1966. His most important book was *Milestones on the Road*. The two most important concepts in Qutb's writings were *jahiliya* and *takfir*. *Takfir*, as mentioned above, means excommunicating, or declaring a Muslim to be a *kafir*. *Jahiliya* is the pre-Islamic ignorance that Islamists accuse present Muslim governments of having reverted to. Governments that have reverted to such a state can be declared infidel, and jihad against them is legitimate.

During the 1970 civil war in Jordan, when the regime battled Palestinians in what came to be known as Black September, Azzam ordered his men to leave

Jordan to avoid killing other Muslims. Azzam was alienated by the dominance of secular nationalism over the Palestinian liberation movement and hoped to internationalize jihad. He studied in Egypt's prestigious Al Azhar University, receiving a PhD in Islamic law and graduating with honors. He went on to teach in Saudi Arabia as well as in Jordan. Following the Russian invasion of Afghanistan, Azzam moved to Pakistan, where he founded Maktab al-Khidmat al-Mujahideen (the Office of Mujahideen Services). The office served as the main clearinghouse for Arab fighters seeking to join the jihad in Afghanistan; it housed, trained, and educated them. Although the top Saudi cleric pronounced jihad in Afghanistan a *fard ayn* (direct obligation), the Jordanian Muslim Brotherhood refused to issue a similar *fatwa,* so Azzam left the movement. Azzam believed that defensive jihad—i.e., defeating infidel invaders in Muslim lands—was a *fard ayn.* He singled out Afghanistan and Palestine as the most obvious cases. (During the war in Iraq, similar declarations that defensive jihad was a *fard ayn* were made throughout the Muslim world.) Azzam's books and sermons formulated his thoughts on jihad, and he mentored Osama bin Laden until 1987, when the Saudi decided to form his own camp for Arabs. Azzam was not radical enough for this new camp; Ayman al-Zawahiri, who would become bin Laden's key deputy and ideologue, virtually excommunicated him.

In November 1989 a car bomb killed Azzam and two of his sons. In the car that followed Azzam's doomed vehicle sat his eighteen-year-old son, Hudheifa, who had been fighting since 1985. In December 2005 I met Hudheifa in a cafe in Amman. Dressed in light blue jeans, wearing a leather jacket and red polo shirt, speaking excellent English, still fit and smiling often, he did not look like an expert in international jihad. Hudheifa, who was light-skinned like his father, with a neatly clipped and groomed beard, ordered a hot chocolate and recounted his tale. When Azzam brought his family to Pakistan, he settled them first in Islamabad, where he taught part-time. He set up the Office of Mujahideen Services in Peshawar in 1983, opening guest houses for mujahideen and training camps in 1984. Hudheifa began his training at the age of thirteen in the Sada (echo) Camp in Peshawar, and in 1985 he trained in Afghanistan's Khaldan and Yaqubi camps. He fought his first battle alongside his father and brothers in Jaji that year. The all-Arab unit included Saudis, Moroccans, and Algerians. When he was not fighting, Hudheifa studied at the Mahad al-Ansar (Supporters' Institute), a school his father had established for the children of Arab mujahideen. Rivals of Azzam condemned him for his friendship with Afghan jihad leader Ahmad Shah Massoud and for his relative moderation. "Al Qaeda separated from Abdallah Azzam," said Hudheifa. "They wanted to fight against the whole world. Our school specialized in defensive jihad: Palestine, Bosnia, Afghanistan, Chechnya."

Hudheifa fought from 1985 until 1992. He befriended Massoud in 1985 and fought alongside the famed hero, taking Kabul with him in 1992. He then went to continue his studies at the International Islamic University in Islamabad, but for the next six years he and some Arab colleagues tried to bring the warring parties in Afghanistan together, shuttling back and forth between Massoud's Northern Alliance and the Taliban's Mullah Omar (he blamed the failure to reach peace on the intervention of Pakistani intelligence). "We were the Arab mujahideen respected by everyone," he told me.

From 1994 to 1995 Hudheifa was in Bosnia, working to funnel money and supplies to the nascent country's beleaguered Muslims, and fighting on their behalf as well. He tried to enter Chechnya, but the Russians had blocked the road and he was forced to turn back. Hudheifa was arrested in the airport when he returned to Jordan in 1996, and again in 1997. He was also arrested in Pakistan, as governments that had supported the jihad began fearing the blowback. In 2000 the Jordanians returned his passport to him, and he was allowed to live freely, selling cars and nuts, importing and exporting, and receiving a license to work as a mobile phone distributor (on his personal multimedia mobile phone Hudheifa showed me films he had saved of Iraqi resistance attacks against the American military). He completed his master's degree in Islamic studies and the Arabic language. When I met him he was working on a PhD in Arabic literature from the classical Andalusian period.

Three days after America's war in Iraq started, Hudheifa and other followers of Azzam crossed into that country, basing themselves in Falluja. "We were trying to convince Muslim scholars to begin the resistance," he explained. "They had no plan. They were sleeping. For one month they did not agree. They said, 'Go back to your country.' We were more than thirty or forty Arabs, without weapons. We went from mosque to mosque, from school to school. People said. 'The U.S. brought us democracy.' They believed the lies of Bush, that he will bring democracy and freedom." Everything changed on April 28, he said, when American soldiers killed seventeen people at a demonstration and twelve more at a subsequent one. Soon after that, rumors spread of four American soldiers raping a seventeen-year-old girl, with pictures distributed on the Internet. "This story was the main cause of starting the resistance in Falluja," Hudheifa explained. "The rape made them reconsider, but there was still no action. I was watching from far only with a smile. In the beginning they said, 'Go make jihad in your country.' After the rape they said, 'Okay, we want to start now or tomorrow we will find our mothers or daughters or sisters raped.' This story exploded the resistance in Falluja. Then they called us for a meeting and said, 'You were right.' We had told them from the first day the Iraqi army abandoned weapons to take them, but they said, 'This is stealing, *haram* [forbidden], looting. You could buy an RPG for three U.S. dollars in those days. The Americans changed the ideology of the people with their oppression. They could have been the best power in the world.'"

Hudheifa spent four months in Iraq imparting his knowledge to the indige-nous resistance. His background gave him immediate currency. "I am the son of Abdallah Azzam," he said, "so everybody wanted to listen, and I have expe-rience in three or four jihads in different countries, and a lot of the Iraqi resist-ance had no plan. We gave them our experience so they could start from where we stopped, so they don't start from zero. Jihad is an obligation as a Muslim. If you can't support jihad with fighting, you can support with ideas or teaching. So we tried and we still do. Followers of Abdallah Azzam helped plan the resistance in all of Iraq, and we had hoped for a united resistance with Shiites. We were aiming to bring unity between Sunnis and Shiites with resist-ance on both sides, but the Shiite leadership was against us and Zarqawi spoiled it, making it fail." The Iraqi resistance requested his father's books, he told me, and beginning in June 2003 they became widely available in Falluja and Ramadi.

He explained that his father "talks about the crimes of Saddam and what real jihad is." His father had also opposed Saddam, he told me, trying to make it clear that Azzam's followers opposed the Baathists as well and were not fighting in support of the former regime. "My father was kicked out of the University of Jordan for opposing Saddam's war against Iran, and he was sen-tenced to death in Iraq for his work against Saddam. We are not with Saddam or the Baathists. We want to support the Muslim population."

Things were more difficult now, he explained. "After September 11 all money-transfer systems changed, but they can't stop financial support for the resistance." Wealthy businessmen from outside Iraq still sent money. "We have Iraqis who were in the Office of Services and are now in Iraq," he told me. But still, the good old days of jihad were in Afghanistan. Back then, "We used to go safely and securely, get a plane from anywhere to Pakistan and find vehicles from different organizations who sent us to rest houses, who took us to safe training camps and then safely to Afghanistan. Now if you want to go to Iraq, there are thousands of dangers facing you. Going into Iraq is very dangerous."

Hudheifa was fiercely opposed to terrorists like Zarqawi, who, he said, gave jihad a bad name. "We say to people who give funds, 'Don't give to Zarqawi. Give to Iraqis, give to the Association of Muslim Scholars. They are the right way. Our school supports them.'"

Hudheifa viewed his support for the Iraqi resistance as consistent with his support for other indigenous Muslim movements fighting in self-defense. "Iraq is a defensive jihad," he said. "Troops from abroad came to a Muslim country." Hudheifa told me he was proud of his work in Iraq. "Praise God, we were suc-cessful. Everything is going much better. Much better than we were planning. It won't take like Afghanistan, nine years, to kick the U.S. out. It will be much faster. If I find a way to go into Iraq, I would go. I told the government. But we must know our aims and goals. Just exploding cars is not enough. We need a plan for the future. When the Americans leave, we will look for the next place."

Although Azzam had opposed attacking Muslim governments, other veterans of the Afghan jihad took a different view, preferring to target what they called "the close enemy" first rather than "the far enemy," such as the Americans. Sheikh Jawad al-Faqih was one such veteran who seemed to want to target all enemies. I met him at the home of a Salafi contact called Abu Saad. Sheikh Jawad was a fearsome Brobdingnagian man with a thick beard and a clipped mustache (en vogue for Salafis); a large head; thick, fiery, protruding eyebrows; immense hands; and a raspy voice. He was a Salafi Hagrid. He wore a black *salwar kameez* and a white *ishmag* (head scarf) without an *eqal* (rope), which was the Salafi way. Like a good Salafi, he strictly adhered to the requirement that one's beard be longer than what a hand's grip can hold. A Palestinian whose uncles had fought the British occupation of Palestine, he had initially been influenced by secular nationalism. In 1982 he found "the correct way," and abandoned his nationalist sentiments. "I looked at all Islamic groups, only praying and fasting," he said. "I didn't like it. To be a real Muslim you have to fight and make the wrong right and hit powers who work against the right and attack Christians, Jews, and the *mukhabarat*."

When he encountered followers of Juheiman al-Utaibi, a Saudi radical who in 1979 had led the seizure of the Grand Mosque in Mecca and was later executed by Saudi authorities, Sheikh Jawad explained, "I found their ideas were what I was looking for." Sheikh Jawad had served in the Jordanian special forces, and he applied the skills he learned when he joined a militant group called Muwahidun, which meant Unitarians, or Monotheists. But in 1985 eight of the members were arrested. Sheikh Jawad was spared arrest because he feigned mental retardation. He was disappointed with his comrades in arms upon their release. "They were afraid," he said. "Their ideas about jihad changed in jail, so they refused to work with me." Disgusted with his fellow Jordanians, Sheikh Jawad was determined to leave. In 1989 he went to Yemen with another Jordanian, and together with seventeen Yemenis they made the journey to Pakistan. He had previously tried to go to Afghanistan but failed. In Pakistan he stayed for two nights in Peshawar's Beit al-Shuhada (home of the martyrs) guest house before entering Afghanistan's Sada Camp, where he received training in Soviet bloc weapons and was sent to the Jalalabad front. "I refused to be with Afghans," he explained. "They had beards, but they were communists or used drugs." He added, "I don't like Afghans except for the Taliban." Sheikh Jawad fought in four battles before being injured and transferred to a hospital. Osama bin Laden, known to friends like Sheikh Jawad as Abu Abdallah, spotted him carrying a heavy mortar across a river. "He liked me and said, 'Sign this guy up,'" said Sheikh Jawad. "He was impressed with my strength. Abu Abdallah was a brother, a jihadi. He was very humble. He helped the jihad with money."

Sheikh Jawad returned to Jordan, and then "a friend of mine asked me to come back to make operations on the other side of the border," meaning Israel, so "we smuggled weapons into Palestine." During the Gulf War he trucked food aid from Jordan into Baghdad. At the time many Afghan veterans gathered in Jordan, preparing to enter Iraq to defend it from American occupation, which would not come for another fourteen years. Instead, together with a doctor called Samih Zeidan, Sheikh Jawad established Jeish Muhammad (Army of Muhammad), and he imposed a strict training regimen on his recruits. Sheikh Jawad admitted to carrying out operations against infidels: attacking a British target, attempting to attack U.S. marines, "killing a priest," and "exploding a Jew." He established cells of fighters he called "families," each of which consisted of five fighters who did not know the identities of any other families. Sheikh Jawad claimed that Jeish Muhammad had cells around the Arab world. Most were veterans of the Afghan jihad. In 1991 a disgruntled member of Jeish Muhammad confessed the names of the organization's members to the Jordanian intelligence. In 1992 members established a new organization called the Jordanian Afghanis, which bombed a movie theater in the city of Zarqa.

Sheikh Jawad disliked living in Jordan and viewed Jordanians as unreliable. "I was jailed thirteen times," he said, "nine times because Jordanians named me, even when they gave their word that they wouldn't." Likewise, he was suspicious of fellow Palestinians in Jordan. "This generation of Palestinians," he explained, "their fathers fled Palestine, so they can't be trusted." Sheikh Jawad was now a car dealer, but he missed the jihad. "I wish I was in Afghanistan now like I wish I was in paradise," he told me. Likewise, he hoped to go to Iraq but worried that the Jordanians would turn him in. "If I reach the borders they will tell the Americans or the *rafidha*, [but] I wish I could go."

> *"Iraq has a different taste. The water, the dates,*
> *the yogurt. It is the country of the caliphate.*
> *I am addicted to Iraq, addicted to jihad."*

Outside, the opulent western Amman homes are unpainted, the cinder blocks still showing, rebar protruding from unfinished rooftops. Hastily constructed square houses are piled one atop the other haphazardly along the hills, an architectural patchwork like in a South American barrio, with narrow alleys covered by laundry hanging between rooftops. Empty lots become trash lots. Thin metal minarets jut up from the cacophony, their mosques mere unadorned squares like all the homes but with a speaker attached to the metal tower. In a maze of narrow treeless streets in Rusaifa, south of Amman, shops cover the heads of female dummies in the windows; on the streets some women wear the *burqa*. Muddy cars drive through roads built in *wadis* (dry riverbeds) and trash collects on cliff sides. In the distance the yellow and red hills and dunes of the desert look cold against the gray winter sky. Like a Jewish settler in the West Bank, Muhamad Wasfi built his home on a deserted moonscape. It too appeared unfinished yet old, the yard covered with garbage, shrubs, a tricycle, and a toy gun.

Abu Muntasar, as he is called, wore fake Nike training pants and a matching blue sweatshirt. He had a strong thick body, with a belly that showed he was not as active as he used to be. His thick beard was unkempt, but his mustache was groomed short like a Salafi's, and his hair was close-cropped. He had a false front tooth. Jordan's winters are bitter, and we sat close to a gas heater in his guest room. Though Abu Muntasar was born in the West Bank in 1963, his father worked for the Jordanian Army. "I still remember the day I left Palestine," he said, "with all the pieces of the Palestinian people. The Jews were raping and killing, so people were scared for their honor and left for Jordan." His family moved first to Amman and then to Zarqa, northwest of the capital, where many military families were based. Abu Muntasar served for two years in the Jordanian military before earning a degree in business management and working as a civil servant. "At that time I generally began learning Islamic thought," he explained. He admired the radical Islamic Group of Egypt and hoped to establish a similar Jordanian movement. "As Palestinian people we want to find a solution for our question," he told me. "Although I was young, I saw no other solution for our problems other than Islam, so I wasn't affected by secular Palestinian movements. I wanted to do something for Islam and Muslims and help establish the Muslim state and make Palestine the capital of our new caliphate." I asked him if he thought this was possible. "I believe it without any doubt," he said. "This has been proven by the Prophet Muhammad in his words."

He viewed Jordan's Islamic movements as contained or co-opted by the government. Like many Salafis, he was autodidactic, reading the works of Abdallah Azzam and the radical Egyptian cleric Omar Abdel Rahman currently imprisoned in America for his role in the 1993 World Trade Center bombing. He read their books and listened to tapes of their sermons, admiring them for going to Afghanistan. In 1989 he went to Pakistan and then Afghanistan "to see the reality of Muslims and their movements, of the Islamic nation and jihad." He dreamed of starting a jihad in Sham (the lands of Syria, Jordan, Lebanon, and Palestine) and liberating his homeland. "I was lucky," he said, because he got to meet his hero Rahman in the Saudi-run Ansur guest house. The sheikh lectured Abu Muntasar and others about jihad: its justification, its history, and its future. "It was the first and last time that I saw the sheikh, but for me it is a rich history," he recalled with nostalgia. Before going to the Jalalabad front, he was trained in the Sada and Salahedin camps, and fought under the leadership of an Egyptian called Abu Uthman. He also fought with Afghan leader Abdul Rasul Sayyaf but complained that "Sayyaf disappointed many people in the final years of the jihad by taking the side of the Northern Alliance against the Taliban. He should have taken the other side."

In 1990 Abu Muntasar reached an agreement with jihad officials in Afghanistan that would allow him to bring his wife and children and work as a teacher with the sons of mujahideen, while continuing to fight during his vacations. Iraq invaded Kuwait upon his return to Jordan, "and my ideas changed," he said. "The war was here." Although a huge international coalition punished Saddam for violating international law, Israel's defiance of United Nations rulings were ignored, he said. "It was a critical point for any Muslim who loves his religion and nation," he said. Together with a Jordanian doctor called Muhammad al-Rifai, who was a leader of Jordan's Afghan Arabs, he "established a jihad fighting movement based on spreading *tawhid* and jihad, and we directed our energies against Israel." Led by Rifai, his movement was called the Organized Movement of Islamic Call and Jihad. The main goal of the organization, which he claimed had thousands of members and supporters, was to establish a caliphate and then to destroy Israel. Abu Muntasar, the organization's speaker, spread its ideas in mosques and schools, although he had no formal religious education. "Islamic thought is something personal," he said. "I taught myself. I was a leader and had to learn more and teach in people's homes and mosques, even funeral houses." Following the Gulf War, the Jordanian government cracked down on Islamic movements, and Abu Muntasar was jailed with many of his associates, since their group was affiliated with the Jeish Muhammad. Abu Muntasar had opposed operations in Jordan. "We knew it would be useless, and we had a much more important goal," he said. In prison he was beaten and tortured. "Torture is how they got information," he said. "Torture is the best way to get information." (I joked that perhaps I should torture him, then, to get more answers.) Following their release from prison, Rifai returned to Afghanistan and then sought asylum in England, while Abu Muntasar worked as a part-time imam in mosques and roved the country to teach and lecture.

Abu Muntasar described the 1990s as his trial-and-error period. He opposed attacking the Jordanian government, explaining that "the near enemy exists to protect the far enemy, but if you attack the near enemy, then you alienate the population. They will say the dead man is a member of this or that tribe, he prays with you, it will get people to hate you. But if you attack the far enemy, you are also attacking the near enemy, but the regime cannot say anything to you because people will hate them. If you kill a Jew or Americans, people will like you." Abu Muntasar was arrested once more for his speeches, and later for his activities with Zarqawi. "What I am concerned with now is continuing the Islamic call and establishing an Islamic way of life and waiting for the correct jihad. The next battlefield is Sham, and we must prepare the people of Sham for this. What happened in Iraq and before in Afghanistan has extension. The U.S. wants to get inside the capital of Islam, which is Sham. This entrance will be through Syria. Syria will be the slaughterhouse of Americans and their supporters, so they are welcome to get inside Syria and be butchered."

Abu Saad called me one night and picked me up from my hotel in Amman. In the front passenger seat sat thirty-seven-year-old Abu Muhamad. Though he was seated in the front and I in the back, lighting my notebook with my mobile phone in order to take notes, I could see from how his head touched the car's roof and his long legs pressed against the dashboard that Abu Muhamad was a giant man. He had a dark *sima* above his prominent brow, and though I could see his thick lips, his face was shrouded by a dark *ishmag* with an *eqal*. He refused to tell me whether he was originally Palestinian, explaining that nationalism was against Islam.

Soon after the fall of Baghdad, Abu Muhamad had made his way to Baquba, a town east of Baghdad near the Iranian border. "I was thirsty for jihad," he explained. "I felt I had a duty to go to Iraq. It's a duty of any Muslim if he can." He had previously lived in Iraq for five years before, and so had established relationships with "good people on the right side," and he knew the country's geography and dialect, so he passed for a local. Abu Muhamad had been married in Iraq in 1989, but when he returned to fight the Americans he had not expected to see his family again. Though at first he and his friends were unorganized, they soon met fighters from western Iraq and became more involved in the jihad. Abu Muhamad had been a sniper during his Jordanian military service. The Iraqis had not needed much training. "Do you know an Iraqi who doesn't know how to fight?" he asked me. Abu Muhamad, who had known Zarqawi before the war, ended up in a group of five or six fighters belonging to Zarqawi's movement but composed mainly of Iraqis. The group was commanded by a former Iraqi pilot. "God's support came and sent us brothers from Ansar al-Sunna who trained us in street fighting," he explained. "Jihad will spread around the world. The Americans are trying to attack Syria, and we are expecting them to attack."

He refused to discuss most of the operations he had taken part in but admitted they had involved shootings and bombs and explained that most suicide bombers were not Iraqi. Jihad was an obligation for Muslims, he told me. "It is not about Iraq. The higher goal is to establish an Islamic state." Referring to Osama bin Laden, he told me, "Sheikh Abu Abdallah said, 'The foreigners and infidels and their interests are everywhere, so anywhere you can hit them you will hurt them.'"

He complained that Jordan was protecting Israel. "If this regime gave the youth freedom they would eat Israel," he said. "They wouldn't even leave their bones. But regimes are trying to protect Israel." Abu Muhamad supported attacks against Iraq's Shiite civilians because he considered them *rafidha*. "The infidel sects are one, if they are Jews or Shiites." He explained that Ibn Taimiya, the thirteenth-century scholar loved by Salafis, had said that Shiites "were worse than Jews or Christians. Shiites hate Islam and hate Sunnis."

Abu Muhamad's days began early, although he and his fellow fighters rarely left the house during daylight, executing most operations at night. During the day, "one of the brothers would lecture, or we prepared for operations." Before his departure for Iraq he had been arrested, accused of being a *mujahid*. "They called us *takfiris*," he complained. "The man who says, 'Don't drink alcohol, don't dance, but pray instead'—they call him a terrorist." Although Sheikh Jawad had spoken a rich Arabic, referring to the Koran, Abu Muhamad's speech was heavily colloquial. He called Egyptian leader Hosni Mubarak a "pimp" for going to pay condolences to Tony Blair following the July 7 London bombings.

Abu Muhamad had not been in Iraq for a year, but he longed to return. "Iraq has a different taste," he said. "The water, the dates, the yogurt. It is the country of the caliphate. I am addicted to Iraq, addicted to jihad."

Yet no one was more addicted to jihad than the "Sheikh of the Slaughterers," Ahmad Fadhil Nazal al-Khalaylah, more commonly known as Abu Musab al-Zarqawi. He hailed from Zarqa, which had been the capital of radical Islam in Jordan since the 1960s and had also produced most of the Jordanian jihadis fighting in Iraq. Zarqa's population of nearly one million is made up mostly of Palestinians who were expelled in 1948 and a second wave of refugees who came in 1967. Abdallah Azzam had also settled there.

Zarqawi, who took his city as his namesake, had been a wild young man, with no interest in religion. A high school dropout, he had a reputation for getting tattoos, drinking alcohol, getting into fights, and ending up in jail. Like many disaffected Muslim youth, he was moved to fight in Afghanistan by stories of mujahideen heroism there. But by the time he arrived as a twenty-three-year-old, the Russians had withdrawn, so he took part in the civil war. His journey to Afghanistan was arranged by Azzam's Office of Mujahideen Services, then run by Azzam's follower Sheikh Abdel Majid al-Majali, or Abu Qutaiba. Azzam's son Hudheifa told me that in 1989 he picked up Zarqawi from the airport in Peshawar and took him to the Beit al-Shuhada guest house. "Zarqawi was a very simple person, silent, he didn't talk. As a witness I can say that he was very well trained in military skills, especially in making bombs. In English you say 'braveheart,' but he had a dead heart—he was never scared. Bin Laden wanted Zarqawi to join Al Qaeda, but he didn't like Al Qaeda's ideology, so he left for Khost. I saw him in Gardez and Khost; if he was alone against a thousand soldiers he would not retreat. He was not a leader at the time, just an ordinary person and a good fighter."

Sheikh Jawad, the imposing former jihadi, had a similar view of his friend Zarqawi, whom he called Abu Musab. "He used to come to my house," he said. "We went to Afghanistan together. Abu Musab was a normal man, afraid of God, a very natural man, didn't have a lot of knowledge." Sheikh Jawad told me that Zarqawi gave two of his sisters as wives to Afghans in order to strengthen his relationship with his hosts. "Afghans took care of him, and he gained experience," he said. Zarqawi was placed in charge of Jordanians arriving in Afghanistan and later led a group called Jund al-Sham (Soldiers of Sham).

In Pakistan Zarqawi met Isam Taher al-Oteibi al-Burqawi, known as Abu Muhammad al-Maqdisi. Maqdisi was a self-taught Palestinian cleric living in Kuwait. Like many Palestinians who relocated to Jordan from Kuwait, he had belonged to an important Kuwaiti Salafi organization called Jamiyat al-Turath al-Islami (The Society of Islamic Heritage), led by the Egyptian cleric Sheikh Abdel Rahman al-Khaleq. Khaleq had come to Kuwait from Egypt in the 1960s, a period when many Egyptian Islamists moved to the Gulf to teach in order to escape government persecution. This persecution persisted until Egyptian clerics like Omar Abdel Rahman, who led the Islamic Group, declared the state itself to be the enemy. This sort of radical Islam was a product of Egyptian prisons, and when these Egyptians were encouraged to take their struggle to Afghanistan they clashed with Abdallah Azzam, who emphasized the importance of fighting defensive jihads. Egyptians such as Abdel Rahman and his followers sought to fight Arab regimes first. Their followers were the *takfiri* par excellence, sometimes viewing all of society as the enemy and demonstrating a willingness to ruthlessly kill civilians. Maqdisi was influenced by this school of thought and brought it back home with him.

Hudheifa Azzam met Maqdisi in Pakistan and was similarly unimpressed. Like Zarqawi, he said, "Maqdisi is also an ordinary person," adding that at first Maqdisi had condemned his father as an infidel, but after Azzam was assassinated he apologized and said he had been mistaken. Upon arriving in Jordan in 1991, Maqdisi led Jordan's Salafi movement, composed of Jordanian and Palestinian Salafis who had fought or trained in Afghanistan. Maqdisi called his organization Tawhid (Monotheism), but he later changed the name to Bayat al-Imam (Oath of Loyalty to the Leader). He traveled around Jordan with his book *Milat Ibrahim* (The Creed of Abraham), which was the most important source for Jordanian Jihadis. The book, also available on Maqdisi's website, discusses some of the main duties the followers of Ibrahim have, such as demonstrating that they are innocent of any infidelity and improper worship of God and declaring infidels to be infidels. Just as infidels are infidels with God, the followers of Ibrahim have to be infidels with the gods and laws of the infidels. Likewise, they have to demonstrate hatred and enmity for the infidels until they return to Allah and renounce their previous infidelity. The followers of Ibrahim also have to renounce tyrants and impious or un-Islamic governments, call them infidels, and call all the people who "worship" them infidels as well. These tyrants include stone idols, the sun, the moon, trees, graves (a reference to the Sufi and Shiite practice of visiting the graves of saints and imams), and laws made by men. It is the duty of the sect of Ibrahim to expose the infidelity of all these forms of worship and idolatry and manifest their hatred and enmity to them as well as showing how silly these things were. Infidels, tyrants, and oppressors all deserve hate and public condemnation.

According to Maqdisi, democracy was a heretical religion constituting the rejection of Allah, monotheism, and Islam. It was a *bida* (innovation), placing something above the word of God and ignoring the laws of Islam. Only God could legislate laws, and God's laws had to be applied to the apostates, the fornicators, thieves, alcohol consumers, unveiled women, and the obscene. Maqdisi held that the regimes that ruled Muslims were un-Islamic and illegitimate. Therefore, Muslims did not owe them obedience and should fight them to establish a true Islamic state.

When Zarqawi returned to Jordan, he sought out former mujahideen he had met in Afghanistan, including Maqdisi. In the summer of 1993 Zarqawi visited Muhamad Abu Muntasar Wasfi. "He sat there, where you are," Wasfi said, pointing to the pillow I was resting on. We sat in his cold guest room as his sons brought in sweet tea and came in to replenish our glasses. Wasfi stroked a cat that wandered in. His children screamed and fought in the next room. His youngest boy, Mudhafer, came in to ask him for some money. "I like to call him Abu Musab al-Khalaylah," Wasfi told me about Zarqawi. "Abu Musab had heard of me. He was a simple Muslim who wanted to serve Islam. He didn't stay long here, and the next day he came with another guy. We sat and we spoke about our hopes and dreams and ambitions to establish the caliphate and raise the flag of jihad against the enemies of Islam everywhere. I disagreed with him on some strategic issues, like his view of Israel and Palestine. He didn't have an idea of making jihad against Jews and Israel. Abu Musab wanted to change Arab regimes."

Zarqawi invited Wasfi to join Bayat al-Imam and offered him the position of emir, or commander, from the Arabic word *amr*, meaning "to order." Wasfi joined but refused the position, claiming that because he was Palestinian he would be subjected to greater retribution by the Jordanian authorities, who were more lenient on Jordanians. Maqdisi, Zarqawi, and Wasfi led the group, limiting their initial activities to proselytizing. "We had no ability to make jihad," Wasfi admitted, "but despite the lack of ability it didn't mean we should stop." Maqdisi had seven grenades from Kuwait, which he gave "to some brothers to make operations in Palestine to kill Israelis," Wasfi said. "The brothers were arrested, and the government uncovered the organization and arrested the leaders, but before that we were fugitives for four months. We were arrested and tortured." Wasfi claims to have suffered "sleep deprivation, beatings, tearing off beards." As a result he has rheumatism and his knees often hurt; he couldn't kneel properly when he prayed for the first year after his release. "When we were put in group prison, we worked on expanding the organization inside and outside the jail. It was my job to organize prisoners. Jail was very good for the movement. Jail enhanced the personalities of prisoners and let them know how large was the cause they believed in. Inside jail is a good environment to get supporters and proselytize. Inside jail is oppression." Wasfi admitted they recruited from criminal ranks. "Even the worst criminal is still repressed because they did not impose Islamic law on him, and when you talk to them with Islam they see the difference between a system of punishment made by humans and a system made by God. This made them supporters of the Islamic call and enemies of oppression."

The Jordanian authorities placed all the Islamist prisoners together and in isolation from other prisoners. They formed relationships, exchanged ideas and knowledge, and established trust in one another. They continued organizing jihadists, especially former criminals like Zarqawi, until their release from the Sawaqa prison in a 1999 amnesty. Wasfi was the movement's spokesman. He explained that even while in prison Zarqawi and Maqdisi reached an outside audience, influencing people in the various cities where they were imprisoned. By then, the awkward and solemn Zarqawi had begun to bloom in his own jihadi way, while Maqdisi, despite the anger and violence of his ideas, avoided conflict. "Zarqawi was very charismatic," said Wasfi. "Maqdisi was calm and passive. We were dealing with prison authorities in a very aggressive way, and Zarqawi was tribal, so his tribal position gave him more power than a Palestinian. If your root is pure Jordanian and you have a big tribe, then you have more power. Prisoners liked a strong representative like Zarqawi, and he fought with the guards. He was very harsh and strong when dealing with members of the organization. He prevented them from mixing with other organizations so they would not be influenced by other ideas, and he prevented them from moving around freely in the prison, even me, but I rebelled against him." Few other jihadis dared to defy Zarqawi save Abdallah Hashaika, who was the emir of the Jordanian Afghans. Zarqawi organized a coup, forcing Maqdisi to hand over control of the movement. When Wasfi told me this, Abu Saad, who was present for the meeting, grew anxious—he didn't want me to learn of tensions within the movement.

Zarqawi's aggressive personality attracted the tough young men imprisoned with him, and Maqdisi was relegated to a theological position, issuing *fatwas*. Like jihadi Salafis outside prison, the jihadis in Sawaqa were embroiled in internal conflicts, declaring one another infidels. "In prison a disagreement of ideas led to problems," said Wasfi. He refused to get into the details but added that "Abu Musab had many wrong decisions that I did not accept, like enmity with other groups." Five months before his release, Wasfi abandoned the movement. After his release he focused on "personal *dawa*," or working to spread Salafism on his own. Though officially forbidden to teach, he still does in secret. "After Zarqawi was released, he asked me to work together, but I refused," Wasfi said.

The men's time in prison was as important for the movement as their experiences in Afghanistan were, bonding together those who suffered and giving them time to formulate their ideas. For some it was educational as well. Hudheifa Azzam was impressed with the changes prison wrought in the men. "Maqdisi returned to Jordan from Afghanistan and educated himself," he told me. "He had a lot of time to read in jail. When I heard Zarqawi speak, I didn't believe this is the same Zarqawi. Six years in jail gave him a good chance to educate himself."

Shortly after his release in 1999, Zarqawi left for Pakistan, where he was temporarily arrested before making it to Afghanistan along with his key followers. Zarqawi was influenced by Egyptian jihadist groups such as Islamic Jihad and the Islamic Group, which held that the leader should be based outside the country in order to avoid harassment by the *mukhabarat*. Maqdisi opposed conducting operations within Jordan.

In Afghanistan Zarqawi found both Al Qaeda and the Taliban insufficiently extreme for him. Zarqawi also criticized Osama bin Laden for not calling Arab governments infidels and attacking them. For Zarqawi, the near enemy was the priority, while for bin Laden it was the far enemy. Hudheifa Azzam explained that bin Laden's Front for Fighting the Jews and Crusaders, established in 1998, required its members to take an oath of allegiance and to fight rival movements, both of which Zarqawi refused to do. Al Qaeda was far more pragmatic; its members negotiated with Pakistan and Iran. Zarqawi was such a strict Salafi that he condemned the Taliban for lack of piety. He criticized them for not being Salafis, insufficiently imposing Sharia, and recognizing the United Nations, an infidel organization. And he condemned Al Qaeda for associating with the Taliban. Zarqawi established his own camp in the western Afghan city of Herat, near the border with Iran. Following the U.S. invasion of Afghanistan in 2001, Zarqawi made his way through Iran to autonomous Kurdistan in northern Iraq—a point worth noting, since the Bush administration claimed Zarqawi's presence in Iraq was proof of an Al Qaeda connection. But Zarqawi linked up with the terrorist group Ansar al-Islam in a region outside Saddam's reach. With Saddam removed from power on April 9, 2003, Zarqawi had a new failed state to operate in. By the summer of 2003 he had claimed responsibility for the devastating attack against the United Nations headquarters in Baghdad's Canal Hotel. Zarqawi allied himself with Ansar al-Sunna, the reconstituted Ansar al-Islam, which was composed mostly of Iraqis, whereas the members of Zarqawi's Tawhid and Jihad group were mostly foreign Arabs.

In October 2004, Iraqi intelligence claimed that Zarqawi's group consisted of 1,000 to 1,500 fighters, foreign and Iraqi. Zarqawi's inner circle was made up of nine emirs, all of whom were non-Iraqi and close friends. The movement had stored weapons in secret depots in Iraq.

Their plan was to turn Iraq into hell for all its residents, to prevent an elected government from taking power, and to create a civil war between Sunnis and the hated Shiites. Zarqawi's group was responsible for the gruesome videotaped beheadings of foreigners and Iraqis accused of collaborating with the occupation. Their bombs slaughtered masses of Shiites as well.

Though Zarqawi had run his own camp independently of bin Laden in Afghanistan, in October 2004 he swore an oath of allegiance to Al Qaeda, renaming his organization Al Qaeda in the Land of the Two Rivers and also joining the Salafiya al-Mujahedia, or Salafi Mujahideen, movement in Iraq. Bin Laden soon announced that Zarqawi was the head of Al Qaeda's operations in Iraq. Either Bin Laden wanted to co-opt a rival jihadi group that was getting most of the attention and actually confronting the Americans, or Zarqawi needed the Saudi financier's help, or at least the connection with the hero of international jihad, in order to attract more foreign fighters and support. On December 9, 2004, Zarqawi's military committee issued a statement about the upcoming January elections. It addressed "all the parties participating in the elections." It threatened Shiites around the world for supporting the crusader occupation of Iraq. It called Ayatollah Ali Sistani the greatest collaborator with the crusaders. It condemned the apostate police, national guardsmen, and army for attacking Falluja. It warned the rejectionist Shiites and their political parties, the Kurdish *pesh merga*, the Christians, and the hypocrites such as the Islamic Party that the Tawhid movement would increase attacks on them.

Though Al Qaeda under bin Laden and Ayman al-Zawahiri had not made Shiites their targets and did not publicly condemn them, Zarqawi held that Shiites were the most evil of mankind. He compared them to a snake, a scorpion, and an enemy spy, like the thirteenth-century cleric Ibn Taimiya, the father of Wahhabism and Salafism. Shiites were polytheists who worshiped at graves and shrines, he argued. They were to be avoided at all costs. They could not be married, they could not bear witness, and animals they slaughtered could not be eaten. Zarqawi defended operations that caused Muslims to die. Martyrdom operations, as he called suicide bombings, were sanctified by Muslim scholars, and defending Islam was even more important than defending the lives of Muslims.

Zarqawi reserved special hatred for the Jordanian monarchy and security forces. He sought to delegitimize the Hashemite kingdom and its claim to power based on its descent from the Prophet Muhammad. It was true that King Abdullah was a descendant of Muhammad, but through Abu Lahab, the Prophet's uncle, who had fought against him. This claim was first made in 1995 by two Jordanian brothers from the al-Awamli family, who sent out a mass fax condemning the regime. They were shot in their homes following a confrontation with Jordanian police. Zarqawi's confrontation with Jordan culminated in the November 9, 2005, attacks, dubbed by Jordanians "our 9/11," in which almost all the victims were Jordanians or Palestinians. By this point his actions were proving too much even for the most radical to stomach.

Hudheifa Azzam viewed Zarqawi and his followers as "against everybody, even themselves. The followers of Abdallah Azzam opposed killing civilians and conducting operations in Muslim countries, he told me. "Our militant activities are only against the military," he said. "No one can give the green light to kill an innocent human being. In 9/11 and 7/7, innocent people were killed." Hudheifa also opposed targeting Shiites. "Abdallah Azzam said Shiites are Muslims," he told me, "and even if they are not Muslims, their blood is still protected."

Shanateh

The war in Iraq galvanized young admirers of Zarqawi and other mujahideen, who frequented jihadi websites and Internet chat rooms, where they could watch filmed encomiums to their heroes and violent depictions of their latest exploits. There were several groups of young men on trial in Jordan when I visited, all failed jihadis, but perhaps more important than succeeding in their quixotic and ill-planned schemes was the time spent in Jordanian prisons, where they could meet their heroes. Like inner-city fans of hip-hop in the United States, where time in jail could be a rite of passage that established street credibility, for these young men in Jordan, jail time proved they were tough enough and dedicated to the cause.

On January 10 I attended another hearing for the ten young men from Irbid. The only two witnesses for the prosecution were set to testify. The courtroom was heavy with blue uniformed security officers. As the judge spoke, the prisoners swaggered and laughed. The first witness was Lieutenant Saud, clad in a motorcycle jacket. He put his hand above a Koran and swore to tell the truth, then stated that he had received information about a group of dangerous terrorists near the Syrian border and was ordered to arrest them. Upon questioning by the defense he admitted that he had found no weapons in their possession. The second witness, with long hair and a long beard, was accused of selling the defendants a Kalashnikov. The prosecutor read the witness's confession, but the witness renounced it, claiming he had never sold any weapons and explaining that the *mukhabarat* had threatened him and ordered him to lie.

The judge ordered him rearrested for perjury. Ashen-faced, he was led away as the prisoners in the cage shouted *"Allahu Akbar!* The way of God is jihad! God is your master and America is their master! Bush is your master! You have the worst master!"* All the accused claimed to have been tortured, and all renounced their confessions. As the session ended the prisoners shouted, "This session we just wanted to hear the testimony, but in the next session we will teach them!"

"Most people here hate and hate and hate the U.S. administration," attorney Samih Khreis told me. "And most people, if anybody has the opportunity to explode the White House, they would." Khreis often represented Jordanians accused of terrorism; his clients had included Azmi al-Jayusi, a close Zarqawi associate, as well as members of Bayat al-Imam and Jeish Muhammad. A high-ranking member of the Jordanian bar association, Khreis remembered seeing mujahideen recruiters on the streets of Amman in the 1980s, working with the support of the Jordanian government and inviting young Jordanians to join the jihad in Afghanistan. "Governments taught them these ideas, Salafi, *takfiri,* to push them to Afghanistan against the Soviet Union, and after the jihad they returned and they compared the government's conduct with what they had taught them, so according to this thinking the governments were infidels. What happens daily motivates anybody to go to jihad. The magic turned against the magician. When they were against Soviets they were good, but against USA they are terrorists?"

Although in the past most recruits to the jihad were uneducated and poor, he said, "after the war in Iraq there was a large increase, and many educated men joined, like engineers. This was new. Most men going to Iraq now are educated and from Irbid, and most are Jordanians, they come from good families." He added that most families of accused terrorists were proud of their sons. Most of them were beaten and tortured during their interrogations, he told me. "Electric torture, sleep deprivation, being tied by hands so you are on your toes. They do it to get confessions." Khreis's youngest client was an eighteen-year-old jihad hopeful. "I take these cases because the American government is against them, and I am not with the USA, and the Jordanian government wants to satisfy USA." Like many Jordanians, Khreis believed Zarqawi was not responsible for the November 9, 2005, hotel bombings in Amman. "The hotel bombings were done by the Mossad, maybe the CIA is involved. There is a secret agreement between the Jordanian government and the USA to bring American forces here to attack Syria, so they want to prepare people for the attack on Syria."

An insider in the Royal Court who studied Jordanian attitudes explained such beliefs as *shanateh,* or schadenfreude. "Whatever is *shanateh* to America, we like it." A June 2005 Pew poll found that 60 percent of Jordanians trusted bin Laden and 50 percent supported violence to get rid of non-Muslim influence. The report stunned the Jordanian government. "We said, No way, our people are not like that," the insider said. But when the Jordanian government conducted its own research it found similar responses. "Even if we assume the Pew poll is exaggerated, maybe 25 percent trust him very much and 35 percent trust him somewhat. The Pew poll is exaggerated, but if Zarqawi wants to recruit here, how many does he need? Even if one-half of 1 percent join, he's okay." Despite the support Zarqawi and bin Laden received in the polls, the insider believed it did not reflect a true radicalization; it was merely *shanateh*. "When it comes to Israel, we are helpless," he said. "Hundreds of millions of Arabs, and we can't hurt Israel or America. So we can be happy with what is happening to America in Iraq."

This inside source also blamed the Jordanian government's tolerance of Salafism. "This is an appeasement from the security services. The church got them to ban *The Da Vinci Code*, but in Abdali you can buy Salafi books. Since the '70s they are turning a blind eye." He added that the requirements for studying Islamic law at the University of Jordan were lower than for any other subject. "Sharia students are the ones who get the worst scores and can't get into other schools, the ones with no critical thinking skills. The Sharia school in the university accepts the dumbest students. They tell them, 'All other majors are closed to you. Become a preacher.'" There are more than three thousand mosques in Jordan, he told me, but one-tenth of them lack a regular imam, which means that "anyone can stand up and do the Friday sermon." In addition, he said, "1,450 imams earn less than one hundred dinars a month, so you can buy them easily. So the quality of the preachers is low."

A Jordanian woman who ran youth empowerment and education programs throughout the Middle East worried that recruits were drawn to Salafism because "they are discouraged and depressed. Across the whole region youth lack dreams because they have been repressed by the system. It's not just poverty. Wealthy individuals are joining the jihad. There is a lack of hope and dreams. The youth feel they are of no value to society and become a burden, so of course they are attracted to these extreme ideologies."

Muhammad Abu Rumman, a Jordanian journalist specializing in Islamic movements and a former Muslim Brother himself, attributed the attraction of Salafism to hopelessness. "The political environment and conditions make them feel bad," he told me. "They have no hope for the future with the political system here, so they try by themselves to do what the government cannot do. They are victims of conditions in Jordan and the Arab world. Political consciousness is born in bad political, economic, social conditions. There is no religious reform. Religious understanding is not supporting democracy and human rights. It always says all the bad things are because we are far from Islam and we don't obey Allah so the U.S. invaded Iraq." He explained that the Muslim Brotherhood, which was Jordan's only opposition movement but refrained from questioning the government's legitimacy, "represents the middle class and shares in the system and government, but in their religious speech they use the same language as Salafis. These youth do what people say and don't do. We all speak of Iraq. The preachers speak of Iraq, and of jihad in Iraq and Palestine. The king would be in danger if he tried to stop this. All of the society speaks the same language."

Hassan Abu Haniyeh, a Jordanian researcher specializing in Salafism and a former reformist Salafi, agreed: "The main motivation for terrorists is unemployment and poverty. The people are between the hammer of the Americans and the anvil of exclusion from participating. If you open an office for volunteers for the jihad in Iraq here you would take a million, and from the rest of the Arab world you would take millions." Abu Haniyeh complained that the American project of reform in the Arab world had given democracy a bad name. "The U.S. terminated us, the reformers," he said, "because now the word 'reform' is a bad word, an American word. If people hear the word 're- form,' they think of Iraq, which became a model of violence. And now the re- form and the reformers are isolated from people, people don't like them. Now the reform project became empty from the inside because the replacement of our regimes is very terrifying, so there is nothing left, only extremist talk."

Yasar Qartarneh was a sharp, raucous, slightly overweight man who jok- ingly called himself an Islamist and liked to provoke. Qatarneh worked for Jor- dan's Institute for the Study of Diplomacy, a think tank within the Jordanian government funded by the Italian Ministry of Foreign Affairs. "Terrorism is linked to events on both sides of the border," he said. "For fifty years Islamist activists and politicians were the regime's main source of legitimacy." Now the chickens had come home to roost. He was concerned that just as America had given reform a bad name, so had Zarqawi tarnished resistance. "We have to draw a line which Zarqawi, Goddamn him, blurred. It was very legitimate to fight occupation. Zarqawi blurred the line, and now you can't distinguish if what he does is terrorism or freedom fighting."

The solution, according to Abu Rumman, was in Iraq. "If Sunnis played a political role in Iraq, Zarqawi would disappear, because who will support him?" Jordan was in a difficult position, watching its neighbor to the east nerv- ously. In December 2004, King Abdullah warned of a "Shiite crescent" from Lebanon to Iraq to Iran that would destabilize the entire region. Iraq's Shiites had demonstrated against Jordan in the past, condemning the country for its steady trickle of suicide bombers who crossed into Iraq and committed atroci- ties against Shiite civilians. In September 2005 Saudi Foreign Minister Saud al- Faisal warned that a civil war in Iraq would destabilize the entire region and complained that the Americans had handed Iraq over to Iran for no reason. From the Jordanian and Saudi perspective, indirectly supporting Sunni violence in Iraq was advantageous, because it would give Iraq's Sunnis greater political leverage. Jordan was dependent on the Saudis. In 2007, when the Jordanian state was bankrupt, the Saudis paid Jordanian civil servants' salaries. Compounding these difficulties, Jordan's fragile authoritarian regime and precarious balance of Jordanian and Palestinian was being tested by the massive influx of refugees from Iraq.

CHAPTER FIVE

Exiles

"YOU HAVE NOW ENTERED IRAQ," MY TAXI DRIVER JOKED. WE HAD, in fact, just entered Seyida Zeinab, a neighborhood on the outskirts of Damascus built around the eponymous shrine to Zeinab, granddaughter of the Prophet Muhammad. This shrine city, long a destination for Shiite pilgrims, had become home to many Shiites among the hundreds of thousands of Iraqis who had sought refuge in Syria from the hell their home had become in Iraq. "Everybody is Iraqi," one taxi driver joked after he stopped to ask several people on the street for directions to a mosque and they replied in Iraqi Arabic that they did not know. "There are more Iraqis than Syrians." Another, after complaining that the Iraqi refugees had driven up prices and insisting that there were four million of them in his city, explained, "Anybody who has a war comes to us: Sudan, Somalia."

It was early 2006, the seventh day of the Muslim month of Muharram, and Shiites around the world were preparing for its tenth day, known as Ashura, in which they commemorate the martyrdom of Hussein, brother of Zeinab, slain in 680 in a battle that crystallized the division between Sunni and Shiite Islam. A vast commercial district had grown around the shrine. Built at first to house and care for the pilgrims and seminary students, the district had become home to so many Iraqis that walking through its streets I was transported back to Baghdad—to Kadhimiya, the Shiite commercial district built around the shrine to Imam Kadhim. "It's like they froze Iraq in 2003 and put it in a museum," exclaimed photojournalist Ghaith Abdul Ahad, who accompanied me. And indeed, we were both struck by the feeling of being in a safe Baghdad. After nearly three years in the war-torn country, I had started to fear Iraqi men; all strangers were potential kidnappers.

All around us the streets bustled with men speaking Arabic in the Iraqi dialect, overflowing indifferently onto the road nicknamed "Iraqi Street." The walls were festooned with posters from Iraqi elections past. Inside a bakery I saw a poster of Ayatollah Muhammad Sadiq al-Sadr, father of populist cleric

Muqtada. There was a mobile phone shop named after the Euphrates River and barbershops called Karbala and Son of Iraq. Ali Hamid, a Sunni barber from Baghdad's Shiite district of Shaab, had been working in the same shop since 2003; he explained to me that many barbers had fled Iraq to Syria because Islamic radicals had forced them to close their shops. "In Iraq there is a sectarian war," he told me. "Here we all get along." He attributed this to the vigilant Syrian authorities. "Praise God, thanks to the Syrian government we have no problems. If anything happens, they deal with it. As shop owners we are not allowed to talk about sectarianism. Word spread to all business owners. You live in a different country, not your country, you have to respect their rules." He added that Iraqi refugees feared the Syrian regime anyway. They had fled to Syria looking for a place to live and were tired of problems. In 2006 Ali began seeing large numbers of Iraqis coming. He noticed many more tea stands springing up and more pedestrians crowding the district.

In one alley, not far away, I found the famous Baghdad restaurant Patchi al-Hati. Patchi is sheep's head, the meal I have dreaded most in my years in Iraq. The restaurant's owner had left Iraq four months earlier, "because of the terrorism and looting," the chef explained over an immense steaming pot boiling with the pungent smell. Anybody with money in Iraq was a target for kidnappers and extortionists. "They heard we were a famous restaurant and thought we were millionaires," he told me.

In another alley I walked past the field office for Ayatollah Kadhim al-Haeri, guarded by plainclothes Syrian security officials. Haeri had been a student of Muhammad Sadiq al-Sadr during his exile in Iran. Following the overthrow of Saddam's regime, Haeri had urged his followers to kill Baathists. He had once been close to Muqtada, but the two had fallen out. Further down the street I found the office of Muqtada's representative, also guarded by Syrian security officials, who were friendly with the Sadr officials and zealous in demanding I provide official permission before entering. That evening I attended the recitation of Hussein's story. Dozens of shoes were piled on the stairway and in a wooden shelf outside a room where men clad in customary Mahdi Army garb—black shirts with black head scarves or headbands—sat listening to Sheikh Ali wail the story of Hussein's bravery and betrayal, ending with the slaughter of his family and finally his martyrdom. The men began to sob, burying their heads in their hands or between their knees. For Sheikh Ali, the story of perfidy and resistance to tyranny was a parable for his community's current oppression, as he saw it at the hands of Americans and Sunnis. "They are doing the same thing with the poor children and people on the streets," he cried out. He concluded by asking God to end the Americans' occupation, free their hostages in Baghdad, and bless the Mahdi Army.

Sheikh Raed al-Kadhimi was Muqtada's representative in Syria. He blamed the American occupiers, along with "people who operate in Iraq under the umbrella of the Americans and former Baathists who aim to destabilize Iraq" and *takfiris,* for the refugee flow into Syria. "They do killings and kidnappings," he said, "and now attacks happen with mortar shells from both sides, so people resort to a safe place and they come to Syria." Sheikh Raed was proud of his leader Muqtada, who he claimed "began the revolt against the Americans and fought them. He made it difficult for the American army." On the eve of the tenth of Muharram a procession organized by Sheikh Raed's office gathered. Dressed in black, they were led by youths wielding immense wooden flagpoles with different colored flags that they struggled to wave from side to side. Others carried framed pictures of Muqtada and his father. It was a *latmiya* procession, in which the men chanted songs lamenting Hussein's martyrdom and vowing fealty to him. "We have chosen our destiny," they sang, "we are the sons of Sadr, soldiers for the Mahdi." The thousands of onlookers waited until dawn for the culmination of the events. By four in the morning hundreds of men dressed in white robes had assembled in tents. They carried short swords, which they cleaned in buckets of soap. They patted their heads for several minutes, perhaps to numb the surface or steel their nerves. After performing the dawn prayer, they lined up and, led by trumpeters and drummers, began a march through alleys lined with shrouded women looking on. The drums and trumpets rang out a martial beat and were followed by chants of "Haidar!" another name for Ali, father of Hussein and Zeinab. The men, and many boys, swung their swords rhythmically, hitting their foreheads and drawing blood, which soon drenched their faces and robes. As onlookers filmed the scene on their phones and the sun rose above them, the men danced in bloody ecstasy. When they reached the shrine the event ended suddenly, and people returned to their homes or hotel rooms. In the Iraqi shrine city of Karbala and Baghdad's Kadhimiya district, I had seen these events end in explosions and terror attacks. In Damascus it felt almost anticlimactic.

The Displaced

As the violence in Iraq caused its population to hemorrhage, Iraqis fled to wherever they could. Millions were displaced, some seeking shelter in Kurdistan, others in safer neighborhoods, cleansed of minorities, or safer provinces. Others fled to Syria, Lebanon, Turkey, Egypt, Yemen, Libya, Denmark, and anywhere else they could. During the civil war between one thousand and three thousand Iraqis entered Syria through the border at Al Tanf, passing through the volatile Anbar province, risking death at the hands of militias and the American military.

"It's the largest refugee crisis in the Middle East since 1948," said Kristele Younes of the Washington-based Refugees International. "Not only is it a regional crisis but it can become international, since Iraqis want to be resettled," she said. "What's especially shocking to me is the level of extreme and indiscriminate violence. Every civilian is at risk. This crisis is growing at almost unprecedented numbers. Fifty thousand are displaced a month, and tens of thousands are leaving. The international response to the refugee crisis was extremely weak until recently. They had not acknowledged the crisis. The only agency that had responded was [the United Nations High Commission for Refugees], and they were doing so with extremely meager resources. One reason why the response has been so weak is because the international community was waiting for U.S. leadership. The U.S. sparked the conflict and should be answering for the humanitarian consequences of the war as well as the political ones."

Those who survived the perilous journey were met by surprisingly friendly Syrian officials led by a captain overwhelmed by the desperate refugees. A thin, energetic man with an air of desperation, the captain politely listened to the stories of hundreds of Iraqis every day, asking for exceptions to be made, for their expired or potentially forged passports to be accepted, and protested. "*Wallahi ma fini*," he would say, "By God, I can't." "*Ma fini, ma fini, ma fini*," until finally he would break and let in the despairing Iraqis. He explained that often his border post was overwhelmed because American convoys or military operations would close down the road in the Anbar province, and when it was reopened huge numbers of Iraqis would descend upon them at once. Dusty and dazed Iraqi families gathered inside and outside his small, drab concrete building, filling out the applications, waiting for their names to be called.

One man waiting for his name to be called, Abu Ibrahim, told me he had left because of the violence. "There isn't an Iraqi here who wants to enter and hasn't lost a brother or father or received a threat," he told me. A Sunni from Seidiya, he complained that the Americans did nothing. "In my neighborhood, the head of the city council was killed just three meters away from one of their checkpoints. His family went to the checkpoint and said, 'How come he was killed just three meters from you?' And they said, 'It is not our duty to go and check why he was killed.' We don't want Iraq anymore—neither itself, not its oil or gas. Let the whole world know that we Iraqis want nothing from Iraq. All we want is to be left alone. The Iraqi leaders go to neighboring countries and ask them to repatriate us to Iraq. Why? So that they will rule and slaughter us." He was called Omar, a common Sunni name that was dangerous to possess. "Omar is not allowed to enter Baghdad," he said. "There is no government in Iraq," just "theft and killing."

Sitting in a column of minivans and trucks piled with suitcases, I found one old woman waiting for her family to return with their passports. She was from Ghazaliya, in western Baghdad. She did not require much prompting to vent her fury. "Is this democracy, to tell people kill and displace people? Walking in the street with fear? Our situation in Iraq is miserable, worse than miserable.

Why is the world silent about Iraq? I don't know. What have we gained from the oil? Nothing. Even in winter we have no kerosene to put in the stove. There is no gas, no security. There is only killing and explosions. We ran from explosions in the streets. The children do not go to school. Even the university students don't go to school. All stay at home." It was her second trip to Syria. She had returned to Baghdad to bring more of her family, which would now reach around thirty people. She began to cry as I parted with her. "Please get our voices to the world," she begged as her voice broke. "What did the United Nations do for us? What did America do for us? Why all of this?"

Past the fortunate Iraqis who had made it out was the no man's land between the Iraqi and Syrian borders, a desolate moonscape stretching several kilometers. Off an escarpment the cold wind battered a collection of neatly ordered tents. Three hundred and fifty Palestinian refugees were marooned here, facing extermination in Iraq but unable to enter Syria. They were refugees for the second time. Most of Iraq's Palestinians had come from three villages—Ijzim, Jaba, and Ein Ghazal, together known as the Little Triangle—which were near Haifa in northern Palestine. As part of the plan to cleanse Israel of its Palestinians, Israeli soldiers bombarded the villages from the air, killing hundreds of civilians. Ground forces then attacked the villages and killed hundreds more civilians. The Little Triangle was defended by a motley group of farmers armed with Ottoman rifles. In July 1948 they were defeated. Many men were summarily executed, while the other inhabitants were expelled to Jenin after the Israeli soldiers relieved them of their money and jewelry and looted their villages. Other Iraqi Palestinians had come from the nearby village of Tira. In one incident, twenty-eight of Tira's civilians were burned alive when they asked their captors for water and were doused in gasoline instead. Others had come from Ayn Hawd, which was also attacked and cleansed under orders of the Israeli leadership in 1948. Iraqi troops fighting as part of a small contingent of Arab volunteers who had come to defend the Palestinians bused them from Jenin to Iraq. By 1949 up to five thousand Palestinian refugees had been granted asylum in Iraq. A minority of Iraq's Palestinians had lived in Kuwait from the time of their expulsion and moved to Iraq following the Gulf War, when Kuwait evicted them. By 2003 the United Nations High Commission for Refugees (UNHCR) estimated that there were up to thirty-four thousand Palestinians in Iraq. Today there are only an estimated twelve thousand left. Thousands fled using forged Iraqi passports. In at least one case, a Palestinian from Iraq landed in Cairo's airport using an Iraqi passport. Because his body bore the scars of his torture at the hands of Iraqi militias, he was resettled with the help of UN officials in a third country.

Under Saddam the Palestinians had received subsidized housing and, in the eyes of Shiites, preferential treatment. Many of these homes were owned by Shiites. Immediately following the American invasion the Palestinians were among the first victims of reprisals by the inchoate Shiite militias. They were expelled from their homes and often ended up in tent communities or in the Baladiyat apartment complexes. The new Interior Ministry revoked the Palestinians' identity papers. They were now obliged to register in Baghdad once a month. But to approach the Interior Ministry was to risk kidnapping, torture, and murder. The Palestinians became illegal, but they could not leave. Their neighborhoods were shelled by Shiite militias, and their men were kidnapped by Shiite death squads. They were being systematically attacked, and they were warned by Shiite leaders that they faced death in Iraq. An Iraqi diplomat in Cairo gave me the typical prejudiced view. He denied that Palestinians were being targeted, insisting that they lived better than most Iraqis. He accused them of supporting Al Qaeda and building car bombs in their neighborhoods. The U.S. State Department was pushing the Iraqi Kurds to accept the Palestinians, but Kurdish officials steadfastly refused, as did the Syrians and Jordanians. "They want to make a point that the solution for Palestinians is not settlement in the region," a United Nations official explained to me.

In May 2006 the Palestinians began arriving at Al Tanf, on the Syrian border. Most came as families. When I visited in February 2007 there were 93 women and 135 children. In the back of the camp there was an area for single men. One tent said "Al Tanf Mosque." That month eight Palestinians with university degrees were taken to Damascus, where they received ten days of training by the UN before returning to open a school for seventy-five children. This was controversial among some of the camp residents, who feared it would make the camp look more permanent. One tent functioned as a bakery, another as a grocery store. The residents were helped by UNHCR and Palestinian organizations in Syria. The Syrian government, already burdened with four hundred thousand Palestinian refugees and a similar number of Iraqis, was hesitant to open the door to thousands more Palestinians. Syrian officials believed that they should not be the only ones sharing the responsibility, but UN officials believed the Palestinians could be absorbed without great difficulty and that the Syrians were also making a political statement about the need to solve the Palestinian refugee crisis. But this debate came at the immediate expense of the desperate refugees, and there were five hundred more stranded on the Iraqi side of the border (known as Al Walid), protected by a local tribal sheikh but still vulnerable to the depredations of the Iraqi Security Forces, who had attacked them in the past. Iraqi Security Forces even entered Al Tanf twice attempting to kidnap people, but they failed. The camp was freezing in the winter, and rains flooded the tents and washed them away, leaving the refugees without shelter for days at a time. During the summer temperatures exceeded fifty degrees Celsius. Children suffered from diarrhea and other diseases from the dirty water. "Al Tanf is a refugee camp on a highway in between borders," said Younes of Refugees International. "There is a lack of funds and very little assistance. People are trading their personal items with trucks for food."

Night fell quickly on the frigid camp. In one dark tent, lit only by a small lantern, I met several men who told me their stories, their voices barely audible over the wind. Hussein, a round young man with a melancholy baby face who wore a tan Adidas tracksuit, was originally from Ein Hawd in Palestine. He had lived with his Iraqi wife and daughter in Baghdad's Hurriya district, a Shiite militia stronghold, where he worked as a taxi driver. "In Iraq before the war we lived without problems," he told me. "The problems started in Iraq as the American occupation began." Hussein was first threatened in 2005, when a letter was sent to his house containing a bullet and two drops of blood. "If you do not leave Iraq, this will be your fate," the letter said. A second death threat was signed by the Badr Brigade, the Iranian-sponsored Shiite militia. "They threatened me to leave because I am a Palestinian," he said. "They think that because we are Palestinians the whole world helps us. But that's not true. If we had an easy life, I wouldn't be working as taxi driver and working in restaurants sometimes. They blew up my car. Then they blew up my house."

Two of Hussein's uncles had been kidnapped and tortured to death with power drills, a specialty of Iraq's Shiite militias. The kidnappers had demanded one hundred thousand dollars in ransom, but Hussein's family did not have the money, and the next day they received a phone call informing them that his uncles' bodies were in the morgue. Their bodies had been mutilated: drills had been driven through their bodies from the neck to the belly, and their genitals had been cut off. Hussein's family was given a CD with a film of the gruesome murders. "We couldn't even have a funeral because they said, 'If you do it we will blow you up.' We had to bury them at night." Hussein was also attacked in his car by a Shiite militia he believed to be the Badr Brigade; he still bore the scars. In March 2006 he heard the sounds of attackers in his house. With his wife and daughter he escaped by way of their roof to a neighbor's roof. The attackers then blew up his house. Two months later, Hussein and his family attempted to flee to Syria after hearing rumors that it was accepting Palestinians. Stranded between the two borders, his wife's family got her to divorce him and she returned to Baghdad.

Ayman was a vegetable seller from Baladiyat. He still spoke in the Palestinian dialect he had inherited from his family, which had been expelled from Palestine when his father was five years old. "My grandfather was my age when he was expelled," Ayman said. "Now it wasn't Jews who expelled us, it was Arabs." Shiite militiamen had attacked his house and killed his mother and brother. Ayman had fled with his wife and two children and hoped to live anywhere as long as it was safe.

Yasser and his father had been arrested by the Iraqi National Guard. "They accused me of being Palestinian," he said. "They said, 'You are a Palestinian terrorist' and 'You Arabs, you destroyed us.'" The two were imprisoned for sixteen days and tortured with electricity. Yasser's nails were torn out. Then his seventy-three-year-old father was electrocuted to death in front of him. The National Guardsmen then gave him twenty-four hours to leave Iraq, and in June 2006 he and his family arrived in Al Tanf. "We paid to get my father's body," he cried, "but they gave me the wrong body." The other men stared down silently as he sobbed. "All I want to know is where my father's body is."

Another man was taken out of his car along with six other Palestinians. All were shot and killed, but he survived. He was denied treatment in the first hospital because he was Palestinian. After he was released from the second hospital, he fled to the border. "Even in another camp right on the border, the Iraqi army came to the camp and arrested five of us for eight days," he said. "They tortured us during that time and robbed us of everything we had. They even took my wedding ring. In Baghdad also they took our houses and cars. Here we have a tragic life, we have gone through cold, heat, dust, and this wind. It is a very bad life. But what is the reason? It is only because we are Palestinians and carry with us Palestinian travel documents. Now we want to live anywhere that is safe and secure. Anywhere. In Iraq they kill us because of our identity."

One family in Al Tanf received a CD with a film of their daughter's gang rape and murder by Shiite militiamen as their final warning to leave Iraq. Three men in the camp with the Sunni name Omar had been followed merely for being called Omar and had survived assassination attempts. The camp provided scant protection, and some men who went close to the Iraqi border to purchase vegetables from locals were captured by the Iraqi National Guard. "They think we are Saddamists," one man told me. "The American occupation didn't protect us." Palestinians who went to get relatives from the morgue were also kidnapped. One baby was born in Al Tanf, and she was named Khiyam, meaning "tent" in Arabic. "We went backward sixty years," one man lamented. "We were born in tents, and our children will be the same. Is this our legacy?"

According to a UN official, Arab governments were reluctant to call the Iraqis refugees because the term is associated with the Palestinians. "The Palestinians are a people without a land," he said. "Iraqis still have a country, although I think it will break up like the former Yugoslavia. It is not positive to be associated with the Palestinians." Jordan, with half its population made up of Palestinian refugees, was afraid of a second refugee wave.

No discussion of refugees in the Middle East can begin without addressing the Palestinian experience. Between 1947 and 1949 up to 750,000 Palestinians were expelled from Palestine by Jewish militias; hundreds of Palestinian villages were wiped off the map. They were dispersed throughout the region, unable to return home and unable to assimilate fully into the countries to which they fled. They soon organized, forming armed groups and trying to return home. These groups were often manipulated by various governments in the region for their own ends, and some even fought one another. Their presence contributed to the destabilization of several countries, while in places like Lebanon, they were preyed upon by more powerful militias, as we shall see in the next chapter. Their cause became a rallying cry. After 2003, radical groups based in the camps exported fighters to Iraq.

In Damascus

The flow of fighters into Iraq, of millions of refugees out of Iraq, the smuggling of weapons and even sheep, and the export of dangerous ideas such as sectarianism and jihadism demonstrated that the Iraqi civil war was close to becoming a regional conflict. One factor militating against such a development was the fact that the Iraqi refugees had not settled in camps but instead had been absorbed into cities like Beirut, Damascus, Amman, and Cairo, which made it more difficult to organize or mobilize them, though also more difficult to help or monitor them. Like the Palestinians, most Iraqi refugees may never return home. The decimated Christian and Sabean minorities had left for good. Sunnis from Baghdad and the south, now cleansed and controlled by Shiites, were also likely never to return. Although the Palestinian cause and its initial popularity in the Arab world eased their integration into Syria and elsewhere, and they were tolerated and even welcomed with generosity by the local population in some instances, this goodwill did not last forever. In Lebanon, Jordan, Kuwait, and elsewhere, it ran out. Jordan and particularly Syria have shown extreme generosity, but they are both straining under the burden.

Damascus became so full of Iraqis that rent prices soared, driving many refugees as far as Aleppo. One hour away from Damascus, in Qudsiya, I found an Iraqi neighborhood with a "Baghdad Barbershop" and "Iraq Travel Agency." Off an alley I entered a hastily constructed apartment building, rough and unfinished, cement and cinder blocks thrown together without paint. The carved wooden doors to each apartment were a stark contrast to the grim hallways. Inside I found Dr. Lujai and her five children. At fifteen, Omar was the oldest; the youngest was two years old. Dr. Lujai, a family medicine specialist with her own clinic, had lived in Baghdad with her husband, Dr. Adil, a thoracic surgeon and professor at the medical college. Both were forty-three-year-old Sunnis who originally came from Ana, a town in the Anbar province. They had been married for fifteen years.

Right after the war Dr. Lujai began to notice changes. Shiite clerics took over many of Baghdad's hospitals following the postwar looting, and they did not know how to manage a hospital. "They were sectarian from the beginning," she said, "firing Sunnis, saying they were Baathists. In 2004 the Ministry of Health was given to the Sadr movement, and the minister was only a general practitioner." Following the 2005 elections the Sadrist ministers initiated what they called a "campaign to remove the Saddamists." The advisers to the minister of health wore the turbans of clerics and mismanaged the ministry. In hospitals and health centers, walls were covered with posters of Shiite clerics. Traditional Shiite music could often be heard in the halls.

Sunni doctors began disappearing. Ali al-Mahdawi, who managed the Diyala province's health department, was said to have gone into the ministry for a meeting and never came out. Several months later, American military raids uncovered secret prisons run by Ministry officials with hundreds of prisoners. Several days after Mahdawi was released, he was murdered on the street. A pharmacist they knew called Ahmed al-Azzawi went in for a meeting with the minister and was killed by his militia.

Dr. Lujai reported that Sunni patients were accused by Sadrist officials of being terrorists. After the doctors completed their operations, she said, the Interior Ministry's special police would arrest the patients. Their corpses would then be found in the Baghdad morgue. "This happened tens of times," she said, to "anybody who came with bullet wounds and wasn't Shiite." Dr. Lujai knew of five Sunni doctors and two Christians who were threatened to leave or fired.

On September 2, 2006, Abu Omar, as Dr. Adil was known, went to work as he usually did in the morning. He had three patients to operate on that day. A fourth came in unexpectedly after he was done, and since no other doctor was available to treat him, Dr. Adil stayed later than usual. He finished work that day at around two in the afternoon. Their home was about fifteen minutes away, on days when the road was open. At 2:15 Abu Omar was driving home when his way was blocked by four cars. Armed men surrounded him and dragged him from his car, taking him to Sadr City. Five hours later his dead body was found on the street, and the next day his body was found in the morgue. I tried to find out the way he was killed, but Dr. Lujai was overcome, crying, and her confused young children looked at her silently. She had asked the Iraqi police to investigate her husband's murder, but an officer told her, "He is a doctor, he has a degree, and he is a Sunni, so he couldn't stay in Iraq. That's why he was killed." Two weeks later she received a letter printed from a computer ordering her to leave the area.

On September 24, Dr. Lujai fled with her brother Abu Shama, his wife, and his four children. Her sister had already been threatened, and had fled to Qudsiya. They gave away or sold all their belongings and paid six hundred dollars for the GMCs that carried them to Syria. Because of what happened to her husband, she said, up to twenty other doctors fled. Abu Shama was an engineer and professor at the College of Technology. He had lived in Baghdad's

Khadhra district. In June 2006 a letter was placed under the door in his office ordering him to leave Iraq or be killed. He stopped going to work after that. One of his best friends, a Sunni married to a Shiite, had been killed in front of the college.

In Qudsiya they paid five hundred dollars a month in rent for the three-bedroom apartment both families shared. Their children were able to attend local schools for free, but Iraqis were not able to work in Syria, so they depended on relatives and savings for their survival. Twenty-five members of their family fled to Syria. Four days before I visited them they heard that a Sunni doctor they knew had been killed in Baghdad's Kadhimiya district, where he worked. He had been married to a Shiite woman. "He was a pediatric specialist," she told me. "We needed him." The people and government of Syria had been good to them, they agreed, and they did not expect to go back to Iraq. Dr. Lujai did not think Iraq could go back to the way it had been. "It's a dream to return to our country," she said.

"First minorities left Iraq, now we get Sunnis targeted by Shiite militias."

Jordan had already closed its borders to Iraqis, and Iran required a sponsor for Iraqi refugees, though for obvious reasons most would never think of going to Iran. "Syria is the only open gate for refugees," said Lorens Jolles of the UN-HCR in Damascus. "At one point Syrian society won't be able to accommodate them," worried a worker from the International Committee of the Red Cross. Syria, with a population of only nineteen million, has a record of extreme generosity to refugees. It houses four hundred thousand Palestinians expelled from their homeland. During Israel's July 2006 war against Lebanon, Syria took in up to half a million Lebanese refugees.

"For us every Iraqi who is here is a refugee," said Jolles. "This takes into account the generalized violence and targeting of most groups in Iraq. And everybody is in need of protection." Because Syria, Lebanon, and Jordan are not signatories to the 1951 Geneva Convention on refugees, the Iraqis did not have the right to work—although those with sufficient money could open businesses, and others worked illegally. UNHCR had signed memorandums of understanding with those countries requiring refugees to be resettled in a third country within a year after UNHCR had declared them refugees. UNHCR had to establish a category of "persons of concern" without calling them refugees in order to avoid getting dragged into battle with the national authorities. It therefore gave the Iraqis the opportunity to register for temporary protection, a legal trick to recognize them as having fled a situation of generalized violence for a temporary period of time. In theory this protected them without presenting the host countries with any formal obligations (though Syria had not deported Iraqis, Jordan and Lebanon had). Most Iraqis had not yet registered with the UN for temporary protection, but hundreds could be found lining up in front of the UNHCR office in Damascus in the early hours of the morning. Between February and April 2007 ten thousand Iraqi families, or at least fifty thousand individuals, had made appointments with the UNHCR.

"First the minorities left Iraq," a UNHCR official told me, "now we get Sunnis targeted by Shiite militias." Until February 2006 the majority had been Christians, although Muslims were represented as well, with Sunnis and Shiites equally represented. Starting in March 2006, though, the number of Sunni refugees shot up, far exceeding all other groups; July through September 2006 saw a sharp rise in Sunnis registering. Between January 2005 and the end of February 2007, 58,924 Iraqis registered with UNHCR in Damascus. Forty-two percent of those registered since December 2003 were Sunni, 21 percent were Shiite, and 29 percent were Christian. In January 2007, 3,144 Sunnis and 901 Shiites were registered. In February it was 5,988 Sunnis to 1,570 Shiites. Only the most desperate refugees bothered to register, so the true figures were unknown. Ninety-five percent of those registered with UNHCR were from Baghdad.

The Shiites were generally single young men, while the rest came as families. For the first two years the Syrians provided free medical care to Iraqis, but they were overwhelmed; in 2005 they ended the practice except for emergencies. Iraqis could attend Syrian public schools provided they were not too crowded, which they often were. Child labor became a problem, since parents were unable to work and children were easier to hide. Children dropped out of school as a result, and Iraqi prostitutes became extremely common. UN screeners reported seeing numerous victims of torture, detention, rape, and kidnapping among newly arrived Iraqis. Most had family members who had been killed, and many were intellectuals.

"The problems of Iraqis have not come to Syria," said Jolles, referring to sectarianism. "The [Iraqi] refugee communities don't integrate, and the government has good control." But he still had his worries. "They are less manageable and understandable because they are not in camps. One million people are uprooted, and they don't know what the future has in store for them. It's normal to have some degree of criminality, violence, and disruption."

According to a Western diplomat, the presence of so many Iraqis gave the Syrian government political leverage in Iraq. Nearly every Iraqi political movement was represented in Syria. Historically Syria had accepted Iraqi dissidents such as those from the left wing of the Baath Party, Dawa leaders like Iraqi Prime Minister Nuri al-Maliki, and even Kurdish independence parties. Iraqi President Jalal Talabani's Patriotic Union of Kurdistan was established in a Damascus restaurant. The Syrians were still playing a complex game. They diplomatically recognized the Iraqi government but also housed members of the former regime, security forces, and Baath Party. They invited Shiite leaders such as Muqtada al-Sadr and radical Sunnis close to the resistance, such as Harith al-Dhari of the Association of Muslim Scholars. Syria saw the Iraqi civil war through the prism of Lebanon, thinking it could manage the conflict through its contacts; thus the Syrians were monitoring and cultivating everybody. But there were also dangerous contradictions in Syrian policy. Syria is a majority-Sunni country, but its close ally is Shiite Iran—which, in the eyes of Sunnis in Iraq and the region, sponsored the very militias that were persecuting Iraq's Sunnis, who were often related to Syria's Sunnis, especially in the border region. "The Syrian government is very capable of managing those issues," the Western diplomat assured me, but sectarianism was at its peak in the region, and Syria, which was once a major exporter of fighters to Iraq, may face its own blowback.

"Their need is enormous," a top official at UNHCR told me. "The temptation is there. The money from bin Laden is there. If the international community doesn't help, then the other groups will, and all hell will break loose. Iraqis are sitting in Syria or Jordan, where the Baathists and Wahhabis are strongest. If 1 percent of the two million can be bought, then that is very dangerous. If they stay on the street you will have youth violence or terrorism. If people are in need they turn to crime or terrorism." He mentioned the North African community of France as a model, some of whom were drawn to Islamic radicalism or terrorism out of frustration and neglect. "They come to the UN and queue at our door for five hours to get a registration card, or they can turn to radical groups for funding," he said, explaining that the money came from Saudi Arabia to Jordan and was disbursed there. "This problem will be with us for a long time," he added, shaking his head in frustration.

Many poor Iraqi refugees settled in the Jaramana district of Damascus. They came to the Ibrahim al-Khalil convent for assistance. The convent was the only white structure amid the graying and incomplete buildings surrounding it, many of which were so hastily thrown together that they were unpainted and lacked glass in the windows. In front of the convent I found a small bakery preparing the typical Iraqi bread known as *samun*, a thick pita with two pointy ends. The owner, Haidar, had left Iraq three months earlier "because of the occupation," he told me. In Baquba he had been a sports teacher.

Sister Malaki, an elderly nun who ran the convent, expressed wonder at how quickly the neighborhood had been built since the Iraqis began showing up. Until 2006 there were no buildings around the convent, she said. It used to take her thirty minutes just to see a taxi on the street, and now she had to wait an hour to find an empty taxi. The first wave arrived in the spring of 2006, she said, but the biggest wave began in the fall of 2006. At first she saw many cases of rape, including boys and girls only ten or twelve years old. "Now it's mostly cases of extreme poverty and people who will never go back to Iraq," she said. "They fully reject returning to Iraq. They will die."

She had worked in a hospital in Beirut throughout the Lebanese civil war and was seeing similar traumas. "The children have a strong fear," she said. When asking her for something many children would threaten her, she said. "If you don't give it to us we will tell the Americans," she repeated with laughter. "Any nation that goes into a civil war," she said, "the pressure makes them bitter. They ask, 'Why us and not you?' Today I was insulted by three different Iraqis. They feel entitled: 'We suffered, you didn't.' The people who really suffer are those who had a lot—educated, university people. Now they are begging. They show me pictures of what they had."

Um Iman worked as a cleaner in the convent. She had come with her husband and three daughters two months earlier. They were Christians and had lived in Baghdad's Dora neighborhood. They had received four letters threatening them with death if they did not leave. One night they took a taxi to a relative's house in Baghdad, and the next morning they joined a convoy of buses heading to the Syrian border. "There were explosions behind us and in front of us," she said. Her husband looked for work every day but could find none. She looked defeated to me. "What can we do?" she asked with resignation. "Even if I die of hunger here I don't want to go back to Iraq. Now there are no Christians in Baghdad."

Lost Amid the Millions in Cairo

As Iraq fell apart its human detritus was scattered throughout the region. Lost amid the millions of Cairo, Iraqis could be found struggling with the bureaucracy in the Mugamaa, the massive labyrinthine edifice where all people's interactions with the Egyptian state began and ended. On the first floor, in the Arab Nations section of the Visa Renewal section, past Somalis and Sudanese sitting and awaiting their turn, was a sign that said, "Booth 23 for Iraqis only." When I visited in late February 2006 the crowds of Iraqis there exceeded the numbers at the nearby section for Palestinian refugees. Iraqis continued to enter Egypt by the planeload. They came on tourist visas at first, but extended them indefinitely or applied for temporary protection at the UNHCR, and settled into the urban sprawl of Cairo.

In the Medinat Nasr district, past the Layali Baghdad (Baghdad Nights) restaurant, I found a small Internet cafe owned by Muhamad Abu Rawan, a twenty-seven-year-old Sunni man who fled Iraq on May 15, 2006, with his wife, Lubna, also twenty-seven. Muhamad walked me to their nearby apartment, where we found Lubna watching a soap opera and holding their three-month-old daughter, Rawa. Their home was sparsely decorated: flower patterns on the sofas and carpets, pictures of a forest, a beach and a lake on the walls. Both Muhamad and Lubna were from Basra. Back in Baghdad Muhamad had worked repairing air conditioners for the same electronic appliance company where Lubna, a civil engineer, worked.

At first they both spoke Egyptian Arabic with me, because, like most Iraqis, they had quickly assimilated into Egyptian culture and had learned the dialect from the country's famous soap operas and films. At the beginning of the American occupation, Lubna told me, "Our lives were normal, like all Iraqis. Every once in a while the Americans would besiege the area, but my father was never politically active, so the Americans never bothered us." One morning in December 2004, Lubna's father, also a civil engineer and structural designer, drove toward the Mansour district to pay his contractors. He took the airport road and got off at the exit that would take him to Mansour, but the roads had been blocked by American soldiers, who were conducting an operation in the area.

In Yarmuk's Qahtan Square American soldiers fired into the air as Lubna's father drove. He sped away to avoid the shots. Perhaps thinking he was attacking them, one American soldier fired at him, and then several others opened fire as well. "He did not have time to close his eyes before he died," Lubna told me, because there were so many shots in his body. She showed me pictures of his bullet-riddled car, with holes in every side. "That year the Americans were killing many Iraqis on the street," Muhamad explained. Lubna, her mother, and her two sisters did not learn about his death until later that afternoon, when Iraqi police contacted them. Their neighbors persuaded them to demand compensation, and they approached one of the lawyers the Americans had authorized to deal with such cases. "After one year the lawyer said the Americans had rejected it twice," Lubna told me as she rocked Rawa steadily and patted her back. The Americans did offer her family seven hundred dollars, but they rejected it as a paltry sum. "My mother had to go back to work as a teacher because my father was the only provider," Lubna told me.

At the time, Muhamad still lived in Baghdad's volatile Dora district, where Shiites and Christians were targeted by Sunni militias. When he picked up a wounded Shiite from the street and took him to the hospital, he found himself targeted by the Sunni militia that had shot the man. They told him they would have killed him were he not a Sunni and forced him to move out of Dora. One year after her father was killed, Lubna and Muhamad got married. They lived with her mother in Hai Jihad, a majority-Sunni district Muhamad described as "very hot." Two days after they were married, there was a joint American and Iraqi operation in their neighborhood. One hundred and fifty Sunnis were arrested, he told me. "The Americans would surround the neighborhood, and the Iraqi police commandos raided the houses. It was our neighbors and friends. They still haven't been released."

"We were afraid to admit we were Sunnis," Lubna told me. "All men stopped going to the mosque to pray because they would have been harassed or killed." Muhamad's sister was married to a Shiite man, he told me, and they had many friends and relatives who were Shiites. "It's the militias of Badr and Sadr," Lubna told me, "they are ruthless." The company they worked for was owned by a Sunni man, and it had branches in Baghdad and Basra. In Basra twenty members of the company were kidnapped. The Shiites were released, and thirteen Sunni employees were murdered. In Baghdad the company's Shiite lawyer was killed by Sunni militiamen, a security guard was kidnapped, and the manager was threatened. The owner belonged to the Omar family, a name that gave them away as Sunni, and his company was known as a "Sunni company." He fled Basra to Baghdad because of threats, and after more threats he fled to the United Arab Emirates. Muhamad was beaten, and his car was stolen. "Every day we heard of people we knew getting killed," he told me.

Lubna and Muhamad chose Egypt because the cost of living was cheap and Syria was threatened by the Americans. They came on a three-month tourist visa and rented their apartment, for which they paid three hundred dollars a month. Lubna felt welcomed by the Egyptians, she said, and Muhamad felt at home because the social environment reminded him of Iraq. After they arrived they were joined by Lubna's mother and her seventeen-year-old sister, Najwa, who attended a private high school. Lubna's grandfather was dying, so her mother returned to Baghdad to see him, but then she could no longer get permission to return to Cairo. Muhamad heard rumors that Iraqis who had tried to renew their visas at the Mugamaa were deported by Egyptian authorities, so he obtained an asylum-seeker registration card from the UNHCR.

The couple ran out of their savings, and in December 2006 Muhamad opened his Internet cafe. Lubna hoped to work when Rawa was older. "Our standard of living in Iraq was much better," she told me. In Medinat Nasr they had Shiite neighbors who had been expelled from a Sunni neighborhood in Baghdad. I asked if the sectarian problems had followed them here. "On the contrary," Muhamad said, "we are happy to see any Iraqi so we can speak our dialect." Lubna added that "the Iraqis who come here are all tired and don't want to organize or attract attention."

Muhamad had to get an Egyptian partner just to open a business. The Egyptian owned 51 percent of the cafe, even though he had not invested anything in it. Muhamad's friend Haidar helped him out at the cafe. A twenty-three-year-old Shiite pharmacist from Baghdad's Khadhra district, where Shiites were under attack, Haidar was married to a Sunni woman. After a local supermarket owner and his two brothers were murdered for being Shiite, Haidar began to receive threatening calls. His uncle's car was stolen and his house burned down, and the walls of the neighborhood were scrawled with notices saying that Shiites' property was forfeit and could be taken by any

Sunni. Haidar's family sold their house, and the new owner was killed. "All the Shiites in the neighborhood fled," he told me. Haidar moved to Cairo in September 2006 to arrange a place to live before his wife arrived. But when she applied for the Egyptian visa it was denied, leaving her stranded in Baghdad. Haidar met Muhamad in Cairo. "We get along better here than in Iraq," he told me. "We feel closer." Hatred of Shiites was increasing throughout the region, and even in Cairo Haidar did not feel fully comfortable. "On the street and in cabs people ask if I am Sunni or Shiite," he told me. "They say we are infidels." One day at the supermarket the grocer heard Haidar's Iraqi dialect and told him, "Your Shiites are infidels."

Egypt had stopped issuing visas to Iraqis, although it was widely rumored that Iraqis who paid bribes at the Egyptian embassies in Syria and Jordan could obtain them. Iraqis in Egypt told me that they had paid hundreds of dollars to visa agencies that managed to obtain visas for their relatives. Egypt had absorbed between two and four million Sudanese, and had refugees from thirty other nationalities. It also had a high rate of unemployment. Egyptians and Sudanese could not find work, so additional Iraqis would further burden the state's weak social services. Between 100,000 and 140,000 Iraqis lived in Egypt before the influx of refugees, but by March 2007 only 5,500 had registered with UNHCR for an asylum seeker's card because, in the eyes of a UN official, "not every Iraqi in Egypt is a refugee." Many of the middle-class Iraqis in Egypt were beginning to run out of resources, and it was only then that they turned to the UN.

Egypt's reasons for no longer letting Iraqis in were twofold. In the post-9/11 world, concern over terrorism justified almost anything. "Tourism is a major industry, so one incident would cost millions in lost revenue," said the UN official. In addition, Egyptians were afraid of Shiites, an Iraqi diplomat told me, "because they think they have links to Iran." Many Egyptians had raised fears of a Shiite wave and of Sunnis converting to Shiism. They also feared making permanent demographic changes to Iraq. "You are taking them from Iraq and implanting them somewhere else, and most of them are Sunnis," a high-ranking Egyptian diplomat told me. "It disturbs me. It means the whole area will be Shiite."

Many Iraqi refugees have carried the sectarian bitterness with them. In an apartment complex that resembled American housing projects, only partially occupied and complete, I found a collection of Sunni Iraqis in a courtyard inside, where a few had opened shops. Ghaith, an eighteen-year-old from Amriya, long since cleansed of its Shiites, had owned a supermarket back home and had opened up a small grocery store on the ground floor of the complex in Egypt. He pointed to his twelve-year-old brother playing soccer with other boys and told me that he had been kidnapped in Baghdad and held for one week. Sitting in the grocery store was Dhafer, a round thirty-five-year-old man with a sharp nose and stubble from a few days of neglect. He had the tired look of a defeated man. Originally from Baghdad's Ghazaliya district, he had been threatened by Shiite neighbors whose sons worked with the Iraqi National Guard and Interior Ministry, he said, and given forty-eight hours to leave. "I brought my relatives for protection and weapons and they escorted us out," he told me. I asked him why he had then left Amriya. "Civil war," he said. "All of Baghdad, all of Iraq, is a civil war. The guy who goes on television and says it's not a civil war is mocking the people." On August 16, 2005, Dhafer came to Cairo with his wife and son. Since then another son had been born. Dhafer and his family regularly watched Al Zawra TV, the Iraqi satellite channel that broadcast resistance operations and was openly pro-Sunni and anti-Shiite. They had recently seen a video of a Sadrist cleric calling on Shiites to kill Sunnis. "I was not surprised," he told me. "I know the Shiite sect. But my wife was crying." Dhafer told me that up to twenty of his friends had already been killed in Baghdad. He had not renewed his residency and instead had applied for refugee status at the UNHCR. Although he missed his family, he never wanted to return to Baghdad. His relatives had also warned him not to return, telling him that it was better to starve outside.

Next door was a hair salon owned by a Sunni couple from Baghdad's Ghazaliya district. It was decorated in pink and red in honor of Valentine's Day, and there was only a chair for one customer at a time. Its owner, Ghada, had taught herself hairdressing after she arrived in Cairo with her husband, Abu Omar, and their three children. Abu Omar, a former colonel in the Iraqi Army, had retired in 1999. After retiring he had opened a stationery shop in the Nafaq al-Shurta district with a friend. The American military raided their home twice. "They said to me, 'You look like an American woman,'" Ghada said, laughing with pride. The military asked permission to use their roof for surveillance, and Abu Omar agreed. "Could we have said no?" Ghada asked.

"After the war I started to feel the Iranian influence," Abu Omar told me. "Before there were no problems between Sunnis and Shiites, but then on television we started hearing people talking about Sunnis or Shiites." Like many former military officers, Abu Omar was actively involved in the Iraqi resistance. "As long as they are attacking the occupiers or those cooperating with the occupiers," he said, the Iraqi resistance was honorable. When talking of the resistance, he slipped and said, "we" instead of "they."

Shiite militias associated with the Iraqi government obtained lists of former military officers and their personal information, he told me. "Every day we heard names of officers killed," he said, estimating that he knew at least one hundred people who had been killed since the Americans overthrew Saddam. He was threatened twice in front of his house, and then his partner was assassinated. "After they killed his partner he told me that we must leave in five days," Ghada told me. She started crying. "They have stolen my house, my furniture. I left everything. Even now I hope to go back. Here we have many troubles. We have no money. It's very difficult. There you feel that you can die every day. Here I am dying every day. Every day you hear bad news. There is no hope. I lost everything. I was a queen in my house before. I had a home, furniture, a BMW. Now I live in a dirty area. What did I do? What did my children do?" Ghada sold most of her jewelry to help support the family. They had been in Cairo since 2005 and had managed to pay for their children's school the first year but could no longer afford to.

Ghada told me that Iraq's sectarianism had followed them to Cairo, causing problems in their children's school. Iraqi Shiite boys beat their son Omar, she said. "He hates Shiites so much," she said, adding that many fights had occurred between Sunni and Shiite Iraqi children. Her son's fight had been provoked by Saddam Hussein's execution, which they watched on television. "We had hoped that Saddam would return to lead Iraq. It was like they ripped my heart out," he told me. "After I saw the images I stayed up all night." Ghada told me that Egyptian customers had cried with her and consoled her after Saddam's execution, and they had recited a prayer together. "The ones that Saddam killed," she said, meaning Shiites, "I would go back and kill more of them. I hate Shiites."

Abu Omar still held out some hope that peace could be restored. "If America comes down from her pride and negotiates with resistance, then maybe there can be a solution. The resistance is very strong and has the best officers." He was not as sectarian as his wife, explaining to me that "there are real Iraqi Shiites, and they have the same feelings we have. It is the Shiites of Iran who are the cause of the problems." Abu Omar often referred to the resistance as "the patriots," explaining that "there are Sunni and Shiite patriots. The patriots can defeat the Iranian Shiites."

Many former Baathists and Iraqi Army officers had settled in Egypt following the war. Harith al-Dhari, leader of the Sunni Association of Muslim Scholars, frequently visited Cairo, where he met with Egyptian leaders, including his friend Mahdi Akef, leader of the Egyptian Muslim Brotherhood. The Association of Muslim Scholars controlled some militias that fought in the resistance. More resistance leaders based themselves across the border from Iraq's Anbar province, in Amman and Damascus, however. Nearly three years into their war against the occupation, many were growing introspective—much like the tribal leader Sheikh Saad, whom I met in Amman in late 2006.

In Damascus in February 2007 I met one of the leaders of the Anbar resistance that Sheikh Saad referred to when he told me they had all fled. Sheikh Yassin was a weathered and frail man with a thick white scarf over his head. He fingered black beads as we spoke. He led a mosque in Hit but had fled a month before we met and left it with his sons. Hit had become deserted, he told me. "The situation there has become disastrous," he said. "They hit my son's house in an airstrike and destroyed his house and killed my grandson. The people of Hit are caught between Americans on one side and Al Qaeda on the other side. And the police and army do not treat people properly."

He too recognized the strategic Sunni error made at the beginning of the American occupation. "That is the origin of the problem: they boycotted. If they had participated with all their weight, they would not have let the Shiite militias take over the government of Iraq." He blamed the Iraqi Sunni leadership for denouncing elections and threatening those who participated. "They made the wrong interpretation," he said. "Shiites wanted to prevent Sunnis from voting, and jihadists did as well. The jihadists fight the Americans on one side and on the other side they destroy the community." Sheikh Yassin had not fled Shiite militias, but rather Al Qaeda. "Sunnis must choose between death or seeking refuge in the Anbar, Syria, or Jordan," he said.

Another opponent of Al Qaeda was Sheikh Mudhir al-Khirbit of Ramadi, a former leader of the Confederation of Iraqi Tribes. The Khirbits had been favored by the former regime, and in March 2003 an American airstrike on their home had killed eighteen family members, reason enough for them to seek vengeance. Sheikh Mudhir had sought shelter in Damascus but made frequent trips to Lebanon for medical treatment. The Iraqi government placed him on its new list of forty-one most wanted, and in January 2007, on a medical trip to Lebanon, he was arrested by that country's Internal Security Forces. His affairs were now being handled by his oldest son, Sattam, who was only eighteen years old but who, according to one Western diplomat, had his father's trust and went on missions for him. I found Sattam in an apartment in Damascus, dressed in a gray suit, wearing pointy leather shoes, and taking business calls from sheikhs well into the night.

In 2004, when he was only fifteen, Sattam and an uncle were arrested in an American military raid on their home. "Every tribal sheikh has weapons, machine guns, missiles, Kalashnikovs," he told me. Sattam was jailed for one month and interrogated about his father's activities. "They treated me badly," he said. "We were tied up for two days, and it was really cold." His uncle was held for three months and was later imprisoned again for one year. Iraq had grown too dangerous for the family's leadership. "In Ramadi you can't drive in a car," he told me. "You don't know if the Americans or Al Qaeda will kill you. Not only Shiites are slaughtering Sunnis; Sunnis are slaughtering Sunnis."

Iraq's Sunnis were beleaguered, he said. He called the initial Sunni boycott of Iraqi politics "a big mistake," one that opened the door to Shiite domination. "Now it's too late," he said. "People here and in Amman feel like they lost." The only way to protect Sunnis, in his view, was to establish a Sunni state that would include the Anbar province, Mosul, and Tikrit. Radical Sunnis in groups like Al Qaeda were now in control of Anbar, and the resistance was taking on Al Qaeda as well as the Americans. "Al Qaeda kills Sunnis the most, and you don't know what they want," he said. His priority was to deal with Al Qaeda in Anbar first, then reconcile with the Shiites, and then work to end the occupation. "When Sunnis in Baghdad get arrested by the Americans, they feel good because it's better than being arrested by Shiite militias." Despite this, he did not bear hostility toward the Shiites. "My father doesn't differentiate between Sunnis, Shiites, and Christians," he said. "We don't have anything against Shiites. Shiites didn't kill eighteen people from our family—the Americans did."

Another longtime resistance fighter was Abu Ali, commander of Jeish Nasr Salahedin (The Army of Salahedin's Victory) in the Tikrit area. A short, stern man wearing a brown jacket, a sweater showing his shirt collar, and green pants, he had a small mustache atop his tight lips and spoke without expression in a low voice. He had arrived in Damascus with two comrades who were wounded and could not get treatment in Iraq. "Our people here said they could help them," he told me. The Americans had raided his home, and he had not slept there for two years, stealing only occasional visits to see his family. I was told that Abu Ali had led a much-publicized attack on the American base in Tikrit on the day American ambassador Zalmay Khalilzad attended a ceremony handing it over to the Iraqi army, and he confirmed this.

"They expressed democracy with bullets against demonstrators," he said of the Americans. "I will keep fighting until the last American and Iranian leaves." Abu Ali added that he anticipated a clash with Al Qaeda as well. Although there was no political leadership in the resistance, he said, "there are politicians, and we express our ideas to them." He worried that the resistance was becoming too public, with many people appearing on television and claiming they led it. "The secret of the success of the resistance is that nobody knows who we are," he said. "If we make it public, then we will be like Palestine, sixty years and no state."

"Nothing positive has come from the Iraqis," he said. "You can't trust an Iraqi."

The prospect of the Palestinian refugee crisis happening all over again is especially worrisome for Jordan. At least half its population of nearly six million people are Palestinians who were expelled from their homes in 1948 or 1967. Following the Gulf War in 1991, Kuwait expelled hundreds of thousands of Palestinians, most of whom ended up in Jordan. Jordan has close and long-standing ties to Iraq, dating back to that country's monarchy.

In a fast food restaurant in Amman I sat with a major from Jordan's powerful General Intelligence Directorate. He insisted that there were more than one million Iraqis in Jordan, though in truth the number never exceeded more than a few hundred thousand. He denied that they were refugees because they had not been forced out of Iraq. When I asked him what he expected a Sunni living in Shiite militia–dominated Basra to do, he told me that the Sunni should merely move to a Sunni area of Iraq. "Nothing positive has come from the Iraqis," he said. "You can't trust an Iraqi." Like most Jordanians he complained that the influx of Iraqis had tripled housing prices.

After Iraqis associated with Abu Musab al-Zarqawi's Al Qaeda movement struck two Jordanian hotels in November 2005, detonating suicide bombs in a wedding, Iraqis began facing interrogations at the border. Beginning in 2006 Jordan imposed strict restrictions on the entry of Iraqis. By the end of that year a sign on the Jordanian border proclaimed that men between eighteen and thirty-five years of age could not enter. Families entering with many suitcases or belongings were turned away as well. Many Iraqis entering Jordan at the border and airport reported being questioned about whether they were Sunni or Shiite. Shiites were more likely to be turned away. Once in Jordan, Iraqis could register with UNHCR for their temporary protection cards.

At first, Iraqis were given three-month tourist visas; but when they left Jordan to renew the visas, they could not return. As a result, many Iraqis chose not to leave and fell into illegal status. Underground, they were unable to work formally and often didn't get paid for the work they did illegally. Many young Iraqi men left their families behind and came to Jordan seeking work. They lived in virtually empty apartments, the only furniture being mattresses on the floor. Their children did not have access to schools or medical care. In February 2006, there were officially fourteen thousand Iraqi children in Jordanian private schools.

Jordanian society was very sympathetic with the plight of Iraq's Sunnis, but Shiites had a hard time there. A young Iraqi Shiite man working with an NGO in Jordan reported being regularly questioned about his identity. Major Jordanian newspapers like *Al Rai* often published anti-Shiite articles, he said. "In Jordan, if you want to work they might ask you if you are Shiite or Sunni, and if you are Shiite you can't work," he told me. "Taxi drivers ask me, 'Are you Iraqi? Are you Sunni or Shiite?'" If he answered truthfully, they would ask him why he was helping the Americans. "After Saddam was executed, they asked me, 'Why didn't Iraqis make a revolution after his execution?' They don't believe Saddam committed crimes. I told one I am Iraqi and Shiite. He asked, 'Are you supporting those Iranians killing Iraqis?' I don't argue, I don't want trouble or to be taken to police station. I bought a bicycle to avoid the taxi drivers."

Dr. Mouayad al-Windawi was a Shiite professor of political science who left the University of Baghdad in May 2005. "In my first lesson after the war, I said this will be a disaster and bring us nothing. We will live in chaos for a long time." A member of the Baath Party until 2001, he explained to me that under

Saddam there was some sectarianism, but it was not overt. A glass ceiling kept many Shiites from advancing too high. "I worked with the Iraqi government for the last forty years," he said. "Not much attention was paid to who you are." I asked him how sectarianism had increased after the war. "Ask Mr. Bremer," he told me, referring to Paul Bremer, head of the Coalition Provisional Authority. "Bremer's system for political parties was good for blocs, not parties. It was good for Kurds and [Supreme Council leader] Hakim. Nationalists boycotted the political process after 2003, but the *hawza* and Sistani told Shiites to wait and see, and Sunnis had no such guy to issue a *fatwa*. The Jaafari government forced Sunnis to see themselves as defending themselves and not the nation. Former Baathists and nationalists like me have no place. I realized there is no future. I told my family we have to stay ten years away from the country."

Mouayad lived in Adhamiya, a Sunni stronghold in Baghdad. Members of Zarqawi's Tawhid and Jihad militia attacked his house. His brother, married to a Sunni woman, was kidnapped and released after a ransom of twenty-five thousand dollars was paid. He then fled to Damascus. "I realized that the country would have a civil war one way or another," he told me. "I still believe the worst is coming, not only to Iraq but in the region. It's the first stage of a conflict that might lead to a Sunni bloc against Shiites. There is no hope for the future." A month before I met Mouayad, his house was occupied by a Sunni militia. Two days before we met, a relative of his was killed when mortars landed on his home.

In Jordan Mouayad was working as a consultant for the political advisory group to the United Nations ambassador to Iraq. "Jordanians were very cooperative until last summer," he said, "but they realized the civil war might lead to new wave. Sixty-five percent of Iraqis in Jordan are Sunnis because Sunni areas in Iraq are under attack." He did not expect the sectarianism to spread to Jordan. "In Jordan security is too strong, and Iraqis here don't want to engage in sectarianism. But over time things might change."

Many officers from the former regime in Iraq had chosen to settle in Jordan. I met two one rainy evening at the home of Maj. Gen. Walid Abdel Maliki, a former assistant to the minister of defense before the war. With him was Gen. Raed al-Hamdani, a former commander in the Republican Guard Corps. Both men, I was told, "had contacts" with the Iraqi resistance. As we sat down, Abdel Maliki's young son burst into the living room. "This is the Mahdi Army," Abdel Maliki told me as he kissed his son, "his behavior in the house." The two former generals were nostalgic for the time before Iraq was overrun with sectarianism. "We never had this sort of fighting before between Sunnis and Shiites," said Abdel Maliki. "Saddam didn't believe in Sunnis or Shiites; he was tribal. Saddam didn't put down the Shiite rebellion because they were Shiite but because it was an uprising. The soldiers who put down the Shiite uprising were Shiites. We never heard from our fathers and grandfathers such a thing as is happening now.

The problem now is from Sunni and Shiite political leaders: Hakim, Dhari, and Adnan Dulaimi are playing the same game." Abdel Maliki blamed Iran for the problems in Iraq. "It's a military idea, to move the battle from your land to the enemy's land," he said, and Iran sought to confront the U.S. in Iraq. "Iranian occupation is worse than American occupation. The only way is a military solution. Al Qaeda, the Shiite militias, the Iranian groups—they have their own agendas but don't want to solve their problems. We have to attack Al Qaeda and the militias. Thousands of Iraqi officers can help Americans."

General Hamdani, Abdel Maliki's former superior officer, had fought and lost in six wars against Americans, Iranians, Kurds, and Israelis. He had been severely wounded in 1991. "The hardest loss was this last one. We were given the responsibility to defend our country. We lost the war and we lost our country." Hamdani also resisted a sectarian approach to Iraq. "It is a mistake to think Sunnis ruled Shiites," he said. "Most of the coup attempts against Saddam were Sunni. If we have a point of view on Iraq, it is as Iraqis, not as Sunnis. There are nationalists and those who are not nationalists."

He did not think the Sunni boycott of the Iraqi government had been problematic. "Many Iraqi Sunnis participated in the government. What was the result? Nothing." Although Hamdani thought the Iraqi resistance should continue its struggle, he too saw a larger threat. "These groups were established to fight the occupation, but now I think the danger from Iran is greater than from America. American national interests and the resistance's interests are the same. The U.S. did itself harm by demonizing the Iraqi resistance and anyone who deals with it. They have prevented the emergence of moderates who can sit and negotiate, and you see now, four years after the invasion, the strongest factions are Al Qaeda and not the nationalists."

Hamdani was involved in a new political party called Huquq, which was formed by Dr. Hassan Bazzaz in August 2006. Bazzaz was a professor of international relations who taught at the University of Baghdad. He left Iraq two months before I met him in February 2007. "I just ran away. I was afraid they will kill me," he said, referring to the Shiite militias. Being a well-known professor was a sufficient reason to be targeted, he explained. When I entered his office he was on the phone with someone in Iraq. "Where did they find him?" he asked. "Who shot him? The Americans?"

Bazzaz was also from Adhamiya. "Good fighters, good people," he said of his former neighborhood. "It never fell."

The Americans had just initiated their new security plan for Iraq, and Bazzaz was trying to be optimistic. "Everything must come to an end, and I don't think this will go on forever," he said. "We are not the first nation to get occupied by a foreign power or the first nation to fight among itself. The Americans are doing it for their own benefit, and we, the Sunni people, can benefit from that." Although he struggled to be optimistic, he still placed hopes in the resistance. "If things get worse, then we, the people who are talking politically, will take the military option," he said. "The Sunni Arab neighbors will have to support us. The worst is coming."

In February 2007 I met Mishan al-Juburi of Al Zawra TV in the offices of a charter airline company in downtown Damascus he claimed belonged to his wife. Two heavy-set thuggish young men stood guard. As I sat down, he began complaining about a recent *New York Times* story about him. "It's completely from a dream," he said angrily. "All the story except my name is not correct."

Juburi told me his version of his life's story. He claimed to have been a busi- nessman in Baghdad's Shorja market. "I knew Saddam personally," he said, "and gave him my full support. Saddam tried to show he was a winner and he didn't care about those who supported him. I lost my son in a car accident and criticized the health minister." Juburi claims that this criticism provoked the ire of the regime. He told me his father had led the Juburi tribe but that since Mis- han had an older brother, he was never expected to lead the tribe. "I like city," he said. "I don't want to be tribal." He also claimed to have been involved in a coup attempt by the Juburi tribe. "I tried to kill Saddam, and he killed thirty- five people from my family: my brother, my cousins. I lost ninety-five people from my family to Saddam, but it's indisputable that Saddam was better. I'm sorry I opposed him."

He had lived in Jordan, Turkey, Britain, and Syria, he told me, and had founded the Iraqi Homeland Party. Before the war he had taken part in an op- position conference in Salahaddin, in Kurdistan. Now he regretted his partici- pation in this conference: "I trusted the American lie of building democracy in Iraq, and I found myself a part of the American destruction of Iraq." He claimed he had come to this realization one month after the war ended, when Bremer declared the American presence in Iraq to be an occupation.

Immediately following the war, Juburi and his militia went down to Mosul from Erbil, where he had been staying as a guest of Kurdish leader Massoud Barzani. "Barzani is my friend. I fully support an independent Kurdistan." He claimed Barzani's militia had helped him take Mosul. I asked him what had be- come of his militia, and Juburi told me, "I think they are resisting."

I expressed surprise at his support for an independent Kurdistan. "I believe it's good for the Iraqi future," he said, though he admitted that the Kurds were planning on cleansing the Arabs of Kirkuk. He told me he had remained in Mosul for one month and then arranged for an election. "I didn't put my name or any name of my family" on the list of candidates, he said, somewhat im- plausibly. After the elections in Mosul, he left for Baghdad and eventually joined the Iraqi government and Parliament. His small party, he said, received 142,000 votes in the first Iraqi elections.

Juburi was known for his sectarian attacks on Iraq's Shiite leaders and mili- tias, whom he called "Safawis," the Arabic way of saying "Safavid," the name of a Persian dynasty that ruled from the sixteenth to the eighteenth century. It is a common epithet used to imply that Iraq's Shiites are not Arabs but are part of an Iranian or Persian conspiracy to gain hegemony over them. "On April 18, 2005, I said the government is Safawi," he said proudly. "I'm the first man to use the word 'Safawi.' Since then I haven't gone to Parliament. The first Jaafari government was Safawi-Persian. We are not against Shiites; we are against Safawis. We fear Iran. The Americans will leave; first we are afraid of Iran."

In November 2005 he established Al Zawra TV. "From the first day we said we are going to say what no one else dares to say," he told me. At first Al Zawra was known for its entertainment programs, but after Juburi's immunity as a Parliament member was lifted following charges of corruption and aiding the resistance, the channel began broadcasting proresistance propaganda. Since most of Al Zawra's target audience in the Middle East did not have access to the Internet, Juburi rebroadcast the propaganda videos that many had seen worldwide online. The videos consisted of members of the resistance preparing for or conducting operations against the Americans. Two commentators, a man in military attire and a veiled woman, occasionally provided news bulletins. Although his channel was praised by the resistance, many also expressed their skepticism about Juburi for being "opportunistic."

Al Zawra received widespread attention throughout the Arab world, and many Iraqi Sunnis in exile watched it as well. One newspaper in Jordan, *Al Arab al-Yawm*, wrote that only Al Zawra transmitted the reports of the resistance without focusing on suicide attacks that promoted sectarianism. The newspaper praised Al Zawra's stance against the occupation and its call for the overthrow of the "puppet sectarian regime." The channel was unique and important, the paper said, because there was otherwise a media blackout imposed on the resistance. The channel showed Arab children the real picture of Iraq, praising the "martyr leader Saddam Husayn."

In April 2006 Juburi absconded to northern Iraq and Erbil, where his friend Barzani provided him with safe haven. "If I stayed in Baghdad the government militias would kill me," he said. "Maliki told me he would execute me if I opposed the government. I am against the Iranians in Iraq, so the authorities accuse me of certain things. Now the office in Baghdad is destroyed." The Americans eventually closed down his station in Erbil too. He explained that he broadcasted from Anbar using mobile transmitters on taxis and other vehicles.

When we met he was running his station from Damascus with the help of his son and publishing a pro-Sunni newspaper. He claimed that he alone funded the station. "I was one of the top-ten richest men in Iraq," he said. Al Zawra was broadcast by the Egyptian satellite network Nilesat. Juburi expressed glee in the distress he was causing as a gadfly. "The Americans pushed me to be against them," he said. "I know how much I give them a headache." He would soon also be broadcast by Arabsat and Hot Bird, a European company.

Juburi maintained that Zarqawi and other Salafis had hurt the Sunni cause. They had sought to provoke a civil war, he said, and they had succeeded. "That's why Sunni society doesn't support them," he said. "There are clashes between Al Qaeda and the Iraqi resistance, which we consider ourselves to be a part of." Al Zawra had become a symbol of the resistance everywhere, he told me. "The resistance are serving us; we have relations with all the resistance in Iraq except Al Qaeda," he said. "We never show anything from them. Al Qaeda is a danger like America in the Middle East. We don't want to make the mistake they made in Afghanistan."

Like many Sunnis, Juburi feared a potential genocide of the Sunnis of Iraq. He believed that Sunni children and women would leave the country. He did not think the Shiites had won yet. "If we are outside the city but Shiites cannot leave their homes, then you cannot say that there is a winner to the civil war," he said. Unlike some Sunni leaders, he did not think the Sunni boycott of the Iraqi government had been a strategic error. "If you push people to join the Iraqi police and army, it means you accept the American occupation."

Although Juburi was ready to criticize Iraq's Shiites and what he saw as their Iranian sponsors, he refrained from criticizing Lebanese Hizballah, a successful Shiite resistance movement. Many Sunni Iraqis saw Hizballah as an Iranian proxy and were thus hostile to the movement. Juburi told me he did not want to talk about Hizballah, possibly because he was a guest of the Syrians, themselves supporters of the movement. He conceded that Hizballah's general secretary was very charismatic and expressed his admiration for Ayatollah Muhammad Hussein Fadlallah, a Lebanese cleric formerly associated with Hizballah. "I love Fadlallah especially," Juburi told me. He agreed with me that it was ironic that in Lebanon the Sunnis supported American policy while the Shiites were opposed to the Americans.

He predicted that Al Zawra would soon go live on the Internet. "We use the Internet the way photography was used in Vietnam," he said. "We will cause Bush a real headache. We will show the reality of American soldiers. America must apologize for what it did to Iraq."

In January 2007 Juburi famously debated Sadeq al-Musawi, a Shiite Iraqi journalist, on Al Jazeera. Juburi came out swinging, asking Musawi to recite a prayer for the soul of "the martyred president Saddam Hussein." Musawi refused, condemning Saddam instead. Juburi called Musawi a Persian, and Musawi responded that Juburi was a thief. Juburi claimed to have evidence that Musawi was an Iranian, and Musawi claimed that Juburi's father had killed Kurds. Juburi called Musawi a "Persian shoe." Musawi stormed off the set, and Juburi continued alone, praising the executed Saddam. Invoking sectarianism and the ancient split between Sunnis and Shiites, Juburi said that the people who killed Saddam were the same people who had killed the caliph Omar ibn al-Khattab and who hated the caliph Abu Bakr and the other companions of the Prophet Muhammad. Although Musawi eventually returned to the set, his exchange with Juburi was no less acrimonious.

In February 2007 Juburi made a speech condemning Al Qaeda for provoking Iraq's Shiites while failing to protect Sunnis from Shiite retaliation, for imposing itself on other resistance groups, for killing Iraq's Sunni leaders, for seeking to create a Taliban state in Iraq, and for killing a messenger sent by Juburi to negotiate with them. Juburi warned that Iraq's Sunnis would fight Al Qaeda. Following his speech, many jihadist websites and forums condemned Juburi. Although the Egyptians had ignored threats from the ruling Shiites in Iraq, in February Nilesat finally pulled the plug on Juburi's channel (other satellite networks continued to broadcast it). The Americans, who had long been pressuring the Egyptians to shut Al Zawra down, finally succeeded.

Others I spoke to disputed Juburi's account of himself. Amatzia Baram of the University of Haifa, an expert on Iraq's tribes and its former regime, was one of them. According to Baram, who also advised the American government: "He is a middle-level sheikh of the Jubbur [tribe], originating from the vicinity of Tikrit. In the mid-1980s he was approached by Saddam to recruit young and uncouth Juburis that would go through a crash (and often crush) course of army officers and then sent to the front with Iran to lead troops in battle. Saddam believed that country tribal boys were tough, very Arab (no mix with Turkish or Persian genes or culture), and imbued with traditional tribal ideals—*murua* (manliness or nobleness), *sharraf* (honor)—and so they will fight the Iranians tooth and nail. Actually, they did prove themselves. Saddam promoted them at a neck-breaking speed in the war. Your man claims that he recruited fifty thousand such, but he is exaggerating. Still, he did a good job. Now, many Juburis were angry at Saddam for other reasons and planned a coup d'état in January 1990. Saddam exposed it and executed many Juburi army officers, imprisoned or just sacked others. It became dangerous to be a senior Juburi for a while. I don't know whether your guy was or wasn't part of the plot, but he felt that the soil was burning under his feet, and fled. He always tried to present himself as far more important than he really was. He returned to Baghdad in 2003 but was not successful in attracting meaningful Juburi support. He always had money, who knows where from. Assad? CIA? Saudis and Gulfies?"

An Iraqi politician close to many Sunni leaders and the resistance who also lived in Syria provided me with another account. My source, who preferred anonymity, explained, "The resistance has doubts about him. They are using him, but they won't give him their trust to speak in their name. When the occupation ends they will judge him for all that he did." He was referring to charges the Iraqi government had made that Juburi had run off with millions of dollars he had been paid for contracts he never completed. He had allegedly used that money to launch his television station.

My source explained that under Saddam's regime Juburi had worked for the *Jumhuriya* newspaper. Juburi then met Saddam's son Uday and fell into his good graces. Juburi came from a poor family, my source told me, but he had made deals with Uday during the sanctions era and had stolen money from Uday before fleeing to Jordan and Syria, taking advantage of the fact that Syria would not hand him over to Saddam. Juburi then pretended he was using money to overthrow the government. My source mocked Juburi for attending the Iraqi opposition conferences in London and Salahaddin before the war, legitimizing the American occupation. When the former regime learned of a coup being plotted by members of the Jubbur tribe, many members were executed, including Juburi's brother, his wife's brother, and many military officers from the tribe.

"When the Americans invaded," my source explained, "he came down with the Kurds to Mosul, and he participated in robbing banks and burning them. He tried to lead Mosul and gave a speech, and people threw shoes and vegetables at him. He bought a lot of votes and got three seats in Parliament. His tribe has rejected him because he came on the back of American tanks." My source explained that Juburi received various building contracts but never built anything. He also received a contract to provide security for oil pipelines. "When he started clashing with the government, they opened his file, and the first file they opened was the pipelines," my source said, adding that some Sunni Iraqi politicians had appealed to Juburi to stop promoting sectarianism. "We told him he serves the American agenda of dividing Iraqis," he said.

CHAPTER SIX

The Battle of Nahr al-Barid: Iraq Comes to Lebanon

IT WASN'T ONLY IRAQI REFUGEES WHO WERE LEAVING THE COUNTRY. Al Qaeda in Iraq was searching for new sanctuaries as well. Most countries in the region were harsh dictatorships with strong security services that would never countenance an influx of the new "Arab Afghans," veterans of the jihad in Iraq, the way they had after the anti-Soviet jihad of the 1980s. But with its weak state, sectarian structure and divisions, foreign interventions, and extreme social inequalities, Lebanon was especially vulnerable to the destabilizing influences of the civil war in Iraq. Best of all, large swaths of it were ungoverned, and there was a Sunni community that felt increasingly insecure. Though there were many differences between the two countries, Lebanon showed a possible glimpse of what parts of Iraq might look like—especially if, as in Lebanon, there was never any process of justice, truth, or accountability to grapple with the civil war and the massacres.

The wave of Sunni extremism and the regional rivalry between Iran and Saudi Arabia were especially felt in Lebanon. Fighting in the northern Nahr al-Barid refugee camp near Tripoli and street clashes in January and May 2008 were a sign that the war in Iraq was spilling over into neighboring countries, with fighters, weapons, tactics, and sectarian tensions all making their way to Lebanon and elsewhere. The clashes were also a sign that America's "New Middle East," based on supporting U.S. client states at the expense of rival movements that had more popularity or legitimacy, was failing. America's support for Sunni regimes that manipulated sectarianism was increasing radicalism in the region and threatening to provoke a larger regional conflict.

While many analysts were promoting a theory of "Shiite revival" in the Middle East, recent events in Lebanon and the region pointed to a Sunni revival. According to a Lebanese political scientist I spoke to, Amer Mohsen, the

Shiite revival, spoken of with fear by Sunni dictators in the Middle East and with pride by supporters, was passé. It had happened in 1979, when the Shah of Iran was overthrown by Ayatollah Khomeini. "If by revival we designate a movement revolutionizing Shiite thought or the way Shiites think of themselves, this already happened in 1979 in much of the Middle East, and that movement reached its apex and is no longer in fashion," he said. "Hizballah in Lebanon is gaining popularity not based on the notions of the Iranian Revolution but as a communitarian movement working in the context of identity politics, much like the other movements in Lebanon. And it is the same thing in Iraq, where Shiite movements have no clear ideological commitment. If by revival we mean increased power for Shiite groups within their countries, that would apply solely to Iraq, where the fall of Saddam supposedly catapulted Shiites to a position of power they had not had since the creation of the country. But this is also a local phenomenon, whose conclusion is still undecided. There is clearly (in the case of Iraq and, to a lesser extent, Lebanon) a phenomenon of Shiites identifying more openly with their sectarian affiliation and building political projects on that basis. But that is a case of the resurgence of identity politics throughout the Middle East in the last years, in which sense, there is a Shiite revival, a Sunni revival, a Druze revival, an Alawite revival, and a Kurdish revival all happening simultaneously."

Amal Saad Ghorayeb, an expert on Shiite movements I spoke to during my time in Lebanon, saw a Sunni revival in the region running on two parallel tracks: "one being the Al Qaeda paradigm, whose sectarianism is religiously, doctrinally, and ideologically based, and which aspires to represent a new resistance, a revolutionary and populist model for the region's Sunnis. While it is not necessarily a reaction to the Shiite Hizballah-Iranian model, it does seek to compete with it. It is insurgent (on a national level) and a resistance or jihadi trend (on the global level). It is a transnational antisystem phenomenon or antiestablishment, anti–world order movement.

"In parallel with this trend is the narrower state-sponsored Sunni sectarian model, which is social and political in nature, is closely interwoven with ruling establishments and personalities, may or may not overlap with the Salafi trend in some cases, but is ultimately a reaction to what is perceived as a growing Shiite threat, as distilled from Arab rulers' discourse and the media. Unlike the Al Qaeda paradigm, though, it cannot compete ideologically with Shiite resistance, nor does it seek to. The Sunni revival is a product of insurgent/jihadist/antiestablishment forces as well as proestablishment forces. In both cases, a revival is taking place insofar as Sunni Islam is seen as being the most effective tool for mobilizing support and achieving objectives."

Mohsen believed that what mainstream Sunni leaders were doing was taking the racist discourse of anti-Shiite extremists (like Zarqawi) and inflating it into a mainstream discourse among Sunni masses. Saad Ghorayeb, on the other hand, insisted that Sunni Arab regimes had appropriated this discourse not so much from Salafis but from the United States, whose leaders and pundits spoke of those who are loyal to Iran and of a Shiite crescent.

Lebanon, in particular, had seen a spectacular revival of Sunni identity and a reshaping of traditional Sunni attitudes since 2005. Order in Lebanon had been maintained by Syrian political and military domination, now referred to as an occupation by opponents of Syria. The Syrians had first intervened in Lebanon in 1976 at the request of the Lebanese president to support right-wing militias against a coalition of leftists and Palestinians who threatened to overturn the Maronite Christian–dominated order. In 1987 they returned, this time in support of Sunnis who had grown tired of the militia wars being fought between the Shiite and the Druze minorities. Both times the Syrian intervention met with American, Israeli, and Saudi approval: first the Syrians marketed themselves as opponents of the coalition between the Palestinian resistance groups and leftists, and the second time they took advantage of American fear of Hizballah, going so far as to attack the Shiite militia.

The Syrian era ended in February 2005, when Prime Minister Rafiq al-Hariri was assassinated, and since then a major divide has emerged between Sunnis and Shiites in Lebanon, with the Christians who had once dominated the country increasingly losing their political significance and becoming marginalized. Lebanon gained independence from France in 1943. Christians and Muslims divided powers and apportioned positions based on sectarian identity, with Maronite Christians benefiting from a six-to-five ratio and Sunni Muslims dominating their Shiite coreligionists. In a sense Lebanon has never had a government but rather a power-sharing arrangement. At first the system of distributing political posts according to sect was merely based on custom. The 1991 Taif Accords, which ended the civil war, enshrined this system while granting a larger proportion to Muslims, allocating seats in Parliament on a one-to-one ratio. The president remained a Maronite Christian, with powers reduced in relation to the Sunni prime minister and the Shiite speaker of the Parliament. The Taif Accords were meant to establish a transitional period that would end with the abolition of political sectarianism, but this never happened. Instead the system became more entrenched, and the Lebanese became more connected to their sectarian institutions. Saudi money and the Syrian military presence in Lebanon helped guarantee that the accords held. While other militias were disbanded, Hizballah was allowed to maintain its armed struggle against the Israeli occupation.

Taif also helped bring to premiership Hariri, a Lebanese Sunni who made his billions working with the Saudi royal family and who used force and bribery to bring the rival factions together in the Saudi resort city after which the accords were named. He had a history of spreading his wealth, granting scholarships to thousands of students, and corrupting the Syrian overlords in

Lebanon, who often seemed like they worked for him. Before the rise of Hariri many of Lebanon's Sunni political and religious leaders had been murdered. Hariri was an ally of Syrian intelligence in Lebanon, and was installed as prime minister in 1992 by Syrian dictator Hafez al-Assad.

Though he is widely credited with reconstructing much of Lebanon, it was the Lebanese who shouldered much of the burden, and under his reign the national debt increased from one and a half billion dollars to eighteen billion dollars. Beginning in 2000, Hariri also contributed to the increase in sectarianism, campaigning more openly on a platform of Sunni power.

Hariri was killed by a massive car bomb. His supporters as well as opponents of Syria established a loose coalition in the wake of his assassination that blamed the Syrians for the murder, demanded the formation of an international tribunal to investigate it, and called for the withdrawal of Syrian forces and influence in Lebanon. The coalition was named for the March 14 demonstration in which Hariri's supporters called for the Syrian withdrawal. The March 14 coalition also became the main vehicle for the Bush administration's agenda in Lebanon and was closely associated with Saudi Arabia through the Future Movement, led by Hariri's son and heir, Saad, who even has a Saudi passport. Most of the March 14 coalition was composed of politicians who had been former supporters and allies of the Syrian regime. One of the most famous chants of March 14 demonstrators was "We want revenge!" That revenge was often taken on poor Syrians who worked as laborers or sold bread on the street. Many of them were beaten or stabbed, and the tents they lived in were burned down in the name of March 14.

Saad al-Hariri was not prepared and had not wanted to inherit his father's mantle. Without his father's achievements to build a popular base he relied on Sunni communal solidarity. Lebanon's Sunnis allied with their historic enemies, the Christians, against the country they had historically identified with more than their own, Syria.

FADIL SHALLAQ was a close associate of Rafiq al-Hariri from 1978 until 2002, heading construction and charitable projects for him, advising him, and finally serving as editor in chief of Hariri's *Future* newspaper. Following the 2006 war with Israel, Shallaq, a Sunni, publicly broke with his former allies, objecting to the sectarian and pro-American turn the movement was taking. He did not view the former Syrian presence in Lebanon as an occupation. "When the Syrians were here, I don't know who controlled who, the Lebanese or the Syrians," he said. "Hariri thought the Syrian presence helped Lebanon," he told me. "I worked with him for twenty-five years." Shallaq rejected the Future Movement's claims that Hariri had been anti-Syrian and argued that the Israelis were more likely to have killed Hariri than the Syrians. Shallaq also re-

jected the reincarnation of Hariri as a Sunni symbol. "Hariri was a Sunni believer," he admits. "He hated my atheism, but he was originally an Arab nationalist, he believed in building the state. He was a Lebanese nationalist, but
he was never sectarian. Sunni sectarianism started after Hariri's death. Sectarianism is not given, it's manufactured. Sunnis were reshaped, reconstituted, reprogrammed after 2005, and became a despicable entity. You needed a corpse.
Without the corpse you could not have reprogrammed their identity. Then
you had a campaign of propaganda. It was well financed." Shallaq blamed a
coalition of neocons and Lebanese allies such as Walid Fares, a former
Lebanese Christian militiaman associated with the American right. He says
they funded the creation of the Future Movement and the sectarian and anti-
Syrian direction it took.

"How could a whole community change like this?" he asked. "Before the
Sunni community was traditional, Islamic, Arab nationalist, a little bit to the
left, with very definite anti-Israeli attitudes about the Palestinian cause. They
had strong feelings about the Syrians, but this wave of hate of Hizballah was
created. It's new."

Shallaq was worried about new Sunni militias being created by the Future
Movement. "There is a not-so-secret militia and security organization. People
are being trained in Jordan; others are trained here by former military men."
Still others were trained by Christian militiamen belonging to the Lebanese
forces, he said. "They are being prepared for civil war. We are in the middle of
a civil war now, or civil conflict. You have to distinguish what happened in 1975
and what is happening now. We won't have the paradigm of 1975 repeated. We
have a civil war without generalized violence. Sectarian feelings are at a maximum point. Militias, arms, preparations, violence—all the elements of civil
war. But will it erupt? And have a green line? I think we will have fighting house
to house, building to building."

One of the people Shallaq blamed for the sectarian tension was his former
colleague Ridwan al-Sayyid, a professor of Islamic Studies at the Lebanese University and speechwriter and adviser to Hariri and his successor for prime minister, Fouad Siniora. On May 3 I visited Sayyid in his apartment. Interestingly,
he agreed with Shallaq on the basic narrative. "There was a repositioning in
the Sunni community since 2005," he said. "They were shocked by the killing
of Hariri." The Syrians had persecuted Sunnis because Sunnis were traditionally pro-Palestinian, pro-Egyptian, and anti-Baathist. "Hariri helped Sunnis
come out of their material, educational, and political crisis, and he made peace
with the Syrians so they would not persecute us. He was a symbol of flourish-
ing Sunnism." After Hariri's killing, the new Sunni feelings were at first only
anti-Syrian, but after the July 2006 war between Israel and Lebanon it became
anti-Shiite as well. He blamed Hizballah and specifically Sayyid Hassan Nasrallah for calling Siniora an agent of the Americans and the Zionists. "Because of

Hizballah, Sunnis feel in danger," he said. Sunni tension increased after the mostly Shiite demonstrators descended upon the government and tried to force Siniora to step down. "Sunnis felt it was against Sunnis and not a political act that Shiites are trying to take the position of Sunnis, the position of the prime minister, which belongs to the Sunni confession, and that Hizballah was trying to destroy the Lebanese state and the Sunni role in the state," Sayyid told me. "Sunnis felt they need to protect the state because the Christians vanished. There is no Christian entity anymore that can mediate between both or make a third party."

Sayyid believed that Hizballah did not act independently but as a tool for Iran to pressure the West. He blamed the July 2006 war on Syria and Iran. "They want to defeat America in Lebanon," he said. "It is a struggle with the U.S., and they waged war against Israel and found that the Lebanese state and Sunnis were on the other side. Sunnis felt that on their side there is Egypt and Saudi [Arabia], and on the other side the Shiites, Syria and Iran." Unlike other Sunni partisans in his alliance, Sayyid did not believe that Hizballah actually wanted a civil war or even that its leaders wanted to impose a Shiite religious state on Lebanon. "But they want to continue the confrontation with Israel without considering the views of the other three million Lebanese," he said. "Hizballah is here with weapons, and accumulating weapons, and they made war with Israel. The country feels threatened, and they don't recognize state institutions—they have their own telephone lines, their own army, their own social networks." Sayyid said he would support Hizballah in the event of another war with Israel. "If Israel wins a war with Hizballah, then Lebanon is destroyed and the Arabs are weakened. How can I, as an Arab, Lebanese, and Muslim, be against Hizballah? I can only say that your program is not good for the country and cannot bring success." Sayyid was not optimistic for the immediate future. "From both sides, Israel and Iran, Hizballah, there is a situation where one will decide to attack. Israel can't wait until Hizballah gets stronger. We cannot win a war against Israel. The Arab countries won't make war with us, so Hizballah will make war alone, and the country will be destroyed."

There were two groups of Salafis in Lebanon, he told me: peaceful ones and jihadists. But he feared that after the appearance of extreme Salafi jihadists the peaceful ones might side with the jihadists. Seyid admitted to me that Sunnis were being trained in Jordan but explained that it was only to work as security guards. Because of Sunni solidarity and the fear that all Shiites have weapons, there were new armed Sunni groups, he said. "Sunnis feel insecure, but it's not a good idea," he told me. "It's not a good situation, but what can you do? The security forces can't protect all those institutions, as the bombings show, so they have to have their own guards."

Facing the Sunni-dominated March 14 coalition was the March 8 coalition, led by Hizballah and aligned with Syria and Iran. Named for the date of the demonstration at which Hizballah thanked the Syrians for supporting the resistance to Israel, the coalition grew to include Michel Aoun, the Christian former Lebanese army general who had spearheaded the fight against Syrian domination. Though Aoun's anti-Syrian credentials were clear, even calling Hizballah pro-Syrian was misleading. The Syrians had fought Hizballah in the past and supported its rivals. It was only in the mid-1990s that they began to support Hizballah, while not allowing it to participate in Lebanese politics, and it was only after the Syrians left that Hizballah entered Lebanese electoral politics. Privately, Hizballah officials disparaged the Syrian system and expressed resentment of the Syrian presence in Lebanon. But their priority was the resistance, and they were grateful to the Syrians for supporting it. Other members of March 8 included lesser Sunni figures such as the late former Lebanese Muslim Brotherhood leader Fathi Yakan, who was sympathetic to Al Qaeda.

The July War and After

In July 2006 Hizballah soldiers captured two Israeli soldiers in a daring raid typical of the tit-for-tat exchanges that were limited to the border region. Hizballah was surprised when the Israelis responded with a massive onslaught, pounding Lebanon and destroying much of its infrastructure, killing about one thousand civilians while laying waste to southern Lebanon and the Shiite suburbs of Beirut. Standing up to the Israeli military might, less than 1,500 Hizballah soldiers lost about 150 of their men. It was the first time an Arab army had achieved a kill ratio on par with the Israelis. The war ended with the Israelis failing to achieve their stated goal of destroying Hizballah or pushing it north of the Litani River. For Hizballah and its supporters, thwarting Israeli goals was a victory—a divine victory, they said. Hizballah shot to popularity with the people, if not the regimes, around the Arab world.

Although Secretary of State Condoleezza Rice described the war and its devastation as the "birth pangs of the new Middle East," it deepened the chasm between the March 14 and March 8 camps, as well as that between Sunnis and Shiites. Hizballah and its allies accused their opponents of collaborating with the Israelis and Americans. March 14 politicians blamed Hizballah for the destruction that had not only ruined the summer tourist season but the economy and infrastructure. If Hizballah accused them of serving Israel and America, they accused Hizballah of serving an Iranian agenda.

Concerned that the Lebanese government, dominated by the March 14 coalition, was attempting to achieve diplomatically and politically what Israel had failed to do militarily (emasculate Hizballah and remove its weapons), the Shiite members of the government resigned. In November the March 8 coalition asserted that the government was no longer legitimate, since without the

Shiites it was in violation of the sectarian division of power. Hizballah sought a national unity government in which it would have a greater share of power. But it was not asking for a larger share of the political pie for the Shiite community beyond the 21 percent of parliamentary and cabinet seats the Shiites were allocated by the Constitution. Instead it wanted a greater share for its non-Shiite allies in the opposition, which collectively represented at least half the Lebanese population. Hizballah wanted a veto-wielding one-third of the cabinet seats so that it and its allies could maintain their influence over "strategic" issues, protecting the resistance, maintaining Lebanon's "Arabism" and centrality in the Arab-Israeli conflict, and preventing Lebanon from falling under American and Israeli hegemony.

In December 2006 Hizballah and its allies in the March 8 coalition initiated demonstrations, and a "sit-in" turned into a tent city in downtown Beirut, an area that symbolized Hariri's costly reconstruction of Beirut and also the seat of the Lebanese government. For Sunnis, this infringement on their territory was perceived as a Shiite "occupation" that had broken the Sunni sense of ownership over this Sunni oasis. In January the opposition called for strikes and civil disobedience. In clashes between Sunnis and Shiites in Beirut, seven were killed and at least 150 were injured. All sides were surprised by the explosion of violent hatred and pulled their forces back. Saudi Arabia and Iran quickly came to the negotiating table. Neither side wanted things to get out of control. Their power was based on the potential for war, not war itself, on playing brinksmanship without being drawn in. During the clashes the army refused to interfere and attack civilians. At the time the army was condemned by March 14 politicians for being insufficiently repressive.

All this was taking place in a region anxious over the civil war in Iraq, in which Sunnis felt threatened by Shiite militias that had profited from the American occupation. King Abdullah of Jordan had warned of a "Shiite crescent" stretching from Lebanon to the Gulf. President Mubarak of Egypt had accused Shiite Arabs of being fifth columnists for Iran. In an unprecedented move, America's Sunni Arab clients in the region, Saudi Arabia, Egypt, and Jordan, had gone so far as to issue formal statements condemning Hizballah, which suggested they were siding with Israel. While the Sunni regimes used the Shiite threat to galvanize their population, nobody wanted an actual conflict between Arab states and Iran. The tense quiet in Lebanon over the next few months was punctuated by bombs and assassinations. But everybody was waiting for what was to come. Saudi Arabia decided that Lebanon was its project, the place in the region where it would confront Iran. But Lebanon was also an Iranian project, and both countries invested large amounts of money and political capital in support of their allies. Unlike Iraq, where their proxies also competed for power, Lebanon was less costly and the consequences less severe. Much as it had in Iraq, Gaza, and Somalia, the United States appeared determined to provoke a civil war in Lebanon. In the conflict over the cabinet seats and over selecting a new president, the Americans were pressuring their proxies not to compromise with Hizballah and its allies, increasing the tension and seemingly denying Shiites the right to participate in the government.

Marooned in Lebanon

Lebanon's twelve Palestinian camps form an archipelago that exists inside and outside the state. Hundreds of thousands of Palestinian refugees live suffocated and marginalized in them. Inside the camps the Palestinian identity is maintained, and the main employers are the Palestinian resistance factions. When the Syrian military was in Lebanon it backed former Lebanese President Emile Lahoud—a Maronite Christian, as was custom, who served from 1998 to 2007. Throughout his presidency Lahoud invoked the threat of *tawtin*, warning that Muslims would grant citizenship to the Palestinians, in order to frighten Christians into backing him and the Syrian presence. Most Palestinians are Sunni Muslims. The Christian minority among them had been granted citizenship long before, since their numbers would bolster the ranks of Lebanon's Christian minority. *Tawtin* was an existential threat, Lahoud warned. It would boost the number of Muslims, and only the Syrians could prevent it.

With massacres of Palestinians committed by Lebanese Christians and Shiites in the past, and most recently with Lebanon's Sunnis having turned against them, sometimes it seems that the one thing that united Lebanese had been their hostility to Palestinians. But in truth the one thing that united them was furthering their sectarian interests. The Palestinians have always been instrumentalized by Lebanese factions. They were used by Sunnis as their militia during the civil war. Shiites in the south joined Palestinian groups in the 1960s to force out their feudal landlords.

Syria sought to maintain the refugee camps as a political card, so Lahoud impeded any way of alleviating Palestinian suffering. In a very cynical policy, Lahoud continued to deny all social rights and representation were denied to them. In the camps, Palestinian clerics deduced that Christians hated Palestinians because they were Sunnis. In 2005, when Lebanese Prime Minister Fouad Siniora spoke of improving the conditions for the Palestinians, he was condemned for invoking *tawtin*. Had they been Christian, no such opposition would have occurred. As a result they had to react as Sunnis and defend themselves as Sunnis. For the clerics it was not the Syrians who were behind the move; it was the Christians. Some Palestinian clerics took advantage of this to mobilize support. If they were rejected in Lebanon as Sunnis, then they would fight as Sunnis.

Radical Sunni groups benefited from this weakened Palestinian identity. Chief among them were Salafis. Salafism is a muscular discourse, and in its most extreme form it sounds like racism when applied to Shiite Muslims. Most Salafis engaged in theology and preaching, and refrained from political or military action. A small minority believed that violence was necessary to achieve an Islamic state. In Lebanon, there were two kinds of Salafis: the traditionalists, who were fully integrated into the political system, and the jihadists, who relied on networks that were not nation-based but had become deterritorialized.

Ayn al-Hilweh, situated in the town of Sidon, a forty-five-minute drive south of Beirut, is the largest of the camps in Lebanon; it houses up to seventy-five thousand people in one square kilometer of squalor. A balance of power in the camp between the two main factions—the broadly secular Fatah, founded by the late Yasser Arafat and the historic core of the Palestinian Liberation Organization, and Usbat al-Ansar (The League of Supporters), a jihadist group particular to the Palestinian refugee camps that was formed in the mid-1980s—prevents fighting from breaking out. Jund al-Sham (Soldiers of the Levant) is another jihadist organization that split off from Usbat al-Ansar. It was named after a group established by Abu Musab al-Zarqawi in Afghanistan in 1999 for militants hailing from the Levant.

In July 2006 Ayman al-Zawahiri, Al Qaeda's second-ranking leader, warned that Al Qaeda would not stand by while Israel shelled Lebanon. Unlike Al Qaeda in Iraq and its founder, Zarqawi, who had declared war against Shiites, Zawahiri sought to establish a common front with the Shiites of Hizballah, who were successfully standing up to the Israelis, but the Shiite resistance organization wanted nothing to do with the Sunni terrorist organization. He linked the struggles in Iraq and Afghanistan with those in Lebanon and Palestine, and blamed "the crusader alliance." Al Qaeda was concerned that the battle against Israel, and the glory, was being monopolized by Hizballah, and it hoped to establish itself in this crucial front. Zawahiri's words were taken seriously by some. Islamist websites and Internet forums carried demands to establish a Sunni jihadist front in Lebanon. Other jihadists fled Iraq, disgusted with the sectarian fighting or pressure from the growing power of the American-backed Sunni militias in the Anbar province. Hunted in Jordan and Syria, they found Lebanon—with its failed state, lawless refugee camps, and sectarian strife—was their only safe haven. Zawahiri's statement in July 2007 praised an attack against United Nations peacekeepers in southern Lebanon.

ONE DAY THAT MONTH, I visited Ayn al-Hilweh for a funeral in the late afternoon. Soon after I arrived calls to prayer echoed from all the mosques in the camp. First built in 1949 to house Palestinians expelled from northern Palestine, the camp had grown into a ramshackle ghetto made of concrete and cinder blocks. Low-hanging electric cables were strung from one building to another, crisscrossing like old cobwebs. Faded political posters were plastered over with newer ones, some for Hamas, others for its rival Fatah, and still others for Saddam, declaring him a martyr for the Islamic nation and a warrior leader. The camp had two main streets and a labyrinth of tight alleys connecting to smaller streets, one of them named after Falluja. At the Shuhada Mosque stood a dozen men in paramilitary uniforms, with walkie-talkies, M4 carbines, AK-47s, scopes, pistols, combat boots, tennis shoes, long beards, and sunglasses. The men had a professional and serious air to them, and they differed from the hundreds of other armed militiamen in the camp who lazily slung their older weapons and were unkempt.

The mosque's second floor connected to the building across the street, forming a bridge. The armed men standing under the mosque were members of Usbat al-Ansar—the leading jihadist group in the camp—and they joined about two hundred other men on the second floor for a special prayer. They were burying one of their comrades, Daghagh Rifai, who had been shot at 9:30 that morning by men belonging to the rival faction Fatah. The armed men lined up with the others in orderly rows, placing their weapons on the floor between their legs. Some of them wore the *salwar kameez* typical in Pakistan and Afghanistan, a jihadist fashion.

Following the prayer, men gathered to gaze briefly at Daghagh's corpse, which was wrapped in the green flag of Islam. A thick man with a large dark beard, he bore fresh wounds on his face. His former comrades carried him down the stairs on an olive-colored military gurney. A procession of hundreds followed them silently around the corner, off the main street, and up an incline. Residents of the camp watched from their doors or from windows and balconies above. As the silent marchers approached the camp's gate, the armed men stayed behind and let relatives take Daghagh's body past the Lebanese soldiers guarding the entrance and on to the cemetery.

One of those paying their respects that afternoon was a cheerful man called Abu Anas, who led me through a maze of dark alleys up to his unlit apartment. We were joined by his friends Abu Salih and Abu Ghassan, wiry, fit men with taut faces and long beards. The power came back on and with it the television, tuned to Al Manar, Hizballah's television station. Abu Anas's wife and children had left the camp to go to the nearby beach, and he was enjoying the quiet, he said, as he served us melons.

Daghagh had been shot outside his home in what they described as an "old story, a chain." A few months earlier Fatah men had attacked members of Jund al-Sham, a rival jihadist group to Usbat al-Ansar. Daghagh was part of a group of Jund al-Sham men who retaliated, killing two Fatah men. "Friends of Daghagh will take revenge on Fatah," they assured me. Two months earlier Fatah had also tried to kill the local Hamas leader but had only succeeded in wounding his youngest son. "Fatah has a bad reputation here," one of the men said. "Fatah was good in the 1970s. They had principles. Now they are dealing drugs, they are opening Internet places with pornography, they just want money and power." The men told me that Fatah men had recently stabbed a member of Usbat al-Ansar as he guarded a school, but he had fought back and they fled. Fatah had also thrown grenades at a mosque, they told me. Fatah and Usbat al-Ansar were the two dominant factions in the camp, they said, but Usbat was stronger. Like many Palestinians, they worried that Fatah intended to abandon the Palestinian refugees who lived outside Israel and the occupied territories, and they insisted that Fatah supported *tawtin* in Lebanon, which they feared would abnegate their right to return to their homes.

Abu Anas and his comrades did not belong to any of the factions. "We have some differences with Jund al-Sham," one told me. "They are a little ignorant. They think with their hearts and not their minds. You need principles, not emotion. Usbat al-Ansar is more open, more educated. They have military expertise."

Abu Salih had tattoos, meaning he had not always been devout. He said he had fought in Falluja in the fall of 2004, staying for about fifty days and taking part in four successful operations against the Americans. "The Americans were cowards," he told me. There had been between 250 and 300 men in his group, he said. I asked why he had chosen Iraq and not tried to liberate Palestine. "It's impossible to go fight in Palestine," said Abu Anas. "The Arabs closed the borders—Jordan, Syria. Here if they open the way to fight Israel, many people would go fight." Hizballah, he said, prevented them from fighting Israel.

I asked the men what they thought of Hizballah, since they supported groups in Iraq that targeted Shiites. "We differ in our beliefs, but we agree on fighting Israel," one said. "Israel is the enemy. We can settle our differences later." Many Lebanese Sunnis resented Hizballah for provoking the last war. "Sunnis who disapprove of Hizballah's war do so because they are allied with America," one of the men told me. They reminded me that a group of Palestinians from the camp who had fought with Zarqawi in Iraq had launched missiles at Israel and that in his final statement, Zarqawi had declared that "we fight in Iraq, but our eyes are on our home in Jerusalem."

Abu Salih met Zarqawi once. I asked him what he was like. "He was a lion," Abu Ghassan interjected. Zarqawi had been very nice to "the brothers" and had cooked for them, Abu Salih explained. It was night when they met in Falluja's Askari neighborhood, and it was very dark. "The earth was burned," he said. "Planes were bombing, but we had cold water, appetizers, grilled chicken." Up to fifty men from the camp had gone to fight in Iraq.

"Usbat al-Ansar is a travel agency and YMCA for jihad," explained Bernard Rougier, an expert on Lebanon's Salafis and author of the book *Everyday Jihad*, "but they are a jihadi group, they must act, so the way of solving the contradiction of being in Lebanon but not fighting Israel or anybody else is by sending jihadists to Iraq and secretly helping other jihadist groups."

I returned a few times to visit Abu Ghassan. Foreigners entering the camp must get permission from Sidon's local military intelligence commander. As I sat in his office I overheard his phone calls. One sheikh called him about releasing a Jund al-Sham suspect from prison. The commander opened the man's file and read the accusations. The man was an extremist: he had helped dispatch fighters to Iraq, was suspected of involvement in explosions, and was inciting against Shiites. With the commander's permission slip I was able to get past the soldiers guarding the gate and drive past the Fatah checkpoint to meet Abu Ghassan. He wore camouflage pants and a knit cap. He led me through more alleys, down rough-hewn stairs, and past a metal door into his apartment. His infant daughter was sleeping in a baby seat.

Abu Ghassan was thirty-one years old and quick to smile, but, like Abu Salih, he always reverted to a hard suspicious gaze when I wasn't looking him in the eye. He had six children, the oldest of which was thirteen. He had a nine-millimeter Glock pistol on his belt. Its price in the camp was two thousand dollars, and it had made its way to Lebanon when some "brothers" returned from Iraq with large quantities of weapons. It was the same pistol the Americans had given to the Iraqi police; I had seen it used by Shiite militias and sold on the black market in Baghdad. An August 2007 report from the American Government Accountability Office stated that 190,000 weapons the Americans had given to Iraqis were unaccounted for. Here was one of them. On a desk was a new Toshiba laptop connected to the Internet. Abu Ghassan told me he worked in a cafe in the camp. "You must have sold a lot of coffee to pay for a two-thousand-dollar pistol and the laptop," I said. He grinned and agreed with me.

He was first trained as a teenager outside the camp by Fatah, before the civil war ended in 1991. In 1995 he came under the sway of Islamic movements, influenced by religious leaders and the recently formed Usbat al-Ansar, listening to mosque sermons and attending lessons held after prayer. Some of the mosques, such as the Shuhada Mosque, also had their own clubs for physical training. The Oslo accords had been signed, and Palestinian refugees felt abandoned—they worried that the PLO was surrendering. Wars were being fought in Bosnia and Chechnya. The first generation of mujahideen—those who had fought in Afghanistan—sought new battlegrounds, and a new generation was galvanized. "I saw Muslims around the world oppressed by secularists," he told me. Now the Lebanese army wanted him on charges of terrorism, "in broad terms for killing and explosions," he said, claiming the charges were false.

He had attempted to sneak into Iraq through Syria to fight six times, but each time the Syrians were patrolling the border. In May the Syrians had killed several jihadists attempting to cross. Crossing the border from Syria had become much more difficult since the second battle of Falluja, he said. "I wanted to go to Iraq to liberate Muslim lands, to fight with the Sunnis. The road was open to Iraq. Palestine was closed." He resented Hizballah for controlling the border with Israel and preventing other groups from conducting attacks. "After Hizballah liberated the south, they became a buffer," he said. "They say they want to liberate Palestine, but on the ground they do nothing, they just wait for orders from Syria or Iran." Unlike many Lebanese Sunnis, he did not feel threatened by Hizballah. "As Palestinians we feel threatened by America and Israel," he said.

"Brothers" in the camp had established a network leading to Iraq. "Young Muslims, enthusiastic, with their own organization, they communicated through the Internet. One guy went and opened the way for others." A guide would lead the volunteers across the border. Some guides did it for money and others because they believed in the cause.

Abu Ghassan first decided to go to Iraq when Zarqawi renamed his organization Al Qaeda, in December 2004. "Before Abu Musab [Zarqawi] appeared, nobody knew how to get people to Iraq," he said. "I want to go fight with Al Qaeda, with the Islamic State of Iraq. The priority for me is to fight America and its allies, and if the Iraqi government opposes me I will fight them too. The Iraqi government is an apostate government." Abu Ghassan had requested to go as a suicide bomber. "Practically speaking," he said, "suicide operations are the best method to kill the enemy. In principle you try as hard as you can to avoid civilians, but sometimes you cannot." He did not believe that Sunnis were targeting civilians, and instead blamed Iran, the Mahdi Army, and Israel. "Zarqawi asked Muqtada to fight the occupier, and Muqtada refused," he said. "We target the Shiites in the government and the militias. The Mahdi Army kills mujahideen and lets the Americans arrest them. Christians have been neutral, not with the occupier, so they have been spared. Shiites are not apostates; their leaders are. Clerics have agreed that the Shiite clerics are infidels, the people are deviants. Hizballah is a Shiite apostate party. The Shiites hate Sunnis."

Another time when I visited Abu Ghassan in his home, Abu Anas was there. They were looking at Google Earth on the laptop while listening to a CD of Salafi chanting called *Commanders of the Jihad*. They showed me another CD, a tribute to Salih Ablawi, known as Abu Jaafar, who had died with Zarqawi in Iraq. He was from Ayn al-Hilweh too, and Abu Ghassan had a collection of his speeches and pictures from Iraq on his laptop. A large picture of Abu Jaafar was on a banner above one of the main streets in the camp.

Abu Anas was originally from the Bedawi camp in northern Lebanon and had grown up in a conservative family. He had fled from the north to Ayn al-Hilweh in 2000 because of his involvement in clashes with the Lebanese army. On December 31, 1999, Islamist radicals battled the Lebanese army in northeastern Lebanon's Sir al-Dinniyeh, led by a Lebanese veteran of the Afghan and Bosnian wars called Basim al-Kanj. Kanj had returned to Lebanon and established his own network, recruiting in the slums of Tripoli and Ayn al-Hilweh and establishing ties with Usbat al-Ansar. With Usbat's help he established training camps in Dinniyeh. Kanj ordered his men to take over a radio station near the camps that had belonged to Lebanon's leading Salafi cleric, Sheikh Dai al-Islam al-Shahal. (His father had first brought Salafism to Lebanon in 1940, but it was Dai al-Islam and his brother who really brought Salafism to northern Lebanon.)

Only months before, churches in Tripoli had been attacked, and some of the suspects had fled to Dinniyeh. Shahal and other Sunni clerics as well as local officials tried to mediate between the army and the militants. When an army patrol passed by, negotiations were suspended. Fighting broke out, and fifteen of the Islamists died along with eleven soldiers and five civilians, although Kanj had not sought such a confrontation. The Dinniyeh group was small, but dozens of Salafis were arrested in Tripoli and radicalized in prison.

The Dinniyeh incident, along with an attack on the Russian embassy and similar incidents, were the first signs that Salafi jihadism was establishing a presence in Lebanon. One lesson of the incident was that the poverty and neglect in northern Lebanon could affect the rest of the country, but this was forgotten until February 5, 2006, when rioters came down from the north in buses provided by the Sunni Endowment and rampaged through Christian neighborhoods in Beirut, seeking vengeance for the Danish cartoons of the Prophet Muhammad. Christians were shocked, as security forces were nowhere to be found despite having advance notice of the demonstration. Those rioters who were arrested were quickly released. Ahmad Fatfat, who was interior minister in 2005, had struggled to release the Dinniyeh prisoners in order to gain the support of northern Sunnis and Salafis. As a concession to Christians the government then released Samir Geagea, the notorious war criminal who had killed Palestinians as well as Christian rivals during the 1980s. Much fanfare met the release of the Dinniyeh prisoners; the episode was televised and used to demonstrate that the government was pro-Sunni. Some of them had belonged to Harakat al-Tawhid al-Islami (The Islamic Unity Movement), the main Islamist militia that fought the Syrian presence in northern Lebanon in the 1980s. In the shifting alliances of Lebanese militias, Tawhid is now considered pro-Syrian.

Abu Anas blamed the Lebanese army for the clashes. "They wanted Hizbal-lah to control the conflict with Israel," he said. "The Lebanese army ambushed them, and during the negotiations they surrounded them and attacked them." Abu Anas had previously belonged to Tawhid. More than fifty Palestinians had belonged to Tawhid, he told me. Many had gone on to other Islamist movements.

In May 2007 members of a new and somewhat mysterious jihadist group, Fatah al-Islam, robbed a bank in Tripoli, provoking clashes with the army. Salafi militants also robbed banks in Sidon and other parts of the country. "Al Qaeda uses credit cards to fund themselves, and they rob banks and companies that are infidel to fund themselves," Abu Ghassan explained. "They don't rob in a criminal way. They don't want to hurt anybody. There is a difference between killing people and taking money that belongs to Muslim people." Although most of the soldiers battling Fatah al-Islam in the north were Sunnis, Abu Ghassan did not blame Sunnis. "The Lebanese army answers to the government, and even though the head of government is a Sunni, the orders come from America. They are not fighting as Sunnis but as soldiers, getting orders, and they think Fatah al-Islam are terrorists." I asked him what he thought. "I think Fatah al-Islam are good people," he said.

The Mystery of Fatah al-Islam

The origins of Fatah al-Islam are nebulous, but based on meetings with Palestinian faction leaders and security officials, as well as documents obtained from their interrogation of the group's members, I pieced together its history. In the summer of 2006 new faces appeared in Shatila and Burj al-Barajneh, the Palestinian camps of Beirut, and in Bedawi and Nahr al-Barid, the camps near the northern city of Tripoli. The men were clearly religious, and they were assumed to be Salafis. They had long beards, and some even wore the Afghan *salwar kameez*. Some were clearly foreign. When camp security inquired about the newcomers, they were told, curiously, that the men belonged to Fatah al-Intifada's "Western Section," a traditionally leftist, broadly secular Syrian-allied Palestinian group that split from the Palestine Liberation Organization in 1983, which was preparing fighters to go to Palestine. Others claimed they were "from the inside," meaning from Palestine itself. During Israel's July 2006 war on Lebanon, more Salafi fighters arrived in these camps, in part because a Fatah al-Intifada camp near the Syrian border in eastern Lebanon was evacuated during the war. Suspicions were aroused because the left-leaning Fatah al-Intifada was known to pay low salaries but some of the newcomers had laptops and went around on motorcycles. The newcomers were led by Shaker al-Absi, a veteran Fatah al-Intifada officer who had been trained as a pilot in Libya and served as one in North Yemen, in addition to fighting in Nicaragua. Absi was in his fifties. A Palestinian born in Jordan, he had spent most of his life in Syrian and Lebanese camps. He was likely disillusioned with the aging and moribund Arab left—which groups like Fatah al-Intifada epitomized—and he was said to have been very religious. In 2002 he was arrested with fifteen others for trying to infiltrate the Israeli-occupied Golan Heights. He spent two and a half years in jail, and was said to have gone to Iraq after his release, eventually making his way to the Helweh camp in the Beqaa Valley, by the Syrian border. There he and his followers trained volunteers, including young men from the slums of Tripoli, to fight in Iraq. Gulf Arabs who flew to Beirut to go to Iraq also gathered there. They were segregated from the rest of the camp and better financed, eating better food like lamb.

When Zarqawi died, some of his men came to Lebanon. Some Salafis were diverted to the Burj al-Barajneh camp to serve as a bulwark against the Shiite suburbs of Beirut, known as Dahiyeh. Many Syrians and Palestinian Syrians who had fought in Iraq and become radicalized there made their way to Lebanon. More than two hundred such men had left Damascus's Yarmuk refugee camp to fight in Iraq with Zarqawi, even though that camp was dominated by the far more moderate Hamas movement. Abu Midyan was one of the foreign fighters who left Iraq because of concerns about the state of the jihad there. He led other comrades in arms from Iraq to Yarmuk, but the Syrians pressured them to leave, so they moved to Lebanon's camps, where they began to recruit from the poor.

Abu Yasser, the Fatah al-Intifada leader for northern Lebanon, was surprised because the newcomers were bearded, prayed five times a day, and abstained from smoking. He asked his superior, the Syrian-based Abu Khalid al-Amli, deputy commander of Fatah al-Intifada, who the newcomers were. "We have new fighters," he said. "We must learn from Hizballah's military and discipline. They are destined for Gaza." Abu Khalid was also sending jihadists to Ayn al-Hilweh. Abu Yasser was surprised and unsettled by the presence of foreigners among them. "Their commanders were Palestinians, and they were independent of us," he said. When other factions asked Fatah al-Intifada who the new men were, they were told cryptically that it was an "internal matter." Shaker al-Absi was the third-ranking official in Fatah al-Intifada, and his authority exceeded that of Abu Yasser's. "I accepted Shaker but didn't control him," said Abu Yasser. Abu Musa, the commander of Fatah al-Intifada in Syria, began to complain that he did not know what was happening in his own organization.

The popular committee for security in Bedawi was tasked with investigating all outsiders who rented apartments in that camp, especially single men. Committee members monitored how much food was being brought into the apartments daily to estimate how many people might be inside. In November a new group of outsiders came to Bedawi and Nahr al-Barid, whom camp residents felt were not part of any Palestinian faction. The committee grew suspicious of newcomers who brought in many bags but had no families. Residents spoke of strange men carrying bags who entered twelve apartments in the camp. One night five strangers came into the camp, and armed members of the resistance asked them what was in their bags, which caused the men to run away. Some of the men were foreigners, including Saudis, Yemenis, Algerians, Iraqis, Lebanese, and an Omani. Fourteen of them lived together in one apartment. When the security committee members first tried to gain access, the Omani, named Ahmad, shut the door in their faces and refused to open it.

On November 23, 2006, an armed patrol of different faction members from the camp security committee was sent to the apartment. They found two Kalashnikovs along with ammunition and grenades and asked the fourteen men to come with them. When the men walked by a Fatah al-Intifada office where Salafi comrades were staying, they erupted in shouts of "God is great! Come to jihad!" and ran inside, throwing a grenade at the security men. An exchange of fire followed, and one of the security men was killed. The security committee raided the other apartments, but the suspects were communicating by radio and some escaped. One Saudi was shot in the leg while trying to escape. When an armed Syrian comrade on a motorcycle attempted to rescue him, he too was shot, and both were taken to a camp hospital. The Syrian had documents signed by Shaker al-Absi. During his interrogation by the Palestinian security officials, the two admitted that they were members of Al Qaeda in Iraq and had come to Lebanon during the July war for training, recruitment, and jihad. Up to eighty men like them entered Lebanon via Fatah al-Intifada, using the organization as a conduit. They claimed to have come to assassinate seventeen Lebanese officials, including members of Parliament, sheikhs, and members of the security forces.

The two men were handed to the Lebanese army. Camp officials found cameras, four computers, and scanners used to make fake identification documents. They also found CDs with footage of training and members swearing oaths of loyalty to Osama bin Laden. "Wherever Muslims are oppressed, we will help them," said one of the men in a film. Other material included maps of the region. Books with instructions on bomb-making were covered by copies of the Koran. They also found a collection of Al Qaeda statements. Abu Yasser told me that he had received a call warning him to leave the computers alone because they were very important.

One young Syrian had left behind a final statement, handwritten with messages to his family; another young jihadist stressed that "this time, I will not go back. I repeat, I will not go back." The young man, who had previously engaged in armed struggle, said, "With all that I have seen the last time, I'm in a serious danger of apostasy—God forbid—if I don't go back there. If the scents of musk and the light in the martyrs' faces and all the other graces we saw and were told of mean anything, they must mean only one thing, that this route is the path of heaven. Moreover, there is no heaven except by this path."

Some of the apartments had been rented by Kanan Naji, a former member of Tawhid who was a liaison between the Future Movement and Fatah al-Islam. Naji was also part of the Independent Islamic Gathering, a group that included prominent clerics in Tripoli such as Dai al-Islam al-Shahal and Bilal Barudi. The Gathering tried to influence Fatah al-Islam, and several of its members were in touch with the group.

In the 1980s Naji's Jund Allah militia of about one hundred had been based in Tripoli's Abu Samra neighborhood. They were known for wearing all-black military fatigues and received some of their arms from Fatah. Once the Syrians took over Tripoli in 1986, Naji fled to areas controlled by a Christian militia. He was underground in the 1990s, but following the Syrian withdrawal in 2005 he became very active, establishing a close relationship with Hariri's Future Movement and the Lebanese Internal Security Forces, and providing arms to Fatah al-Islam. Four Palestinians affiliated with Naji's militia rented some of the apartments in Tripoli. They brought in sniper rifles, M-16s, and other weapons more advanced than what was usually found in the camp. Naji was one of the officials who hoped to use jihadist Salafis to serve the purposes of the anti-Shiite Future Movement.

The camp's leading factions prepared to rid themselves of the Salafis, but the Salafis—who until then were identified as the Salafist wing of Fatah al-Intifada—absconded to the nearby Nahr al-Barid camp. On November 26, 2006, they declared themselves under the new moniker Fatah al-Islam, calling for their supporters from other camps to join them and calling for the death of Abu Yasser, the leader of Fatah al-Intifada in northern Lebanon, for his role in turning over two of their men to the Lebanese army. Abu Yasser sent a message to his boss, Abu Khalid al-Amli, in Damascus, accusing him of putting camp security in danger by sponsoring the Salafis initially. Abu Yasser was incensed to learn that about thirty Salafis posing as Fatah al-Intifada also came up to Nahr al-Barid from Beirut's refugee camps. Abu Fadi, the commander of Fatah al-Intifada for all of Lebanon, had even used Salafis as bodyguards. He was expelled from the group and fled to the United Arab Emirates.

Abu Yasser claims that he had been deceived by Abu Khalid. "He tricked the organization," he says. "Abu Khalid was a dictator, and he is a secular man in every meaning of the word. He was preparing groups to fight the Americans in Lebanon, and maybe he was making a connection with Al Qaeda. The Syrians didn't know the details of Abu Khalid's plan, but they knew in general about the ideology of the fighters and that they were coming to Lebanon to fight America, and the Syrians did not know of the connection between Abu Khalid and Al Qaeda. Abu Khalid was expelled from the organization." Abu Khalid was jailed by the Syrians, but because he was seventy-five years old and had a heart condition, he was placed under house arrest.

The camp's security committee began to investigate Fatah al-Islam and its associates. One Syrian suspect, born in 1980, had entered Lebanon in March 2007. He had come up to Bedawi from Ayn al-Hilweh, where he joined Fatah al-Islam. Despite his ties to the jihadists, he was released because some of the camp officials worried about upsetting the Islamists in the camp. Another suspect confessed that he too belonged to Fatah al-Islam. When the raid took place, he had been in touch with a man from Jund Allah via his walkie-talkie. He was spirited away to Tripoli, where he stayed in an apartment belonging to Kanan Naji. When he returned to Bedawi he was arrested by the security committee and was found to be carrying an American-made pistol. Another prisoner, born in 1986 in Syria, had been in touch with Fatah al-Islam via the Internet. He was given an address near a mosque in Bedawi and told to go there. He took money from his father, telling him it was to cover the cost of his university tuition, but instead he went to Lebanon, hoping Fatah al-Islam would help him get to Iraq "to resist the Americans, because the Americans are the enemies of Islam." The young man's cover in the camp was that he was studying Islam.

In November 2006 things got worse in Taamir, an area between Sidon and Ayn al-Hilweh. Jihadist Salafis took control of the neighborhood and imposed Islamic law. At the entrance to Taamir a banner signed by Zarqawi called for the defeat of America in Iraq. Many Lebanese families left, fearing for their lives. That month a statement signed by the "Al Qaeda Organization in Lebanon," allegedly based in Nahr al-Barid, threatened the Lebanese government, announcing that Al Qaeda had arrived in Lebanon and would work to destroy the government, which was commanded by the Americans. They would fight the enemies of God until victory or martyrdom, the statement said.

In Nahr al-Barid, however, Fatah al-Islam found a welcoming environment. Pictures of Saddam Hussein were on the camp's walls and in its homes and shops. Graffiti in support of the jihad in Iraq was also evident. When the Syrians pulled their troops out of Lebanon and lost direct control of the camps, the vacuum they left was filled by mosques, which gained in influence as the leftist resistance groups weakened and money from the Gulf came in. Islamists were seen driving expensive cars. Nahr al-Barid was more conservative and religious than other camps, with the most clerics (about fifteen) and the most mosques (about ten). Even before the July war inhabitants began to notice religious men moving into the camp who spoke in foreign dialects and whose wives were veiled. Up to seventy of them arrived during the war, a phenomenon similar to what occurred in other camps. Following the flight of Fatah al-Islam to Nahr al-Barid, these various groups joined their leader, Shaker al-Absi, openly taking their weapons with them. Up to fifty-six people came to Nahr al-Barid from the Burj al-Barajneh camp in Beirut.

Fatah al-Islam had been planning to establish itself anyway, but in more than one camp at once, at a time of its choosing. In Nahr al-Barid group members took over the offices and weapons depots that had belonged to Fatah al-Intifada. They replaced Palestinian flags with Islamic flags. "When they took down Palestinian flags we knew they had no Palestinian agenda," said Abu Yasser. New weapons arrived—American M-16s, M4s, and even missiles, unlike the Kalashnikovs that the Palestinian factions were accustomed to. In a meeting with all the camp factions Fatah al-Intifada insisted that whereas before they had been suspicious of the newcomers, now they knew the men were dangerous. Fatah agreed that they should be expelled. Other groups, nervous about potential strife, refused to have any bloodshed in the camp. Fatah al-Intifada warned that Nahr al-Barid had been hijacked by Fatah al-Islam and all would bear responsibility for what would happen. Estimates for the initial size of Fatah al-Islam varied from forty-five to seventy. Some of the men had brought their families; others married local women. Only a minority of them were Palestinians. Most were Lebanese, Saudis, Yemenis, Syrians, and even Iraqis. Many came openly, in vans. Wanted Palestinian and Lebanese men from Ayn al-Hilweh and Taamir made their way to Nahr al-Barid as well, despite the many checkpoints along the way, leading camp officials to suspect senior Lebanese official involvement in the move, since the Interior Ministry was in the hands of pro-Hariri Sunnis. Although Usbat al-Ansar never publicly endorsed Fatah al-Islam, it did dispatch fighters to join the group in the north.

Jihadists with a more violent and nihilistic agenda took over Fatah al-Islam's leadership council and influenced its leaders, shifting their focus away from Palestine and toward global jihad. Abu Laith, the son-in-law of Shaker al-Absi and one of the founders of Fatah al-Islam, grew frustrated with the group's change; he left for Iraq but was killed by Syrian security forces at the border. Other members also disagreed with the more extreme elements. Abu Midyan, who was said to have orchestrated the February 2007 bus bombings north of Beirut, refused to fight the Lebanese army because his enemy was Israel. In Nahr al-Barid, Shaker al-Absi linked up with a powerful arms dealer called Nasser Ismail in order to improve his power base in the camp. Ismail helped recruit members, including the more radical Abu Hureira, a Lebanese member of Jund al-Sham. Abu Hureira helped push Fatah al-Islam toward a more extremist position, and he brought many other Lebanese Salafi jihadists with him. These radicals began to alienate the residents of Nahr al-Barid. Abu Midyan and Abu Hureira disagreed about the new direction the group was taking. While Absi did not share the views of these radicals, he needed the military support they brought, and so he could not afford a rift with them. A Saudi cleric linked to Al Qaeda called Abu al-Hareth took over the leadership council. He helped bring more foreign fighters and create cells outside the camp. Some of the newcomers spoke of creating an Islamic state in northern

Lebanon. Others didn't even know they were in Lebanon; they thought they were in Iraq.

In December in Nahr al-Barid a committee from Palestinian factions told Absi that his new faction was not acceptable and that he had to return the Fatah al-Intifada offices, disband his organization, and stop making announcements to the media. Absi did not respond to their demands. At the same time, Abu Khalid, the deputy commander of Fatah al-Intifada based in Syria, was arrested by the Syrians. His boss Abu Musa gave a press conference stating that he was very upset at Abu Khalid, but the notion that the Syrians were completely ignorant of the actions of a faction they controlled strains credulity. For Abu Khalid to take such steps independently of the Syrians would have been foolhardy.

Bernard Rougier speculated that the Hariri strategy was to "control and enlarge the Islamist coalition, which could be used to fight Hizballah on the communal level. The Syrians wanted to impede the Hariri strategy by creating division in the Hariri ranks, so they inserted a Salafi jihadist group that wants to fight Israel because it would take Sunni support from Hariri. Then it took on its own life and the Syrians don't have to do a thing. And it had a magnetic effect on Islamists in the country. It began to have influence in Tripoli." Rougier distinguishes the communal agenda, which "views the real enemy as Shiites," from the jihadist agenda, which "views the real enemy as the West, and Shiites are third or lower on the list of priorities." But the Syrian regime, dominated by the Alawite sect—which is related to Shiism and which rules a Sunni majority and has crushed Islamist movements in the past—would not encourage an ideology that despises its own Baathist government. While the Syrians had allowed Arab volunteers to pour into Iraq to fight the Americans for the first two or three years of the occupation, the main opposition to the Syrian Baathist regime is a Sunni Islamist one. So it would not likely support the growth of Salafi jihadists so close to its own border. Moreover, Syria would not introduce anti-Shiite and anti-Hizballah elements into Lebanon. A Salafi attack on Israel would be Hizballah's worst nightmare because it would drag the powerful guerilla army into a war with Israel at a time and place not of its own choosing.

"When Fatah al-Islam took down the Palestinian flag and vandalized posters of Hassan Nasrallah, they started getting a lot of money," said Abu Yasser. "Their main goal was to be the Sunni military force in Lebanon. The north has a rich history of Salafis, and they wanted to declare their emirate. Those who empowered them were not Palestinians. We let them enter as a baby chicken and they became an elephant. How did they get these advanced weapons? When they were part of Fatah al-Intifada, they were only seventy. They became five hundred. With us they were very poor. We gave them spare clothes. How did they get so much money? And how did they buy all the grilled chicken in Nahr al-Barid?" According to Abu Jaber of the Popular Front for the Liberation of Palestine (PFLP), once a leading resistance movement within the PLO but now completely marginalized, the financial situation of the Fatah al-Islam members suddenly improved as more foreign faces appeared. "They were probably there, but people didn't see them," he said. "How did they live for six or seven months?" he asked. "They used to buy three hundred loaves of bread a day. They bought apartments, rented land, buying very advanced weapons, spending a lot of money." People in the camp grew worried, and some refused to rent them homes. Some said that they were Muslims who were not bothering anybody, while others said that they did not belong in Palestinian society. As Fatah al-Islam began to spread throughout the camp, it seemed to many that the group was preparing for something. It was also clear that its members could get in and out of the camp without harassment by Lebanese security officials.

"The Fatah al-Islam picture got more and more clear," said Abu Jaber. "In their first announcement their goal was to liberate Palestine and correct the errors of Fatah al-Intifada. And they called men in the camp to join them in liberating Palestine in an Islamist way. After a while their speech changed. They said they came to fight Israel in the name of Sunnis. They said, 'We won't fight those who fought Israel [meaning Hizballah], but we have differences with them.' They did not have their own mosque. They were moving around in all the mosques." The leader of Al Qaeda in Iraq sent Saudis and other fighters from Iraq to Nahr al-Barid but warned them not to provoke Lebanese Shiites.

Ensconced in Nahr al-Barid, the Fatah al-Islam militants grew in number. Their headquarters had a yard for military training. Above it flew a black flag with an Islamic slogan. Some walked around camp with scarves concealing their faces. Shaker al-Absi insisted that they were independent of Al Qaeda even though they had a similar ideology, and that they had no ties to Lebanese or Syrian officials. He explained that "Muslims" were funding his organization. The secular approach to the struggle had failed to achieve its goals, he argued, and they now rallied under the flag of Islam. He explained that his organization's main goals were to liberate Jerusalem and oppose the U.S. project in the Middle East. He refused to be involved in internal Lebanese affairs. Fatah al-Islam's main criticism of Hizballah was not that it was a Shiite party but that it denied other groups the same right to resist Israel. Importantly, Absi denied being a *takfiri*. (*Takfiris* typically single out Shiites, as did Zarqawi in Iraq, and sometimes call for their deaths.)

Members of Fatah al-Islam claimed to have "brothers" in all the camps in Lebanon, as well as in Syria, Jordan, and Palestine. But according to an informant with Lebanese army intelligence, the group clashed with mainstream factions in the camp three times and achieved dominance. Fatah al-Islam's ranks were bolstered by Lebanese Sunnis reacting to the increasingly aggressive steps being taken by Hizballah supporters, whose actions were viewed by many Sunnis as an attack on Sunni power, an occupation of Beirut, and an attempt to seize control of Lebanon. Clerics in Tripoli reported being asked by followers if they were permitted to join Fatah al-Islam. Dai al-Islam al-Shahal, the founder of Lebanese Salafism, explained that Lebanese Sunnis felt targeted, alienated, and punished, and as a result some were joining Fatah al-Islam and others were sympathizing with it. Shahal had maintained direct dialogue with Fatah al-Islam from its establishment in an attempt to influence its ideology and actions.

"Fatah al-Islam was very different after they declared themselves," said Abu Yasser. "At first their goal was to fight the Americans in Lebanon. But their first enemy was [Fatah al-] Intifada, and they fought us and we had two wounded and they had one killed and three wounded, and then Shaker al-Absi made some new channels with groups in Lebanon." In March 2007, following accusations by the Lebanese interior minister that the Syrians were backing Fatah al-Islam, the Syrian interior minister responded that Fatah al-Islam was an Al Qaeda organization that was also targeting Syria and had been discovered in August 2002 when several of its members were arrested, including Shaker al-Absi. He added that Absi had coordinated with Zarqawi in Iraq to conduct terrorist attacks. But the Future Movement insisted that Fatah al-Islam was a Syrian tool, and the Movement's leader, Saad al-Hariri, described the organization as "the gang of Asef Shawkat," referring to the head of Syrian military intelligence and the brother-in-law of the Syrian president. The television station and newspaper controlled by the Movement also initiated a campaign to convince Lebanese of the links between Fatah al-Islam and the Syrians. Others in the opposition claimed it was a creation and tool of the Future Movement. Both were wrong.

Some members of Fatah al-Islam had fled from the Rashidiyeh camp in southern Lebanon after the UNIFIL forces boosted their activities following the July war. Others came from Taamir and Ayn al-Hilweh. A Syrian volunteer seeking to engage in jihad made his way to Bedawi by accident and asked for Fatah al-Islam at a Fatah al-Intifada checkpoint. He was in his twenties and was carrying a laptop and three thousand dollars. The security committee interrogated him for twenty-four hours. The man had been invited via the Internet by Fatah al-Islam to come fight jihad and "liberate Lebanon." It was not clear who he was supposed to liberate it from. After Lebanon there would be many steps, the invitation said.

In February up to twenty armed men from Jund al-Sham took over a kindergarten that belonged to the Hariri Foundation and was overseen by Bahiya al-Hariri, sister of the slain prime minister. The area was controlled by Usbat al-Ansar, and the move was seen as an attempt to pressure local officials, improve the group's financial situation, and obtain housing. Jund al-Sham was already known as Jund al-Sitt (The Army of the Lady), because Bahiya al-Hariri was a financial backer of the armed group. She paid up to one hundred of the men to leave, and they went north to Nahr al-Barid. Some of them were veterans of Iraq. It was a move typical of the "Saudi" mentality of the Hariri family, an attempt to pay off potential troublemakers and buy loyalty. Mustafa Allush, a Parliament member from the Future Movement, confirmed that the transport of the men had been facilitated by Hariri's people for "humanitarian reasons." Once Fatah al-Islam was set up in Nahr al-Barid, officials close to the Future Movement and the Independent Islamic Gathering courted the group, hoping it would side with them. To their chagrin, Shaker al-Absi and others insisted on maintaining their independence.

In March Lebanese Interior Security Forces arrested suspects behind the February 13 bus bombings, which killed three and injured twenty-one in the village of Ain Alaq, north of Beirut. The twelve men, including four Syrians and four Saudis who were accused by the Lebanese interior minister of belonging to Fatah al-Islam, confessed to setting the bombs. The four Saudis claimed to have been deceived by Fatah al-Islam. They said they had been planning to go to Iraq and instead found that they were expected to remain in Lebanon. The Saudi ambassador requested that the Saudis be extradited back to their country. Fatah al-Islam representatives denied involvement in the attacks and denied that the detained men belonged to their group. As the heat on the group increased, spokesman Abu Salim Taha warned that if Fatah al-Islam had to respond militarily, it would. Abu Jaber of the PFLP worried that if military steps were taken, the results would be catastrophic. The bus bombers had not actually belonged to Fatah al-Islam, but they had spent one night in Nahr al-Barid before the attack and were said to have called the Fatah al-Islam leadership afterward.

Nabil Seyid, a PFLP official who coordinated the security committee in Bedawi and was secretary general of the factions in the northern camps, explained that the factions did not have control of the camps and had no way of dealing with Fatah al-Islam. "We are under Lebanese authorities, and the Palestinian factions aren't united, and when they want to make a decision they have to consult." Abu Jaber, also of the PFLP, admitted that there had initially been poor communication and many disagreements among the Palestinian factions. When suspicions first arose, the factions decided that they could not interfere in the internal affairs of Fatah al-Intifada. Nahr al-Barid had a conservative culture, so Islamists were welcome while Fatah's men were known for being thuggish and even drunk. "People in the camp had no problem seeing Muslims—they were praying, they didn't bother anybody," Abu Jaber said. "The PFLP was suspicious, though. By the time they had declared themselves Fatah al-Islam, they were stronger, situated, stable, they had brought families.

A committee of the factions spoke to them and told them to leave the camp, but these people were very strong." Abu Jaber explained that following the Oslo accords the factions had progressively grown weaker. Less money was coming into the camps. There was no powerful Palestinian regime to dislodge the four hundred well-armed Salafis. "Whoever let them in should kick them out," he said. "All the camp is surrounded with Lebanese army checkpoints, and these people were coming in and out." Fatah al-Islam had brought two vans full of weapons in broad daylight, without obstruction, he said. There were popular demonstrations against their presence. Many of the Palestinian faction leaders insist that prominent Lebanese Sunnis and members of the Future Movement tried to co-opt Fatah al-Islam. "What is for sure is that all sides tried to benefit from them, but no one can control them," a Hamas official from Nahr al-Barid told me. "The Syrians tried to use them, and Future tried to use them in their war against Hizballah. They made many promises, but in the end they did their own program."

The Lebanese army increased its presence around the camp, surrounding it and establishing checkpoints at the entrances. Nahr al-Barid had been one of the main markets in northern Lebanon, but the security measures put the camp's economy in a stranglehold. The army searched cars and checked identification papers, causing traffic jams leading to the camp and reducing the number of visitors to the market.

Fatah al-Islam's men refused to heed calls for their removal or disbandment. They were Muslims, they said, on Muslim land, and they recognized no borders. Their persecution was a necessary result of their ideology and was akin to the persecution the Prophet Muhammad faced when he first began preaching. Absi warned that he had more than two hundred men and that they were observing the army's movements around the camp. If Fatah al-Islam felt under attack, then it would respond violently, he said. Absi was becoming increasingly influential in Tripoli, especially among youth. Following a bank robbery in Sidon, the Lebanese interior minister gave a press conference on March 13, 2007, stating that Fatah al-Islam was self-funded and relied partially on bank robberies.

In March two Fatah al-Islam members were killed in a clash with Fatah that also brought injuries on both sides. Fatah al-Islam made a show of force in the camp and removed pictures of the late Fatah leader Yasser Arafat. In another clash more grenades were thrown and more men were injured. At the funeral for one of the slain men, a Gazan who had come to Lebanon via Germany, a large number of people turned out, including Salafis and clerics from Tripoli. "We were surprised by how popular they were," said Abu Yasser. Many Salafis from Tripoli swore oaths of allegiance to the group. By then Fatah al-Islam numbered 150, its ranks bolstered by members of other groups such as Usbat al-Ansar and

Jund al-Sham. Some called them "strangers in the camp." They kept to themselves and spoke in classical Arabic, perhaps to conceal their foreign accents.

In April at least seventy residents of Tripoli, including Saudis and other foreign Arabs, were arrested in Tripoli. Most of them were from the Abu Samra district, which housed important Salafis and their institutions. The suspects were accused of belonging to Al Qaeda. They were said to be linked to a man who had been arrested in Saudi Arabia for allegedly trying to collect money to fund militias in Lebanon. Anger increased among the Salafis of Tripoli at what they felt was their persecution by government forces. Others resented what they perceived as a double standard allowing Hizballah members to have arms but denying Sunnis the same privilege. That month Hamas held commemorations in honor of Ahmed Yassin and Abdel Aziz al-Rantisi, two leaders who had been assassinated by the Israelis. They played religious and nationalist songs. Fatah al-Islam members complained about the music, which they considered un-Islamic, but Hamas prevailed. Fatah al-Islam also accused Hamas of following Anwar Sadat's path of negotiation with Israel.

Abu Yasser claims that forty Saudis flew to Beirut and were taken to Nahr al-Barid, where they were kept for months until the tensions with the army began. One of the Saudis called his family back home, and they arranged for his surrender to Lebanese authorities. Many Salafi clerics and state religious officials came to visit Fatah al-Islam, their vehicle license plates indicating that they were from Dar al-Ifta, or the Sunni Endowment, a state body, which was headed by the Grand Mufti, or the Mufti of Lebanon. In May eyewitnesses claimed that large deliveries of new weapons were brought into the camp for Fatah al Islam. In July Abu Salim Taha explained that pressure had been placed on his group to take a side in internal Lebanese conflicts but they had refused to do so they were being targeted.

Accusations were exchanged throughout 2007 between the two opposing coalitions about who was responsible for Fatah al-Islam, with some even speculating that Saudi Arabia and the United States were collaborating with the Future Movement to sponsor jihadists who would confront Shiites.

The March 14 coalition accused the Syrians of backing Fatah al-Islam and similar groups. On August 20, 2007, Democratic Senator Joseph Lieberman made similar accusations, claiming that "the road to victory now requires cutting off Al Qaeda's road to Iraq through Damascus." Most of the support for Al Qaeda in Iraq came from Syria, he asserted, as did the actual fighters. The majority of Al Qaeda's foreign fighters made their way into Iraq by first flying into Damascus International Airport, he claimed, "making the airport the central hub of Al Qaeda travel in the Middle East." It was time to demand that "the Syrian regime stop playing travel agent for Al Qaeda in Iraq," he said, calling for an international boycott of that airport.

According to Syria's ambassador in Washington, the urbane Imad Moustapha, these accusations were laughable. "We have in Syria organizations that might be very similar to Al Qaeda in ideology and approach," he said. "Al Qaeda is not one single organization that has headquarters in Afghanistan. It has inspired groups all over the Islamic world. We have had serious incidents in Syria, some not publicized." He blamed U.S. policy in Iraq for the spread of these groups. "When the U.S. changed Iraq into this lawless state, Iraq became fertile ground for every extreme organization. The flow of terrorists is not unidirectional. It's bidirectional. At an early stage we told the U.S., 'Stop the accusations that we are helping Al Qaeda.' If they go and fight in Iraq, they will continue their holy war against other regimes. Only yesterday we extradited some Saudis to Saudi Arabia. This is a very burdensome task, and it needs lots of cooperation. In Damascus airport any young man who arrives alone, especially from Saudi Arabia, we don't let them in. They are very upset about this, and we receive many complaints." Every few weeks Moustapha received a copy of a list from Syrian intelligence of individuals rejected at Syrian entry points for security reasons. He showed me several months' worth of the lists, which were marked "top secret" and contained the names of thousands of individuals denied entry, some of whom were Egyptian and Algerian. "Borders can't be controlled by one country," he said. "It needs exchange of intelligence, cooperation, the diligent effort of the other side."

On May 19 a bank belonging to the Hariri dynasty was robbed southeast of Tripoli, apparently by men from Fatah al-Islam. Credible sources from the Palestinian factions and Hizballah and its supporters maintain that Fatah al-Islam received monthly payments in this bank, which were suddenly halted. When the payments stopped they demanded their money and returned armed to rob the equivalent of one hundred thousand dollars, their monthly stipend. Absi told Muhammad al-Haj, the Hamas negotiator, that they had come to receive their transfer, but problems had arisen and they did what they had to do to get the money.

Early the next morning Lebanese security forces raided apartments in an affluent district of Tripoli belonging to Fatah al-Islam members, some of whom were foreigners. The conduit for renting the luxury apartments was said to have been the Mufti of Tripoli. One of the militants called Sheikh Dai al-Islam and asked him to tell the authorities not to arrest them. The response from the security forces was that they would not negotiate and were going to finish them off. The militant threatened to attack the army. Haj, who is also head of the council of Palestinian clerics, claimed to have been surprised by the clashes. Before the bank robbery, he said, "there had been an agreement between Fatah al-Islam and the authorities that Fatah al-Islam would not be involved in Lebanese politics or harm peace and stability, and would not expand its activities outside the camp, and that the thirty foreign Arabs with Fatah al-

Islam would be deported." Despite the close proximity between the Internal Security Force base and the Lebanese army base, and the fact that the army was surrounding the camp, the ISF did not notify the army that it was conducting the raids in Tripoli. The ISF did, however, notify two Lebanese television stations.

The following day a group of fighters led by Abu Hureira, one of the most militant figures in Fatah al-Islam, attacked a Lebanese army location and slaughtered the soldiers. Shaker al-Absi was said to have been uninformed about this in advance and to have emerged from his home in his pajamas at the sound of fighting. Humiliated and angry, the army struck back. Abu Hureira and his followers refused to negotiate. It seems Absi was frustrated that things were getting out of control and felt that he had been forced into a battle. Rumors spread throughout the country that the soldiers had been brutally slaughtered and mutilated, provoking a wave of hatred that targeted Palestinians in general, despite the fact that Fatah al-Islam was composed mostly of non-Palestinians and all the Palestinian factions condemned it. On May 20–21 bombs exploded in a Christian and Sunni neighborhood in Beirut, igniting fears that the fighting might spread.

Shaker al-Absi claimed that he never wanted to target the Lebanese army but was forced to do so by the raid in Tripoli. In the chaos of the first day, said Muhammad al-Haj, it was not possible to establish a dialogue. Once negotiations led to a cease-fire, armed Sunni civilians from the area descended upon the camp to support the army and attack the Palestinians. Haj blames these civilians for reigniting the battle. He was shot by Fatah in a failed assassination attempt after the group grew concerned over his success in mediating between the army and Fatah al-Islam and what it meant for their role in the camp. "They thought that what was being achieved through negotiations would prevent Fatah from forming its security committee to control the camps," he told me.

When Future Movement leader Saad al-Hariri called upon his forces to support the army and security forces, this was interpreted by his forces to mean that they should join the fight. Hundreds of armed Sunnis from the region descended upon the camp. When fighting began, it became very difficult for civilians to leave because they had to endure artillery fire as well as snipers from the army and Sunni militiamen from the north. Fatah al-Islam took advantage of the armaments of the PFLP-General Command—Ahmed Jabril's Syrian-sponsored split from the PFLP—and the Fatah Revolutionary Council, commonly known as the Abu Nidal Organization. Members of these ostensibly secular groups—with a reputation for once performing spectacular acts of violence—were helping Fatah al-Islam out of solidarity on the local level, but not on orders from their officers. Interestingly, the Salafi leaders in the camp who had initially welcomed Fatah al-Islam disavowed them now. Dai al-Islam al-Shahal maintained contact between Fatah al-Islam and the Lebanese authorities. When the fighting started Syria closed two border points in the north.

On May 25, Hizballah leader Hassan Nasrallah gave an even-handed speech commemorating the liberation of southern Lebanon from the Israeli occupation in 2000. In that speech he discussed the clashes in the north and spoke of two "red lines." The army and the security agencies in Lebanon were a red line that should not be crossed by attacking them. Likewise, the Palestinian civilians and their camps were a red line, and the security forces should not kill civilians in the name of a war on terror. The Future Movement seized on these statements to accuse the Shiite leader of supporting Palestinian terrorists against the army. Anger swept throughout the north and other Sunni areas in the country. At the same time Lebanese security forces cracked down on local Salafis in Tripoli, and rumors circulated that some were being tortured.

Clerics in Tripoli had to calm many of their followers who sympathized with Fatah al-Islam. Some began to feel betrayed and persecuted by the government. The Future Movement began to lose ground among Salafis. Its leaders had campaigned as protectors of Lebanon's Sunnis but instead were perceived by some as having launched *fitna* (strife) in the north. In the slums of Tripoli, resentment was growing against Lebanese security forces, who were picking people off the streets even if they were innocent, beating them, and releasing them as an example to others. Some people in Tripoli felt that Fatah al-Islam members were well-intentioned mujahideen who had been forced to fight in Lebanon when they should have been fighting in Iraq. The majority of the soldiers fighting with the army against Fatah al-Islam were Sunni Muslims from northern Lebanon. Many in the north were not sure how to react. When the first few dead soldiers arrived in their hometowns for burial, some of them were not buried as martyrs because they had died fighting fellow believers. The majority of Sunnis embraced the army, however, and a propaganda campaign in support of the army began in earnest, with one bank issuing credit cards with a military camouflage motif, advertisements on television showing the nation saluting a soldier, and bumper stickers stating allegiance to the army. It was a cathartic experience after the previous year's war and the divisions it had reinforced in the nation.

Members of the Abu Nidal Organization also provided assistance, including weapons, to Fatah al-Islam in Nahr al-Barid, and some of the Abu Nidal men who were wanted by Lebanese security forces even stayed behind and fought alongside Fatah al-Islam. Over the next three months the Lebanese army regularly announced that it had vanquished Fatah al-Islam, but despite destroying the camp and making forty thousand Palestinians homeless, the fighting continued, and Lebanese soldiers continued to die. Absi had not been seeking a confrontation with the Lebanese army, but once the fighting started he might have hoped that other supporters and Salafis would rise up throughout

Lebanon and its camps. Negotiations faltered over the demand to hand over wanted Lebanese men among his ranks. Abu Salim Taha, the Fatah al-Islam spokesperson, blamed the Future Movement for inciting hatred against them. He admitted that there were many foreign Muslims among them. Even though they had no organizational ties to Al Qaeda, they considered them their brethren.

In early June it was Jund al-Sham's turn to clash with the army, in Ayn al-Hilweh. There had been fears that the fighting in Nahr al-Barid would spread south, and now it was happening. Usbat al-Ansar, which was already part of the camp's executive committee, played a key role in securing the camp. The Lebanese government gave Usbat al-Ansar a new status by recognizing it as a power broker and partner it could deal with. This negotiated solution allowed the Palestinians to continue policing themselves. It was a stark contrast to the military solution offered in Nahr al-Barid.

In June Lebanese security forces arrested four people in the Beqaa Valley in eastern Lebanon. They also found a large amount of explosives and money. One of the suspects was a Saudi carrying fake Iraqi identity papers. Two Syrians and a Palestinian were found with him. By then another thirty-two Fatah al-Islam prisoners had been captured, most of whom were Lebanese. The Saudi authorities asked for their citizens to be repatriated so that they could learn more about similar groups in the Kingdom, and Lebanon consented. South of Tripoli Lebanese security forces killed five Islamist fighters, at least two of whom were Saudis. In July, after Fatah al-Islam began firing missiles outside the camp, Abu Salim Taha, the Fatah al-Islam spokesman, explained that the group was targeting the army and some missiles had reached Lebanese towns because of miscalculations. He asked the Sunnis to accept his apology. Lebanon's many Salafist jihadist groups refused to back Fatah al-Islam, as did Al Qaeda. Their focus was fighting Israel, and none of them wanted to jeopardize their position in Lebanon by provoking the authorities.

By late June most of the Palestinian refugees from Nahr al-Barid had fled to the nearby Bedawi refugee camp. In a schoolyard there I was stopped by Abu Hadi, born in Haifa in 1946. "I am a person without an address," he told me. "I wish I was a donkey or a horse so I would have doctors and lawyers for my rights." He pulled out a notebook. "My office is my pocket," he said. He showed me a plastic bag with a sponge and a towel. "My bathroom is in my hand." A peaceful demonstration of hundreds of civilians, including women and children, marched from Bedawi toward their former homes, asking for the right to return there. Lebanese soldiers opened fire at close range, killing two demonstrators and wounding at least twenty. As the demonstrators fled they were attacked by Sunni civilians from the region, beaten and stabbed. Palestinian families seeking to recover the corpses of their relatives killed by the army's indiscriminate shelling were told to sign statements affirming that the men had been with Fatah al-Islam or were killed by the group. At the Interior Ministry's Qibba base near Nahr al-Barid, where many Palestinians were inter-rogated, at least one of the officers had graduated from an American military program in interrogation described as "debriefing, interviewing, and elicita-tion." Numerous Palestinian men reported being detained and tortured for many days. Palestinians throughout Lebanon were beaten at checkpoints.

A SENSE OF FOREBODING united people in Lebanon and throughout the re-gion in response to the destabilizing occupation of Iraq. It also made Sunnis feel vulnerable. North of Tripoli, by the village of Qubat Shamra, where a boy was selling watermelons off the side of the road the day I visited, there was a stretch of broken wall with two lines of graffiti. "We tell you, oh rulers, of treachery and tyranny, the blood of the martyr Hariri is not to be forgotten," said one. The other listed the successors of the Prophet Muhammad whom Sunnis revere and warned that "the blood of Sunnis is boiling." It was signed by an unknown group called the Mujahideen Battalions of Tel Hayat, in refer-ence to a nearby village. Further up the road toward the Syrian border, past tall pine and eucalyptus trees, one side of an apartment building was covered with a large painting of Rafiq al-Hariri. "They feared you so they killed you," it said. "Truly they are pigs." It quoted from the Koran as well, an example of the strange juxtaposition of Islamism and the Hariri cult. I stopped at Kusha and met a twenty-three-year-old third-year law student called Muhamad, who had learned English from listening to rap music. Muhamad had joined the In-terior Ministry's new Information Branch earlier that year as a volunteer "be-cause of the Shiite campaign against this government," he said. "You have to do something." His responsibility was to "keep an eye open for anything strange in town."

According to Muhamad, Lebanon's Sunnis had finally come to believe that Lebanon was their country. "After they killed Hariri we woke up," he said. "Shiites hate us. After Hariri's death I started feeling hatred of Shiites. I hate Shiites after they thanked Syria in the demonstration." He also hated Shiites for reacting positively to Saddam Hussein's execution. "At the end Saddam was a Sunni," he said. "I love Saddam. He subjugated Shiites. He was a leader in every sense of the word." Muhamad believed he was helping to defend Lebanon from the "Shiite crescent." "They're trying to extend their principles through all of Lebanon. The biggest danger is coming from Shiites, not Israel. The priority is Shiites, to confront their project. I would take a gun and face Shiites, not only me but many people here."

In the village of Masha I drove by the main mosque, which had a large pic-ture of Hariri on one wall. Above the mosque a large blue sign said, "Palestine and Iraq are calling you, boycott American products." Elsewhere in town a small shop had the obligatory picture of Saddam with his two sons at his side. A local sheikh had praised Fatah al-Islam as mujahideen.

Throughout Sunni towns in the north and Sunni neighborhoods in Tripoli and Beirut one finds images of Saddam and graffiti praising the executed former Iraqi leader. "The nation that gave birth to Saddam Hussein will not bow," said one in the Beqaa. In Beirut's Sunni stronghold of Tariq al-Jadida I found posters of "the martyred leader" Saddam with the Al Aqsa Mosque in Jerusalem behind him. On the road to Mishmish, a small mountain town in Akkar, I passed a wall where someone had written "Long live the hero Saddam Hussein." Entering the town I drove under many banners honoring the army. "Only your pure blood draws the red line," said one, in reference to Nasrallah's recent speech. When I visited in late July 2007, the all-Sunni town had already lost three of its men to Fatah al-Islam; eight other soldiers from Mishmish were wounded. "People are very angry at the Palestinians," mayor Hanzar Amr Din told me. He did not believe the anger would subside after the fighting. "If they think of coming back to the camp, people will destroy it," he said. "People here were very upset at Nasrallah's words about red lines," he said. "Last summer people were happy with Nasrallah for fighting Israel, but saying that the camp is a red line means he is backing Palestinians against the army."

That summer I found similar sentiments in the Sunni town of Bibnine. A laborer in a sandwich shop compared the situation to the 1970 Black September fighting, when the Jordanians had gotten rid of Palestinians. "I swear on the Koran," he told me, "if I see a Palestinian I would slaughter him and drink his blood." I asked him what he thought of Hizballah. "I hope they get rid of them too," he said. The walls of Bibnine were plastered with pictures of the ten soldiers killed in the fighting, and I was reminded of the similar pictures festooning Shiite towns a year before in honor of the Hizballah soldiers who had died. On a wall near children playing on a road, someone had written with chalk, "Saddam Hussein is the martyr of the nation." Khuzaimi, a twelve-year-old boy, told me that "we all want to grow up to join the army to destroy this infidel al-Absi." But since Fatah al-Islam would be destroyed by then, he said, "then we will all go fight Israel."

Most of the townsmen had taken their weapons to Nahr al-Barid in the first days of the fighting to "help the army," I was told by Qais, a member of the Internal Security Forces from the town. "Anybody above sixteen went down," he said—122 soldiers in all. "There is no family in Bibnine without somebody down there," he said, adding that his family had fifteen men there. "There is a big anger at the Palestinians," he said. "We consider them responsible for this." When I visited Bibnine on July 31 the shelling of Nahr al-Barid echoed up to the town. Many of the townsmen worked as fishermen off the coast of Tripoli, but since the fighting had begun they had been forced to stay at home.

"They should be put on the border in the south so they can smell Palestine soil and remember it," said Abu Muhamad, whose son Osama, a twenty-six-year-old soldier, had died in Nahr al-Barid. He blamed Syria for sending Fatah al-Islam to Lebanon. "My son the martyr, from childhood he wanted to be in the army. He grew up in a military house. I am a retired soldier. I am proud of him. He was brave, not a coward." Abu Muhamad had two other sons in the army, one of whom was wounded in the battle. "Our first martyr was Rafiq al-Hariri," he told me. "He was a martyr to the nation, and we all want to be martyrs to the nation."

From his balcony Abu Muhamad could view the camp smoldering down on the coast. His face was lined and weathered. He looked tired but tried to smile. "The people won't allow the camp to be rebuilt," he said. "As soon as the fighting stops, people will go down to prevent it from being rebuilt." Another guest, the father of a soldier still fighting in the camp, repeated an oft-heard slander that the Palestinians had sold Palestine to the Jews in 1948 and now had sold Nahr al-Barid to the jihadists. "That gang bought their camp," the man said. He had been among the first armed men to descend on the camp, he told me. "All towns around the camp went down and took the arms of soldiers who were killed," he said. "Now there is a blood feud between Lebanese and Palestinians," said Abu Muhamad. "The big problem is not with the Palestinians." The real problem was not the Nahr al-Barid camp but the one in downtown Beirut, he said, meaning the Shiite protesters. Like most Sunnis in the north, he had been angered by Nasrallah's "red lines" speech in May. "Call it red lines or green lines or whatever you want," he said. "Your lines won't stop us."

The forty thousand homeless Palestinians of Nahr al-Barid were housed in local schools in the nearby Bedawi camp and in Tripoli, watching from afar as their homes were obliterated. Nahr al-Barid was a thoroughly urban camp, with many low apartment buildings. It was located right off the Mediterranean beach, and the view would have afforded its residents some respite from their fate. At least forty-two Palestinian civilians had been killed by September 2, when the army and media declared a great victory—some even called it a victory over Nahr al-Barid rather than Fatah al-Islam. It was only on October 10 that the army finally began to allow a trickle of Palestinians back to their homes, and only in the so-called "new camp," a small area that had housed two thousand families on the outskirts of the original camp. The army had been in control of the new camp, and fighting had not taken place there.

About one thousand families obtained the permits from the army and passed through the checkpoints, where soldiers and Lebanese demonstrators heckled them. They found only destruction. It was as if a giant plague of locusts had ravaged the camp. Every single home, building, apartment, and shop was destroyed. Most were also burned from the inside, and signs of the flammable liquids the soldiers had used abounded on the walls. The empty fuel canisters were left behind on the floors. Ceilings and walls were riddled with bullets shot from inside for sport. Lebanese soldiers had defecated in kitchens, on plates, bowls, and pots, as well as on mattresses. They had urinated into jars of olive oil. Most homes had been emptied of all their belongings. Furniture, appliances, sinks, toilets, televisions, refrigerators, gold jewelry, cash—all were stolen. Even the charred walls the Palestinians had been left with were not spared: insulting graffiti had been written on them, along with threats, signed by various army units. The media were not permitted in, and with few exceptions they were ignoring the plight of the Palestinians, if not reveling in it. The army's behavior confused observers. While it seemed to ignore Fatah al-Islam targets, it systematically destroyed other parts of the camp. Following the battle the army continued to treat the camp as a military zone and imposed an army engineer onto the committee planning the reconstruction, informing other members of what the army wanted done.

The army, which had never been used to defend Lebanon from external threats such as Israel, only to suppress internal dissent, and which had struggled to defeat a small band of extremists, had systematically gone through every bit of the camp and ravaged the infrastructure, destroying six decades of life to render it impossible for the Palestinians to return. All the windows were broken, electrical wiring was pulled out, copper wires stolen for resale or reuse, water pumps removed or destroyed, generators stolen or shot up. The columns typical in the camp, which supported homes, had been shot up so that the concrete was turned to rubble and the rebar exposed. Those few computers that were not stolen had been picked apart, and the RAM and hard drives were all missing. Photo albums had been torn to shreds. Every car in the camp was burned, shot up, or crushed by tanks or bulldozers. Much of the looting and destruction had taken place after the fighting ceased, or in areas where fighting never occurred. The many businesses and shops that had served much of northern Lebanon had been looted of their wares, as had pharmacies and health clinics. Palestinians reported seeing their belongings on sale in the main outdoor market in Tripoli. The camp had once been imbricated into the local economy and culture. Now the Palestinians were unwanted and rejected. For some it was not just the second time they were refugees. Apart from 1948, in 1976 many arrived from Tel al-Zaatar, a camp near Beirut that had housed twenty thousand refugees until Lebanese Christian militias besieged it, massacred many of its inhabitants, and then leveled the camp to prevent the Palestinians' return. "It is our destiny," one man said without emotion in his blackened home in Nahr al-Barid, standing by excrement the Lebanese soldiers had left behind on the kitchen floor. The total loss of life from Nahr al-Barid was fifty civilians, 179 soldiers, and 226 suspected Fatah al-Islam militants. About six thousand families lost their homes.

Palestinian children's art from this period depicts the Lebanese soldiers and Lebanese tanks destroying the camp as Israelis. Videos filmed by Lebanese soldiers circulated on the Internet, showing medical staff from the Civil Defense brigade abusing corpses and beating prisoners. Hundreds of Palestinians had been abused or tortured in Lebanese detention, and some had died from medical neglect of treatable wounds. Although still facing harassment and the occasional beating by Lebanese soldiers, hundreds of Palestinians were at work emptying their homes of rubble. One woman stood on her balcony throwing rubble from inside her home onto the broken street, where it was piled up on the sides. The majority of the Palestinians were still unable to access their homes, and could only wonder what was stolen, broken, and excreted upon. On the roof of a taller building in the new camp, I found Farhan Said Mansur, a sanitation officer standing with his wife and gazing silently across to their distant home, whose broken roof they could just make out—as if looking at Palestine, where he was born. "It is a calamity to all Palestinians," he said.

Many Salafi jihadists had escaped to the Bedawi camp. Other cells had remained in Bedawi during the fighting. The camp's security committee still had them under surveillance. Outside Bedawi I stopped with my photographer as he shot a bony horse grazing on a hill. Palestinian mechanics in the area surrounded him, holding his hand and warning him not to take pictures, because it was a Palestinian military position. We noticed concrete bunkers on the top of hills belonging to the pro-Syrian PFLP-GC. Just beyond was the army. In November the influential American-allied Lebanese leader Walid Jumblatt threatened that the Burj al-Barajneh camp in Beirut would be the next Nahr al-Barid, and the Palestinian community felt even more vulnerable. That month the Lebanese cabinet warned that Islamist militants were infiltrating other Palestinian camps. The phenomenon would be dealt with as it had in Nahr al-Barid, said the minister of information, Ghazi al-Aridi. Nobody thought to address the actual condition of Palestinians in the camps.

As the Lebanese Army celebrated its "victory" over Fatah al-Islam, its commander, Michel Suleiman, was to become the next president. He would not be the first president to have punished the Palestinians. Between 1958 and 1964, President Fouad Shehab created an elaborate, ruthless secret-service network to monitor the Palestinian camps. During his 1970–76 reign, President Suleiman Franjieh clashed with Palestinian factions, even using the air force to bomb a neighborhood thought to be pro-Palestinian. I've heard followers of assassinated president-elect Bashir Gemayel, whose Maronite Christian militia massacred Palestinians in 1976, brag that he was stopped at a checkpoint in the early years of the country's 1975–90 civil war with a trunk full of the skulls of dead Palestinians. And the leading opposition Christian leader is Michel Aoun, a retired general who participated in the 1976 killings.

"Social confinement is leading the youth to religious radicalism," says Bernard Rougier. "Youngsters are socialized by religious clerics who tell them how to understand the world and the 'true reasons' of their social exclusion. To end that situation, refugees should be allowed to work in the Lebanese society, in order for them to live under new and different influences (with a restriction: nothing should be done to naturalize them, because it could upset the Lebanese balance of power, and Palestinian refugees would be, once again, caught in the Lebanese inner contradictions; in addition to that, such naturalization would dissolve the negotiations about the right of return). So what needs to be done is to distinguish between the issues, between what is social (the right to work), what is political (and should be discussed at the regional level), and what is linked to the legal situation of Palestinian refugees in Lebanon. In order to do that, Lebanese parties would have to stop frightening the Lebanese society about the risk of *tawtin* (a condition almost impossible to meet in Lebanon)."

As Iraq became a less hospitable place for jihadists and foreign fighters, or as there were less American targets to go after, these veterans, experienced at fighting the most advanced army in the world, were looking for new battles. Andrew Exum is a former U.S. Army officer who led a platoon of light infantry in Afghanistan in 2002 and then led a platoon of Army Rangers in Iraq and Afghanistan in 2003 and 2004. He lived in Beirut from 2004 until 2006, and now researches insurgencies and militant Islamist groups at the Center for New American Security in Washington, D.C. "The fighting in Nahr al-Bared is, unfortunately, just the first round in what I fear will be a series of battles fought in the aftermath of the Iraq War," he says. "On Internet chat rooms, we're seeing militants turn away volunteers to go fight in Iraq and promising the next fight will be in Lebanon and the Gulf. Lebanon, especially, is a magnet for Sunni extremists. You not only have a haven for these groups in the Palestinian camps—with security services from rival Arab states competing for their loyalty and attention—you also have two tempting targets: both the pro-Western ruling coalition in Beirut as well as the opposition, led by a powerful bloc of Shiite parties. How can we not expect these Sunni militants, who have spent the past four years waging war on the Shiites of Iraq, to try and carry that fight onto the large, politically active Shiite population in Lebanon? Or onto the pro-Western regime that precariously hangs onto power?"

FOLLOWING THE CIVIL WAR Iraq became a less prominent topic on the jihadi web forums. In part the novelty factor wore off. But Iraq was a loss for the jihadists, and as it grew bloodier, with more civilians being targeted, it was less inspiring for aspiring jihadists than merely fighting against the crusader and occupier. But there was very little soul-searching on the forums; jihadis seemed to have moved on without a lot of serious public discussion of what went wrong. This was partly because fighting picked up in other places after 2005, especially in Afghanistan, Lebanon, and Somalia.

And while America's militaristic ambitions will likely engender violent resistance movements regardless of the ideological environment, a major reason for the growth of Al Qaeda is now something beyond anti-Americanism. It is the internal war between Sunnis and Shiites in places like Lebanon, Iraq, Pakistan, and even Yemen. Al Qaeda can no longer be seen as just a force against U.S. encroachments; it is now part of these local phenomena. In this internal war in the Muslim world, Al Qaeda has become a major driving force of Sunni-Shiite hatred. Al Qaeda in this case means something more general than the actual organization. Even in moderate Lebanon, sectarian Sunnis have been Salafized. They may not have been religious beforehand, but they view Al Qaeda as an effective way to combat perceived Shiite expansion and a potent symbol for them to reclaim their masculinity. One of the many ramifications of this is that the United States is yet again involving itself in forms of spiraling violence whose outcomes are unpredictable and whose unintended consequences will be keeping it busy for decades to come.

Part Three

◆◆◆◆◆◆◆◆◆

THE SURGE

CHAPTER SEVEN

"Iraqi Solutions for Iraqi Problems"

BY LATE 2006 IRAQ SEEMED LOST, A FAILED STATE, HEADING TOWARD Rwanda and threatening to provoke a regional conflict. There was finally a sense among Americans in Baghdad that things were going wrong. The First Cavalry Division of the U.S. Army—known as the "First Team"—took over the headquarters of Multi-National Division Baghdad (MND-B), the major U.S. military unit responsible for the city of Baghdad, in November 2006. Before its arrival, military policy was directed to handing over more authority to the Iraqi Security Forces. As one embedded planner with the Fourth Infantry, who were previously in charge of Multi-National Division Baghdad, told me, "[We were] struggling to control violence when the prime directive was to downsize and turn over responsibility to the Iraqi Security Forces as fast as humanly possible. Al Qaeda and the Mahdi Army filled the void and were trying to 'cleanse' the opposing sect from their perceived areas of influence." But the Iraqi Security Forces were hugely compromised. I was told that every new Iraqi army unit being deployed to Baghdad would first spend two weeks in the Bismaya range in Diyala to train. While training there, the Mahdi Army would contact these units and tell them to leave them alone. "The Iraqi army couldn't do the right thing if they wanted to, because politicians would pressure them," one deputy brigade commander told me.

Maj. Gen. Joseph Fil, commander of the First Cavalry Division, who in November 2006 became the commanding general of MND-B, told a subordinate in September 2006, "I don't know what we are going to do in Baghdad. I do know we are not going to keep doing what they're doing." "We were all very vested in Baghdad," a key author of the change in American strategy from the First Cavalry told me. "First Cav felt very possessive of the place and realized it was burning and that the old ways weren't working."

The new priority was to focus on protecting the Iraqi population from violence and slow down the transition to the Iraqi Security Forces. The increase in troops that would become known as the "surge" would be much more than an additional thirty thousand American troops. It heralded a change in doctrine and tactics. The Americans would live in the neighborhoods, not merely in massive Forward Operating Bases (FOBs) cordoned off from the general population, from where they would "commute to work." They would implement population-centric counterinsurgency, designed to secure, or control, the population and win their allegiance at the expense of rival guerrilla forces.

Before the surge the Americans would take Iraqi National Police (INP) units offline for extra training, including on the rule of law and human rights. It was called a "reblueing exercise," but it never worked. The Americans would go in and clear an area, leaving the INP there. In operations such as Together Forward I and II, from 2006, the American unit would report that it cleared one thousand houses and twenty mosques, and confiscated twenty AK-47s. Then they would leave the INP, and violence would get worse, as happened in Ghazaliya. It took Zarqawi to push the Iraqi Security Forces to take their work seriously, and they did this with the help of power drills and death squads, punishing Sunnis en masse until the will of the resistance was broken. It wasn't in the counterinsurgency manual, but it worked.

Baghdad was the sine qua non for everything the Americans were trying to do, but at the National Security Council they realized it was falling apart. Brett McGurk, the NSC's director for Iraq, was writing daily reports for President Bush about security in Baghdad, arguing that the military strategy was not working. In August 2006 National Security Adviser Stephen Hadley asked McGurk and Meghan O'Sullivan to work on a review of Iraq policy. All the Iraqis McGurk knew from his time in the country in 2004 were fleeing, hiding in the Green Zone, or dead. The son of one Iraqi judge he was friends with was killed right outside the Green Zone.

McGurk looked at past similar civil wars and concluded that it took a neutral force to provide a presence and stabilize the country, but the ISF wasn't neutral (and neither, of course, were the Americans). McGurk believed that the Americans did not have enough troops to achieve their ends, that their mission was not properly resourced. In the summer of 2006, he made his position clear to the president. Hadley knew that McGurk and O'Sullivan were advocates of a troop surge, but he didn't want the media to say the NSC supported such a surge, because it would immediately form antibodies before they could even do a review. He told them never to use the word "surge." Gen. John Abizaid, the commander of U.S. forces in the Middle East, was opposed to an increase in troops, as were Secretary of State Rice, Defense Secretary Rumsfeld, and Gen. George Casey, commander of U.S. forces in Iraq.

McGurk and O'Sullivan challenged Abizaid's assumptions. They saw that in battles during 2005, in the mid-Euphrates, in Al Qaim, Tal Afar, Heet, Haditha, and elsewhere, whenever the U.S. military stayed, the population turned against the insurgency and became cooperative. The Marines told them that mayors of towns had asked them not to leave. The pair were also skeptical that the Iraqi Security Forces could handle the levels of violence in Iraq, and proved that they couldn't. The Interior Ministry was mistrusted, and the Iraqi army was at risk of fracturing or disbanding, as it had in 2004, when the Americans had to restart it.

In the spring of 2006 President Bush gave a speech highlighting Nineveh province's Tal Afar to show that American strategy was working, but Tal Afar—where the Third Armored Cavalry Regiment had cleared, held, and built—was not part of the American strategy; it was an exception. McGurk and O'Sullivan were cynical that political reconciliation could end violence. People on the street were not fighting each other because the Iraqi Parliament could not agree on an oil law, they argued. They felt they could show empirically that more U.S. forces, with a different strategy, could stabilize the country and lead to security. They spoke to old Iraq hands at the CIA and saw that the agency's findings supported their position. To them a troop surge was not intended to open a space for political reconciliation; it was about building up the Iraqi Security Forces so they could hold the line and allow politics to take its course. Although many CIA analysts thought a surge would be throwing good money after bad, and was coming too late to be effective, McGurk and O'Sullivan were zealous about the need for more troops.

By the end of the summer of 2006, Bush was finally focused on changing course in Iraq. He no longer trusted Casey and Abizaid, and he wouldn't defer to the generals anymore. Although Bush was briefed every morning by a CIA official about events around the world, he asked for a special briefing by the CIA every Monday only on Iraq. But he didn't want his regular briefer from the agency; he wanted a young analyst. It was unusual for a young analyst to have that kind of access to the president. A typical analyst was a geek in an argyle sweater who was terrified by the idea of briefing the president, especially since an analyst might approach Iraq as an intellectual challenge, while Bush often flaunted his anti-intellectual credentials. When he was briefed about how the Mahdi Army was providing services to its supporters and beginning to resemble Lebanese Hizballah in its early stages, Bush was not curious and did not inquire how and why. Instead he asked, Should we kill Sadr? And what do we do to stop it? But Bush was also beginning to understand Iraqi political dynamics. He talked to Maliki regularly, one on one, through a translator. He gave Maliki advice. Bush wanted to build a special relationship with Maliki, as one leader to another leader. Others in the administration said he should not engage so frequently because he would lose leverage.

In November 2006 Bush met with Maliki in Amman. He told Maliki he would send more troops to stabilize Baghdad, but he needed his Iraqi counterpart's support. U.S. military leaders were skeptical of Maliki. They said he was sectarian and knew what was going on in the streets. But McGurk sympathized with his position; he knew Maliki would lose if he took on the Mahdi Army. Maliki wanted to work Shiite politics and weaken the Shiite militia before taking them on. The Iraqi prime minister gave Bush his commitment.

EVEN THOUGH THE SURGE was controversial at its inception, its success would become something of a proverbial truth, and the proponents of the new counterinsurgency strategy—known by its acronym, COIN—would soon become very influential over the American defense establishment. Gen. David Petraeus, with whom the surge would become identified, had spent the course of 2006 reshaping how the U.S. military thought about counterinsurgency. He effectively had a yearlong graduate course in COIN while based at the U.S. Army Combined Arms Center (USACAC) at Fort Leavenworth, Kansas, where he served as commanding general. There, along with Conrad Crane, John Nagl, Marine Gen. James Mattis, and others, he wrote the U.S. military's manual on COIN. According to the manual, called FM 3–24, the purpose was to "relearn the principles of counterinsurgency," create better learning organizations in the military, and change the Army and Marine Corps. It was not just about winning Iraq and Afghanistan; it was written "to help Army and Marine Corps leaders to conduct COIN operations *anywhere in the world*" [emphasis added].

Some in the CIA and the National Security Agency were wary when Petraeus was appointed to run the war in Iraq. In 2004 he had been in charge of training the Iraqi Security Forces. The Iraqi army had performed poorly in the battles of Najaf and Falluja, even though Petraeus was still briefing the U.S. government about how great the Iraqi Security Forces were. Battalion-level commanders were complaining that 80 percent of the Iraqi army were absent without leave and that the ones who did show were incompetent. Petraeus was considered a liar by these figures within the CIA and NSA—typical military, refusing to admit there was a problem. But Petraeus could be candid among his fellow military officers, so it was likely that in his briefing to civilians he was constrained by Rumsfeld's worldview, which obstinately refused to see the reality of disaster in Iraq.

Petraeus was not one to publicly undermine policy. He would be hailed as a "warrior scholar," but in 2004 he was still part of the "stay the course" school. In fact, in 2004 he wrote an optimistic op-ed in the *Washington Post* about the war in Iraq, which was perceived to be entering the political debate during an election year, something usually taboo for someone so high in the chain of command. In the op-ed, titled "Battling for Iraq," he listed the numbers of recruits and graduates from the Iraqi Security Forces. "I see tangible progress," he wrote. "Iraqi security elements are being rebuilt from the ground up. . . . Iraqi leaders are stepping forward, leading their country and their security forces courageously." Though he admitted there were setbacks, he insisted there were "reasons for optimism." "Iraq's security forces are, however, developing steadily and they are in the fight. Momentum has gathered in recent months. With strong Iraqi leaders out front and with continued coalition—and now NATO—support, this trend will continue. It will not be easy, but few worthwhile things are."

Perhaps a clue to Petraeus's real thinking is the fact that by the end of 2005 he was back in the United States working on the new counterinsurgency manual, which turned out to be a scathing critique of how the military had been fighting the war in Iraq. Similarly, between 2003 and 2004, he had opposed Bremer's de-Baathification, dismissal of the Iraqi army, and free-market reforms in Iraq. He e-mailed his men, telling them to ignore Bremer, basically urging insubordination. Petraeus wanted to provide stability in Iraq and knew Bremer was destabilizing the country.

Petraeus was a masterful bureaucrat. He took an Army that was focused on fighting a conventional war—whose standard practice, in the words of a State Department official I spoke to, was to place their boots on the heads of Iraqi men they were detaining—and got it to "turn on a dime to fight an insurgency." Petraeus would become the most influential U.S. general since George C. Marshall. The surge would also be seen as a panacea to U.S. problems in Afghanistan. The story I tell in the next chapters is more complicated than both Petraeus's hagiographers and critics claim.

ALMOST ON ARRIVAL in February 2007 Petraeus headed straight to Ramadi, capital of the Anbar province, to see Col. Sean McFarland of the First Brigade, First Armored Division. McFarland's brigade had been in Ramadi since June 2006. Before that they had been in Tal Afar, where soldiers were practicing an approach called "clear, hold, and build" and living in combat outposts (COPs) with the townspeople. While these outposts initially suffered heavy attacks, in battle the Americans usually dominated, and attacks fell after the first summer.

(Capt. Robert Chamberlin believed the real reason Tal Afar was pacified was the cleansing of its Sunnis and the tacit American support this received. After serving in Tal Afar he wrote an article in *Military Review* in 2008. "Shiites now dominate a community that was formerly 70 percent Sunni," he explained. "Shiites made up 98 percent of the applicant pool in a July 2007 recruiting drive for the local police. The Sunnis moved to nearby villages and sought shelter with families and tribes, but they still think of Tal Afar as 'their' city.")

Living in COPs allowed the Americans to have greater access to Ramadi's infrastructure and to reach out to local leaders. In the early days of the U.S. invasion, these leaders had generally supported the resistance. They eventually turned against Al Qaeda, but their attempts to expel the group in 2005 failed.

The tribes were crushed, killed, and forced to flee. This time they had American support; that made a difference.

McFarland initially found a city dominated by Al Qaeda–linked groups with almost no Iraqi Security Forces. He set up tribal militias called provisional auxiliary police and stationed them so they could protect their own area. The Americans protected the homes of collaborating tribal leaders. Instead of warning that they would soon be leaving, the Americans promised to remain as long as it took. McFarland believed it was his attempt to recruit thousands of locals to the Iraqi police that led to what would be called the Sons of Iraq program—known in Arabic as Al Sahwa (the Awakening)—in which previously antagonistic Sunni militias began to cooperate with the Americans. Brutal Al Qaeda retaliatory attacks on police and the tribal leaders who backed them increased local hatred of the group.

The Americans found a young "sheikh" called Sattar Abu Risha. He was not exactly a tribal leader, and he was not exactly fighting for freedom, but he was willing to fight Al Qaeda in return for American support. Unlike past rebellions against Al Qaeda, this time the Americans propped up their new ally. They had two Marine battalions in downtown Ramadi, and they parked a tank in Abu Risha's front yard and visited him twice a day. In September 2007 Abu Risha held a conference establishing the Anbar Awakening. More and more tribes in the area joined. When Awakening tribes were attacked, the Americans provided air and armor support and rescued them.

"The enemy overplayed its hand and the people were tired of Al-Qaeda," McFarland wrote in a 2008 article in *Military Review*. "A series of assassinations had elevated younger, more aggressive tribal leaders to positions of influence. A growing concern that the U.S. would leave Iraq and leave the Sunnis defenseless against Al-Qaeda and Iranian-supported militias made these younger leaders open to our overtures. Our willingness to adapt our plans based on the advice of the sheiks, our staunch and timely support for them in times of danger and need, and our ability to deliver on our promises convinced them that they could do business with us. Our forward presence kept them reassured." Petraeus supported the introduction of the Awakening phenomenon elsewhere. Paying people who used to shoot at Americans was a radical step, but he did not consult his chain of command. "Petraeus did what he wanted to do and sought approval after, and he had enough clout to do it," an American intelligence official told me.

IN DECEMBER 2006, when Washington began to push new troops to Baghdad, General Casey, the head of Multi-National Forces Iraq (MNF-I)—the U.S. military formation that provided overall command and control for operations in Iraq—summoned the Iraqis and laid out the new "surge" plan with Prime

Minister Maliki, Defense Minister Abdul Qader Muhammad Jassim, Interior Minister Jawad al-Bolani, and the First Cavalry team. The Americans called it the Baghdad Security Plan, while the Iraqis called it Fard al-Qanun (Imposing the Law). Maliki approved the concept and committed to bringing in more Iraqi troops and letting the Americans "target all criminals," which included Shiite militias and Sadrists. It was a momentous step for Maliki, whose collaboration with Shiite militias was viewed by the Americans as an obstacle to their goals.

Proponents of counterinsurgency obsessively study the history of so-called "small wars," such as the British war in Malaya, the American war in the Philippines, the French war in Algeria, and the wars in Vietnam. Their doctrine emphasizes using the least amount of violence against the enemy, becoming familiar with the occupied country's culture, and working to remove support for the insurgents. While this requires killing those who cannot be "reconciled," it also requires creating local proxy forces and finding political solutions that the civilian population can see as a better alternative to backing insurgents. Proponents of COIN strategy realized that American tactics in Iraq had until then relied on brute force and killing.

COIN theorists never answered (or even asked) questions such as, Should the Americans have invaded Iraq or Afghanistan in the first place, or should they be occupying other countries? Instead they focused on practical matters such as implementation. To them the American reliance on brute force was counterproductive, and the numerous "decapitation operations" in which insurgent leaders were assassinated were not useful. They exhorted less violence, fewer "kinetic operations," which only alienated people. They urged military and civilian agencies to collaborate and to understand the concerns of the people and address them, providing security and responding to their grievances.

American casualties peaked when their forces were involved in clearing insurgents from the belts. Once they transitioned to the hold-and-build phase, U.S. casualties declined drastically. But the extent to which the Americans protected the Iraqi population during the surge has been romanticized. American airstrikes killed more than 250 civilians in Iraq in 2006 but more than 940 in 2007 and another 400 in 2008. Thus, Americans killed more civilians in 2008 than in 2006, at the peak of the civil war—this despite the fact that the much-lauded scripture of the military's COIN manual states, "The employment of airpower in the strike role should be done with exceptional care. . . . Even when justified under the law of war, bombing a target that results in civilian casualties will bring media coverage that works to the benefit of the insurgents." In addition, artillery was used often during the surge for the purpose of "terrain denial," even when that terrain was a populated area. This must not have felt very population-centric to the population.

On January 11, 2007, the "Crisis Committee" had its first meeting in Baghdad, at which the Baghdad Operation Center was set up and Lieut. Gen. Abud Qanbar was designated as its commander. The BOC was formed to give the Americans a counterpart in the battle of Baghdad, to be Maliki's face in Fard al-Qanun.

Initially, the Americans didn't want the BOC to be under Maliki's direct control; they wanted it to be under the Defense Ministry's command. Nor did they want Qanbar to lead it at first. The Iraqi general seemed too Soviet in his style and was too close to Maliki, but Qanbar proved flexible and able to learn. Brig. Gen. John Campbell, deputy commander of the First Cavalry Regiment, mentored Qanbar and also played a vital role in the success of the Awakening. He took Qanbar to meet some of the Awakening men, and Qanbar realized he knew them from the Saddam-era military. "Brigadier General Campbell had exceptional rapport with our Iraqi partners," observed Maj. Andy Morgado, who served as a division maneuver planner and later as a combined arms battalion operations officer.

Multi-National Forces-Iraq—headed by General Casey at the beginning of the surge, then by General Petraeus, and then by Gen. Raymond Odierno—was the overall strategic headquarters for U.S. coalition forces. Multi-National Corps-Iraq (MNC-I), the tactical unit responsible for command and control of operations in Iraq, was supposed to coordinate the actions of its subordinate divisions: Multi-National Division-Baghdad and Multi-National Division-Center, which was responsible for area south of Baghdad.

Lieut. Col. Steve Miska, who served as a deputy brigade commander throughout Baghdad during the surge, told me that the additional soldiers provided a greater density of troops for more effective partnership with the Iraqi Security Forces. But another factor was important. In Baghdad, before the surge, none of the boundaries separating American forces matched those used by Iraqi forces, and none of those boundaries matched the political lines of *baladiyas* (local municipalities). As a result it was difficult to synchronize with local politicians or security forces, and there was little American integration or coordination with the ISF. The surge realigned the military boundaries with the political boundaries. "That allowed for sustained relationships between the Iraqi army, coalition forces, and political leaders," Miska explained. "It restored confidence among the populace in many cases. The overall surge strategy realigned the Iraqi army boundaries to match the district boundaries in Baghdad. We did the same for the U.S. boundaries. The effect was that now the same U.S. and Iraqi commanders would work with the same local politicians to resolve issues."

The lines for the ten Baghdad "security districts" were drawn on a map by Lieut. Col. Douglas Ollivant, chief of plans for MND-B, and Major General Ali of the Iraqi Ministry defense staff, who had studied at Sandhurst (in 1971), the Indian Staff College, and the NATO staff college in Italy, and who spoke English well. Each of the districts would be under the authority of an Iraqi army or Iraqi National Police headquarters. This was a key meeting, where strategic boundaries were being drawn, and yet nobody from Corps, as Odierno's staff was called, was present except for a very junior major who was there only as a note-taker. The surge plan was drawn up by Brigadier General Campbell, Colonel Toby Green, and Lieutenant Colonel Ollivant with little guidance from Multi-National Corps-Iraq. General Casey was present, however, giving very specific guidance. It was Casey who suggested creating joint security stations in Baghdad.

In addition to the role played by McGurk and O'Sullivan, two outsiders played a crucial role in the push for more troops. Fred Kagan and Gen. Jack Keane are controversial figures: the former is a neoconservative military historian with no experience or specialization in the Middle East; the latter an imposing and intimidating retired general with a forceful personality. But they were effective because they provided a public voice arguing that a troop surge could work. While working on this book I met American officials who loved them or hated them, who attributed the whole surge to them or denied they had any significant role. "Success has many fathers," one lieutenant colonel explained, and the surge was the only positive development anyone could point to in America's catastrophic occupation of Iraq.

In 2006 there were many voices calling for either an American withdrawal or an increase in American troops. Colin Kahl of Georgetown University and then the Center for New American Security visited Iraq in the summer of that year. Based on his experience he called for more troops or for a withdrawal, but he was ignored as an outsider and a Democratic partisan. (President Obama would later install him as Deputy Assistant Secretary of Defense for the Middle East.) There was a joint push for more troops coming from the NSC and the Keane/Kagan duo. Keane, who looked at Iraq from a purely military view, was the most consistent and longstanding advocate of a troop increase. "He was always poking," one NSC member told me. J.D. Crouch, the deputy national security adviser, hosted an Iraq review in December 2006. He convened small groups in which he appeared neutral, but he steered skeptics to the surge—and then convinced his boss, Stephen Hadley. One lieutenant colonel involved in the surge described Kagan as "just a blowhard who could be counted on to give the party line in print when he returned from each of his Petraeus-sponsored trips." But another lieutenant colonel described him as a brilliant and rigorous thinker. "Kagan is the main guy behind the push for more troops, and Keane is an idiot," he told me, adding, for good measure, that Casey and Fil were also idiots. Although neoconservatives have traditionally been advocates of increased reliance on airpower, Kagan broke with this neoconservative predilection for "shock and awe" tactics. Instead he believed that war was about influencing people on the ground, and thus required more troops. Kagan provided Bush with an alternative to the Senate's Iraq Study Group report, which advocated a reduction in troops.

An internal NSC review and Keane's force of will persuaded the president to change course in Iraq. The push out of Washington for more troops was then utilized by Multi-National Division-Baghdad, with some oversight from General Casey, to secure Baghdad. General Odierno had a very different concept, his critics told me. "He wanted to use the troops out in the 'Baghdad belts' to go kill Sunnis," one senior American officer said. Odierno's role was "totally blown out of proportion," according to one of the architects of the surge in Baghdad, "and I don't think he really figures in the picture." Major Morgado strongly disagrees: "Though Baghdad was a large problem set, it was not the only problem set," he said.

There was a serious and heated internal debate among the Americans in Baghdad, both between different headquarters and within them, over whether they should focus on population security or continue to capture and kill. Advocates of the latter approach, of which Odierno apparently was the champion, saw which way the wind was blowing, aped the new COIN language, and called their method "clearing," as in "clear, hold, and build" or "clear, control, and retain."

But Morgado disagreed with this description of Odierno's philosophy. "Maliki wanted to go and kill Sunnis," he told me. "By putting a larger American presence in the belts, it stopped Maliki from pursuing this aim, and it allowed Americans to effectively interdict lines of communication and thereby stop accelerants of the violence. The Awakening would have been hard-pressed to happen if Maliki was allowed to unleash a one-sided assault on the Sunnis in the belts."

General Petraeus and the bulk of MND-B were focused on providing security to the Iraqi population. Odierno and some other elements—most notably the Third Stryker Brigade combat team, Second Infantry Division, under the command of Steve Townsend—wanted to keep "clearing," the most violent part of the "clear, hold, and build" process. Odierno tasked the Third Infantry Division to lead the organization of Multi-National Division-Central and facilitate the fight in the belts outside Baghdad. As airpower advocates have noted, more bombs were dropped in 2007 in MND-C's area of operations than at any time earlier in the war. While Baghdad was focused on population security (despite some internal dissidents and occasional lapses), MND-C was still killing and capturing until much later, when the Awakening groups were established there too.

Odierno wanted to reduce the influence of MND-B (the major institutional proponent of executing the surge) and transfer terrain to the other units that shared his focus on killing and capturing. Odierno could never directly say,

"Don't secure the population," since Petraeus would overturn that, but he could nibble away at MND-B's influence. (Morgado denied that his old boss had any obsession with killing. "I believe General Odierno sensed weakness in General Fil," he said. "Odierno used to talk about reconciling with various parties back in 2003 to 2004. This was not a new concept for him.")

Most interlocutors I dealt with from the military and National Security Council agreed that Odierno was neither a visionary nor a strategist. "Petraeus is an A who hires A-pluses," one American intelligence analyst dealing with Iraq told me. "Odierno is a B who hires Cs." Petraeus also had the star power to handpick whomever he wanted, which led to the creation of a coterie of West Point graduates and within that a smaller group of graduates from West Point's social sciences department. Petraeus made COIN the universal policy, and thanks to his status he was able to sell an increase in troops to the American people and Congress despite their growing antiwar mood.

Though the surge was Baghdad-oriented, the increased troop numbers also allowed the Americans to operate in the "belts" that surrounded the city. Odierno's role in the belts was a key element. He took the concept of the surge and decided where to put troops. "He is not a bright guy, and he didn't have bright guys around him, but he figured out how to fight the battle of Baghdad," one insider told me. If Doug Ollivant and others at First Cav were the architects of the surge, Odierno was the builder, the operational realizer. Morgado served in Balad, north of Baghdad, between July and November 2007. "Al Qaeda in Iraq had freedom of maneuver in the belts," he explained. "This gave them unlimited opportunities to marshal resources in the hinterlands, use multiple avenues to infiltrate supplies and weapons into Baghdad, and conduct attacks. Al Qaeda, with this latitude, was free to conduct attacks on Shiites and act as an accelerant for retribution by the Mahdi Army or other Shiites.

"While U.S. and Iraqi forces kept the Shiites under control in Baghdad, U.S.-led efforts in the belts kept the Sunnis/Al Qaeda off-balance. Both efforts depended on the other, but the belts clearly supported the efforts within Baghdad. I thought it was critical for U.S. forces to lead in the belts. We stood up the Sons of Iraq and brought the Sunnis into the 'good guy' side of the ledger. I don't think this was feasible or desirable by a Maliki-led effort. His solution to the Sunni problem would have been 'Kill them all' and only would have exacerbated the problem. Though the Sons of Iraq pose a political problem now and in the future, these are much better conditions."

Balad is a Shiite-dominated town surrounded by rural Sunni communities. By the time Morgado arrived in Balad, the Mahdi Army had been largely put down, while most Sunnis within the town had been chased out or killed. Morgado's principal threat remained Al Qaeda in Iraq and associated groups. "We were tight along the Salahaddin/Diyala fault line," he said. "Their lines of communication ran from Samarra and Anbar in the west, from Baquba in the east, and Mosul to the north. In turn, they would use the Balad area to stage attacks in Baghdad/Taji area in the south."

The first Sons of Iraq group was "stood up" in Balad in August 2007. Morgado's battalion cultivated six of these groups, putting about 200 individuals on the payroll. "They were extremely effective. Once these groups stood up, Al Qaeda went after them hard, but they remained resilient. With largely Sons of Iraq influence, we began capturing or killing every major high-value target we had, and attacks in our zone decreased dramatically. It was clear with the Sons of Iraq that part of their motivation was monetary, but largely they were tired of the violence. Their allegiance with Al Qaeda only brought them death and instability. By working with us, they realized they could stabilize the community. Knowing that we were providing support to these groups, monetarily and operationally, gave them a lot of confidence."

When Bush announced his surge in January 2007, I thought it was too late for the Americans to make a difference. I had spent four years writing about the oppressive nature of the American occupation, and I didn't see how enlarging it could make things better. General Petraeus himself asserted that military gains would be ephemeral if Iraq's factions did not reach political deals. It seemed as if more troops might only provoke further resistance, or if not, that a few thousand more troops couldn't possibly halt the civil war and affect the situation in Iraq strategically. But the addition of more American troops also forced other armed factions in Iraq to change their plans and actions.

According to Lieutenant Colonel Miska, the introduction of combat outposts, smaller bases inside neighborhoods, and joint security stations where Americans lived and worked with Iraqi security forces allowed the Americans to integrate the Iraqi army, Iraqi police, and U.S. forces into an overall security plan. "We were commuting to work, but an insurgent lives among the people, so you must do it too," he told me. "We started doing this in Ghazaliya before the surge. Ghazaliya was a killing field. The Mahdi Army was attacking from Shula and the north, Al Qaeda was attacking from the south. The first combat outpost we put in was on the sectarian fault line between the two sides. We set it up with the Iraqi army, and within a week some stores opened up, people came in. We were there in a sustained presence and wouldn't leave them. It helped set up Sons of Iraq; people realized Americans could be an ally."

Miska said that the Sons of Iraq were originally organized to fill a gap in local security, predominantly because the local police would not provide security to the Sunni population areas. During the surge, the Americans started placing combat outposts (COPs) and joint security stations (JSSs) along the sectarian fault lines and right in the Sunni areas because the need was greatest there. "Al Qaeda held the Sunni population hostage in neighborhoods like Amriya, where the flagpole of Al Qaeda of Mesopotamia was planted," he said. "I think part of the reason the Sons of Iraq came to us in Amriya and Ghazaliya was that they saw the Americans were committed to protecting the Sunni people. Nobody else had a stake in the game—not the police, not the Iraqi army or the Iraqi government."

More than the surge itself, the declaration of the surge forced armed factions in Iraq to change their calculations. Sunni militias who resented Al Qaeda or were already in conflict realized that the Americans were no longer aiding the "Iranians" whom Sunnis saw as their fundamental enemy. Instead they saw the Americans acting to limit Iranian influence. They saw that the Americans would back them against Al Qaeda and would not abandon them, as they had previously done with Sunni collaborators. Controlling the Anbar province and cutting it off from Sunni strongholds in western Baghdad denied Al Qaeda some of its strategic depth and access to its hinterland. This weakened it and allowed Sunni groups opposed to Al Qaeda to take advantage of the opening. These Sunni groups might have been more skeptical of the Americans had they not seen the success of their Anbari brethren, who began collaborating with Americans against Al Qaeda groups in the summer of 2006 and helped turn one of the most dangerous parts of Iraq into one of the least violent.

There had always been infighting between Sunni resistance groups, but they tried to minimize these publicly to maintain the appearance of a united front. Al Qaeda tried to Iraqify itself after the death of Zarqawi, with Iraqis as its official leaders, controlling the Mujahideen Advisory Council. The increased sectarian violence and aggressive Shiite push forced Sunni groups to rally together and work with Al Qaeda. But Al Qaeda members acted like gang leaders, terrorizing local populations more than fighting the occupier. Local religious, tribal, and traditional leaders, as well as educated elites, were either killed, co-opted, or expelled. Often the population followed them out, turning areas into ghost towns.

In October 2006 Al Qaeda announced the creation of its Islamic state in Iraq. It was not about liberating Iraq from the occupation; it was about a larger global war. But most of the Iraqi resistance had no appetite for this sort of global jihad. Resistance groups began to feud with Al Qaeda, as leaders were assassinated. In 2007 the Islamic Army of Iraq publicly broke with Al Qaeda, condemning its tactics and claiming that thirty members of the Islamic Army had been killed by Al Qaeda. These clashes began in Amriya. That year three leading resistance groups established the Jihad and Reform Front, which condemned Al Qaeda's tactics (such as targeting civilians) and goals.

Al Qaeda men condemned tribal traditions for being un-Islamic, and actively undermined or usurped traditional authority. This alienated local communities. During the modernizing era of the 1970s, tribes were marginalized as the state asserted itself. But in the '80s tribes were co-opted and armed in the war against Iran. Tribalism was used by the regime, and tribal leaders who proved loyal servants were empowered. Although tribal leaders were initially ignored by the occupation, the Americans also began to co-opt and collaborate with them during the surge, empowering them to rebel against Al Qaeda.

Sunnis in Anbar might have opposed the occupation, but they also wanted stability, and Al Qaeda brought only chaos. The Sunni tribal "Awakening" began in Anbar, led by Sheikh Sattar Abu Risha. Soon other tribal leaders joined him. Many were not important or powerful until the Americans empowered them. Abu Risha himself was widely known as a highway robber, operating on the highway between Baghdad and Amman. His conflict with Al Qaeda might have had more to do with a dispute over looted goods than ideology. But when Al Qaeda killed his tribesmen, a blood feud between it and the tribes started. Al Qaeda taxes on smuggling also made tribal leaders chafe. The explicit American shift in emphasis from killing the enemy to protecting the population allowed it to be more subtle when dealing with resistance groups. By the end of 2006, the Syrians had also cracked down on illegal border crossings, closing some of the routes Al Qaeda relied on for personnel and supplies. As for Sheikh Sattar, shortly after meeting President Bush, he was blown up outside his home in September 2007, which was probably convenient for both the Iraqi government and the Americans, who now no longer had the problem of disposing of him once he outlived his usefulness.

At the same time, the Sadrists were facing a backlash from fatigued Shiites who saw them as an onerous gang. An increase in American troops focusing on Baghdad was guaranteed to lead to a crackdown on the Mahdi Army, and Muqtada al-Sadr always retreated before the Americans could defeat him, a lesson from his 2004 experience in Najaf. But if his people could lie low and wait for the Americans to reduce their troops once more, they could emerge unscathed and even benefit by letting the Americans cull his ranks of disobedient and criminal-minded elements, strengthening his control.

By the summer of 2007, tension between Maliki and the Sadrists had increased. Though the Sadrists had backed Maliki's rise to power, they now withdrew from the government, hoping to weaken him. Maliki went so far as to compare Sadrists with Baathists. On the other hand, many of the Sadrists in the government were viewed as corrupt and brutal, so it is also possible that Muqtada withdrew them to clean his movement's image. The year 2006 was supposed to be the year of the police, according to the Americans. Instead it was the year the police and Mahdi Army became one. The rank and file were dominated by Sadrists. Officers were terrified of their own men. The Mahdi Army took for granted its authority over certain areas. Nobody could challenge the Sadrists—not the Iraqi Security Forces and not the Americans. Just like Sunni criminals using *fatwas* to justify their crimes under the guise of Al Qaeda, so too did Shiite criminals profit from the booty they seized from Sunnis under the guise of Mahdi Army activities. As a result of its criminal activities, seizure of Sunni property, and control over essential services such as gas and benzene distribution, the Mahdi Army was well funded. Its wealth also allowed it to provide social services so as to maintain and even increase its base of support from urban youth to the many families it now assisted, especially among the displaced.

Control over its men was always a concern for the Mahdi Army leadership. As leaders were arrested, younger, less-disciplined fighters gained more control. Different Mahdi Army units fought each other. As Mahdi Army territory increased, its leadership lost control over local units. Splinter groups terrorized and preyed on people in the name of the Mahdi Army. Even supporters of the Sadrists began to resent the Mahdi Army.

In the summer of 2007, six months into the surge, the Mahdi Army was still cleansing Sunnis in areas like Hurriya. Although Hurriya was majority-Shiite, its Sunnis were well organized and strong. Shiites were initially on the defensive, with many of their civilians killed on a daily basis. To defeat the threat of Sunni militias, the Mahdi Army systematically cleansed all the areas and began to encroach on the nearby majority-Sunni Adil neighborhood. The assassination of businessmen and religious leaders struck fear into the community, weakening it and facilitating its flight. Following attacks on Shiites, the Mahdi Army would pile Sunni corpses on streets in revenge. Amriya and Ghazaliya were the last two neighborhoods in western Baghdad still fully in Sunni hands. Dora was still contested. In eastern Baghdad, only Adhamiya remained in Sunni hands.

In late August 2007, Mahdi Army men clashed with opponents from the Supreme Council in Karbala. About one hundred people were killed and much property was destroyed while hundreds of thousands of pilgrims were in the city to mark the Mahdi's birthday. An outraged Maliki, who considered Karbala his town, flew down and made it clear he was the boss, wearing a pistol and giving orders to his special forces to secure the city and arrest Mahdi Army men, in some cases leading his own men into neighborhoods. Maliki realized that the Mahdi Army could threaten his authority. On August 29 Muqtada declared a *tajmid* (freeze), ordering his army to halt its operations for six months. Soon after he turned on unruly members of his movement, killing or expelling them.

The Mahdi Army cease-fire was the most important factor in the decline in violence. Until the freeze, eight months into the surge, the civil war was still raging and Sunnis were being cleansed from Shiite neighborhoods that had already been walled off. The militias were still advancing on the west side of the Tigris, far from their base in the east, until the freeze halted their advance all at once. The freeze would cost the movement dearly, because in a way its expansion was its purpose. Sadrists had few firm principles except being opposed to the occupation and federalism. The movement represented the angry, dispossessed poor, and it had to express their anger in some way. By the time of the freeze the sectarian killings were beginning to decline. But now the Mahdi Army was in control of areas where it did not have a natural constituency, such as with middle-class or better-educated Shiites. With the increase in American troops and change in their tactics, the Mahdi Army was also less necessary for self-defense, and its excesses were harder for Shiites to tolerate.

A lesser-known element in the new counterinsurgency approach was increased attacks against the Mahdi Army's key nodes, support zones, and capabilities. Protecting the population through bases inside neighborhoods and erecting concrete walls were the most obvious and essential elements. But the Americans also increased their offensive action against the Mahdi Army both inside and outside Baghdad. This was a key reason for Muqtada's cease-fire. From February to August 2007, the Americans and their allies arrested an average of one thousand suspected Mahdi Army men per month, and killed many as well. This had a chilling effect on the Shiite militia. The Mahdi Army cease-fire held despite attempts by the Supreme Council and other rivals to provoke the Sadrists into confrontations.

According to Miska, the cease-fire was not declared because Muqtada had a change of heart about the United States. "He did it because most of his militia was fragmented and out of control," he said. "In order to regain control, he issued the cease-fire. Any elements that did not obey the cease-fire would be subject to discipline. Discipline was sometimes doled out by elements we called 'Golden JAM' [U.S. military used the acronym JAM—for Jaish al-Mahdi—to describe the Mahdi Army] coming from Najaf to kill rogue leaders and elements. Sometimes the U.S. forces collaborated with the Golden JAM to get the same targets. We also coordinated with moderate members of JAM against more extremist elements. The majority of JAM would never admit this, but it did happen in very subtle and discreet ways. There are many different flavors of the Mahdi Army, its many different members acting for different motives, using the name of the organization."

Not all factions were so cooperative. Miska described a 2007 battle by the shrine in Kadhimiya in which the American unit called Iraqi Security Forces for help but none of them came. A Sadrist Parliament member, Baha al-Araji, was sitting in the Iraqi brigade commander's office telling him not to assist the Americans. "The next day Araji introduced a resolution in Parliament to prevent Americans from coming within a certain radius of the shrine to create a sanctuary for JAM to operate," Miska said. "It didn't pass, but it set back American relationships."

Mahdi Army fighters from different areas would come in to place explosively formed penetrators (EFPs)—a more powerful type of IED—targeting the Americans and the Iraqi general in charge. Normally they would warn civilians to leave beforehand. "There was one particular period after a firefight with the Mahdi Army in Kadhimiyah in April 2007," Miska said. "Prior to the firefight we did not have an IED in six months in the neighborhood. After the firefight we were getting banged with EFPs right outside our gates. We were able to prevent most of the attacks, but some still achieved success. The people were very frustrated about all of the Mahdi Army attacks in Kadhimiyah. But Mahdi elements played on the fears that the infidels were threatening the sanctity of the shrine. Finally in August, my truck got hit with an EFP during a combined patrol. Eleven people hit the ground wounded when the bomb went off. Eight ambulances pulled up to the scene within thirty seconds of the blast. Casualties were quickly hauled away. No U.S. or Iraqi soldiers were wounded. The backlash from the people was quick. A senior leader approached us and asked to broker a deal. If we would agree to bring a former Mahdi Army leader back from hiding in Iran, he would promise to keep the 'bad' Mahdi Army out of Kadhimiya. We gave the former leader thirty days to make a difference. He lived up to his end of the deal, since no further Iranian bombs [EFPs] went off in Kadhimiya. We promised not to detain him as long as he did not conduct extremist activities against the Iraqi people or our forces."

Unlike the Mahdi Army, Al Qaeda took longer to change its calculations. Its ranks were reduced as the Americans targeted them with better intelligence, the Iraqi security forces attacked them, Awakening men turned on them, and they outstayed their welcome in most Sunni areas. American commanders on their third tour of Iraq were beginning to figure out how to do things better; crucially, they demonstrated an improved ability to take advantage of social dynamics in Iraq. The increase in troops also allowed them to take more action without the same limitations. "It's unclear if the surge would have worked a year earlier," John Nagl told me. "Sunnis didn't realize they had lost and the American military wasn't ready."

The Americans called these new Sunni militias neighborhood watch groups, concerned local citizens, Iraqi Security Volunteers, or Critical Infrastructure Security guards. These groups were paid by the U.S. military and operated in much of the country, employing former fighters and often empowering them, to the fury of the Shiite-dominated government as well as the Shiite militias, who thought they had defeated the Sunnis, just to see them trying to regain power through the backdoor. The Americans euphemistically called it "Iraqi solutions for Iraqi problems." General Petraeus paid these former insurgents without first getting approval from Washington. Control over the war had devolved to the field.

Another key dynamic that was fortuitous for the Americans was the success of the sectarian cleansing operations. Militias had consolidated their control; clear front lines were developing. Many Sunni neighborhoods were depopulated. There was nowhere for Sunni militias to hide. The majority of the Iraqi refugees abroad were Sunnis. The Shiites had won the civil war. In 2007 the Bush administration and the U.S. military stopped talking of Iraq as a grand project of nation building, and the American media dutifully obeyed. Any larger narrative was abandoned, and Iraq was presented as a series of small pieces. Just as Iraq was being physically deconstructed, so too was it being intellectually deconstructed, not as a state undergoing transition but as small stories of local heroes and villains, of well-meaning American soldiers, of good news here and progress there. But it was too early to tell if the whole was less or greater than the sum of its parts.

Ghost Town

I decided to visit those parts to find out for myself. In December 2007, I took advantage of the lull in Iraq's civil war to visit areas that had been no-go zones a year earlier. Baghdad's neighborhoods were walled-off islands, but Iraqis could now visit areas outside their own for the first time in a year or two. The checkpoints manned by the Iraqi Security Forces were no longer as feared, but a foreign journalist was still a tempting commodity. Iraqis knew to make jokes when stopped, to assess if their interlocutor was a Sunni or Shiite, and to use the right kind of slang. For $250 in Baghdad's Sadr City I purchased two fake Iraqi National Identity cards: one Sunni name and one Shiite name. It was something many Iraqis had done as the "killings over identity" got worse.

I started in Dora, one of Baghdad's most fearsome neighborhoods. Dora was a formerly mixed area in southern Baghdad with a majority-Sunni population. It was once a good place to live, with many expensive villas; but their prices had fallen dramatically since 2005, when Sunni militias began to expel Shiites and Christians. The Sunni militiamen who cleansed much of Dora lived in the surrounding rural areas, such as Arab Jubur and Hor Rajab. Criminal gangs took advantage of the chaos to target anybody with money for kidnapping and ransom. As the Iraqi Security Forces strengthened and were populated by supporters or members of sectarian Shiite militias, Sunnis from the Shiite areas of southern Baghdad were cleansed. Soon Sunni and Shiite areas exchanged volleys of mortars, and front lines were drawn between neighbors and friends. Shiites moved into empty Sunni homes and Sunnis moved into empty Shiite homes, creating a further incentive for violence that was part criminal and part sectarian. As Sunni militias radicalized and became more anti-Shiite, Sunnis grew to depend on Al Qaeda and the Islamic State of Iraq's fighters for protection against the Shiite militias. Motivated less by nationalism or any interest in the notion of Iraq, and more by grander Manichaean ambitions to fight the West or establish an Islamic emirate, these radical jihadist groups became a golem, terrorizing the very Sunnis looking to them for protection and often acting like criminal gangs. Dora was easily accessible from the southern belts of Baghdad, allowing Al Qaeda to cross the Tigris and enter Karada and other Shiite areas. Dora was also on the highway to Baghdad from the south and adjacent to the still-contested Seidiya neighborhood.

Dora was undergoing a radical transformation that I could not clearly see when I visited in late 2007. Much of Dora, it seemed to me, was a ghost town. I walked down Sixtieth Street in an area called Mekanik with one Sunni militia. Tall concrete walls built by the Americans divided parts of it, separating warring factions. Lakes and rivers of mud and sewage choked the streets, with mountains of trash dividing them. Most of the windows of the one- or two-story homes were broken. The wind blew through them, whistling eerily. House after house and block after block were deserted, bullet holes pockmarking their walls, their doors open. Many were emptied of furniture; in others the furniture was covered by a thick layer of the fine dust that invades every space in Iraq. Apart from our footsteps, there was complete silence.

My guide was a thirty-year-old man called Osama, who grew up in this neighborhood. He pointed to shops he used to go to, now empty or destroyed, a barbershop that had belonged to a Shiite man, a hardware store that had belonged to a Sunni man. "This is all my neighborhood," Osama told me. He wore jeans, a sweater, and a baseball cap, and had a slight baby face concealed by stubble. The previous U.S. Army unit had not been active in his area, he told me. "They were really cowards," he said. "They let Al Qaeda and the Mahdi Army fight."

We passed by the Ibn Sinna elementary school, which had served as a dividing line between Al Qaeda and the Mahdi Army. We continued and he showed me a Shiite mosque that in previous incarnations had been a cafe and before the war a Baath Party office. He pointed to the destroyed mosque. "The Mahdi Army was killing people here," he said. "They were torturing people and the people destroyed it. They were shooting on our neighborhood. The Americans raided it; it was a great day. If I find somebody from the Mahdi Army I would kill him right away, not give him to the coalition forces."

Osama had lost many friends and relatives in the civil war. When we drove past the nearby district of Baya, he pointed to the gas station. "The Baya fuel station is all Mahdi Army," he said. "They killed my uncle here. He didn't accept to leave. Twenty guys came to the house, the women were screaming. He ran to the back, but they caught him, tortured him, and killed him." The Mahdi Army also targeted men with Sunni names. "I have three friends called Omar," Osama told me, "all killed."

Osama said the Mahdi Army freeze was "bullshit." In the nearby area of Seidiya, he said, "two days ago they blew up the Sunni Ibrahim al-Khalil Mosque. The Mahdi Army is still killing people. Twenty days ago they killed three Sunni civilians who came back because they heard it was safe." The

Mahdi Army was Iran, he told me, the Quds Force. "The Mahdi Army is not listening to Muqtada and Muqtada is lying," he said. "The Mahdi Army made Al Qaeda come here to defend people, but then Al Qaeda was worse. The government sucks; you know they are all corrupt. Then after a few months Al Qaeda became corrupt."

Osama had been a translator working with the Americans; then he had moved on to sign lucrative construction and sanitation contracts with the American company KBR. Al Qaeda got wind that he worked as a contractor for the Americans, and he felt threatened. He and a network of friends of his in the neighborhood started acting as sources for the Americans, sometimes riding along in U.S. Army vehicles with their faces masked to point out suspects.

Osama and his men were first contracted by the American military under Lieut. Col. Jim Crider, who commanded the First Squadron, Fourth Cavalry of the Fourth Infantry Brigade Combat Team, First Infantry Division (1–4 Cav), during the surge in 2007 and 2008. They took over the East and West Rashid security districts in January 2007. In May 2007 they took over the northeast sector of East Rashid and attempted to apply the principles of the new counterinsurgency field manual.

"Anyone who was openly Shiite was already gone by the time we got to Dora," Crider recollected. "We found a few people who were Shiite but posed as Sunni for their own protection. It was common for our troops to find three military-aged males with no furniture living in a house. That is not good enough evidence to detain them, so we would demand that they produce a legitimate rental contract within seventy-two hours or move out. More often than not, we would revisit the house to find it empty again.

"The government of Iraq back then was very sectarian. They were terrified that Sunnis would take back what they had gained." Crider cited the installation of Dr. Bassima al-Jadri as head of the government's reconciliation committee as one example. Jadri was a thirty-eight-year-old former senior official in Saddam's military industry ministry, where she had worked on improving Iraq's conventional weapons capacity. Even then she was connected to the Sadrists, and after the war she was in Parliament allied with Muqtada al-Sadr. Her formal relationship with the Sadrists began in 2004, when their opposition to Bremer intensified. They sought her out, and she agreed to advise them, meeting with religious and tribal leaders. She later established a relationship with the Dawa Party and became close to Jaafari and then Maliki. By this time her bodyguards had split off from the Sadrists. She was very suspicious of Sunnis and Americans, believing that neither wanted to allow Shiites to rule Iraq. She was very forceful, and when Maliki established his office of the commander in chief, meant to advise him on military matters, Jadri was put in charge of it, in part because of her fierce loyalty to him.

Under her the office developed a fearsome reputation for issuing secret sectarian orders, advising Maliki on military matters and overruling the Defense and Interior Ministries, circumventing the chain of command to order officers to attack targets. She helped Maliki create his own praetorian guard. Jadri wanted to purge all nonsectarian officers and those not loyal to the ruling Shiite parties while promoting sectarian officers by removing Sunni names from lists of recruits to the army and police. She viewed all Sunnis as Al Qaeda supporters. When Maliki established a national reconciliation committee, the Implementation and Follow-up Committee for National Reconciliation, Jadri was put in charge of it.

IN ITS FIRST MONTH in Dora the 1–4 Cav was attacked fifty-two times. Sunni militias used deep buried IEDs to destroy American armored vehicles. In response, starting in June 2007 Crider initiated a twenty-four-hours-a-day, seven-days-a-week presence in his area. This curtailed Al Qaeda's ability to move about freely. People began to stay outside later into the night.

A fellow officer was reading David Galula's 1964 treatise *Counterinsurgency Warfare: Theory and Practice,* which "emphasizes the importance of conducting a census right away," Crider said. The 2–12 Infantry, from whom Crider adopted the idea, called it Operation Close Encounters. "I knew a good idea when I heard one," he said, "so we began to conduct this operation daily in order to map out who lived in our neighborhood, what they thought, and who was not supposed to be there."* The goal was also "to build a real relationship with the population one family at a time," he would later explain in an article he wrote for *Military Review.* "We found that while people would not talk to us on the streets, they would often speak freely inside their homes. Since we went to every home, no one felt singled out. Galula points out that a census can serve as a 'basic source of intelligence.' We found that it was a tremendous source of intelligence that gave us an in-depth understanding of how people

---

*Another soldier told me: "I spent a lot of time thinking about COIN prior to leaving the U.S. I read U.S. Army Field Manual FM 3–24 Counterinsurgency, as well as books by David Galula, Roger Trinquier, and Sir Frank Kitson, and thought long and hard about how to apply these lessons to our area of Baghdad, especially in terms of how intelligence was central to successful COIN. Of course, once we arrived in Baghdad, a lot of this was put aside, unfortunately, as we were taken away by events. Soldiers were being injured and our area seemed to be out of control, so the emphasis shifted from applying good COIN techniques to just responding to what was happening. We never really gained the initiative in that first area. Indeed, it took us about sixty days or so to really get back to the COIN basics that we had read about. Once we began to apply these lessons, things changed in our favor, and never turned back."

felt. We came to understand that Al Qaeda in Iraq was supported only by a small minority of the population. We discovered issues around which we could build an alliance based on a relationship of trust and respect. We could shape our talking points, information operations, and psychological operations to have the effect we wanted because we knew our target audience well."

The 1–4 Cav visited every home in the area, talking at length with every family. Using handheld biometric data collection tools, the Americans were able to document who lived in every house and made it difficult for the Al Qaeda men to know who was informing on them. By June and July of 2007, the 1–4 Cav was able to use local sources and terminate Al Qaeda cells that dispatched car bombs and planted IEDs. The removal of these cells allowed for the Awakening men to begin operating in the area.

Although an occupation is always onerous, the 1–4 Cav and other units that implemented COIN did not conduct mass arrests in which all men were targeted randomly, as had units before 2007. Officers from the 1–4 Cav visited families of arrested men, explaining to them what evidence they had. In August Al Qaeda men from Arab Jubur infiltrated Dora, bringing their families so that they would appear to be internally displaced persons. As the 1–4 Cav cooperated with the American unit in Arab Jubur, they were able to arrest the Al Qaeda men, frustrating the group's attempt to reinvigorate itself.

Crider insists that the twenty-four-hour presence in the neighborhoods produced immediate results, with IEDs and murders dropping off significantly. He also suggested that because his unit was made up of young soldiers who were in Iraq for the first time, they were not encumbered with the attitude that the Iraqi people were the enemy. "A platoon would go out and do an eight-hour patrol, handing out microgrants, cutting loose wires, talking to Iraqis," Crider said. He was struck at the familiarity his lieutenants developed with the neighborhoods and local families. Using a computer program called Tigernet, they could plot the information on who lived in every house, their job, skills, ability to speak English, and other details into every location on the satellite maps of his area.

Back then the only concrete barriers in Dora were smaller "Jersey" barriers around the Mekanik area. "They didn't stop movement as good as we wanted to," Crider said. "We were trying to get walls as soon as we could. It forces the population to funnel through checkpoints and protects from gunfire. It took three or four months to put up the walls. Dora was the first place in southwest Baghdad that got walls. There was one protest when walls went up by guys we believe were involved in the insurgency. The insurgents hated those walls. Over the course of a few weeks we saw the impact." The farmlands that had been used to smuggle weapons or fighters into his area were now cut off.

In September 2007 there was a murder campaign in Dora, with more than nineteen killings. The first victim was Haji Sattar, a local council member. His killers entered the District Advisory Council in broad daylight and asked for him by name. Then they shot him in the head and walked out. "The murder campaign was an attempt to shake up the neighborhood," Crider said, "They were trying to kill people who they thought were sources for us." It briefly succeeded. Haji Hashim, the deputy head of the Rashid district council and a close ally of the Americans, fled for three months. "Sattar's death got Hashim shaken," Crider told me. Hashim had been collaborating with the Americans since 2003 but had managed to stay alive and stay respected by many people in Dora. "Hashim would give us tips: 'Don't drive down this street for a couple of days,'" Crider said.

By July 2007 Crider's men had cultivated thirty-six new local Iraqi sources. "In August the number of detentions skyrocketed, and soon enemy activity fell down," Crider said. The last attack that killed one of his soldiers happened on September 9. "The last IED was September 27. When Shiites returned to Dora in early 2008, there was some increase in violence but no killings." Crider's unit arrested more than 250 Al Qaeda suspects, with 80 percent of them sent on to long-term detention, although most never faced any court or due process to establish their guilt.

Nick Cook, a captain serving under Crider in Dora and the neighborhoods south of it, helped set up the first Awakening groups in his areas. "In Dora we were approached by a guy named Zeki, an old source of ours, who wanted to help stand up the SOIs," he told me. They wanted their headquarters set up along the boundary between his troop and the other American troop in Dora. Cook was introduced to Zeki and his partner, who stated emphatically that they had hundreds of fighters ready to take up arms against Al Qaeda. A lot of their members had come from Arab Jubur. As Cook got to know Zeki's group, it became clear that many had relatives living in Dora, and that they wanted to help their families.

At first it seemed that the group was making little difference in Dora. At the beginning of Ramadan in 2007, however, Zeki's group received information that the mosques were going to be attacked by Al Qaeda. They asked permission to set up security. "About two dozen guys in red and black jogging suits took to the streets," he said. No incidents occurred during that time, and the "neighbors seemed happy to see their sons taking to the streets." From then on the Sons of Iraq were a constant presence. Many members of the group told Cook that they had joined resistance groups right after the invasion because they wanted to get the Americans out of Iraq. Later, though, they felt disenfranchised and identified the selfishness of the groups as the cause.

Cook was also the one who first established a relationship with Osama. "Osama came to me in April of 2007," he said. "He had run into me the day before, and I had given him my phone number." The father of one of Osama's friends had been kidnapped that night, so Osama decided to bring his friend to the combat outpost in Mekanik. Cook met with Osama and heard his friend's story. Then he immediately directed a patrol to try to find where the father had been taken. Unfortunately, the search was unsuccessful. But Cook said that Osama never forgot the encounter.

About two weeks later, an IED hit and destroyed a Humvee, killing one soldier in Cook's troop and badly injuring two others. Three days later Osama called Cook and told him he was parked outside a house; inside it, he said, the man responsible for the IED was having lunch. A patrol was sent to investigate immediately. When the troops arrived Osama guided them to the house and pointed out the insurgent. Once the man was brought back to Forward Operating Base Falcon, the unit discovered that he was one of the top-ten "high-value individuals" for a cavalry regiment a little to the south of where Cook was stationed.

From then on, the unit forged a close relationship with Osama and relied on his intelligence. He even helped a patrol surprise a couple of insurgents emplacing an IED in the middle of the night. When Cook and his troops were moved north into Dora, they handed Osama over as a source and friend to the unit that replaced them. But the new unit did not manage the relationship well, and Osama started calling Cook's fire support NCO to tell him how he was tired of working with them. He said he was planning to start the SOI in Mekanik because he hated what Mekanik had become.

At the beginning of August Cook's Tactical Humintelligence Team received a phone call. Approximately sixteen members of Al Qaeda were being held by Osama and his fighters in Mekanik. This was no longer Cook's area of operation, but the unit whose jurisdiction it was said they could not help. So Cook's troop received permission to go and link up with Osama's fighters. They joined forces and later transferred the sixteen men into U.S. custody.

Col. Jeff Peterson commanded the 1–14 Cavalry Squadron, which was attached to the 3–2 Stryker Brigade Combat Team. He was in Baghdad from July 2006 until September 2007, operating both in Haifa Street and areas in the neighborhoods of Saha, Mekanik, and Abu Dshir, just south of Dora proper. Peterson worked with the regular police and the national police in East Rashid. "They were over 90 percent Shiite and infiltrated with Mahdi Army members or at least sympathized with them," he told me. "I had evidence that their leadership compromised our missions, and I suspected they at least cooperated with the enemy attacking our forces. Some members of the national police were guilty of sectarian violence, and we arrested some officers. The Sunni population was so distrustful of the national police that I built a barrier around the Mekanik neighborhood and didn't allow the national police in the area.

"The security situation improved somewhat. There was significant improvement to the national police as we more effectively partnered with them down to platoon level. Additionally, the commander was replaced and we arrested several officers that we think were the primary source of corruption in the battalion. Over time they became much more competent, professional in their behavior, and successful in their operations. They also began gaining the trust of the local population.

"The biggest challenge I faced was the sectarian nature of the Shiite-dominated local government structures. They had significant influence over the decisions about resource allocation and controlling essential services like benzene, propane, and kerosene distribution, and medical clinic and school resourcing. They gave priority to the Shiite neighborhoods and neglected the Sunni neighborhoods. This made it very difficult to build legitimacy in the eyes of the Sunnis who were being marginalized by their local government. In general, the Shiites, in conjunction with the national police, would attempt to displace Sunnis from their homes and then take physical control of the vacant house. In response, the Sunnis would defend their homes or counterattack into Shiite areas. I never sensed the Sunnis were trying to expand; it was the Shiites that were trying to take control of more area."

Something I was told by Capt. Jim Keirsey, who served in East Rashid between October 2006 and December 2007, confirmed the endemic sectarianism of the Iraqi Security Forces. "A large number of the national police brigade and battalion charged with securing the population of Dora persecuted the population," Keirsey said. "They were often very antagonistic toward the population of Dora. It became a vicious cycle. Extremists within Dora would attack Shiite residents to drive them out. The national police would execute reprisal detentions or allow Shiite extremists to attack Sunnis in Dora. Or they would detain Sunnis from Dora outside of the community. Dora Sunni extremists would then seek additional reprisals, perhaps capturing a passing taxi driver and beating him near death. Then the national police, enraged, would charge into the *mahala* en masse with little fire discipline, terrorizing the populace."

As I walked the desolate streets in December 2007, it was hard to know if things were improving. But with few killings occurring in Dora, the conflict seemed frozen in place. A man and his daughter walked hurriedly by. I asked them why the area was empty. "It's a good neighborhood," they assured me. "People left because there is no electricity." In another home I found a man shaving a friend. They told me there had not been electricity in the area for a year and a half. The Mahdi Army controlled the electrical station in the area, they explained. "People will come back when electricity comes back," they said. "We're afraid to go out at night." The Mahdi Army fired mortars at this area from the nearby Shiite neighborhood of Abu Dshir, people told me, and launched attacks from there, engaging Al Qaeda in firefights in Dora. I asked one man why he had not fled like everybody else. "Where will I go?" he asked me. Many Shiite homes in Dora were burned down, to prevent the owners from ever returning. Poor Sunnis who were expelled from Hurriya and Shaab or other poor Shiite areas had moved into the homes of better-off Shiites who had been expelled from well-to-do Sunni areas such as Dora, Ghazaliya, and Amriya.

Osama ran three hundred Iraqi Security Volunteers but resented the restrictions placed on him by the Americans. In Seidiya, Adhamiya, Amriya, Ghazaliya, and other volatile Sunni neighborhoods in Baghdad, ISVs were allowed to patrol freely and carry heavy-caliber machine guns. "We use our own guns," Osama told me. "The Americans didn't give us anything." Osama had a contract to provide a certain number of men at ten dollars per day. He was paid every other week, and he paid his men and provided uniforms and whatever else they might need.

"The only reason anything works or anybody deals with us is because we give them money," Adam Sperry told me when I visited his office in Forward Operating Base Falcon. A bright twenty-three-year-old who majored in creative writing in college, Sperry was an Army intelligence officer from the Second Squadron, Second Cavalry Regiment. Capt. Travis Cox, his colleague, explained to me that at higher levels a lot of money and time was being spent trying to figure out how to transition the ISVs into other jobs. "To a large extent they are former insurgents," Cox admitted.

The 2–2 SCR was patrolling Osama's area in Dora when I visited. The unit's Major Garrett had to figure out what to do with all these militiamen. He placed his hopes on vocational training centers that offered instruction in automotive repair, carpentry, blacksmithing, electricity repair, and English. But adults who were part of a militia were not likely to want to abandon their weapons. "At the end of the day they want a legitimate living," Garrett told me. "That's why they're joining the ISVs." I didn't think anybody was working for a paltry ten dollars per day merely for a legitimate living. These were men who had fought the American occupation as well as the Shiites of Iraq. They had not done so for profit, as the Americans insisted. "The ideological fight, forget about it," Captain Dehart, the unit's senior intelligence officer, said when I suggested this to him. "We bought into it too much. It's money and power." Peace would come to Iraq "if they just realized they would make more money with us through construction contracts than fighting us."

In Dora the Americans were the government, building electrical power stations because the Shiite-dominated government didn't care about supplying electricity or other services to Sunnis. The 2–2 SCR was spending thirty-two million dollars on construction contracts signed with Iraqis and on salaries for Sunni militiamen they hired to be ISVs. They spent twelve million dollars alone building walls around neighborhoods. Sperry complained that American counterinsurgency strategy "is to spend millions of dollars and build walls to make Iraqis more divided than they already are." But his boss, Lieutenant Colonel Reineke, felt very strongly about building walls around neighborhoods and didn't care if some people were cut off as a result. He was frustrated that a wall he was paying local contractors to build around Mahala 860 was taking too long. The wall was meant to keep Al Qaeda fighters out and cut off arms smuggling routes. Some locals left outside were upset that they were not being included inside the walls. Often it seemed as if the American strategy was merely to buy Iraqis off temporarily, and they distributed "microgrants" of three thousand dollars to all the shop owners in their area.

I WONDERED what would happen when this massive influx of American money stopped pouring in. Would the Iraqi state become a bribing machine? Would the ruling Shiites even want to pay Sunnis whom they had been trying to exterminate until recently? Sunnis they believed had been trying to kill them? The British occupation of Iraq in the early twentieth century was described as "colonialism on the cheap." The British did not spend much money on the occupation, and relied on the use of airpower as an alternative to a large standing army. The British bribed tribes and tried to mold the political system in a way that benefited their local allies and enriched them, turning them into feudal lords. This was nothing compared to the billions of dollars the Americans were throwing into Iraq. Adding up all the men employed by the Interior Ministry, the Defense Ministry, the other security branches, the Awakening militiamen, and others working for private security companies that contracted with the American departments of State or Defense, there were more than a million Iraqi men in the security sector. This was more than Saddam had. But for the Americans, spending billions of dollars bribing Iraqis was a pittance compared to how much they spent per year just keeping their military in Iraq or the cost of repairing their damaged vehicles, let alone the cost of injured soldiers. But loyalty that can be purchased is by its nature fickle. Would these maneuvers lead to a real or stable political process in Iraq?

Osama was the English-speaking diplomatic face, but behind him were tough men of the resistance. One, called Salah Nasrallah, or Abu Salih, had dark reddish skin, a sharp nose, and small piercing eyes. The Americans required that each *mahala* have two ISV bosses, so Osama gave half of his three hundred men to Abu Salih's control. ("We know Abu Salih is former Al Qaeda of Iraq," an American Army officer from the area told me.) The day I met Abu Salih he was wearing a baseball cap with the Iraqi flag on it. Turning off Sixtieth Street we walked up to the Batul School for Girls. A soldier with the 2–2 SCR had been shot in the throat and killed in front of this school, presumably by Al Qaeda. Abu Salih explained that the Mahdi Army kidnapped Sunni girls from the school and that during final exams they had attacked it and shot it up, then looted it. Osama blamed the Mahdi Army but added, "When I say Mahdi Army I mean the Iraqi National Police." Abu Salih picked up Korans and other religious books that were strewn about the dusty floors.

A thick muscular man called Amar, or Abu Yasser, was the other brawn behind the operation. Handsome and jovial, Abu Yasser wore a green sweatshirt and matching sweatpants with a pistol holstered his under arm. "Amar is the real boss," an American Army intelligence officer from the area told me. "That guy's an animal, he's crazy." Osama explained that nobody from Mahala 832 knew that he was in charge of the ISVs in the area. "They think Abu Salih and Abu Yasser are in charge, because my family is still there." He added that they were still arresting Al Qaeda infiltrators from among the ISVs. Osama was trying to arrange for Abu Yasser to manage his own ISV unit in the nearby Mahala 834, where he actually lived.

Abu Yasser had worked for the General Security Service until 1993 and then joined the Iraqi military industry. In 2004 he joined the Army of the Mujahideen, a resistance organization operating in Mosul, the Anbar province, and southern Baghdad. Although he claimed to have joined to protect Sunni areas from the Mahdi Army, in 2004 that Shiite militia was still cooperating with the Sunni resistance and was not targeting Sunnis. In fact, he had fought the American occupation, operating mostly out of Arab Jubur, he said, where the organization "was young people, mostly to defend the area." He had not resigned from that organization, he added, but decided to work with the Americans and the ISVs "because of Iranians getting more power in Iraq," he told me. "They are occupying Sunni areas. They are the bigger enemy." Like many others, Abu Yasser admitted that Sunnis had made a strategic blunder by boycotting the Iraqi political process in the early days of the occupation, and Sunni clerics had made a mistake issuing *fatwas* prohibiting Sunnis from joining the nascent security forces the Americans were creating.

Abu Salih had belonged to the 1920 Revolution Battalions. He had decided to work with his former enemies the Americans and join the ISVs because of the Iraqi government. "It's an Iranian government," he said, "and the people are its victims." A colleague of his, Abu Yusef, averred, "Maliki is Iraqi, but he lived in Iran a long time, he works for them." Referring to Maliki's political party, Abu Salih added, "The Dawa Party is the first enemy of Iraq." Unlike some of his associates, Abu Salih did not think it had been a mistake for Sunnis to boycott the security forces. "If Sunnis had joined they would have been killed or fired," he said. Abu Salih admitted that some men from Al Qaeda joined the ISVs so that they could have the identity card as protection should they get arrested. If the Iraqi government did not allow the ISVs to join its security forces, "it will be worse than before," he said.

Abu Yusef, who was sitting with Abu Salih, was a former investigator for Saddam's Special Security Service. Like all members of the security forces, he had been fired when former American proconsul Paul Bremer issued an edict dissolving them in May 2003. Many joined the resistance after that, though Abu Yusef denied having done so (but he told me he fought the Mahdi Army and killed many of them). The Mahdi Army killed twenty-seven members of his family, he said, adding that on one day, earlier in 2007, forty-seven Sunni corpses were found next to the nearby Sunni Tawhid Mosque, presumably murdered by the Mahdi Army. He denied being anti-Shiite, though. His wife was Shiite, and many of the officers he worked with in the security service were Shiites from throughout Iraq.

The Hero House—the sobriquet the Americans gave to Osama's headquarters—was located behind a tall concrete wall that stretched the length of a highway the Americans called Route Senators. The Americans paid Iraqis to build these walls, Osama said. Before they were erected, he said, the Iraqi National Police had fired on the neighborhood from the highway. Now his guards manned a checkpoint at a gap in the wall that allowed vehicles to enter the area. The house belonged to Abu Yasser's cousin, a doctor living in Britain. It was also surrounded by concrete barriers and manned by men in civilian clothing casually slinging Kalashnikovs. Inside the mostly empty house was a room with mattresses and another with some chairs, a desk, and a large satellite image of Dora that the Americans had given Osama. As we drank tea in the office, one of Osama's sources entered and pointed to a spot on the map where an Al Qaeda agent was residing. The suspected Al Qaeda man was called Walid. "He is harmful to people," Osama told me. "I just want to kill him. Now he is back in the area. His cousins are Al Qaeda also." But he said he would watch him instead, to see who he worked with. The Americans had recently required the ISVs to wear uniforms, and Osama was annoyed that most of his men were still in their civilian attire.

Inside I met Hussein, a lanky twenty-one-year-old wearing a blue tracksuit. He was one of Osama's original partners, though he was from Mahmudiya, south of Baghdad. He was working as a guard in a local Sunni mosque when the Mahdi Army, backed by the Iraqi National Guard, expelled his family and other Sunnis from the area. They killed his uncle and cousin. His family fled to Arab Jubur, but Al Qaeda pressured him to join them and came to his house looking for him, so his family told them he had gone to Syria, and he started to work with Osama in Dora. "Al Qaeda and the Mahdi Army are the same thing," he told me, "two faces of the same coin."

Hussein was the fourth-ranking member of Osama's unit, after Abu Yusef and Abu Salih. He took me with him as he drove through the area to inspect the twenty checkpoints their men were maintaining. We drove through the mostly deserted neighborhood, with its shattered homes. Most of the graffiti on the walls had been painted over, but some still said, "Long Live the Mujahideen." On various corners two or three men stood or sat with their

Kalashnikovs. "Al Qaeda and the Mahdi Army destroyed a lot here," Hussein said as we surveyed the devastation, but he added that "Al Qaeda destroyed the area, not the Mahdi Army." We were stopped at the checkpoints, and though some of the men recognized Hussein, many cautiously gripped their weapons and questioned us. "We're a patrol from the central headquarters," Hussein told them. Some of the men were teenagers, others were in their fifties. One of them covered his face menacingly with a red checkered scarf. The local market, previously shut down, was partially reopened, and as ISV checkpoints were being established some of the Sunnis who had fled the area, though none of the Shiites or Christians, were returning. "Clean Shiites can come back," Osama told me. While I was there a Sunni family from the city of Samarra, north of Baghdad, arrived at the checkpoint. They hoped to stay in one of the homes in the area. The ISV men questioned them and demanded copies of the identity cards of all the people who would live in the house. "Anyone else I will arrest," said Osama. A woman approached the gate to ask for information about men who had been arrested, but the guards could not help her.

One of the men prepared lunch for us: mushy cooked tomatoes; mushy fried potatoes; and kibbe, ground meat fried in dough. Osama called an American sergeant from a nearby base. "Your guys detained this guy," he said. "He is seventy years old. What's wrong with this guy, is he bad? Oh, he's fifty? They told me he was very old. If you know for sure he is Al Qaeda, then fuck him." Then he asked about a series of men who were detained and warned about an Iraqi who worked with the Americans. "He is a bad guy," he said. "He threatens people."

Osama received a phone call from representatives of the Awakening Council boss Ahmad Abu Risha in Ramadi, the brother of the slain Sheikh Sattar Abu Risha, summoning him and his men to a meeting. He was very excited and hoped to discuss what would happen in six months, when the ISV program was scheduled to end. He wanted the Awakening groups and the ISVs to form a government for Sunnis with Abu Risha, he told me, "because the Iraqi government doesn't do shit." If the U.S. Army left or once more took to remaining within their FOBs, he said, violence in the area would return.

Haji Hashim was the deputy head of the Rashid council who had collaborated with Crider. In 2003 Hashim and others volunteered to set up the local council. Before the war he had been in the Ministry of Education. "I spoke in mosques," he said, "and said we have to work with the Americans. Dora became very bad in 2005. We were considered collaborators." Al Qaeda came in, he said, and then it became dominated by locals and was joined by other resistance groups. "Then sectarianism started," he said. "Al Qaeda killed Shiites, the Mahdi Army and Badr killed Sunnis and former officers. Things got worse after Samarra. Most police were supporters of the Mahdi Army, and Dora was a target for the Mahdi Army. In Shiite mosques they spoke out against Dora. Many Sunnis were killed in Abu Dshir."

The people of Dora collected their government-provided propane tanks in Abu Dshir. In 2006 "Sunni agents from here went there to get them, and four were killed," he told me. "After that nobody could get propane, so people had to use wood to cook. So American patrols went to collect the propane, and now it's better, but there are still lingering fears about being attacked." Hashim was shot in the head once when he left the house to collect his propane. The Americans took him to the hospital in the Green Zone, but he lost his vision in one eye.

"I have seen dogs eating dead bodies," Hashim told me. "Al Qaeda and the Islamic State of Iraq killed any Shiite, any government employee, and Shiites killed any Sunni. The Iraqi National Police used to shoot randomly when they were attacked. The leadership of the Iraqi Security Forces was sectarian at the time. They made random arrests, would shoot randomly and kill innocent people. The Rafidein Brigade of the INPs made random arrests. They took sixty-eight people from shops, and after that we found their bodies in Abu Dshir. Police shot at electrical stations so people wouldn't have power."

One especially vindictive unit came through with PKCs (heavy-caliber machine guns) and shot up the area the day before they were replaced. "They had a strong hate," Hashim explained. "Anybody who crossed the street was shot. Only cats crossed the street." He attributed the improved security to the Americans. "One of the most important things they did was walling off the areas," he said. "It's true it bothered people, but it worked." The Americans also helped release innocent Sunnis who had been arrested by the Rafidein Brigade.

A new commander took over the Rafidein Brigade and improved relations with the people, Hashim told me. But the commander was later replaced by another who "did bad things, made random arrests, he made problems instead of solving them." This one was later punished and transferred to the traffic police. "Then the Wolf Brigade came in 2007," said Hashim. "They arrested people in mosques right away, tortured people. Boys from the area fought the Wolf Brigade. I asked them why they were fighting. They said, 'It's better to die fighting than to end up arrested with holes drilled in our bodies.'"

ONE DAY I ACCOMPANIED men from the 2–2 Stryker Cavalry Regiment, a unit based in the nearby FOB Falcon, on a mission as they met up with Osama and his men as well as Hamid, or Abu Abdel Rahman, head of the Hadhir Neighborhood Advisory Council (NAC). Hamid had been in the Iraqi army for twenty-two years. Now he represented the six *mahalas* in his area. The

Americans were establishing NACs and DACs (District Advisory Councils), institutions separate from the Iraqi government and funded by the U.S. military. Three Sunnis of the ten members in Hamid's council had been assassinated. Five others had fled the area to avoid death. Hamid explained that because Sunnis had boycotted the elections for the provincial councils, Shiites dominated them and were trying to appoint Shiites to the local councils. The members of the Baghdad provincial council were mostly from Shiite neighborhoods such as Sadr City, Shaab, and Karada, he said. The NACs and DACs were an American attempt to compensate for the electoral disparities, though as with the Awakening and the ISVs, they were creating separate independent institutions that did not answer to the central Iraqi government. NACs and DACs were loosely tied, and though they were only meant to "advise" the Americans, the goal was to get them to "implement." Hamid knew Osama and had helped him receive the ISV contract.

The Americans met up with Hamid, Osama, Abu Salih, Abu Yasser, and Abu Yusef at an Iraqi National Police checkpoint and walked down Sixtieth Street to the Tawhid Mosque, followed by their Stryker armored vehicles. The Tawhid's Sheikh Abu Muhammad wore a green *dishdasha* with a brown vest. An older, bearded man, he had thick glasses and wore a white cap, topped by a red scarf. Shawn Spainhour, a civil affairs officer with the unit, asked the sheikh what help he needed. The mosque's generator had been shot up by armed Shiites, and the sheikh asked for three thousand dollars to fix it. Spainhour took notes. "I probably can do that," he said. The sheikh also asked for a NAC to be set up in his area, "so it will see our problems." Two bearded middle-aged men in sweaters walked up to the Americans in the mosque and gave them a tip on a Mahdi Army suspect. The soldiers quickly got back into the Strykers, as did Hamid, Osama, and his men, and the Stryker vehicles drove up to a street in Mahala 830, where they found a group of young men with electrical cables. Some of the men ran away when the Americans showed up. Those who stayed were forced into a courtyard and made to squat facing the walls. They all wore flip-flops. Soldiers from the unit guarded them and took their pictures one by one. "Somebody move!" shouted one soldier. "I'm in the mood to hit somebody!" Another one pushed a prisoner against the wall. "You know Abu Ghraib?" he taunted him. Unlike in the nearby Shiite area of Abu Dshir, in majority-Sunni Mekanik it was standard practice to arrest all "military-age males" for "processing."

As other elements of the American unit raided nearby homes, the two men who had tipped off the unit came up to me, thinking I was the Americans' translator, and explained that the men in the courtyard were Sunnis and that some belonged to the Awakening. Some of the men had been involved in tipping off the Americans to the Mahdi Army suspect down the block. I tried to tell the soldiers, but the electrical wires on the ground caused the Americans to think the men had been trying to lay an IED, so they blindfolded and hand-cuffed all eleven of them. "If an IED is on the ground, we arrest everybody in a hundred-meter radius," I was told, though here it was only an electrical cable, and most likely the men had been trying to connect a house to a generator. In the house the two tipsters had identified, the soldiers found Mahdi Army "propaganda" and arrested several men, including one called Sabrin al-Haqir, or "Sabrin the Cruel," an alleged Mahdi Army leader.

The Strykers took the prisoners to the nearby COP Blackfoot. Inside, Hamid and the Sahwa men drank sodas and ate muffins. Osama and Abu Salih shook hands with the Americans and thanked them for arresting Sabrin, who they said had a lot of blood on his hands. Once the misunderstanding was cleared up, the Sunnis from the first house the Americans raided were released, three of them being taken to sign sworn statements implicating Sabrin. An American captain instructed them to list who did what, what they did, where, when, and how. Abu Salih walked by and quickly told the men in Arabic to implicate Sabrin in some attack. None of the Americans noticed this coaching. Osama met with a sergeant from the unit and asked him if he could put a PKC on top of his pickup truck. "No," the sergeant said. "But we can hide it," Osama pleaded. Sabrin was soon moved to a "detainee holding facility" at FOB Prosperity. "We were able to confirm through independent reporting that he was a bad Mahdi Army guy," said an American Army intelligence officer. "He was involved in EJKs," or extra-judicial killings, a euphemism for murders.

Osama's main competition for contracts with the Americans was another local Sunni power broker called Muhammad Kashkul, or Abu Tariq. A former bodyguard for Saddam, he was now a contractor too. "He knows that when security is stabilized contracts will come in," Captain Cox said, explaining Kashkul's motivation for collaborating with the Americans. In one meeting with the Americans, Kashkul bragged that while working as a bodyguard for Saddam he had slept with 472 women. "Is that a lot in America?" he asked. Kashkul and Osama tried to play different American units against one another, but Cox helped arrange a meeting where the two were forced to work out what he described as "their turf war." Osama was not convinced. "Coalition forces like Kashkul, so I have to be his friend," he said. "They told me I have no choice. I have to be his friend. For two years they were looking for him. Showing his picture. Then they arrested him, took him to Blackfoot, and released him after two hours and said, 'He is working with us.'"

The Americans were obsessed with the concept of "reconciliation," which Cox defined as "Agree to quit fighting and talk about problems and get U.S. contracts."

"Osama hates reconciliation," Sperry told me. "He doesn't feel that he has anything to reconcile. He hates that these other guys get contracts." Osama had recently lost face when he accidentally discharged his Glock pistol and nearly hit an American soldier while in a meeting. Some of his men were proving unruly as well. "A couple of Osama's guys were caught outside their sector," the officer told me, "so we detained them and brought in the leaders. Abu Salih was really pissed." When I was visiting Falcon FOB to discuss the ISVs, a major stuck his head through the door. "Are you tracking that the Heroes beat some guy up?" he asked Captain Dehart. "The Heroes' usefulness is almost over," Captain Dehart grumbled. He defended the reconciliation process. "It's an overt process," he said. "You can't be in the shadows. We take *mahalas*, the Critical Infrastructure Security guards, the local leadership, provide us names." As a result, he said, the men with real power in the area emerged from the shadows. "I've heard them tell me, 'I will give you a hundred men, you give them weapons, and you will have no problems.'" But the process they called reconciliation required some community vetting in theory. It seemed that the Americans were turning themselves into a commodity sought after by Iraq's warring factions. The Americans were a way to obtain contracts, influence, weapon licenses, identity cards. "They love ID cards," joked one Army intelligence officer.

When Osama drove me home from Dora we stopped at an Iraqi army checkpoint near Qadisiya. He noticed a familiar Audi parked on the street and then saw a man he knew as Naseem walking past the soldiers. Naseem was Al Qaeda, he said, and was responsible for many attacks against civilians and the Americans. Osama put his cap on and called a soldier over. The soldier had a green bandanna masking all but his eyes as though he were a bank robber. "That guy is called Naseem, he is with Al Qaeda," Osama said. The soldier seemed annoyed and I was worried that he would arrest us instead. "I'm with the Awakening," Osama said, he showed several badges he had been given by the Americans. The soldier told him to keep going but Osama insisted. "What do you want me to do?" the soldier asked. Osama tried to convince them, but the soldiers were indifferent. Frustrated, he drove away.

Osama's part of Dora, which included Mahalas 830, 832, 834, and 836, was called Hadhir. Though each *mahala* had its own ISV unit, Osama hoped that eventually all of the Sunni Awakening militias would be united under one leader so that they could attain political power too. We were in Mahala 830. The Mahdi Army used to attack from Mahala 832. Iraqi National Police, who cooperated with the Mahdi Army, would drive up to Sixtieth Street and spray houses with gunfire, Osama told me as we walked by a solitary INP checkpoint. "I want to kill them," he said, "really, but the Americans make us work together." Since his men had been granted legitimacy by the Americans they were taunting the national police, telling them that just days before they were shooting at them.

"There was definitely a link" between the INPs and sectarian forces, Nick Cook told me. "I am not sure how deep it went, but you could tell the INP definitely treated the Sunni neighborhoods with a lot of indifference and disdain. Many times I heard the national police refer to the neighborhood as lived in by dogs or criminals, referring to the residents. To the national police every person was a suspect. I never did see outright prejudice, but when you moved from Mekanik, a Sunni area, to Abu Dshir, a Shiite area, you definitely saw a change in personality with the national police." Captain T recalled, "I remember several instances of units in predominantly Shiite areas actually catching [INPs] in the act of planting IEDs."

Lieutenant Colonel Miska was based in Kadhimiya's Forward Operating Base Justice. It had three detention centers in it: the Kadhimiya prison; the Ministry of Justice prison, where the government executed condemned people; and an Iraqi army detention center. Miska worked closely with the Iraqi Security Forces, and at one point he had six brigades' worth of Iraqi National Police or army men working with him. I asked him about the abuses he saw. "The Kadhimiya prison run by the national police was the most notorious," he said. "This was Saddam's former military intelligence facility. Senior members of the national police reportedly tortured, extorted, and killed prisoners, mainly Sunnis. The prison was made to hold about 350 prisoners. They had about 900 there when we first began putting pressure on the NP. At first we would conduct inspections and bring in teams that would write reports. The NP would complain that all the Americans talked about was human rights. They would also do a good job of stonewalling the investigators and making it difficult to gain entrance. We eventually started cycling reporters into the facility and getting front-page stories to embarrass the NP. The prisoner population quickly dwindled as a result."

One of Miska's closest colleagues was an Iraqi army brigade commander who was going after both the Mahdi Army and Al Qaeda. As a result, he was put under intense political pressure. Miska accompanied him to numerous meetings with senior Sadrists and other politicians who were trying to get him to back down. But every time he would keep the heat on. The Iraqi commander eventually left Iraq after four attempts on his life, and Mahdi Army hit squads were hunting for his family. "It took me eight months to finally get through the bureaucracy of immigration, UNHCR, and other agencies to help him relocate to the U.S.," Miska said. "Today his family is safe and living much more comfortably than they did in Iraq."

The Iraqi government, it seemed, would come up with every possible excuse not to send help to Dora. "When we would go to the Green Zone and ask ministers and deputy ministers to help out, they would claim that Dora was too dangerous," Captain T said. "We would protest and say that we would take them there to see it themselves and would, of course, protect any government workers or contractors who were working in the area. To them, this was impossible because the area was unsafe!

"It was ridiculous dealing with the Iraqi government. This was particularly clear when we were setting up the Iraqi Security Volunteers as paid security forces in our area. We were attempting to integrate them into the Iraqi security forces, but the government stonewalled this at every turn. They would ask for ridiculously detailed information from the ISVs, which they were, in turn, unwilling to provide to a government they didn't trust. The government would demand that the ISVs meet standards far above what the ISF themselves had to meet.

"Dr. Bassima al-Jadri was a particular problem in this regard, as she was extremely sectarian. She saw the ISVs as the armed forces for the Sunni political parties. We tried our hardest to make sure that the ISVs were security oriented, not politically motivated. In fact, this led us to deny a small group of low-level informants our sponsorship as ISVs. They turned against us and went 'rogue.' They were sponsored by the Iraqi Islamic Party. We eventually had to detain several of them to convince them that we would not permit the politicization of our ISVs. Anyway, Bassima saw the ISVs as a threat to Shiite domination and would try to throw every possible obstacle in our path against ISV integration into the ISF. And this woman was the [government's] lead on reconciliation!"

Saddam Hussein designed Baghdad with a circle of loyal neighborhoods around it. With its many officers, Seidiya was a place he could count on. But it had become a vital battleground during the civil war. Sunnis and Shiites both wanted it, since it opens up into Sunni strongholds like Dora. Shiites wanted to block whatever was coming in. It was located between Shiite-dominated Amil and Sunni-dominated Dora, and it was on the important road that Shiites took to go south to Karbala and Najaf. The Mahdi Army rained mortars down from the Baya district and destroyed Sunni mosques. The neighborhood was originally 55 percent Sunni and 45 percent Shiite, but by the end Shiites would have the upper hand. Seidiya went from being a relatively peaceful middle-class neighborhood to a deserted and broken wasteland, all under the Americans' watch. Most of the residents had fled, and abandoned homes were used by militiamen and insurgents.

"The Shiites were definitely winning," said Captain Noyes, a platoon leader in Seidiya. "They were on the offensive and the local Sunnis were on the defensive, but it was a very violent and contested battle. The Shiite groups were attempting to kick Sunnis out of Seidiya and move Shiites in. The Sunnis were attempting to defend themselves, but some of them had Al Qaeda ties and were targeted by coalition forces, so they were fighting a two-front battle." Most of the murder victims he remembered encountering were Sunni. "Many were killed with a single shot to the head, and signs of torture were on their bodies. The bodies were placed in areas to intimidate locals. Sometimes IEDs were placed under the bodies targeting whoever tried to recover the body. The

Shiites were more effective and organized. They were part of the government, Ministry of Interior, the IP, and INP working there. Sunnis were isolated."

Noyes lived and worked with the 321 INP, or the Wolf Brigade, which was responsible for Seidiya. "They were extremely sectarian, regularly involved in and committing crimes," he said. "The Wolf Brigade and Iraqi police were an arm of Shiite extremists, filled with Shiite militia members. I frequently found the Wolf Brigade involved in outright sectarian activities in cooperation with Shiite militias. The Iraqi police were so often tied to attacks on coalition forces and locals that it went beyond complacency or incompetence.

"Eventually an Iraqi Army battalion took over Seidiya, but they were still under the INP brigade command responsible for West Rashid. We got 321 INP kicked out over a long period of documenting and reporting their crimes against the people of Seidiya. Their battalion commander was LTC Haidar. At one point we found him and General Mundher stealing furniture from an abandoned apartment. They claimed it was General Mundher's apartment and they were moving it out."

The Americans arrested more than seventy members of the Wolf Brigade, who had been found expelling Sunnis and moving displaced Shiites into their homes. The Wolf Brigade was replaced by the Iraqi army's Muthana Brigade, itself feared by Sunnis, and the Muthana Brigade clashed with the Seidiya Guard, the Awakening Group established by Noyes and his team. "The Seidiya Guard were by far superior to the INP as a counterinsurgency force. Their leaders were much more competent," Noyes observed. "They conducted operations to win the support of the population; the INP did the exact opposite. The Seidiya Guards captured people occasionally. They would then turn them over to ISF or CF. Shiites that they handed over to INP were usually released. They understood their legitimacy was on the line, and so they were careful in how they handled people they captured. I encountered only support for the Seidiya Guard with the local populace. However, their relationship with the INP was horrible. They each viewed each other as illegitimate sectarian actors, and probably rightly so. The Seidiya Guard was disbanded after I left, under Iraqi government pressure."

Not everyone was happy about the new militias being created by the Americans, especially the Shiite-dominated ISF. More a paramilitary force than a team of street cops, the Iraqi National Police resembled the National Guard in the United States, compared with the more local Iraqi police. Both types of police units were dominated by Shiite supporters or members of the Mahdi Army or Badr militia and had fought in the civil war, often targeting Sunni civilians and cleansing Sunni areas. I accompanied Lieutenant Colonel Reineke of the 2–2 SCR to a meeting at the headquarters of the INP's Seventh Brigade, in the former home of Ali Hassan Majid, the notorious Chemical Ali. It was now a joint security station (JSS), staffed by Iraqis and Americans. This station was feared by Sunnis, who were often kidnapped by the national police and, if they were lucky, released for ransom. It was rumored to be a Badr militia base for torturing Sunnis.

Brig. Gen. Abdel Karim, the INP brigade commander, sat behind a large wooden desk surrounded by plastic flowers. Behind him was a photograph of Iraqi President Jalal Talabani. To his side was a shotgun. Karim controlled three INP battalions and was the senior Iraqi security official in the area. Even the Iraqi army officers in his area were under his authority. Lieut. Col. Jim Crider was partnered with Karim's Third Battalion, Seventh Brigade, or 372. "Every time we went on patrol with them, we got shot at," Crider told me. "Every time we patrolled with national police, we were introducing an irritant" into the Sunni neighborhoods. Sometimes Sunni militiamen would let the Americans pass, only to blow up the INP vehicles. Although Crider's men at the JSS with Karim always had a list of all the prisoners held there and inspected the jails, Crider admitted that abuses probably still took place outside his men's gaze. Iraqis were relieved when they learned that the Americans, and not the INPs, had detained their sons. "In the context of the surge, our policy was not to turn prisoners over to the INPs," he said. "I remember Karim as very sectarian. I hated being around him. I once brought an Iraqi army commander from Mahmudiya, south of Baghdad, to our JSS to show him our setup. Karim was furious and brought us all into his office, where he sat and stared at the wall. It was weird, so I got up and left. I could tell he was a sectarian stooge from a long way away. Guys like him are the greatest threat to the stability of Iraq. They push regular Sunnis into a corner and then are surprised when they fight back."

In December 2007 the delegation of Americans led by Reineke was greeted warmly by Karim and his men. Five or six of his officers were with him, all Shiites. Reineke acted with exaggerated deference, saying *"naam seidi"* (yes, sir) repeatedly when addressing Karim. They discussed where they would place checkpoints and conduct joint patrols. Karim sought assurances that the ISV recruits had been properly vetted by local leaders, the Iraqi National Police, and the U.S. Army. Reineke mentioned that General Mustafa, a local ISV leader from Arab Jubur, had requested to open an office at the JSS. Karim grew tense. "The Awakening is a path for these individuals to get recruited by Iraqi Security Forces for jobs in the government," he said. "More than that we don't agree, the government is worried that these groups will be a militia or will be used by political groups." Reineke tried to assure him that "the volunteers are only a short-term solution until they find jobs in the government." Karim responded that "we have information that the Baath Party and Al Qaeda have infiltrated the Awakening. It's very dangerous." Reineke mentioned that in nearby Seidiya, the Awakening had opened an office. "The Awakening in Seidiya was killing people," Karim said. "They are not yet in the government. We don't accept that the Awakening will open an office. There is only one government. Those who qualify can join the police or the government, but the Awakening is temporary. There are two commands in this area: American and Iraqi. We won't accept another." The Iraqi general won the showdown.

A stern man named Abu Jaafar had been observing the exchange. Wearing a dark suit and a dark shirt buttoned up, with no tie, he had two thuggish companions in leather jackets who were very friendly with Karim. A Shiite known to the Americans as Sheikh Ali, Abu Jaafar had his own ISV unit of about 100 men in southern Dora's Saha neighborhood. The Americans said he was unofficially in charge of that area. He was also a Neighborhood Advisory Council representative for Mahala 828. "He may not be Mahdi Army, but he has a lot of Mahdi Army friends," Maj. Jeffrey Gottlieb whispered to me. He also had a lot of access to Karim's headquarters.

"We've got a sectarian fault line in the Saha area," Captain Cox explained to me that night, back at his base, drawing a line on the satellite image on the wall. "Saha was a battleground between [Al Qaeda in Iraq and the Mahdi Army]. We took over on September 8, 2007. The drop in violence is thanks to our unit moving in and patrolling every day." Sunnis had been forced to rely on Al Qaeda for self-defense, he explained, and though northern Saha had been "an absolute killing zone before," rich Sunnis were now trying to return.

Victims of sectarian killings were down by half since the 2–2 SCR had arrived, Cox said. "We can have meetings and agreements between prominent Shiites who had ties to militias and prominent Sunnis who had ties to AQ." He sounded triumphant, but I couldn't help noticing myself that attacks against Americans were also down to nearly zero when I was there.

But not far away, in Mahala 836, Cox admitted, a Shiite man was murdered when he went to check out his house after hearing it was safe to go back. The 2–2 SCR also noted a spike in criminal killings, they told me. I wondered how they could distinguish. The Mahdi Army cease-fire and the withdrawal of Al Qaeda forces to northern Iraq in order to avoid the surge created a power vacuum that allowed criminals to operate more freely.

A few days later I returned to meet with Karim without the Americans present and found him talking to several senior Shiite army officers about the forced displacement of Iraqis and what to do with the displaced. An Awakening member was living in a house that the original owner had sold to somebody else, and now the Awakening man refused to relinquish it to the new owner. "We need a mechanism to solve these problems," one officer said. A colonel called Najam who spoke with a Shiite southern Iraqi dialect worried that displaced Sunnis had taken over former homes of Shiites in Dora. "We need to bring back the Shiites, but the Sunnis are in the houses," he said. "This battle is bigger than the other battles—this is the battle of the displaced." Eavesdropping, I could hear Najam angrily condemning somebody, presumably the Awakening. "They are killers, terrorists, ugly, pigs," he said.

Karim's phone rang, and he spoke with a superior officer about a clash the previous day between the Awakening and armed Shiites. "American officers took Awakening men to a sector where they shouldn't be," he said. "Residents saw armed men not in uniforms and shot at them from buildings. Four Awakening were injured. My battalion was called in to help." In truth, they had clashed with the Mahdi Army, but Karim downplayed their role and blamed an American captain for establishing an ISV unit in an area where he should not have. "Yes, sir," he said, "the Awakening will withdraw from that area. They started the problem."

Gen. Abdul Amir, another man present, was the commander of the important Sixth Division of the Iraqi army. He warned that men were joining the Awakening for political purposes. "They want to be prominent in their neighborhood so that they will get elected. The prime minister said, 'I don't want this to be about politics, I want this to be about security.'"

The sectarian Shiite parties ruling Iraq worried about the Awakening becoming a pan-Iraqi movement. If it succeeded in being nonsectarian, it could displace them from power. Najam joked that 98 percent of the Awakening was Al Qaeda. Just then a U.S. Army major walked in and met with Karim outside the office. An embarrassed Karim returned and said he'd been informed he could not talk to me.

"Gen. Abdul Karim was a completely sectarian individual who was more interested in consolidating Shiite influence and power via his police than in really solving the problems that plagued the area," an American captain confided to me. "He was also incompetent in that he did not at all understand how to run operations or how to collect and use intelligence. People were fairly scared of him, especially his own subordinates, which suggests he was connected to one Shiite militia or another, though this was never confirmed. I think it was unlikely that he was intimately involved in any particular militia, but only because that might create a problem for him. I remember once, while visiting our AOR [area of responsibility], his personal security detachment, a ridiculous thirty-plus policemen, provoked our ISVs into a confrontation and hauled several away to the INP HQ. It was a near nightmare getting them released, but the event was indicative of Karim's belief that he controlled Dora and that only he would influence the security situation there."

I returned on a different day to meet Abu Jaafar, who suggested Karim's headquarters as a good location. Karim showed me a plaque on his wall that he said was an award from Prime Minister Maliki for being nonsectarian, and he pointed to medals on his desk that the Americans had given him—also, he said, for being nonsectarian. Next to them were a couple of traditional rings worn only by Shiites.

Before the war he had owned some minivans, he said. After the war he built the Shiite Imam al-Hassan Mosque in Saha. "When terrorist activities started in the area, I wasn't involved," he said, because it was not clear who was responsible. "When things got clear I saw that people needed somebody to lead them and command them according to God." He explained that his men had taken the homes of "bad Sunnis" (meaning Al Qaeda) and inventoried their contents. "They don't want to come back because they were killers," he said. Problems in his area had started two years earlier, he said, with random assassinations. "My cousin was a school principal and a local council member, and he was shot to death walking home. And others were killed, and we didn't know why or who killed them. After a while I knew that my neighbor was informing for the killers. Most of the dead were Shiites. I talked to the young men in our area and said, 'If we don't cooperate, we will be killed one by one.' We started to guard our area." Abu Jaafar and his militia used old refrigerators, cinder blocks, and earth to wall off their area. His enemies—Al Qaeda but also the 1920 Revolution Battalion and the Army of the Mujahideen—were, he claimed, these same people in the Awakening. Shiites did not need an Awakening. "We are already awake," he said, smiling icily.

Abu Jaafar pulled out a list of forty-six people from Saha. "Criminals in the Awakening," he said. "For two years I was naming these people." He singled out Hamid, the Neighborhood Advisory Council boss in Hadhir. "Shiites could not join the local council," he said. "They would be killed." He blamed Hamid for dividing Saha in two, with Shiites controlling the south and Sunnis controlling the north. But in fact Shiites had pushed Sunnis out of northern Saha, and that area became a key front line in the civil war. Abu Jaafar pointed to two other names. "The Americans told me, 'If you see these two men, you can kill them or bring them to us.' Now they are wearing the Awakening uniform in Mahala 828. They said they have reconciled. I have to be patient. We are awake and our eyes are open."

Al Qaeda had changed its name and now called itself the Awakening, Abu Jaafar insisted. He claimed that Sunnis were acting weak so that they could attack once they regained strength. I asked him about Awakening Council founder Sattar Abu Risha, who had incurred the wrath of Al Qaeda. "He was just a robber in the street, and they made him a leader," Abu Jaafar said dismissively. I told him that many Awakening members claimed they were fighting Al Qaeda. "How did they fight Al Qaeda?" he scoffed. "Fight themselves? Fight their brothers? And where is Al Qaeda? Did it evaporate overnight? We know everything, but we're just waiting." I asked him how he knew Karim so well. "General Karim is a good guy," he said. "During the battles I was here every day."

Ghost Police

I visited JSS Cougar at the Walid INP station, where the First Battalion, Seventh Brigade, Second Division (172 INP Battalion) worked with a U.S. Army National Police Training Team (NPTT). This team, led by the cynical Major Gottlieb, covered the area of Baghdad the Americans called East Rashid. I turned up dressed very casually, in a T-shirt and jeans. Seeing this, American officers from the 2–2 SCR admonished me to wear my body armor to protect myself from accidental INP discharges. "I did convoy security in the Sunni Triangle and was hit by numerous IEDs, complex attacks, small arms, but I never felt closer to death than when I was working with Iraqi Security Forces," joked Captain Cox.

A tall and lanky tank officer, Gottlieb underwent about seventy days of training with his men to prepare for this mission. "We don't know as much as we could know because we don't know Arabic," he said. "The INPs here are almost all Shiites. Orders from their chain of command are usually to arrest Sunnis, not Shiites. But they don't go on 'Sunni hunts' like the Second Brigade in Seidiya and a lot of other brigades." The battalion he worked with was mostly from southern Iraq, especially Basra, and many were more loyal to the Badr militia. "At first they were encouraged to resign or given dangerous missions and were replaced by guys from Sadr City." I asked him if he had any evidence of Sadrist sympathies among the men. "Today I was sitting in the office and the brigade finance officer's phone rang, and the ring tone was a Sadr song," he said. Pointing to the newly painted walls, he said, "It's all cosmetic. They know if everything has fresh paint and looks squared away, we'll think they're squared away." Local Iraqi National Police were resettling displaced Shiite families in empty Sunni homes in this area. Gottlieb called them "United Van Lines missions": "The national police ask, 'Can you help us move a family's furniture?' There are people coming back, and we don't know if they were originally from here. Official U.S. policy is, we do not take part in any resettlement activity. I could make up a deed."

Gottlieb conducted an inventory of the weapons that were supposed to have been assigned to the base. Five hundred and fifty weapons were missing, including pistols, rifles, and rocket-propelled grenade launchers. "Guys take weapons when they go AWOL," he explained. "It was funny how they always expended four hundred rounds of ammunition. They would have fake engagements and transfer the ammunition to militias." There was also a problem of "ghost police," he said. Although 542 INP men were assigned to his JSS on paper, only about 200 would show up at any time. Some would be on leave and some simply did not exist, their salaries pocketed by officers. "Officers get a certain number of ghosts," he said. He looked at an American soldier nearby. "I need some ghosts. How much are you making?"

I accompanied the NPTT on a joint raid with the INPs. Captain Adil, a trim thirty-year-old with a shaved head and sharp gaze, led the raid, despite his rank and position as a battalion staff intelligence officer, because only 25 percent of the INP's officer positions were full. As a result, INP officers end up doing a lot of things that American noncommissioned officers do. Adil briefed his men on the mission using cardboard and Styrofoam on the floor to replicate the vehicles. All the men wore the same blue uniforms, but with a variety of helmets, flak vests, and boots. "Today we have an operation in Mahala 830," he said. "Do you know it? Our target is an Al Qaeda guy." Adil would be riding in the Reva, a South African armored vehicle. The rest would follow in Hummers and pickup trucks. His men repeated the instructions; he ordered them to shout the answers.

The targets were two brothers, Salah and Muhamad, suspected of working for Al Qaeda. They occasionally visited their family in their brother Falah's home. Falah was known as Falah al-Awar, or Falah the Blind, because he had lost an eye. He belonged to the Islamic State of Iraq and had been arrested two weeks earlier by the Americans. Under interrogation he revealed that his brothers were involved in similar actions, attacking the Americans, kidnapping, and killing. "He dimed his brothers out," an American officer said.

Thirty-five Iraqi National Policemen took part in the raid. The INPs climbed over the wall and broke through the main gate. They burst into the house, ordering the women and children in one room while tying the hands of two young men with strips of cloth. One of them was Muhamad, one of the brothers they were looking for. The other young man was Mustafa, Muhamad's young brother. He wasn't on the target list but was picked up anyway. Salah was nowhere to be found. Mustafa started crying. "My father is dead," he said. Adil reassured him, holding the top of his head with his hand, as if he were palming a basketball. Seated in the living room, the women asked how long the two would be taken for. Adil told them they were being taken for questioning, and explained where his base was.

Then it was over. The INPs sped away. The Americans followed, surprised at the hurry. "We just picked up some Sunnis, we're getting the fuck outta here," joked one American sergeant. "Yeah, the moral ambiguity of what we do is not lost on me," said Gottlieb jocularly in response. "We have no way of knowing if those guys did what they say they did." Gottlieb later said that the Interior Ministry "uses 'Al Qaeda' as a scare word for Americans," describing all Sunni suspects in this way.

Back at the base Muhamad and Mustafa were seated on the floor in the operations room, blindfolded, with their hands in plastic zip ties. Sergeant Costa, an American, high-fived Adil's deputy, Lieutenant Amar. The names on the prisoners' ID cards were compared to what Costa and Major Fox had on a printed document of their own. Both were brothers from the Harfush family.

These were the guys they wanted. Their pictures were taken, including of their front and rear torsos, to look for scars or wounds and to compare their physical condition then with how it might end up later, in case of future abuse. The older brother had a leg injury, which they photographed. The two were then separated. The older prisoner sat in Adil's office, which had a locker, a plastic table, two beds, and a television playing an old Egyptian film. Costa and Fox sat on one of the beds with a translator. The prisoner, Muhamad Abdallah Harfush Gertaini, of the Garguri tribe, wore a blue tracksuit. After his blindfold was taken off, he was taken outside to throw up. He came back shivering. "Why are you shivering?" Adil asked with a smile. He gave him Amar's jacket to stay warm. Adil showed him a picture and asked him who it was. "My cousin Qasim," he said, and gave his address in the Mekanik neighborhood. "But he was arrested a few months ago." Qasim was being held in an American prison. "This family, all of them work for Al Qaeda," Adil said with a laugh.

Adil began a long lecture. "We can do this the hard way or the easy way," he said. "You're an Iraqi citizen and you want to serve your country and repent. . . . How many checkpoints were bombed? How many of our men were martyred? We are the state, we put the law above all else regardless of sect. Why didn't we go after your neighbors, why you?" Muhamad denied any wrongdoing. "I have four sources," Adil said. "I know everything. I'll advise you right, I have people I trust who told me about you and your brother. A source saw you with his eyes." Adil showed him a picture of another man and asked who it was. Muhamad answered and told him that the man had been martyred. "Martyred?" shouted Adil. "He was a terrorist!" Adil showed him a picture of a one-eyed man. "He is my brother," Muhamad answered. Adil listed people his brother had killed. Both brothers had volunteered for the Awakening. "The Awakening won't help you," he said. "I'll get all of you. You're a liar. Four sources swear against you." Muhamad meekly protested. "Ask people," he said. "I did ask," said Adil. "I know you. I have a source who will talk for a whole hour about how you were injured in your leg. This is your last chance . . . you have until the morning." He asked about Muhamad's brother Salah, who they failed to find on their raid, and called Muhamad a liar when he said he had gone to work in construction up north.

Mustafa was brought out. He had long matted hair and wore matching jeans and a jacket. He stretched uncomfortably. "My hand," he winced in pain. "My haaand," Adil mocked him, and asked him about Salah. Mustafa said he worked in a bakery in the north. Adil believed he was in Baghdad. Mustafa was taken out, and Muhamad was brought back, his blindfold removed. "Good morning," Adil said. "Do you know your religion? You guys are always talking about Islam." He lectured about Islam and quoted Condoleezza Rice. "These guys are destroying Islam," he told us, and looked back at the prisoner. "You say we are Iranian. We are Iraqis, we are building your country." The brothers were accused of expelling Shiites and killing civilians. "No criminal will say, 'I am a criminal,'" Adil said. "They all say, 'I'm innocent.'" Adil's source claimed that Mustafa was wounded while attacking an INP checkpoint.

The next day Sunni leaders from the area met with the American soldiers and claimed the brothers were innocent. Hamid, the Hadhir NAC boss, would not vouch for them, however. When the 2–2 SCR first arrived they had imposed discipline on the 172 INP Battalion, some of whom had gone on forays into Sunni neighborhoods just to punish civilians. "We arrested a whole checkpoint, nineteen guys, in the beginning, from the 172," Captain Dehart told me, "so they don't use checkpoints as staging points, so there will be no more shenanigans." Still, some local Sunni leaders asked that the two brothers be transferred to American custody.

Getting to Know Adil

I met with Captain Adil several times in 2007 and 2008, and we became friends. Adil had been an army infantry officer before the American occupation. His father was a Shiite former Army officer and his mother was Sunni. Adil's sister married a Sunni man and they fled to Syria, because she feared Shiite militias would kill him. Adil's wife was Sunni. He had lived in the majority-Shiite and Mahdi Army–controlled eastern Baghdad district of Shaab, but he moved after the Mahdi Army threatened him for refusing to obtain weapons for them. He paid a standard $600 bribe to join the police, but was cheated and denied the job until a friend helped. "Before the war it was just one party," he said. "Now we have one hundred thousand parties. I have Sunni officer friends, but nobody lets them get back to service. First they take money, then ask if you are Sunni or Shiite. If you are Shiite, good. The army is not sectarian. I dream to get back to the army. In Saddam's time nobody knew what is Sunni and what is Shiite," he said. He rejected the notion that most officers had been Sunni or that most of the Baath Party had been Sunni. "If someone tells you, 'I was not in the Baath Party,' he is a liar. All Iraqis were in the Baath." The Americans made a mistake by dissolving the Iraqi army and security services, he said. In Dora the army had a good reputation, and there were many stories told about how soldiers helped people go to the hospital and get through roadblocks.

Typical of an officer who graduated from the military academy before the American occupation, Adil viewed the new sectarianism that dominated inter-Iraqi relations as anathema. The Iraqi army was the least sectarian force in Iraq, he said. In the Seidiya district it had battled the police, and at Dora's Thirtieth Street checkpoint Iraqi soldiers came to blows with local INPs and IPs from the Balat station in Saha, Mahdi Army men who had gone through the

Police Academy. Some of these Mahdi Army policemen were involved in the recent clashes with the Awakening men in the Kifaat area of Mahala 828. A U.S. Army intelligence officer told me that from a Sunni perspective, the Balat station was "problematic." It was commanded by Lieutenant Colonel Muhamad and Sergeant Ali Faqr. Muhamad had his hands tied; a Mahdi Army leader had entered his office and threatened him with a gun to his head. Muhamad asked the Americans to arrest Mahdi Army suspects for him.

Adil admitted that attacks against his people had gone down since the establishment of Awakening units. "The Awakening has the right to join the Iraqi Security Forces," he said, "but they should be cleaned so we won't have terrorists inside government. Just like we were cleaning the INPs, they are cleaning up the Awakening." But he was also suspicious of the Awakening members. "Awakening in Dora is the same people who used to be attacking us, and now they taunt us, saying, 'We used to attack you.'" He told me that Abu Salih was a former insurgent who had made IEDs. He suspected Muhammad Kashkul, Osama's rival, of working with Al Qaeda and helping the group to infiltrate the Awakening. I asked him about Osama's men. "All these people before were shooting us," he said. He admitted that INPs from the Sixth Brigade had shot at Sunnis in Dora, but not his INPs. He accused Hamid of being an Al Qaeda terrorist. "I have an order from the Ministry of Interior to arrest him," he said.

The Americans were pressuring him to target the Mahdi Army as well as Al Qaeda. "It's better if the Americans go after the Mahdi Army," he said. "If we arrest them, then the chain of command will release them. The sectarian issue is powerful." Adil did not trust his own men. "Three-fourths of them are Mahdi Army," he said, locking his door before we spoke. "Sadr and Badr officials controlled the leadership of the INPs, and the Iraqi police—all of them are Sadr." Although the Interior Ministry's leadership was dominated by the Badr militia, he said, the majority of its employees were still Sadr supporters. Adil's best friend and lieutenant, Amar, was Sunni. "I was fighting to get him," he told me, and was threatened as a result of their friendship. "An officer is a brother of an officer. I want to work with something not for Sunnis or Shiites, just for Iraq."

Adil was repeatedly threatened by the Mahdi Army. He dismissed the freeze. "No one cares about Muqtada," he said. "A week ago Mahdi Army guys threatened an INP checkpoint . . . and then sniped at the checkpoint, so the INPs arrested three of them." The men worked for a Mahdi Army leader called Wujud, who lived in Sadr City. Wujud worked with another Mahdi Army leader called Amar al-Masihi, and together they fired mortars at Adil's base after the arrests. In nearby Abu Dshir he warned that the Kadhimayn Mosque was an office for the Sadrists, and it ordered the people of Abu Dshir not to join the ISVs. The Americans wanted Adil to go after the Kadhimayn Mosque, but he could not do it.

Adil was summoned to meet Lieutenant Colonel Fadhil, the former brigade intelligence section commander. Wujud and another Shiite militiaman were there. "They stole our vehicles and weapons," he said, "and Wujud told INPs to be careful because you give Americans information. In front of Lieutenant Colonel Fadhil, Wujud told me, 'Adil, be careful, we will kill you.' My boss was sitting there and didn't do anything." I asked him why he had not arrested Wujud. "They know us," he said. "They know where we live. I'm not scared for myself, but I'm scared for my family."

Wujud worked with Ziyad al-Shamari, a leader of what the Americans called a "special group" because of a poor translation of what may be better termed a "private group," as Iraqis called Shiite militias and gangs not loyal to Muqtada. Adil added that a man called Abu Yusuf, a contractor who was working with the Americans in Combat Outpost Blackfoot, also worked with Wujud and owned the car used in a recent attack. Adil warned that Wujud and Abu Yusuf stole cars and might blow them up to make it look like Al Qaeda was responsible. Wujud once lived in Dora but now lived in eastern Baghdad's Ur neighborhood, and he was in charge of dispatching men to Iran for training. General Karim was also from Ur. "He is Mahdi Army," Adil said, claiming Karim had cleansed Sunnis from other parts of Baghdad and its surrounding towns when he was with the Fourth Brigade. "No one can talk about the Mahdi Army in our battalion or police or in the Ministry of Interior."

Lieutenant Colonel Fadhil was replaced by Lieutenant Colonel Majid. Majid asked Adil to collect the ransom for a Sunni man whose release had been ordered by the Iraqi courts. "He was not Al Qaeda," Adil said. Majid wanted four thousand dollars, but the prisoner was related to Lieutenant Amar, and his family told him. Like most officers accused of pro-Shiite sectarianism, Majid was promoted out of the position where he caused trouble and moved from division to brigade. "No orders come to us to arrest Shiites, but many gangs from the Mahdi Army are kidnapping people for money," Adil said, "If he is Sunni, they take money and kill him."

"Our command," he said, referring to General Karim, "wants to work with the Mahdi Army." Karim praised the Mahdi Army when the Americans were not around, he said, and complained when others criticized them. Adil knew Karim's friend Abu Jaafar as well. "Abu Jaafar is a bad guy," he said. "He has groups fighting in Mahala 828. He knows Ziyad al-Shamari. He always puts his nose in our operations and tells our commanders where to open checkpoints. Abu Jaafar was a mechanic before the war, so how is he a sheikh? He worked with special groups and made deals with them to fight. Abu Jaafar calls every Sunni Al Qaeda." Adil believed Abu Jaafar worked for the Badr militia. "Badr came here [from Iran] and took the government and assassinated former Baathists, officers, and pilots," Adil said.

One day I met Adil in his neighborhood. Though it was not far from where he used to live and still dominated by the Mahdi Army, he was less known there. He grew nervous as we approached an INP checkpoint. He didn't want them to know who he was, in case his men had informed the Mahdi Army about his attitude, which could make him or his family a target. At home his two boys watched television in his small living room. "I have decided to leave my job," he told me. "No one supports us." Lieutenant Amar, a former Republican Guard officer, also wanted to quit; together they would try to join the army. He was feeling pressure from his chain of command, and had been accused of being Sunni. A few months earlier he was accused by the Interior Ministry's internal affairs department of selling cars to terrorists, and five days before I met him he heard rumors that the ministry had issued an order to fire him. When I mentioned Adil's concerns to Gottlieb, he said that Adil was always threatening to quit.

I visited Shaab, Adil's old neighborhood in eastern Baghdad, to attend Friday prayers at the Shurufi Mosque, a center for Muqtada's followers. My friend Firas picked me up, the same friend who a year earlier had been too scared to let anybody at the Mustafa Husseiniya know that he knew me. To avoid certain checkpoints we drove through a former Iraqi air base that had been looted after the war and was full of indigent Shiite squatters. It was called the Hawasim neighborhood by locals, a reference to looting. Small children with matted hair played barefoot in mounds of garbage. Sewage flooded the roads. Donkeys and sheep dug through trash searching for something edible. "Long live Asa'ib al-Haq," said graffiti on a wall, referring to a Sadrist resistance group that split from the Mahdi Army. My friend put a cassette of Mahdi Army songs in his stereo. As the chanting and wailing began, he joked, "Now we are Mahdi Army." The song was a refutation of rumors that Muqtada fled to Iran when the surge started. "He prefers death over leaving his home," the men sang.

We drove past local Shiite ISVs the Americans had hired to pressure the Mahdi Army. The men wore masks to conceal their faces and avoid retaliation, and they were protected by Iraqi police manning the checkpoints with them, defeating the purpose of having them there. Graffiti on the walls called for death to the Awakening men.

We arrived before the noon prayers so we could talk to the imam and listen to the sermon. I met Sayyid Jalil Sarkhi al-Hassani in a green guest room. He was seated on the floor reading a religious book. He had a beard with no mustache and wore wire-framed glasses and a brown cloak. As we spoke his men prepared him for his sermon, placing a white funeral shroud around his shoulders, a symbol that he was ready for martyrdom. On one side of the room was a large painting of Muqtada's father, Muhammad Sadiq al-Sadr, who was Sayyid Jalil's teacher. Sayyid Jalil lived in Sadr City and normally ran a mosque there, but for the past year he had led Friday prayers at the Shurufi Mosque.

When I spoke to him, he denied that the reduction in violence was the result of the Mahdi Army freeze. "That might mean that the Mahdi Army was the cause for the violence, and that's not true," he said. "The political situation is not in the hands of the government, it's in the hands of the Americans. The American forces needed some security. They can increase the violence or decrease it. The Mahdi Army froze because of rumors that it is the source of violence and the Mahdi Army is the reason for the sectarian fighting and the fighting between Shiites, especially after the Karbala incident. That's why Muqtada saw that it is necessary to re-educate the army and keep them away from the field, and despite this the violence is still occurring and the fighting between Shiites is still occurring. After the Mahdi Army freeze it appeared that they were not responsible for the war among people, so now we see that the Mahdi Army is working on education and leadership. Muqtada ordered his people to pray, to worship, to read, and to preach to general education so that they will show the real picture of the Mahdi Army." He stressed that the Sadrists opposed injustice and were nationalists. In truth, however, the significant decrease in violence immediately following the Mahdi Army cease-fire belied his assertion and proved just how responsible the Sadrists were for the fighting.

Inside the mosque was painted light green. About five hundred men sat on straw mats. Fluorescent lights and fans hung down from the ceiling. There was a curtained-off section for women. The dome of the mosque was still damaged from a 2006 car bomb attack. The first *hossa* (slogan) that was shouted asked the men in the crowd to pray for Muqtada, for the release of prisoners, and for death to the Americans and their agents. Another one asked God to grant victory to Muqtada and the Mahdi Army. "Death is an honor to us, arrest is honor to us, resisting the Americans is an honor to us!" went another. Most of the sermon dealt with religious matters and the upcoming month of pilgrimage to Mecca. Sayyid Jalil asked his followers to "pray for other Muslim people in Palestine, Afghanistan, and in all the world, and curse the occupier and the Israelis, and grant victory to all Muslims, to get rid of the Americans, of dictatorships and secularism." He asked the people to raise their hands in prayer "for victory for all mujahideen in the world" and for freedom.

After the sermon and the prayer that followed, lunch was brought for Sayyid Jalil and other mosque staff. Firas and I were offered food by a famous Mahdi Army IED maker. As Sayyid Jalil walked to his office, men came in and said that an American patrol was in the area and he was ushered away. As we left several young men in the courtyard asked us to join them for lunch. After my friend returned me to Mansour, his friends from the Mahdi Army asked him suspiciously if I was a foreigner and a friend of his. He said I was. They asked him if I drank alcohol, and he said I did not. They asked him if I slept with Iraqi women, and he said I did not. Apparently, they wanted to kidnap me and were looking for a proper pretext to justify it.

We ended up having lunch that day at Mustafa Husseiniya in Ur. Its imam, Sheikh Safa, had fled to Iran to avoid arrest and had not returned. I sat with the caretaker, Abul Hassan, and his assistant, Haidar, in Abul Hassan's home. (Haidar had been expelled by Sunni militias from the town of Abu Ghraib, west of Baghdad. His brother was killed working as a policeman.)

Born in Sadr City in 1972, Abul Hassan, whose real name was Adil, was a muscular and voluble man. He had a raspy voice, permanent stubble. He was jocular and warm and spoke in colloquial Iraqi Arabic because he lacked education. His grandfather had moved to Baghdad from the south when Abul Hassan's father was still a child, and President Abdul Karim Qasim gave the family land in Thawra (Revolution) City, which would become Saddam City and later Sadr City. Abul Hassan did not attend high school, and after his military service he worked a number of odd jobs, like driving a taxi and small trade. He had always been a Sadrist, he said with a smile, and had followed Muqtada's father. Following the elder Sadr's murder, Abul Hassan and his friends established a small underground armed resistance cell but failed to engage in any successful operations. After the war he and Sheikh Safa took over the Baath Party office and were the ones who converted it into a *husseiniya*. Now Abul Hassan informally led the Ur district.

The Mustafa Husseiniya, which had been demolished after the previous year's raid, was now being rebuilt. Abul Hassan maintained his office in an adjacent one-room structure, where he sat on the floor behind a desk and received guests and supplicants. The mosque still provided help to poor families and IDPs. "Only Sadrists help the displaced," he said. They also helped families of martyrs and other needy people, giving them bags with basic requirements such as milk, oil, rice, sugar, and similar items. "The government doesn't do it," he said.

The Mahdi Army in the area assisted the families of one thousand martyrs and three thousand prisoners with stipends, the size determined by whether they were married, Abul Hassan said. The family of an unmarried Mahdi Army martyr received seventy five thousand dinars a month (about sixty dollars), as did the family of an arrested man; and the family of a married Mahdi Army martyr received twice as much. Most of the displaced families they helped lived in other people's homes, he said, but many still lived in tents in the nearby Shishan (Chechen) neighborhood, thus named because Iraqis thought Chechnya was very poor.

Haidar brought lunch in: mushy cooked tomatoes with kabob and bread. As we ate, two women in *abayas* came in and asked for bags of supplies and children's clothes. Haidar went to fetch them.

Already in December 2007, before the March 2008 clashes, Abul Hassan was comparing the Supreme Council, which dominated the government, with Saddam Hussein. "Why did Saddam kill Shiites?" he asked. "He was also afraid of Shiite masses. The Supreme Council wants a secular Islam; they don't reject occupation or even talk about it." Under Saddam supporters of Muqtada's father walked to Karbala for pilgrimages. Abul Hassan complained that people walking to Karbala were still targeted because they were viewed as Sadrists. "The Sadr Current represents 75 percent of Iraqi Shiites and is a popular movement," he said. "Only the Sadr Current helps the poor and represents them."

Some materials and labor were donated to help with the mosque's reconstruction, but the government-run Shiite religious endowment was controlled by the Supreme Council. "We always have problems with the Supreme Council," he complained. "They always instigate it. The Supreme Council are untrustworthy and just want power." Abul Hassan was suspicious of the Sunni Awakening militias. "There is an Awakening group in the Fadhil neighborhood," he said. "There is a man called Adel al-Mashhadani, he killed hundreds of Shiites, he beheaded many Shiites. He is well-known by people for his terrible crimes. Later they put him as head of the Awakening in that neighborhood. He is a criminal, he should be prosecuted. This is not logical."

Since members of the Mahdi Army had committed to the freeze, he observed, they had been arrested, their families displaced and their savings stolen. "Now the freeze is ongoing and the arrests continue. I think it's better to lift this freeze," he said. "With things happening like the night raids, I don't think the freeze will continue. The followers of the Supreme Council displace the families of arrested Mahdi Army members in the city of Diwaniya."

I told Abul Hassan that Sunnis accused Sadrists of being Iranians. "This is nonsense," he said. "We are Iraqis. Did you see Iranians or hear us talking the Iranian language? We are the followers of the first and the second martyred sayyids."

The War Inside the Mahdi Army

The Golden Group—Golden JAM, in U.S. military parlance—was established, composed of trusted Mahdi Army men led by Abbas al-Kufi. The group was tasked with cleaning up the Mahdi Army in Baghdad and killing rogue militiamen. Shiite militias called assassins *sakak*, the equivalent of "ice men," maybe because corpses were put on ice. *Sak* meant to "get iced." ("*Ahmed sak Hassan*" means "Ahmed iced Hassan"—or, if he was in New York, "Ahmed whacked

Hassan.") While the ice men were doing their job, it was not clear if Muqtada had miscalculated with his freeze, allowing his Shiite and American rivals to gain the momentum. On the other hand, he may not have had a choice but to flee to Iran, as he did in 2007. "We would have killed or arrested him if he had stayed," one National Security Council Iraq expert told me.

But the cease-fire was allowing the Mahdi Army to reorganize. In Baghdad it was split into two commands: eastern and western Baghdad. Eastern Baghdad had three subcommands: north, east, and Sadr City. They were further divided into sub-subcommands, each consisting of about three hundred men. At the top of this chain of command was a council in the southern town of Kufa, near Najaf, which Muqtada chaired. In Shaab there were about three thousand Mahdi Army fighters, led by a man called Adil al-Hasnawi. They were required to be devout, lest they be expelled. They did not receive a salary or training; instead they manned checkpoints, attended Friday prayers, protected pilgrims traveling to holy cities such as Karbala, cleaned the streets, and guarded mosques.

Nominally the Mahdi Army responded to Muqtada or his designated representatives. But there were highly criminalized elements that were displaced from Sunni areas and occupied Sunni houses in Hurriya; these elements resorted to a protection racket in order to support themselves and their families. "This was done at the behest of the community civil leadership and clerical leadership to protect against Sunni incursion and attacks," noted a major who served with the First Battalion, 325th Airborne Infantry Regiment, Eighty-Second Airborne Division. But then, according to the major, there was the Mahdi Army sent from Najaf—the so-called Golden JAM—to clean up the criminalized elements and bring them in line with Muqtada's office. At the same time the Iraqi Security Forces leadership either worked in conjunction with the Mahdi Army or independently to conduct offensive actions against coalition forces and sectarian cleansing of Sunnis. The ISF was an "institutional sanctuary" for Mahdi Army members; the Shiite-majority police and national police in that area were actively targeting the Sunni population. Furthermore, the major said, the Office of Muqtada al-Sadr conducted its own census by collecting ration cards, effectively forcing Sunni displacement by preventing Sunnis from receiving goods and services within Hurriya and sending displaced Shiites into evacuated Sunni houses. The Office and Mahdi Army elements funded operations by intercepting propane shipments and conducting their own delivery operations, raising the price of propane and preventing delivery to Sunnis. At the same time, clerical and tribal leadership meddling into socioeconomic affairs allowed the Mahdi Army to become criminalized and terrorize the Sunni and Shiite population. "Most of the Sunni population had been displaced to the district south of the Hurriya DMZ [demilitarized zone], so to speak, when my company arrived in Hurriya," the major told me.

"There were some Sunnis who lived there, but were mostly women without husbands and lived pretty low-key. My southern border was lined with bullet-riddled and burned houses that distinguished the line between Shiite Hurriya and the Sunni district south of Hurriya."

The major told me about Operation Seventh Veil, which was aimed at targeting the Shiite militias, no matter the political risk. Dagger Brigade initiated an operation to investigate, track, and detain "radical or criminal ISF leadership to disrupt this longstanding government sanctuary." Many were confronted with evidence of their criminal links and warned to behave. A major coup resulting from this operation was the arrest of Ghazaliya's police chief as well as officers from the Iraqi army.

By June 2007 Golden JAM had killed or captured rogue Mahdi Army elements, and the major's battalion had disrupted the militia's lines of communications, resources, and leadership, denying them sanctuary and killing "high-value individuals."

In Dora, the main headquarters for the Sadrists and the Mahdi Army was the Kadhimayn Mosque in Abu Dshir. Its loudspeakers were within listening reach of Falcon FOB, where the 2–2 SCR was based. According to that unit's senior intelligence officer, Captain Dehart, "We are actively targeting rogue elements of Shiite extremists that have not complied with Muqtada's cease-fire and the remnants of Al Qaeda." When Dehart first came into this area, it was Al Qaeda's top stronghold in Iraq; but after successful clearing operations the leadership fled and the ones left were low-level thugs, young Sunni males with nothing better to do than to call themselves Al Qaeda, string together fellow thugs from the neighborhood, and try their hand at extortion and murder.

On a map Dehart showed me Saha and Mahala 828, or Kifaat, in northern Saha. He pointed to southern Saha, the majority-Shiite area ruled by Abu Jaafar, General Karim's ally. It had large government-built apartment complexes. The north had villas he said had belonged to mostly Sunni government officials. "In the last few months Shiite militias moved up. Now the north is largely abandoned; it has a 10 percent occupancy rate. That's where the fault line was. We called it 'the arena.' Sunnis from Mahala 830, or Hadhir, would come across and Shiites would come up and fire mortars into Sunni Mahalas 822 and 824 and randomly kill people. We have been able to cut that a lot. I can't even say we—the surge, as Iraqi institutions have started to stand up and get more efficient. And it comes down to the people too, tired of the violence. We've had only one indirect fire incident in the last two weeks, directed at the FOB. It's been a month and a half since we've had anything shot neighborhood to neighborhood. When we first got here it was several times a week. We specifically targeted that, and captured or killed mortar teams on both sides."

First Lieut. Adam Sperry was Dehart's tactical intelligence officer. Walking back from the chow hall to the tactical operations center one night, we heard celebratory gunfire and a speech blasting from the Kadhimayn Mosque's loud-speakers, which he called "the propaganda phone." Sperry said it was for the death of the Ninth Imam.

A week before my visit three Shiite NAC members who led three *mahalas* in Abu Dshir had been kidnapped just as ISV recruiting was set to begin in the area. They were taken to the Kadhimayn Mosque and released within twenty-four hours. The mosque's previous imam, Sheikh Majid, had been arrested a year earlier but was later released. I asked why he was arrested. "Because he was a scumbag," Sperry said. "The mosque was raided eight months ago. Weapons and a torture chamber were found. We should have raided that mosque a month ago."

Sperry described Ziyad al-Shamari as the bane of his existence. "He's the rogue special groups commander of Abu Dshir, responsible for EFPs [explosively formed penetrators] that have killed lots of our soldiers. This guy is not, nor was he ever, a Sadrist. He is funded entirely by Iran." Sperry explained that Shiite militias did not attack the Americans in Abu Dshir, because it was their command-and-control location. "They don't want to fight there or draw attention to themselves," he said. Instead, they placed EFPs in other parts of Dora.

"Abu Dshir is stable," Sperry said. "We don't want to disturb that by breaking down doors. The guys we target in Abu Dshir are transiting there." (The night before 2–2 SCR had gone on a raid to pick up two Mahdi Army suspects. When they showed up, one man drank a few gulps of motor oil and the other swallowed three pills of Viagra and passed out.) Thanks to the cease-fire and reconciliation, Sperry was having a hard time doing his job. "It's impossible to determine who is good or who is bad," he said, explaining that the only men the 2–2 SCR targeted were those who attacked the Americans after the cease-fire. "We can't target anyone based on any evidence before that date."

In December 2007, on my first Friday with the 2–2 SCR, an imam called Sayyid Abbas spoke at the Kadhimayn Mosque. He condemned killings and expulsions of people. "We are all brothers," he said, and explained that Muqtada had imposed a cease-fire on his men "to correct all the mistakes and remove the bad members who joined the Mahdi Army without knowledge or religion. "They are just killers and thieves," he said, "so if you know of somebody from the Mahdi Army trying to do something bad in the name of the Mahdi Army, please tell the mosque. We will take care of him by reporting his name to Kufa, and we will let the government know." The government would arrest the renegade men, he said, granting the Iraqi Security Forces the Mahdi Army's approval. The American forces were infidel forces, he said; they were trying to provoke a civil war, and Iraqis had to fight that. "We can't kill our own brothers and our own people just because they are Sunni and Shiite," he said. Not long after that, the Americans and Iraqi National Police raided the mosque again and found IEDs, mortars, and rockets.

Mahdi Army leaders were livid about the attempts to recruit Shiites for the Awakening and used the mosque to conduct investigations. They posted a "final warning" on the walls addressed to "the good people of Abu Dshir" and in "honor of the blood of our noble martyrs," asking people to protect the souls of their sons and not join "the conspiracy known as the Awakening." Abu Dshir's main street, known as Rashid al-Tijari (the Americans called it Market Street), was lined with signs on light poles that bore pictures of Muqtada, his father, and various Mahdi Army "martyrs." A slogan said that not all men were real men, which implied that these really were. A faded poster on one light pole said, "Bush and Saddam, two faces on same coin" in English. Graffiti on the walls warned *takfiris* that the Mahdi Army would declare them infidels deserving of death.

Sunni militias from the nearby Arab Jubur area had fired mortars at the Shiites of Abu Dshir. Walking through the neighborhood I found a man called Hisham working on his house. He had lost two brothers to the violence. Mortars from Arab Jubur had also landed on his neighbor's house. "If it wasn't for the police and the Americans, Al Qaeda would have destroyed us," he said. "We are poor people, we just go to work and come back. We had no problems with our Sunni neighbors—it was all Al Qaeda." People expelled from Arab Jubur and the Furat district had settled in the area. Muqtada's local office and the Kadhimayn Mosque were providing assistance to them, including homes (emptied of Sunnis) and a stipend. Locals complained that the Mahdi Army freeze had hurt them. The militia had guarded the neighborhood and provided propane and kerosene, which they had trouble getting now. I asked who was protecting the area. "Its people," I was told. "People sit in front of their homes."

In Dora the Mahdi Army was under the command of the Karkh, or western Baghdad Brigade. The leader for western Baghdad and many of his local commanders were recently replaced for ignoring the freeze, and the Sadrists were trying to provide social services and help local municipalities. Some Sunni families who had been displaced by Al Qaeda in Arab Jubur were received by the Sadrists in Abu Dshir and provided with assistance. Mahdi Army men complained that the cease-fire was paralyzing them and causing them to lose respect or authority in their areas. In the nearby Bayya district, the Sadrist office was furious when an unknown corpse turned up on the street; several days were spent investigating whether somebody had disobeyed Muqtada's orders. But the Mahdi Army was unable to control the rogue groups; sometimes, in fact, they received help from them.

In Abu Dshir the Mahdi Army relied on lookouts who watched for the Americans on rooftops and street corners. They also released pigeons from coops when American patrols approached. In the past this had led Americans to shoot innocent pigeon keepers. Apart from going on raids in Abu Dshir, the

Americans conducted "presence patrols" in which they walked through the streets and interacted with people. I followed a platoon of soldiers from the 2-2 SCR around Market Street and spoke to the local shopkeepers about them. Flocks of sheep were herded through the streets, a common sight in the city. The Americans walked past furniture shops, waved to shopkeepers, and bought roasted chicken and fresh bread at inflated rates. "The Americans don't have a strategy," one local observed. "They don't know who is with them or who is against them, and they've been here for four years." I asked a group of men if Muqtada was powerful in this area. "It's a Shiite neighborhood," one said, as if it were obvious. "JAM has lookouts on streets dressed just like that," an American officer said, pointing to a young man in a matching tracksuit. "It's funny, you can look at these guys and know that they're bad and have nothing to detain them for."

Shopkeepers whose shops were destroyed during the fighting were supposed to receive money from the Americans. "Why did some get money and some didn't?" I was asked by men who assumed I was a translator for the Americans. A group of men called the American officer over to show him an old man's leg that was injured in an explosion. "Can't anybody help him?" they asked. Another man asked if the Americans could help his unemployed son find a job in the security forces.

Platoon leader Lieutenant Cowan decided to visit a random house and ordered his men to "clear" it. Uninvited, they pushed open the outer gate and the door to the house. As the translator was elsewhere with Cowan, I had to explain to a frightened and bewildered woman and her two sons that the officer merely wanted to talk to them and they needn't worry. The younger boy clung to his mother's *abaya* and whimpered in terror. A soldier gave him some candy, and he stopped crying. "I feel bad walking on these people's carpets with my shoes," one major said. "My wife would kill me." He went back outside. Cowan came in with his Iraqi translator, who wore a mask and sunglasses. He asked the woman how much electricity she received per day, about her water and sense of security. Cowan asked her if she knew who Ziyad al-Shamari was and how much influence the Mahdi Army had over the area. She laughed sheepishly with her older son. "We don't go outside, we close the door," she said. "You don't hear rumors?" asked Cowan. "You don't hear whispers? Do you know if there is JAM activity in the Kadhimayn Mosque?"

In a different home Cowan encountered an old man in a wheelchair who was a retired Iraqi colonel. "All Shiites here love the U.S. Army," the man told him. "Yeah, well, we love you," Cowan said with a smile. "In the beginning the Mahdi Army protected us from Al Qaeda," the old man said. "Then they joined the police, they are all police. They protect us from mortars, Al Qaeda in Arab Jubur."

One day I accompanied twenty-two-year-old platoon leader Rob Johnston as his men took two masked Iraqi "sources" from the Badr militia to identify Mahdi Army suspects. The Americans had been collaborating with this militia since 2004, when they teamed up with Jalaluddin al-Saghir, the Supreme Council cleric and politician. Saghir would send his security chief, known as Haji Dhia, to the Americans. Haji Dhia would wear a ski mask, point out the house, and tell the Americans what they would find there. He once escorted an American unit to a house at 2 a.m. They found an arms bazaar inside, with more than one hundred Kalashnikovs laid out in neat rows around the walls, along with ammunition, Glock pistols, and two MP-5s. Though at first the information was directed against Sunnis and helped the Americans arrest Al Qaeda cells, the Supreme Council provided information about the Sadrists as well, especially during the 2004 fighting in Najaf.

That morning in December 2007, the Americans descended from their vehicles and entered the main covered market in Abu Dshir. People tried to navigate around the large soldiers, looking at them quizzically as they squeezed through the tight alleys of the market. The Iraqi sources stayed in the vehicle. As women bought vegetables, fish, and clothes in various stalls, the soldiers rounded up all the men in the market, as well as those entering or leaving, pushing them back and holding them by their shoulders, ordering them to obey. One by one they led dozens of men to the street so the sources could identify them. One young boy started crying. A man hurrying back to his stall was halted. "Fish, fish," he said in Arabic.

I wandered off to buy some popcorn from a stand. As I returned men warned me to go in a different direction because the Americans were stopping people. Sergeant Bowyer, charged with carrying out psychological operations, distributed an Arabic-language newspaper published by Americans and asked people inane questions. "So, how is everything here?" he asked one man. "What's your sense of the people? Are people really happy in regards to reconciliation?" "Do you think JAM feels threatened by reconciliation?" he asked another. "When JAM tries to influence the people in Abu Dshir, how do they do it?" he asked another. "We can't talk about this openly," one man replied. "I'll take that as a sign that it does happen," Bowyer said. His vehicle was equipped with speakers, and as he drove through Market Street it blasted an announcement in Arabic calling on the people to continue with reconciliation and ignore those who would "take them back."

The men raided a house and found some bewildered men working. "We're laborers," the men protested as they were taken to be identified by the sources, who had pointed out the house. They were pushed against the walls. One soldier held one of them by the back of the neck. The three men were quickly interrogated one by one. "What do you think of the way he talks," the lieutenant asked me. "Do you think he's honest?" Their stories were consistent with the obvious—they were mere laborers. "Can I go?" the last man asked me. "They're not taking me away?" As I said no, he smiled and kissed my cheek. "We appreciate the time you gave us," Lieutenant Johnston told them.

Children chased after the soldiers asking them for candy and teasing them. When they learned I spoke Arabic, they pointed to the pigeons that were flying above homes. They had been released by Mahdi Army lookouts. All the children liked Muqtada. "The Americans are dogs and Muqtada will defeat them," one boy said. "The Americans are donkeys and the boys who take candy from the Americans are donkeys," another boy said. "When they are here we say, 'I love you,' but when they leave we say, 'Fuck you,'" he told me. Another boy showed me his watch, which had a picture of Muqtada's father on its face.

Johnston's platoon raided Abu Dshir one night. The soldiers broke down the gate of a home and rushed into the house. "We are not Mahdi Army, we are in the Iraqi army," an old man protested. "We are not Mahdi Army or anything." It was a middle-class home with no overt signs of religiosity and none of the typical things associated with Muqtada's supporters. The five women and one child were herded into the living room as three men were interrogated. "Mister, I am no Jaish al-Mahdi," one man protested in English. "Okay, okay, *uskut, shukran*" (be quiet, thank you), said a soldier. "We hate the Mahdi Army," said an old woman, "believe me." Thinking I was a translator, the residents looked at me and begged me to explain that none of them had anything to do with the Mahdi Army. The women were made to stand, empty their pockets, and pat themselves down, starting with their arms, down their chests to their legs.

One man, it turned out, was a laborer who had signed up for the Awakening. Another worked in their father's pastry shop. Their father was seventy years old, and a brother who was absent was in the Iraqi army. The men's pictures were taken. They were shown pictures of Mahdi Army suspects and asked to identify them, but they recognized none of them. "We are not terrorists," the old man said. "We like the government." Most of their protests went untranslated. "Why do you think automatically I'm looking for the Mahdi Army?" Johnston asked. "Because you have been arresting people and accusing them of being Mahdi Army lately," the man replied. He was handcuffed and complained that they were too tight. Johnston put his finger between the cuffs and the man's wrists. "If I can fit one finger, it's okay," he said. The two sons were also handcuffed, and they were all taken away. Their phones, computer, and cash were also taken, as were their personal papers, CDs, and other objects of interest that had Arabic writing on them. "They probably got some propaganda in there," a sergeant explained as he carried off a hard drive.

Neighbors who rushed into their homes when the Americans arrived provoked American suspicion, and they too were brought in for interrogation.

One old man started crying, fearing the Americans would take his son away. On the way back the tired soldiers bantered in the Stryker. "You know what I hate most about detainee duty? Watching those motherfuckers shit," one complained. "I bet there's an Iraqi rap song about being arrested by us," another said.

The Reconciliation?

In Virginia, sometime after my trip to Iraq in December 2007, I met P.J. Dermer, a former Special Forces aviator who had been a Middle East foreign area officer in the U.S. Army since the late 1980s and had traveled independently through much of the region. In 2003 he worked with the Iraqi army; subsequently, he returned to work under Petraeus. "Sunnis realized they were in trouble—we were killing 'em, the Shiites were killing 'em," Dermer observed. "As we saw the Awakening develop, we realized we can't kill our way out of this. But some guys were afraid to come out, and we had to make sure Maliki was soothed."

Even in 2004 and 2005 American commanders established relationships with Sunni tribal leaders who were tired of the Al Qaeda presence in their area. But there was no systematic approach to transition these temporary alliances on the battlefield into a normal relationship with the Iraqi government. In July 2007 Petraeus established the Force Strategic Engagement Cell (FSEC). Its task was to reach out to the resistance and "reconcile" them with the Iraqi government. Typical of the military, the unusual name for talking to resistance leaders was "key leader engagement." According to Petraeus, the goal of KLE was "to understand various local situations and dynamics, and then—in full coordination with the Iraqi government—to engage tribal leaders, local government leaders, and, in some cases, insurgent and opposition elements." This was a challenge for the military, which needs a formula or system for everything it does, even building relationships. Petraeus formalized KLE because developments like the Awakening were occurring with little involvement or support from the Iraqi government. As a result the government was very suspicious of the Awakening and the Americans' motives. In addition, Petraeus had no body of his own through which to coordinate these local developments or approach them strategically.

"You cannot kill or capture your way out of an insurgency," Petraeus said. He hoped to establish a dialogue between members of the resistance, or at least influential supporters, and the Iraqi government. This would facilitate the American and Iraqi forces' takeover of areas controlled by the resistance without requiring combat in village after village. Of course, those in the resistance, whether Sunni or Shiite, who were "irreconcilable" would be killed or captured. FSEC was composed of a few dozen mostly military officers, although the American ambassador appointed a civilian from the State Department to work with them. "Engagers" working for FSEC developed "lanes" to reach out to the Iraqi government and resistance.

"We gave insurgents a place to come see us, to realize we weren't ogres," Dermer said. "The Awakening was also a movement within Sunnis at large, but they didn't realize what they wanted. Some wanted to take over from the Shiites, others just wanted to go back to normal life. We were getting deeper and deeper [with the Sunni resistance], further up the hierarchy, and having more success. But Sunnis were way too divided." Dermer met leaders of the Islamic Army of Iraq, Ansar al-Sunna, the Jihad and Reform Front, and some people connected to the 1920 Revolution Brigades.

Dermer would meet these resistance men in Jordanian hotels. In Jordan and Syria he also met with Iraqi businessmen and expatriates who were in touch with the resistance but were not driving it. In 2003 he had been involved in the creation of the new Iraqi Defense Ministry. Many of the former military officers he had met then were now influential in the resistance.

The Iraqi government's Implementation and Follow-up Committee for National Reconciliation (IFCNR), led by the notorious Dr. Bassima al-Jadri, was set up by Maliki to work on "reconciliation" issues with the Americans and to deal with the Awakening movement. "The Awakening wasn't a reconciliation with the Iraqis but with the power to be in the battlefield," Dermer explained. "The purpose of Maliki's reconciliation committee was also to thwart whatever we wanted to do. The reconciliation committee was all Shiite except for a couple of token Sunnis. They did a good job of making us believe we were making progress. It was clear to me from dealing with the Iraqi army, Bassima, Adnan [a Shiite former intelligence officer under Saddam], that they [the Awakening] were doomed from the beginning. We kept a nice face on it with all this talk about jobs, yeah yeah, blah blah. The Iraqi government was flabbergasted when we told them how many [Awakening men] we had on the payroll. But it worked. It settled down the killing to a manageable degree. Abud Qanbar hated tribal sheikhs. He's urban. 'They had their chance,' he said. The Iraqis wanted to arrest all the Awakening leaders, and the minute space developed they went after them. Maliki was smart; he created the reconciliation committee. He was building tribal councils, the mirror image [of the Awakening] but Shiites. Bassima and Adnan were involved in building the tribal councils. You could get something done if you had a good relationship with Bassima and Adnan. The tribal support councils were meant to manipulate tribes to be on Maliki's side, like the Ottomans and Saddam. Bassima was Maliki's watchdog to mitigate the Awakening and the Sunnis. Some senior insurgent guys were FREs [former regime elements], generals I met in 2003."

Though Jadri was a friend and confidante of Maliki, everybody else around her hated her. "Bassima had issues being a woman in a man's world," Dermer

told me. "Iraqi generals kissed her ass." Jadri and Adnan wanted to meet the
Awakening men, so the Americans brokered it. "Sunnis wouldn't engage with
the Iraqi government without American interlocution," Dermer said. "The
Shiites wanted us out of the way. We brought in Raad from Ghazaliya, Abul
Abed from Amriya, and Abu Azzam al-Tamimi from Abu Ghraib." These were
important Awakening leaders in Baghdad. "We brought them into the palace
to meet Bassima and Adnan," he said. "It took a lot of work."

Dermer mocked the notion of "key leader engagement," which in practice
meant trying to have as many meetings as possible and using that as a measure
of progress. FSEC was originally led by Graeme Lamb, a British general who
was Petraeus's deputy and who had experience establishing a dialogue with
armed groups in Northern Ireland. "Lamb was replaced by an idiot British
general and an idiot State Department guy," Dermer complained bitterly.
"The guys in charge of FSEC didn't get it. It takes very unique people for this
office. These fuckers are killers. You can't be a starry-eyed thirty-year-old or
Harvard grad, but it was a lot of PowerPoint briefings, six-month rotations—it
was bureaucratic. People hated success, like getting high in the insurgency.
The agency [CIA] fought us, State [Department] hated us. Once you put it in a
bureaucracy, it won't work. It was a brilliant idea, but we didn't know what we
were doing."

FSEC also saw the prison population as a group with potential to be "reconciled," and also as a possible source of intelligence on the resistance. Some
prisoners were resistance leaders and could actually encourage their supporters outside to reach an accommodation with the Americans or the Iraqi government. In American prisons Dermer and his colleagues met with leaders of
the Mahdi Army and special groups.

Throughout the American occupation the majority of Iraqis seized and imprisoned by the Americans were innocent, even innocent of conducting attacks against the Americans. Few of the tens of thousands of Iraqis detained in
the American-run gulags were ever even charged with anything. Few Americans question whether they had a right to invade a foreign country and arrest
scores of its men every day on scant evidence. When the men were eventually
released, the Americans staged shows of fanfare and magnanimity.

In December 2007 the 1–28 Infantry Division, which controlled the Jihad
district, staged one of these slightly absurd "reconciliation" ceremonies when
it released fifteen Shiite men. Col. Pat Frank of the 1–28, who supervised the
ceremony, explained to me that Jihad was part of what the Americans had
named Northwest Rashid, and was about 42 percent Shiite and 58 percent
Sunni. There were a little over 1,800 ISVs in Northwest Rashid. There were
also 985 Shiite police recruits and 834 Sunni police recruits; 850 of them came
out of the ISVs. "Moderates have gained the momentum in the area and over-
taken extremists," Frank said.

Frank's men staged a reconciliation accord between Sunnis and Shiites as a gesture and requested a list of local men they had imprisoned that the district's leaders wanted to be released. "They were suspected of Shiite militant activity," Frank said, but were screened by the Americans and Iraqi government before their release. "Some people on the list were rejected at senior levels" by the Americans, he told me. Only fifteen men had been approved. The Americans built a "reconciliation hall" for the "Reconciliation Committee." Frank showed neighborhood leaders charts in which he gave them red stars or green stars depending on whether violence had gone down in their area. He gave a metal emblem of the black lion, which symbolized his unit, to a female American correspondent in case she ever had problems. "The Iraqis know us and love us," he said. "Just show it to them and you'll be fine."

The fifteen prisoners were brought in to the building in handcuffs. The few journalists present were ordered not to take pictures until the cuffs were removed. The event was clumsily choreographed. Journalists, council members, and local dignitaries were herded into a separate room and guarded by soldiers. Tahsin Ali Samarai, of the Reconciliation Council's security committee complained that they had given the Americans a list of 562 prisoners from their area that they wanted released. The Iraqi army colonel in charge of the area told me that all the men were innocent. Another tribal sheikh agreed. "The Americans arrest people randomly," he said, adding that some of the men had been imprisoned for nearly two years. Sheikh Awad Abdul Wahel, also known as Abu Muhammad, was president of the tribal sheikh council, which had submitted seven hundred names of prisoners from the Jihad district alone. "I serve my people, not the Americans," he said. "They were never accused or found guilty," Sheikh Hussein Karim al-Kinani said. "American accusations and arrests are random."

Outside one angry young woman called Leila waited with her two children. Her husband, Muhammad, was arrested sixteen months earlier while sleeping on his roof to avoid the summer heat. A neighbor was shot and Muhammad was rounded up with all the other men of military age in the area. Their son was born while he was in prison. Leila blamed the Americans for the civil war and did not want to talk about reconciliation. One woman in an *abaya* came because she heard men were going to be released. Her son was captured by Abul Abed, the notorious Awakening leader in the Sunni district of Amriya.

Inside the prisoners were boisterous. They were seated in alphabetical order, and behind them sat "guarantors" for a "bond" they would have to sign. "It's not an oath on the Koran," Frank explained. "It's on their honor. A guarantor is a mentor, just like in the U.S., when an individual runs in trouble with law and somebody steps up to mentor them. The reconciliation committee wants to see these fifteen men do well." The Iraqis seemed uninterested and amused by the American show. They endured speeches given by Frank and

Captain Ducote. "We want to make this a special event," Frank said, and asked the men to quiet down. "Thank you for being patient, but this is for you." Prisoners and guarantors got up pair by pair to each sign their "bond." The Iraqi colonel played his part. "The government is in control now," he said, "not like before. There is a state and there is law." He told them to join the police or the army. Frank was uncertain how to describe the prisoners. He could no longer call them detainees. "We will now ask each individual to stand," he said. "Guarantors stand too. You raise your right hand. Guarantors put your left hand on the shoulder of the individual."

"I acknowledge that recent signings of the Reconciliation Agreement have ushered in an era of peace and partnership between Shiite, Sunni, Kurdish, Christian, the Mahdi Army, Iraqi Security Forces, and American Forces," the oath said somewhat optimistically. Interestingly, the only militia that was mentioned was the Mahdi Army, though the Americans were granting it a role as a legitimate actor. "Based on my arrest record, Iraqi Government and Coalition Force leaders have agreed that my immediate release would be beneficial to the Reconciliation process. I pledge to not commit any violations of the Reconciliation Agreement's 12 points, violate Iraqi Law, or attack Coalition Forces." The men were not told what those twelve points were. "As a proud Iraqi citizen living in Northwest Rashid, I will become a contributing member of the community in the historic effort to rebuild this proud nation." The Iraqis might have wondered where Northwest Rashid was, since they never used this designation. They might also have considered that they were rebuilding a proud nation the Americans had helped destroy. The guarantors took a similar oath stating that they were "bound by honor" to notify American or Iraqi authorities if the "individual" violated the oath. "As an Iraqi living in Northwest Rashid, I am proud to guarantee the mature and peaceful future actions of this citizen," they said.

Then Frank spoke. "The coalition would like to welcome all the members of the free Jihad community," he said. "The area of Jihad has been changed a lot. Violence has been reduced tremendously, and this reconciliation is proof." He did not explain who the men were reconciling with. "With your release from detention we expect that you will become part of the reconciliation, and we look forward to working with you and the guarantor, the person behind you. All the citizens of Baghdad are watching Jihad now." It was unlikely that any of them were, because the only Iraqi journalist present was a lone freelance cameraman. "Welcome back," said Captain Ducote. "Jihad is not the same place that you left. You were released based on your ability to join the reconciliation process. I look forward to seeing you on the streets as we patrol."

It was a reconciliation between the Americans and the Iraqis, not between Iraqis, just as the Awakening was a reconciliation between Sunnis and the Americans. By December, up to eighty thousand men were part of the ISV program in eight Iraqi governorates. Nearly all were Sunnis, though there were a few thousand Shiites as well, in separate units. The Awakening program peaked at about one hundred thousand men. Though it was meant to compensate for the sectarian imbalance resulting from Sunnis' boycotting the security forces and being blacklisted by the Shiite government, the creation of new Sunni militias seemed to be promoting sectarianism and a fissiparous future. The drop in violence resulting from the decision of Sunni militias to cooperate with the Americans, the Mahdi Army's decision to regroup, and the "surge" in American troops was meant to buy time for reconciliation between Iraq's warring parties and bickering politicians, but there was no political progress. Apart from the security forces, the Iraqi government was nonexistent outside the Green Zone. The Americans *were* the government. Walls created small fortress neighborhoods in Baghdad, preventing militias from fighting one another directly. Shiite militias battled one another in the south over oil and control of the lucrative pilgrimage industry. Everybody waited for the civil war between Kurds, Arabs, and Turkmen to start in the north. Sunnis and even some Shiites had quit the government, which couldn't pass laws or provide services anyway. The prime minister's office circumvented Parliament to issue decrees and sign agreements with the Americans that Parliament opposed.

Iraq was still under a foreign occupation. American soldiers were not mere policemen walking their beats on patrol, helping old women cross the street and working on reconstruction and beautification projects.

A foreign military occupation is a systematic imposition of violence and terror on an entire people. When I visited Iraq during the peak of the surge, at least twenty-four thousand Iraqis languished in American prisons. At least nine hundred of them were juveniles. Some were forced to go through a brainwashing program called the "House of Wisdom," in which American officers arrogantly arranged for prisoners to be lectured about Islam—as if a poor understanding of Islam, not the occupation itself, was the cause of the violence. The Americans were supposed to hand over prisoners to Iraq's authorities, since it was officially a sovereign country, but international human rights officials were loath to make this recommendation because conditions in Iraqi prisons were at least as bad as they were under Saddam. One American officer told me that six years was a life sentence in an Iraqi prison, because that was your estimated life span there. In the women's prison in Kadhimiya female prisoners were routinely raped.

Conditions in Iraqi prisons worsened during the surge because the Iraqi system could not cope with the massive influx. Prisoners arrested by the Americans during the surge were supposed to be handed over to the Iraqis. They often were not, but those were the lucky ones. Even in American detention, Iraqis did not know why they were being held, and they were not visited by defense lawyers. The Americans could hold Iraqis indefinitely, so they didn't even have to be tried by Iraqi courts. A fraction were tried in courts where Americans also testified. But observers were yet to see an Iraqi trial where they were convinced the accused was guilty and there was valid evidence that was properly examined, and no coerced confessions. Lawyers did not see their clients before trials, and there were no witnesses. Iraqi judges were prepared to convict on very little evidence. If Iraqi courts found prisoners innocent, the Americans sometimes continued to hold them anyway after their acquittal. There were five hundred of these "on hold" cases when I visited in early 2008. Often the Americans still arrested all men of military age when looking for suspects.

As politics and power became more and more local in Iraq, the Iraqi state itself seemed as though it were an American protectorate. As long as the new militias and security forces in Iraq fought Al Qaeda, they had the backing of the United States, much as dictatorships during the cold war enjoyed U.S. support as long as they fought communism, regardless of human rights abuses they might commit. The same logic applied to dictatorships in the Muslim world that collaborated in the war on terror. For sure, violence in Iraq was down, but there were still at least six hundred recorded attacks by resistance groups every month and about six hundred Iraqi civilians being killed in violence related to the civil war and occupation as well as more Iraqi soldiers and police. Since the surge began, nearly a million Iraqis had fled their homes, mostly from Baghdad, which had become a Shiite city. One reason fewer people were being killed was because there were fewer people to kill, fewer targets for the militias (which was why they turned on their own populations). The violence was not senseless; it was meant to displace the enemy's population. And if war is politics by other means, then the Shiites won. Opinion polls showed that the overwhelming majority of Iraqis blamed the Americans for their problems and wanted them to leave. American officials tried to put a positive spin on this, explaining that at least it united Iraqis, but Iraqis had opposed the American occupation from the day it began.

In early 2008 I met Captain Adil again. The Americans were threatening him, saying he would lose his value to them if he didn't pursue the Mahdi Army more actively. His chain of command wanted to fire him for the feeble attempts he had made to target the Mahdi Army. He picked me up in his van, and for lack of anywhere safe and private we sat and talked as he nervously scanned every man who walked by. He complained that the Americans called every Shiite suspect Mahdi Army and every Sunni suspect Al Qaeda, and that the Awakening was raiding houses without the permission of the Americans or Iraqi Security Forces. Now the Mahdi Army worried that the ISVs and Awakening were a new force meant to target them, he said, and that they would replace Al Qaeda. He worried that the Mahdi Army could start fighting again out of fear of the Awakening. "No one can control these guys. Abu Jaafar, the ISVs—the coalition must be tough with them. The situation won't get better. If someone kills your brother, can you forget his killer? You work hard to build a house and somebody blows up your house. Will they accept Sunnis back to Shiite areas and Shiites back to Sunni areas?"

Pilgrimage to Ramadi

Early in the morning on February 2, 2008, I joined Osama's comrades Abu Salih, Abu Yusef, and other ISV leaders from their area as they gathered to depart for Ramadi, the national seat of the Awakening Council, the political movement led by Abu Risha. They hoped to translate their military success into political power, but rivals from Dora had pre-empted them and appealed to Abu Risha to grant them recognition. We left in a three-car convoy. Abu Salih drove the car I was in. He explained that he named his son after his uncle Salih, who was killed by the Mahdi Army. Close to the Hero House we were stopped at an Iraqi army checkpoint. A soldier ordered Abu Salih to open the trunk. "I'm Abu Salih," he said. "Open the trunk," said the soldier. "Dog, son of a dog," Abu Salih muttered. "They have shitty manners." We passed by workers putting up new concrete walls. "They closed off Baghdad, but they didn't close the Iranian border," he complained.

Driving west, we entered the Anbar province. Looking at the desolate flat desert with a few trees, Abu Salih said, "Iraq is beautiful." Past the town of Abu Ghraib we saw a pickup truck with a large Russian anti-aircraft gun called a Dushka affixed to its back. The Dushka was often used as a heavy-infantry machine gun. Somali warlords had made it famous by placing it on their "technical" vehicles. "Now that's the Awakening," Abu Salih said, wistfully gazing at the Dushka. "How can we stand up to Gen. Abdul Karim with only Kalashnikovs?" We drove by more Awakening Council men with American Hummers and Russian PKCs, or belt-fed machine guns. "Ooh, look at that PKC," Abu Salih said.

We drove by the large yellow Awakening Council flag. The flag bore the Bedouin coffee pot as its symbol, stressing the group's Bedouin origins, of which some Sunnis were proud. Some Shiites, in turn, prided themselves on a settled farmer heritage. "Hopefully we will have this flag today," said Abu Salih. We were meticulously searched before entering the Awakening Council headquarters, our pens checked, our candy squeezed. Inside a large opulent guest hall, supplicants sat on long sofas lining the walls. Abu Risha, brother of the slain founder of the movement, sat on an ornate throne under a picture of his brother Sattar. We were served tea by Bangladeshi servants, and he ignored us. Eventually he turned to our group and asked, "How is Dora?"

We followed him into a smaller office, where three of the rival men from Dora were sitting. They referred to Abu Risha with deference, calling him "our older brother" and "our father." It was a strange phenomenon, urban Sunnis from Baghdad pledging their allegiance to a desert tribal leader, looking to the periphery for protection and representation, a reversal of past roles. But the Americans had empowered Abu Risha, and Baghdad's Sunni militiamen hoped to unite with him to fight their Shiite opponents.

Abu Husam, one of the rivals, told Abu Salih that his men were merely guards, not the Awakening. "You are military and we are political," he said. Abu Jawdat, the elderly leader of ISVs in an area adjoining Abu Salih's, bristled. "We are a political entity," he said. "We are not mercenaries." Abu Risha's political adviser attempted to calm the increasingly loud men. "Dora is big and can't have one leader," he said. "Are we in the time of Saddam Hussein?" He explained that the Awakening Council was preparing for national elections and that they should have elections in Dora as well to decide who will represent the Awakening there.

"Who fought Al Qaeda in Dora?" demanded Abu Yasser. "We all fought," said Abu Husam. "No, you didn't," Abu Yasser snapped. "I fought and I won't let somebody who I was protecting and was behind me come in front of me and say he fought. I was in the Army of the Mujahideen."

Abu Husam stood up and accused Abu Salih of having been an Al Qaeda member. Abu Salih turned red and waved his arm over his head. "Nobody lies about Abu Salih!" he shouted. One of his companions jumped to his defense and explained that he belonged to the 1920 Revolution Brigades and was wanted by the Americans. "No, he wasn't," laughed Abu Husam. All the men spoke with respect of the resistance and jihad. To them this was merely a *hudna* (cease-fire) with the American occupation while they fought the Iranian enemy, meaning Iraq's Shiites.

The men who fought Al Qaeda believed they deserved to be the new leaders. Abu Yusef explained that he had defended Dora's Tawhid Mosque from the Mahdi Army and the Iraqi National Police. "I won't let somebody who was behind me come in front of me," he said. He was backed by Muhammad Kashkul, Osama's former rival and a former officer in Saddam's feared intelligence service. Kashkul fought alongside several resistance groups in the area, and still clashed with his American paymasters over his hatred for the local INPs.

Abu Salih was forced to kiss Abu Husam, but in the end Abu Salih and his men, and not their rivals, left with the Awakening Council flag. They would be the new political bosses for their area. On the way back they listened to Bedouin music about Arabs standing together even when the whole world confronts them. Abu Salih recited the songs. In one of them a guy swore he would get in his GMC and use his PKC and marry an Iraqi woman.

The previous night Osama received a phone call from the Americans. They had decided to appoint him head of a new tribal advisory council, something Maliki had just created, even though the makeup of the councils was vague. Osama didn't know he was even a candidate, and he was not sure he wanted the added responsibility, though he knew it would help him protect his men. He explained that he made good money as a KBR contractor and that his wife wanted him to quit this Awakening business. In December he only made one thousand dollars from the ISV contract, and in January he made two thousand dollars. It was not a lot, he explained. He was also increasingly frustrated with the Americans. They were one week late paying him, and his men were agitated. Some suspected that he had been paid but kept the money for himself. A few days earlier Brig. Gen. Abdel Karim's men had opened fire on Osama's neighborhood and beat some of his men with their rifles. When the Americans did nothing, Osama threatened to quit and withdraw all his men. He argued with Lieutenant Colonel Reineke. "Reineke keeps telling me Abdel Karim is a good guy, he is the government," Osama said. "I said, 'Fuck the government. If I leave Al Qaeda will take over Dora.'"

CHAPTER EIGHT

The Battle Over Amriya

Part 1

Amriya, in western Baghdad's Rashid district, was one of the first neighborhoods to feel the full blast of civil war and mass population displacement. Long a resistance stronghold, it soon became as fearsome as Dora. The Samarra bombings of February 2006 accelerated this, as Shiites in Baghdad, particularly those in the Iraqi Security Forces who were linked to the Shiite militias, saw Amriya—with its large Sunni population, former links to the Baath Party, and current links to Al Qaeda along with Sunnis from Anbar—as a prime target for attack. The Sunnis, in turn, fought back ferociously. As it turned out, Amriya was the first place in Baghdad where the Awakening phenomenon of the Anbar was replicated. American collaboration with Sunni militiamen—many of whom were former resistance fighters—succeeded in radically changing the neighborhood.

Lieut. Col. Gian Gentile's squadron had been based in the west of Rashid district since January 2006. He and his men were among the first squadrons to go through the newly created COIN Academy in Camp Taji, just north of Baghdad. "The week course was essentially a course in Galula 101," he told me, in reference to the French theorist of counterinsurgency. "We used what we learned at Taji often in the months ahead. I never thought that more troops were needed, since I concluded early on that there were limits to what American combat power could accomplish and at some point Iraqis had to take over for the destiny of the country."

Gentile had been leading counterinsurgency operations with a primary focus on transitioning security responsibilities to the Iraqi Security Forces. However, after the Samarra bombings, it became clear to him that their primary purpose was to try to arrest the violence and protect the local population.

Gentile began to grasp after the Samarra bombings that the orgy of violence unleashed by it was actually a civil war. "The Sunnis regarded the government as their mortal enemy," he said, "and in many respects, they were correct. For the first half of 2006, when we were in West Rashid, we worked only with national police and the local police. After Samarra, within days, their links to Shiite militias and sectarian killings became clear. We did our best to curb this, but it was very difficult to do so."

In June 2006 he moved up to northwestern Baghdad—principally Amriya, Ghazaliya, Shula, Mansour, Kadhimiyah, Khadra, FOB Justice—and took over from an infantry battalion from Tenth Mountain Division. "It was an exceptionally large area," he said, "but I focused on Ghazaliya, Khadra, and Amriya, with the latter being the primary focus. This move was part of the Casey drawdown plan [General Casey's plan to transition power to Iraqi Security Forces], which was in full swing until things fell apart in Baghdad in July 2006."

The expanding sectarian warfare was made evident with the daily dumping of dead bodies on the streets of the district. The Iraqi army battalion commander who served with Gentile speculated that the bodies were Sunnis, killed elsewhere in Baghdad and then dumped on the streets of Amriya to intimidate the Sunnis there. "I saw it differently," Gentile said. "They were mostly Shiites who were still living in or coming into Amriya, and the Sunnis killed them as a way of 'cleansing' their district. Any semblance of trust had broken down completely between Shiite and Sunni, and the Sunnis in Amriya, I believed, saw any remaining Shiite in the district as a threat and link to marauding Shiite militia that could still enter the district and kill, since they were aligned with Iraqi Security Forces.

"The Iraqi army battalion in Amriya had turned Route Cedar, the main market street, into a kinetic civil-war attack zone," Gentile said. The Iraqi soldiers had two checkpoints on either end of the street and fighting outposts on roofs and inside buildings on nearly every block. The constant fighting, IEDs, suicide bombs, and car bombs had shut down all the businesses. Gentile thought that he could win "local hearts and minds" if he improved conditions on the road. He was authorized to remove the two checkpoints and the other outposts. He stationed one of his cavalry troops on the street and focused on reopening businesses. In mid-August 2006 he started building short concrete barriers—Jersey barriers, in American military parlance—around the entire district, with a single entry point run by the Iraqi army. "I initially started to build it in order to try and prevent Sunni insurgent infiltration into the district bringing in IED, car bomb materials, etc., from Ghazaliya to the north and Abu Ghraib to the west. But after it went up—especially the southern wall, which isolated Amriya from the Shiite-dominated West Rashid to the south of it—I found that the locals actually liked it because it prevented marauding Shiite militias from entering into it." All of this led to a much-improved state of security for the local Sunnis,

Gentile said, but the increased security for Sunnis made the area more lethal for the remaining Shiites because it gave the Sunni militias greater freedom of movement. They no longer had to fear Shiite militias.

This was the beginning of the massive population transfer: Sunnis from areas of Baghdad being taken over by Shiites were moving to Amriya. Any family moving out from Amriya was Shiite. "I knew it was going on, but there was no way to stop it," Gentile said. "We tried through moral suasion, but the locals and their leaders denied to us that it was happening. We tried driving bans, but that became impractical. How does one stop a civil war at the barrel of a gun with only a seven-hundred-man cavalry squadron in a district of close to a hundred thousand people?"

I spoke to Gentile some time after his tour in Amriya. I was curious to know what difference the new counterinsurgency doctrine made. "People like Tom Ricks will tell you that during the surge, units operated differently and adopted new COIN tactics. That just did not happen. What was decisive and made the fundamental difference in Amriya was the co-opting of our former enemies—the non–Al Qaeda Sunni insurgents who became known as the SOI, the Sons of Iraq."

Amriya came to be seen as a critical piece of terrain because it physically linked the western parts of Baghdad with eastern Anbar. It was also important because it was so close to the Baghdad International Airport and a relatively easy and safe trip for Sunni leaders coming back to Baghdad from the west. "But for the Sunnis in the area, after I built the wall around the place, and after we got the main market street back up and running, and after I established close operations with the Iraqi army battalion, it did actually get better," Gentile says.

Gentile says he had enough troops to "secure Amriya" but that he was challenged by an enemy that was a mix of Al Qaeda and other Sunni insurgent groups. But since he did not have the Sons of Iraq on his watch—they would emerge later, after Gentile left Baghdad—he never had the local intelligence to discover who set off an IED or fired a sniper round. His efforts were also complicated by the fact that Sunnis were using their increased security to attack the remaining Shiites in the district. The Sunnis also saw the Iraqi army battalion that Gentile was partnered with as an enemy.

Although Gentile was in Baghdad before the surge, he insists he was using the COIN principle already and that every time he was visited by Admiral Giambastiani and Generals Abizaid, Casey, and Chiarelli, he briefed them on how he was using "clear, hold, and build." "The notion that method started with the surge of troops in Baghdad is hokum," he says.

The Iraq army battalion Gentile's squadron partnered with in Amriya was "an exceptionally strong outfit," he said. "The battalion commander, a Sunni and a professional army officer who served in Saddam Hussein's army for twenty years prior, was highly competent, professional, and principled. Tactically the battalion was effective too: it could move, shoot, and communicate, and had competent leaders. Yet the problem with it was that aside from its battalion commander and a handful of soldiers, it was almost completely Shiite." Gentile never believed that there were active links between this battalion and Shiite militias, unlike the police units he had worked with in West Rashid, where the links were clear. "But one could not get away from the fact that they were Shiite and when you boiled it all down with them, especially at times when they were angry over a killing or attack, they saw every Sunni resident in Amriya as their mortal enemy. How would a more robust MITT [military transition] team, more combined patrols with me, more parts for their Humvees, change that basic condition?"

Though Gentile was skeptical that COIN was a cure-all, he knew that he could not kill his way out of the problems he was facing in the district either, so he started fraternizing with local religious leaders, even those with strong links to insurgent groups. He met regularly with Sheikh Walid of the Tikriti Mosque, Sheikh Khalid of the Abbas Mosque, and the imam of the Hassanein Mosque. "I spent a lot of personal time with them, and I think it made a difference in terms of how we were perceived in the area," he says. "I actually became close to them and considered them my friends." He even visited two mosques—close to where his battalion was often pounded by IED strikes—that were considered to be strongly influenced by Al Qaeda and befriended Sheikh Hussein of the Maluki Mosque.

"Sheikh Walid and Sheikh Khalid both were extremely important to me and my squadron. I did not consider them anti-American at all. Both of them became key conduits for me for information in the area and in resolving problems." Khalid's influence and importance in the area became clear to Gentile. He spent many hours in discussion with Khalid, to the extent that Khalid began to start hinting to him that things were slowly changing. "It was becoming clear to the Sunnis in Baghdad that the Americans were finally starting to understand their position. He and Walid and I had agreed on the opening of an Amriya police station that would be manned by local Sunnis from Amriya," Gentile said. The problem was getting this approved by the Shiite government. This plan was clearly a forerunner of what would become the Awakening.

In October 2006 Sheikh Khalid said something to Gentile that caught his attention at the time and that he has never forgotten. "For some reason I asked him about insurgent attacks in the area and about Al Qaeda," Gentile said. "He then pulled me off to the side a bit, out of earshot range of his mosque guards, and my troops knew what to do by placing themselves between me and the imam and his guards. He then very breezily dismissed Al Qaeda as an important factor in the future of the area and the country. I thought that odd at the time, since AQI seemed to be behind so much of the violence. But it later occurred to me that what he was essentially saying and reflecting were the early and fundamental changes that were occurring in Anbar with the Awakening and his sense that it would very possibly be soon spreading to Baghdad."

As it turned out, Sheikh Khalid was a key player in the eventual link of U.S. forces in Amriya with the Sons of Iraq. Gentile's successor, Lieut. Col. Dale Kuehl, commanded the First Battalion, Fifth Cavalry, in Amriya from November 2006 until January 2008. "Amriya was pretty violent when we got there, as was Khadra just to the north," he told me. "Soon after we took over the entire Mansour Security District, which includes all of Mansour area except Ghazaliya, which 2–12 Cav was responsible for. Most of the violence seemed to be directed at the Iraqi Security Forces, especially the Iraqi police. They could not come into Amriya without getting attacked. A lot of violence was also directed at the populace, especially against the Shiites. Kidnapping was also common. The going rate for ransom was between thirty-five thousand and fifty thousand dollars. Civil society had completely broken down. I think many people responded with random and vengeful violence. However, I also believe that JAM special groups working with elements within the Iraqi government were trying to push the Sunnis out of Baghdad. I also think that AQI and other extremist groups were trying to establish a Sunni enclave to stop the JAM encroachment."

It was Kuehl's first deployment in Iraq, but he was well schooled in counterinsurgency. He had written his master's thesis on civilians on the battlefield in the Korean War and had studied Mao Zedong's theories on guerrilla warfare. Just before taking command of the 1–5 Cav, he read *Learning to Eat Soup With a Knife: Counterinsurgency Lessons From Malaya and Vietnam* by Lieut. Col. John Nagl. Nagl had been his roommate at West Point and would go on to play a crucial role in writing the U.S. Army's new manual on counterinsurgency. Nagl's book emphasized the importance of the military becoming a learning organization, adapting to the needs of a different type of war. "Of course, prior to deployment we had a number of leader teaches and seminars to discuss the fight we were going into," Kuehl said. "This study culminated with the COIN Academy in Taji, which I thought was an excellent course."

The first large IED to hit one of Kuehl's patrols occurred one February morning in Khadra. The IED was planted at an intersection and tore off the driver's door. The driver lost both legs. After securing the site Kuehl took his patrol to a nearby street and started questioning locals. He talked to one man who asked him if the patrol was a combined one with the Iraqi National Police. "I told him it was not, it was a U.S.-only patrol. His response was a bit startling. He said, 'That is not supposed to happen.' I pressed him to explain. He just repeated that our patrols were not supposed to get attacked. He also asked why the INP observation post on a nearby bridge did not see the IED go in. It should have been able to. He was a bit upset himself, showing a piece of shrapnel that landed in his yard where his daughter was playing."

Kuehl left him to see for himself, passing through the same intersection that had just been bombed. Just as he was looking up to see the window from the observation post that overlooked the intersection, his vehicle was hit by another IED. "It flattened a couple tires and took some chunks out of our windows, but everyone was okay. From this incident I realized that there were definitely different insurgent groups working in the area. The locals knew what was going on with at least one of these groups, and it sounded like they were not targeting U.S. troops. But this other group definitely was." He did not know it then, but this was the start of Al Qaeda flexing its muscles in the area. They had been pushed out of other areas, like Haifa Street and Anbar, and were trying to take over Mansour. Compounding this was the influx of displaced people from Hurriya to the north and Amil and Jihad from the south. "Locals kept complaining that the violence was coming from people outside the area. We kept dismissing this, but to a large extent I think they were correct," Kuehl said.

At the COIN Academy in October 2006, General Casey informed Kuehl and his team that the goal was to hand security in Baghdad over to the ISF by the summer of 2007 so that the Americans could depart as soon as possible. This was based on the not-unreasonable notion, advocated even by Centcom commander General Abizaid, that the American presence in Iraq was the cause of most of the violence in Iraq. But once in Baghdad, Kuehl was convinced that Casey's goal was unrealistic because of the sectarian violence and the sectarian nature of the government and ISF. He began to focus on protecting the population, even before General Petraeus arrived and formalized the new approach.

Previous attempts had been made to rid Amriya of Al Qaeda, such as Operation Together Forward in August 2006 and Operation Arrowhead Strike 9 in April 2007. Yet in May 2007 Amriya was even more violent. According to Kuehl, previous operations had failed because of poor intelligence, which led to imprecise targeting. Once an area was cleared of Al Qaeda there were not enough troops to hold it, and Sunnis did not trust the ISF. During Operation Arrowhead Strike 9 Al Qaeda men fled or blended into the population, avoiding the operations. As a result of the Americans' inability to provide security, they could not move on to rebuild the area. When Kuehl and his men changed their focus from handing over authority to the ISF and instead tried to protect the population, he said they began to see gains in security.

In January 2007 the Mahdi Army seized the Hurriya neighborhood and moved on to the Amil and Jihad districts. "We couldn't do anything and the Iraqi Army chose not to do anything," Kuehl later wrote. "Instead, we watched helplessly as thousands of Sunnis were forced out of their homes get-

ting pushed into Mansour." Sunni militias were forced to collaborate with Al
Qaeda to protect their areas from the Mahdi army, but the Americans offered
an alternative that, in the short term at least, proved more tempting. Kuehl hy-
pothesized that Al Qaeda controlled Amriya but only as an active minority
that intimidated the neutral majority. In February 2007 he began to have clandestine meetings with clerics in Amriya late at night. Sheikh Walid was already
organizing against Al Qaeda, but he was not ready to act. That month Kuehl
also met with community leaders and assured them of his commitment to defeating Al Qaeda and protecting Amriya from Shiite militias.

Kuehl inherited Gentile's wall around Amriya, but it was too short and had
a lot of holes in it. "We fought to keep it closed, and AQI fought to keep it
open," he said. "Our first casualty was a sergeant killed while trying to put one
of these barriers back in place." Kuehl spent a couple of days in personal reconnaissance figuring out how to get from Abu Ghraib to central Baghdad
without running into a checkpoint. It was all too easy, he found. One evening
he traced out this route to his boss, Colonel Burton. From there the brigade
developed a plan to wall off a good portion of northwest Baghdad, starting
with Route Sword, south of Ghazaliya. Then they built blast walls along the
airport road. By June Amriya was closed up. "The final point was establishing
the entry control points into Amriya," he said. "I knew they would be targets,
so I wanted to make it look formidable, like the Green Zone."

A similar approach had proved useful in the rural Anbar province, which
had been dominated by Al Qaeda and foreign fighters. American Special
Forces reintroduced a tough police chief whose tribe was disliked and feared,
and they built a vast earthen berm around the city, restricting all vehicles.

At first the locals of Amriya did not like it, "but they grew to appreciate the
security that it helped to bring," Kuehl said of the walls he built. "I especially
had trouble with the shop owners at the entrance to Amriya. We were able to
accommodate some of their concerns, but I left them up. I did want to open
up Amriya to more vehicle traffic through the checkpoint, but I met resistance
from many of the locals. This was not completely resolved before we left."

The local police were also a hindrance to Kuehl's ambitions to improve the
security environment: they were, he said, "incompetent, poorly led, poorly
trained, poorly equipped." Stationed in Khadra, its leadership was Sunni and,
to make things even more difficult, may have had Al Qaeda links. The lower
ranks were filled by Shiites, generally from outside Baghdad. "No one was local, which was one of the biggest drawbacks to the police," Kuehl said. "They
pretty much spent most of their time in the station and collected reports and
statements from people who came in. We would take them with us in patrols
in Khadra, but they could not come into Amriya without getting shot at."

The Iraqi National Police were another problem, Kuehl said, lacking strong
leadership skills. "It was like having three hundred privates, no sergeants, and

only a dozen officers. They were not equipped as well as the Iraqi Army, which was a challenge given the lethality of the environment. We conducted joint patrols with them, but their primary focus was on conducting checkpoints, which was a sore point with the locals." The INPs were also known to do the sectarian bidding of their political superiors. Kuehl recalled being approached by a group of imams because ten Sunnis were suddenly detained after someone from the Shiite-dominated Interior Ministry turned up at a couple of checkpoints with a list of people to detain. When Kuehl went to the local police headquarters to find out what was going on, no one could produce the list. Eventually Kuehl managed to get a copy of the names of all the men detained. He went to the holding cell and talked to each one. "A couple months after their arrest I inquired on their status," Kuehl said. "It took over a week for someone to figure out that they were still being held. I finally was able to get their families to be able to see them. I suspect this was all sectarian-driven. They were then pushed up to the jail at FOB Justice, an ironic name, and were still being held when we left over six months later."

The Iraqi army, Kuehl said, was the most competent of the security forces they worked with. Of the army battalions he worked with, Second Battalion, First Brigade, Sixth Division, was the most competent. But, he added, the battalion "went through a string of commanders, and their performance directly correlated with the quality of battalion commander. The first commander I worked with was Colonel Ahmed, a Sunni. Very competent, I really respected him. Although his formation was mostly Shiite, I think they respected him." Ahmed was being targeted by Al Qaeda, though, and after his sons were attacked, he requested and received a transfer. "The guy who replaced him was basically honest but not a great commander. He was replaced in May by Colonel Sabah, who was previously in Ghazaliya. He had a terrible reputation among the Sunni population, and there was a lot of concern about him. He was basically competent, but he was ruthless and crooked. We suspected him of extortion, coercion, and rape. We got the reports on Sabah from people in Iraqi Family Village, which was just outside of Liberty. Sabah kept an apartment there. We got a lot of reports on him. Must caveat to say that none were proven, just lots of reports." Another regarded him as "the worst Iraqi battalion commander I have ever seen. He clearly had a sectarian agenda and was implicated by locals in a weapons-selling scheme where he would sell weapons found in weapons caches, potentially back to the Shiite militias." In contrast to Sabah, Lieutenant Wael, his replacement, was a true professional, according to Kuehl. "He was smart yet lacked the arrogance I saw in most Iraqi officers. Initially he was a bit wary about working with the SOI, but I think he quickly saw how effective they were. Wael was a solid officer and another Sunni, which was a plus to the area. I do not think Brigadier General Ghassan [a local Iraqi army commander in western Baghdad] liked him working so close with Abul Abed [the founder of the Sons of Iraq in Amriya], so he got transferred to Washash, and Lieutenant Hassan was brought in from there in December 2007, just before we left. Hassan was okay, but not as smart and creative as Wael."

IN FEBRUARY 2007 there was an effort by the Iraqi Security Forces to go after some of the Sunni leadership in Mansour. In a forty-eight-hour period three of the top Sunnis Kuehl was working with were targeted by the Iraqi army. This included Adnan Dulaimi in Adil, a powerful politician belonging to the Iraqi Accord Front who lived along the border between Hateen and Yarmuk, and Sheikh Khalid in Amriya. Part of the problem with the politicians, as Kuehl recalled, was that they had well-armed security detachments and the Iraqi army was very suspicious of them. One night Kuehl had to position himself between Dulaimi's security force and the army to prevent a confrontation. Soon after he was called to an incident at another politician's location, where he kept him from getting arrested. Two days later the 2/1/6 Iraqi army battalion raided Khalid's mosque in Amriya.

After these incidents Kuehl met Ghassan and his commanders at his headquarters in the Green Zone. "I told them that I thought they needed to be a little more aware of the appearance of their actions to include excessive detentions and the targeting of these political figures. The commander responsible for Yarmuk took offense at my remarks and did not like me interfering with his operations. We got into a nice little shouting match, and he later stormed out. Ghassan did not appreciate this, and our relationship was never the same."

Staff sergeant "Yosef" (his preferred nickname) was an American soldier who served in the First ID, Second Brigade Reconnaissance Troop (Second BRT), which was outsourced to Kuehl's 1–5 Cav. Under their platoon leader, Capt. Brian Weightman, the troop set up a joint security station in an abandoned shopping mall in the Adil neighborhood in February 2007, at a point where two freeways met close to Dulaimi's home. Yosef worked with Dulaimi's bodyguards, a variety of Iraqi Security Forces, and eventually with the Awakening group in Amriya.

On one occasion, Yosef recalled, he was on the roof of a police station in a Sunni neighborhood, talking with a police guard who spoke great English but initially didn't want anything to do with him. Yosef managed to establish a rapport with him. The guard confided that every policeman at the station was off-duty Mahdi Army. This made sense to him.

On another day Yosef's patrol group heard a loud exchange of gunfire. They got a report that a police truck had been blown up on the ramp, just southwest of the mall they were patrolling. When Yosef's men showed up, "the police were shooting the shit out of an apartment building." Under a colonel's direction, the police seemed to be systematically shooting along every story of the apartment complex, story by story. "He was standing out in the middle of the street, pointing and yelling to gun trucks that were more or less on line with one another, pumping the building full of rounds. When we asked him if he needed any help, he kind of blew us off," Yosef said. When the group asked the colonel what the police were doing, the colonel reported they had taken fire from the building and were returning fire, but it seemed to Yosef's men that they were just shooting the whole side of the building up.

"We inquired where he was taking fire from, and he answered with a kind of a grin and said that they had it under control," Yosef said. This was at a time when the military were harping on Iraqi Security Forces taking responsibility, so Yosef's men left the scene, knowing there were probably no insurgents in the building.

Like Kuehl, Yosef was impressed by the professionalism and nonsectarianism he found among some who served in the Iraqi army. Yosef told me of a lieutenant called Mustafa, who epitomized this. He was, Yosef reported, a physical giant, with the physique and face of an old boxer: strong legs, big belly, broad shoulders, and a beat-up face with a crooked, mashed nose. He was a Sunni who had been in Iraqi Special Forces before the war. He spoke perfect English, but never around his men or other Iraqis. He carried a short AK-47 with a hundred-round drum.

"We patrolled with him on and off for a couple of months," Yosef said. "One day he found something my whole platoon passed up: a nervous-looking taxi driver in a long line of cars waiting for gas, who had an IED initiator under his driver's seat. Mustafa choke-slammed the poor dude with one hand and calmly restrained him under one of his heavy boots pressed down on the dude's back." His techniques in the neighborhood worked well—perhaps too well, Yosef suggested. Under Mustafa's leadership the neighborhood had become relatively peaceful, but he wasn't arresting enough people to satisfy his command. They had him moved into another neighborhood.

When Yosef next saw him, a few months later, he was further north, in a demilitarized zone between Shiite forces in Ghazaliya to the north and established Sunni forces in the south. Yosef was with his boss, Captain Weightman, when they joined Mustafa in his office, a barren room in a large house on a block of other large houses looking north from Mansour. He told them that his name had been leaked to some Al Qaeda forces near his home, and they had kidnapped his brother and tortured him extensively to get to him. "He showed us the pictures of his brother's back with lashings and his brother's battered face," Yosef said. "In the end they accepted a ransom from Mustafa for his brother. I think the amount was ten thousand dollars." Mustafa told them that when his command had moved him up to the neighborhood, they removed all of his Humvees, so he had to patrol his neighborhood on foot. "It was obvious that his good intentions weren't appreciated by his command. But Mustafa didn't hide, and he was out on foot with his men every day," Yosef said. Observed Weightman, "We worked well together, and he genuinely tried to help the people of the areas he was assigned to. He was not sectarian. He couldn't get promoted above second lieutenant."

ONE DAY, EARLY ON in their deployment, Yosef and his men were the first to the scene of a devastating vehicle-borne IED strike on an army checkpoint at the intersection of what the Americans called Phone Card Road and Route Huskies, just southeast of Adil. The blast was so large that it destroyed two Humvees, took the front off three stories of two buildings, and sent another Humvee deep into the coffee shop in the same building. The planners of the VBIED had timed it to explode as the army unit was changing guard. Seventeen soldiers were killed. Yosef discovered that that the son of Sunni politician Adnan al-Dulaimi was a VBIED builder in the area of the bombing and was suspected of being involved.

Dulaimi was the leader of the largest Sunni bloc in Parliament at the time. He had been living in Hurriya but had left—along with thousands of other Sunnis—because of Mahdi Army intimidation and killings of Sunnis, and moved to Adel. Before Kuehl's company established a combat outpost in Adel, Dulaimi's thugs prevented sectarian killings of Sunnis in the area by their mere presence. His house—modest by an Iraqi politician's standards, protected by low concrete barriers, with a small yard in the front—sat in the center of the neighborhood and provided a good view of the area.

At this time Kuehl's company was stretched thin and thought Dulaimi could be co-opted because of his participation in government. "We just couldn't be there all the time with such a large area, having only three platoons, and the active portion of the insurgency that was combating our troop in Jamia." But Dulaimi was known, in the words of an American major, to be a "sleazeball," even though Kuehl's company had no specific evidence to detain him. "Even if we did, politicians had complete immunity with respect to U.S. forces. We weren't allowed to search his house," the major said.

Dulaimi's compound was right down the street from the joint security station established at the Adil mall. It was there that Yosef tried to establish a relationship with the guards stationed outside the compound. Yosef's company had moved into the deserted five-story mall with the hesitant approval of Dulaimi, who remembered the help Weightman's platoon had offered a few months earlier when they responded to a firefight on his street between Mahdi Army forces and Dulaimi's guards and helped repel the Mahdi Army.

Soon after they were settled at the new joint security station Yosef was out patrolling with Weightman in a convoy of four Humvees when Uday, Dulaimi's head bodyguard, requested a meeting. At the time Dulaimi was having trouble with the Iraqi police patrolling the neighborhood. There were accusations from the police that Dulaimi was harboring insurgents among his staff and that his family members were attacking police checkpoints and patrols. However, there were also allegations that the police were behaving aggressively toward Dulaimi's neighbors and arresting innocent people.

During the conversation with Weightman, Uday became angry and stated, "If by the next night, you don't convince the IP to get out of the neighborhood, then all you have done here will be ruined!" Weightman's response was measured and without anger. "I think this impressed Uday. Even though Uday had pressure on him from the extremists among his ranks to go to war with the Americans living in their neighborhood as well as to continue their open war with the Iraqi Security Forces, Captain Weightman's response diffused the situation, and we ended up having a relatively safe, although sometimes rocky, working relationship with Uday and Dulaimi's compound security forces."

One day Yosef, who was building a rapport with Uday, accompanied him as his guard and escort on a visit to a prison. While there he witnessed one of the most disturbing manifestations of sectarianism when he realized that 90 percent of those jailed were Sunni. The prison was so full, Yosef speculated, because the police "had rounded up every male in the neighborhood of fighting age." Uday was using the cover story that he was visiting the prison as a humanitarian observer. In reality, Yosef noted to himself, "he's just trying to track down his brother and the other eight members of Dulaimi's bodyguards who've been arrested and lost in the system."

The prison was a vision of bedlam. The cells were so crowded that half the prisoners had to stand while the other half sat or lay down. The paperwork documenting the accusations against some of the prisoners was said to be lost. Other prisoners had been in jail for up to six months without a trial. The legal system was swamped. Sexually transmitted diseases were rampant, often spread by the guards. Guards were providing condoms and medical care to the detainees only if the detainees either paid them money or submitted sexually. In his notes from his visit, Yosef observed, "I don't care if 90% of those Sunnis are Al Qaeda. When all of the guards are Shiite, and most of those Shiites are in the Mahdi Army, it gets ugly."

"There are reports of released prisoners mysteriously dying shortly after their release, perhaps by poisoning," Yosef recorded in his notes. "Some prisoners' records show 'transferred' next to their name, but no mention where to. In-processing records are recorded in a book, and inaccessible to public. Once they have a trial they are recorded into a data base and that is accessible to the public. This means that when they get arrested, they virtually disappear from their family and friends."

There were three big rooms where the prisoners were crammed in like slaves. Yosef noticed some of the guards silencing the prisoners when Uday came by. So when they went to the maximum-security wing, "with its short dead-end corridors and lazy guards," Yosef and two fellow soldiers filled the doorway and spoke loudly so Uday could discreetly ask questions and take notes about the guards' abuses. "The guards finally caught on after a couple of wings, but we were late for Uday's next meeting, so we took off," Yosef said.

CAPT. BRENDAN GALLAGHER initially served in the western Baghdad neighborhood of Khadra, which was where Kuehl initially set up his first combat outpost alongside the Iraqi police. "In April and May 2007 at our first combat outpost—the Khadra police station—we would have IEDs hit us as soon as we left the main gate," Gallagher said. This happened repeatedly over the course of weeks. The IEDs would strike them within one hundred meters of a local police defensive position. "The police on guard should have been able to see the IEDs being emplaced," he said. "They were in plain view of his position. This was infuriating to me, because it seemed so evident that at least some of the guards were in collusion."

When Gallagher confronted the police chain of command, they were generally dismissive of his concerns. He began to suspect that they were either incompetent or collaborating with insurgents. "In retrospect, I believe some of them were probably being pressured by AQI to keep quiet and passively let us get attacked," Gallagher said. Soon after that, he decided to move his company's combat outpost to a different part of Khadra, co-located with 2/5/2 National Police. "When I told the local police I had decided to move, they practically begged us to stay," he said, but by that point he had lost confidence in them.

A month later Gallagher's company was reassigned to Amriya. Most residents there thought that the Shiite-dominated government was conspiring against them, intentionally denying basic services to an area dominated by Sunnis. "There appeared to be a lot of circumstantial evidence to support this," Gallagher said. They heard reports that the national police or the army was forcibly removing people from their homes because the inhabitants were Sunni.

By early 2007, Khadra and Amriya were overwhelmingly Sunni, yet the Khadra police had Shiites throughout their ranks. "This helped create a significant credibility gap with the Sunni population," Gallagher said. "If the police had been exceedingly competent they might have been able to overcome that obstacle, but that was hardly the case." In early 2007, the Khadra police essentially refused to patrol on their own because they were prime targets for the insurgents. "Police inherently symbolize stability and order, and for that reason Al Qaeda wanted them dead. The fact that that many of these IPs were Shiites only made things even more dangerous for them," Gallagher said.

To make matters worse, their vehicles had almost no armor. Therefore the police tended to stay in their headquarters at the center of Khadra. "We tried to get them to investigate murders and other crimes that were happening on a regular basis, but it was like pulling teeth to get them to leave their HQ building. They would only leave the police station when we personally escorted them, and even then they were little value-added," Gallagher said.

"There was serious sectarianism and collaboration throughout some sectors of the ISF," he said. "However, there were also many good and honest Iraqi soldiers and policemen who were doing the best they could. The challenge was determining who was who. In some ways it was like trying to play poker with many different players at the table, all with varying motives (some good, some not so good), and we were trying to figure out what was going on. But unlike poker, this was not a game—lives were on the line."

As had been the case with Lieutenant Mustafa, some of the most effective people working in the Iraqi Security Forces could be punished by their superiors, or face the wrath of insurgents, if they seemed to be working too well with the Americans. "One of the most effective 2/1/6 Iraqi army battalion commanders had his family threatened," Gallagher recalled. "He was forced to leave his post and depart the area as a result. This was a setback for us, because he was extremely competent, impartial, and nonsectarian. He was only able to stay in command for a relatively short duration."

One Iraqi army commander that Gallagher met with, who was responsible for the Hurriya and Adil neighborhoods at the time, admitted that if it came down to fighting for their country or the Mahdi Army, most of his soldiers would fight for the Mahdi Army. He was a Sunni commander. People were extremely fearful that the security forces were collaborating with Mahdi Army operatives to carry out assassinations, either by letting them through checkpoints or providing information or other assistance.

The process of sectarian cleansing started before the 1–5 Cav got on the ground in Amriya, Gallagher told me. "Within the first few months of our deployment, virtually all of the Shiites had effectively been driven out or killed," he said. "Once the Sunni volunteers stood up, things eventually started to calm down in our area of operations."

The Iraqi Security Forces maintained checkpoints outside Amriya to avoid being attacked. Consequently, the walls that trapped Al Qaeda in Amriya also meant they focused their attacks on the Americans, since they were deprived of other targets. Kuehl moved forces from elsewhere in Mansour to focus on Amriya, and he asked for more troops, which allowed for more patrolling. He also increased the concrete fortifications around Amriya and imposed curfews and bans on vehicles.

But just as he was trying to establish a permanent combat outpost in Amriya, close to the Maluki Mosque, an IED attack on May 19, 2007, killed six of his soldiers and one interpreter. Kuehl called Sheikh Walid that night and demanded his help in getting rid of Al Qaeda. He was convinced that the sheikhs of Amriya knew who the Al Qaeda men were but were too scared to act. In the past American soldiers had retaliated brutally after suffering such losses, and there were many soldiers who wanted to "do a Falluja" and respond with extreme violence. But Kuehl restrained them. Locals, also expecting the Americans to "do a Falluja," were apparently impressed when they didn't. Sheikh Khalid later said that this restraint was a key factor convincing locals of the Americans' good will.

According to Kuehl, the Awakening men in Amriya approached him first. "I think it was something the Sunni leadership had been setting up for some time, and I had been encouraging them to work with us," he said. "I just did not think it would happen in this way. I believe many of them were former insurgents. Looking back, I think one of the imams was hinting at it for a while but was a bit secretive in our discussions. I figured that there were things going on in the background that I could not see. Sheikh Walid called me on the night of May 29 to tell me they would attack Al Qaeda the next day. We had a heated discussion for about twenty minutes. I was trying to convince him to give us the intel and let us take care of it. He insisted that they had to do it themselves."

Kuehl warned him that if they threatened American soldiers or civilians in any of their operations, they would be shot; then he ordered his men to back off and let events transpire. The next night Sheikh Walid called Kuehl up to tell him of their success, and the next day Al Qaeda responded.

"They were pretty cocky after the initial success, but Al Qaeda came after them hard on the second day, which is when they asked for my help." The Americans responded quickly, driving to the Fardus Mosque to back up the rebels. Dead and wounded fighters lay sprawled in the mosque. The Americans also lost one soldier in the battle.

In a letter sent home to family and friends later that year, Staff Sergeant Yosef wrote, almost wistfully, of the time in May 2007 when Abul Abed, a charismatic and enigmatic Sunni militia leader previously unknown to the Americans, entered their midst. "Abul Abed saw some Al Qaeda men placing a roadside bomb on the side of the road near his house," Yosef wrote. "He confronted them and asked why they were placing it so close to his house. Adul Abed told them, 'That is a big bomb. It could kill me and my family.' Their reply? 'It's okay if you die. This is jihad.' Abul Abed walked directly back into his house and did what I hope any of us would have done under the same circumstances: he grabbed his AK-47, walked back outside, and shot the three men to death in his front yard."

Abul Abed was a former officer in Saddam's army. "After that event, he feared for his life," Yosef wrote. "He did have connections though, useful connections, connections with guns. They consisted of Iraqi Sunni men, who up until then, had been fighting 'American invaders.'"

Yosef empathized with these men, even though some of them had fought in Falluja against comrades in Yosef's platoon. "Last May these local men from Amriya decided that they couldn't live with Al Qaeda anymore," Yosef wrote, "and since they couldn't rely on the Shia-run government for help, they called us and literally asked us if we would allow them to start a war against Al Qaeda. We said yes. When my platoon first got the word that we had been selected to work with the 'Freedom Fighters' of Amriya, we couldn't believe it. We had just finished a five-month mission living out of a four-story abandoned mall at the intersection of two highways in Western Baghdad. We were exhausted, and I remember one of my Army friends saying, 'Great, now we're going to train more terrorists.'"

In early June Yosef's platoon went into Amriya for the first time. They took five Humvees and about twenty men. "So, there we were driving slowly down a narrow Amriya neighborhood road, trash and rubble on either side," Yosef wrote. "No one was around. We made it without incident to the temporary headquarters of the AFF [Amriya Freedom Fighters] at an abandoned school. A few of their men met us at the gate. They all had guns. We really didn't know what to expect. We left our Humvees with drivers and gunners in them. We had about ten dismounted soldiers when we went inside the compound."

The school, as Yosef describes it, was situated in the middle of a fairly upscale Iraqi neighborhood, complete with the familiar abandoned two-story houses, electrical wires bunched together and hanging low from telephone poles, and trash on the side of the streets. Yosef's company commander, his interpreter, and two other soldiers went into the main meeting room with Abul Abed, the AFF leader. Yosef, his platoon leader and his section sergeant walked into a room next to the main meeting room.

"At the end of an outer corridor was Abul Abed's office, one door short of his office was another classroom with some sofas, and tables. Both rooms had fans, and since it was the beginning of June, CPT Weightman, SSG Kirk, and I waited in the other room while CPT Mitchell and Abul Abed introduced themselves, and started planning. It was in this other room, short of Abul Abed's office, where I met Ali, and Muhamad. Ali was younger than me, in his early twenties—a short skinny dude, with thick well kept hair, sly eyes and a smile that probably drove women wild. He wore a t-shirt, sweat pants, and interestingly enough had a hand grenade in his pocket.

"Muhamad on the other hand was in his late teens, tall, with a sharp strong jaw, and big eyes. He wore a tank-top, had on shorts and carried a thick sheep herding stick. He too had a grin on his face, and unlike Ali, Muhamad could speak English. They seemed comfortable enough with us, and so we started joking around with them. We already had our helmets off, which was disarming in and of itself. But something was bothering me. The hand grenade that Ali had in his sweat pants pocket, he kept on taking it out and rolling it around in his hands. I, being the most uptight of the three Americans, was kind of worried and asked if Ali would let me see the hand grenade. He seemed slightly taken aback by my worry, but he handed it to me none-the-less. I looked at it. Sure enough it was a Russian made fragmentation grenade, slightly less powerful than the American made ones, but still deadly especially in a confined space such as this room. I showed it to CPT Weightman, who was much less impressed with it and told me to give it back to Ali. I did, and we continued our light hearted exchange of jokes and jabs.

Mitchell picked up on Yosef's ability to build a rapport with Iraqis early and assigned him to gain intelligence on the different men in Abul Abed's group. Yosef did this by hanging out with them whenever they were there. Some of the younger AFF, like Muhamad, still attended school, and then patrolled with the AFF when they were out of school. The relationship, as Yosef reported, developed from caution to common respect and friendship. "Watching Abul Abed lead his men was educational. It showed me the reality of the old saying, 'A company is the long shadow of a single man.' They were professional because he was professional. If there were lapses in some of his soldiers' performance, it was because they were moonlighting as AFF, when in fact they worked for other forces in the neighborhood."

A few months later Al Qaeda came for Muhamad at his high school. They raided his school while he was in class, bribed the school guards and took him away from his classmates. They kidnapped him, kept him for the afternoon, and tortured him. They ended up beheading him and leaving his head in a tree. Two years later, when I spoke to Sergeant Yosef about this, his anger was still raw. In a note to his family, soon after Muhamad's death, he wrote: " I feel slightly guilty for Muhamad's death. I thought at the time, and still think that there was an Al Qaeda spy within the AFF who fingered Muhamad. Perhaps by befriending Muhamad, and encouraging him to be friendly with me I effectively made him a target. Perhaps they kidnapped him out from his high school and beheaded him, specifically so that other young AFF would understand that being friends with American soldiers was a sin punishable by death. Any fear Al Qaeda was attempting to instill in the AFF was trumped though by Abul Abed's swift vengeance. I don't want to be too specific, but I'll say this, Mohamed's death was avenged at least 4-fold within a day. The practical result of this brought confidence back to the AFF as quickly as it had wavered."

AFTER THE INITIAL SUCCESS of establishing Abul Abed and his men, Kuehl found that the harder part was working out a longer-range partnership and then maintaining it. "There were a couple of things I wanted to ensure," he told me. "First, we had to work with the Iraqi army. Second, I wanted to have some civil control of this movement. Getting the Iraqi army on board was the first challenge. I met with Brigadier General Ghassan for about two hours trying to convince him this was a good idea. He had already helped by providing Abul Abed's men ammunition, but he was a bit hesitant to get directly involved. He finally agreed to meet with Abul Abed, who was cooling his heels outside along with another leader. This was probably the most important negotiation I ever had to do."

"I don't think Abul Abed and the Iraqi army relationship was ever good," Sergeant Yosef added. "I remember Colonel Sabah, who Abul Abed was supposed to work with. The first time I saw them butt heads was one night when the AFF and the Iraqi army were supposed to do a patrol together. Colonel Sabah wanted to head the patrol, with the AFF acting as neighborhood advisers. Abul Abed refused. He wanted the patrol to be conducted by AFF, with the Iraqi army acting as observers, because there had been accusations by the neighborhood residents that the Iraqi army had been too aggressive. The other issue was that Colonel Sabah didn't want Abul Abed on the ground with his men. Colonel Sabah wanted to be in command of all the men, both Iraqi army and AFF."

This argument took place in Abul Abed's office at AFF HQ. Colonel Sabah had two other officers with him, one younger and one very gray one, who would take turns trying to persuade Abul Abed to play by their rules. Abul Abed's skill as debater was apparently brilliant, said Yosef. He would listen to Colonel Sabah and officers yell until they were exhausted, and then he would quickly answer with sharp responses.

"After about fifteen minutes, the oldest of the three Iraqi army officers basically gave up," Yosef reported. "He had a look on his face like, 'This really isn't my fight.' Then the younger one slowly sputtered out of steam. It was obvious that this Iraqi army officer was not very intelligent. Abul Abed really didn't even acknowledge him. Colonel Sabah ended up nudging him out of the argument. Finally, it was Colonel Sabah against Abul Abed. Colonel Sabah laid all his cards down with what he thought was the final blow. He said the following, and I remember because I asked my interpreter what he said: 'If you don't patrol under my command, then you will be considered an enemy force, and I will arrest you and your men.' Abul Abed stood there for a minute thinking, then took his pistol belt off and threw it into his closet and said, 'Fine, if I have to patrol under your command or else get arrested if I command my patrol, then I will not patrol, and neither will my men. You are on your own,' and then he walked to the door, as the three Iraqi army officers stood there dumbfounded, and yelled to his men, 'No one is going anywhere tonight!' Colonel Sabah and his guys stormed out infuriated, and some heated words were said with lots of pointing and angry eyes.

"Abul Abed was obviously furious. But he knew that Colonel Sabah wouldn't do the patrol alone. Abul Abed knew where the enemy forces were hiding. It was his AFF intelligence on Amriya that had gathered the Iraqi army and even the Americans here tonight. If Abul Abed didn't go out, then the Iraqi army would be blind. Colonel Sabah came back, he compromised, and said that it would be a joint command that night. During the patrol, if I remember correctly, the AFF and the Iraqi army men worked well together, but the rift between Abul Abed and Colonel Sabah grew greater as the night went on. I was on patrol so I don't know exactly how it happened, but I remember hearing afterward that they continued to argue throughout the patrol. It makes sense, too. Abul Abed was about Colonel Sabah's age, and Abul Abed was an officer under Saddam. These two men should have been peers in the same army, but one was excluded from the mainstream security forces, and the other was not."

The relationship between the Iraqi army and Abul Abed's Awakening group was always contentious, especially at the leadership level. Gallagher said that they always had to a walk a tightrope to maintain the support of the Iraqi army. There was one incident that nearly shut down the whole effort. Four bodies had been found in the southeast corner of Amriya. Gallagher was in Sabah's office at the time, and Sabah was convinced that Abul Abed was behind it. This was on a day when a number of local contractors had been invited to Abul Abed's HQ to start generating projects to repair the infrastructure and get some money flowing in the community.

When Sabah arrived at Abul Abed's headquarters, he started shouting at the Fursan (as the AFF were called, taking their name from the Arabic word for "knights") while ten of his security detachment formed a tight, protective circle around him. Sabah's men had weapons drawn on the Fursan, and the Fursan had weapons drawn on them. Gallagher managed to get into the center of his tight circle with his interpreter. "Sabah was yelling that there was only one army in Amriya and that it was either Abul Abed or him. It turns out that some knucklehead in the Fursan had refused Sabah's security detachment entry into the HQ building."

Yosef was also present, filming with his video camera. "I guess the day before the IA wouldn't let one of Abul Abed's food trucks into Amriya and then called the AFF 'sons of animals.' When the Iraqi army showed up at the AFF HQ, Abu Bilal, one of Abed's lieutenants, ordered his men to get their guns and grenades and get ready for a fight, and they all started running out to the gate with their AK-47s."

Abu Bilal apparently was in a terrible mood. His brothers had just been kidnapped by Al Qaeda. But when Abul Abed emerged from his building, he was furious as he tried to stand down his men, especially with Abu Bilal. "I set my camera on the gate's wall and videotaped the whole thing," Yosef noted later. "Major Daniels came running out into the street from his meeting with Abul Abed, without any armor or helmet, just sunglasses. He and his men positioned themselves between the IA trucks and the AFF at the gate. It was a zoo. Finally, the IA left. Luckily, before I turned my camera off, I recorded Abu Bilal striding out after them, with his shirt untucked. His shirt is never untucked. In the video, it's apparent he's got multiple weapons under his shirt. I wonder if he ever caught up with the IA patrol and took some pop shots at them."

"This incident," Gallagher said, "set us way back, and I spent the next forty-eight hours dealing with the fallout. From this incident we hammered out a written agreement between us, the Iraqi army, and the Fursan. While it put more restrictions on the Fursan, they were generally positive and a step toward rule of law. It also placed more emphasis on the Iraqi army to conduct joint operations with the Fursan."

Kuehl's own relationship with the Awakening men in his area was tentative at first, but eventually they grew close. "For a long time I was not sure how far I could trust Abul Abed," he said. "I knew he was a bit of a hothead. Some members of the group were just thugs. I believe some were brought in by Abul Abed and Sheikh Khalid to gain local political support for the movement. There were times where I had to discipline members of the group. At one point I arrested one of the leaders of one of the factions. I never trusted the guy because we suspected him of pushing people out of homes and stealing their furniture. I had even detained him and three of his brothers during an operation just before the Fursan came forward. One brother we kept, the others we released due to lack of evidence. I ended up detaining this guy after we connected him to an attack on Abul Abed and excessive use of force. I think we also got some other incriminating evidence on him."

Over time Kuehl developed closer relationships with the Awakening men at his level and also at subordinate levels. Abed's men were brought into the planning and targeting process along with the Iraqi army. "In a sense, each of us gave legitimacy to the other," Kuehl said. "Not everyone trusted the Fursan, nor did everyone trust us or the IA. When we did operations together, complaints went down." Initially Abed's men, who could move easily within the population and were not burdened with heavy equipment, conducted missions with U.S. oversight. They identified five targets on their first mission. Kuehl provided an outer cordon with his D Company, consisting of tanks and Bradley fighting vehicles. These vehicles were fitted with great optics so they could keep a close eye on what was going on, even at night.

Abul Abed and his men went in and captured their five targets without firing a shot. They questioned them and turned two over to Kuehl. "They wanted to release the other three, which is an interesting part of this," Kuehl said. "In our negotiations Sheikh Khalid asked for the ability to give amnesty. He said many of the AQI fighters were the young boys of the community. He wanted to release them after they signed an oath to not fight for Al Qaeda and for their parents to also sign for them. I thought this was a great idea and agreed. I think this did a lot to undermine AQI's base."

The other part of destroying Al Qaeda involved local civil oversight, which was also risky. Kuehl saw Sheikh Khalid as the most legitimate local leader. The Neighborhood Advisory Council was seen to be ineffective and had links with AQI and corruption. On the other hand, Kuehl suggests, Sheikh Khalid seemed to be respected by many in the community. Sheikh Khalid was a strong critic of the Maliki government. He shared the perception with many in Amriya that the Maliki government was intentionally denying services to Sunni areas. He was fairly soft-spoken, but despite his quiet exterior he had strong opinions and definite influence in the community.

Sheikh Khalid's mosque was located next door to Gallagher's company's combat outpost, which helped facilitate communication. He would provide recommendations to Gallagher on how the locations of concrete barriers should be less obtrusive to the local pedestrian traffic, particularly for Iraqi children who walked to the nearby school. "We therefore adjusted the barrier locations to meet his request. I believe following through on such reasonable requests helped sustain a positive working relationship, which in turn helped sustain our credibility and respect in the area," Gallagher said.

Abul Abed seemed to respect Khalid. "I tried to get Khalid to sign the security contract we were establishing, but he kept delaying," Kuehl said. "He never said no, but there was always some new demand. I think he was also getting pressure from other people behind the scenes. After months of haggling I finally made the decision to have Abul Abed sign the contract. In retrospect, I think Khalid wanted to keep out of direct involvement. Still, I thought it important that we get some voice of the people. We asked Khalid to organize the local leaders within the community. He formed a local council from the community to include tribal leaders, former military officers, and other professionals. He took great risk in doing this since it would have no official government legitimacy. However, he was politically connected, and I think he did a great job of adding legitimacy to the effort. One group that never really got on board was the Iraqi Islamic Party. They were jealous of the power that this movement was gaining, and I think they saw it as a threat."

"Money was not the primary motivator for Abul Abed," Kuehl later wrote, noting that Abed's men were not paid for the first three months. When they did get paid in September 2007, Kuehl described the sum as a "pittance" compared with the risk they were taking, much less than what Al Qaeda were paying their men. "[Abed] was driven by a desire to protect his family and bring stability to the Sunni areas. While he was very much against [the Mahdi

Army], I would not label him as sectarian. Several of his closest aides were Shi-ites. I would classify him as a nationalist if anything."

Over time restrictions had to be put on the Fursan's operations. All opera-tions had to be conducted with the Iraqi army. The problem was that the army had difficulty keeping pace with the Fursan. But multiple security outposts were established throughout Amriya with the Fursan, protecting key infra-structure in the community. "Between their outposts, the Iraqi army outposts, and our two combat operation posts, you could not move two blocks in Am-riya without running into someone involved in security," Kuehl said. "Vio-lence dropped significantly."

With Abul Abed's intelligence as well as information coming from other sources, Kuehl was able to map out the insurgent network. "The information provided by Abul Abed and his men allowed us to target much more accu-rately," he said. "We had names and in some cases pictures. We posted wanted posters that proved very effective. Tips from locals increased significantly. We hit Al Qaeda pretty hard, detaining some, killing others. Those that remained fled. Civilian deaths pretty much ceased."

Other than a couple found dead in their home in August, Amriya did not have any other murders until Christmas Day. IED attacks dropped off com-pletely, as did small-arms fire and indirect-fire attacks. The last IED, a deep buried one that went off on August 6, ended up killing the driver of a Bradley. Within thirty-six hours of the attack, Abul Abed and his men were able to de-termine that it had been carried out by a cell from an insurgent group that was brought into Amriya for a joint operation. "We had never been able to do this before," Kuehl said.

Like many I spoke to, Gallagher characterized the initial relationship be-tween the Americans and the Fursan as tenuous; many U.S. soldiers were skep-tical of working with men who had been their enemy. "Some of the volunteers had almost certainly been emplacing IEDs against my soldiers just a few months earlier," he said. But trust was built over time. Gallagher de-scribed a turning point for him and his men: "We were conducting a company cordon and search in northeastern Amriya, Mahala 630. We received a report that there was an IED just a few meters from one of our Bradleys on an exte-rior blocking position. I began to call up EOD [Explosive Ordinance Disposal] to destroy it," Gallagher recalled. But before anyone could react, one of the new volunteers, a daring young nineteen-year-old named Ali, got out his small pocketknife, walked over to the location, unearthed the IED with his bare hands, and disconnected it. "He came back with a smug look of contentment on his face. To this day, this still strikes me as fairly crazy. Obviously he knew what he was doing, but at the same time it was extremely reckless. Events like this demonstrated that the volunteers were technically competent. It also demonstrated that they were not afraid to risk their lives to defeat AQI and gain our confidence."

But there were strains and rivalries within Abul Abed's organization. One of his lieutenants, Abu Sayf, operated mainly in Mahala 634. Gallagher's team began hearing reports that he was acting far too aggressively. He was alleged to have been stealing people's belongings, stealing cars, forcing people from their homes. This culminated in a brief power struggle with Abul Abed in September and October. "One day Abu Sayf pulled me aside at his operational post and started making wild accusations against Abul Abed. His underlying implication was clear, that Abul Abed needed to go away and he should be the rightful leader of the volunteer organization. He asked me not to tell anyone about what he had just told me. However I felt I could not keep that a secret from my battalion commander, Lieutenant Colonel Kuehl, so I informed him." The battalion was able to substantiate the rumors that Abu Sayf was corrupt and had been stealing property. His suggestion that he should replace Abul Abed caused him to lose even more credibility. "We rapidly detained him," Gallagher said, "and Abul Abed kicked him out of his organization." Some of Abu Sayf's comrades, led principally by his brother, threatened to quit if he was not released. The brother was subsequently expelled from the organization.

KUEHL BELIEVED THAT Abul Abed was controversial because he was a charismatic leader who inspired others. "He had kind of a Robin Hood reputation within the populace and became quite popular in a short period of time. I think his rise in popularity was seen as a political threat both by the government and by the Iraqi Islamic Party. Overall he did pretty well with the press. Part of the controversy is his shadowy past. I know he was in the Iraqi army before the war—still not sure what rank, either major or captain. He claims to have been a sniper during Desert Storm. I believe he was in intelligence. His family lived in Baghdad and owned some bakeries. The biggest thing that concerned me about his behavior was his volatile temper and his violent tendencies. He used to beat his subordinates when they crossed him."

The *Guardian* journalist Ghaith Abdul-Ahad wrote an article about his time with Abul Abed. "I think Ghaith embellished a bit, but the behavior he describes was a concern for me," Kuehl said. "We got a lot of reports about his behavior, and it is true we were not with him 24/7. But we were with him a lot, and he came to rely on our presence to ensure that he was not targeted by the government. In some cases we could deny reports because I had someone with him at the time he allegedly did something. In general his behavior was pretty consistent with what I saw from IA officers. I saw him on several occasions work to get Shiite families back into Amriya. Over time I think he learned that he had to tone down his image, since he had become a public figure. I think he grew with the increasing responsibility he gained from leading a large organization."

In late July 2007 a captain serving under Kuehl wrote to his father, reporting that within two months the Fursan had virtually eliminated Al Qaeda from Amriya—an area, as the captain observed, that had been declared "the capital of the Islamic State of Iraq" two months earlier. "These guys are from the neighborhoods, they know the people, and they are primarily concerned with making their neighborhoods safe again," the captain wrote. "They conduct joint operations with us and the Iraqi Army. Unlike the IA, these guys are actually a pleasure to work with. Most of them are ex-military from the Saddam era and several are former captains, majors, or lieutenants. They have discipline and know how to plan and execute a mission. The month before the movement started, we lost fourteen American soldiers in Amriya. In the two months that the movement has been going, we have lost zero American soldiers in Amriya."

The captain noted that people all the way up the chain of command had visited to see the project. Everyone realized the strategic importance of the Fursan, even the Maliki government, which was wary of the Sunni militias. But when Fursan members were seriously injured, their options were limited: "They are paying a heavy burden for their relentless pursuit of AQIZ," the captain said, using a common acronym for Zarqawi's Al Qaeda in Iraq. "We can only treat them at U.S. facilities if they are in danger of losing life, limb, or eyesight. Otherwise, they must be treated at an Iraqi facility. This works just fine for the ISF, which are predominantly Shia. The Ministry of Health is dominated by the Sadrists. I have personally been in the three hospitals that these guys would be treated at and all have pictures of Muqtada al-Sadr hanging on the walls. If I send my Freedom Fighters to these hospitals, they will not last a day. Obviously, my only option to maintain the fighting force is to get these guys seen by Americans. To this point, we've been unable to provide these guys much in the way of legitimacy, money, or weapons, but we have been able to care for them. They are doing the work that we could not do and they are paying the price for it. Knowing that they will be properly treated if they get injured is an incredible morale boost for them, not unlike any warrior. I can't emphasize enough how this whole endeavor could go either way at this point. In three years of doing this, this is the first endeavor that's actually given me hope."

According to a major who served under Kuehl, "An unsung hero of this entire time period was the commander of the combat support hospital in Baghdad. More than anyone else he kept our sometimes tenuous relationship with the SOI on good standing, simply by admitting their casualties to his facility and treating them. The rules on this were somewhat in the gray area, and lesser men or those who did not see the strategic situation would have been justified refusing care and turning them away. I had one such conversation with a doctor on Camp Liberty who was discussing the practical reasons for not treating them, that they wouldn't have enough beds for the American casualties. I told him that if he wanted to quit treating American casualties altogether, all he had to do was to treat these SOIs when they were injured."

From August 7, 2007, until Kuehl's battalion departed in January 2008, there were no serious attacks in Amriya. In the second half of 2007, the murder and kidnapping rate dropped from at least thirty a month to four. By the time Kuehl left, two hundred shops had reopened. Kuehl does not credit the surge itself for the reduction in violence, nor does he think that violence dropped because the battalion paid off a Sunni militia. But the increase in troops let him defeat Al Qaeda in his area and halt the Mahdi Army advance into northwest Baghdad. The joint security stations and combat outposts that Kuehl set up in neighborhoods, increased foot patrols, improved understanding of the communities his men patrolled, construction of concrete barriers, as well as improved cooperation with the Iraqi Security Forces were all factors that helped reduce the violence, Kuehl believes.

In September the captain wrote once again, reflecting on the contribution played by Sheikh Sattar Abu Risha of the Anbar Awakening and Abul Abed, his Baghdad counterpart. He noted that both were charismatic leaders, uncompromising in their beliefs and corresponding actions—the types who start movements, excite people, and bring them together. But he cautioned: "They burn bright and they burn fast." Up until the end of July, he noted, if they had lost Abul Abed, the movement in Baghdad would have died. "If he'd died before that point, I believe that many of his men would have gone out to Anbar and fought with their brothers there, while the locals would have gone back to what they were doing before . . . attacking the Iraqi Army, and us occasionally, and trying to figure out a way to feed themselves and their families." But once Amriya was rid of Al Qaeda and the Awakening was legitimized, Abul Abed's role seemed, paradoxically, less vital. "At this point, the show will go on with or without him." The traits that the captain identified in Abul Abed were central to his success and what made him "such a joy to work with": the honorable warrior, his charisma, the passion and principle that "rubbed off on his men . . . don't necessarily lend themselves to usefulness in the current environment." The same could have been said for Sattar Abu Risha, whose death, the captain suggested, was a "blessing in disguise, as now there's a martyr for the cause."

"Unless they topple the current regime, they're going to have to compromise," the captain explained. "They're going to have to work with others. They're going to have to follow principles like due process. It's not efficient, but that's the point. Democracies are messy and slow and they put an emphasis on negotiation and accommodation. Those aren't really traits that Abul Abed possesses. That's why I like him."

"As we handed over eastern Amriya upon our departure in January '08," Captain Gallagher said, "I told my replacement that this would be his number-one challenge: to ensure the volunteers were formally integrated into the security framework. I did not want to see us, or the Iraqi government, turn our backs on these men, because the blowback could be significant."

Part 2

I returned to Amriya in December 2007. My friend Hassan pointed to a gap in the concrete walls the Americans had built around the Sunni bastion. "We call it the Rafah Crossing," he joked, referring to the gate to besieged Gaza that another occupying army occasionally opened. Iraqi National Police loyal to the Mahdi Army had once regularly attacked Amriya, and Sunnis caught in their checkpoints, which we drove through anxiously, would have once ended up in the city morgue. Police had recently put up Shiite flags all around western Baghdad, which the residents of Amriya viewed as a provocation. Our car lined up behind dozens of others that had been registered with the local Iraqi army unit and were allowed to enter and exit the imprisoned neighborhood. It often took two or three hours to get past the American soldiers, Iraqi soldiers, or the Fursan (most people called them the Thuwar, or revolutionaries). When it was our turn, we exited the vehicle while Iraqi soldiers searched it and an American soldier led his dog around the car to sniff it. I was patted down by one of the Sunni militiamen, who asked me if I was a bodybuilder. Not knowing I was American, he reassured me: "Just let the dog and the dog that is with him finish with your car and you can go." He laughed, and we laughed with him.

We drove past residents who were forced to trudge a long distance in and out of their neighborhood, past the tall concrete walls, because their cars had not been given permission to exit. Boys labored behind pushcarts, wheeling in goods for the shops that were open. One elderly woman in a black robe sat on a pushcart and complained loudly that the Americans were to blame for all her problems. Cars could not enter Amriya after 7:30 p.m. Once inside, we drove along roads scarred by massive IEDs.

I met with Um Omar, a stern woman who ran the Ethar Association, an independent NGO that provided aid, housing, and education to vulnerable families. She wore a tight head scarf and gloves on her hands as a sign of modesty. Um Omar had a degree in chemistry but had been a housewife before the war. "After the invasion, there were many needs," she said. "My sister's husband was killed and two of my uncles were killed. My sister's husband was killed by random American fire. One of my uncles was killed by an American tank, which drove over his car while it was driving on the wrong side of the road, so he crashed into it. My other uncle was killed by the mujahideen during the battle of Falluja while he was providing aid to Falluja. The mujahideen suspected he was a collaborator with the Americans because they saw him talking to the Americans when they stopped him at the checkpoint and let him through." Um Omar's husband was a former Awakening man affiliated with the Islamic Party. He had been arrested by the Americans and was in a feud with Abul Abed, and so he lived outside Amriya.

Kuehl knew Um Omar. "If you have already talked to her, I am sure she had an unfavorable opinion of me," he told me. "Her husband, Abu Omar, was one of Abul Abed's lieutenants from the start. The two had a bit of a love/hate relationship, and we had to step in on a couple occasions. I had to counsel Abu Omar once for excessive use of force, and he was also arrested outside Amriya with a couple of weapons in the vehicle he was in. He was held for a couple days and then released. From the start I was convinced that Abu Omar was representing some other faction. For a while I had even considered him as an important counterweight to Abul Abed. However, he also happened to be the brother of Hajji Salman, our primary AQI target."

The confrontation came to a head when the Americans, acting on a tip from a rival Fursan member, found a large weapons cache behind a false wall in Abu Omar's house, Abu Omar claimed that they were put there by his brother. After he was arrested, the Iraqi Islamic Party pressured Kuehl for his release. Community leaders, including Um Omar, asked to meet. "I knew of her through her charity work but had not met her up to now," Kuehl said. "She was pretty impressive. She was obviously well educated and passionate about getting the release of her husband. After about two weeks he was eventually released. Part of the condition for his release was that he would no longer work for the Fursan. Through this I pretty much determined that his affiliation was with the Iraqi Islamic Party, which had been trying to take control of the movement from the start."

Um Omar's main office was in Amriya, but the NGO also operated on the outskirts of Baghdad, Samarra, and Nasiriya. Most of its funds came from generous Iraqis. In Iraq a child was considered an orphan even if he or she had lost just one parent. The organization had registered 4,317 orphans. In Amriya alone it had 2,034 orphans. Before 2006 it had only 600 to 800 orphans in Amriya. "Their fathers were killed, their houses were burned," Um Omar told me, "some of them were left without either parent." Most of Amriya's Sunnis were too scared to go to the Yarmuk hospital outside Amriya. "It's a sectarian hospital," Um Omar told me. "By sectarian, I mean this hospital has militias in it and people are afraid to go there. If you live in Amriya, you have to go to private hospitals, which are expensive for orphans, widows, and displaced families."

When I first met Um Omar in January 2008, she had three thousand displaced families registered with her in Amriya alone. They were supposed to receive payments from the government, but she knew of no one who had. The Ethar Association had once received help from the Red Crescent, but now that aid was going to the local Awakening group. Since Amriya's security was improving, many Sunnis who had fled to Syria were coming back, even if some of them were not originally from Amriya. At least 50 percent of the families in Amriya could not access their monthly rations, and Um Omar knew of families who had not received any rations at all during the previous year. "We experienced the most difficult five years," she told me. "Iraq went through wars, the Iran war, the Kuwait war, the sanctions, but it wasn't as hard or unmerciful like the days of the occupation. The number of orphans is so high, and as much as we find some people to adopt them, we see there are more orphans coming. We have many children whose fathers were arrested, and it's been a long time that nobody knows where they are. There are the families of detainees: the husband has been arrested for three or four years, and nobody knows where he is. The Americans are easier in providing information and allowing contact with the detainee. In the first days of the occupation the detention by the occupation forces was ugly, as you saw in Abu Ghraib, but in the last year and now it's preferable to be in the custody of the occupation forces than the MOI [Ministry of Interior]."

Ethar provided orphans with rations, blankets, and heaters for the winter—and medical care, thanks to volunteer doctors. Orphans also could attend their nursery school and subsequent education. Widows received medical care and vocational training as well as educational assistance, including university tuition. Ethar had a kitchen project where widows made pastries and sold them in local markets.

Um Omar took me to her nursery school. Among the orphans was a boy whose mother was killed beside him in cross fire. At first he did not talk to other students and remained isolated, but the teachers succeeded in making him more social. Um Omar had books full of files and photos of children in need of medical assistance, from a two-year-old bloated from cancer to a teenager who was shot by Americans and paralyzed. One seven-year-old girl called Hadia Abdallah had lost both her parents. Her father was killed by random American gunfire and then her mother was killed when Iraqi National Guardsmen opened fire indiscriminately. When the mother was shot she dropped Hadia on the ground, and the child was paralyzed from the waist down. Of the two thousand orphans Um Omar had registered in Amriya, 60 to 70 percent had lost a parent to fire by occupation forces, she told me. The rest were killed by terrorists.

Uday Ahmad was shot in the jaw. The boy's jawbone was shattered, and he needed a simple operation so that he would not have to be fed through a plastic tube, but his family was afraid to visit hospitals because of the threat from Shiite militias. Another boy in her album was shot below the eye by the Americans.

"Every day I listen to the widows and see their tears, and I can't get them enough help," she said. "This morning a widow came in, her donor stopped providing help. Some donors get killed or got arrested and some of them got displaced. So they stop paying the help. She was waiting until the end of the month to come here to get paid. She came crying, saying it has been a month that she is feeding her children soup only. She did not buy fruit or vegetables for a month. She said yesterday the children were crying, 'We don't want soup anymore,' and her neighbor heard their cry and gave them a plate of food. This is one case out of thousands of widows."

Two weeks earlier she delivered school uniforms to orphans in Abu Ghraib. "A little boy came to me shivering, without a coat and shoes," she said. "I can't explain now how I managed to stop myself from crying, and the look in his eyes and his happiness while I was putting the new clothes on him, and he was looking at the new bag and new books."

I told Um Omar that I could see the children were still afraid. "How do you want them not to be afraid after they saw the terrorist militias raiding their areas, killing their fathers, killing their brothers, and destroying their houses? I know a displaced woman who told me that she saw two of her neighbors being dragged away just because they were Sunnis. She said they dragged the father and his son and killed them. How do you expect the young children to forget them easily? Obviously these kind of things have more impact on the spirit of children than they do on older people, and I don't think that it will just go away and the wounds will heal quickly."

Um Omar complained that Amriya's population had once been prosperous and very educated: a neighborhood for lawyers, doctors, and teachers. She estimated that 40 percent of those educated people had been displaced. The families who replaced them in Amriya were less educated and from poorer neighborhoods.

Since 2006 Um Omar had registered 5,520 displaced families in Amriya, and they hadn't yet returned to their homes. "They are not willing to return because their areas became 100 percent Shiite areas, and their houses were either destroyed or burned, and their sons were killed. They can't return anymore though they want to return home." They would never be able to return, though Shiite families had returned to Amriya, she said.

Um Omar admitted that there had been some security improvements, but she did not attribute it to American efforts. "It happened by the Awakening's efforts. The tribal men's efforts were the reason for improving the security. In the past, our areas were always raided by the militias and interior commandos, arresting many of our guys and taking them to unknown destinations. This is not security, right? We couldn't stop the militias from doing this. I think security was improved when the Awakening guys joined the security forces."

Forty percent of Amriya's homes were abandoned, their owners expelled. More than five thousand Sunni families from elsewhere in Iraq had moved in, mostly to Shiite homes. Of those who had fled to Syria, about one-fifth returned in late 2007 when their money ran out. The Ministry of Migration, officially responsible for displaced Iraqis, did nothing for them. The Ministry of Health, dominated by sectarian Shiites, neglected Amriya or sent expired medicines to its clinics. Like elsewhere in Iraq, the government-run ration system, upon which nearly all Iraqis relied for their survival, did not reach the Sunnis of Amriya often, and when it did most items were lacking. Children were suffering from calcium shortages as a result.

Seventeen-year-old Ahmad Maath was a student who helped support his family by leaving Amriya and collecting people's rations and fuel for them. Amriya's citizens were afraid of the INP who guarded the fuel station. "They are with the militias," he said. "They say, 'Fuck you, Sunnis, you are pimps'— you know, such silly things. But what can we do? We tolerate that because we want to feed our families." He and his friends would bring the tanks at night and wait until the morning to collect the government-supplied kerosene. One day Ahmad saw the Mahdi Army surround the station and take ten thousand liters of kerosene and one hundred and fifty cooking gas cylinders without paying. They said they needed it to cook for the Muharram ceremonies.

I had heard of corpses being dropped at garbage dumps, where dogs would feed on them. Twelve-year-old Abudi, my friend Hussein's son, had seen many corpses in one of the main squares. "I saw people executed by Al Qaeda," Abudi told me. "I saw a woman here being executed. I felt scared from them. I feel afraid from both, the Americans and Al Qaeda. They attacked my father, a car rushed and shot my father. I felt sad. My father got injured and he was bleeding, but he is okay now. The Americans killed a child in Amriya because he was playing with a toy gun."

I visited Abudi's elementary school in Amriya. It was overcrowded because of the many displaced children. Its population had grown from 400 to about 769 students. Each class contained fifty-five students, with three to four students to a desk. One boy lost his father in Amriya when a bomb landed on their house. There were children displaced from Jihad, Shuhada, Furat, Shula, Turath, Amil, Hurriya. The teacher asked them if they wanted to go back home. "We can't," a child said. "We are threatened by gangs." Sabrin was a small girl whose father was murdered in a drive-by shooting in the Muhamin neighborhood of Amriya. Abdurahman was a sixth-grade boy from New Baghdad. The Mahdi Army had threatened his family and kidnapped and killed his brother. His family's house in New Baghdad was occupied; now they were renting a home in Amriya. To help support his family Abdurahman worked in restaurants and sold black-market gasoline on the streets. When Al Qaeda still controlled Amriya, one of his brothers was arrested by the Americans because a *mujahid* came to his shop to change the oil in his car, and his brother was accused by the Americans of working with them. One boy's father was killed by the Mahdi Army in the Jihad district.

"When the children first came here they found themselves in a different environment than the one they used to live in," the school principal told me. "The way they behave and the way they are is all different. Gradually, they started to adapt to here. Of course, they were very afraid as a result of what they had seen in their areas. Some of them wake up at night. When they hear gunfire they just keep screaming. When a Hummer passes by they scream, even when they are inside the class. They are hurt from the inside. But you know they are children, so they occupy their time with playing and other stuff."

The school guard, who had not been paid in months, told me neither the Americans nor the Iraqi army brought security to Amriya. "Let us be realistic," he said, "our brothers from the Thuwar secured us. They are better than the army and the Americans. The Americans don't do anything when you go complain about something. They just put it down on a paper, while the Awakening, when you go complain to them, they do something. They go to those who did wrong and punish them. They are our sons, from the same area and we know them well, while the Americans and the army are not."

Um Omar took me to visit the family of Saad Juma, who had been displaced from the Amil district by Shiite militias more than a year earlier. I found them in the burned-out house of a Shiite family that had fled with only their clothes. When Saad and his family moved in, the house was torched and dirty, full of tires and other flammable items that had been used to burn it. The Shiite militias had expelled all the Sunni families from the area using loudspeakers on police cars to warn them. They cursed Sunnis and said they would kill anyone they saw on the street. "I remember one of our neighbors who lived nearby was killed there," Saad said. "They killed him immediately. Another one was killed with his two little children in his garden. The militias called him by his name and shot him with two, three shots in the head, and they left the house after that."

Saad insisted that before the war, relations between Sunnis and Shiites in his area had been good. "We were like one family. Those militias came from outside, not from our area. Maybe from Shula or from other areas. They might come from the other side of the city." Um Omar added that "the militias knew who the families were, and they knew the area well. They must be helped by the others in this area." Saad agreed, adding that the local Sadrist office was near their area.

Saad owned his previous house and had shared it with ten other relatives. He was a construction worker before he was displaced, but now he relied on the Ethar Association for food and aid. "The government is busy with itself," he said. "It doesn't care about people. It only cares about itself." I asked him if he wanted to go back home. "Is there anyone who doesn't wish to return to his home?" he asked me. But he didn't think it was safe enough.

Abasya Aziz was from the Sunni Mashhadani tribe. She and her family were expelled from the house in Hurriya they had lived in for thirty-five years. For two days Shiite militiamen shot at their house and called on them to leave. The men left to find a new house, but the women stayed another four days until one was found. "We were very scared alone," she said. "I was scared to take all the furniture at once. So every day I take some of the furniture, and I also had to leave some furniture there." Their new house had no electricity, so she had to show me around with a flashlight. The landlord originally wanted rent to be 350,000 dinars but because they were poor he reduced it to less than 250,000. "I wish to return [to Hurriya] and live a stable life," Abasya Aziz said. "That's what we are looking for. Now we can't go back there because it is not safe. Also, I am afraid for my other sons. I can't go back. It has been one year, and it's still not safe there."

On the outskirts of Amriya, on a muddy field, I found a Sunni family in a makeshift brick home. I spoke to twenty-two-year-old Haidar, who lived there with eleven other family members. He told me that they were expelled from Amil by the Mahdi Army in 2006. His eighty-three-year-old grandfather had owned their house in Amil. Now Mahdi Army men were living in it. Haidar was on crutches, his legs amputated after a car bomb exploded too close to him when he was working as a mechanic in Bayaa. "Honestly, I don't wish what happened to us even on my enemy," Haidar told me. "We were displaced from our area. We left our house without any reason. It was a big house with two floors. We don't have issues with anybody. We left our house and came here to live in this dirty house while they came and lived in our house. We suffered lots of damages. Before I used to go with my brother and sell gas to earn a little money. Now I can't anymore."

I returned often to Amriya and saw a lot of Um Omar. Of the 104 students in her school, ten received free education, fourteen were orphans, thirteen had fathers in detention, and most of the rest had been displaced within the past year. "It is a very bad life," Ms. Rasha, one of the teachers, told me about her students. "Our students, especially last year, we told them to study and focus on their school, especially the ones in the last year of the high school. They say, 'What is the benefit? Let's say we got into a good university, can we go study in that university?'" The students couldn't go to university because of security problems and bombs, she told me, but also sectarianism. "Most of our students are named Omar. They say, 'My name is Omar. When the teacher reads my name on the exam papers, they will mark it as failed and throw it away.' Last year they canceled the results of the final high school examinations. Specifically they canceled the results of the students of Amriya, they didn't mark their exam papers. The students made a second attempt on the exams and even a third attempt, but they've never received their results back."

ABUL ABED WAS KNOWN for his brutality. He was a short, thin thirty-five-year-old who had broken his knuckles beating prisoners and suspected members of Al Qaeda. He destroyed the homes of Al Qaeda men and hung pictures of their dead bodies on the walls of Amriya. He claimed four of his brothers had been killed by Shiite militiamen, and he kept pictures of their broken and tortured bodies on his phone. He and his men blasted through Amriya, letting everybody know they were its new rulers. According to some stories, Abul Abed had been working with a network of informers for the Americans, targeting Al Qaeda and Iranian spies, finally infiltrating Al Qaeda in Amriya. Abul Abed also had a good relationship with politicians Saleh al-Mutlaq and Ali Baban, a Sunni Kurd who was minister of planning and who had been expelled by the Islamic Party. Many of Abul Abed's men were displaced Sunnis from Mahdi Army–controlled areas like Hurriya, yet he claimed he helped seventy-five Shiite families return to Amriya.

I first met with Abul Abed in what looked like a school or ex-Baath Party headquarters that had been converted into an office, and I later interviewed him several times in his lavish home. (One morning I found him drinking a can of nonalcoholic beer.) The street where he lived was manned by his guards, who stood at roadblocks. He traveled in convoys of pickup trucks and SUVs with his men hanging out of windows, their rifles and pistols waving about, sirens blaring, a pale imitation of the Blackwater style. He was a former military officer and leader in the Islamic Army of Iraq, but much of his biography was apocryphal, and he had labored to construct a heroic legend about himself.

He claimed that in 2006 he and others from the Islamic Army decided to fight Al Qaeda, which had declared the Islamic State of Iraq and was trying to control other Sunni groups, insisting that they pledge allegiance to Abu Omar al-Baghdadi, who would be the future caliph, and demanding a portion of their loot. The Islamic Army refused, and Abul Abed and his men began a clandestine war on Al Qaeda. The conflict started with assassinations but soon escalated into open warfare. Abul Abed claimed he had spent months collecting intelligence on Al Qaeda fighters who had sought sanctuary in Amriya after fleeing from other parts of Baghdad or the Anbar.

In May 2007, fourteen American soldiers were killed in Amriya. Until then Lieut. Col. Dale Kuehl had lost only three men in Amriya. On May 29 Sheikh Walid of the Fardus Mosque called Kuehl up and told him Abul Abed's men would be attacking Al Qaeda in Amriya. They attacked an Al Qaeda base at the Maluki Mosque, and the next day Al Qaeda men struck back at Tikriti

Mosque. Sheikh Walid contacted the Americans, who sent Stryker vehicles to assist Abul Abed's fighters. The Americans helped defeat Al Qaeda in that battle and then provided medical assistance to Abul Abed's wounded men. That first week Abul Abed and his men, along with the Americans, killed about ten Al Qaeda suspects and captured another fifteen.

The official name for Abul Abed's Awakening group, the first of its kind in Baghdad, was the Fursan (Knights) of Mesopotamia. But Abul Abed and his men referred to themselves as the Thuwar (revolutionaries). Part of Kuehl's deal was that he would help Abul Abed's men if they did not torture prisoners or kill people who were not from Al Qaeda. They would be allowed to hold prisoners for only twenty-four hours. Kuehl knew that as an American, he would never know the area or its people as well as the local Awakening men. At first Kuehl's men asked the Fursan to wear white headbands and sit in the American vehicles to identify Al Qaeda locations. But soon Al Qaeda men took to wearing white headbands. Riding along with the Americans also didn't work because the windowless vehicles left the Fursan disoriented and unable to locate targets. The Fursan were given special reflective armbands that the Americans could see as well as handcuffs and flares to help send signals to the Americans. Kuehl collected their biometric data and agreed to provide them with some weapons.

At first Abul Abed believed he could spread his control into other Sunni areas in western Baghdad. When Iraqi Vice President Tariq al-Hashimi, of the Sunni Islamic Party, visited Amriya without coordinating with Abul Abed, the Fursan leader was furious and nearly clashed with Hashimi's bodyguards. Abul Abed felt threatened by the Islamic Party, and that same night he raided the home of Abu Omar, Um Omar's husband, and a subordinate commander who was allied with the party. Shots were fired and civilians were threatened. Abu Omar was not home, but Abul Abed arrested several of his men.

In November 2007 Abul Abed was interviewed by the London-based, Saudi-owned *Al Hayat* newspaper. Al Qaeda had turned into Iraq's biggest enemy, he said, and so he had to ally himself with his erstwhile enemies, the Americans, against whom he claimed he had once fought "honorably." He claimed to have six hundred men under his control, each of whom got paid about $360 a month, and three hundred of whom had become Amriya's police force. He called for further integration of Awakening men into the government.

When I met him again in early 2008 he had switched from wearing military uniforms to suits. "The situation is different now," he said. "We have destroyed Qaeda. It is safe now, and it is very good for me—I am number one on the hit list of Qaeda. Just after the assassination of Sheikh Sattar, the next primary goal for Qaeda became me. If my fate is to die, then that is okay." He repeated his claim that he had six hundred men in Amriya, and many outside. I asked where. "All of Baghdad," he said. I asked how many; he said "a lot." His main target was anyone who broke the law, he said, whether they were Al Qaeda or not. "We are against criminals, against killers, against the ones who make bombs and against the ones who destroy." In the past his men had clashed with the Mahdi Army as well.

"Our areas and our sect were marginalized, which is what Al Qaeda used to initiate a sectarian war. Now we are working on fixing this and rehabilitat[ing] our areas in order to take our real positions in the government and in the country." He would not run in elections, he said, but Iraq's national security adviser had taken the surprising step of offering Abul Abed a position in the government. "I have been offered many positions from different big political parties. But I refused them. I explained from the beginning to the journalists that I didn't come for money, nor for political reasons. I know lots of scornful people who put themselves in front of others and step on people's shoulders to go up the ladder and take a chair or a position in the government. This is not my goal, and I have explained that to the channels that visited me. I am not running for any position, not going to take part of the political process. I have a goal that I would like to achieve, not only in Amriya but in all of Baghdad: re-instate the security in our areas and save innocent people's lives. Only when I achieve these goals I will leave.

"Everybody knows how Al Qaeda used to control our areas. They de-stroyed the area, they killed civilian families, they filled the streets with bombs. Their work became barbaric, killing people for their identity, on suspicion. They started by killing Shiites, then they started killing Sunnis, then finally they started killing Christians with the excuse of establishing the Islamic State of Iraq. They said, 'Since you are a Christian, you must pay a ransom.' If the man had money to pay the ransom, he paid and lived in his home. If he didn't, they killed him and threw his corpse in the trash. People advised them that this is destruction and far away of jihad, so they killed the ones who gave such advice. They acted like a gang—they kill and steal, and they look for new mod-ern cars. They killed people under the name of jihad."

Abul Abed told me that jihad had four conditions: to preserve the religion, the land, the honor, and the money. "These are four conditions, all of which Al Qaeda breached. Qaeda claimed that they are fighting the occupation. If you fight the occupation, why would you kill civilians? If you are fighting occupa-tion, why would you steal the water pumps? If you are fighting the occupa-tion, why would you take down the mobile telecommunications towers? If you are fighting the occupation, why would you steal from the shops of the Muslims? They did that with the excuse, this is Shiite and that is Christian. Did the Prophet do that? The Prophet had a Jewish neighbor, and he never did that to him. Is taking rich people's money a form of jihad? Is this against occupa-tion? No, it is not." Al Qaeda, he said, is a dirty gang using the cover of Islam. They dragged people from their cars and filled the streets of Amriya with corpses. The smell of these bodies was everywhere, but people were prohibited from removing them because IEDs were placed just underneath them. "This is not jihad, this is destruction!" Abul Abed said. "All the shops were closed, food never entered the area because people were afraid to come into the area. If a man looks at them in a strange way, they killed him, and many other issues that we can't count. The garbage accumulated and made mountains two meters high in the streets of Amriya. The government was about to attack Amriya. Day after day they said, 'We must attack Amriya, we must bomb Amriya.'

"It started when Al Qaeda kidnapped two young guys from the Dulaimi tribe in Amriya. The father of the two guys came into the mosque and was crying. Two days earlier Sheikh Walid was passing by the Munadhama Street when he saw a very old woman. She was a Christian, white, and she was wearing a skirt that was not long, and she was fat. The woman's husband was taken by Al Qaeda, and his body was in the back of their car and his leg was outside the car. The woman was holding her husband's leg, not letting it go. The woman was on the ground and they were hitting her with their pistols. The sheikh and I were asking if this was jihad. No, this is not jihad. We knew then that fighting these people is the jihad itself, in order to protect people from them, to protect their money and to protect their honors. Al Qaeda destroyed people's lives."

What actually sparked the war between the Islamic Army fighters and Al Qaeda in Amriya was the murder of an Islamic Army leader called Zeid, or Abu Teiba, who was a good friend of Sheikh Hussein of the Maluki Mosque. Abu Teiba was a law school graduate who also provided security for the Maluki Mosque. Sheikh Hussein had been detained by the Americans, and Al Qaeda had taken over his mosque. Al Qaeda men captured Abu Teiba and brought him to the mosque, where they filmed his torture and accused him of being an infidel. "Zeid, he was one of the best guys in Amriya," Abul Abed told me. "He was an Arabic teacher, he was teaching the Koran, he was teaching Islamic religious beliefs and Islamic religious law, he was popular in mosques, he was popular in the area. They tortured him until he died. He was in the Maluki Mosque, he was in the house of God. When I started the fight, Zeid used to always protect the mosques. We have a video of him being tortured, tortured according to the Sharia law. A guy from the Islamic State of Iraq was slapping him while he was bleeding. He was not allowed to discuss why they tortured him because in their view he was an apostate. They were telling him, 'You are a criminal. Abul Abed told you to fight the mujahideen.'"

Abul Abed was in the Dubat neighborhood of Amriya, supplying his men with weapons and vehicles, when one of his men told him about Sabah, the so-called "white lion," who led Al Qaeda in Amriya. Sabah was standing on a corner with his assistant. Abul Abed walked to him accompanied by three or four of his men, carrying his charged pistol. They stood face to face.

After Abul Abed challenged him, Sabah stepped back, pulled his pistol, and shot at him, but his weapon didn't work. Abul Abed pulled his pistol too. He shot Sabah, and Sabah ran. While he was running he charged his weapon again and pulled the trigger, but again it didn't work. He was using Iraqi bullets. Abul Abed kept shooting at him until he fell; then he took his gun. "I always carry it with me," Abul Abed said. "I replaced the bullets with good foreign bullets."

Abul Abed recited the names of other Al Qaeda leaders he had fought and killed. "Let me tell you one point. They have announced themselves as an Islamic country. They all came up as leaders. Some of them presented themselves as a minister of defense, minister of interior, and mosque leaders, and security and intelligence and army and patrols. They were all known to the people of Amriya. We knew their names and their faces. We knew them all. They were not working only secretly but also publicly. They didn't even cover their faces. The Iraqi and national forces were unable to enter the area." Abul Abed told me his unit lost about twenty martyrs in the battle of Amriya. The day before I met him the Iraqi National Guard and the Thuwar raided a home and confiscated weapons.

Abul Abed no longer bragged about being a former resistance fighter. He had become more cautious after Ghaith Abdul-Ahad's controversial profile of him appeared in the *Guardian*. I told him that everybody said he was in the Islamic Army of Iraq. "Is this something to be ashamed of?" he asked. "Allow me to let you know that we have corrected the attitudes of many of the jihadist battalions. Many of them have put their guns down and said, 'Enough.' Some media are trying to make this a point against us, to make a problem between us and the Iraqi government."

I told him that the government maintained that the Awakening men were former insurgents and that it did not trust them. "Let's say I am strong and you are also strong and I want to fight you but you can't fight me, and I have caused you so many injuries, and made you dizzy, and you can't win the fight with me despite your capabilities," Abul Abed said. "And then I tell you I won't fight you anymore and give you my hands. I ask you to put your hands in mine, and I say, 'Let's build Iraq and forget our problems.' If you are a nationalist and love your country and don't have loyalties to neighboring countries, you would accept me as a friend, not because you are weak. But if you are loyal to a neighboring country and you have an interest in this fight, when I give you my hand you will beat my hand. That is fine, let's fight again. This is Iran's interest. I'm giving an example that if there were, as they say, armed resistance groups who offered their hands to the government, the government should accept them. If I push the resistance groups in the corner, they will give up and become more violent than before."

I asked him if Al Qaeda was the only threat to Iraq. "Not only Al Qaeda," he said. "We have the Mahdi Army. I think the Mahdi Army has a very short life." I asked him if he trusted the Mahdi Army cease-fire. "No," he said.

Abul Abed believed there was an Iranian occupation in Iraq. "The American occupation in Iraq is 20 percent, and the Iranian occupation is 80 percent in Iraq. We started being terminated. I experienced this during the time when Bayan Jabr Solagh was the minister of interior. I saw fifty police cars equipped with big machine guns. They entered Amriya from 4 a.m. till 7 a.m. They took my four older brothers. Since then they said they are in the ministry for interrogation. We went there and found their names in the detainee list. We went there more than once. After a while we heard there were more than twenty-one bodies found in the Iraqi-Iranian border in a town called Badra wa Jasan. When they transferred the bodies to the morgue, my four brothers were among the corpses. Their arms were cut, their eyes were taken out, their fingers were cut, their skin was burned with acid. Why? This is a question that I always direct to the Iraqi government. I say, Why? Because they are Sunnis, they always accuse us of being terrorists. If we were terrorists, what have we done? Why were my relatives terminated? Because Iran wants to terminate us."

I asked him if he was accusing the Iraqi government of being Iranian. He smiled. "I never said the government. I said Iran has the bigger hand in Iraq. . . . I am not accusing the journalists, but journalists often make problems for us with the government, and there are some parties in the government who want these problems. I am sure you understand my concerns. Journalism is a two-edged sword: one edge that can cut with it and the other edge might cut the user. I have been visited by a journalist from the *Guardian*, Ghaith Abdul-Ahad. I hosted him for four days in my house with my family. He ate my food, I satisfied all his wishes, and then in his article he said I am a mafia man. He made a big mess for me."

When I mentioned the walls that Kuehl had erected in Amriya, Abul Abed denied that the walls made it like a prison. "Keep in mind that it is not only our area that is walled. Amriya is walled, Khadra is walled, Dora is walled, Hatin is walled, Adhamiya is walled. If we take off the walls, you will see how many car bombs will attack civilians. Qaeda attacked children and women in Ramadi with massive trucks filled with chlorine." But he expected that the walls would shortly come down. "We are planning to open a police station manned by local inhabitants of this area. An official police station. Khadra police station is manned by Khadra people, Adhamiya police station is manned by Adhamiya people. Dora the same, and Fadhil the same."

Of his 600 men only 333 received salaries under the American contract, he said. "We are not here for the money. Ask any soldier of the Awakening if they have come for money. Is he risking his life, his family's life, his children's life, his wife's life, for two hundred dollars? He might get killed, slaughtered, killed in car bombs for this simple amount of money. No, he is here for his beliefs and his principles." Abul Abed told me that he planned to open a police station in Amriya. Only 233 of the 600 candidates he had offered to the police academy had been accepted. He complained that his men were abused there. "The officers in the training center take our guys every night at about 2 a.m. into interrogation rooms. It's like they were in a detention center, not a training center. The officers tell our guys that Abul Abed is a criminal and a terrorist. They ask them, 'What did you do before coming here? Why did you sabotage Iraq?' They harass our guys a lot. Yesterday I paid a visit to the center and met with the guys. They were afraid to talk to me in public, and the majority of them said, 'We want to leave this country.' A first lieutenant from the national police who works in the center goes into their room every night and takes four or five of them and keeps interrogating them until the morning. The guys were asking me if they were detainees. We have very deep wounds. Let me tell you something, if you see all these fighters, every one of them has lost his brother, his uncle or his father, most of the guys have lost members of their families."

I asked him how he could work in a government that was made up of the same militias that killed his brothers. "This is a very complicated subject. Iraq has gone through bad conditions in the past, much worse than this. Is the government going to last forever? The answer is no. There will be another stage where there will be other elections, so if we abandon our roles in Iraq, falsification will happen again in the elections, and we won't enter the elections because of the destruction, the fighting, and this will be a success to Iran, primarily. I follow the law. We have lots of supporters, even including Shiite brothers. Yesterday we had a meeting with the tribes of the south. We are dealing with each other as Iraqis. The strife that happened between Shiites and Sunnis is being reconciled now. Yesterday we had a visit here in Amriya from tribal leaders of the south, from Yusifiya, Mahmudiya, Mahawil, Karbala, and Hilla. We had tribal leaders of big Shiite tribes. They were our guests, and we even had reconciliation between towns and neighborhoods, Sunni and Shiite neighborhoods. Is this bad for the government? If Iraq doesn't get a professional government that is not sectarian, that doesn't belong to only one sect, then this county will fail."

Abul Abed appeared on television and called for Shiites to return to their homes in Amriya. "My first principle is reconciliation, stopping the sectarian fighting across Baghdad neighborhoods. We wanted to make a model for others to follow, and we wanted the others to do the same initiatives, but unfortunately, this didn't happen. There was a Sunni family from Amriya that went back to the Amil neighborhood. The day after they got there, the father, the mother, and two sons were killed. One of the brothers survived and gave me his mother's phone number, so I called. A man answered the phone. I said, 'Hello, how are you, my brother?' The guy said, 'Hello, who are you?' I said, 'I am Abul Abed, the leader of the Thuwar in Amriya.' He said, 'And what do you want?' I said, 'My brother, our area was a red zone. Shiites used to be killed in our areas, and we took the responsibility of returning Shiite families into their homes in our areas, and now we protect them. This is an innocent family. Why did you take them? What did they do?' He said, 'We are the Mahdi Army, there can only be killing between you and us.' I said, 'Let me tell you something, if you are a real man, the brave man and the real soldier who considers himself a brave fighter doesn't kill a woman, nor does he kidnap a family. I am a soldier, and I only fight the ones who carry weapons against me. I fight men. This is a manly point of view, and if you want the Islamic point of view, the Prophet said, "Don't cut a tree, don't kill an animal, don't kill a woman, and don't kill an old man, this is if you were a Muslim."' He said, 'You are filthy, and there can only be blood between you and us.' I hung up the phone. The next day the surviving brother was told that all his family were killed." Abul Abed said that similar things happened to many Sunnis who returned to Hurriya.

"I am a Sunni. I'm sure that 80 percent of Shiites are not satisfied with the United Iraqi Alliance. I have Iraqi friends from Sadr City—they visited me with presents, they cried for the good old days when we were all together. The politicians are the reason for this problem, whether they are Sunnis or Shiites. Neither the Sunnis in the government represent us and help us, nor did the Shiites in the government help the Shiite population. People got tired from the situation. They want to breathe and go out freely. Two bombs exploded by my house targeting me, planted by Al Qaeda to kill me. I was transferred to an American hospital and had operations and survived. One of my sons was burned, and the other was injured."

After I last saw him, Abul Abed began to seek alliances with other Awakening men in preparation for the upcoming provincial elections. This attempt to become legitimate might have been his undoing. In April a bomb targeting Abul Abed in Amriya wounded him, and he went to Jordan for medical treatment. In June 2008 while he was at a reconciliation conference in Sweden, his house in Iraq was raided on the suspicion that he had been involved in sixty murders or abductions. He never returned to Iraq, settling in Jordan instead. Al Qaeda's predictions that the Awakening leaders would be disposed of after they served their purpose were proven correct, he said. Abul Abed blamed the Islamic Party, with whom he had a longstanding feud (as Um Omar's husband could attest). Abu Ibrahim, Abul Abed's former close aide, took over for him and was perceived by many as a stooge for the Iraqi army who arrested anybody who opposed him.

"I am aware that Abul Abed is in Jordan," Kuehl told me. "I have had contact with him from time to time and am concerned about his safety as well as that of his family. I am hoping that he will be able to come to the U.S. at some point under refugee status. I do not know the details of why he had to leave. I am pretty sure it was politically motivated."

Staff Sergeant Joe Hartman had expected Abul Abed to rise in Iraqi politics. "I never thought that he would be betrayed. However, after reading some of the reports about his disrespect for current political leaders when they tried to visit with him, it seems to me that any political savvy he once had was corrupted by the tough military work he performed in Amriya. I can't imagine anyone remaining unaffected after having to defeat such a ruthless enemy as Al Qaeda, all the time still being persecuted by the Iraqi army for his past. He must have slept with one eye open every night. I hope he finds some peace."

AMRIYA WOULD BECOME a battleground again, but this time it involved senior U.S. officers, long after they served in Iraq, who quarreled over the efficacy of the surge doctrine. Lieut. Col. Gian Gentile, who preceded Kuehl and went on to teach at the U.S. Military Academy at West Point, became the most strident and outspoken voice within the military decrying the cult of counterinsurgency.

Gentile admitted that violence in Amriya had dropped precipitously starting in July 2007. "But the primary condition for that lowering of violence in Amriya was the deal cut with Abed and the SOIs," he maintained. "Was Dale Kuehl instrumental in that role? Yes, most certainly he was. Might another battalion commander less savvy to the area have missed that opportunity? Sure. But did the opportunity arise because Dale and his battalion were doing things in terms of COIN tactics and methods that were fundamentally different than mine? No. The COPs [combat outposts] didn't go into Amriya until after the deal had been cut."

Kuehl was unwilling to criticize Gentile publicly, but he believed that his time in Amriya during the surge did involve new and innovative tactics that led to success. "In general they were doing COIN operations," he said of Gentile and his men, "but we did change some things based on training and lessons learned that were pretty standard throughout the Army during our preparation, [placing a] heavy emphasis on COIN. Some of the criticism Gian has received is a bit unfair. He and his men were not hiding out on the FOB [Forward Operating Base], and they were patrolling every day. However, Gian's assertion that we did nothing different is false. He cites a lieutenant in my battalion who says that we had not really changed anything. At the platoon level, it may not have been much different, but I think it was different at the battalion and brigade level."

The two men had admirers and detractors. I spoke to one captain who served under both in Amriya. He described Gentile as "an intelligent, thoughtful, and caring leader who lost a lot of soldiers and took each of their deaths very, very personally. He was a pleasure to work for, and in the short time I worked for him, for two months, he took the time to mentor me. Unlike many of our senior leaders, he actually had some useful knowledge to pass on. I believe that his current arguments hold merit, but I wish he would quit responding to everything like it was an ad hominem. I truly believe he took his command so personally that he feels underlying guilt for the deaths of his soldiers, and this is the manifestation. He takes it personal now and is poor at conveying his beliefs, which is sad. Violence didn't go down under Kuehl until the SOI. May 2007 was the most violent month in the war in that area, as I recall. Gentile and Kuehl both kept lines of communication open with the extremists and local insurgents. Gentile was more conventional when I got there, but it was a conventional high-kinetic fight. He understood the concept of COIN, but the timing and resources weren't there to execute it."

This captain told me that Kuehl was "an arrogant though intelligent ass" who "did not understand the fight until late, if at all. He was very, very concerned that any misstep by Abul Abed's guys would have ramifications on his career . . . not its effects on his soldiers, Iraqis, or the outcome of the war. He was able to act dispassionately and rationally despite all of the losses his unit faced because he did not care about his men. I also believe that General Petraeus understood his sector better than he Kuehl did . . . he probably spent more time there."

On the other hand, Capt. Brendan Gallagher told me, "That is an extremely harsh and unfair criticism of Lieutenant Colonel Kuehl. I am not sure who said it, but I can verify it is 100 percent false. I can say with absolute confidence that Lieutenant Colonel Kuehl cared extremely deeply for each and every soldier in 1–5 Cav. I have nothing but positive things to say about him. I think in combat he was willing to accept certain risks in order to achieve success, which is what any good commander must do. If you take zero risks, you hunker down your forces in extreme force-protection mode, then you will not succeed in this kind of war. Consider for a moment: if you follow the bunker mentality to its logical conclusion, then you might as well not even leave the FOB at all—or better yet, never even deploy to Iraq in the first place. That way you are guaranteed not to incur any casualties. However, you also are guaranteed not to accomplish any of your strategic objectives. I think this marks perhaps the most important way in which we blazed a new path in Amriya. We were willing to take calculated risks into unchartered waters in order to make progress. Secretary of Defense [Robert] Gates said it best himself: we cannot kill or capture our way to victory. If we focus only on killing the enemy and force protection as our overriding objectives, then we effectively ignore history

and disavow counterinsurgency doctrine. Dismounted patrols, the establishment of COPs, getting out on the ground and gaining the trust of average
Iraqis—all these things involve inherent risk. But if we take prudent steps to
mitigate each risk, we stand the best chance of success. Compare the security
situation in Amriya when we departed [in January '08] to the security conditions previously. The results speak for themselves."

According to a major who served under Gentile, "Despite Lieutenant Colonel
Gentile being depicted in the media as a 'conservative' who only wants to focus
on high-intensity conflict, he set the groundwork for Lieutenant Colonel Kuehl
extremely well in one of the most important aspects of counterinsurgency.
COIN is about people, and people are about relationships—especially in Arabic
and Muslim culture. Gentile spent all of his time, in the very brief time that I saw
him, talking, negotiating, and working with the local imams in Amriya. Kuehl,
the beneficiary of this initial relationship building, continued the relationship and
allowed the SOI to emerge with the support of the local imams."

I asked Gentile what he thought Kuehl did differently from him. "Other
than rightly capitalizing on the changed conditions that presented to him the
opportunity to cut a deal with the SOIs, not much," he said. "His organizational structure as a combat battalion was a bit different than mine, since I was
an armored reconnaissance squadron—which meant that he had a greater dismounted capability, which might have produced more dismounted patrols.
But in terms of tactics, I don't believe there was much difference at all, although I am sure he would disagree with that statement. My outfit did dismounted operations, we engaged with the local population, etc. The notion
that I 'commuted' to the area and stayed inside my vehicles as put forward by
the surge zealots is a chimera. Dale did not put his first combat outpost in until late May '07, and it was a tactical one in the sense that its purpose was to facilitate movement into and out of the area. The first Galula-like COP did not
go into the district until late June. So the notion that during the first five or six
months of the surge—which arguably was the decisive period—that he was
doing things on the tactical level radically different from me is not correct.
What happened is that after the violence began to drop, and American soldiers
and marines stopped dying in large monthly numbers, folks looked back onto
the first period and superimposed the coherence of [the COIN manual] FM
3–24 that they believed was there at the time but actually was not."

"Probably the biggest difference," Kuehl said of his approach as opposed to
Gentile's, "was in taking a broader, long-term perspective of the problem. One
of the things that was highlighted in our staff training was the need to develop
a 'campaign plan' at the battalion level. This plan is intended to be long-term,
with objectives six months to even a year out. In contrast, the campaign plan I
got from Gian looked out about two weeks and really was nothing more than
a patrol schedule.

"I visited Gian's squadron in July 2006, and they were stretched pretty thin. If other parts of Baghdad were like his area, I am sure it looked like there were barely any U.S. soldiers on the ground. To be fair, I do not think that this type of planning or creating of a vision was part of the train[ing] Gian would have had, so [it is] not necessarily surprising that they did not have one. Even now we continue to adapt, and units that are there now are probably doing things I never thought of. There were two long-term projects that Gian left me with. The first was the Amriya Bank, which he laid the groundwork for. The other was the establishment of a police station. This second one did not happen until after we left."

Gentile wrote an article in the September 2007 issue of *Armed Forces Journal* called "Eating Soup With a Spoon," the title being a reference to John Nagl's influential book on COIN, *Learning to Eat Soup With a Knife*. In the article Gentile criticized the COIN manual and especially the paradoxes of "Tactical success guarantees nothing" and "The more you protect yourself, the less secure you are." Kuehl would later write accounts of his time in Amriya in part as a response to Gentile's criticism. "I think in this article Gian underestimates the abilities of our officer corps to use the manual as it is intended, as a guide as opposed to dogma," Kuehl told me. "I think the article also provides some insights into Gian's way of thinking. In his mind the new manual takes the enemy out of the equation and tries to make COIN sound easy by winning over the populace. I think one quote by Gian is relevant: 'I was angry and bewildered because the paradoxes, through their clever contradictions, removed a fundamental aspect of counterinsurgency warfare that I had experienced throughout my year as a tactical battalion commander in Iraq: fighting. And by removing the fundamental reality of fighting from counterinsurgency warfare, the manual removes the problem of maintaining initiative, morale and offensive spirit among combat soldiers who will operate in a place such as Iraq.'"

I asked Gentile about this. "I don't think that a center of gravity, theoretically, even if there can be such a thing, should be predetermined and turned into a rule for any type of stability or counterinsurgency operation," he said. "In modern counterinsurgencies certainly the population is an important consideration, but the American Army has turned the notion of the people as a center of gravity into an immutable rule, which then determines a prescribed set of tactics and procedures, which ultimately calls for large numbers of American combat soldiers on the ground. This kind of approach might be the right choice in certain circumstances, but it should not be the only way. If it is, then we can expect many more adventures at nation building to come."

Kuehl told me that "Gian tried to maintain the initiative while maintaining the morale and fighting esprit by his men by doing periodic large-scale cordon-and-searches to keep them focused. He also established small kill teams in houses, some of them occupied by residents. These teams generally consisted of a six-man team, usually including a sniper, emplaced to counter enemy IED efforts. I remember Gian telling me that many of these operations were to maintain the morale of the unit. What baffled me was that they served no real tactical purpose. In fact, I think in some ways they hurt the effort because they were not focused on good intelligence, so we were stumbling around inconveniencing the local populace.

"I banned the use of occupied homes for small kill teams right after we took over. I read a couple patrol reports from Gian's unit that made clear to me that these operations were not going to win over the populace. We continued with the cordon-and-search operations (we called them 'block parties') for a while. However, as we gained more intel, we relied less on them and focused more on targeted raids and eventually did away with them altogether."

I asked Gentile if he thought his cordon-and-search operations and small kill teams had been counterproductive. "Well, this is certainly the stock question that any population-centric counterinsurgency expert would ask," he said. "Sure, they can be, but we should not assume a priori that they will be all the time."

These operations could serve a purpose that outweighed their potential to alienate the population, he said. "It depends on the situation and what strategy has been created as the political object of war and the necessary military means to accomplish it. In other words, if you are a New American Army Way of War proponent, then the absolute and unequivocal answer to the question is that they are never productive and can never work in *any* counterinsurgency operation. But depending on the policy objective and a realistic approach to strategy, such methods might be effective. And arguably, during the critical months of the surge, it was just these types of operations that reduced Al Qaeda, fueled by the former Sunni insurgents who we bought off."

Kuehl found it ironic that Gentile focused on offensive operations to maintain the initiative and morale, he said, because "Gentile did not have the initiative when he turned over the area to us. The initiative belonged to the insurgents. Gian's patrols would not go on the two main streets in town due to the IED threat, and there was one area where they would not dismount due to the sniper threat. He had very little information on the nature of the threat in the area. While there were perhaps a dozen individuals that they were looking at, there was no clear understanding of the nature of the insurgency. At least none that he passed on to me."

Kuehl's operation officer, Lieut. Col. Chris Rogers (who was then a major), wrote a response to Gentile in the January 2008 issue of *Armed Forces Journal* titled "More Soup, Please." "Gian had been criticizing the surge and the change in focus for some time," Kuehl said. "To be honest, it really pissed me off. Here we were trying to make this work, and he, a commissioned officer, was openly critical of the effort. I found this very unprofessional on his part.

Furthermore, not once did he ask my opinion on what had changed and how we were trying to do things. In fact, he never once contacted me while we were in Iraq. I think he took some of my comments in the press as personal criticism of how he did operations, which was never my intent." (Gentile responded in *Armed Forces Journal* with an article titled "Our COIN Doctrine Removes the Enemy From the Essence of War.")

"Several times I have heard Gian say that we had done nothing different from his formation," Kuehl told me. "He uses a platoon leader from my battalion as a source to back up his argument. This platoon leader said that he did not think we did anything different, and he was critical of my decision to put an outpost in northwest Amriya. I am pretty sure I know who this was, and he was not exactly one of my stellar performers. It seems a bit odd that Gian would rely on the opinions of a lieutenant who had a lieutenant's view of operations, as opposed to the experiences of the commander and XO of the formation, who had a broader perspective."

I asked Gentile if he might have been stretched too thin. "Not in Amriya from August until the end of November—I made the conscious choice to concentrate almost all of my squadron in Amriya, because it was such a critical district. The notion that the surge brigades greatly increased the amount of combat power on the ground does not work in Amriya. In fact, what Kuehl brought into the area was roughly the same with what I had there. Kuehl did not increase the overall amount of combat power relative to what I had there, so the premise to this question is flawed based on actual conditions." Gentile did not have a strong presence in other parts of Baghdad that were technically under his authority, and as the next chapter, on Washash, will show, the paucity of troops did allow militias to operate without hindrance.

Kuehl ended up expanding the area under his control. "Shortly after taking over, we expanded our area to include all of Mansour," he said. "This gave me a broader perspective, since we had a much larger area to be concerned about. Gian was focused almost exclusively on Amriya, with one company in Khadra. The rest of Mansour was under the control of a Stryker unit for a couple months, but they were not permanent. The expansion to include all of Mansour under our responsibility allowed me to see the problem of Al Qaeda and other insurgent movement more clearly. Along with intelligence I was getting I was able to trace the infiltration routes used by Al Qaeda into western Baghdad. One of these was along the road to Abu Ghraib. AQI could easily bypass all the checkpoints and get into central Baghdad. The result of this was the improved walls along this road as well as around Ghazaliya, Khadra, and Amriya. This severely restricted the movements of AQI. Gian did put walls around Amriya, but it was very ineffective, consisting only of the shorter Jersey barriers. Insurgents could easily move them, go over them, or around them. The barrier we put up was much more comprehensive and effective."

I VISITED SHEIKH KHALID AL-OBEIDI, president of the Council of Notables, so vaunted by U.S. occupation forces. I found him in a large hall receiving a long line of supplicants seeking food or help with medical problems or with finding missing loved ones. In another office I saw a similarly occupied Sheikh Hussein of the Maluki Mosque. I was curious to hear Sheikh Khalid's views on why security in Baghdad had improved. "The U.S. Army has given the chance for these areas to be protected by their own," Khalid told me. "Thus many people of these areas have volunteered to protect their own areas. This has helped to impose better security in the areas. This experience was successful to a large extent, but it needs a further investment, and we are afraid it might fail at the end. What pushed the people to accept such a project and even pushed the U.S. forces to support and allow it was the resistance operations against the U.S. forces. The U.S. forces need the people in order to protect themselves and protect the people. The people were suffering from militias in these areas in addition to the military operations in these areas. People have been asked to help and have been given the chance to protect themselves. In terms of future outlook, this is not going to help build a government, but in the meantime, people feel it is safer now than then, since they have the opportunity to protect themselves."

But Sheikh Khalid was extremely cautious about the future. "The Iraqi people find themselves passing through a time much worse than any other time," he said. "Much worse because nothing has changed for the better. Iraqi people have no life. They are insecure and incapable, even to leave their house safely. They have very few sources to earn money and even the political elite that came now didn't bring anything better than the previous one. There is no real project that helps people. Iraq is a very vital place for the security of the entire world. A stable Iraq means stable oil prices and a stable economy. An unstable Iraq means a bigger Iran that imposes its control over the Gulf region and threatens all neighboring countries. Help will only come through reconsidering the political process and giving a better chance to Iraqis to choose who represent them. The political project in Iraq didn't start right from the beginning. It was built on a sectarian basis, and thus some parties have gained control of decision making in Iraq. They have marginalized lots of skilled people, those who would have helped to shape and lead the Iraqi state. In order to let Iraq exit its ordeal, we all need to reconsider the political process and give an opportunity to the Iraqi people to choose their government without the pressure factors that were used in the previous elections. The current changes in Iraq's security situation have shown the American administration that peace has only been gained with the people's help and the help of the key figures—only through the help of Sunnis. If the same marginalization stays in Iraq, I think it won't be good for anyone at the end, and the political and democratic process in Iraq that the West is hoping to achieve won't be accepted in our communities because people won't believe in it."

CHAPTER NINE

The Eclipse of the Mahdi Army

ONE DAY IN EARLY 2008, I WAS ON PALESTINE STREET IN EASTERN Baghdad, heading to a meeting at the Interior Ministry. My driver stopped to buy some black-market gasoline from a man selling containers on the sidewalk not far from where a national police pickup truck was parked. I gave the man a twenty-dollar bill, but he thought it was fake, so he took it to the police to see what they thought. They saw my beard in the distance and the American money, and so they came to my side of the car to ask for my ID. Upon hearing my foreign accent they panicked; then I showed them my American passport and the press ID the U.S. military had given me, and they panicked even more, unable to read English but aware I was a foreigner. Pointing their rifles at me, they ordered me out of the car and tried to handcuff me. One of them poked me in the ribs with his rifle, searching for a suicide vest. I asked them if I could call my friend at the Interior Ministry, who would tell them who I was, but they worried I would detonate my bomb with the phone. We struggled as I refused to let them handcuff me, afraid that they were members of a militia who would kidnap me. My driver told them I was Iranian. When they heard that, they relaxed somewhat and swore on Imam Ridha that they would not harm me. "We are the state," they told me. "We are all Shiites."

Eventually, I told them I would go with them, but not if they handcuffed me. They put me in the back of their truck, and we drove to their headquarters. The officer stared at my IDs for several minutes, not saying anything. He was probably worried about having to deal with all the officials I was naming in case I was telling the truth, and in the end he let me go. His men told me to shave my beard so I wouldn't look Saudi. In retrospect, despite my fear, they were not abusive. It was a change, a sign that they took their role as "the state" more seriously. I would see more and more of this in the next two years.

I waited for my friend at an Interior Ministry safe house. Inside, a barber agreed to give me a "Mahdi Army"–style shave. Televisions were all tuned to Shiite religious channels showing Muharram processions. In the lobby of the ministry itself, and in the minister's reception area, the Shiite TV channel Al Furat was showing live images of religious processions in Karbala. My friend, who was the minister's secretary, showed up late and explained that as he was driving to the office he saw men in a pickup truck belonging to the Facility Protection Service (FPS) stop on the street, grab a young man, blindfold and handcuff him, and throw him in the back of their truck. The FPS was a government militia that protected ministries and other Iraqi government offices but was notoriously lawless and loyal to sectarian Shiite militias. My friend complained that it was impossible to control these FPS guys. As I left I saw that Shiite religious flags were placed on the roof of the Interior Ministry across the street.

The televisions in the lobby and waiting room at the Interior Ministry were tuned in to the Shiite religious channels. Shiite religious music blared from radios of police vehicles. Shiite religious banners hung on the walls of the Interior Ministry and other ministries, while Shiite religious flags waved in the wind above the nearby Oil Ministry and other government buildings. It may have seemed harmless, but it made Sunnis feel like they did not belong and were not wanted. It was a way of letting them know that the state now belonged to sectarian Shiites. But while Shiites seemed to be firmly in control of the establishment, one group that had been marginalized by Saddam was beginning to feel similarly marginalized by the new order. The angry, poor revolutionary Shiites who found a political voice in Muqtada al-Sadr and whose influence peaked during the civil war had found that their power had started to wane after the Mahdi Army cease-fire.

Like many mass movements, the Sadrists were misunderstood and reviled. Muqtada was often mischaracterized as unintelligent or boorish, despite surviving a Baathist regime that killed his father and brothers and an American occupation that swore to kill or capture him. The Mahdi Army was often described as a militia, but it was also a people's army. All Iraqi men have at least a rifle and some ammunition in their homes, and Muqtada's force was composed of such volunteers, who could never be fully demobilized or disarmed because they armed, and in many cases mobilized, themselves. At one time the Sadrists were probably also the largest humanitarian organization in Iraq, providing sustainable assistance to more Iraqis (albeit Shiites) than anybody else. No other movement or leader in Iraq had such devoted and inspired followers. In a volatile and fissiparous Iraq, the Sadrists were there to stay. Muqtada represented the anger of many people. He was oppressed and angry like them; he had suffered like them. He did not lead them; they led him. He was only as popular as he was angry, and when he stopped being angry, stopped being "anti," his popularity went down. After he ordered his militia to freeze, it was common to hear Mahdi Army men say, *"Assayid jundi wasarahna"* (the sayyid [Muqtada] is a soldier, and we have relieved him of his duty).

In February 2008 I revisited Abul Hassan's office in the Mustafa Husseiniya. When I had last seen him he had been brooding over the efficacy of the Mahdi Army's cease-fire. But now he seemed absorbed by more mundane pressures of sustaining the social welfare network that the Sadrists had built for their base of supporters in the slums. During one of my visits I found him distributing, in his rarely empty office, bags of clothes and rations to poor women in black *abayas*, many of whom were from displaced families, expelled by Sunni militias. Most Iraqis had depended on the Public Distribution Service, an extremely efficient ration system that provided essential staples for all Iraqi families under the former regime. But the system had stopped functioning because of security problems, corruption, and sectarianism. Most families did not receive even half of what they used to, and displaced Iraqis, especially Sunnis, received nothing at all. The Sadrist movement was supplementing the rations for Shiites as well as it could, although some of that assistance may have come from extortion and other militia activities.

When I visited Abul Hassan another time, his office was still crowded. Two young men from the Iraqi Security Forces were among those visiting him. One was a member of the FPS; the other belonged to the Iraqi National Guard. Both proudly told me they were also members of the Mahdi Army. "We want you to know that most of the Sadrists are working for the government," said the FPS member. They listed their many friends who had been killed by Sunni militias. "Many of my friends got killed in Adhamiya, Sleikh, and Bab al-Muadham when they were heading to their work," he told me. "One of my friends got killed, and they burned his body. His body stayed in the street for two days. It was only when the security forces intervened that his family was able to get his body." "I'm a soldier in Iraqi army, the Iraqi National Guard, for three years," said his friend. "We saw that none of the political parties or movements are working for the benefit of the people except this movement. The Sadrists are devoting their time and effort to help Iraqi people. I thought the best way to help the people is by joining them."

One man had absconded to Abul Hassan's office because the Americans were looking for him. "They came to our house," he told me. "They arrested my brother after destroying our furniture. They said that I'm wanted by them. They took him because he is my brother. If they do not find the one they are after, they will take the brothers. Sometimes they take the father." Several men were seated on the floor awaiting Abul Hassan's arbitration services. He was to adjudicate a legal dispute over real estate. "We can't reach the registration directorate," they told me, because it was in Adhamiya, a Sunni stronghold. "We might get killed if we go there because of the sectarian problems."

Abul Hassan's faithful assistant, Haidar, was always present. He had the dark skin of southern Iraqis. He was thin and muscular, and always wore a cap. He sedulously did Abul Hassan's bidding, and was in charge of feeding the guests and making tea for them. Haidar and his family had lived in Abu Ghraib. He insisted that there had been no sectarian tensions in the area before the war, and said he had played soccer with Sunnis. Things got worse after the battles in Falluja in 2004, he said, when foreign radical Sunnis killed people they accused of being spies and threatened to slaughter Shiites. In 2006, because of these threats, he and his family were forced to leave Abu Ghraib and come to Shaab.

I persuaded Haidar to show me his new home in Shaab and introduce me to his family. His mother told me about the fraught circumstances that led to her family's flight. "Abu Ghraib was a Sunni area," she said, reflecting on her old neighborhood, "the Sunnis are good people. After one of my sons joined the police, we were told to leave the area, but there was nowhere to go. I accepted my son joining the police because we needed money. His father was a police sergeant, and after the war there were not enough jobs. Seven months after he took the job, we were one of about seventeen houses that received letters threatening us to leave the area. My two sons came to Shaab and found us a house to rent, and we stayed for a year there. My other son, the policeman, was killed during the course of duty. That house was not good enough for us."

"This house belonged to a [Sunni] terrorist," said Haidar, who joined the Mahdi Army soon after the American invasion. "He became a *takfiri* and was killed. Then the house was given to the Sadrist Current. There were a lot of *takfiris* here, and they committed a lot of killings in the area. Then the Mahdi Army came and finished them. There are no Wahhabis in the area anymore." Three other families also shared the house; the home received about thirty minutes of electricity a day from the national grid, so they paid to receive more from a local generator.

"I wish peace will be upon everyone," Haidar's mother said. "We are getting tired. We just need a decent house to live in and decent food to live off of, and that America gets out so the Sunnis and the Shiites get back together without any differences. I wish for my sons to get an education and to be teachers or lawyers, and for the girls to grow up and get marred with a good future. I am a believer in God, and to die in dignity is better than another kind of death."

"I don't think I'm able to go back," Haidar said of his old home, "because the tribes there now are against Shiites." Although the Anbar province was more stable because of the powerful Awakening militia there, Haidar and his family, like other Shiites, did not feel reassured. "The Awakening are the same," he said. "They were with the terrorists before, and they are the Awakening." He told me he would like to take revenge for his brother's death.

Haidar took me to the nearby Saddah area on the outskirts of the city, where hundreds of impoverished Shiite Iraqis, many of them displaced by

Sunni militias, lived in makeshift homes. There were about three hundred such homes in the area, with ten to twenty residents in each one. Locals complained that they were harassed by the Americans. The only help they received was from the local Sadrists.

Jasim Muhamad was an Iraqi army veteran who was wounded during the American invasion of 2003. He and seventeen of his relatives, including eight children, now lived in three adjacent shacks. They were from Haswa, near Falluja. They said that no one had returned to Haswa since some women went there to transfer their children's school papers to Baghdad and were killed. "No one from the family tried to get us back to our homes," said Jasim's wife. "If I go back, I will get killed." Up to three thousand families from Haswa were displaced, they told me, their homes looted. The Iraqi army had told them to leave Haswa because it was unsafe. They believed that the Awakening members were the ones who had expelled them and that these same militiamen would threaten them if they dared to return.

Previously Sunnis and Shiites had lived together in the area. Jasim and his family blamed outsiders for instigating the problems. They received a letter from the Tawhid Brigade, stating that because Sunni families had been killed and expelled in Baghdad, infidel families (meaning Shiites) had five days to leave or face death. Those who ignored this warning were killed, including Jasim's brother-in-law, whose body was never found.

The Ministry of Displacement provided Jasim and his family with beds, blankets, and a small kerosene cooker, but nothing else. After one year of trying, they succeeded in transferring their ration cards from the Public Distribution Service, but they received rations only every few months, and only a small share of what they used to receive. The Sadrist movement provided them with food such as rice, flour, and sugar. There was no running water in the area, so they relied on a nearby well. Although they had been connected to the national power grid, they rarely got electricity. They had to break apart a bed to use it for firewood because they had no cooking gas or kerosene. On some days they had no food. Jasim was unable to register for his pension as a wounded veteran because the ministries were not functioning properly.

Jasim's brother found an occasional job working in the sewage system, and he would sometimes bring money to the family. Only their older children attended school. The family members had voted in the most recent elections for the Shiite Iraqi Alliance list, but they complained that they had not received anything from the government, not even security. "My message to the American people after five years," said Jasim's wife: "They destroyed us and didn't help us, they didn't reconstruct the country, they even added more destruction to us. The days during Saddam were better. Now there is killing and nothing good. Before there was security and life was going on easily, while now there is nothing. Now things are getting worse and worse, killing in the streets, and there is no life. Strangers come to our homes and threaten us. I feel life is miserable now and our country is destroyed."

The neglect in Sadr City and other neighborhoods on the outskirts of Baghdad was shocking. But Washash, in central Baghdad, was stark for its contrast to the upscale Mansour district adjacent to it. Of course, much of Mansour was deserted when I visited because of Al Qaeda and the Mahdi Army, but the district's clothing stores and restaurants were once packed, its shopping boulevard and ice cream parlors open until late at night. The streets of the majority-Shiite Washash remained unpaved dirt, many flooded with water or sewage. It was quiet and removed from the nearby bustle.

Washash was a staging point for Mahdi Army attacks against Al Qaeda and forays into the Mansour district. It was one of the few Shiite neighborhoods I saw that was surrounded by concrete walls, with only one road left open for cars, guarded by Iraqi soldiers. Elsewhere a few narrow openings between the concrete blocks allowed pedestrians to enter one at a time. About five thousand families lived in Washash, but most of its Sunnis had fled or were slaughtered, and the Mahdi Army men there were notorious, even among other Mahdi Army units, for their brutality. In Washash I saw more posters and banners in honor of Muqtada and his father than anywhere else in Baghdad.

When I first visited Washash in April 2003, sewage flooded the streets and there was a thriving arms market nearby. About sixty thousand people lived in an area not much larger than one square kilometer. When American vehicles approached, the weapons dealers would hastily conceal their wares. The revenge killings started in Washash soon after Baghdad fell, and it didn't take long for the murders to take on a sectarian tone. In October 2003 three Sunnis were killed in Washash: Sheikh Ahmed Khudeir and his brother Walid Khudeir were killed along with a teenage assistant as they walked home from the Sunni Washash Mosque after the morning prayer. The three were riddled with bullets. Locals believed militiamen from the Badr Corps had killed them. Hospital officials reported seeing many similar cases in the area. In August 2004 a police chief and a patrolman were killed in an explosion in Washash. In December 2004 several members of a Sunni Salafist group in Washash were killed, and Sunni gunmen tried to kill a Shiite sheikh called Razaq; they missed Razaq but killed his wife and wounded his son, who remained paralyzed. Following the killings, Sunni and Shiite clerics issued a joint edict banning sectarian fighting. By the summer of 2005, sectarian violence was a common occurrence. Sectarian violence targeting Sunnis was so bad that in July the Sunni *waqf* (endowment) complained about the targeting and arrest of Sunnis.

Washash and the nearby Iskan were located in northeast Mansour on an important sectarian front line between Shiite-controlled Hurriya and Kadhimiya and Sunni-controlled Khadra, Jamia, Adil, and Mutanabi. In October 2006, during Operation Together Forward II, American soldiers raided a house in Washash while searching for a death squad and found documents recording the cleansing of Sunnis from the area. The documents included a list of nearly seventy homes where Sunni families had been expelled and Shiite families were brought in to replace them. There was also a list of "good" families who would not be expelled. American soldiers discovered letters threatening Sunnis as well as DVDs with the same message from the Mahdi Army, with images of exploding houses and threats to kill a male of the house. That month Washash notables asked the Iraqi government to intervene in a crime wave that had led to the discovery of sixty corpses and the threatening of many families by militias. In November a journalist working for the state-run *Al Sabah* newspaper was killed in Washash. In December, gunmen assassinated a news editor for an Iraqi radio station as he left his home to go to work. In April 2007 four women accused of being informants for the Americans were killed in Washash.

In the summer of 2007, as American forces pushed the Mahdi Army out of Hurriya, some members of the militia moved to Washash, resulting in an increase of militia activity and murders. In July of that year Sunni politician Adnan Dulaimi publicly accused Shiite militias of cleansing hundreds of Sunni families from Washash and added that soldiers from the Iraqi army's Sixth Division had cooperated with the militias. Dulaimi's bodyguards had clashed in the past with men from the Sixth Division, and Dulaimi accused the division's Colonel Rahim of an attempted assassination. That same month, Tariq al-Hashimi, leader of the Islamic Party and the Sunni vice president, complained about Shiite militias in Washash. In August a car bomb exploded close to a coffee shop in Washash. Later that month the First Battalion, Sixty-fourth Armor Regiment, set up a combat outpost nearby. A Sunni Arabic teacher at the local secondary school was shot on the street. Men were killed for drinking alcohol. In September a U.S. airstrike during clashes with the Mahdi Army killed between fourteen and thirty-one residents, some of whom were civilians. Several homes were destroyed, including one that belonged to an expelled Sunni family whose teenage son had been murdered earlier that summer (they had moved to Ghazaliya).

Later that month gunmen assassinated Washash's notorious Mahdi Army commander, Hamudi Naji, along with two of his associates, leading to reprisals against Sunnis. (Several months earlier Naji and his men had struck a truce with Sunnis in Washash.) Locals believed that two of the assassins were from the Iraqi Islamic Party. Some blamed the small Ugaidat clan; others said Naji was killed by the relatives of a man he had killed two years earlier. Hundreds of Sunnis fled Washash after the reprisals. Many were killed, including whole families, and several homes were destroyed. One car carrying a fleeing Sunni family was hit by an RPG before they escaped. Many Sunnis who fled to nearby Adil complained that American and Iraqi forces had facilitated their displacement by directing them to the highway and escorting them. That month a car bomb exploded in Washash and killed two civilians. The Mahdi Army manned checkpoints and kidnapped Sunnis without American interference.

In the fall of 2007 the bodies of murder victims were often found in Washash. In October more than one thousand men marched to protest the new wall the Americans were planning to build around the area. Their chants rejected the wall and America. Small Jersey barriers were already up, but the Americans were constructing a larger wall that would seal the neighborhood more effectively. In clashes with the Iraqi army after the protest, two locals were injured. That month the Mahdi Army and the Iraqi army fought openly in Washash.

In November four Mahdi Army commanders were killed in Washash. It was suspected that the Mahdi Army itself might have been responsible for the assassinations, and that the four were negotiating with the Americans to establish a Shiite Awakening group. In late 2007 Mahdi Army men from Washash declared that they were operating independently of the militia's hierarchy as a result of disagreements with the local leadership, based in Shula.

In 2006 Washash was technically a battle space "owned" by Lieut. Col. Gian Gentile, but from July to November of that year he did very little there because he was concentrated in Amriya. Gentile told me that no other American combat unit conducted systematic COIN operations there in 2006—the result of low troop numbers, perhaps. By the time an American unit eventually got there, a brutal Shiite militia was running rampant. Lieut. Col. Ed Chesney commanded the First Battalion, Sixty-fourth Armor, Second Brigade, Third Infantry Division, from Fort Stewart, Georgia. They arrived in late May 2007 and controlled their area of operations from June 15, 2007, to July 3, 2008. The battalion's area of operations encompassed a large portion of the Mansour district, including the neighborhoods of Khadra, Jamia, Adil, Iskan, Washash, Mutanabi, Andalus, and Mansour. Chesney was on his third deployment to Iraq; he had been an executive officer in Bayji from 2003 to 2004 and a deputy brigade commander in eastern Baghdad from July 2005 to January 2006.

"The battalion and our brigade prepared for the deployment by focusing on our core war-fighting fundamentals and skills," Chesney said. "We did not focus on COIN until late in our preparation. Most of my senior NCOs and officers had at least one Operation Iraqi Freedom deployment as experience, and we used the collective experience."

"Washash was the poorest area we were responsible for," Chesney said. "It was also heavily Shia, with the neighborhoods to the south being mixed to heavily Sunni. The walls were not in place, other than some Jersey barriers on some of the streets. The area was dominated by a criminal JAM element under the control of Hamudi Naji. The Sunnis to the south were petrified of him and his element and did not trust the army. What police there were in the area were from the Kadhimiya district, which did not engender trust in the Sunni population. There had been sectarian killings and intimidation in the mixed and Sunni areas around Washash; all of this was attributed to Hamudi's group. There was no JSS [joint security station] close to Washash.

"By this time there were not a lot of mixed neighborhoods," Chesney continued. "Consequently, when the army arrested people in Washash they were almost always Shia, so the people thought they were sectarian. But in Jamia, they arrested all Sunnis and were sectarian. When there was sectarianism it usually took the form of disrespect to the people or had a criminal aspect to it. Also, at times the Iraqi junior leaders performed poorly and were afraid to confront either JAM or Al Qaeda elements—this fostered the notion of sectarianism. The army around Washash, especially the rank and file, was sympathetic to JAM. . . . Lieutenant Colonel Hassan, the battalion commander, did not trust them to conduct cordon and searches properly if U.S. forces weren't there to watch over them. We suspected corruption in many areas but were unable to prove it."

Because it was so dangerous for outsiders, my driver, whose cousin lived there, arranged for us to be met by the head of the local tribal council, Sheikh Kadhim Khanjer Maan al-Saedy, who guaranteed my safety. A Sadrist, he introduced me to Mahdi Army men who surrounded us as we strolled through his neighborhood's dirt streets. Many displaced Shiites from wealthier majority-Sunni neighborhoods had been forced to flee to Washash and work where they could. "We are helping the people who have been displaced from other cities," he said. "Some of the help is with stipends, salaries, or places to live in. Also we are trying to provide gas and kerosene as much as we can." Graffiti on the wall behind him said, "Long live the hero leader Muqtada al-Sadr." The men told me that Ahmad Chalabi had visited the area and promised to help. "He only sat for thirty minutes, drank his Pepsi, and left," a sheikh told me.

I met one man displaced from Dora. "Shiites were the minority there," he said, "and they started killing them in their houses. They did not get my son because he was at his college, and we came to this area because it has a Shiite majority." One month after fleeing to Washash, he said, "the Americans and the Iraqi army came to our street, and they blew up the door to our house, and they arrested us and some of our neighbors, we don't know why. I was arrested by the American army with my son for eleven months and six days— without any charges. They accused me of being a terrorist, and they don't have any proof. They released me and they kept my son, and we don't know for which reason. If anybody says the Americans came to liberate the country, we say it is not true. If they came to liberate us, they should show some respect to us. There are no human rights."

Sheikh Kadhim introduced me to an elderly man in a head scarf whose home had recently been raided by the Americans. "At 11:30 p.m. they raided our house after breaking our doors," the man said. "They beat the men, women, and my daughters-in-law. We asked them, 'What do you want?' but they said nothing. We don't know what they wanted."

As Sheikh Kadhim and I walked down the street, we were surrounded by throngs of Mahdi Army men and other residents of Washash desperate to voice their anger. "As you know, we consider the Iraqi army to be our sons and brothers," Kadhim told me. "Unfortunately the army unit here which is surrounding the area is giving false information about us. They said we are doing many bad things and the neighborhood is unsafe. When the Iraqi army raid houses, they steal the mobile phones and money, attack the elderly people, and falsely accuse people. For example, some of our young guys were accused of planting bombs. After the investigation, they discovered it is not true. Some of them were accused of killing people; they said such and such killed ten or fifteen. After the investigation they released him. So there are false accusations against those innocent people."

Kadhim and the people of Washash spoke of the Iraqi army unit in charge of their area much the way Sunnis spoke of the Iraqi police. "They are dealing with us in a sectarian way," Kadhim said. "Most of the prisoners are Shiites, most of the arrests are of Shiites." The Iraqi police were different, he said. "The Iraqi police can come without weapons and see if anyone would shoot one bullet. We will be responsible for them as the tribal leaders council. . . . The police are peaceful people. If anyone files a complaint they will respond to him properly. We don't have any problem with the police." I would soon find out just how close they were with the police.

We passed men wheeling in goods for sale on pushcarts, and at an intersection I found a tractor used as a garbage truck to clean the streets. "Our sons collect trash with this car," one tribal leader told me. "The Sadrist Current collects the trash," a man corrected him.

On the corner sat many women in *abayas* by dozens of colorful jerricans. They were waiting for kerosene that the Mahdi Army was supposed to bring in, but, they claimed, the Iraqi army was besieging their area and preventing the kerosene from coming in. The women had been waiting for four days.

I approached the women hoping one might agree to talk to me on camera and was surprised by how eager they all were. "My dear," said an elderly woman with tribal tattoos on her chin, "we don't have electricity, kerosene, or gas, and we are surrounded and we have been insulted. Where should we go? To whom should we complain? We are waiting for a month to get some kerosene, but we got nothing. Only the Mahdi Army used to bring us kerosene, but now the Iraqi army is not allowing them. It is not true that the Mahdi Army are terrorists," she said. A tribal leader interrupted her. "The Americans are the real terrorists," he insisted. "They are bringing Al Qaeda and the terrorists to Iraq!"

A younger woman explained to me that "without the Mahdi Army, our women or girls could not go outside. We are under a lot of pressure. They are defending us like they are defending their own sisters." She and her daughters had been expelled from the majority-Sunni town of Mahmudiya, she told me, after two of her sons were murdered. "The Mahdi Army are the only ones who gave me a shelter, and they are protecting me and my daughters. The terrorists killed my sons with a car bomb. One of them was married, and he left behind four children, and I have twelve people to look after. May God bless the Mahdi Army. Now I feel safe to go to the market. We are going out only with the protection of the Mahdi Army. Anyone who says they are terrorists is lying."

Another young woman, holding her baby, told me that "the Americans are ruining people's lives. We don't have electricity, and we don't receive our rations. They are raiding the houses every night. What we have done? The Americans and the national guards are raiding our houses every day, and our sons are not sleeping there at night. Tell me, what we have done?"

A thick, muscular Mahdi Army man explained that an Iraqi army captain named Salim was preventing the kerosene truck from entering the neighborhood. Another man insisted Salim was a Sunni and was punishing them for sectarian reasons. I found out later that he was, in fact, a Shiite.

"We haven't had electricity in Washash for four months," one man told me. "Sewage floods, and there is no water, no electricity, and we are surrounded. It is like a prison inside Washash. Tell me, what is the difference between here and prison? We are surrounded by a wall that prevents us from going to other neighborhoods. Our sons and daughters can't go to the schools in the Arabi neighborhood, which is the closest area. Our conditions are very bad, and there are random arrests. The services we have are only through the help of the Sadrists, may God bless them. They are cleaning, they are helping the ones who need some money. They are bringing the kerosene and giving it to families."

A tribal leader warned, "If it is going to be like this for a long time, the young men will lose their minds. Maybe we will too. We can't control our sons. It will be very bad. We can't keep our sons quiet anymore."

"We receive electricity for half an hour a week," another tribal leader told me. "What about shops, factories, and workers? What is the reason? They should say it clearly on TV: 'This neighborhood is a target. We don't want to give them services; we want to humiliate them.' The other neighborhoods around us all have electricity. We were bombed by aircraft. More than fourteen houses were destroyed."

One man who had served in the Iraqi army's special forces for twenty-three years said the Iraqi army had just raided his home. "They insulted me and my honor!" he shouted at me. "An Iraqi soldier came with an American standing beside him. He said to me that I am the brother of a whore! I have only one AK-47, and he took it. Why did he take it? It was only an AK-47 with thirty bullets. They destroyed my furniture and stole my money. My son has a lung problem and I don't have money to buy kerosene, and the soldier is calling me the brother of a whore! I spent eight years fighting in the war with Iran, and a soldier came to me yesterday and called me the brother of a whore! If there is security, as Mr. Bush is saying, then American or Iraqi soldiers wouldn't come at seven o'clock and shoot randomly. We lost many people because of those injuries."

A tribal leader led me to the rubble of a home the Americans had bombed two months earlier. Seven of his relatives had been killed there, some of them children. "What do they want?" he demanded. "Do they want us to fight? We don't mind. If you try to strangle a cat, it will scratch you. We are trying to control our sons, and each one of us has seven to eight sons. If the situation continues like this, we will have to make a decision. We are losing our patience."

They led me through the market, which had once served the neighborhoods around Washash. "We are paying rent and we don't have work," one shopkeeper told me. "This wall ruined our life and our business," another said. "Would you accept to walk in this mud?" a man asked me. "People are holding their sons in order to cross the pools of water on their way to the schools. It's as if Washash is not on the map. Even the government doesn't care about it."

They showed me more shops without customers. "The policy of walls is wrong," a tribal leader told me. "The Americans think that they are providing security for the people. Even if they achieved that, what is the use of safety if a man is hungry? When they closed the area people lost their living." We approached the walls that separated Washash from Mansour. "We are like Palestine," one of my guides said. They showed me the narrow opening between the barriers. Behind it was an Iraqi army checkpoint. A soldier spotted me filming and began to approach. "He won't dare come in," one of the men said of the soldier. "We will fuck him."

Nevertheless, I was ushered away by Mahdi Army men, who consulted one another about what to do with me before the Iraqi soldiers came looking. One offered to drive me to a different opening in the back of the neighborhood, where there was a friendly Iraqi National Police checkpoint. He assured me that the police were "good," and I got in his car alongside another Mahdi Army member, who then led me through a fence to a gap in the barrier. "They are from our group," he said of the police, meaning they were with the Mahdi Army. As I waited for my driver to circle around and come pick me up, he explained to the police officer what had happened, and the police protected me from the Iraqi army.

I returned the next day to resume filming in the area, spotting unarmed Mahdi Army men sitting on steps and standing on street corners. As soon as I began, men from the Mahdi Army told me that someone had alerted the Iraqi army and a patrol was looking for me. We snuck past them again, avoiding the vehicles that slowly searched the streets.

I MET WITH SALIM, the Iraqi army captain so loathed by the Mahdi Army supporters who guided me through Washash. He was an intelligence officer in Mansour, thirty years old, with a round face and a short military haircut. I told him the men in Washash had accused him of being a Sunni and targeting them for sectarian reasons. "I'm a Shiite," he replied with a laugh. "How can I be sectarian?"

Before the war Salim had been an artillery officer living in Bayaa. In September 2003 an American lieutenant colonel based in Camp Falcon, asked Salim about his job. The American, who also happened to be an artillery officer, asked Salim to join the new Iraqi army. He became an officer in the Iraqi Civil Defense Corps, commanding a company in charge of the airport road.

In early 2004 the Americans established the Defense Ministry and Salim became part of the new Iraqi army. "At the time there was only Al Qaeda, not Mahdi Army," he said. "We confiscated a lot of weapons and car bombs. This was before the sectarianism started. I was trained to be an intelligence officer." When Salim joined the Iraqi Civil Defense Corps, there were very few Sunni officers, he said. "Sunni officers were afraid because they were worried that the Americans think Sunnis are terrorists, but Americans judged people on whether they were good." On the night of the Samarra shrine attack in 2006, Salim's unit had orders to protect all Sunni mosques and the Islamic Party headquarters. "But the Iraqi army, not all of it was clean," he said, "and some officers told their soldiers to let the Mahdi Army operate freely, especially in Rusafa [eastern Baghdad]. Samarra made officers sectarian, but even before that the Iraqi National Police was infiltrated with militias. Most officers were in a dilemma: if you act like a real officer and be a patriot, you will lose your family and your house, because you live in a Shiite area—this happened to me."

Salim first clashed with the Mahdi Army in Washash when it was commanded by Hamudi Naji. Much of the government supported the Mahdi Army and had access to good information, he said, so Hamudi managed to obtain Salim's phone number. "In the end of 2006 we captured a lot of Mahdi Army guys," he said. "But we got orders from the prime minister's office and Baghdad Operations Center to release them. Once we captured four armed Mahdi Army guys with Glocks—they had masks. It was next to the Buratha Mosque. An army lieutenant captured them. He was punished, and they were released an hour later. So the officer requested to be transferred to Iraqi special forces."

"I was on patrol next to Maamun College in the Iskan neighborhood, on Street Twenty-three, and I saw two guys with a pistol and MP5 take a man and put him in the trunk of their car. We went after them. The men ran away and left their weapons. The man in the trunk was Sunni. His family came to get him, and we kept the vehicle and guns." This was when Salim's conflict with the Mahdi Army began. Hamudi Naji called him. "You are Shiite, one of us," Hamudi said, according to Salim. "We don't want anything from you—just return the car and the weapons." Salim responded that if Hamudi gave him the name of the two fugitives, then he would return the car. "These men are in the Mahdi Army," Hamudi said. "How can I give them to you?" Hamudi used religious language and appealed to Salim as a Shiite. "I said I am secular," Salim told me. "I don't care if you're Sunni or Shiite or Hindu—I have orders."

In 2007 Salim and his men stopped a government vehicle at one of their checkpoints that was leaving Washash and heading to Sadr City. The men wore tracksuits and had two Glocks with three magazines each. The Americans said they were Mahdi Army leaders and detained them. One of the suspects was called Ali Kadhim. The Americans had a picture of him wearing a turban. Hamudi Naji called Salim again and demanded their release. Salim told him that they were wanted and that the Americans had them in their custody. "You arrested them, so you bring them back to us," Hamudi said. "You have twenty-four hours to get them back to me." Hamudi called Salim again that night. "What have you done about them?" he asked. "You're crazy," Salim replied. "The Americans have them." I expressed surprise at the Mahdi Army's audacity. "The state was on their side," Salim said. "We were afraid of the Mahdi Army; they weren't afraid of us."

Hamudi Naji arranged for Mahdi Army men in Bayaa to join with members of the Iraqi National Police Fifth Brigade and go to Salim's house. They mistakenly went to the house of his neighbor Anas, who was an army captain as well. The Mahdi Army men insisted that Anas was Salim with a fake ID card and put him in the trunk of their car. Hamudi called Salim's phone and was surprised to hear Salim answer. "Who are you?" he asked. "Salim," the captain replied. "So who is the lamb we have here?" Hamudi asked, referring to Anas as a victim about to be killed. Anas was released after being terribly beaten. Salim sent his family to Hilla and his wife and children to Egypt. "For one year I visited them every two months," he told me. "It was very expensive."

A week after the failed raid on Salim's house, the Mahdi Army killed his uncle in the Amil district. "I decided to terminate the Mahdi Army in Washash," he told me. The Americans had a new captain and colonel in the area, and in mid-2007 they had a meeting with Salim about the Washash, Iskan, and Tobchi neighborhoods. The Americans brought their intelligence officer, and Salim gave him all his information.

The Americans, Salim told me, decided it was time to rid the area from Amriya to Mansour of Al Qaeda and the Mahdi Army. The Iraqis and the new American troops worked on a plan. The colonel told Salim he had heard good things about him and that his captain would give Salim whatever help he needed. They built the walls around Washash and set up a joint security station next to it, with a quick reaction force to counter the Mahdi Army. The previous American base had been too far away. Salim met with the American platoon leaders and NCOs, and introduced them to his team. He suggested that they first target Al Qaeda so that locals wouldn't think that they were only going after the Mahdi Army. The first target was Abu Zeinab, an Al Qaeda leader in Mansour. "Too easy," the Americans replied.

"I had strong intelligence sources in Mansour," Salim told me. "It was a great operation. We found a car bomb and an IED factory. The intelligence was all ours. The Americans were new and had no sources." Abu Zeinab wasn't there, but the Americans gained crucial information from the ID cards they found in his house and arrested him in Bab al-Muadham one month later. The next week Salim's source told him about a Mahdi Army weapons depot. He told the Americans, who set up a decoy mission to a Sunni area in Mansour and then sent a small force to Washash to get the real target. In a garden behind the house they found four explosively formed penetrators (EFPs), two sniper rifles, as well as PKC machine guns. But there were no people in the house, which belonged to displaced Sunnis. Salim told the Americans that this was a great opportunity; they turned the house into an Iraqi army base and used it to conduct night missions. During one of them they detained the *sakak* (assassin) Ihab al-Tawil. After he was interrogated, he led the Americans to six or seven houses with a total of nine buried bodies belonging to Sunni and Shiite victims. One of the victims was a six-year-old boy whose father was Sunni and whose mother was Shiite. The killers couldn't find the boy's father, so they killed him instead.

The day after the raid, an Iraqi soldier named Hussein Naas was killed by Muhamad Karim Muhamad, a sniper from Washash, while on a foot patrol. Muhamad was a former Iraqi National Police officer who had been trained by the Americans. A source gave Salim his location, and a force of Iraqi and American soldiers closed off the area for five hundred square meters, conducted dismounted raids, and captured the suspect while he was in bed with his wife. At first he denied killing Naas, but Salim showed him all their evidence. He, in turn, led them to a house with four sniper rifles, sticky bombs, rockets, IEDs, and ammunition.

During Ramadan in late 2007, while Salim was visiting his family in Egypt, he learned that a small team of American and Iraqi special forces had ambushed Hamudi Naji and killed him. Mahdi Army guys were up very late, eating and loudly playing games. An Iraqi member of the team called Hamudi Naji and pretended to be a neighbor complaining about the late-night noise. Hamudi came with three of his security men to see what his men were doing. The Americans killed him and one of his guards. Salim told me that Hamudi's body was riddled with sixty bullets. After this ambush, the Americans increased their raids in Washash and Iskan.

At that time the Mahdi Army was at its peak, according to Salim. Two people in the prime minister's office supported the Mahdi Army, he explained.

One was Maj. Gen. Adnan al-Maksusi, an intelligence officer, and the other was the notorious Dr. Bassima al-Jadri. "They used to fire all officers who were against the Mahdi Army or who arrested the Mahdi Army," Salim told me. "Petraeus told Maliki, 'Either you fire these two people or we fire you.'" The Mahdi Army was taking over Sunni areas, Salim explained, "so the Americans came up with the Awakening—former insurgents but officially armed, so it created a balance. We knew the Awakening men, we had their names, we knew that they were wanted. The first time I heard about it I was against it, armed men on the street. The Americans said, 'Cooperate with them, use them now, and we'll arrest them later.' The Awakening created a balance between Shiites and Sunnis in early 2008." I told him about my Awakening friends in Dora being arrested. "It's just like what they did in the Jamia district and Amriya," he said. "Every Humvee that went to the airport road, Abul Abed would place an IED against it—so later they arrested the bad Awakening men. We found dead bodies of Shiites in Abul Abed's house in Amriya."

With Hamudi Naji gone, Salim's campaign against the Mahdi Army began in earnest. There were orders to arrest all Mahdi Army leaders, he told me. The Iraqi army closed off the Iskan, Tobchi, and Washash areas for four days. "In Washash we arrested over seventy men," he said. "In Iskan we arrested twenty men. In Tobchi we arrested twelve senior men with weapons." Naji was replaced by his nephew Hikmat Hussein Maan. Hikmat, known as Hakami, had a brother called Hossam al-Awar, or One-eyed Hossam, who was the main *sakak* in Washash. These two men escaped to Rusafa in eastern Baghdad. "The Mahdi Army freeze is a lie," Salim told me. "It's just information operations, like when the Americans said they stopped operations in Falluja but they continued them." Hakami fled to Ur, which was outside Salim's area of operations, but the young captain was determined to get him.

Salim had a female source in Washash. The Mahdi Army had killed her husband and left her with six children. Hakami had been in love with her, Salim told me. Salim arranged to meet her at a restaurant in Mansour, "like civilians," he said. "Next we met in an apartment, but nothing happened," he joked. He told her he wanted her to resume her relationship with Hakami, and she called him in Ur. "They met in Najaf and fucked," he told me. The next time they met in Zafraniya at her friend's house. The third meeting was arranged to take place in Karada. Salim called a military transition team (MTT, pronounced "mitt") whose captain he liked. "Hakami had been in Iran the week before," he told me. "He got six thousand dollars and the names of a cell to organize in Shula. It was to be an assassination cell."

Salim met the American intelligence officers in charge of his area. They wanted Hakami too, but Salim's source did not know the Americans were involved; she thought it was only the Iraqi army. Salim agreed on the plan with her the day before, but he didn't tell her that U.S. Special Forces in civilian clothes would arrest Hakami. On the day of the meeting in Karada, she would be wearing an *abaya* and carrying a yellow government file so that she could claim to be going to a ministry. She would meet Hakami at her friend's house at 7 a.m. She would write a text message but send it only when she saw Hakami.

"The Americans don't trust anybody, so they came at midnight," Salim told me. They had a Lebanese translator with them and told Salim to wear civilian clothes. They drove in a black GMC and covered Salim's eyes with black goggles so he couldn't see. He was offended, but one of the American intelligence officers said he would wear them too. After driving around for thirty minutes, they took him to a room with two beds and a couch and removed the goggles. American Special Forces men with beards came in. One spoke Arabic. Then Iraqi special forces came in. Salim told them the details. They left him at 3 a.m. and came back with more questions, as well as food and drinks. At 5 a.m. they told him that they could not conduct the operation because they didn't have enough information. "Special Forces didn't trust anybody," he said. "They thought it was an ambush for them." Salim was frustrated. He asked them if they could at least give him permission to operate in Karada. They told him they would send regular forces and he could sit with them in a Humvee.

At 6 a.m. they blacked out his eyes again and drove him to the checkpoint, where he found the MTT team and an African American lieutenant waiting for him along with four Humvees. They gave Salim an American uniform and a pistol. The interpreter working for the Americans did not speak English well, he recalled. They waited for the woman's message at the Jadriya JSS. She called at 7 a.m. to say that Hakami had not yet appeared. The convoy of Americans acted like a normal patrol in Karada and stopped in Dalal Square. At 7:20 a.m., the message came: Hakami had arrived.

The Americans came very fast. They arrested Hakami and the woman. The MTT team was very pleased, Salim recalled. "Hakami thought I was an interpreter because I was wearing an American uniform," Salim said. "He said to me, 'Please, brother, help me, it's not me.' I said, 'Do you know who I am? I'm Captain Salim.' He started crying."

In detention in Washash, Hakami revealed his bases and arms depot. The Americans then took him to Camp Bucca. Hossam al-Awar was never caught, but it was widely rumored that he worked as a bodyguard for a general in the Interior Ministry in Kadhimiya.

"Many people were deceived by the Mahdi Army," Salim said. "We Iraqis are not well educated. The Mahdi Army manipulated." Salim insisted that I had to distinguish between the Mahdi Army and the Sadrist Current. "The Current defended Shiites from Al Qaeda," he said. "The Mahdi Army used bad guys for personal gain. Al Qaeda was the same. They said, 'We have to protect your area from the Mahdi Army and the Americans,' and then they turned on the people and harmed the area. But we good people were the victims."

One hundred and forty Sunni families returned to Washash, he told me. Salim also returned sixty-four Shiite families to Mansour's Dawudi area, formerly an Al Qaeda stronghold. IDPs took their papers and identification cards to the returnee center in the Harthiya district. When they received a letter approving their return to their house, they gave it to the local unit in charge of the area. The family occupying the house had three days to leave, he told me. "If they don't leave, they are treated like terrorists," he said. "They must go back to their house." Some families had agreed to exchange their houses.

The Mahdi Army was finished, he said, but its supporters were still in the government. Salim was jailed for two months, he claims because of his aggressive pursuit of the Mahdi Army. "They made fake charges against me," he said. "They accused me of killing Shiites." Others say Salim beat a Mahdi Army suspect to death. He told me that he paid thirty thousand dollars in ransom to the man's family and he was released. But he was kept off active duty for several months as a result, which he viewed as additional punishment.

SALIM ALSO BELIEVED that Gen. Abdel Karim in Dora was associated with the Mahdi Army. He told me that the Badr Corps had been active only for the first two years of the occupation. "Their first goal was to kill Iraqi pilots and high-ranking Baathists, Saddam supporters, Iranian targets," he said. "Then they worked with the government." Salim believed that men who had fought the Americans were also criminals. "The Americans didn't come to destroy the country," he said. "If it wasn't for the resistance, the Americans wouldn't have stayed even for one year. We are all afraid—if the Americans go, who will fill the vacuum? Maybe the Iranians. Sectarianism is still there. An officer targeting Sunnis is promoted, but if he is targeting Shiites they will harm him or wait until the Americans leave. Shiites have power in the government and know they will take over Iraq. Sunnis want to overthrow the government and have Sunnis in power. Nobody can do anything now because the Americans are here."

Capt. Clarence "Wes" Wilhite worked closely with Salim. Wilhite was the Commander of D Company (nicknamed the Black Knights), of the First Battalion, Sixty-fourth Armor Regiment. Wilhite's battalion arrived in Iraq in late May 2007 and departed in July 2008. He took over as the commander of D company in August 2007 and served throughout his deployment in that position. His area of operation included Washash, Iskan, Arabi, Dur Sud, Mutanabi, Hai Draq, Mansour, and Andalus. This put him on the eastern side of the battalion's area. Unlike much of the 1–64 AR's terrain, his area had not only an Al Qaeda presence but also Shiite militias, and in much of the area, these militias were the main threat.

"Dur Sud was where we established the JSS on August 25," Wilhite said. "This became known as the Sunni-Shiite 'fault line' for most of our battalion meetings. For lack of a better analogy, this was our line in the sand, where we wanted to prevent JAM expansion to the south. To the south of these areas, we faced the Sunni-insurgent threat, AQI. This area was unique because it was not necessarily as disputed as Amriya or Jamia. Often patrols encountered the deep-buried IED threats in Amriya and Jamia; however, this threat was not present in Andalus. Primarily, I saw this as a support zone where AQI used to facilitate operations in Amriya and Jamia. In the vicinity of the Grand Mosque was another interesting problem due to the high number of displaced persons, embassies, abandoned dense market areas, and high-level foreign officials in the area. Al Rawad Square had just suffered a vehicle-borne IED [VBIED] strike following a soccer game that killed over forty Iraqis in late July 2007."

I asked Wilhite what the area was like when he first arrived. "'Desolate' was the one word that came to mind," he said. "My first patrol over eastern Mansour prior to assuming command of D Company was an eye-opener. I had hopped on a few patrols with my battalion commander's security detail, but actually having the opportunity to walk the streets of these places and getting a back brief from some of my platoon leaders really opened my eyes. As I look back at my notes and video, specifically on Washash, the smell of raw sewage running through the streets in 105-degree heat, sights of Muqtada al-Sadr pictured everywhere, Naji graffiti everywhere, few people in sight, and young guys in tracksuits watching us at every corner and disappearing around the next corner come to mind. At the time, it was a nightmare, but an opportunity."

Wilhite explained that among his challenges were getting the Iraqi army to buy in to their plan and the persistent image of security in his area. "In July, prior to taking command of D Company and establishing the JSS, the company arrested one of the company commanders in the IA [Iraqi army] battalion who was actively working with Naji in Washash. We identified the IA company commander as being complacent and facilitating JAM operations in Washash and Arabi. He was detained and replaced."

Iraqi army cooperation with the Americans in the fall of 2007 prevented further collaboration with the Mahdi Army, he said. "Seeing the pure dissatisfaction and anger in their face at having to dig up their own people from shallow graves, having JAM kill a few of their soldiers or attack their checkpoints, affected their leadership—which, in turn, directly influenced their soldiers. Also, the IA's first battalion commander we had to work with was terribly ineffective. The establishment of relationships, much like with any person in Arab culture, was absolutely critical. The relationship I had with Captain Salim and his second battalion commander, Lieutenant Wael, was a great one. Whenever we had good information, we shared it. When we detained someone, we made sure we both got the information from questioning. We made it a point to have all of our subordinate patrol elements do every patrol possible together after January. We took IA patrols to their FOB and did training exercises on dismounted patrolling techniques, marksmanship, vehicle search, home search (we actually learned more from them on this one), and room clearing. We made it a point to bring all of the leadership, IA officers and NCOs, to our planning sessions and patrol briefs. Often IA checkpoints would get in brief firefights with JAM. We always made it a point to get a patrol there as soon as possible to support them."

Another problem was the lack of effective local government leaders, Wilhite said. "There was no one—at least, very few. Literally, everyone had stepped down, fled the area, or been killed as a result of AQI attacks in the south, JAM in Mutanabi and Washash. When we didn't have leaders we (us and the IA) asked around and made them to eliminate the perception of an area under martial law. I inherited a company that had great, ambitious small-unit leaders, but the vision and direction of where we were going was not clearly articulated. I wanted to compartmentalize the different lines of effort against Sunni and Shia insurgents and the effort to support the Iraqi population."

There were many different kinds of Iraqi police in Wilhite's area, such as traffic, local, regional, and a quick reaction force. "Most of them were useless and corrupt," he told me. "The local ones based out of the Yarmuk area for the Mansour district were by far the most reliable. Our liaison in our JSS proved very helpful at times during the Sons of Iraq integration." With respect to the Iraqi army, he said, "competence varied here considerably, but collectively they were and became the most reliable, active, and trustworthy of the whole lot. This was, along with all ISF organizations, very officer-centric—the opinions, actions, and demeanor of the battalion commander drove the pulse of the whole organization. Our first battalion commander struck me as wishy-washy, lethargic, and not a strong leader. He rarely provided us good feedback or buy-in about his area and was reserved to let the IA company commanders do what they saw fit with little back briefs. Lieutenant Colonel Wael came in with great ideas, a strong personality, and an open mind. A few commanders out there, I would go so far as to trust my soldiers to be led by them. Others should have been rooted out and fired. Sectarianism was present in their ranks.

"The Sons of Iraq turned out to be an excellent gamble yet arrived with a lot of baggage. Inspired from the Anbar Awakening and the success of Lieutenant Colonel Kuehl's integration of the neighborhood watch in Amriya with 1–5 CAV, we adopted a program for recruitment of the concerned local citizens program, later known as the Sons of Iraq program, to support the Iraqi army security efforts in the area. The ability to get these guys on checkpoints inside the *mahala* and regularly talking to their neighbors increased the effectiveness and saturation of security in the area threefold and completed the 'oil spot' of security in the area. Being able to add upwards of three to six checkpoints and a constant patrol walking inside the *mahala* during this critical time of transition helped everyone out. At its peak we had enrolled over four hundred local residents in this program."

Wilhite's area "was less of an Al Qaeda stronghold and more of a transitory meeting area based on the terrain," he explained. "In the fall, mainly in Dawoodi and Andalus, we would usually use just one platoon with an IA company and conduct meet-and-greet 'soft knock' patrols." Most of the area was abandoned or had Sunni IDPs moving into the area. By searching abandoned homes for explosives and engaging local religious leaders, Wilhite's troops kept a pretty good pulse on the situation. For the most part, except for some questionable embassy areas that were off-limits, things remained quiet. Typical insurgent tactics remained ineffective—they used "soda pop" IEDs (which had little or no effect against U.S. vehicles) and murdered government officials to little avail. "Our biggest worry," Wilhite told me, "was that AQI would attempt to turn the area into a mini Amriya and Jamia." This was doubtful, however. By that time most AQI fighters had fled from Baghdad because of pressure in those areas. Winter was very quiet. In the spring insurgents regrouped and began using different tactics. The standard IEDs became slightly larger and targeted only the Iraqi army, not U.S. forces. Insurgents began intimidating new markets that were popping up in the area by creating a diversion (usually an argument), leaving behind a satchel on time delay, and blowing up a store. They also began using stationary VBIEDs to target passing convoys and busy market areas.

In light of the shifting tactics, Wilhite said the Sons of Iraq provided vital intelligence. A few found out information about Al Qaeda cell meetings and even possible attacks in the area. "As you can guess," Wilhite said, "Salim had a personal stake in running these guys down. Some informants led us to higher-level folks." But, he said, he had been barred from discussing the details of these cases. AQI's most effective attack targeted one of Wilhite's dismounted patrols at a marketplace in southeastern Mutanabi. It was a suicide attack—the first and only time this method was used in the area.

Expulsion, displacement, and intimidation had been rampant before the JSS was built, but AQI's ability to dump bodies and intimidate the populace decreased as U.S. forces established themselves in the area. Wilhite said they monitored the return of many families through the neighborhood council in the winter and spring of 2008, as conditions improved. The process for expulsion and displacement was fairly simple. Families were made to pay protection and rent to the Mahdi Army. If they didn't pay, they were evicted, and if they didn't leave, they were killed. Additionally, the Mahdi Army controlled propane, heating gas, and fuel in and around the *mahala* by forming a monopoly on the services provided to the populace. Local Shiite government complacency and corruption enabled this to occur.

Wilhite said he would characterize the Washash tribal leaders as Sadrists, or "White JAM." They had full knowledge of the killings that occurred in 2006 and 2007 but did not act on this knowledge for fear of their own lives and well-being. During his tenure in eastern Mansour, Wilhite said, he always considered the Washash sheikhs' council fairly useless and ineffective. "When they showed up at the neighborhood council meetings it was, 'I want,' 'We need,' 'Give me this,' 'We are important,' 'No, there is no JAM in Washash,' 'No, I will not commit to anything,' 'Tell Americans to stop coming into Washash.' Pretty frustrating." U.S. forces eliminated the Mahdi Army's influence by putting the pressure on early. They were assisted in this effort by the assassination of Mahdi Army militiaman Hamudi Naji, and by other counter-measures such as the construction of the wall to restrict movement, the establishment of Sons of Iraq to the south to prevent further expansion into Mansour, and the IA's desire to patrol the area. Hakami's indecision also helped—most reports showed him growing paranoid over not wanting to end up like Naji. "In the end," Wilhite said, "I think JAM was dissolving when we left, not necessarily directly because of our actions but also because of the situation."

Wilhite explained that he erected the walls around Washash in order to isolate the neighborhood and the Mahdi Army there from the rest of the population, and to prevent them from moving south. "We occasionally told Washash folks that the walls were to keep Al Qaeda out. Usually, we pushed this information campaign when AQI would detonate a car bomb in a Shia neighborhood. We told the people, 'See, the walls keep you safe!' We would say, 'There are only two ways in, and the IA will not let a car bomb through the checkpoints.'" Concrete was the order of the day during that time; walls went up around Khadra, part of Jamia, and Amriya. "If I was a cement contractor," Wilhite said, "I'd be rich." He ended up using concrete in Iskan, Dur Sud, Arabi, and part of Mutanabi as well. Wilhite felt that the walls were effective. Some Washash businessmen complained about losing customers, but he viewed this complaint skeptically. Iskan, Arabi, and Dur Sud all had cheaper prices and, Wilhite said, better products than Washash in the first place. He asked around about where folks went for food in the areas adjacent to Washash Market area.

Hamudi Naji had owned "Black JAM," and it owned Washash, Wilhite reported. Naji's men had their hands in everything. They had systematically taken over almost every Sunni home in Washash and rented it out to a Shiite family. Sunnis were given three options: pay an exorbitant amount of protection money and live there until Naji's men told you to leave; leave in the next twenty-four hours to avoid being killed; or lose your house and your life immediately. Wilhite's troops later found Sunni families murdered and buried in their backyards in different states of decomposition.

Naji's group patrolled Washash much like a mafia gang. They had lookouts, and when the Americans would come on patrols or late-night raids, they used their own observation posts to describe the activity. When Wilhite's group got too close, Naji's group would often attempt to distract them with runners, gunfire, or distant explosions. Wilhite said his initial strategy was to stop focusing on Naji the individual (the agent of terror, the small-time warlord) and more on his apparatus (the organization itself). All intelligence always pointed to Naji, and Wilhite saw this as a liability. However, applying Petraeus's COIN strategy to Dur Sud seemed new and made a lot of sense.

In Washash, numerous raids had failed to capture Naji. Wilhite wanted to weaken Naji's network instead of constantly trying to catch the one guy who would supposedly make everyone's problems go away. He attempted to identify all the unknown midlevel managers taking orders—weapons traffickers, IED makers, financial supporters, shift managers (including sergeants of the guard)—and used a JSS hot line to get information from Iraqis. Wilhite said his troop would sometimes take informants out with them and conduct raids to get information about a Naji-led killing. For the most part, they were successful.

"I remember," Wilhite said, "after a raid, an old man even gave us a big smile and a thumbs-up sign. I felt we were starting to gain momentum because the population of Washash saw us pulling these guys off the streets." Whenever possible, they also tried to bring the Iraqi army out with them too, though initially "buy-in" was difficult. Then, on the night of September 20, Naji was killed on the streets of Washash and all hell broke loose. Immediately, there were a few retribution killings of Sunnis. Elements of Wilhite's Red Platoon drove headlong into a firefight while attempting to gather information on what had transpired. The next three days were "days of madness," he recalls.

The Iraqi army moved three companies into the area and left them there to keep the peace. Those loyal to Naji wanted to kill and provoke every Sunni left in Washash and everyone connected to them. Several Sunni families piled everything they could carry and attempted to leave the first day. "I remember on the third day JAM attempted to intimidate anyone from leaving the area by detonating an IED on a group of males trying to leave the *mahala*," Wilhite said grimly. "For the next eight days, we patrolled Washash heavily until a balance was restored."

"In the fall of 2007," he continued, "we continued our strategy of attacking JAM's network." His troops did more raids, captured more low-level guys, and started building the wall around Washash. The purpose of the wall was to prevent them from having free access in and out of the *mahala* without submitting to searches at IA checkpoints. It also served as a physical barrier to contain

Mahdi Army movements south into Mahala 615. After they completed building the walls in Mahala 617, they began building in Mahala 615 to measure the effects of the sectarian violence and Shiite expansion into mixed areas. They were also waiting to see who would emerge as the "next Naji."

The last Black JAM assassination was carried out in early November of that year. "An Iraqi army soldier had actually stopped a kidnapping from occurring and killed one of the midlevel managers of the Washash JAM network," Wilhite said. "Unfortunately, he was killed in the process. What we were missing was a persistent presence in the area that could remain on the streets." On the national level, the Awakening movement came to full steam. U.S. forces began recruiting Sons of Iraq in eastern Mansour. "Ultimately," Wilhite explained, "the constant presence of the Sons of Iraq working with the Iraqi army in Dur Sud and Arabi prevented any more JAM movement into these areas to the south. Additionally, it motivated many families to work with our local neighborhood council members to bring displaced families, Sunni and Shiite, back into the communities." At that point, the Mahdi Army was effectively contained through physical barriers and the presence of security in the southern *mahalas*.

Wilhite's low-intensity campaign against the Mahdi Army operations continued until Muqtada al-Sadr's "falling out" with the government in late March and early April 2008, when Prime Minister Maliki declared full-scale war on the Mahdi Army. "At this point, things transitioned very rapidly to a kinetic fight, and for a few brief moments all hell broke loose," Wilhite said. On March 27, the Mahdi Army began attacking symbols of the government of Iraq (like Iraqi army safe houses and checkpoints), and verbally threatened and intimidated workers in several government buildings in the area. Just about every predominantly Shiite community experienced a skirmish of some kind that day. At midday the Third Company safe house was attacked with small-arms fire and three RPGs from inside Washash. Wilhite's company teamed up with their attached military transition team and the remainder of the Iraqi army to respond. Unlike previous engagements that were short in duration, this one continued even after U.S. forces moved in to support the Iraqi army. "By the end of the day," Wilhite said, "all four of my platoons, the 'mitt,' my sniper assets, and half of the IA battalion had been involved in what turned into a five-hour engagement." Under orders from his Iraqi army superiors, Wael, the local IA commander, was prevented from entering Washash to root out pockets of resistance. As the Mahdi Army drew short on ammunition and it got dark, the firefight petered out. Similar to the September 2007 operation in which Naji was killed, this one continued with persistent security operations for several days after the fighting subsided, with no new contacts except for when a Mahdi Army sniper killed an IA soldier the first night. It was a turning point—Wael and the Iraqi army wanted the Mahdi Army out of the area for good.

Naji had operated in a very brutal manner, freely using torture and aggressive intimidation tactics to hold on to power. He had used contacts in Kadhimiya, Shula, and Sadr City to assist and support his operations in the first few months of the U.S. presence in the area. For the most part, under Naji, the Mahdi Army operated fairly independently from a "higher headquarters." There were occasional clashes within the Sadrist community, but outside Washash, no real divisive internal disputes were monitored. By the time Hakami replaced Naji as leader, his power base was not nearly as extensive and his ability to expand to the south was limited.

"Salim never saw Naji's body, nor did I," Wilhite said. Word on the street was that he had been killed by rival members of the Ugaidat tribe from another *mahala*. With everyone fixated on Naji, Wilhite found it strange that Salim had recorded conversations with him on his cellphone. Some questioned whether Salim was actually colluding with JAM, though it became clear, as Wilhite got to know him and his family situation, that he was not. "He walked a thin line in the beginning," Wilhite said. "He dove pretty far into the deep end to find out critical information. He often got in trouble with his brigade, division, or Ministry of Intelligence for his actions. I have to say, he was keenly aware of second- and third-order effects of what we were doing at the time. I am happy to see he came out fairly unscathed."

THE CONSTANT HARASSMENT by U.S. forces was putting pressure on the Sadrists, and in early 2008 Baha al-Araji, the Sadrist member of Parliament, privately complained that "we lost our respect on the streets. We can't stay like this anymore with everybody attacking us." It was the holy month of Muharram when I spent much of my time with Abul Hassan in the Ur district. During this month Shiites commemorate the singular event in their history, when Hussein, grandson of the Prophet, and his followers were slaughtered by the hated Yazid. Ceremonies culminate on Ashura, the tenth day of Muharram, the anniversary of Hussein's martyrdom in Karbala. Shiites continue to lament Hussein's martyrdom and view his battle as a struggle against injustice and tyranny. Ayatollah Khomeini declared the Shah of Iran to be Yazid before the Iranian Revolution and Shiite militiamen declared Israel to be Yazid following its invasion of Lebanon in 1982. Abul Hassan and his followers now agreed that America was even worse than Saddam. He compared Hussein's battle against Yazid with the Sadrist battle against America. "They rejected what we reject today," he explained, reminding me of the expression "Every day is Ashura and every land is Karbala." "In every time there is a Yazid and a Hussein," he told me, adding that America, Israel, and Great Britain were the new Yazid.

I revisited the Shurufi Mosque after Ashura in February 2008. It was a Friday, and straw mats were placed outside for the overflowing crowds. I saw a pistol partially covered by one man's prayer carpet. Fans hung down from the ceiling. Hundreds of men strolled in. Many were fit young men in tracksuits, members of the Mahdi Army. As they sat to listen to the sermon, men would periodically stand up and shout a *hossa* in hoarse voices, to which the audience would respond, "Our God prays for Muhammad and his family!" One man called for freeing the prisoners from American prisons. Another shouted, "Death to spies and the Americans!" Other *hossas* I heard were: "He sacrificed his life for us, death is an honor for us, arrest is honor for us, resisting the Americans is honor for us!" and "Pray for Sadr, release of all the arrested people, and in a loud voice, death to the Americans and to their agents!" and "Pray in a loud voice, please God, give victory to Sadr's son and the Mahdi Army!"

After the prayers I spoke to Sayyid Jalil, the imam of the Shurufi Mosque, and asked him to explain the importance of Imam Hussein and the story of Ashura. "Hussein was the father of freedom and free people, who defended the rights of the working class and poor people," Sayyid Jalil told me.

"Today's Yazid is Bush and those who follow Bush," he said. "They are all Yazid. There is a Hussein and Yazid for every era. Everyone who oppresses people, steals their freedom, and forcibly shuts their mouths is Yazid. Anyone who attacks people, occupies their land, and claims he came to free them is Yazid. Yazid's wish was for everyone to kneel before him so he could keep his seat forever." Muqtada had said no, Sayyid Jalil told me, which was exactly what Imam Hussein had said, "and also what our father and the father of all Muslims, Muhammad Sadiq al-Sadr, had previously said—he said no to Saddam. This word came from Hussein when he said no to Yazid. This impressed people and attracted them to the leader." Unfortunately, some politicians were supporting the occupation, he said, and therefore were supporting Yazid. "The leader," as he called Muqtada, was popular because he opposed the occupation and supported Hussein's revolution. I asked him how Muqtada could lead without the proper religious degree. Muqtada was a Hojatullah, he told me, a clerical rank that entitled him to lead "the biggest group in the Iraqi nation," meaning the Sadrists. Hassan Nasrallah of Lebanese Hizballah was a great leader, but he didn't have a high religious degree either, Sayyid Jalil told me. "A degree is not necessary to make a leader," he said. "Many leaders don't have degrees, and that doesn't make them unpopular."

"We have not seen anything of this alleged democracy," he continued. "We have seen destruction, we have seen pain. Now our young sons are living under the force of occupation, they are suffering the pain of prisons, not for any guilt they have but because they said, 'Allah is our God.' This is something that everyone should have the right to say. The occupation doesn't want that. They don't want anyone to say no to the Great Satan. If the occupation came for the sake of Iraq and Iraqis, we wouldn't see these massacres that are carried out in the name of freedom, humanity, and democracy. In fact, we would have seen the opposite of that. We view Hussein's revolution as a revolution for all humankind. It includes old people, children, and young people who are filled with passion and believe in their cause. Every honest man should believe in the revolution of Hussein if they oppose occupation, oppression, and slavery."

FIVE YEARS AFTER a war launched allegedly to liberate Iraq's Shiite majority, American planes bombed Shiite neighborhoods in Baghdad and Basra while dispatching their weak Iraqi proxy forces in a failed attempt to crush the Sadrists. Curfews were imposed and American snipers killed Iraqi civilians. The fighting between Muqtada's supporters and rival Shiite militias backed by Prime Minister Maliki's Dawa Party, as well as the large Iranian-created Badr Organization of the Supreme Iraqi Islamic Council (formerly the Supreme Council for the Islamic Revolution in Iraq, or SCIRI), signaled the end of the civil war between Sunnis and Shiites.

Until 2007 the Sadrists had tacitly cooperated with the Badr Organization to purge Sunnis from Baghdad and the Iraqi state. There had been exceptions, as the two groups were rivals and represented different classes among the Shiites. But during the civil war, the tacit alliance between the two Shiite factions was very effective, and that success was one of the main reasons violence was down in Iraq. There were fewer people dying because there were fewer people to kill; the cleansing had nearly been completed, with Sunnis and Shiites inhabiting separate walled enclaves run by warlords and their militias. The security gains American officials bragged about were largely the result of the expulsion of millions of Iraqis from their homes and the construction of walls to divide or imprison them. But the inter-Shiite fighting opened up the possibilities of cross-sectarian alliances between Shiite nationalists opposed to the occupation and federalism and Sunnis who had virtually the same goals. The one factor militating against such an alliance was the deep hatred many Sunnis felt for the Sadrists after two or three years in which the Mahdi Army slaughtered Sunni civilians without discrimination. At a minimum, Sunni militiamen could sit back and enjoy watching their Shiite opponents getting weaker. The peak of cross-sectarian unity was in the spring of 2004, when Sunni and Shiite militias collaborated in fighting the occupation in Falluja and the south. Tragically for them, sectarianism divided them and weakened resistance to the occupation, ending in a costly civil war that tore Iraq apart. In February 2008 leading Sadrists warned that the freeze would not be extended later that month, but Muqtada did extend the Mahdi Army freeze.

Between the winter of 2007 and the winter of 2008, Maliki's premiership transformed. Maliki won the trust of many Sunnis by making a surprise move and targeting Shiite militias. The Mahdi Army had overextended itself; Muqtada was not in control, and many Shiite militias had become mere criminal gangs. Nowhere was this more true than in the southern port city of Basra. Not only is Basra Iraq's second-largest city; it is also where most of the country's oil is concentrated, and it is from there that most of the oil is exported as well. A variety of Shiite militias and gangs controlled it, imposing an extremist reign of terror and letting the city and its port fall into the hands of mafias as the British, who nominally occupied the city, did little. In late March 2008 Maliki launched Operation Sawlat al-Fursan, or Charge of the Knights, dispatching fifteen thousand soldiers to Basra. There they attacked Mahdi Army fighters in the Sadr City–like slums of Hayaniya, Gzeiza, Jubeila, and Jumhuria, hoping to arrest those they described as criminals. Similar operations occurred throughout the south. Maliki described the targets as outlaws, not mentioning the Mahdi Army by name. Muqtada did not lift his cease-fire, but he did not tell his men to disarm either, and fighting spread throughout Shiite parts of Iraq. Iraqi Security Forces were unable to defeat the various Shiite militias in Basra, and it seemed as if they might even be repelled by the well-armed fighters. American armored vehicles and airstrikes were necessary to rescue the beleaguered ISF. Maliki's seventy-two-hour deadline for the Mahdi Army to disarm was extended by several days, and his government even announced a weapons buy-back program. Maliki himself flew down to oversee the operation. Curfews were imposed in Shiite towns throughout the country, and the security forces acted with brutality. Up to 1,500 members of the ISF refused to fight, while about one hundred surrendered their weapons to the Mahdi Army. Rockets and mortars fell on the Green Zone in Baghdad. Many Iraqi civilians were also killed in the American airstrikes in Basra and Baghdad. The fighting spread to Washash, where the Mahdi Army fought the ISF for five days before deciding to abandon the neighborhood. The next month a few Sunni families returned to the area.

Before the operation was initiated, Hassan Hashem, secretary to Interior Minister Jawad al-Bolani, carried a personal message to Muqtada in Iran, telling him to evacuate his people because they were about to get hit. But Maliki's decision to target unruly Shiite militias, regardless of his motivations, was one of the most important factors ensuring the civil war would end. Sunnis like my Awakening friend Osama in Dora suddenly changed their mind about the prime minister and started supporting him.

Maliki's move was also a surprise for the Americans. A British general in Basra complained to me that the Iraqis had appropriated a British military plan for attacking the Shiite militias in the city, but he may have been looking to restore a wounded ego. "Charge of the Knights was a British-inspired plan," he told me eight months later. "It caught everybody by surprise. We were going to do it later. Charge of the Knights was written by the Royal Marines, but it was predicated on the Iraqi military being where they are now." Ambassador Ryan Crocker and General Petraeus had only twelve to twenty-four hours' notice of the offensive. "It is an open secret that it did not go well in the first few days and only turned around when the U.S. started to provide support, mostly intelligence, airpower, and planners," a senior American military official working on Iraq told me. "But I think Maliki started to realize that if his security forces didn't control the country, then he wasn't really the leader. I think it was a purely institutional move to assert the primacy of the prime minister. How Maliki became a nationalist is a long story that I don't totally understand myself. I think part of it was just growing into the job. I also think that there was a seminal moment in Basra when his personal bodyguard—and I understand the two were close—was killed by a Sadrist round."

An American intelligence official dealing with Iraq told me that the Mahdi Army's attempt to take over Karbala had affected Maliki, especially when Mahdi Army rockets landed too close to Maliki's house. "The Basra offensive caught us by surprise," the official told me. "He had no logistics, no plan, only General Mohan [Mohan al-Freiji, Maliki's chief of security in Basra]. No food, no place for them to sleep. Petraeus and Crocker took advantage of it and saved his ass. Maliki also wanted to go to Sadr City and Maysan, but the U.S. felt he wasn't ready. Maliki realized he could be a nationalist leader." Importantly, it was Iran that brokered the cease-fire between Maliki and the various Mahdi Army groups.

The Iraqi decision to go into Basra was made independently; the Americans heard of the operation only after it started, when Maliki flew down with the key leadership of the Iraqi Security Forces to oversee it. Petraeus and Crocker were extremely worried when Maliki did this, but Bush, apparently, was supportive and said, "He's finally doing it." "Maliki goes to Basra and takes on Iranian-backed stooges," an American intelligence official told me. "He is the one Arab leader who has taken on with force an Iranian-backed group." But there was a tense seventy-two-hour window during which Maliki's forces were surrounded. When Americans came to Basra, with Navy SEALs and air support, they came in lightly, but they turned the tide. But once the Americans helped swing things in favor of the ISF, "they gave us the finger," Lieut. Col. P.J. Dermer complained to me. Dermer worked closely with the Iraqi army; even when the Americans were rescuing them, he said, the Iraqis just did whatever they wanted. "Maliki committed his men to battle knowing there was an American corps on the ground," Dermer told me. "What Maliki did [seizing the initiative against the Shiite militias] was brilliant, but his guys sucked. We bailed them out, so when [Gen.] Abud [Qanbar] entered Sadr City, he entered without a shot being fired at them."

Having the Americans come to the rescue may have seemed like a failure at first, but it won Maliki the support of more Iraqis, who saw it as a move against sectarian militias and demonstrated that he could take the initiative. He capitalized on his success by establishing tribal support councils throughout the south whose members benefited from his largesse and often acted as Maliki's own Awakening councils, even arresting Mahdi Army men. It was a naked attempt to steal support from Shiite groups that had a deeper grassroots base than the prime minister, and it worked. Maliki was beginning to expand and assert his control. He was at once targeting Sunni areas and Shiite areas. Following his successful challenges of the Mahdi Army in Baghdad and Basra, albeit with substantial U.S. support, he turned to Mosul. At the same time, he was consolidating control over the Shiite Maysan province and planning to target Al Qaeda in Diyala. The American victories in Najaf and Falluja in 2004 taught Iraqi groups that they could not remain for long under American bombardment, and it was better to disperse. Following Maliki's American-assisted victories, he wisely adopted a key element of counterinsurgency theory and tried to establish the credibility of his government as the nonsectarian group that could protect the population.

Dermer lived in the Baghdad Operations Center (BOC), working with General Abud Qanbar every day. In the beginning, the Americans led the briefings, but by the spring of 2008 the Iraqis had taken them over and would ask the Americans if they had anything to add only at the end. "Abud was a good man," Dermer told me, "great for Iraq—a nationalist above religion. He ran his shop single-handedly; everything had to go through him. He didn't rely on his staff enough. But he learned the importance of the media. Abud's primary staff guy who handled the media was Maj. Gen. Qassim Atta. Abud called him first thing in the morning and last thing at night—what other military commander in the Middle East focuses on media so much?"

One morning Dermer was with Abud in the BOC. Abud saw an announcement on the news that the Sadrists were going to hold a demonstration in Baghdad in response to the battle in Basra. "I'm not going to let this stand," Abud said, according to Dermer. "I won't allow it. The militias have to be stopped." Dermer had hoped to contain the demo, but Abud said, "No, I'm going to stop it." Dermer asked him if he needed Maliki's permission. "I'm the commander of Baghdad," Abud said. "I don't need anybody's permission." Dermer realized Maliki had not given him guidance and that Abud was going to war.

Without telling the Americans, Abud started moving battalions to the site of the demonstration. He knew he had Maliki's blessing, but he was making the plan up by himself. Dermer and the American leadership were taken aback. "I have a core patch," Dermer told me, "with a direct line to Petraeus, and I have battlefield responsibility with General Hammond [of the Fourth Infantry Division, which replaced the First Cavalry Division]. I have to translate this to the coalition, so I have to let Petraeus know."

Dermer persuaded Abud to sit down with the Americans and come up with a plan. Maliki then gave permission for the Americans to shoot into Sadr City,

Ur, Shaab, and other areas, but the Americans were not allowed to enter Sadr City. Sadr City, and to some extent the Sadrists, had been off-limits to the Americans. In 2004 the Americans were about to kill Muqtada in Kufa, but he was with Iraqi National Security Adviser Mowaffak al-Rubaie, so the American canceled the hit. Later Maliki would prohibit the Americans from operating in Sadrist areas or targeting the Mahdi Army. During the surge Americans had to get Maliki's permission to kill or capture Mahdi Army men. Sometimes they wouldn't tell him whom they were targeting because they were worried his people would inform the targets. Later there would be full coordination with the Iraqis about the target lists. In March 2008 the Americans were granted permission to use snipers and helicopter gunships, even if they couldn't bring troops inside these areas.

But the National Security Council's Brett McGurk and other Americans were worried. Sadr City was home to three million people. Maliki assured them he knew the street, and it turned out that he did, which created a sense that the ISF could handle security. American sniper teams positioned on the edges of Sadr City proved to be very effective in the battles, though many civilians were also killed.

"As a military Middle Eastern guy, Abud couldn't fathom a militia," Dermer told me. "Under Saddam he had despised the fedayeen [Saddam's guerrilla force]. The Iraqi army is fighting to regain their honor. It's not about fighting skills. Iraqi fighting skills were terrible. It's about regaining their place in society. We lost a lot of American lives because of Iraqi incompetence. The Americans wanted to take over the operations during the Battle for Baghdad but didn't. We were telling the Iraqi army what to do, and they wouldn't listen. They didn't pair with us in the battlefield. When it was time to advance up an avenue or cross a line, the Iraqis didn't; the Americans did, so American soldiers got killed. They wanted our logistics, Apaches, and ISR [intelligence surveillance reconnaissance]. We tried to get them to use their own shit, but why would they when they had our shit? We had to prevent them from failing so we won't look like we failed."

After one battle Dermer and the Americans visited an apartment building in Ur that the Iraqi army had just destroyed. "It was a bloody mess," he told me; the Iraqis had opened fire on the entire building, but the Americans had no choice but to tell them they did a good job.

"IEDs scared the shit out of them," Dermer said of the Iraqis he worked with, "so our guys would go down the road and they wouldn't. We lost two majors. We were having heated arguments in BOC, yelling and shouting. We would plan for two hours and then they wouldn't execute. Iraqi commanders were not being held responsible. Abud finally fired the Rusafa commander, but nobody would replace him, so Abud rehired him. We had one or two Iraqi brigades disappear off the battlefield, but that's not bad out of five or six divisions in Baghdad." I asked Dermer what made some units good. "It was the personality of the commander and his relationship with the American commander that determined whether a unit was effective," he said. "Abud was good at building civil infrastructure after the fighting," Dermer added. "He would take the minister of electricity, of water and power, of education—anybody in charge of building stuff, they wouldn't go without him. Abud didn't want the Iraqi military leading the effort; he wanted Iraqi civilians to do it."

The American and Iraqi surge, along with Charge of the Knights, emboldened Iraqis to resist militias. While Captain Salim attributed the improved situation in Washash to his efforts, and not the Americans', Abu Karar, a leader in the Khazali tribe, also claimed responsibility. When I met Abu Karar he had big Shiite rings on his fingers. He was a large, grave man with dark reddish skin and a stain on his forehead from praying. He worked as an accountant in the Housing Ministry.

Before 2006 there was no displacement in Washash, Abu Karar told me, and no explosions. Until that year the Mahdi Army was an army of principles and creed that fought the occupation. "They did a good job, and everybody liked them," he said. "They improved Shiite areas. Before Samarra, I supported them. But after the Samarra explosion, their way of thinking changed. They became gangs, they took money from people, and each house in Washash paid five thousand dinars a month. If you didn't pay, they blew up your house. Only Mahdi Army families didn't have to pay. When militias took over, displacement started, and all the Sunnis left. Shiites came here from Ghazaliya, Dora, Jamia. Some stayed in empty Sunni houses, some paid rent. The pious IDPs paid rent to the Sunni owners, while militias also charged IDPs rent for the houses they were squatting in. There were no Sunnis left and they started to kill Shiites."

On August 14, 2008, Abu Karar led a "revolution" in Washash, he told me. As he describes it, his tribe coordinated with the Iraqi and American armies and carried weapons with their permission. They attacked the Mahdi Army at 6 a.m. "We had an intifada," he said. "We knew where they stayed, and we arrested sixteen of them. I arrested [Mahdi Army leader] Ihab al-Tawil with my own hands. After the arrests, we found twenty-seven bodies, and twenty-five were Shiites." I suggested this sounded like the way the Awakening groups started, and he bristled. "We don't believe that," he said, dismissing the Sunni resistance. "Most Sunnis supported Al Qaeda and turned on them because of pressure from the government." To him the Awakening was made up of former Al Qaeda men, but he was not a former member of the Mahdi Army. "When did Ramadi start to resist?" he asked me, answering that it was when the governing council gave Shiites more seats than Sunnis.

Soon after his uprising against the Mahdi Army, Abu Karar was elected to head the local tribal council. "My service to the area caused me to be elected," he said. In the eight months since Charge of the Knights began, nobody was killed in Washash, he bragged. Five days into the campaign, Abu Karar met with the representatives of forty Sunni families from Washash in the nearby Arabi neighborhood. "It was my personal effort and my tribe's effort," he said. "I told them, 'We want your return to be peaceful, without vengeance. Use the law or come to me to do it the tribal way, and anybody carrying weapons will be expelled again.'" The forty families returned. But Sunni areas were still dangerous, he said. "Sunnis are safe coming back to Shiite areas. But Shiites are not safe to come back to Sunni areas. Shiite IDPs have not left Washash to return to their homes. Some Sunnis can't come back to Washash; they are wanted for crimes. We have four or five wanted families. They killed more than thirteen people from my tribe, and we will avenge them."

Hassan Abdel Karim and his brother Fadhil Abdel Karim were cousins of Abu Karar who also lived in Washash and were popular in the area. Both were thick and muscular. Hassan was a boxer. "Militias wanted us to work with them and carry weapons, but we rejected it," he told me. "My wife is Sunni. My neighbor is Sunni." One evening Mahdi Army men knocked on his door and asked him to go knock on his Sunni neighbor's door; his neighbor trusted Hassan and would open it. But Hassan refused. He warned his Sunni neighbors, who were from the Zowbaei tribe, that they were in danger. He told them he too would be leaving. But they insisted on staying. Three brothers from that family were killed. He also warned neighbors from the Sunni Mashhadani tribe, and they fled. After this, Mahdi Army men shot at his house and accused him and his brothers of being spies. He fled with his brother, his wife, and daughters to Syria, where they lived in Damascus's Seyida Zeinab area. After they had fled, Mahdi Army men opened fire on their home, damaging it with hundreds of rounds and later charging the family for the expended bullets.

Hassan remained in Syria for two years and nine months. In 2008, after Charge of the Knights, his cousins called him and asked him to return. "Let's fight the Mahdi Army," they told him. "They are killing Sunnis and Shiites. The people are strong but scared, and you are popular here, so they will follow you." Hassan returned and initially joined an Awakening group in the Mansour district. After the Mahdi Army threw a grenade at his cousins' house, Hassan and his brother captured Ihab al-Tawil, he told me. "The neighborhood was with us," he said. "We gave Ihab to Captain Salim. We had an intifada against them in Washash." A Mahdi Army member called him up angrily, demanding to know why he did this and why he was letting Sunnis return to Washash. "We began to uncover bodies and weapons," he told me.

"Mahdi Army members called me up to tell me because they didn't want the army to raid their homes and get their families in trouble." The Badr militia of the Supreme Council asked him to join them, he said, but he refused. "We rejected to carry weapons," he told me.

IN DECEMBER 2008 I flew Royal Jordanian from Amman to Basra. Most passengers were Iraqis. Because of the Muslim holiday Eid, embassies were closed; we did not have time to get visas, but a contact in the British military promised to obtain them upon arrival. The Iraqi customs officials did not take kindly to the violation of procedure and were offended by the British presumption, but a letter from the British commander persuaded them to relent. The Iraqi officials made it clear they were doing us and the British military a favor. Five Iraqi policemen stood at the exit examining all luggage. My colleague had a copy of Patrick Cockburn's excellent book on Muqtada, and when they saw Muqtada's glaring visage on the cover, they turned giddy. They were amazed that a foreigner would have a book in English all about their beloved cleric. One of them kissed the cover and asked if he could keep it. My friend agreed. I was surprised, not by the sentiment but by the comfort in which the men publicly expressed it.

The Iraqi translator accompanying the Royal Marine who met us at the airport dismissed Muqtada's supporters as merely poor and uneducated. It was the same mistake the occupiers had made from their arrival but was equally typical of middle- and upper-class Iraqis. After years of war and devastating sanctions imposed on Iraq, most Iraqis were poor and uneducated. But so what? Did this delegitimize the Sadrists or in any way reduce their popularity? On the contrary. Unfortunately, the man expressing it this time was the personal translator and adviser to the British commander in Basra, and sequestered as he was in Basra's airport, he was getting scant information about Basra's realities. The British commander had never heard of Thar Allah, one of the most lethal Iranian-backed militias in Basra. And when I asked him about the Mahdi Army, he was confused; he knew them only by their American-designated acronym, JAM.

I found a city largely under the control of the Iraqi Security Forces, with little sign of the British presence except for the occasional patrol. The local economy was thriving, and women could once again walk on the streets without wearing the veil if they chose to. A trickle of Sunnis had returned. Over and over again, when I spoke to civilians they told me the same thing: "Now sectarianism is finished in Basra." I spoke to officials of the once-formidable Communist Party. They blamed the Americans and British for introducing chaos into Basra. "Any foreign army is not good," one official told me. "The British army is less violent than Americans, but they let militias rule and made deals with them." The Communists also backed the prime minister. "Maliki is an Iraqi nationalist," they told me. "He went from being a man of a party to a man of state. He said only the state can have weapons." They agreed with me that the Sadrists were still the most popular movement among Shiites and worried that the Mahdi Army had sleeper cells. "The sectarian project failed in Iraq," one of them told me. People in Basra spoke of "before March" and "after March" to describe their lives, and in the city's middle-class areas, the Charge of the Knights campaign won only praise.

I attended a conference in a large auditorium at the local chamber of commerce that had been planned by local officials to explain how they spent the hundred million dollars Maliki had given them after Charge of the Knights. There were no foreign soldiers there, and I was the only foreigner. Representatives of local businesses, civil society, and the local media attended. The conference was a hosted by a woman and started with a prayer and recitation of the Koran. The national anthem was played, and everybody stood up. The host and others read poems. The conference had a decidedly Shiite tone: every time the host asked the crowd to pray for the Prophet Muhammad and his family, as was the Shiite way, the crowd responded loudly. Grandiloquent speeches about Basra and Iraq followed. There was no mention of the British or the Americans. It felt like a postoccupation Iraq.

I met with Jassim Ahmad, deputy head of the Sunni Islamic Party in Basra. The party's previous headquarters was destroyed after Samarra with the help of local police, and it was now based in an unmarked building across from police headquarters. The Islamic Party had sixty-eight martyrs in Basra, he told me. Many Sunni sheikhs had been murdered as well. Sunnis began returning after Charge of the Knights, he said. Although the security forces in Basra had been closed to Sunnis, there were currently about four hundred Sunnis in the local police and army. "Now the Sunni sect doesn't have problems in Basra," he said.

In stark contrast to downtown Basra were the slums of Hayaniya. They were far removed from the heart of the city, as if the population was segregated, and surrounded by sewage and garbage dumps. Streets were unpaved, and many houses were made of mud. An Iraqi army brigade surrounded them and had bases inside. The brigade, a mixed unit of Sunnis and Shiites that was headquartered in Ramadi and trained by the Americans, had arrived in Basra on April 13. I visited a school they were occupying in Hayaniya and met with two officers: one was a Sunni from Falluja, and the other was a Shiite from Baghdad's Shaab district. They sat on beds in a room with no door. Their men played volleyball in the yard. "The enemy was anybody illegal," they told me, "anybody carrying weapons." They had clashed mostly with the Mahdi Army and Thar Allah, but now the city was quiet, they said, adding that "we don't need help from the British." Hayaniya had the most problems, they explained—it was like Sadr City. The officer from Falluja joked that in the upcoming elections, the Saddamists in his city would win because the Awakening groups backed them. Both officers praised the Awakening's Abu Risha. "Petraeus is wrong," the Sunni officer told me. "The Americans caused the problems. The army and the people and the Awakening brought peace." His Shiite friend agreed. "We are the highest authority," he said. Many locals complained that the Iraqi army's occupation of schools and heavy presence in their neighborhood was oppressive and made them feel occupied.

One evening I met with four Mahdi Army men in the Gzeiza slum, adjacent to Hayaniya. One commanded one hundred fighters, one commanded forty fighters, and the other two were mere fighters. Their more senior commanders had fled to Iran. They had all taken part in the 1991 uprising against Saddam and a smaller one in 1999. They insisted that both uprisings had been influenced by the Sadrists. There were about 1,500 houses in Gzeiza, they told me. The Iraqi army occupied four schools, they said, complaining that soldiers mistreated children, wore shorts, and were inappropriately dressed in front of women. The army also stole from homes and harassed people, they said. They still supported Maliki despite his crackdown, but they insisted that Muqtada was popular throughout Basra. The Sadrist Current was under extreme pressure from the British forces, the Iraqi government, and the ISF, they said, but added that the Sadrists had no problem with the people or the government. They didn't think that the Americans would leave Iraq. "The Mahdi Army is not weak," one of them told me. "We obey Muqtada, and whatever he says we do, and he said, 'Don't fight the government.' We are not against the government or the people, just against the occupation. We are giving the government an opportunity. Before Charge of the Knights the Mahdi Army controlled Basra. We can be more than the army. We can get rid of them in two days. There is pressure from the government now. There are provocations, but we were ordered not to have arms on the street."

The men conceded that killings were down, but they still complained about crime. "We are sitting on oil, and we don't have electricity," one of them said. "In the summer for an hour or two. Now it's three hours on, three off." The Mahdi Army was loyal only to Iraq, they told me, which was the same thing the two Iraqi army officers had said. The street in Iraq was Sadrist, they said, and the Mahdi Army was the *muqawama* (resistance). "The Mahdi Army made the government strong," one said. "Baghdad had terrorism, but the Mahdi Army and the government got rid of it together. There is resistance of the pen and resistance of the gun. After the occupation the Mahdi Army will be cultural. The government is now arresting people randomly. Now all countries pursue their interests in Iraq." Thar Allah had no links to the Mahdi Army, they said, but belonged to the Supreme Council, and the Supreme Council belonged to Iran. They blamed Thar Allah for the expulsion of Sunnis and Christians. Elections were coming up soon, and I asked whom they would vote for.

"A week or two before the elections in the Friday prayers they will tell us who to vote for," one of them told me.

On my last day in Basra, a British armored vehicle was stoned by a group of local men. One brave man climbed on top of it and was persuaded to go down only when a British soldier emerged and pointed his weapon at him. There was little sign after more than five years of occupation in Basra that the British had built or improved anything in the vast slums where most of the population lived. And when the British tried to encourage the local government to increase services in Hayaniya and similar areas, the local officials said that these poor Shiites didn't belong in Basra anyway, since they were from Amara, from the marshes. British officers told me the provincial council had a condescending attitude toward the residents of Hayaniya and its neighboring areas, and that they were desperately trying to get services to these areas. Little had been learned after five years. The poor Shiite majority was still neglected, just as it was under Saddam. Only Muqtada carried their voice.

In late December 2008 I visited an Iraqi Christian family in East Beirut that had fled Baghdad only two weeks earlier. A small Christmas tree was in the corner of the room. "My husband couldn't go to his shop, the children were without school because of the bad situation," the mother explained. There were less kidnappings in Baghdad now, she admitted, but there were still explosions. "It's difficult to be away from my country," she said, switching back and forth between the Lebanese and Iraqi dialect. I told her about the book I was working on, a project about Bush's legacy in the Middle East. Bush had only brought them war, not freedom, she said bitterly. "Why should I thank Bush?" she asked. "For the war we experienced in Iraq? For our displacement from our homes? For the year we couldn't send our children to school and the year my husband couldn't go to his shop to work? Why will I thank him? We just now left Iraq. Where is the democracy? Where is the security?"

When the family moved into their small apartment in Beirut, they found a pencil drawing of Saddam Hussein on their wall, beneath which was written "the brave martyr." The mother said she kissed it when she saw it. "I love him," she said. "In Saddam's time Iraq was safe. We could go to school and work safely—there was no displacement. We were Christians living with Sunnis and Shiites, one next to the other. Since Bush came, the Sunnis left their homes. We have not seen any changes in Iraq. We don't expect change because of Obama. He's American."

I asked Saramand, another Iraqi Christian, the same questions. He had arrived in Beirut six months earlier and now worked in a local church whose congregation was made up entirely of Christian refugees. Two weeks earlier forty families had arrived, he told me. "Before, if there were five or six people in a house and one worked, they could live," he said. "Here they all work just to survive. Work is not allowed, but people work." He too blamed Bush for his plight: "What do you expect to happen in an occupation? The democracy that Bush sent us is killing, theft, settling of scores. Where is the democracy? Where is the freedom? Where are the promises he made? Garbage has reached up to our heads in Iraq. Children are dying every day in Iraq—for what? If there was no Bush, I would not be here. If you see a refugee laughing, it's a lie. Inside, he is full of memories."

IN MARCH 2007 the surge was still nascent, but the legal basis for the American occupation was expiring. United Nations resolutions effectively let American troops do whatever they wanted, but the Iraqis wanted that to end. The Americans needed a bilateral agreement to anchor their presence in Iraq. Bush wanted a policy to hand to his successor, knowing he would be under a lot of pressure to leave. In the spring of 2007 the Americans began to discuss their options. The U.S. military said it needed a Status of Forces Agreement, but civilians in the government were skeptical that a typical SOFA could be passed.

In the Middle East, most American SOFAs are secret, their terms hidden from the population, because the governments the Americans deal with are dictatorships. If citizens from these countries knew what was in a typical agreement, they would be outraged. But Iraq was sort of a democracy, and the SOFA would have to go through Parliament and be made public. The 1948 Treaty of Portsmouth, between Iraq and Britain, was on the minds of many Iraqi politicians. When the terms of Portsmouth became known in Baghdad, there were massive protests led by a movement known as Al Wathba (The Leap). The treaty was abandoned. President Lyndon Johnson's 1968 treaty with the Shah of Iran was also on Iraqis' minds, since Iranian anger at the treaty helped lead to the rise of Khomeini. Most SOFAs grant immunity to American military personnel. But the Iraqis were afraid that immunity could fuel the Mahdi Army and the resistance. It would look like the politicians were giving Iraq away.

The fall 2007 declaration of principles signed between Maliki and Bush set the atmosphere. It described cultural, economic, and diplomatic ties and laid out the terms of the partnership and security relationship. "It was very hard," an American official told me. "Maliki didn't want to sign. He was timid politically, and the other parties would stab him for it even if they agreed with it. Bush wanted him to sign it in the U.S., but he balked, so they signed it via video conference." In February 2008 the State Department hired Ambassador Robert Loftis, a senior basing negotiator and an expert on drafting SOFAs, but who had no Iraq experience. His draft gave the Americans full authority and control. Ambassador Ryan Crocker and NSA's Brett McGurk said it wouldn't work, it was an impossible dream. The terms leaked, the Sadrists protested, and Maliki opposed it. This was not what he got on board for.

The Americans fired the entire SOFA team. McGurk arrived in Iraq in mid-May and worked directly with Maliki, meeting him twice a week and also working with Maliki's close advisers. It was a small American team: McGurk, Crocker, and David Satterfield. They had a direct line to Secretary of State Condoleezza Rice, National Security Adviser Stephen Hadley, and President Bush. The timelines set by the SOFA were very controversial within the U.S. military. It set a June 2009 withdrawal of American troops from Iraqi cities and a full American withdrawal by 2011.

The Iraqis were making maximalist demands, but the Americans assumed Maliki was just posturing because of domestic politics. The Iraqis rebranded it the Withdrawal Agreement because the original draft had so poisoned the atmosphere. Immunity for troops was the hardest issue, but eventually the two sides came up with a hypothetical situation that was impossible to imagine. Perhaps if an American soldier went to a bar and raped an Iraqi woman or committed some other unlikely but egregious act, then he would be prosecuted under Iraqi law. Otherwise the Americans would try him. "During the SOFA they played us like fiddles," an American official told me. "The prime minister's office got exactly what they wanted, a presence in the country that protects them and which they have oversight over and which they can use as a stick against opponents."

Maliki's Law and Order campaign against militias resonated with the middle class. His confrontation with Kurds galvanized Iraqi nationalist support, and the SOFA poured water on the Sadrist flames. There was now a timetable for withdrawal; it looked like the occupation would end. But a different iconic moment will be forever associated with the trip Bush took to Baghdad to sign the SOFA.

THE YEAR 2008 ended with Muntadhar al-Zeidi reminding President Bush and the world for only a moment about the Iraqi victims. During a press conference on Bush's last visit to the country, Zeidi spoke for the masses in the Arab world and beyond when he shouted, "This is a farewell kiss from the Iraqi people, you dog!" as he threw his first shoe at the American president. Zeidi was a secular, left-leaning Shiite from Sadr City whose work as a reporter for Baghdadiya television had won him local acclaim because of his focus on the suffering of innocent Iraqis. He had been arrested twice by the American army and kidnapped once by a militia.

He remembered, as did all Iraqis, that the American occupation had not begun with the surge. The story of the American occupation was not one of smart officers contributing to the reduction of violence and increase in stability. That was only one chapter in a longer story of painful, humiliating, sanctions, wars, and bloody occupation. Those with short memories, such as *New*

York Times columnist Thomas Friedman, might remember the American occupation as "a million acts of kindness." But to Iraqis and anyone else sensitive enough to view them as humans, the occupation was one million acts of violence and humiliation or one million explosives. There was nothing for Bush to be triumphal about during his farewell press conference. Even the surge had exacted a costly toll on Iraqis. Thousands more had been killed, arrested, thrown into overcrowded prisons, and rarely put on trial, their families deprived of them. The surge was not about a victory. With a cost so high, there could be no victory. COIN is still violence, and the occupation persisted, imposing violence on an entire country. As Zeidi threw his second shoe in a last desperate act of defiance, he remembered these victims and shouted, "This is for the widows and orphans and all those killed in Iraq!"

Part Four

❖❖❖❖❖❖❖❖❖

AFTERMATH

CHAPTER TEN

Lebanon: Toward Zero Hour

ONE EVENING IN THE SPRING OF 2008, I WAS SITTING ON A STOOP ON a dark street and speaking to several Sunni "concerned local citizens," the new euphemism for American-backed militias in the Middle East. The young men were speaking of the danger coming from Shiites when I interrupted one of them, who was wearing a white sleeveless shirt, and said, "Don't take this personally, but would you let your sister marry a Shiite?" In an instant he flattened his hand and moved his arm like a blade, slicing into the air the way he would slice her throat. I was not in Baghdad, where this might have been commonplace—I was in Beirut, where, as in pre-occupation Iraq, once it would not have been out of the ordinary for a Sunni and a Shiite to marry. In the early years of the American occupation of Iraq there were concerns about the Lebanonization of Iraq; but now it seemed Iraq was coming to Lebanon.

Sunni neighborhoods in Beirut felt insecure. Thuggish Shiite Amal supporters regularly zipped through on their scooters to shoot in the air and taunt them. Leaders from the Sunni-dominated March 14 coalition were being blown up occasionally, and it was clear the security forces could not protect them. The Future Movement's leaders felt pressure to protect themselves and their anxious constituency, so they created a private security company to protect Future leaders and local militias in various Sunni neighborhoods throughout the country, established under the leadership of Salim Diab, former general coordinator of the Future Current.

Lebanon had no history of strife between Sunnis and Shiites. There had been class conflicts in the past—Sunnis were condescending to Shiites the way urban people often are to rural people, and Sunnis reviled Shiite religious traditions, which Shiites resented—but the divide had not been violent. Lebanese Sunni racism against Shiites was an artificial sectarianism, seeming to come out of nowhere. Lebanese Sunnis had never seen themselves exclusively as Sunnis. Even former Prime Minister Rafiq al-Hariri was not seen as a Sunni leader before his death. Until then he had not even had the support of most

Sunnis, and Sunni leadership was not centralized. His death was exploited for political and sectarian reasons.

The first Sunni show of force was the Future Movement–backed demonstrations in February 2006 against the Danish cartoons of the Prophet Muhammad, which turned into a riot targeting Christians. Hariri's son Saad was very embarrassed by this. Sunni power often seemed to be devoid of specific goals except keeping Shiites out of power. Historically Shiites were called the epithet *"mutwali."* But following Hizballah's victory in the 2006 war, some urban Shiites reclaimed their victimization as a source of pride and made *"mutwali"* cool, in a way that resembled the African American reappropriation of the word "nigga." Hizballah has never exploited sectarianism and has always gone out of its way to ease tensions. Hassan Nasrallah warned that the Americans were trying to drive a wedge between Shiites and Sunnis. But Hizballah could not escape the fact that it was a Shiite party.

From May to September 2007, the army had to contend with the crisis at the Nahr al-Barid Palestinian refugee camp, which left some 420 people killed, 168 of them soldiers. On September 4 of that year, Lebanese Defense Minister Elias Murr announced the cessation of 106 days of fighting against Islamic militants in the camp. It was the second war Lebanon had seen in two summers (see Chapter Six). The Lebanese army, which had stood by impotently in the summer of 2006 as the Israeli military destroyed much of the country in the name of fighting Hizballah, this time destroyed a refugee camp housing forty thousand people in the name of the war on terror. The three months of fighting with the jihadists from Fatah al-Islam, the worst the country had seen since its fifteen-year civil war ended in 1990, had been a distraction from growing internal divisions in Lebanon. These divisions had brought the country dangerously close to civil war once again in January 2007, when Sunnis and Shiites clashed on the streets.

There was a sense of foreboding that summer, a feeling that something worse was about to happen. The July war with Israel was still on everyone's mind, and with it the fear that neither Israel nor Hizballah viewed the previous summer's denouement as conclusive. Another war was ongoing in the north, with the interregnum punctuated by the occasional car bomb or assassination. And a third war, "the next civil war," seemed to be on the horizon. Meanwhile, according to Lebanese political scientist Amer Mohsen, Lebanese politicians seemed like Shakespearean actors on a stage, "tragic characters who follow a path that was already charted for them—i.e., they have no agency in what is happening." These politicians, Mohsen explained, "are clearly aware that, no matter what they do, events that control their country and destiny are decided by parties that are far larger than them."

In November 2006, six Hizballah and Amal ministers resigned from the government coalition to protest violations of the agreed-upon rules by

Prime Minister Fouad Siniora and his March 14 allies. They called for the government to uphold the tradition of cabinet consensus, which dated to the end of the civil war. The opposition began planning for street demonstrations, which were called off after a Christian politician was assassinated. That month a young Syrian man detonated his suicide vest on the Syrian border with Lebanon after he was denied permission to cross because his papers were discovered to be fake. He was said to belong to the Al Qaeda–linked Tawhid and Jihad organization. On December 1, 2006, the opposition condemned the government as illegitimate and staged a "sit-in" in downtown Beirut, establishing a huge tent city in Martyrs' Square, the same place where anti-Syrian demonstrators had launched their March 14 "intifada." Key roads were blocked, and traffic became unbearable. Numerous shops and boutiques in the downtown area went out of business. Some Sunnis began to view the sit-in as a Shiite occupation. Three days later, a Shiite supporter of Amal was shot dead. The Lebanese army was deployed on the city's streets. On January 24, 2007, three young men were killed following a strike called by Hizballah, as opposition supporters blocked roads and burned tires. The next day four Lebanese were killed and more than 150 were injured in clashes at the Arab University of Beirut, near the Tariq al-Jadida neighborhood. It was left to Iran and Saudi Arabia to get involved and postpone further conflict. This was the nature of Lebanon's sectarian system: it could never be stable; it was impossible to achieve ideal harmony. Lebanon was not a viable state.

Hizballah was the biggest party in the March 8 coalition, and its patron was Iran. Future, the Hariri family's movement, was the biggest party in the March 14 movement, and its patron was Saudi Arabia. In a November 29, 2006, op-ed in the *Washington Post*, titled "Stepping Into Iraq; Saudi Arabia Will Protect Sunnis If the U.S. Leaves," Nawaf Obaid, a Saudi foreign policy adviser to Saudi Prince Turki al-Faisal, warned that the Saudis would have to defend Iraq's Sunnis from the Shiites of Iraq and Iran if the Americans did not. The Saudis were worried that the Americans were allowing the Iranians to win in Iraq and Lebanon. Along with the Jordanians, they would provide Iraq's Sunnis with weapons and financial support. The Saudis had already commenced construction of a multibillion-dollar barrier between them and Iraq to isolate them from the violence they had helped foment. The Saudis also assumed the role of defenders of Lebanon's Sunnis. Two years later I met Prince Turki— who had been the ambassador to Washington, intelligence chief, and liason to Osama bin Laden—and asked him if he really feared Iran. "Iran wants Mecca and Medina," he said. "They want their ideology to control it." Hizballah in Lebanon was completely an Iranian tool, he said. "The Saudi interest is for Iraq to maintain its Arab identity and not fall under Persian influence. Iran views Saudi Arabia as the little Satan, not Israel—read Khomeini's work." But he added that Iran's vulnerability was its ethnic minorities: the Kurds, Baluch, and Azeris.

The Saudis were getting nervous, watching their proxies throughout the region weaken. In the 1960s Egypt's pan–Arab nationalist Gamal Abdel Nasser was the main competition with Saudi influence in the region. The Saudis and Americans both tried to undermine Arab nationalist and leftist movements. The result was an increase in the power of fundamentalists and the weakening of Arab progressives. The Saudis now had no Arab rivals for their influence with the less powerful exceptions of Qatar and Syria. But Hizballah (and Hamas in Palestine) represented resistance to the Saudi, Israeli, and American project in the region, and the Saudis would not tolerate it.

ON AUGUST 10, 2007, four days before Hizballah was to commemorate the "divine victory" over Israel (as they called it), I visited the Salam Mosque in Tripoli, a northern coastal city—Lebanon's second-largest—and its Sunni bastion. Hundreds of men filled the mosque and overflowed onto straw mats outside. They sat in the heat listening to a fiery sermon with apparent indifference. Sheikh Bilal Barudi, a Sunni cleric close to the March 14 coalition and also part of the Independent Islamic Gathering of Sunni clerics, gave the sermon. Arabs were once again in conflict with the Persians, he said, a conflict he saw as age-old and also between Sunnis and Shiites. "We ask the Iranians and Americans to withdraw from Iraq," he said. "Iran is our historic enemy. Throughout history Iran always had an ambition of controlling Arab countries around them." He spoke of the Shiites of Lebanon occupying Beirut, mocking Hizballah's "divine victory" and calling its members enemies of Islam. The war had started after Hizballah captured two Israeli soldiers, hoping to exchange them for four leftist Lebanese resistance fighters held by the Israelis. Barudi condemned Hizballah for destroying Lebanon to rescue leftists whom he called "infidels." This was a refrain I would hear repeatedly over the next year.

One of those attending the prayer that Friday was Samir Jisr, a member of Parliament with the Future Movement, the Saudi-backed political movement clustered around Saad al-Hariri, which he inherited from his father, Rafiq. I met Jisr in his home a few blocks away. He explained to me that just as Sunnis had felt threatened during the Syrian era, so now they felt threatened by Hizballah. "Most people here were with the resistance to Israel," he said. "People looked at Hizballah as the resistance, but after the Israelis withdrew and they practiced politics and shifted to inside Lebanon, people considered it a threat." He explained that it was the presence of pro-Hizballah demonstrators "in the heart of the streets . . . the way they threaten to stop the country," and their possession of weapons, that "scares people." Jisr had criticized the army publicly for allegedly torturing Lebanese Sunnis suspected of militancy. Now Sunni militants were afraid, he said.

He blamed poverty and oppression for increasing extremism and complained that after the civil war Beirut had gotten all the attention in the reconstruction while the north was neglected. The Syrians were hated, he said, because of their shelling of Tripoli in the 1980s, which he claimed killed up to 1,200 Sunnis. "It's a big wound for people in Tripoli," he said. The war in Iraq had negative effects on Lebanon too: "They are not spreading democracy. It's obvious that they are trying to divide Iraq and steal its resources. Everybody believes the Americans are responsible for Sunni-Shiite problems. There is a fear among people that what is happening in Iraq will affect Lebanon."

Dai al-Islam al-Shahal, Lebanon's most important Salafi cleric, blamed Shiites and Iran for the civil war in Iraq. Many Salafi clerics like him were obsessed with Shiites; Shahal was rabidly anti-Shiite. "The Sunnis in Iraq are oppressed by Shiites, and Iranians are allying with Americans there," he told me.

I met Shahal in his office in Tripoli's Abu Samra neighborhood, where many Salafis are based. It was August 14, or "Victory Day," according to Hizballah. As I waited for Shahal to arrive in the morning, his devoted young male secretary assured me that my heart would race when I saw him. Shahal had a white beard and wore a white robe, with a white cap and a white scarf on his head.

Like most Sunnis, he did not think that the war with Israel had, in fact, ended with a victory—he wished it had not happened. He viewed Hizballah as a threat to the Lebanese government and the entire country. "There is an old Shiite project to control Lebanon," he told me, mentioning the canard of the "Shiite crescent," first described by Jordan's King Abdullah. "Iran is exporting its Islamic Revolution," he said, and "the project of controlling Lebanon is being implemented. A minority rules Syria, allied with Shiites here and Iranians in Iraq."

Although Sunnis were being targeted, "Sunnis are more powerful," he told me. "If, God forbid, a civil war happens, they know how to defend themselves and are prepared." Sunnis were engaged with the state, he explained, but in the event of a civil war they would require militias. And while Sunnis in the government were allying with the Americans, "people on the street are totally against the Americans." Sunni Islamists had allied with the Future Movement and the Lebanese government because they defended Sunnis, he explained, but relations between Sunnis and the government had been damaged by the fighting in Nahr al-Barid.

Shahal had been one of the key negotiators between Lebanese authorities and Fatah al-Islam. "Fatah al-Islam used Fatah al-Intifada as a passage into Lebanon to set up a movement to fight Israel," he said. "Most of Fatah al-Islam are not Palestinian." Fatah al-Islam's ideology had been close to that of

Al Qaeda, he said. Muslims were under attack, he said, explaining that the American administration wanted to strike Islam and was trying to establish bases in Muslim lands to take their resources. "The defense of Muslim lands from America and the West is better than attacking Americans and the West in their countries," he said. Al Qaeda's mistake was "moving the battle to Western territory. When Muslims are under attack, it is right to defend themselves but not to move the battle to the West."

IF THERE IS A RED LINE separating Sunnis from Shiites in Beirut, it is the Tariq al-Jadida neighborhood, a Sunni bastion close to Dahiyeh, the southern Shiite suburb dominated by Hizballah. Entering the neighborhood, one passes a Saudi flag, a Lebanese flag, and the flag of the Future Movement. Large posters of Saudi King Abdullah hang above the streets. Beginning in early 2007 various local militias began to appear, their names changing often. One was called the Panthers. Every night the streets of Tariq al-Jadida were patrolled by men who did not carry arms in public. They were recruited and paid by the Future Movement. Typically they were young men sitting on street corners, smoking water pipes, eating pistachios, and demanding that passersby present their identification papers. Sometimes they had lists of wanted men. They were supervised by older men, veterans of the Lebanese army, security forces, or militias from the civil war. Just in case, Interior Security Forces sat in armored personnel carriers in the center of the neighborhood. On my first visit, in 2007, I asked some of the young men who they were protecting the neighborhood from. "*Zaaran*," said one muscular youth, referring to hoodlums, or thugs. I asked which *zaaran*. "From Dahiyeh," he said. "We will chop them up." During this visit, I was stopped by chubby young men on scooters who zipped over and took me to what they called on their radios Checkpoint One. Fortunately I had befriended a local militiaman named Fadi, a small man who owned a barbershop close to the edge of the neighborhood, who vouched for me. Fadi had a ponytail, wore tight black clothes, and had a huge shiny watch on his wrist. He patrolled his street on behalf of the local Future militia and was paid four hundred dollars a month by the Secure Plus company, which he said was the same as the Future Movement. Fadi had not done his military service, but he had received one month of training in Akkar.

Tariq al-Jadida, a mostly middle-class Sunni area, was the heart of Sunni power in Beirut. In contrast, Bab al-Tabbaneh, a district in Tripoli, in northern Lebanon, was poor and marginalized; many of its unemployed youth were used by the Sunnis of Beirut as shock troops to intimidate rivals. Unlike poor Shiites, impoverished Sunnis in Tariq al-Jadida—and elsewhere in Lebanon—do not have a powerful movement to provide for them or protect them. Instead, rival politicians compete for popularity by occasionally dispensing favors, usually before elections. Crumbling buildings torn apart by shells and bullet holes, with laundry drying outside the windows and balconies, look down over rows of garages and small workshops for wooden furniture. Black flags with Islamic slogans wave in the sun. Salafis helped clean up Bab al-Tabbaneh from gangs and drugs, improving its reputation. Many former gang members and drug addicts had become Salafis and even jihadists; the only evidence of their past delinquency was their remaining tattoos. In the 1980s, the Syrian army had been stationed in the Jabal Mohsen neighborhood, which towered above Tabbaneh. Thirty thousand Alawites lived there. From there the Syrians punished the recalcitrant Sunnis of Tabbaneh, and the scars had never healed.

I found a group of men drinking tea outside a shop. Mustafa Zaabi sat with his brothers and friends. "Everything is a lie," he said. "There is no electricity, so everybody is on the street. If we talk, who will listen to us? What are we, Palestinian refugees? I wish we were Palestinians so we had care from the UN or the government." They blamed the Palestinians for the fighting in Nahr al-Barid. "The people fighting in the camp are mostly Palestinian, just pretending to be Fatah al-Islam," said Mustafa's brother Muhamad. "It's impossible that they will rebuild the camp," said Mustafa.

Mustafa had been an active member of the Future Movement and had voted for the party in the past, but he had stopped giving his support. "They did nothing," he said. "Many people feel betrayed. Those who said we are sons of Tabbaneh, where are you now? We don't want the hundred dollars that you paid on election day. If we knew what was waiting for us, we wouldn't have voted for the entire Hariri list. For three years I didn't see anything from the house of Hariri." Mustafa still had high hopes for Saad al-Hariri. "First because he is the son of Rafiq al-Hariri," he said. "We saw how Hariri made Beirut. We hoped he would build Tripoli and create work opportunities for youth."

Mustafa and his two brothers had all been accused of acts of sabotage against the Syrian military and had been jailed and tortured by the Syrians. Mustafa had belonged to the Murabitun militia in the 1980s. He spent six months training in Libya but had left in disgust because Lebanese weren't trusted with weapons. Mustafa had been injured in the civil war when a shell landed nearby. His entire body had been burned, and his hand was still maimed. His brother Hussein was paralyzed and in a wheelchair, a result of being beaten on the back of the head with a gun while imprisoned.

Seated with Mustafa and his friends was a thin nineteen-year-old named Ayman. Like many young men, he was marked with crude tattoos and had scars up his entire arm that he had inflicted on himself. "He learned it in prison," explained Mustafa. Ayman had spent seven months in prison "for a simple problem," he said.

One way sectarian leaders in Lebanon distribute favors is by covering legal fees or helping people get out of prison. Ayman had many friends who had been to prison. "Most guys go to jail because of street fights with blades," said Mustafa, "not for robberies. There is nothing to steal here." Another thin young man, also called Mustafa, had similar scars from self-mutilation on his arms, which he had created with razors. I asked him why he had done it. "Depression," he said. "There is no work—we take it out on ourselves." The older Mustafa explained that young men like him used drugs and sniffed paint thinner.

They led me around the neighborhood, down dirt-strewn alleys with electrical cables hanging low and blackened walls ridden with bullets. I saw posters of Saddam on the walls next to posters of Rafiq al-Hariri. "Saddam is considered to be oppressed," Mustafa told me. "The Americans took him to kill him." Everybody in the area had been saddened by the news of Abu Musab al-Zarqawi's death as well, he told me: "He was somebody liberating Muslim land." A group of young men stood beneath posters of Saddam and Hariri, alongside a picture of Khalil Akkawi, the slain founder of the anti-Syrian Tawhid movement, which was militarily active in the 1980s. After Akkawi's assassination and the arrest or killing of most of Tawhid's members, there was no powerful group remaining to fill the vacuum in Bab al-Tabbaneh. I asked the young men why they liked Saddam. "He was a Muslim," they all agreed, "a hero, a real Arab." They had all been sad and angry when he was executed.

I asked them what they thought of Saad al-Hariri. "He is a Sunni Muslim, clean," they said. I asked about Hizballah. "No! No!" they shouted, waving their hands. "*Kish! Kish!*" one added, making the sound he would make to shoo a dog away. "Nobody likes the Palestinians," they told me. "They are pimps. They are the cause of all these problems; they let Fatah al-Islam into the camp. They should go back to Palestine."

Several hundred Palestinian refugees had been housed in the Bab al-Tabbaneh Elementary School, and others were in seven other schools in the area of Tripoli. Locals had demanded that one of the school gates facing their neighborhood be kept locked. Blue plastic sheeting had been used to divide halls and create private spaces for families. They stood around or sat on chairs that students would soon need, just waiting. Hosam Ilmir, the principal, worried that the school year might be canceled if alternative housing was not found.

"Bab al-Tabbaneh has the poorest people in the country," Ilmir told me. "They are strangers in their country. The basic requirements of life are not here. Most students in school are not concentrating because at home their brother or father is on drugs, drunk, beating their mother. They can't sleep at home, so they sleep in class. There is sexual abuse of children." The Future Movement paid poor Sunnis when they were needed for voting, protests, or demonstrations in Beirut, he said. Many people came down from Bab al-Tabbaneh for the Beirut protests over the Danish cartoons in February 2006, he said. The state mufti called for people to come down, the Sunni Endowment provided buses to transport some of the protesters, people were paid for their presence in Beirut, and gasoline prices were also covered for the ride. "One guy is responsible for many other guys," he said, "and he distributes the money." This was the case in all the main March 14 and Future Movement demonstrations in Beirut, he said.

"We Sunnis of Lebanon never had a militia," Ilmir said. "The Sunni army was the Palestinians. Sunnis were businessmen." Now Sunnis wanted their own militias, he said. Unlike the Future Movement, which offered only money when it needed manpower, "Hizballah always looks after their people." The Future Movement had influenced people in Tripoli "to think Hizballah started the war and destroyed the country," he said. He blamed the Lebanese media outlets associated with the Future Movement and March 14, such as LBC and Future TV, for inciting people. "For Sunnis in Lebanon, Hariri was seen as a Sunni leader, and his killing enraged Sunnis," he told me. "Going back to the postwar period, the Sunni street was divided in two. Some Sunnis supported anybody who fights Israel, and some Sunnis said Hizballah will turn their guns on Sunnis." He insisted that Sunnis were being armed under the guise of private security companies set up as legalized militias by the Future Movement. People were also joining Salafi movements, he said, because "people need work. If there is money, people will follow you all the way to China."

Ilmir agreed that since the fighting began the heat had been turned up on Salafis. "There is a lot of pressure by security forces," he said. "People with beards are arrested for no reason, like in the Syrian days. They hold you for a week and give you two hundred thousand liras. Getting tortured by your people is worse than being tortured by strangers. As a Sunni, if anybody comes and throws a stone at Israel from Tanzania, I will kiss his hand. This is not just my view, this is the view of the silent majority of Lebanon." After I left he ran after me and clasped my hand. "Don't be surprised from what you heard from me," he said. "This is the view of all educated Sunnis."

It certainly was not the view of several taxi drivers I met. One driver who took me from Bab al-Tabbaneh to downtown Tripoli explained the difference between the March 14 and March 8 coalitions. "The opposition thinks we are agents of America and Israel," he said, and did not disagree with the notion. "We are with America and Israel, and they are with Iran and Syria." Abu Ali, a taxi driver who picked me up in Tripoli, complained that politicians were destroying the country. "I have twelve children, and I can't feed them," he said, not wondering if perhaps he should have had fewer. "They ask me if I'm with Syria or America. No, sir, I'm with America. They freed us from Syria. I don't hate Shiites because I'm a Sunni. They destroyed the country. Hizballah is the party of the devil. The Palestinians are pimps. The Palestinians are killing our army." It seemed to me as though Lebanese Sunnis were becoming the new Maronite Christians, no longer interested in Arab nationalism but only in a narrow Lebanese chauvinism, looking to America for protection and hating the Palestinians to the point of sympathizing with Israel.

The army, long condemned by March 14 politicians, had become a rallying cry for them—so much so that in Marj, a small Sunni town in the Bekaa Valley, I passed under a banner that declared, "The Army is the solution." It was a sharp contrast to the rallying cry "Islam is the solution," which one often heard from various popular Islamist movements in the Middle East, such as the Muslim Brotherhood. Although Marj had once been a bastion of Arab nationalism, it had also produced 9/11 hijacker Ziad Jarrah. Not far from Marj was the town of Majd al-Anjar, from where at least a dozen men had gone to fight in Iraq. Salafism was introduced to Majd al-Anjar by Zuheir Shawish, a Kurd married to a local woman. Sheikh Adnan al-Umama was backed by Saudi funds and increased Salafi education. He was also on the Future payroll.

Minutes after I drove into town, in early August 2007, the mayor and a local police officer arrived to ask me who I was. I arranged to meet the *mukhtar* (town headman), who lived across from the Bilal Bin Rabah Mosque.

Graffiti on a wall by the mosque read, "They say it's a war on terrorism, but it's a war on Omar," referring to the Prophet Muhammad's companion, an important figure to Sunnis. Mukhtar Shaaban al-Ajami had held his position for nine years. A muscular man with a long red beard, he practiced martial arts and bragged about his strength. At forty-six years old, he was a leonine figure. He lived with his wife and four children and had his own farm. He proudly showed off his deep well, sheep, chickens, geese, vegetables, and fruit.

His grandfather had been *mukhtar* for forty years, in the days of Ottomans and the French. There were twenty thousand residents in the all-Sunni town, he told me. It had never had strong political parties, and parties never had more than ten people. There was almost no immigration from the town, and since 1985 it had become very religious, with everybody over fifteen attending one of the six mosques.

The Syrians had occupied Ajami's house for ten years, and he had taken part in anti-Syrian military operations. "The Syrians tried to remove Sunnis from their role in the country and raise the status of Shiites," he said. After the Hariri assassination, Sunnis had grown more extreme. "They made us feel this way. Shiites hate us and want their revenge after a thousand years. They killed Hariri and they don't want a trial for the killers. Before Hariri died, Sunnis were not so extreme. They made us like this. Everybody supports Saad al-Hariri because of the sectarian conflict. It began when Iran entered Lebanon through Hizballah. Shiites consider themselves oppressed historically, and now it's the chance for them to achieve what they want. Only Bashar al-Assad is stopping it, because if it starts here it will spread there between Alawites and Sunnis, and Alawites are the minority. Shiites made themselves different, spe-

cial, always. Go back in history; they are obsessed with Hussein and want revenge. Hizballah is an Iranian party, that's it—it serves Iranian interests."

Ajami had encouraged young men to go fight in Iraq in the past, but no
longer. "The situation is confusing, and you don't know who the resistance is,"
he said. "Al Qaeda is fighting people, people are fighting each other." Ajami acknowledged that the March 14 movement, which he supported, was cooperating with the Americans. "The Americans are working for their own interests,"
he said. "In Lebanon they are with the Sunnis. Their interests in Iraq are with
the Shiites. The Future Movement is looking for protection from Syria, so it is
allying with Americans and French." He insisted that Fatah al-Islam had been a
ploy to make Sunnis look like terrorists. "They made Fatah al-Islam terrorists
and Shiites resistance. Making Nasrallah the hero is serving the Shiite agenda.
Give me half the money they got, and I will form a much better resistance."

Ajami took me to meet the mufti of the Bekaa Valley, Khalil al-Meis. Meis
had been mufti since 1985. He had been famous for his strident sectarian
speeches, which many identified as pro–Al Qaeda, until he was co-opted by the
Future Movement in the 2005 elections. He too agreed that Sunnis felt targeted
following the killing of Hariri. "They killed Hariri and now they are surrounding [Prime Minister] Siniora," he said. "Siniora represents the Sunni presence in
the state, so they are trying to weaken him." In his view, common among Sunnis, Hizballah was part of Iran, and the group had used its victory over Israel to
dominate Lebanon and try "to make Shiites feel less like Arab patriots and
make them feel Iranian." Such accusations had grown increasingly prevalent;
even Egyptian President Hosni Mubarak had called Shiites fifth columnists for
Iran. "Sunnis are not allied with America, but the Americans are fighting Iran
in Lebanon," Meis said. "In Iraq America is allied with Shiites. In Afghanistan
the Shiites benefited from the Americans. Americans are Americans—but they
always look for their interests, with Sunnis here, with Shiites in Iraq." Saddam
had become a symbol for Sunnis because of the way he was executed and the
timing, which coincided with the day on which Sunnis celebrated an important holiday. "Saddam is not the Iraqi Saddam anymore," he said, but a Sunni
symbol.

IN JANUARY 2008 the mufti of Mount Lebanon, Sheikh Muhamad Ali Juzu, attacked clerics who wore "black turbans," meaning Shiite clerics. In April he
warned that Hizballah was implementing an "armed invasion" of his majority-
Sunni area and called on the government to allow Sunnis to carry weapons so
that they could defend themselves.

I drove down to Juzu's ornate home, on a hill overlooking the Mediterranean. It was guarded by a German shepherd and men wearing sandals and

the uniform of the Internal Security Forces. Juzu was notorious for his anti-Shiite vitriol. Born in 1927, he had been mufti since 1962. Problems between Sunnis and Shiites were new, he said. He blamed them on Ayatollah Khomeini's Iranian Revolution and the rise in the 1970s of the Lebanese cleric Imam Musa Sadr and his Amal Movement. "He divided people," he said of Sadr. "Before, Shiites were in all parties and didn't have this extreme *assabiya* [esprit de corps]. After the Iranian Revolution the Iranians began purchasing the loyalty of Sunnis throughout the Muslim world, he insisted. "Here in my area some Sunnis go with Hizballah because they get paid," he said. "They want Sunnis against Sunnis, like what happened in Nahr al-Barid. It served Shiite interests."

Juzu repeated the common observation among Sunnis that the Americans had changed the regional balance, empowering Iran and Shiites. "The destruction of Saddam and Iraq helped Iran," he said, "Now Iran controls Iraq." Juzu himself was a friend of Sheikh Harith al-Dhari, head of Iraq's Association of Muslim Scholars. Dhari was among Iraq's most sectarian Sunni leaders. The resistance organizations he backed had cooperated with Al Qaeda in attacks against Shiites. "Sheikh Harith fights and defends his country and his identity, and is fighting Iran and the Americans," Juzu explained.

Juzu defended the need for Sunnis in Lebanon to arm themselves. "It's natural when a man feels he is in danger to protect himself," he said. "It's easy to make war in Lebanon. The army would split in two if a civil war happened. If there are two equal poles, it's good, it will prevent war; if one side has more power, there can be war." Despite all this, he said, "If there is a war against Israel I am with Hizballah. Anybody who fights Israel—an Iranian, a communist—the Arab people will support him."

The Sunnis of Lebanon are, of course, very diverse and not at all monolithic in their values or motivations, and the struggle within their community, as well as within Lebanon, is not between radicals and moderates. It can more accurately be described as a competition between haves and have nots. In Lebanon, as elsewhere, the poor have only two choices: to accept their fate or rebel. While rebellion in the 1960s or '70s might have come under a leftist, secular, Marxist, or nationalist guise, today the language of rebellion is often that of Al Qaeda.

Although Lebanese Maronites—Syriac Eastern Catholics—have a mythology of being victimized by the Syrians, the Sunnis of Tripoli suffered much more when their city was bombarded. The Syrian presence was more pronounced in the north as well. In the 1980s there was a major face-off between Salafis and Syrians in the north. In 2000 Najib Mikati, a Sunni politician competing with Rafiq al-Hariri, began to rehabilitate Sunni Islamists from Tawhid and elsewhere. He even tried to free the prisoners from Dinniyeh, though he failed to do so—this maneuver was left to Saad al-Hariri in 2005. Mikati began his campaign to court Salafis when he feared the Muslim Brotherhood would

not support him. It was only in 2004 that the Future Movement approached
northern Salafis, and their relationship remains ambiguous to this day. The
Future Movement had turned the formerly anti-Syrian elements of Tawhid
into their street gangs in Tripoli, while other Tawhid veterans sided with pro-
Syrian politicians such as Mikati. Lebanon's Salafis were divided, and Hariri
did what he and other rich Sunni politicians usually do: he bought people's
loyalty and calm.

Clerics close to the Future Movement such as Bilal Barudi tried to buy Fatah al-Islam off, but the group was neither a March 14 creation nor a Syrian
one. State sponsors were no longer needed for these sinuous, nonstate entities.
This pattern of buying support was not unique to Tripoli; in Sidon, in southern Lebanon, the Future Movement co-opted the Communists. "They were
indiscriminate in accepting support as long as they received votes or loyalty,
whether from Al Qaeda or former Communists," says As'ad Abu Khalil, a
Lebanese-American professor of political science at California State, Stanis-
laus. "Mikati capitalized on longstanding fanatical Sunni sentiment. Mikati
and Rafiq al-Hariri had the same problem: yes, they did have the support of
Syrian intelligence, but they wanted to institutionalize their bases of support.
They needed permanent sources of support so they . . . went to areas where
they fielded candidates and tried to co-opt existing forces on the ground."

Salafis typically rejected the very notion of elections, viewing democracy as
an alternative to religion and hence apostasy. But in Lebanon, especially beginning in 2005, Salafis campaigned and voted despite the fact that the system required a Christian president. Their motivation was to protect Sunnis, and
clerics advised their followers to vote for the March 14 coalition. Traditional
Salafis perceived the Hariri assassination as an attack on Sunni power. They received money from Saudis as well as the Hariri network and justified their interpretation of Islam in terms of defending Sunnis against an alleged Shiite
threat. The Saudis had been battling a domestic Al Qaeda franchise since 2003,
and as a result they had cut off support for jihadist Salafis. This allowed Future
to come in and provide funds in exchange for moderation and cooperation, regarded by some of the rank and file as a betrayal.

ACCORDING TO A FORMER military commander of the Tawhid movement
who had spent eleven years in a Syrian prison, "Tripoli is a reservoir for Sunni
jihadists in Lebanon." Hundreds of men had left Tripoli to fight in Iraq, and
veterans of the Dinniyeh incident from Tripoli who had been released had also
joined Fatah al-Islam. A veteran of Islamist movements, he believed that Fatah
al-Islam was not allied with Syria or the March 14 coalition. There was a con-
fluence between the interests of Syria and some of the Salafis, he said, but
March 14 supported the "official Salafis" such as those in the Independent

Islamic Gathering. He attributed some of the motivation to statements by Ayman al-Zawahiri, who had declared Lebanon a land for jihad and described the UN peacekeeping mission in the south as a crusader occupation. The Mujahideen Shura Council in Iraq had decided to fight the Americans in Lebanon, he said, and dispatched fighters there as well.

While Fatah al-Islam was not a creation of Saudi Arabia, or the Future Movement, or even Syria, as various parties in Lebanon allege, it did find a welcoming environment in northern Lebanon. Tripoli has a tradition of armed militancy and is full of armed groups and experienced veterans. When a Saudi militant named Juhayman al-Utaibi took over the Grand Mosque in Mecca in 1979, a key moment in jihadist Salafi history, three of his accomplices were from Tripoli. In addition to the Tawhid movement and Kanan Naji's Jund Allah, there is also Suyuf Allah, or the Swords of God, founded by a judge in a religious court. As a result there was no need for Sunni leaders to turn to jihadists, since they had an available pool of veterans from the 1980s Tawhid experience. While conspiracy theorists have blamed Sunni leaders in Lebanon for arming their people, and there have been some independent initiatives of this nature, it is just as likely that the Sunnis were responding to pressure from below. Not responding would mean losing ground and popularity. The Muslim Brotherhood, embodied in the Jamaa Islamiya movement in Lebanon, was weakened in Tripoli because it failed to propose any solution for the events in Lebanon, according to Patrick Haenni of the International Crisis Group in Beirut. Haenni, who has also studied the Brotherhood in Egypt, explained that it normally operates under the slogan "Islam is the solution," but in Lebanon, as the Shiite Hizballah movement had also conceded, this cannot be offered. As a result people have been pushed toward private initiatives, while the traditional Salafis have lost ground because they are too close to power and too moderate. In late 2006, in the Bab al-Tabbaneh slums of Tripoli, one banner that went up above the streets called for Saad al-Hariri to "arm us and leave the rest to us."

Tripoli was once the main city in Lebanon; in the nineteenth century, Beirut was a backwater in comparison. The main publishing houses and intellectuals were all in Tripoli. When Lebanon was cut out from Syria, Tripolitans protested in opposition. Traditionally Lebanon's Sunnis were hostile to the idea of Lebanon itself, which many viewed as a Christian project at odds with Arab nationalism. Tripoli's economy suffered after it was separated from Syria. Rafiq al-Hariri helped spread Saudi money to buy votes in the north. Young people who might have gone to study in Jordan or Egypt instead went to study in Saudi Arabia. Saudi money also made its way to traditional Salafis as long as they avoided overt politics. When the jihadists appeared there was a sense among some in the March 14 coalition that the newcomers were their friends and could be political allies. The increasingly sectarian rhetoric used by

Lebanese politicians and clerics provided the space for jihadist Salafis to feel at home. Tripoli, Lebanon's second-largest city, is a majority-Sunni city with few other groups represented. During the civil war Sunni militias battled the Syrians there. The quality of life in some parts of Tripoli, and in the poor villages of Akkar nearby, resembled the Palestinian camps.

In June 2007, a Sunni member of Parliament called Walid Idu was blown up. He had been very pro-Syria until 2005, like many of the Future Movement's members. When Idu's body was brought to the hospital, sectarian chants could be heard. "Allah, Hariri, Tariq al-Jadida!" some shouted, modifying the Shiite pro-Hizballah chant "Allah, Nasrallah, and all of Dahiyeh!" Others chanted the names of early Sunni leaders like Omar and Uthman, and warned that the blood of Sunnis was boiling and that they wanted revenge on President Lahoud, Syrian President Assad, and Hizballah's Nasrallah. At Idu's funeral procession some mourners chanted for Hariri, Saddam, and Zarqawi, while others chanted for the United States. "Sunni! Sunni! Sunni!" they shouted. Some also shouted support for Libya, apparently because Libya was implicated in the death of the Amal Movement's founder, Imam Musa Sadr. "My dick, Nasrallah, and all of Dahiyeh!" others shouted, and "We don't want sectarianism, but God is with the Sunnis!"

According to Omar Nashabe, a Sunni journalist with the leading independent paper *Al Akhbar*, "March 14 created the environment by supporting Sunni *assabiya*." He told me that when Lebanon's mufti, the main Sunni cleric appointed by the state, spoke at the government headquarters in Beirut following the initiation of the Shiite sit-in the downtown area close to the Prime Minister's office, he had called Siniora "our prime minister" (meaning the Sunnis) and stated that nobody (meaning the Shiites) would be allowed to remove him. Nashabe mocked the bogeyman of the Persian invasion. "Traditionally Maronites were said to be closest to the West," he said. "After Hariri's death it was the Sunni sect. The Saudi government pushed this to show that Sunnis are close to the American agenda, but most combatants of Fatah al-Islam were Saudis." Nashabe explained that groups like Fatah al-Islam are not necessarily linked to any regime, nor do they have to be state-sponsored. Instead they benefit, like other criminal groups, from the tensions and organized crime in Lebanon. Like the Sunnis in Iraq, the Sunnis of Lebanon feel weak and on retreat compared with the Shiites, with no clear identity. As a result it often seems as if they support a hodgepodge of different and contradictory causes, like the disparate chants heard at Idu's funeral.

According to As'ad Abu Khalil, "Hizballah's arms existed from the 1990s until 2005, and back then it was praised by the same Sunni voices who were aligned with them. The Hariri Saudi alliance has been successful in alarming Sunnis in the wake of Hariri's assassination. After the failure of Israel they tried to drive a bigger wedge between Sunnis and Hizballah. The Saudis surpassed the success of Al Qaeda in deepening the Sunni-Shiite rift—they are the heirs of Zarqawi in that regard, utilizing their media and defining every political issue in pure Sunni-Shiite term. The Saudis are the pillar of the American agenda in the Middle East and want to further American interests. The U.S. wants to weaken Hamas and Hizballah. So they make Hizballah seem not as a resistance movement (as it was perceived by Sunnis up until 2005) but portray it as a sectarian force that furthers Iranian interests in the region through their media, publishing houses, statements of their politicians. They control the culture industry in the region. Saudis control Arab newspapers in the Arab world and outside."

To understand the point of view of Hizballah's policy-makers, I met with the cerebral Nawaf al-Musawi, a key adviser to Nasrallah, as well as one of Hizballah's most ubiquitous public faces and head of its foreign policy unit. Just recently Ahmad Fatfat, a key Future Movement figure who was the former interior minister and current minister of youth and sport, had described Nasrallah's May 2007 statement on red lines (see Chapter Six) as the worst political mistake the Shiite leader had ever made. I asked Musawi about this. Nasrallah had been concerned about three issues, he told me. "First, protecting the Lebanese army, because it is the guarantee that prevents civil war from happening. If it is weakened, the pro-American faction in Lebanon will ask for the deployment of multinational forces. Second, preventing a new 'War of the Camps' in Lebanon and preventing Palestinians from being targets of new massacres and tragedies. This would destroy Lebanon and deepen the suffering of Palestinians, and would disperse the Palestinians and negate their right of return. Third, preventing Lebanon from becoming a place of war for Al Qaeda. This would transform Lebanon into an oven, and the coals of this oven would be the bodies and property of Lebanese and Palestinians. The Bush administration transformed Iraq into a place of war with Al Qaeda, and now it is a place of massacres, and we don't want our country to become a place of massacres. So let the Bush administration solve their problems away from Lebanon."

He rejected the notion that Sunni ideology had changed. "The new thing that happened with Hariri was the increase of Saudi influence in the Sunni environment," he said, "And this happened with Syrian approval and cognizance, because without Hafiz al-Assad's approval, Hariri would never have been prime minister. The Lebanese Sunni position reflects the Saudi position. The sectarian tension in Lebanon is enhancing Saudi influence in Lebanon. And the other way around as well: Saudi influence is enhancing sectarian tensions in Lebanon."

Musawi insisted that the Future Movement, which dominated the Interior Ministry, was supporting jihadist Salafis in Lebanon. "These were the Sunni reserves to fight the Shiites," he said. "Until Nahr al-Barid, the Ministry of Interior characterized the Palestinians as part of the Sunni reserves that would fight with them against Shiites. This idea of building a Sunni militia to fight Shiites began after the killing of Hariri. Since 2005 I was warning European officials on a constant basis and let them know that we see what the house of Hariri is doing with Sunni extremists and Salafis, and this is a very dangerous game and it will be against he who plays with it, as it happened in Afghanistan. As for us, we are not looking for any war with anybody, internally or externally. Our only objective is to defend and protect our country and preserve its stability." He blamed Bandar bin Sultan, the former Saudi ambassador to Washington, for the creation of groups like Fatah al-Islam. "It is Bandar's project to take Saudi Salafis and bring them here to fight Hizballah."

Musawi dismissed the notion that Hizballah wanted to impose a Shiite state. "We understand the political reality of Lebanon very well," he said. "No single group can rule by itself. The Lebanese can't be governed except by consensus, and we want a democratic and consensual country."

In recent months a military alliance backed by the United States had been established in the region, and U.S. Secretary of State Condoleezza Rice had even explained that American arms shipments to Saudi Arabia were meant "to counter the negative influences of Al Qaeda, Hizballah, Syria, and Iran." "It's an illusion," Musawi said. "Even the countries allied with the U.S. know Bush will not stay long. So these allies are not serious. The Saudis have their own concerns, Egypt and Jordan have their own concerns. If Rice says this, it doesn't mean the Saudis will do this. They will do what's in their best interest." But like other Hizballah leaders, Musawi was concerned about the role of Jordan. Its intelligence agents were said to be in Lebanon, and Sunni militiamen were being trained in Jordan.

He rejected accusations that the demonstrations in downtown Beirut were an "occupation." "Beirut is a cosmopolitan city in the international sense," he said, "and a city for all Lebanese and its demographic fabric is proof of this. It's not true that Beirut has one sectarian identity. It has Orthodox, Maronites, Shiites, etc., and Beirut is our capital. The Shiite presence in Lebanon is an old one. We are not refugees or guests. If they don't like it, they can go find another place."

Nothing was unique about Hizballah possessing an armed wing. "All the sectarian militias have weapons," he said. "The only thing we have that they don't have is missiles, and these cannot be used in a civil war." But Musawi conceded that Hizballah might not have succeeded in explaining its position on Syria to the people of the north, who had suffered under the Syrian occupation, but he reminded me that until the mid-1990s the Syrians had supported Hizballah's rivals. "I won't defend the military, political, or security performance of the Syrians. We were the first victims of the Syrians." He also reminded me that most of the so-called anti-Syrian politicians had collaborated closely with the Syrians politically and financially until the Hariri assassination.

They had thanked Syria in 2005 for one reason, he said: their support for the re-sistance. "We are friends or enemies based on the position on Israel, not a struggle for power or sectarian differences."

Superglue and Sectarianism

As the Americans tried to galvanize Sunnis in the region to view Iran and its allies as a threat, they showed more signs of succeeding in Lebanon than any-where outside Iraq. Events in Beirut in early 2008 reminded me of Baghdad in 2004, when the civil war was just beginning and every morning we would hear of small sectarian incidents. New militias were being formed, such as the all-Sunni Tripoli Brigades in the north. In Beirut, street fights regularly occurred between members of the Future Movement and the Shiite Amal Movement. Amal's young men were more thuggish, and the movement was less ideologi-cal and disciplined than Hizballah, which normally avoided being drawn into internal conflict.

In December 2007 Brig. Gen. Francois al-Hajj was killed by a car bomb. It was the twelfth political assassination in the past three years but the first tar-geting an army officer. Hajj was expected to be the next commander of Lebanon's army, but he had also been in charge of the army's operations in Nahr al-Barid. He had been the army's liaison with Hizballah and was not at all close to the March 14 camp, so it seemed unlikely that opposition forces were behind it. On the other hand, it may have been the hand of Fatah al-Islam reaching out for revenge. At an opposition demonstration, the army shot and killed seven Shiites who were protesting extended power cuts, com-plaining that the pro-opposition area of Dahiyeh had more cuts than pro-government Christian and Sunni areas. Neglect of Shiites was the whole rea-son Hizballah had created its so-called "state within a state."

In the first few months of 2008 small clashes between Sunni and Shiite mili-tias occurred regularly. A January roadside bomb targeted an American diplo-matic convoy, but it was less newsworthy than the increasing sectarian polarization—which grew worse following the assassination that month of the Sunni Internal Security Forces official who was himself investigating Lebanon's numerous political assassinations. At his funeral crowds chanted, "The blood of Sunnis is boiling!" The next month Saad al-Hariri seemed to move the country closer to a civil war. "If they are after a confrontation, we are up for the job," the Future Movement leader announced. Sunni thugs then took to the streets and shot into the air in celebration. One Friday the sheikh of the Dhunurein Mosque, in Beirut's Ras al-Nabaa neighborhood (formerly a front line between Christians and Muslims, now a front line between Sunnis and Shiites), declared that Beirut was occupied and Sunnis had to defend it. The implication was that Shiites were occupying Beirut and that they were the threat. The following day young men from the Shiite Amal militia vandalized the mosque. Graffiti warned Shiites to beware of Sunni rage and invoked the names of early Islamic leaders whom Shiites revile, such as Omar and Muawiya.

In Tariq al-Jadida's main shopping street, Afif al-Tibi, there was a huge commotion one Monday morning following weekend clashes. The streets were lined with about two dozen retail and wholesale clothing stores owned by Shiites, who are a minority in this largely Sunni enclave just north of Shiite southern Beirut. At least five of these shops had their locks clogged with superglue by Future members. Earlier anti-Shiite slogans had been spray-painted on the Shiite-owned shops. After the superglue incident some Shiite shop owners felt threatened and left their shops closed, choosing to stay home. That weekend there had been intense clashes in the Ras al-Nabaa district. Members of the Future Movement had attacked an Amal Movement office. Following the fighting Future supporters stood guard at every street corner in the surrounding area. Many carried chains, metal clubs, or M-16 automatic rifles. They included Lebanese Kurds. After one young man concealed his M-16 from a passerby, another shouted at him, "Why are you hiding it? Show it, we don't care! Let them know that we have guns too!" Shooting could be heard all night, and in Tariq al-Jadida supporters of the Future Movement destroyed the locally famous Ramadan Juice shop, which was owned by a Shiite man from Dahiyeh and had been open in the neighborhood for twenty years. Future members claimed he was a spy for Hizballah. One Future member explained why they were harassing local Shiites. "We don't want them in Beirut," he said. "Beirut is only for Sunnis."

At the time of the superglue incident, the head of the local Future militia on Afif al-Tibi Street was Abu Ahmad. He had prevented hotheaded militiamen from burning down the Shiite-owned shops. He had also previously refused to arm his men or allow them to maintain a weapons depot because he sought to avoid problems with Shiites. He explained that Sunnis had been living side by side with their Shiite neighbors for many years and that they should solve their problems peacefully. He was replaced, however, by a more aggressive man, said to hate Shiites and love weapons, who armed the young men.

Although the Shiites of Tariq al-Jadida were not overtly political, it was becoming clear that they were not trusted or wanted. Militiamen assigned to intelligence duties stood watch on street corners all day long. Young men worked on various shifts, usually at night, getting paid a few hundred dollars a month, with the promise of a bonus if they took part in fighting. Some were posted in other areas, where more bodies were needed to confront the Shiite Amal movement, a less ideological and more sectarian group than Hizballah. Sunni militiamen coordinated with members of the security forces and army. The Future Movement also mobilized Sunnis from Akkar, who were considered more aggressive than Beiruti Sunnis. Other "real Sunnis" were imported from Din- niyeh and the town of Arsal in the Bekaa Valley to defend the Sunnis of Beirut. Numerous apartment and hotel rooms around the city were rented for them. The Future militias were also recruiting retired army and intelligence opera- tives. There was even a Future security company in Tariq al-Jadida, its office fes- tooned with posters of Rafiq and Saad al-Hariri. Senior March 14 leader Walid Jumblatt confided to me that Sunnis were joining militias and training in Jor- dan. He disapproved of this and said they should join the security forces.

Shaqer al-Berjawi was one of the new militia leaders in Tariq al-Jadida. His movement was called the Arab Current. Berjawi had once belonged to the Murabitun militia and fought in west Beirut during the civil war. After Hariri was assassinated, he began forming his new movement (with support from the Future Movement) because Sunnis felt leaderless and weak. He recruited Fa- tah supporters from the Palestinian camps to fight alongside Sunnis, a growing phenomenon. Hamas members in Beirut blame his people for clashes that oc- curred between rival Palestinian factions. Berjawi participated in the January 2007 clashes and is rumored to be among the Sunni snipers who were target- ing Shiites. He was arrested afterward and accused of weapons smuggling but soon was released.

I met a nineteen-year-old black-market weapons dealer in Tariq al-Jadida who had been selling guns illegally for nearly three years. "Its very profitable," he told me. "You can double your investment, especially in these times, when all gun prices are getting more expensive lately and everybody is worried about themselves and getting ready for the 'zero hour.' People will defend their sect." He explained that he sold to Sunnis, and occasionally to Christians or Druze, but never to Shiites because "these are the people we want to fight and they have a lot of weapons." He admitted that until 2005 he had never heard sectar- ian language. "Now everybody is speaking about sectarian conflict," he said. "Now even a four-year-old or a six-year-old kid speaks of Sunnis or Shiites."

Business started getting good for him after the so-called "Tuesday incident," which is how many Lebanese refer to the January 2007 clashes, and it im- proved again after the "Thursday incident," when Amal and Future supporters clashed in 2008. "After those incidents, people demanded guns in a big way," he told me. The Kalashnikov was in highest demand, with people often opting for a package deal including an ammunition vest and ammunition for eight hun- dred dollars.

Most of his customers were in Tariq al-Jadida, where he said three-quarters of the people were now armed. The majority of his clients were men between the ages of twenty and thirty, though women were also purchasing small pis- tols. Almost all of his clients were with the Future Movement.

The young gun dealer, thin and tattooed, also belonged to the local Future militia and worked as a guard. He explained that he had received paramilitary training on a base in Akkar for twenty days along with about sixty-five other young Sunni men. Retired army sergeants had done most of the training, though foreigners, including an Australian of Lebanese descent, had trained them in close protection. The training was conducted under the cover of the Secure Plus security company, one of several owned by Saad al-Hariri. The Interior Ministry was stacked with Sunnis loyal to Hariri, and its Internal Security Forces were viewed by Hizballah as a Sunni militia. Pro-Hariri control of the ministry has eased the way for legalizing these companies-cum-militias.

By the spring of 2008, it seemed as though there were two Lebanons: a Sunni one and a Shiite one, with less important groups just bystanders. The youth, not remembering the violence of the 1980s, seemed eager for another civil war. It was a good time to join Sunni militias, the gun dealer said, because there were several groups recruiting, and this was driving up prices for new recruits. The Murabitun, a civil war–era Sunni militia that had been reactivated, allegedly paid its men nearly three hundred dollars a month. Some Secure Plus recruits guarded installations such as the Saudi embassy. Others wore civilian clothing and monitored Sunni neighborhoods or stood on standby, well armed and uniformed, in case fighting erupted. If recruits proved especially capable, my young interlocutor explained, they were sent to front-line areas such as Ras al-Nabaa, where there were many Shiites. Some were selected for more advanced training in Jordan, which lasted longer. His brother had gone for this training, but graduates were secretive about what they were taught.

I asked him if he wanted to fight Shiites. "Definitely," he said. "I want to defend my sect. Shiite areas are different. There are no police there, they train kids from an early age and put hatred in their hearts from an early age and teach them that Sunnis killed their leaders. I feel threatened leaving Sunni areas. Iran and Syria have a plan to control Lebanon but so far have not succeeded." He drank alcohol and was not religious, so I asked him why he was fighting for Sunni Islam. "My identity card says I am a Sunni Muslim," he said, "and I have to defend my sect. Before I didn't know the difference between Sunnis and Shiites. Shiites made us hate them by their acts." He expected that there would be a war with Shiites, and he hoped so, not just because it would be good for business. "Sunnis can win only if they are united," he told me with obvious approval, but he explained that they were not relying merely on the Sunnis of Lebanon but on the help of Saudi Arabia and other Sunni countries. "The Saudis will help. The Saudis are funding all this, not Hariri. Tariq al-Jadida is the castle of Sunnis. If it falls, Lebanon falls."

The May Events

On May 1 Walid Jumblatt, the most prominent Druze politician in Lebanon and the leader of the Progressive Socialist Party, called a press conference and announced the discovery of cameras that were monitoring Beirut International Airport. He implied that Hizballah was planning an operation and that it might fire shoulder-launched rockets at planes on the runway. He also warned that Hizballah had its own communications network. Two days later Jumblatt called for the Iranian ambassador's expulsion and asked that flights from Iran to Beirut be banned to curtail the delivery of financial and military aid to Hizballah. Jumblatt then attacked the airport's security chief, Gen. Wafiq Shuqair, accusing him of conspiring with Hizballah to install the secret cameras. Two days later, on May 5, Lebanese judicial authorities announced that they had ordered an investigation into the affair. Coincidentally or not, statements from American military officials were published in the Western media that day accusing Hizballah of training Iraqi Shiite militias.

On May 6 the government reassigned Shuqair. Given Hizballah's angry reaction to his removal, it appears the charges against him were true. Then the Council of Ministers questioned the legality of Hizballah's parallel communications network, which was a key element of the group's military command and control ability. The government called the communications network "an attack on state sovereignty." It was the first time Hizballah's military was challenged internally; until then the weapons of the resistance had been off-limits. The government's moves were conducted in coordination with the Americans and the UN envoy, who warned that Hizballah "maintains a massive paramilitary infrastructure separate from the state," which "constitutes a threat to regional peace and security." Nasrallah's deputy Sheikh Naim Qasim said the network was an integral part of the resistance. It seemed like a culmination of a process beginning in September 2004, when the UN Security Council passed Resolution 1559, which supported Hizballah's rivals' call to disarm the resistance.

The General Federation of Labor Unions called for a strike and demonstration on May 7 to demand that the government raise the monthly minimum wage, which had not been changed since 1996. Hizballah and its supporters planned their mobilization for the same day. Early that morning Shiite demonstrators blocked bridges and roads throughout the city, including the important airport road, with burning tires, vehicles, garbage containers, cement blocks, and earthen mounds. The airport suspended flights. Many of the demonstrators were masked; some were armed.

A grenade exploded in the Corniche al-Mazraa neighborhood, wounding several people. As it became clear that the situation was getting out of control, the General Federation of Labor Unions called off the demonstration and strike it had planned for that day. As Sunni and Shiite *zaaran* clashed, throwing stones at one another, Lebanese soldiers separated the two sides by firing into the air and using tear gas. Upon hearing that the Future Movement's office in the Nuweiri district was destroyed, Sunni supporters of Hariri in the north and the Beqaa gathered to come to Beirut and face the opposition. Small armed clashes occurred throughout the city.

I hurried toward Ras al-Nabaa with some local journalists searching for where shots were coming from and spotted Amal fighters hiding behind street corners and Sunni fighters huddled in front of Future offices. As armed men materialized from behind corners on both sides, I suddenly realized things were potentially more lethal than I had thought. I wanted to leave immediately, but Nada Bakri, a fearless stringer for the *New York Times*, went charging ahead, so I followed her, not wanting to appear to be cowardly. In the end, an armed man with a revolver in front of a Future office told us to go away, which I did with relief. That evening Hizballah supporters fortified barricades to block the road to the airport. Tents were brought in preparation for a long stay.

On May 8 I returned to Corniche al-Mazraa, to the divide between Barbir and Tariq al-Jadida. Hundreds of disorganized Shiite youth, mostly teenagers from other areas, were gathered on the road. Lebanese soldiers prevented them from crossing to the other side. The call to prayer blared from the nearby Sunni Jamal Abdel Nasr Mosque. The Shiite *zaaran* stood up. "The blood of Shiites is boiling!" they shouted, adding religious slogans. Some were holding stones or chips of cinder blocks; others had knives, clubs, and plastic bottles full of gasoline. They threw their stones and cinder-block chips across the road at the soldiers and the Sunni neighborhood. The soldiers threw the stones back. One of them was filming the Shiite youth. Some soldiers pleaded with the youth to stop, while others loaded and aimed their M-16s. I was surprised by how provocative the Amal supporters were. For them it was just a show of force to intimidate Sunnis. Older men, with serious faces, well-groomed stubble, and shirts buttoned all the way up, herded the boys. Whenever it seemed as though the boys were about to cross to the Sunni side, they were reined in. I felt as though Hizballah had Amal pit bulls who were foaming at the mouth, eager to attack, and that Hizballah was letting them bark and bite a little to show the other side that it was holding the leash and could let go at any time.

Many of the families living in Barbir had packed up and left for the mountains or their villages, expecting things to get worse. That afternoon, a few hundred Shiite *shabab* (youth) were organized in rows. Many Amal men wore combat boots and combat pants. They squatted and peered across the road at Tariq al-Jadida, squinting and pointing, looking for snipers in the buildings. Most of them were the same young men I had seen the day before. I saw a few men wearing the gray Internal Security Forces uniforms working together with the Amal men, who set up checkpoints and demanded identity papers in plain sight of the Lebanese soldiers. I sat on the street next to a few *shabab* who were resting, waiting for something to happen. One of them was from Dahiyeh. "Hamra Street is for them," he said of Sunnis, and told me that there were Sunni volunteers from Akkar there. We discussed buying arms. The *shabab* told me that AK-47s were coming in from Iraq. I asked them why they were there. "We are here to defend the weapons of the resistance," one of them said. "We as the Shiite sect are targeted. They are removing high-ranking Shiite officers from their positions." We discussed which identity mattered most to them. Three agreed that they were Shiites only, not Arab or Lebanese, much to my surprise. "We are here to fight Qabbani," one said, referring to the mufti of Lebanon. In the afternoon sandwiches were brought for all the *shabab*. I noticed men appearing with AK-47s and other rifles, sitting on corners, talking among themselves, getting ready for something.

That day the order came down from the Future leadership for the presenter on Future TV to begin the news segment on Nasrallah's speech with the inflammatory "How the resistance became the occupier." In Barbir we sat around listening to Nasrallah's speech from car radios. Everybody cheered. Nasrallah said that the cause of the crisis was the attack on Hizballah's military apparatus, which was "a declaration of war . . . against the resistance and its weapons for the benefit of America and Israel. The communications network is the significant part of the weapons of the resistance. I said that we will cut off the hand that targets the weapons of the resistance. . . . Today is the day to carry out this decision." The opposition-led activities would not cease until the government revoked its decisions, Nasrallah concluded. Saad al-Hariri then responded in a speech calling the opposition actions a "crime" and warning, "We will not accept that Beirut kneel before anyone." By Beirut, he meant Sunnis.

As the speeches ended, shots could be heard. The Lebanese army retreated as if on command, their vehicles rumbling away. The boys shouted in triumph and jumped. More and more armed men emerged from a building—some with ammunition vests, some in designer clothes with carefully gelled hair. They stood behind corners emptying their magazines into the buildings across the street without discrimination, firing from RPGs. The troops of boys who had been calling for blood until then fled, some started crying. The local commander, a dark-skinned man in his forties called Haj Firas, was a former Amal fighter who was now with Hizballah. He was frustrated with his men for not aiming properly. He took one fighter's AK-47 and demonstrated, shouting, "Aim and shoot!" Shots were being returned from buildings and street corners on the other side, but nobody was aiming at anything. "It's open now," one Amal fighter told me. "It will get worse. I hope so, so we can win." Reinforcements were brought in from Dahiyeh. A commander arrived and reported that Amal leader Nabih Beri had ordered them not to shoot too much. One of the men cursed Beri. "He wants us not to shoot too much, but they are shooting a lot at us," he complained. Suddenly I recognized one of the Amal fighters. A fit young man, with gelled hair like the rest of them, he worked at the juice bar in my health club in the evenings and was a geography teacher during the day. We paused for a moment in surprised mutual recognition; then I sprinted across the street, ducking to avoid sniper fire. As fire from automatic weapons, sniper rifles, and the occasional RPG went back and forth, I was trapped on one block. I wound up spending the night in the lobby of an apartment building nearby with local journalists from Al Jazeera and other media.

The next morning, May 9, I walked home past armed Amal men on patrol, some of whom waved their party's flag as they passed indifferent Lebanese soldiers and headed into Sunni areas. Clashes continued in much of Beirut, and the occasional RPG explosion could be heard. The Future newspaper office was attacked and burned. Hizballah surrounded the Future News television building, and the Lebanese army advised the station to halt all broadcasts, which it did. Ash Sharq radio, also belonging to the Future Movement, was taken off the air. Future TV offices containing archives were burned down after militiamen from the Syrian Social Nationalist Party (SSNP) clashed with at least thirty-five armed Future supporters there. The SSNP looted the Future media office and hung pictures of the Syrian president. Shutting down the main news outlet may have been wise from Hizballah's point of view—it prevented Future's ability to mobilize supporters and probably helped prevent more violence—but it looked ugly, even if people were reminded that former Prime Minister Rafiq al-Hariri had shut down many opposition media outlets himself. Beirut residents were stunned to see Hizballah soldiers patrolling the streets and manning positions. They were in control of Hamra and Verdun, and there were a few last gun battles in the Sadat area as the Hizballah soldiers surrounded Hariri's headquarters in Qoraitem.

In the morning March 14 officials were summoned for an urgent meeting in Maarab at the home of Samir Geagea, the leader of the extreme right-wing Christian Lebanese Forces. They decided to escalate the conflict in the north, where Hizballah and its allies were weaker. The mountain road from Beirut to the Beqaa Valley was closed, as was the main highway in Tripoli and the road to Halba in Akkar. The road leading to the Masnaa border crossing with Syria was blocked by angry Sunnis from the Beqaa, especially the town of Majd al-Anjar.

I walked on west Beirut's Hamra Street and approached a group of soldiers wearing beards and irregular uniforms. I realized it was a mix of Hizballah soldiers and the Lebanese army. Some Hizballah soldiers had sacks of RPGs on their backs. A commander sat on a chair in front of the Crowne Plaza hotel. The streets were empty and shops were closed. A platoon of Hizballah soldiers patrolled in formation down Hamra, scanning the rooftops in all directions and covering one another. They wore knee pads and had gear like American soldiers. Their professionalism reminded me of the times I had patrolled the streets of Baghdad with Americans, except that some of these young men wore sneakers. They shooed away journalists and politely but firmly detained a friend and me; they removed his camera chips but for some reason allowed me to walk alongside their patrol all the way down Hamra Street. Once Hizballah secured locations throughout the city, it handed them over to the Lebanese army. It was clear the army—historically always a weak force—had taken sides and was collaborating with stronger side, the resistance, under the guise of appearing neutral.

In Tariq al-Jadida, I went looking for the Sunni reaction and ran into three men I had seen earlier. One had long hair, one was skinny, and one was fat. "You're talking about Amal and Hizballah, man," one told me when I asked him why they had given up so quickly. "There is no creed here. Sunnis fight for money. We were doing it for a hundred dollars. We're only good for waving flags and singing songs. We were betrayed by our own leaders, even by Saad al-Hariri himself. We thought we had guns and ammunition, but when we went to ask for bullets and ammunition, our organizers and leaders abandoned us." The Secure Plus headquarters had been burned down. One man denied they had surrendered to Hizballah. "We handed Tariq al-Jadida to the army ourselves," he said. "If they come back, our *shabab* are ready." Hizballah had twenty-five years of experience, one man told me, while local fighters in Tariq al-Jadida were getting high on pills. Close to the smoldering Secure Plus headquarters, a suspicious boy working security for Future checked our IDs. Angry youths surrounded us, but he assured them I was American and not working for Al Manar, Hizballah's television station.

Checkpoint One, where I had been stopped before the fighting, was now closed—nobody was there. "Here it's frustration," one Future militiaman man told me. "They laughed at us. All the leaders are liars. Saad is a liar. The army is with them." The volunteers from Akkar all ran away, they said. The fighters on the other side had all been Amal, they said. "If it was Hizballah, they would destroy us in a minute." I asked one man if he wanted a national unity government. "I didn't say yes and I didn't say no—nobody asked me," he said. "Ask them, the men with the guns."

The feelings of shame and betrayal were palpable on people's faces. "Beirut fell to AKs and RPGs," one man said. "We won't attack Shiite civilians, but they attacked Sunni civilians," said another. "Our allies inside and outside didn't help." "They're going to provoke us now; they want to make a Persian state." "We are calling the people of the world: we are under siege. We were five hundred fighters facing fifty thousand fighters."

The army had taken their weapons, the men complained. "We don't trust the army. The army was against us in the battle." They were worried that Shiite militias and their allies would come in now. "Secure Plus turned us down when we asked for weapons," many people said, explaining that they were also worried that their names were in files inside. So local Sunnis burned it down.

"We are frustrated and everybody is cursing Saad," one man said. "All militias in Lebanon, they pay money for their guys to prove themselves on the field," said one. "Our militia didn't support us. Now anybody who gives money or arms, everybody will support him." They complained that the Future militia leaders had turned off their phones the previous night, not answering when they called for help.

HIZBALLAH MEN were patrolling the streets of Beirut, calling into question their commitment never to use weapons inside Lebanon, though they justified this by claiming they were defending the resistance's weapons and that they sought no political advantage in the standoff. As Nasrallah explained at a press conference, Hizballah had used its weapons to defend its weapons. By the morning of May 9 all of west Beirut was in the hands of Hizballah or its armed allies. The government headquarters, called the Sérail, was surrounded, as were the homes of key March 14 leaders like Hariri and Jumblatt. It was the coup that never happened, but it galvanized the more militant Sunnis of the Beqaa and northern Lebanon. Even if Hizballah's motives were not sectarian, the group could not evade the fact that one side was Shiite and the other was Sunni.

That evening Sahar al-Khatib, a relatively unknown presenter on Future News, appeared on the right-wing LBC TV. She broke down and spoke emotionally, condemning the army for taking Hizballah's side. "We were driven out of the Future TV building," she said. "We did not want to surrender." Then she addressed the leaders of the opposition and the people of Dahiyeh and Baalbeq, meaning Shiites. She had given them a voice, she claimed. Now who would be the voice of the people of Beirut (meaning Sunnis)? Sunnis, she implied, were the people who said, "There is no god but God," meaning they were the real Muslims. She directly addressed Shiites, who she said wore ski masks on the streets of Beirut. "People who are proud of their actions do not wear ski masks," she said. Sunnis had opened their homes to Shiites in the July war. "They took you into their hearts," she lectured Shiites. "We prepared food for you with love during the July 2006 aggression, but you threw it on the ground." Shiites, she said, "have made me regret my objectivity" for reading the names of Shiite martyrs from the 2006 war. She had defended Shiites, she said. Who would now defend Sunnis when Future TV was shut down? Shiites had broken the hearts of Sunnis, she said, who loved them. It was rare to hear such openly sectarian language, but she grew more explicit. "Why do you hate us?" she asked. "You have awakened sectarianism in me. . . . You kill the people who build this country."

The Bush administration promised to provide the Siniora government with whatever support it needed against what it described as a Hizballah "offensive." March 14 officials described it as a coup.

The Sunni Response

On the night of May 9 the mufti of Akkar, Osama Rifai, went on television and radio and called indirectly for the Syrian Social Nationalist Party to be attacked, as revenge against the SSNP activists who had burned down the Future TV office in Beirut. Attacking Hizballah's weak ally in the north was a safe way to send Hizballah a message. "We'll teach them a lesson," he said. SSNP leaders and their allies believe that the Future Movement leadership, including Saad al–Hariri, gave an order for a response. Khaled Dhaher, a former member of Parliament and leading Islamist politician allied with the Future Movement, and Musbah al-Ahdab, an independent Tripolitan member of Parliament, helped to organize the response in the north. The decision was made to send a warning to the March 8 coalition in Halba. The SSNP had a weak presence in the north, and Halba was a small, majority-Sunni town whose people supported the Future Movement. The two parties had clashed three years earlier. On the night of May 9 armed supporters of the Future Movement took positions around Halba.

Halba is the capital of Lebanon's northern region of Akkar. Many of the towns sitting on the mountainous region afford views looking down all the way to the Mediterranean Sea. Green fields surrounded the town, with houses scattered on the green hills above it. Like most of Lebanon outside Beirut, it is a lawless region, at least in the sense that the state's presence is not strongly felt or seen. Shortly after 9 a.m. on the morning of May 10, young men set tires on fire and parked trucks to block the roads leading into Halba. Bright red flames rose from the tires and black smoke billowed up, concealing the low apartment buildings. The wind carried the stinging rubbery stench. Members of the Internal Security Forces, in their gray uniforms with red berets, strolled around next to the crowds of young men who stood around the burning tires. Others in the army's green uniforms took a look as well. They were not armed. More and more young men gathered, many carrying clubs and metal bars. Some zipped back and forth on scooters. They disappeared into the smoke. The rain that started to fall did nothing to slow the activities or the flames. Some dragged sandbags to fortify their roadblocks. Tractors came with tires piled on them and young men sitting on top. In Lebanon there always seem to be tires available to burn at roadblocks. Cars approaching turned around to look for a different route. At first traffic continued as normal—these armed acts of civil disobedience are normal in Lebanon, and the culprits are rarely punished.

Sunni leaders in the north used the loudspeakers on local mosques to call people together, and thousands of men gathered in the center of town for a demonstration. By now the sun was out again, shining on the sky-blue flags of the Future Movement as well as the green-and-black flags with Islamic slogans that men waved. Others carried posters of Rafiq and Saad al-Hariri. Many men clapped; others just watched. An Arab nationalist song from the 1960s blared from loudspeakers, sending the message that God would defeat the aggressors. Perhaps the organizers were trying to claim the mantle of Arab nationalism and deny it to their opponents. A speaker proclaimed that theirs was not a project of militias; it was the project of Rafiq al-Hariri, the project of education. Hariri did not graduate gangs or militias, he said. On one poster a man had written that Sayyid Hassan Nasrallah, whom he called Ariel Sharon, was fully responsible and should take his thugs and tyrants out of Beirut. Another sign said, "Saad is a red line."

Men shouted to God. Others chanted, "Oh, Nasrallah, you pimp! Take your dogs out of Beirut!" (which rhymes in Arabic). "Oh, Aoun, you pig! You should be executed with a chain!" "Tonight is a feast! Fuck Nasrallah!" "Nasrallah under the shoe!" "Who do you love? Saad!"

Suddenly in the distance shooting started. Some men ran away, while others ran toward it. One man in a loudspeaker shouted, "Fight! The order is yours!" Another man called for caution. "The Internal Security Forces should take the proper position so there won't be any attack here, and we ask the army to control the situation," he shouted. "The mufti is coming. Brothers, we need to control ourselves. We are delivering the wrong message to the others. We did not come to fight."

Armed men stood on the top floors of apartment buildings, looking down from balconies. Others on the street with M-16s and AK-47s used buildings for cover. Exchanges of fire echoed through town. Men gathered in corners and peered over to see where the shots were coming from. Crowds remained in the center of town, and religious leaders from Akkar's Sunni Endowment hurried to the scene to take part in the demonstration. Some were guarded by armed men in civilian clothes. Some members of the Internal Security Forces and Lebanese army also stood watching.

That morning fourteen members of the SSNP were manning the local party headquarters, which was in an apartment building off the main road, surrounded by trees. Founded in 1932 by Antoine Saadeh, the SSNP is an Arab nationalist party that calls for the establishment of a Greater Syria uniting all the countries of the Levant. It is one of the smaller parties in Lebanon, but it had allied itself with the powerful Hizballah and Amal-led March 8 bloc, and its militiamen were known for being more thuggish than most. It is not clear exactly what happened in the first moments of the battle, but one version suggests that around ten o'clock that morning hundreds of armed Future

Movement members and supporters attacked the SSNP office with automatic weapons and rocket-propelled grenades. The SSNP members had some light arms in their office, and when they returned fire, two of the attackers were killed. Another version, equally plausible, is that a mob armed with sticks and clubs began to attack the SSNP office, and it was then that two of the Future Movement supporters were killed by the SSNP men inside. Armed attacks against the fourteen men inside the office followed. Trucks brought more men from the area into town. Many of the vehicles belonged to Future Movement officials or allies such as Khaled Dhaher.

Sporadic gunfire soon turned into steady volleys and exchanges. After a few minutes the first RPG hit the building. Two hours later the fire was so intense that the SSNP men asked their leadership in Beirut to help them get out. The Beirut office tried to coordinate with the Lebanese army and Internal Security Forces, attempting to negotiate the peaceful surrender of the SSNP men to the army. The building had been set on fire, and by then the smoke was making it difficult for the men to stay inside.

Muhamad Mahmud Tahash was one of the SSNP men inside. A low-ranking member of the party, he had gone to the office that morning completely unaware of what the day had in store for him. "RPGs were coming down like rain," he later told me. "There was heavy shooting, and no army outside." He went out of the building, hoping to seek the army's protection, and was shot in the shoulder. "It shattered my bone," he said. "I started walking in between people to go out, then the rest of the men went out as I was walking. I was beaten by people with rifle butts and screwdrivers." He would later receive fifty stitches on his head. "I fell on the ground and they dragged me away to the Future Movement office, where they beat me," he said. The other men who followed Tahash out of the building were all unarmed. They had reached an agreement with the Lebanese army, and they assumed that the Future Movement supporters and militiamen were part of the agreement. The local Future Movement leader, Hussein al-Masri, who was present for all the day's events, had indeed told the army he agreed. But when the SSNP men emerged, one was hit with three shots and killed; another pretended to be dead; the others were all captured. Among them were other low-ranking members, guards, administrators, and a member of the local management committee. The Lebanese army was not there, but hundreds of armed men were. The SSNP men were beaten with stones and sticks, stabbed, burned, and shot in their legs to prevent their escape. The mob's attack was filmed by many of the participants.

The men were sprawled on the ground, swollen, bloody, and barely conscious. Hundreds of men continued to beat and taunt and shoot at them. "Mahmud, shoot him!" one man called out as somebody cursed a victim's female relatives and shots were fired. "We are Islam!" someone else shouted.

"God will make us victorious!" "Shoot him! This is for Beirut! Fuck his mother! You think we are Jews that you're shooting at us? Shoot the fucker! We are the rulers, you brother of a whore! Are you proud of yourself for shooting a Muslim?" "This guy shot Hariri's picture! This guy, this guy!" the man was then beaten with a stick. "God won't give you mercy! I'm going to shoot you like you shot my cousin! God is great!" One man in the crowd pleaded for the attackers to stop. "Enough, he's dead, enough! Oh, Muslims!" Others continued to attack and shout. "You infidels! You Jews! By God, I'll fuck your sister." "Bring the flagstick," somebody shouted. One of the victims was stabbed with a stick. "God is one! Pray for the Prophet!" The same lone voice continued to plead, "We are Muslims! In our religion this is forbidden! If they don't know the religion we know the religion! Act like Muslims! Guys, act like the Prophet has told you guys! Guys, we are Islam, God will give us victory . . . please, please!" One young boy asked to be allowed to abuse the wounded men. "I don't want to do anything, I don't want to do anything," he said. "I just want to break his arm." "We have four men in here and we have one inside as well! Guys, burn them! Burn them now!" "By God, I'll fuck your sister!" One of the wounded men moaned, "Oh, God! Oh, God!" One man pointed to one of the victims' necks and said, "I'm going to shoot you here! You're not going to die alone!" "Enough, Nabil, leave him!" Someone pleaded, while elsewhere the attack continued. "This is the first bastard that started shooting at us! And this one too, he shot at us directly, this one! Film me while I put my slipper in his mouth, film me!" "Make us proud, guys!" One young attacker with a Future Movement headband shouted to the men, "We want to fuck your sisters!" "Shoot the second one, come on!" "Fuck his mother!" "Guys, burn them!" "I'll fuck your sister!"

Two adjacent buildings were also attacked. Hundreds of men surrounded them and shot from all sides. "God is great!" they shouted as they burst into apartments and ransacked them. Residents were terrified; there was nobody in charge. They broke into one family's house and threatened a mother and her children, pointing their guns at them. "We will kill you," they said. One of the boys was nine years old. As one group of attackers left the apartment another would charge in, and the terror would begin again. As the families from the apartments fled down the streets, they walked past bodies and pools of blood. One of the apartments belonged to a Christian Lebanese army officer and his family. Like their neighbors, they watched their furniture get destroyed, their clothes flung about, their apartment shot up. "When there is so much violence and hatred, it's impossible to build a state," the officer later told me. The eighty-year-old father of one of the Christian SSNP members was also in a nearby building. Despite being weak and sick, he too was detained for much of the day and threatened with death. The office of Arc en Ciel, an aid organization that helped the handicapped and was located above the SSNP headquarters, was looted and destroyed. A nearby gas station whose owner was affiliated with the SSNP was also torched.

Survivors of the attack on the SSNP office who made it to local hospitals were attacked by mobs that were waiting for them. Nasr Hammoudah was killed when a fire extinguisher was shoved into his mouth and emptied into him. Mohamad Hammoudah, Abed Khodr Abdel Rahman, and Ammar Moussa were also attacked on their way to the hospital and upon their arrival.

Khaled Dhaher was one of the leaders of the mob. Witnesses implicated him in ordering some of the executions and even of shooting the SSNP prisoners himself. Dhaher protected Muhamad Tahash from execution and interrogated him, asking him how many men were in the office and what kind of weapons they had. One of the men approached and shot Tahash in the belly. Dhaher's bodyguard, who was Tahash's childhood friend, helped spare his life. He prevented a man from executing Tahash, so instead the man kicked Tahash in the face and broke his teeth as Dhaher looked on. While in captivity, Tahash observed Dhaher giving detailed orders to the mob. Dhaher told his men to attack the local Syrian Baath Party office. They told him it had been closed for three years. "I don't care," Dhaher responded. "Break in and burn it." Muhamad al-Masri, a local Future Movement leader, was also present. Dhaher's bodyguard locked Tahash in a room and called the Internal Security Forces to pick him up. They drove him to the hospital in a white civilian Mercedes-Benz. Tahash saw the mob waiting to kill survivors of the massacre. "I was left in the Mercedes by myself," he said. "Men came and tried to cut my arm off. They couldn't, so they twisted it and broke it. Then they emptied a fire extinguisher in my mouth and all over me. While they were attacking us, they accused us of defending Hizballah and the Shiites." Tahash's wife learned of the attack in Halba from the news. She called her husband's mobile phone, but a stranger answered. "Muhamad was burned to death," he told her. "Fuck you and fuck Antoine Saadeh [founder of the SSNP]."

As the men lay dying on the dirt, their attackers and other gleeful onlookers filmed them with their cellphones, bringing the lenses in close and squatting to get better angles. The men were kicked in the head. Some of them were forced to reveal their genitals so the attackers could determine if they were Muslim or Christian. All but two of the victims were Sunni Muslims. Some had been beaten to death; others were still struggling to move or breathe. Their bodies, turned to bloody pulps, lay strewn on the ground. The attackers disappeared. Fires continued to crackle inside the building. One of the men still had his shirt pulled up and his pants open. By 5 p.m. eleven men were dead, crushed, beaten, and shot to death. Soon crowds came to view the bodies. Old men and young boys filmed the dead. The Lebanese Red Cross finally arrived, and then the Internal Security Forces and the Lebanese army. The bodies were taken away in ambulances. Army vehicles rumbled into town, taking positions on the streets. As in January 2007, the offices of the SSNP were attacked because it was an easy target with no sectarian base and less immediate consequences. But the SSNP had a long memory and a history of seeking revenge, party members in Beirut warned me. They believed that the mayor of the Akkar town of Fnaydek and his brother were among the leaders of the mob and that the attacks had been ordered by senior Future Party men and Sunni politician and Parliament member Musbah al-Ahdab.

In Tripoli that day I saw a banner that said, "No to Wilayat al-Faqih," a reference to the Iranian system of government. That evening I interviewed Ahdab in his ostentatious Tripoli apartment. He had a small militia of dozens of fit armed men protecting him. One of his security guards belonged to Afwaj Trablus, the Tripoli Brigades. He was paid by Secure Plus. There were six or seven thousand men like him, he told me, who had been trained but not in the use of RPGs. A few had received advanced training in Jordan. "It would be better if the Syrians were here," he said ruefully. "At least there was security." Ahdab's eyes were bloodshot and wide in near hysteria. His breath smelled strongly of alcohol. An Iranian militia had taken over an Arab capital, he told me. As we spoke, we got word of clashes in the slums of Bab al-Tabbaneh.

I raced over with a Lebanese friend. There was no power, but the buildings were illuminated by the occasional thunderous flashes of RPGs. At a nearby traffic circle, we saw dozens of men running toward Bab al-Tabbaneh carrying launchers and RPGs. They had long beards and were obviously Salafis. We stopped to talk to several men who stayed behind. They were fighting the Nusayris, they told me, using the pejorative term for Alawites, in the hilltop neighborhood of Jabal Mohsen, which overlooked Bab al-Tabbaneh. "They've hated us for 1,400 years," one man told me, referring to Shiites. "The rich are in Beirut," a garage owner who was watching the fighting said. "We are the poorest area of Lebanon." "They are afraid of Tabbaneh. They are afraid of Sunnis," another man told me. "We have *assabiya* for our sect."

Hundreds of fighters rushed into the blackness. "This fight is revenge for Beirut," one man said. I asked them why they didn't go and fight in Beirut. "We are waiting for permission from Sheikh Saad," someone told me. "Saad realized he didn't want to fight Shiites, he doesn't want a military conflict. Future is a moderate current. If Future disappears, then Sunnis will die. If you cut our wrists, the blood will come out and spell Saad, and spell Sunnis."

My friend was a Sunni from the Ras Beirut area of the capital, which is identified as Sunni. He was stopped by several irate armed Salafis who demanded to see his ID card to confirm his address. "If you are not from Ras Beirut, I will slaughter you now," the leader of the group barked at my friend." One of the men disparaged the Sunnis of Baghdad, who had failed to stand up to Hizballah. "The Sunnis of Beirut want to have nice jackets, nice cars, and nice apartments," he told my friend. "They like to go out on a Saturday night and stay out. Here we are day laborers, and we save money to buy guns because we know we will need them. That's why we blame you." As I left I realized Saad al-Hariri was actually a moderating force, preventing Sunnis from pursuing further violence.

The next morning I returned. One woman had been killed in the clashes, but no fighters had been hurt. I visited the home of nineteen-year-old Ibrahim Jumaa, who had gotten married a month and a half earlier and had just moved in. An RPG had gone through his wall, through his living room, and into his toilet. The Lebanese army was on the streets of Bab al-Tabbaneh. They had also been there before the previous evening's clashes started. Like in Beirut, the fighting was preceded by youth throwing stones at one another. When the army withdrew, the shooting started. "We all fight," one man told me. "It's our neighborhood, our land. We are on fire after the battle of Beirut." Some of the people tried to console my friend, who was a Sunni from Beirut. Others asked him why Tariq al-Jadida had fallen so quickly. Their radios crackled. "Hide your weapons, the army is coming," somebody said. The men told me they hid their weapons when the army showed up for the sake of the army's feelings. "The problem with the army is as soon as they hear a shot, they leave," said one man.

Most of the bearded men in Afghan attire were gone in the morning, save a few of their leaders, who sat in a cafe and coordinated with their men by radio. Locals were hostile to the media, and warned that they would not accept Al Jazeera or the local Lebanese channel, New TV, which were perceived as pro-Hizballah. The Saudi-owned Arabiya network was welcome, though. They demanded that Future TV be allowed to operate again and that the siege on the airport be removed. "Hariri airport is not Nasrallah airport," one man said. "We are mad because Sunnis were broken," another said, but they were not angry at Saad. One man who had fought in Iraq in 2003 told me it was part of the same conflict.

Mustafa Zaabi, the man who had guided me through the area in the past, told me that "Sunnis here won't be quiet." I walked by a cafe with a poster of Saddam at his trial, in which he was holding the Koran. It said, "Long live the Muslim community, Long live Palestine, Arab freedom." Mustafa had led his own group of fighters during the clashes. He carried an RPG launcher. He and the older men knew how to fight, he said, but the younger guys didn't. He seemed ecstatic. "It's an experience, fighting," he said. "We felt as if they took us back twenty-seven years. We went back to the same positions we were in before."

Hundreds of Tabbaneh residents had been massacred by the Syrians and their allies in the 1980s. The civil war had never ended there. The bitterness remained and occasionally erupted into violence, but with the influx of Salafis and jihadists and the interpretation of local conflicts through the paradigm of a regional conflict between Sunnis and Shiites, it was becoming more explosive. The Salafis played a crucial role in the latest battle. "We depend on them," Mustafa told me. "They have a creed."

Local militiamen scrounged their money and relied on donations from wealthy Sunni patrons and politicians. All the Sunni leaders in Lebanon had provided them with assistance, including Najib Mikati, Omar Karameh, and Saad Hariri. And their various supporters all fought together against the Alawites. They bought many of their weapons from the Palestinian camps. "If we had part of Hizb Ashaytan's [the devil's party] weapons, I would be talking to you from the mountaintop," Mustafa told me. Musbah al-Ahdab was particularly loved in the area for his public anger and financial support. "Musbah was 20 percent popular before he went on TV and said that people should organize themselves and get their weapons so what happened in Beirut won't happen here," one man told me. "Then his popularity became 100 percent." Some people told me that Ahdab had also provided them with weapons and ammunition. Khaled Dhaher was a good guy, they all agreed. ("He didn't abandon us," Mustafa told me. "He took care of us.") Many of them had footage of the Halba massacre on their mobile phones. Dhaher's people had been involved, everybody said proudly; his people were well armed. Mustafa bragged that Dhaher had killed some of the victims himself. It was rumored that the families of the two Sunni supporters of the Future Movement who were killed in Halba during the clashes each received one hundred thousand dollars from the Hariri family. Locals told me that Dhaher's people had distributed ammunition to the militias of Tabbaneh. "Jund Allah dazzled us with their weapons and the amount of ammunition that they had," Mustafa said of Kanan Naji's militia. Two Future officials, Muhamad al-Aswad and Khalid al-Masri, also had armed groups in Tabbaneh.

The way the clashes erupted sounded familiar. Nobody knew who started shooting first, Mustafa told me. *Zaaran* from both sides were insulting one another and throwing stones, and then the shooting started. It was a result of an old anger in their hearts, he told me, which went back to the Syrian occupation. "It's an old war," he said. "There isn't a house or a family in Tabbaneh that doesn't want revenge on the Alawites, that doesn't have a blood debt with the Alawites," another man told me.

People had been told to expect a battle that day, so they had prepared for one. And indeed, a battle happened in Tabbaneh and other poor areas around it. Suddenly all the old armed groups that had once dominated Tripoli reemerged, but their men were too old and the young men on the streets lacked proper training. As a result Sunnis often turned to current or former members of the security forces. An Alawite leader claimed that the first RPG had been fired by a pro-Syrian Sunni group.

The army had come the previous night during a truce, but when fighting resumed it withdrew again. Mustafa's area was a front line. He broke a hole in the back of his building so his men could sneak out to the other side. One of his men showed me a wad of cash he had just received to buy more ammunition. The price for a hand grenade was now seventeen dollars. Before the fighting it had been four dollars. A rocket-propelled grenade was now seventy dollars. Mustafa would buy weapons from Palestinian dealers in the Minyeh area close to Bedawi.

One of his men had gone down to Tariq al-Jadida with several hundred others from the north for the Beirut fighting. They were only given clubs, he complained, not guns, and had barely been fed. He felt betrayed. "No," said another, "Saad didn't want bloodshed."

"There is a strong Sunni awakening in Lebanon," Mustafa's younger brother Khudhr told me. "We all became terrorists," another man said. "Hassan Nasrallah made us all terrorists. We don't want to fight Israel." Instead, they told me, they would fight the Shiites with all they had.

"We as the *shabab* of Tabbaneh are fighting as Islamists, not as the opposition or the majority," Mustafa explained. "We are in solidarity in defense of our religion." He told me that they feared a repeat of the massacres they had faced in the 1980s by the Syrians and their allies.

Whenever power was used against Salafis and Islamists, they became more devout and defended their religion, Mustafa told me. There was no area in Lebanon that had poverty and neglect and didn't have people embracing their religion. "The comfortable citizen doesn't think about the gun," he said. "In this area it's like you're in a Palestinian camp." If they could have left their area, they would have gone down to Beirut to defend Sunnis, he told me. They were resentful of the Sunni leadership, which had betrayed them. "During Nahr al-Barid they accused the *shabab* of belonging to Fatah al-Islam because they were Sunnis. They killed who they killed and imprisoned who they imprisoned just because they were Sunnis. But Hizballah did what they did in Beirut, and nobody questioned them or confronted them."

"If we close the airport road, they will say we are terrorists," one man said. "Yesterday I started to pray because I felt like I am in the hands of God. And that's how I became a terrorist. They pushed me and abandoned me, and I am alone. What can I do? I seek shelter with God."

One day I showed up in front of Mustafa's shop and found him wearing a new military vest he had just purchased for twenty dollars. The other guys wanted one too. His Salafi cousin Shadi Jbara gave him money to purchase more. There had been fighting the night before. One of the men bragged that in all their fighting ten civilians had died in the clashes but none of the fighters had been killed.

Shadi had just been released from prison two weeks earlier and was opening a bakery. Along with several other Al Qaeda wanna-bes, he had tried to blow up a local Kentucky Fried Chicken. Shadi's father had been assassinated during the battles of the 1980s, and he bragged that his mother had become a mujahida, carrying an AK-47 and shooting RPGs at the Alawites of Jabal Mohsen. Shadi had known some of the Fatah al-Islam men in prison. One of them, an Algerian, told Shadi he had come to Lebanon to defend Sunnis from Shiites.

At first Shadi wasn't sure if he could talk to me because he hadn't received permission from the sheikh he followed. He had once been like any other guy, he told me, going out at night, chasing women. In 1991 he met a man who led him to the right path—the path of God. He went to Saudi Arabia in 1993 and met with Afghan Arabs and leaders of Salafi movements. He worked in a restaurant, and at night he would study there. After five years he returned from Saudi Arabia. Osama bin Laden gave orders to attack U.S. businesses; the easiest targets for Shadi and his friends were restaurants, so they decided to attack a Kentucky Fried Chicken. They placed one kilogram of TNT by the restaurant early in the morning so nobody would get hurt. They didn't want to cause casualties, just damage to the restaurant to gain media recognition.

Shadi explained that his friends had made a tactical error when they attacked a McDonald's. Before leaving their explosives, they had sat down to eat and were captured on the security camera. Most of the men from the group were from Tabbaneh. They were rookies and confessed to the police immediately, informing on the KFC group as well. Prison was like a university, Shadi said. He spent five years behind bars and met men from different groups. At their peak Salafis like him numbered 420 in the prison. They were categorized as terrorists and separated from other inmates. In prison they had access to DVDs and CDs with lectures by Zarqawi and other famous jihadists. "Zarqawi, God have mercy on him, influenced the *shabab* more than bin Laden did," he told me.

Fatah al-Islam was not a Syrian creation, he insisted. Many of its men had fought in Iraq or Bosnia. Some had belonged to Zarqawi's Al Qaeda in Iraq. Most were Palestinians from Syria's Yarmuk camp. Syria was like a reservoir for these groups, he told me, but thousands of men had been arrested there. Lebanon was a small country, and it was hard for Al Qaeda to operate there, he explained. Most of the Al Qaeda men in Lebanon weren't planning operations in Lebanon but were looking to Iraq.

Sunnis in Lebanon were very weak, he said. "The Sunnis of Beirut are not fighters; they are traders. If there were fifty Salafi jihadi guys in Beirut, then Hizballah would have lost a lot. The only people who can face Hizballah must have an ideology and a military. We were very angry at Saad. Hizballah is a military party; you can't fight them with politics." Shiites in prison were celebrating and shouting for Ali after the Hizballah victory in Beirut. But Salafis in prison were happy when they heard about the Halba massacre. I asked Shadi where I could hear a strong sermon. "Sermons don't affect people," he told me. "It's the small studying sessions that affect people. The guys who talk about jihad in the sermons tell people to stay home and not go to jihad."

Shadi thought Prime Minister Siniora was an infidel, apostate, and ally of the Americans. But the Hizballah-led siege of Siniora's government was not about Siniora, he said; it was about the sect. Shadi had friends who had fought in Iraq, but it was harder than ever to go there. Because there was so much pressure on veterans of the jihad in Iraq once they returned to Lebanon, many mujahideen preferred to die in Iraq, Mustafa approached his Salafi brother and Shadi and gave them instructions. "We need you sheikhs to take the mountain in the front, and we will follow." Shadi responded that they were lacking ammunition and needed to better organize themselves. Shadi told me he understood that the people of Tabbaneh were being used by the Sunni elite in the country. And he knew that when that elite pressed a button again, the fighters of Tabbaneh would once more be activated.

The walls of Tabbaneh were covered with posters of Khalil Akkawi, the slain leader of the Tawhid movement. In the early 1980s he had been an ally of Kanan Naji. Together they had fought the Syrians. Akkawi was assassinated in 1986. I spoke with his son, Arabi, who remained very respected and connected throughout Tripoli because of his father's legacy of resistance. Arabi had been nine years old at the time of his father's death. Policemen smuggled him out of Tabbaneh with his mother and sister in the back of a pickup truck because the Alawites were looking for them to kill them.

The people of Tabbaneh did not view the Beirut fighting as a political dispute, Arabi told me. To them it was simply Shiites attacking Sunnis. They felt they were slapped in the face and had to react in Tripoli. If the Future Movement was weakened, then the Salafis would take their place. "Salafis are raging, and it's the right environment for Salafis and Al Qaeda to grow," he told me. Some Salafis had brought weapons to Tabbaneh with the support of officials from the Interior Ministry such as Gen. Ashraf Riffi. "On the street people are saying, 'We wish Fatah al-Islam still existed.' Al Qaeda became acceptable now. The environment is welcoming."

There was no alternative to the Future party for Sunnis, he told me, and Future had not lost popularity. "Whenever sectarian conflict increases, then Future gains in popularity." Arabi believed it was his father's former ally Naji who had started the most recent battle with Jabal Mohsen. He told me that Naji's men launched RPGs at the Alawites and opened fire on their neighborhood, so the Alawites thought the Sunnis were attacking them. Naji was backed by Dai al-Islam al-Shahal, Lebanon's most prominent Salafi.

I returned regularly to the neighborhood. Tensions would occasionally increase, the army would withdraw, and people would return to their fighting positions. One explosion took down much of an apartment building. Men with military vests and AK-47s materialized suddenly. One of them had a body full of tattoos: "Because I love you," said one; another said, "I'm not afraid of death but my mother's tears kill me."

I returned to see Shahal again, in his office in the Abu Samra area of Tripoli. There was a more obvious armed presence outside and inside his office than before. On his desk next to plastic flowers was a leaflet that said, "The Salafi Current in Lebanon is calling for the Sunnis to organize to face any danger." Before we started, he closed his eyes and recited a long prayer. Then he opened his light blue eyes and started talking. A big *fitna* (internal strife) had happened, he told me; if it wasn't contained it would open the door to danger-ous events. Sunnis in Beirut were under heavy pressure because it was the cap-ital and they were weaker than Sunnis in the north. There was a plot against Sunnis, but the north was their real stronghold, where the *shabab* were Salafis and stronger and disciplined. That's why they could give balance to the Sunnis and halt the conspiracy against them. All Sunni forces in Lebanon united. "In Beirut and here there are weapons, personal weapons, and it isn't enough. But we have faith. We don't need Al Qaeda. The Salafi Current is on the ground. It has forces."

As long as the Salafi movement existed, there was no need for Al Qaeda in Lebanon. "The Salafi street in Lebanon has its presence, its strength, and we will hopefully work on strengthening it," Shahal said. "Salafis in Lebanon are intelligent, and they know the ground. They know the Lebanese situation, and they can play the game by its internal rules [meaning they had a local agenda], and they are not incapable of military conflict when it's needed. We don't need human support from outside Lebanon. What we need is psychological support and financial support. This is not a call to jihad. It's a call to self-defense. We don't expect any support from the regimes but from those who are convinced in our religion and our call."

Sunni militias were beginning to form, and in Majd al-Anjar, a Sunni strong-hold in Lebanon's Beqaa, irate *shabab* closed the key Masnaa border road to Syria. On May 12 I drove there to check it out. Few roads led into the tightly connected narrow streets, where the plethora of mosques and the austerity and solidarity, among other things, reminded me of Falluja. I stopped to see if the *mukhtar*, Shaaban al-Ajami, was home. He was not. A muscular policeman with long hair stood in front of a mosque across the street, watching us. Suspi-cious locals stopped me to ask who I was. A hardened woman led us to a road-block, just past a large intersection leading to the Syrian border crossing at Masnaa. Lebanese soldiers perched indolently atop their armored personnel carriers, phlegmatically watching anarchy as several hundred men with auto-matic rifles, rocket-propelled grenade launchers, pistols, and hand grenades manned roadblocks of earthen barriers and fires. Some wore masks. There was nobody in command—it was a mob, not a militia, and so even more frightening. The men were angry, afraid, suspicious, shouting at strangers and one another, each one an authority unto himself. They carelessly swung their weapons around, oblivious to where they were pointing. Some rested the barrels of their rifles on top of their feet, a sign they had no professional training. A car approached with a family inside. They surrounded it, shouting at the passengers. A woman inside shrieked in fear. Local police showed up in an official pickup truck; the young muscular policeman with long hair emerged and greeted the armed men, warmly kissing and embracing them.

When strangers approached, the men immediately demanded to know if they were Sunni or Shiite. Hundreds of Syrian laborers carrying bags and baskets descended from buses and walked between the earth barriers on their way to the border. Two old men were detained, their identity cards revealing them to be Shiites. Locals sitting in the shade by shops quickly descended when they heard Shiites were found. Rifles were loaded and a *frisson* passed through the mob. The harrowed Shiites were finally released unscathed.

Nabil Jalul, a redheaded thirty-four-year-old local leader, carried a tiny pistol he could hide in his pocket. He wore a ski mask but raised it above his brows so we could talk. He used the language of the *takfiris* I had met in Iraq, those extreme Sunnis who declare other Muslims who do not share their austere practices (especially Shiites) to be *kufar* (infidels). He called Shiites *rafidha* (rejectionists), an anti-Shiite slur, and told me they had been armed by the Nusayris, a slur for Alawites, meaning the Syrian regime. Shiites were agents of the Israelis, he said, and they had not liberated their holy sites in Iraq from the American occupiers, so who could take Shiites in Lebanon seriously when they spoke of liberating Jerusalem from the Israeli occupiers? "We fight based on a creed," he said, while "they" (meaning Hizballah) used weapons against other Lebanese. "Resistance is not about entering Beirut and oppressing its people. This roadblock is for victory in Beirut and the Sunnis. We won't open the road until they open the airport."

Nabil referred to Hizballah (which means Party of God) as Hizb al-Lat (Party of Lot), meaning the party of sin. Like many other Salafis, he also called them Hizb Ashaytan (Party of the Devil). "We are the *shabab* of Majd al-Anjar," he said. "We fight the *rafidha*. We ruled for hundreds of years. We have many mujahideen and martyrs in Iraq. If the Sunnis of Beirut call us, we will come." He told me many jihadist websites published calls for Sunni volunteers to come to Lebanon. Some required secret passwords, but he wouldn't give me his.

Nabil had no formal military training, but, like many in the Beqaa, he began handling weapons at a young age. His life changed when he fell under the influence of Abu Muhamad, a local of Kurdish descent who had been one of Zarqawi's deputies. Abu Muhammad's real name was Mustafa Ramadan. An ethnic Kurd from Beirut who had once been a hoodlum who drank alcohol, he married a woman from Majd al-Anjar and moved to Denmark. He returned a

Salafi and recruited some youth from the town to his own network, finally going to Iraq with his sixteen-year-old son. Abu Muhamad was trained in Afghanistan and was part of Basim al-Kanj's Dinniyeh group. He was arrested in 2002 in a mosque in Majd al-Anjar. After four months in prison he used his connections and paid his way out. In Iraq he was said to have dispatched the car bomb that killed SCIRI leader Muhammad Bakr al-Hakim in 2003. He died fighting in Iraq, in an attack on the Abu Ghraib prison that nearly breached its walls.

Nabil's brother-in-law was killed fighting in Rawa, a town in Iraq's Anbar province, in June 2003. I visited the town the morning after dozens of Iraqi and foreign fighters had been slain in their desert camp by Americans. Locals buried them by a mosque, placing their ID cards in bottles that served as tombstones. Other youths from Majd al-Anjar were buried in Rawa that day. One of them was the son of Abu Muhamad, which was why he was also known as Abu Shahid, or father of the martyr. At least seven young men from the town were martyred in Iraq, and Nabil had a plaque in their honor in his guest room.

Nabil was jailed from 2004 until 2005, accused of plotting to bomb Western embassies and other targets. He later proudly showed me the many articles about his arrest and release. He was released with other jihadists at the same time as Samir Geagea, a Lebanese war criminal and leader of the right-wing Christian Lebanese Forces. The release of the radical Sunnis was meant to placate Sunnis and bolster the Sunni credentials of the Future Movement.

Majd al-Anjar was an important smuggling center. After the American invasion of Iraq, Nabil smuggled weapons and fighters into Syria and Iraq. Smugglers from the town relied on dirt roads through the mountainous border. All of Lebanon's political factions relied on smuggling through Syria, Nabil told me. Many of the Lebanese officers at the border received salaries from smugglers that could reach five thousand dollars a month. Smuggling was still a good business, but it was more difficult now. Only special explosives were smuggled from Lebanon to Iraq, such as C4 and TNT. He showed me a picture of himself from the early days of the Iraq War, with a beard down to his chest. Back then he was so religious he refused to own a television.

Abu Muhamad would come from Iraq and meet Nabil in Damascus, where they rented apartments. Nabil delivered truckloads of weapons to him: bombs and explosives as well as missiles and silencers for pistols. They bribed Syrian customs officials and used clandestine dirt roads. Nabil's friend Ismail Khatib purchased the weapons, sometimes with his own money, and handled communication with their brethren in Iraq. "We were a very tight group," Nabil said. "We couldn't be penetrated." Ismail's cousin Ali was among the dead in Rawa in 2003. After another fighter was killed in Iraq and two trucks of weapons were seized, the authorities began to watch their network. The Syrians, who still maintained bases in Lebanon at the time, had an intelligence headquarters nearby. Nabil was arrested on September 19, 2004, two months after his last delivery of weapons to Syria. The Syrians were the ones who sent Nabil to prison. "They decided to stop the flow of foreigners into Iraq," Nabil told me, "just like all the Arabs who changed their policies suddenly and decided to look good for the Americans."

Majd al-Anjar was also an important stop in the network that smuggled fighters to Iraq from Lebanon and its Palestinian camps, especially Ayn al-Hilweh. Dozens of men from that camp were martyred in Iraq. Among its most famous martyrs was Abu Jaafar al-Qiblawi. His poster hung above one of the main roads in that camp. Nabil was his friend and had smuggled him into Syria. Ismail took him on to Iraq. In the last film showing Zarqawi, Abu Jaafar was the one who handed a machine gun to him. He was killed with Zarqawi in June 2006. After his death a thirteen-minute video, filmed in August 2005 on the banks of a river, showed his last will. In the video he held a machine gun and addressed his parents, calling on his father to remain steadfast and his brothers to join the jihad. The mujahideen would be victorious, he said, in their fight against the greatest power in the world, America, which was the leader of nonbelief. America had to be destroyed, he said, and Muslim lands had to be liberated. He sang songs for his mother and to his beloved. One of Abu Jaafar's brothers was killed in the Nahr al-Barid battle in 2007, and another was arrested in 2008 by the Lebanese army while attempting to smuggle a Saudi fighter out of Ayn al-Hilweh.

When Nabil and the men in his network were arrested (they were found with fifty kilograms of TNT and five kilograms of C4), they were tortured by members of the Interior Ministry's Information Branch. During the interrogations Nabil was hit in the back of his head with a club; his legs were bruised for months after the beatings. Nabil was accused of being the number-two man in the group. Ismail was tortured to death, and his funeral in Majd al-Anjar was an occasion for massive demonstrations. With Ismail's death, Nabil lost his connections to Iraq and no longer smuggled on behalf of the jihad. Nabil bragged about those days. "We are Al Qaeda," he told me. "We had connections to Abu Shahid." Nabil knew seven or eight men who had returned home to Majd al-Anjar from Iraq, and he knew there were others. In town I met a middle-aged Iraqi Baathist who, I was told, had been in the resistance, though he refused to discuss his past except to say he had served the state. "I'm wanted in Syria for terrorism," he told me, adding that he was also wanted in Lebanon for opening fire in a fight. Sheikh Dai al-Islam al-Shahal from Tripoli visited Nabil after his release from prison. "Dai al-Islam is a friend of mine," he told me. "He knows the truth, but he won't speak all of it." It was clear Nabil didn't think highly of him, and he made a contemptuous face.

Back at the roadblock Nabil and others set up in Masnaa, a convoy of expensive cars drove up, and Sheikh Muhamad Abdel Rahman, head of the
Sunni religious endowment in the Beqaa, emerged. Hundreds of men surrounded him as he gave a speech with a loudspeaker. An establishment figure,
he came, like others, to try to influence the men. The Sunni elite feared young
men like Nabil, whom they could not control. Representatives from the Future Movement had asked them to open the roadblocks, Nabil said, as had the
municipality. Although locals voted for the Future out of Sunni solidarity, they
did not belong to the party—which had opposed the initiative taken by local
youths to close the road.

Sheikh Muhamad addressed them directly. "You represent Majd al-Anjar,"
he said. "The decision to open the road is yours. It's impossible to open the
road without your agreement. The decision must protect the interest of the
town and the people of the town and the *shabab* of the town." He warned that
there were some infiltrators among them. "You are not here for stealing. If
there are people among you stopping and stealing, it's harming your dignity."
The issue was protecting Sunnis' dignity and autonomy, he said; they would
open the road if it was in the interests of the sect. "The Islamic Sunni resistance begins today," he said. "We work for Lebanon, and they work for Iran."
Young men shot into the air as he spoke.

"The sheikh, the municipality, the Future Current, the world came to open
the border," one of the young men said triumphantly, "but the *shabab* of Majd
al-Anjar who closed the border refused to open it."

The following Friday I visited the Abdel Rahman Auf Mosque in Majd al-
Anjar, also known as the Wahhabi Mosque. Nabil met us at the entrance to
town and guided us to the mosque, handing us over to a chubby bearded
friend before going home. Expensive cars were squeezed in around the
mosque, which was full of young men and boys. It had two floors, with a
screen on the second floor so people could watch the imam give his sermon.
Sheikh Adnan al-Umama, a local, spoke of Hizballah's "barbaric raid" on
Beirut and condemned Iran. In Iraq the mujahideen were called terrorists, he
said, while Hizballah's Shiite brothers in Iraq helped the Americans.

The battle was one of creeds, he said, meaning between Sunnis and Shiites.
"These people who came against us are secular and infidels. If they were honest about what they say, then we have to be ready to fight them. We saw them
invading Beirut with hearts full of hate and accusing us of the murder of Hussein. If they have a problem with the government like they claim, why did
they attack civilians and humiliate our women and our Muslim homes in
Beirut?" Hizballah "terrorized us in our cities. Their friends in Iraq are friends
with the Americans. We are the real people of the resistance. Sunnis are the
real resistance." The battle against Israel was a Sunni battle as well, he said.

"I'm not agitating for a sectarian conflict. But, on the other hand, we won't stand still if they try to humiliate or insult our homes and our women." The Lebanese army would fall apart soon because of the sectarian division inside it, he said. It was time for Sunnis to stop being afraid of Shiites to start rising up. "Until the government is able to defend us, we insist on carrying our guns," he said. "And we will resist [the Shiites] with our women and children and all the power we have. I praise our heroes who blocked the road. Yes, they did the right thing. We are the pure, noble Muslims, and we are merciful, and we won't stay silent about the attack on the people and our women in our cities."

As I listened to the sermon with a friend, a man turned to question us suspiciously, but Nabil's friend explained that we were with him. Then suddenly a thick older man with a long gray beard took my friend's notebook from his hands and demanded mine as well. After the prayer ended he interrogated us as others surrounded us. He tried to read the notes and ordered Nabil's friend to make copies of our identity cards.

I later went to meet Sheikh Adnan at his home. Landscape paintings and gaudy European art decorated his guest room. Given the tone of his sermon, he was younger, quicker to smile, and more jovial than I had expected. He began by apologizing for the men who had interrogated us at his mosque. He normally preferred not to give political sermons, he told me, focusing instead on religion, because politics was always changing.

Majd al-Anjar, with its twenty thousand residents, was unique, he said, because it was close to the border, was populated only by Sunnis, had a large number of graduates in Islamic studies educated all over the Arab world, and had no secular political parties. Sheikh Adnan was not optimistic. "Outside powers determine events here," he told me. Shiites were doing the same thing in Lebanon that they were doing in Iraq, but Iraqi Sunnis were stronger because they had weapons from the former regime at their disposal and a better geographical location. Bin Laden and Zawahiri were wrong when they called for Al Qaeda to operate in Lebanon, because they did not know the nature of the country, he said. It was too divided and mixed, and Al Qaeda could never establish a stronghold.

He did not want *fitna* in the Muslim community, he said; he wanted to fix the problems of arms in Lebanon and the dangers they posed for Sunnis. After seeing what happened in Beirut, Sunnis understandably wanted to arm themselves too. The Future Movement had no creed, he said. Its people worked only for money, unlike Hizballah. Sunnis were looking for a leader to represent them, but the Mufti Qabbani was too close to the Saudis and the Future Movement, and he was weak, having done nothing in response to the events in Beirut. There was an opening now for Islamist movements, but the experience of Nahr al-Barid had made Islamists wary of organizing. He wondered why the Americans had abandoned the Siniora government and asked me if I had any insight.

We drove to Nabil's house. He lived with relatives on the second floor of a compound. Nabil's guest room was a shrine to jihad. He had a large collection of ammunition shells and grenades on display in his cupboard. Upon entering his house, guests were greeted by framed pictures of the 9/11 attacks—the Twin Towers aflame and a smoldering Pentagon. "We are not in line with Sheikh Adnan," Nabil told me. "He is moderate, as they say." Instead Nabil and his friends took *fatwas* from scholars associated with Al Qaeda. Nabil asked his little boy what he wanted to be when he grew up. "A mujahid!" his son grinned. A tall man wearing jeans and a T-shirt that were too tight (in true Lebanese style) burst in the room. His name was Hossam, and he was one of the organizers of the roadblock. Seeing the pistol on his belt, I asked if he was a cop. "No, I'm a mujahid," he said. He explained that closing the road was a spontaneous decision taken by the *shabab*. "Our conscience and our honor made us close it," he said. "I smoke hashish, I'm not religious. It was something from the inside."

I visited often in the spring and summer of 2008. Nabil always had his 9-millimeter Glock pistol in his hand, on his lap, or on the table beside him. Like many Glocks I had seen in Lebanon, it had been smuggled in from Iraq, an American gift to mostly Shiite Iraqi Security Forces now in the hands of radical Sunnis in Lebanon. Once, as I sat in Nabil's guest room, he received a phone call. He grabbed his pistol and ran out. Three unknown cars with tinted windows had entered the town. He called Hossam. "Three cars came in," Nabil said. "They might be military. Park your car and I'll send someone to pick you up. . . . They're raiding your house. . . . Don't worry about me. I'll start shooting if they get close to my house." Nabil took out a walkie-talkie and contacted other men in their network. Hossam, sweating and out of breath, walked in with a thuggish-looking friend. Hossam wielded a new AK-47 equipped with a scope and flashlight as well as a drum magazine to hold far more ammunition. He wore an ammunition vest laden with extra ammunition and several American hand grenades that he said cost fifty dollars apiece. His friend carried a PKM, a belt-fed machine gun. "If Saddam Hussein was alive he would help us with ammunition," Hossam said. "That's why they killed him."

Hossam's father had killed a man, and the two families were feuding, which was why he always carried a pistol. But in the battle against Shiites the two families were together, he said. "I never carried a rifle before," he said, "but since the Shiites attacked I started carrying one." Hossam had taken part in sectarian clashes between Sunnis from the nearby town of Saad Nayel and the Shiites of Talabaya. A few days earlier Sunnis and Shiites had fought each other in the nearby town of Sawiri as well. Hossam claimed he had forced Shiite officials at

the Masnaa border crossing to stop working there. This was why security officers were paying a visit to the town. "We and the state are opposed," said the
thuggish man.

"Before May 8 I used to love life," said Hossam. "I would never sleep. I was
into women, drugs, alcohol—I was living life to the fullest. Something happened in my heart I can't explain to anybody. Since May 8 I am a different person. I started praying five times a day, feeling more confident when I'm
fighting." Now he fantasized about becoming a suicide bomber. "I should be
doing martyrdom operations too," he told me, his eyes darting to Nabil, looking for approval. "I would like to blow myself up during Nasrallah's speech
when there is a large group of people." He got so much pleasure from shooting, he said, and he surmised that if he went on a martyrdom operation his
soul would feel even better. Nabil expected suicide operations like those in
Iraq to occur in Lebanon, targeting Shiites. "I won't be surprised if it happened," he said.

Nabil didn't seem to have a job, but I soon realized he had a lucrative underground business selling weapons. I asked him why he always carried a pistol
with him. He quoted a hadith about how one must always be armed. I asked if
he was not worried about the authorities. "The army is not allowed in here,"
Nabil said. I asked who didn't allow them. "We don't allow them," he said.
"None of them will survive. Do they want another Nahr al-Barid?" Likewise
the police were not allowed to come into town, he said: "If they do, the whole
town will fight." I was reminded of the accusations that Hizballah was a state
within a state. Outside Beirut there was little sign of any state willing or able
to assert itself, and unlike Shiites, the Sunnis of Lebanon had no comparable
social movement to fill the vacuum.

As we drove through the narrow alley leading to Nabil's house, a man asked
him to sell him two thousand rounds of ammunition. "Come to my house,"
Nabil said. One day when I visited Nabil I found his living room converted into
an armory. He had an RPG launcher, many boxes of ammunition, and eight rifles, including AK-47s, a PKM, and a Degtyaryov machine gun. In a box that
originally contained a Syrian dress, Nabil had stuffed an assortment of
grenades. He took some out to play with, to my displeasure, and showed me
how to take them apart.

Nabil introduced me to Marwan Yassin, or Abu Hudheifa, a gentle,
friendly man he called his sheikh and emir. Abu Hudheifa was not formally
educated in Islam, but he studied Sharia at home and memorized the Koran
at the late age of twenty-five. He had six children. He had just been released
from prison after serving ten months. I asked him if he had been tortured.
"Not this time," he said with a smile. In 2004 the Syrians arrested him trying
to enter Iraq. He spent eight months in a Syrian prison before he was trans-

ferred to a Lebanese prison, where he served three more months. He was tortured in both countries.

Majd al-Anjar was special, he said, because it had a lot of religious people of the same color, meaning Sunni. "We have a lot of people who went to Iraq and were killed there, so we have people who love jihad," he said. "Iraq is under direct American occupation. Here, it's an indirect Iranian occupation." Sunnis in Lebanon were in a weak position, he said.

One night in June Nabil called around midnight to tell me he had just received word that two local boys, Abdallah Abdel Khalaq and Firas Yamin, had blown themselves up in Iraq on two consecutive days. Twenty-year-old Abdallah, whose nickname was Abu Obeida, called his family the night before to say goodbye and explain that the next day he would either park the car and detonate it or, if there was too much security, detonate it while driving. At noon the next day he blew himself up while driving in a crowded Baghdad street. Two hours later his companions called his parents to let them know the happy news about their son's martyrdom. The family was religious and proud of him, and distributed candy. Firas, who was called Abu Omar, had gone to Iraq with Abdallah without telling anybody in town. Nabil had a film of them both with a Kuwaiti fighter who had been to Afghanistan. "If I had a chance I would go," Nabil said.

Nabil took me to meet a group of friends in an office. They were drinking tea. Several had long hair and long beards. One had the physique of a bodybuilder. I asked them what they expected to happen. "Very bad things," said one. Nabil spoke of prophecies in the Koran about a final battle occurring in Sham, or Greater Syria. The American invasion of Iraq was one sign of it. I had heard many jihadi Salafis in the region predict this imminent final battle, one that would be fought with swords. An older man in traditional Arab dress was the father of a young man who had been martyred in Rawa. As I chatted with the men, Nabil played absentmindedly with the pistol on his lap.

One morning one of Nabil's friends drove me around town. He spoke on his cellphone to a woman. "We are ready," he told her. "We didn't sleep since last night." The night before, Nabil said, the Lebanese army had arrested the father of one of the guys in their group in Masnaa. There were regular clashes with local Shiites, whom the men called Hizballah, probably inaccurately. "Last night we went down to Marj," Nabil's friend said, "patrolling with our cars with tinted windows, driving back and forth in the main streets of Majd al-Anjar and Marj. We had guns, we were ready."

Nabil introduced me to a friend they called Dr. Saadi because he had a PhD in history from the University of Damascus. Only in his thirties, Saadi had a guest room well stocked with books on Islam. He'd been imprisoned for alleged involvement in the 2000 "millennium plot" to blow up the American

Embassy in Jordan. After his release, he traveled to Falluja at the height of the jihad in 2004 and met Omar Hadid, a famed fighter in that town.

There was no Sunni party in Lebanon with a creed, Saadi complained, only those who fought for money. The Future Movement had become mercenaries without belief, he said. They controlled Lebanon's Sunnis but obeyed the Americans, and Salafis were marginalized. But one day soon only the Salafi ideology would survive, and they would raise the Sunni flag in Lebanon. The May event had given a fillip to extreme movements in Lebanon such as Al Qaeda. The country's unique diversity had moderated Saadi's extremism, like it had for all of the Salafis I met in Lebanon. The variety of sects living in Lebanon meant that no single group could dominate the others, he said.

As we spoke, AK-47 shots suddenly erupted not far away. All the men burst out laughing, especially when they saw me flinch. A friend had just been released from prison and he was shooting into the air. "Army intelligence captured him," Nabil explained, "and we threatened to block the roads. Now he is shooting into the air in celebration for himself."

Like many Salafis I had met, Saadi was envious of Hizballah for confronting Israel but at the same time dismissive because Hizballah limited its activity to liberating Lebanese territory. "Hizballah protects the Jewish border with orders from the Syrian regime," he said. Moreover, by respecting UN resolutions, Hizballah proved that it had no genuine commitment to liberating Palestine. Hizballah had proved it had no principles, he said, by forming an alliance with a Christian party, the Free Patriotic Movement. The goal of Hizballah's "takeover" of Beirut was to weaken Sunnis in the Arab world, he said. The group was acting like the Mahdi Army in Iraq, proving it was only a Shiite militia. "Sunnis around the world are mad after what happened in Beirut," he said. "The result will be a thousand Zarqawis coming after Hizballah." Nabil was a great admirer of Zarqawi. "Behind the sword was a merciful heart," he said, "an eye that cried for the whole Islamic nation. There will be thousands of Zarqawis now."

I went with my friend to see Khaled Dhaher at his mountain redoubt in Bibnine. When we arrived in town we called Dhaher, who told us to give a few thousand liras to any taxi driver and ask him to lead us to his house. "Everybody knows where it is," he said. A taxi driver agreed, and suddenly a man in civilian clothes approached the driver's window, asking who we were and why we had weapons. We said we didn't have any. He called Dhaher to see if we were authorized. Then he flashed his wallet open and told us he was an undercover officer for the Interior Ministry, but there was no government ID card in it.

Four fit young men slinging AK-47s stood outside Dhaher's house, which was also a school. Inside there were three older men in a courtyard who were also armed. Dhaher was making and receiving phone calls when he arrived.

"Tell them to stay away, and let's wait until the dialogue is over because we might have to do to them what we did in Halba," he told somebody, referring to the negotiations in Doha, Qatar, to resolve the crisis and threatening another massacre. "Let's tell the brothers to gather and we can visit Mufti Rifai. At this point there is no turning back," he said in another phone call. Then he called a lieutenant named Arabi and thanked him for his cooperation. Finally he spoke to an associate. "Stay in your position even if there is shooting at you," he said. "Keep your eyes wide open. Never retreat, never surrender. An attack might happen tonight." Dhaher's brother was also there; he had come to ask about obtaining a gun license for somebody. "Who needs a license?" Dhaher asked. "Send some bodyguards to my center. There is no need to carry a license these days."

Dhaher was a short, chubby man with dark skin and a beard. He was a spokesman for the Independent Islamic Gathering, which had been established in December 2006. Now the Gathering had a presence on the ground, he said. "In Akkar we have twenty thousand retired soldiers from the Lebanese army ready to put their efforts and experience in order to protect the Sunni reservoir of Lebanon here in the north," he said. The recent fighting was a result of an Iranian, Safavid, Persian project, he told me, echoing a familiar litany. The Sunnis of Beirut were the people of bureaucrats, education, business, he said. They weren't fighters like the people of the countryside. Now Sunnis were arming themselves in the north and the Beqaa and establishing a national Islamic resistance to create an equilibrium. "Now we are getting ready, we are arming ourselves so we can confront them and challenge them. Don't forget that 60 percent of the army is Sunni. There are more then ten thousand trained and retired soldiers here, around us in Akkar. Sunni officers have resigned from the Lebanese army." He was getting calls from sheikhs, he told me, adding, "Now we are all fighters."

He explained that the Halba incident happened after the mufti of Akkar, Osama Rifai, called upon the Sunni street in the north to demonstrate against what had happened in Beirut. The Syrian Social Nationalist Party wanted to control Akkar, he said; they opened fire on the demonstration, killing two. The fighting wasn't led by the Future Party, he told me; it was the citizens and sons of the area reacting to what happened in Beirut. "It's only a simple reaction to what happened in Beirut. I personally protected the prisoners and gave them to the army," he said. "We won't give our weapons to the state until they do, and we will add to them and buy more arms. It is forbidden for Hizballah to occupy Sunni Beirut."

Sunnis had lost their trust in the security forces, he told me, especially after seeing the Lebanese army side with Hizballah. "We will defend ourselves," he said. He had met with members of the Lebanese army who supported what they were doing and would join them to fight by their side when needed, he told me. Dhaher's brother chimed in: "The Sunnis of Beirut were hit, but we will hit back one hundred times." Another brother added, "We don't have a choice but to defend our honor." They were disappointed in Saad al-Hariri, who hadn't supported the sect enough. Dhaher added that they were coordinating with Sunnis in the Beqaa and in Arsal.

I went to Arsal, a town bordering Syria that I had not heard of before talking to Dhaher. I saw more posters for Saddam Hussein on the walls than for Rafiq al-Hariri. "We all sacrifice ourselves for you, Saddam," read graffiti on the road approaching the town. Elsewhere I saw "We are all yours, glorious Saddam," "All the Muslim community is for Saddam," and "Saddam and 100 million Saddams." The town was sprawled across a valley, invisible at first beyond desolate hills. Its homes were unpainted, incomplete, with rebar sticking out. The land around it was arid and barren.

We stopped at a cellphone shop and asked a man there to guide us to the *mukhtar.* Arsal was surrounded by a sea of Shiites, he bragged, disparaging other Sunni towns for being "faggots." He got in his van, which had a Saddam sticker on it, and led us to the home of Basil al-Hujairi, the mayor. Hujairi was also a teacher who ran an Islamic school. His home overlooked the town from a hill. It was incomplete but ostentatious, with columns at the entrance. As we climbed the steps to the house, numerous calls to prayer echoed back and forth across the valley.

Hujairi had been mayor for four years. He was a supporter of the Muslim Brotherhood, he told me, but he admitted that in the recent fighting the Brotherhood had not had a strong stand. Only the Salafis had been strong. His town had forty thousand people, he told me, and they all had a strong Sunni identity. It was a poor town that relied on farming and smuggling. The Syrian border, only twenty kilometers away, was not controlled. Before 2005 the townspeople had clashed with the Syrians.

The town had at least ten mosques. Another was being built in honor of Ismail Hujairi who was martyred in Iraq the day Baghdad fell. His brothers, who brought his body back, were paying for it. Others from the town had fought in Iraq and returned.

Only three officers in the army were from Arsal, though many townsmen were enlisted. There were no government services in town. Electricity was four hours on, four hours off. I was thus surprised to learn that townspeople from Arsal still identified enough with the state to go down to Beirut and demonstrate so often. They had gone to protest the Danish cartoons and to show support for Saad Hariri. Sometimes on the way to and from these demonstrations, townspeople would clash with Shiites in the neighboring villages.

Shiites want revenge for the death of Hussein, Hujairi told me. They believed they would go to paradise if they killed Sunnis, he said, but Sunnis would defend their dignity. "Life without dignity or death—people will choose death."

Although many Western journalists live in Beirut, and many others descend on it whenever there is a crisis, few venture outside Beirut. This is despite the fact that Lebanon is such a small country. So the neglected Sunni population and the anger of that community are relatively unknown. Likewise, most Lebanese don't venture outside their areas, let alone into the areas of other sects or the slums and villages of the poor. In many of these towns, there is little electricity or other services, and people rely on remittances from relatives abroad for survival. Despite the presence of several Sunni billionaires in the country, there was no party equivalent to Hizballah that could provide social services to poor Sunnis.

Continuing my travels through the Beqaa, I visited the hillside town of Qaraun. Its houses were made of white stones with red roofs. In the town square I found a poster for Prime Minister Siniora and Rafiq and Saad al-Hariri. The town did not appear overtly religious, and I did not get the same hostile looks that I had received in Majd al-Anjar and Arsal. It had three *mukhtars*, and I met the most important, Nasr Dabaja, at the gas station he owned. His father had also been *mukhtar* and was famous for resisting the Israelis when they occupied the town in the mid-1980s. The town's population was 8,500, he told me. A quarter were Christian, and the rest were Sunni Muslims. There were only two mosques in town, and only one was in regular use. The Future Movement had no local office.

Before we began talking, Dabaja asked us if we were Sunni. He eyed my friend from Beirut suspiciously and asked if he prayed five times a day. As we spoke a Shiite man walked into his office, and Dabaja told us to stop talking until the man left. Muslims in the town supported the Salafis, he told me.

During the Dinniyeh events of 2000, Lebanese intelligence arrested seven or eight men from Qaraun while three or four others absconded. They were accused of fighting the army. Five eighteen-year-old boys from the town had gone to fight in Iraq in 2003, he told me. He and his brother were excited to learn that I was going to Iraq. They asked me to inquire about the fate of the young mujahideen from their town.

All Sunnis felt threatened and were uniting, he said, whether with the Muslim Brotherhood or the Future Movement. The Brotherhood was gaining in popularity in town because Sunnis felt marginalized. When they asked the Future Movement for weapons, they were turned down, he complained. "The Islamists will protect the Sunnis," he said, and the Salafi movement would emerge stronger after these events. Dabaja's brother agreed. "People are moving to extremism," he said. "Before they were supporting Future, which is moderate, but now we cry for Nahr al-Barid. We could have used those people." Dabaja agreed: "Last year we supported the army in Nahr al-Barid, but now we regret killing the extremists. People are thinking of weapons. We are threatened now. Are we going to sit with our hands tied?" Hizballah was afraid of the Salafis, they said. Dabaja liked Dai al-Islam al-Shahal, who was a "big thinker." He asked me for Shahal's phone number. As mayor Dabaja used to be invited to Shiite villages, but now that sectarian feelings were hardening he was not visiting them anymore. Roads between Qaraun and nearby Shiite towns were blocked.

Heading out we picked up an old Bedouin man called Hassan Fayad, who lived in the town of Shaabiyat al-Faur. Fifty men from the town had gone to fight in Beirut, but they had only been given sticks. There was a strong sense of Sunni solidarity now, he said, and they wanted weapons. "Shiites exposed that they are against Sunnis," he said. He cursed Hariri for betraying Sunnis' trust and humiliating them. "If Hariri wants to gain Sunnis back, he has to arm us. Without dignity there is nothing. We won't accept to be humiliated."

I continued visiting Tariq al-Jadida in late May and early June. The Muslim Brotherhood had put up new posters, one of which said, "The people of Beirut will only turn their weapons on the Zionist enemy. Peace in Beirut is the red line." All local shops owned by Shiites were now closed, even those that had been in the neighborhood a long time. Sunni shop owners who had been friendly with their Shiite colleagues did not help them. The brother of one man from Tariq al-Jadida who had been killed in the fighting had come back after the funeral and shouted, "We don't want Shiites here!"

"The *shabab* are upset," said Fadi, the local militiaman I had befriended. "Future brought us down to the street but could do nothing. Future is popular because there is no Sunni alternative." Fadi and his men had asked Secure Plus for weapons but were told they didn't have any. It seemed as though the leadership had sold the weapons for profit. Provocations were occurring on a nightly basis. One night a car drove down Fadi's street blasting Hizballah songs. Before that motorcycles drove through the area with flags for Amal and Hizballah. They caught one man, beat him up, and burned his motorcycle.

"We know who was on the street and who was at home," he said. Those who fought were told they would receive a hundred-dollar bonus. "This battle changed our thoughts. We returned to our religion, to our sect. I won't die for the [Future Movement]. I will die for my home, my sect. I am a Sunni. Now there is no Sunni living who likes Shiites." But Fadi still drank and didn't pray five times a day. Like many other Sunnis, he was proud of the Halba massacre. "It's our right to do what we did in Halba," he said. "They shouldn't have been involved in the game."

I found it ironic that the neglected and often impoverished Sunnis of Lebanon identified so closely with the state and with the Sunni elite. I returned to visit Hossam Ilmir, the principal at Bab al-Tabbaneh Elementary

School. I found Mustafa Zaabi sitting in Ilmir's office. Ilmir had 1,082 children in his school this year. The yard was dirty and smelled of urine. He complained that his students had to drink dirty water. He had not changed his mind about supporting the resistance following the clashes, he told me, because the weapons of the resistance had been targeted and the government had tried to make it a sectarian issue.

Ilmir blamed poverty for the fighting between Tabbaneh and Jabal Mohsen. The youth of both neighborhoods were unemployed. The elite, he thought, wanted to keep them poor. Ilmir and Mustafa agreed that the origins of the conflict were not sectarian but economic—rich against poor, with the elite making it seem sectarian. The people of Tabbaneh were ignored by politicians because most of the neighborhood's thirty-five thousand people were originally from Akkar and so did not vote in Tabbaneh. Only five thousand of them voted in Tabbaneh, so politicians had little to gain from helping them.

The people of Lebanon were still divided while their leaders drank coffee together, he said. "The more the leaders agitate the street, the more power they get. Some young kids don't want calm. They hope it escalates. They can go to the leaders and get money from them. The leaders hire men from Tabbaneh to be their armed bodyguards." The ideologies of both sides were bankrupt, he told me. Politicians escalated sectarian tensions in order to reach their goals. Leadership was based on creating fear and tension. Without fear and tension, they wouldn't be leaders.

Mustafa agreed that the communities were being led by elites. He remembered throwing rocks at Jabal Mohsen when he was seven years old. "The rivalry goes back before the massacre," he said. "We Sunnis oppressed the Alawites," Ilmir admitted. "They were garbage collectors, then they got educated, and we couldn't believe they changed." When he tried to arrange a reconciliation involving youth soccer, he was discouraged. "The police said it would end in stabbings."

For once the Palestinians had emerged unscathed, having wisely chosen to abstain from involvement. A local Hamas official told me that there had been a joint Palestinian decision to stay out of the fighting. Some Fatah men had been involved in the Tariq al-Jadida fighting, and others had shut the road from Saida to Beirut. Dai al-Islam al-Shahal asked Palestinians in the north to join him, but nobody responded. "Dai al-Islam is another kind of Salafi. We don't trust him, and we don't share his point of view," the official told me. "There is a general feeling that Sunnis in Lebanon were insulted in this battle," he said. Hizballah knew that if the conflict lasted any longer, it would spread in the region.

Some Sunnis were beginning to question their support for Saad al-Hariri. The Muslim Brotherhood had mediated between Hizballah and the Future Movement, so the Hamas official expected the Muslim Brotherhood would benefit from an increasingly influential role. Hizballah didn't want bloodshed, the Hamas official told me, because every Sunni killed was a danger to the group. "Hizballah was very smart to end it in a short time."

Fatah al-Islam had spread outside the camps and might seek a role as the defender of Sunnis, he told me, even though Shaker al-Absi, who was still alive, had not sought a fight with Shiites. "The atmosphere is very welcoming for these groups," he said. "Sunnis felt that they were caught without their underwear on." Now some Sunnis asked why they had supported the war on Fatah al-Islam, because they could have used them in the recent battles.

In Bedawi Palestinian officials told me that the Palestinian leadership in Beirut took a united stand and decided not to take sides. The pro-Syrian and pro-Fatah groups worked together, coordinating and refusing to get involved. Hizballah also met with Palestinian leaders and urged them not to participate. The Bedawi officials told me that Salafi clerics and leaflets had recently appeared in the camp, using the language of Iraq (such as referring to Shiites as *rafidha*), and Lebanese Salafi groups were active in the camps again. Representatives of Khaled Dhaher and Mufti Rifai were encouraging people to fight the Alawites of Jabal Mohsen. Shahal was openly calling for this, too, asking for Palestinians to fight Hizballah. There were rumors that Fatah al-Islam men were fighting the Alawites at his behest. Shahal and his fighters had allied with Dhaher and the Future Movement.

The officials believed Absi was alive and living in the Beqaa. One of the Palestinian intelligence officials had known him. Absi had come to Lebanon without Syrian backing, he told me. He had not wanted to fight Shiites, only the UN peacekeepers and Israel. But Abu Hureira, the Lebanese Fatah al-Islam member from Akkar, had wanted to take up the fight. The intelligence official had been in Nahr al-Barid when Abu Hureira attacked the Lebanese soldiers. Absi hadn't known about it in advance and had emerged from his house astonished. Before the attack Abu Hureira had called Sheikh Bilal Barudi in Tripoli and told him that if his men from the bank robbery were not released, then they would attack. Fatah al-Islam had been more than one group. During the Nahr al-Barid fighting Mufti Osama Rifai issued a *fatwa* allowing for Palestinians to be killed and for their belongings to be looted. There was a backlash following the fighting with Fatah al-Islam. Many of the older sheikhs in the camp were resented and replaced by young ones. The Lebanese army still manned checkpoints around Nahr al-Barid and was still humiliating people.

Entry into Ayn al-Hilweh was harder than ever, but I managed to get the army's permission to meet Abu Ahmad Fadhil, the Hamas leader in the camp. The various Palestinian factions had formed an emergency committee headed by Kamal Midhat of Fatah. "There was a Palestinian consensus against interference," he told me. "Even Usbat al-Ansar is in it. We as Palestinians won't get involved in internal Lebanese affairs, we told the opposition and the government."

Fadhil worried that Al Qaeda in Iraq was sending fighters to Lebanon. "These guys, their situation in Iraq is difficult, and they can't live in Syria either." As a result, some of them were coming to the camp and to the Beqaa, especially Majd al-Anjar. Both sides had an interest in getting the Palestinians involved in the fighting, Fadhil said, and attempts to draw them in had been especially forceful in Beirut's Shatila camp. But Palestinians had rejected Fatah al-Islam, and even the most extreme groups like Jund al-Sham and Usbat al-Ansar did not have an anti-Shiite reaction following the May 8 clashes. Ayn al-Hilweh was different from Nahr al-Barid. Nahr al-Barid was far from Tripoli, while Ayn al-Hilweh was part of Saida. In Nahr al-Barid, the Palestinian factions were weak and could not stand up to Fatah al-Islam, but in Ayn al-Hilweh, Palestinians "are very strong and have the ability to prevent groups like Fatah al-Islam from appearing."

I went to see Abu Ghassan in the camp, with whom I had spent so much time in 2007. The last camp member to go fight in Iraq had left four or five months earlier. Now the border between Lebanon and Syria was hard to cross, and the Syrian Iraqi border was even harder. "We had nothing to do with the Beirut battles," he told me. "Neither side likes us; they would all have blamed us. Hizballah sent people here and said, 'These guys killed you last year in Nahr al-Barid, fight with us.' Future said, 'These guys killed you in the war of the camps, join us.'"

Attacks on Sunni mosques were evidence of sectarian hatred on both sides, he told me, but he regretted this. "We have doctrinal differences with them, but we have an enemy, Israel. I am speaking as a Muslim: if sectarian war happens here, like in Iraq, then Palestinians would get involved. In the end, we are Sunnis."

I asked him which jihadist ideologues were most influential in the camp. He named Abu Muhammad al-Maqdisi, a Saudi called Sheikh Khalid Rashid, Ayman al-Zawahiri, and Abu Musab al-Zarqawi, but "Sheikh Osama" bin Laden was the most important, "because he renewed jihad in our century." Although many "terrorism experts" in the West were excited that several prominent jihad ideologues had recanted, Abu Ghassan confirmed my view that most people knew they had been forced to change their mind.

He had sold his Glock pistol recently. Weapons prices in the camp were related to the prices in Syria and Iraq, he told me. He now had a CZ75 pistol, which cost $1,500. As we spoke, we heard shots fired outside. He told his son to come in the house.

Back in Tripoli, Musbah al-Ahdab publicly stated that if Hizballah had a right to fight, then so too did Salafis. If the army could not protect Lebanese citizens, then he could not ask Salafis to disarm. If Hizballah did not lay its arms down, the whole north would become Salafis, he warned. "The only solution is to put Hizballah's arms on the table and find a solution; otherwise, the whole north will become Salafists, and I can only sympathize with them," he concluded.

In early July 2008 I returned to the Salam Mosque in Tripoli to hear Bilal Barudi speak. People sat smoking a *nargila* at a nearby cafe. I sat at one of the tables as Barudi's sermon blasted throughout the area. Sunnis were in danger, he warned; they wanted *tawtin*, the granting of citizenship to the Palestinians. "We are in a rage now and we should take advantage of that rage," he said. "We have to keep our sect together. Why are they afraid of *tawtin*? Because Palestinians are Sunnis. . . . There is a conspiracy against us Sunnis." Why, he asked, did Armenians in Lebanon have citizenship when their homeland was stable but the Palestinians, who had nothing, were denied it?

I interviewed Barudi in his office. He was born a sheikh, he told me, explaining that his family had provided sheikhs for seven hundred years. Barudi had met Shaker al-Absi when Absi first arrived. "He started attracting young men with a call to defend Sunnis," he told me. "I told him you are all going to get killed." Barudi claimed he had gone to Beirut to meet Hassan Nasrallah and other Shiite officials after the 2006 Samarra shrine attack, but he said that Nasrallah had been very aggressive with him. He also claimed that Iran and Hizballah operatives blew up the shrine, and stressed that two hundred Sunni mosques in Iraq were destroyed on the same day.

"There is no alternative to Hariri," he told me. "Hizballah is trying to control us and remove us from the Lebanese equation, but we asked the mufti and Saad al-Hariri to arm the guys on the street, and we know that the guys on the street are capable and ready to fight. There is no solution but the armed solution. This period of time will be dangerous. There is a chance for Al Qaeda to appear in Lebanon. We expect suicide bombers in Lebanon soon." Barudi described the Islamic Gathering as "a national Islamic resistance against the Iranian plan in Lebanon," warning that the Shiites would make him don an *imama*, as a Shiite clerical turban is known.

I asked Nawaf al-Musawi of Hizballah if he expected Al Qaeda to establish itself in Lebanon. "Saad won't stay in Lebanon if this happens," he said. "They will pay the price for this. The Al Qaeda agenda has other priorities. Musbah al-Ahdab will be the first victim."

Musawi was feeling triumphant. "We are always thinking about how a threat can become an opportunity," he told me. "The situation in Lebanon is different than Iraq. The Future Movement doesn't have a future without an agreement with us. Experience shows that facing us is a losing battle for them. If they threaten us with Salafis, they are committing suicide. Dai al-Islam works for the Saudis, but his environment is an incubator for killer *takfiris*. We avoid any form of sectarian conflict."

Future had a plan to control Beirut, Musawi explained. It was a good plan, he admitted: Future wanted to seize neighborhoods, isolate Dahiyeh from

Beirut, surround Shiite neighborhoods, and close the roads around Dahiyeh and the Beqaa. The Future plan was not to occupy opposition areas but to besiege them and have an extended period of street fighting so that the government would tell the UN that Hizballah was an outlaw group. Then there would be an excuse to invite international forces into Lebanon and press the issue of Hizballah's arms. "We had a quick operation, and we caused this plan to fail," Musawi said. "As an organization we had good intelligence." He explained that Hizballah had the centers of power in Beirut surrounded. "We had the head. The Saudis lost on the battlefield."

Hizballah and its allies did not seek to change the government by force, nor did it seize control of government officers. Its demand was merely the revocation of the government's two decisions targeting the resistance. On May 13 the government finally relented. Following the clashes in Beirut, a delegation from the Arab League managed to establish a truce. Roadblocks were removed, the country was reopened, and militias removed their weapons from the streets. Then the parties to the conflict were flown to Qatar, where the national dialogue resumed to resolve the crisis. For the Saudis it was a double humiliation: not only had their proxies been defeated in Lebanon but they had lost their lead diplomatic role to their rival Qatar.

March 14 proved itself utterly dependent on the Bush administration and the neoconservatives, widely perceived as closer to Israel and more anti-Arab than any other American regime. But Hizballah also suffered a blow to its credibility because it had violated its longstanding commitment never to use its weapons internally. In this sense American and Saudi proxies scored a victory by portraying Hizballah as merely one more sectarian militia in Lebanon, and no longer the national resistance.

"Backed by Syria and Iran, Hizballah and its allies are killing and injuring innocent citizens and undermining the legitimate authority of the Lebanese government and the institutions of the Lebanese state," said Secretary of State Condoleezza Rice. "Seeking to protect their state within a state, Hizballah has exploited its allies and demonstrated its contempt for its fellow Lebanese."

The May incidents demonstrated the futility of Future adopting any kind of armed program. Hizballah's brief takeover of Beirut demonstrated how little the Saudis, Americans, and French were willing to do for their local proxies in Lebanon, and in Doha March 14 was forced to conform to most of the opposition's stipulation.

Sectarian Hatred Spreads Across the Region

In Palestine the Americans had pushed Fatah and Hamas to the point of civil war, and then in Lebanon they had also managed to push political tension to armed conflict. In both cases the goal was to discredit overwhelming popular movements, subverting democracy and ignoring the popular will. In Lebanon the Bush administration pressured the ruling coalition not to compromise with the opposition. In December 2009 Nasrallah condemned Arab states—not for being silent, he said, but for their partnership with Israel in the murder of Palestinians. He called on the Egyptian people and army to protest and pressure the Egyptian dictatorship to open the siege on Gaza. It was the first time Hizballah had ever singled out an Arab state. Even during Israel's 2006 war on Lebanon, the movement had not gone this far. The next month Nasrallah stated that although Hizballah had not made enemies of Arab states that supported Israel in the 2006 war it would make enemies of those that collaborated against Gaza and the Palestinians. If the Egyptians opened the border, he said, then food, medicine, and even weapons could reach Gaza—and the victory of the resistance in Lebanon could be repeated.

Sunni Islamists resent Hizballah for monopolizing the struggle with Israel and denying them access to fight the Zionists. The American invasion of Iraq gave them a worthy enemy for the first time since the Soviets invaded Afghanistan. It must have been galling to Al Qaeda leaders to see Hizballah regularly praised on Arabic satellite networks while it was condemned, to see that Nasrallah was the most beloved individual in the Arab world while bin Laden and Zawahiri were reviled or ignored. In September 2008 one of the Muslim world's most prominent Islamic scholars, Yusuf al-Qaradawi, who had condemned Al Qaeda in the past, denounced Shiites as heretics and warned that they were trying to penetrate the Sunni world.

In 2006 a poll of majority-Sunni Egypt revealed that Nasrallah, Iranian leader Mahmoud Ahmadinejad, and Hamas leader Khalid Meshal were the three most popular figures in the country. But following the execution of Saddam there was a backlash against Shiites. Some Fatah supporters took to labeling Hamas as Shiites because it received help from Iran. Iranian nuclear intransigence has led the Americans to seek an alliance with Sunni Arab dictatorships. The Americans and Israelis campaigned to convince regional governments that Iran was their real enemy. The notion of "moderate Sunni" states was propounded by the Americans, but the people of these states hated their regimes.

Throughout the region the Iraq War reinvigorated pre-existing sectarianism and provided a new framework for reviving sectarian politics. Since the mid-1970s Kuwait had been the most important center of Shiite radicalism and organization in the Gulf, with movements there reaching out to Shiites in Bahrain and Saudi Arabia. Kuwait had historic tensions between Shiites and Sunnis, which occasionally flared. Sunnis would gang up on Shiite candidates in parliamentary elections to sabotage their electoral chances. The social contract in which the ruler protected Kuwait's Shiites from persecution collapsed after the Iran-Iraq War, but after the Iraqi invasion of Kuwait it was restored because of the exaggerated role of Shiites resisting the Iraqi occupation. Some said that Shiites hadn't fled from Kuwait like others because the Saudis wouldn't let them across the border. Following the American invasion of Iraq tensions increased, fomented by members of the royal family. Given regional fears of a Shiite revival, Kuwait was vulnerable to these machinations.

After the February 2008 assassination of legendary Hizballah commander Imad Mughniyeh, up to two thousand Kuwaiti Shiites marched in his honor, including two Parliament members. They were met with anger and political maneuvering because any expressions of sympathy for Hizballah, Iraqi Shiites, or Iran were seen as disloyal.

Like in Kuwait, sectarian tensions in Bahrain had been a regular feature of the political landscape since the 1980s. They were typically initiated by the government but there were also flare-ups initiated by Shiites, who are the majority. Following the American invasion of Iraq the ruling family in Bahrain, like that of Kuwait, was better able to play the sectarian card—warning of a powerful Iran, a Shiite-dominated Iraq, and a fifth column at home.

In July 2009 Egypt charged twenty-six men with spying for Hizballah and plotting to attack tourists. "Iran, and Iran's followers, want Egypt to become a maid of honor for the crowned Iranian queen when she enters the Middle East," Egyptian Foreign Minister Ahmed Abul Gheit declared. The next month Jordan put six of its citizens on trial for fomenting religious sectarianism and promoting Shiism. The Moroccan dictatorship severed its ties with Iran after accusing it of spreading Shiism in Morocco. Yemen accused Hizballah of training Zaydi rebels in the north. The Yemeni dictatorship was in the midst of two civil wars: one against southern secessionists and one against Zaydi tribesmen in the north. Zaydis, who ruled Yemen for centuries, are related to Shiites but are also very close in their beliefs to Yemen's Sunnis. The Yemeni dictatorship had manipulated its sects, supporting Al Qaeda–like Salafis and veterans of the anti-Soviet jihad in Afghanistan when it suited it, and then supporting Zaydis to counterbalance the Salafis. Now it was invoking the phantom Iranian and Hizballah threat as well as an exaggerated Al Qaeda presence to bolster its weak status, with American and Saudi help. Hizballah did admit to supporting Hamas, but it denied getting involved in conflicts between regimes and their people.

The Shiite belief that succession to the Prophet Muhammad should run through his bloodline through his cousin and son-in-law Ali is viewed by the Saudi clergy and royal family as a threat to their power. Shiites in Saudi Arabia are considered subhuman, an official view that is promoted in state schools; they are not allowed to practice their religion in public. During Israel's 2006 war on Lebanon, leading Saudi cleric Sheikh Abdallah bin Jabrin banned support for Hizballah. In December 2008 Saudi security forces fired rubber bullets at crowds of Shiites demonstrating in solidarity with the Palestinians of Gaza.

In 2009 the imam of the Grand Mosque in Mecca attacked Shiite clerics, call-ing them heretics. Even ordinary Shiites had no excuse for the ignorance and error of their beliefs, he said.

In Lebanon nothing has been resolved; the crisis has been merely further postponed. The 2009 elections were a slight setback for Hizballah's Christian allies, but Hizballah lost no popularity, and all its candidates were elected. Al-though Hizballah's Christian allies, led by Aoun, received the most votes among Christians, they were defeated thanks to some clever gerrymandering, which allowed Sunni voters to tilt the balance in favor of March 14 in Christian districts. But when the time came to apportion ministries, the Aoun move-ment received five, while Hariri's Christian allies received only three.

In June 2009 Saad Hariri was sworn in as prime minister. The Syrians sup-ported his election. The Saudis, who had begun their rapprochement with Syria earlier that year, pushed Hariri to visit Damascus and reconcile with the man he accused of killing his father. Hariri was now head of a national unity government, with Hizballah as his partner. But although Lebanon's elites were governing together and even playing football matches, their constituency had not reconciled and remained at odds with one another. Sunnis, in particular, were still feeling humiliated and resentful. After the elections Dai al-Islam, Fu-ture's main Salafi ally, expressed disappointment with the disrespect and neg-lect they felt Hariri was showing them.

The country's volatile sectarian structure remained, as did its underlying so-cial and economic injustices. The sectarian leaders who profit from the system—which forces these injustices to be expressed in sectarian and xenopho-bic language—remained too. The Palestinians remained without rights or hope. Nahr al-Barid remained under siege. No Palestinians had returned to the original old camp, while up to twenty thousand returned to the new one. The camp was now run by Lebanese army intelligence, which still arrested people and accused them of Fatah al-Islam membership. Humiliations and harassment continued at the checkpoints. Lebanon's Sunnis remained bitter, though the state did begin taking aggressive action against my friends in Majd al-Anjar. Meanwhile, people waited for the next war with Israel.

CHAPTER ELEVEN

A Guest of the Taliban

ZE TALIBANO MILMAYAM: I AM A GUEST OF THE TALIBAN—IMPORTANT words to remember in Afghanistan. One Saturday afternoon in August 2008, two Taliban commanders met me in Kabul to take me to the Ghazni province, south of Afghanistan's capital. The plan was to spend a week with various Taliban groups in areas they controlled. A well-connected Afghan friend I trusted had made the introductions. He knew many groups of fighters in Afghanistan, he said, but he would trust my security only with a group who knew that if anything happened to me, then they and their families would be killed. Contact had been made through a well-respected dignitary from Ghazni who connected us with Mullah Abdillah, a midlevel Taliban commander, who then contacted Mullah Baradar, the Taliban defense minister, and approved my trip.

Mullah Abdillah was a thin man with dark skin and a wispy beard that was long and tapered beneath his chin. He was quick to smile and looked like Bob Marley. He walked with a limp and was bandaged from a recent injury. He had come to Kabul to meet me a week earlier. I explained what I wanted to do. He promised to submit the request to his defense minister, but he was then called away on a mission to the north. I waited impatiently and nervously in my Kabul hotel to receive word about my trip, contemplating the many dangers and trying to ignore the admonitions of friends with more experience working in Afghanistan. Journalists had been able to access armed groups in the 1980s and '90s, but now it was more dangerous. Afghan journalists were killed by the Taliban or arrested by the government if they succeeded in meeting the Taliban. In 2007 an Italian journalist was arrested by the Taliban; he was released at a price, but his driver and fixer were both murdered. In 2008 a British filmmaker, Sean Langan, was held for three months with his fixer, but both were eventually released. David Rohde of the *New York Times* also spent seven months in the company of the Taliban. Lack of access meant that very little was known or understood about the Taliban, one of the most important groups resisting the U.S. occupation.

The origins of the Taliban are in the jihad against the Soviets, who invaded Afghanistan in 1979. The United States, Saudi Arabia, and Pakistan backed seven Sunni Islamist parties who fought the Soviets. Many of these mujahideen were extremists, but there was a preference for radical Muslim groups over nationalist groups. Gulbuddin Hekmatyar's Hizb-e-Islami (Islamic Party) received the most backing. Jalaluddin Haqqani was another commander who received backing from the West. Both were now fighting the Americans and their allies in Afghanistan. The mujahideen were eventually successful, after the Soviets withdrew support for their quislings, and then the West forgot its proxies, who took to fighting among themselves and preying on the population. Into this postwar chaos stepped the Taliban.

The Taliban came from religious schools set up across the border in Pakistan. These schools provided a free religious education to millions of Afghan refugees and Pakistanis. Many of them helped to spread a radically strict form of Sunni Islam combined with Pashtunwali, the Pashtun tribal and social code of behavior. From a small core of devout religious students with rudimentary military skills, the Taliban grew into a vast state and military movement that controlled all but a fraction of Afghanistan. As the warlords were busy fighting one another and terrorizing Afghans, the Taliban seized their first town in 1993. Three years later they took Kabul. In 1998 the Taliban took the last major city in the north, Mazar-i-Sharif. The Pakistanis abandoned Hekmatyar in favor of the Taliban when they saw how successful the movement was. By 2001 less than 10 percent of Afghanistan remained in the hands of the Tajik Mujahideen, who continued a losing struggle against the Taliban until the Americans came to their rescue.

The Taliban have been portrayed as coming out of nowhere and rescuing a war-weary population that welcomed them because they were terrorized by warlords. In truth, most of the country was not in an anarchic state, although Kandahar and its environs were. In much of the country the Taliban had to fight its way into areas that were already at peace and where local services were better than anything the Taliban could provide. The Taliban even engaged in rape, murder, and massacres to conquer some areas. Some of their violence was ethnically motivated. In some places they violated Islamic laws of war with a scorched-earth policy. They even had a sex trade in Tajik girls. And while Kabul was not at peace, residents of the capital certainly did not welcome the arrival of the Taliban, who also bombarded the city. According to Afghan expert William Maley, "While the Taliban attempted to legitimate their power by reference to their provision of 'security,' with the passage of time it became clear that . . . they had made a wilderness and called it peace."

The austere mix of strict Islam and Pashtunwali was harsh. But Western NGOs were able to work in Taliban-controlled Afghanistan, though subject to draconian conditions, and the United States had a civil relationship with the group through diplomatic back channels until 1998. The Taliban had little interest in the West but instead cracked down on local practices they viewed as un-Islamic, including music and flying kites. The Pashtunwali code of hospitality forbade the Taliban leadership from handing over the Al Qaeda leadership, as the Americans demanded after September 11, and NATO, which was seeking a new reason for its existence after the demise of the Soviet Union, united to expel the Taliban from Afghanistan and install a friendlier government. The UN-brokered Bonn conference in December 2001 established an interim administration led by Hamid Karzai, a Pashtun with no power base of his own. Pashtuns are the largest of Afghanistan's fifty-five ethnic groups, but the government was dominated by Tajiks, many of whom had battled the Taliban. In 2002 a *loya jirga* (grand assembly) was held, which established a transitional administration dominated by Tajiks. For the first four years, the NATO-led International Security Assistance Force (ISAF) was restricted to Kabul, where it protected the Karzai government but ignored the fires spreading throughout Afghanistan. After September 11, the Pakistanis played a double game, joining the U.S. "war on terror" while continuing to back the Taliban. The Pakistani dictatorship backed Islamists to help it confront its more secular and popular democratic opposition. But these Islamists were allied with the Taliban. Just as American neglect of Afghanistan after the Soviet withdrawal led to the Taliban and secure bases for Al Qaeda, so too did American neglect of Afghanistan after it removed the Taliban and moved on to Iraq lead to a resurgence of the Taliban and Al Qaeda. Following the defeat of the Taliban, the American strategy was centered on a "light footprint," relying on Special Forces to turn Afghanistan over to local leaders, with a weak central government in Kabul. Warlords were paid to run things and fight Al Qaeda. A continuous flow of U.S. funds was necessary to maintain the local militias and prop up anti-Taliban elders.

I had first come to Afghanistan in 2004, after my time in Falluja, seeking respite from the war. It was an idyllic time for me. Afghanistan was still the forgotten war; the mood in the country was optimistic. I drove up to Bamiyan in the north and went swimming in lake Bandi Amir. South of Kabul, I took road trips through villages in Logar and Paktiya all the way to the Pakistani border. I watched the first presidential elections in Gardez. But by 2008 the distance between Iraq and Afghanistan seemed to have closed. It was as if Afghanistan had become Iraq's neighbor. The foreign military occupation was now killing and arresting innocent civilians, always denying initial reports that turned out to be accurate. The insurgency was increasingly sophisticated, learning from Iraq; its IEDs and suicide bombings were devastating.

The alleged success of the surge in Iraq seemed to confirm the notion that more American troops could solve other problems. For American politicians and the complacent news media, the U.S. was on the verge of victory in Iraq, even if it had taken five years, the destruction of the country, a civil war, hundreds of thousands of dead, millions displaced, communities divided by concrete walls, and the creation of new militias to reduce the violence from its highest points. As I showed in previous chapters, this is not the case, and the reduction of violence, falsely attributed to the increase in American troops, was leading many to draw the wrong lessons from Iraq and then apply them to Afghanistan.

Seven years after the Americans overthrew the Taliban, the movement was gaining confidence, able to control territory right up to Kabul's backyard, while the American-backed government was weaker than ever. President Hamid Karzai was unable to extend his control beyond the capital. CNN was calling Afghanistan the "forgotten war," and it had indeed received less attention than Iraq from the international media and even from the Bush administration. The 2008 presidential campaign changed that.

For Republicans the military has traditionally been the chief tool of foreign policy, but Afghanistan became a much more central issue for Democratic presidential nominee Barack Obama than it did for John McCain. Obama wanted to legitimize his call for a withdrawal from Iraq by increasing troops in Afghanistan. The Democratic narrative was that the United States should have stayed in Afghanistan and needed to swivel the cannons back to the original target. The Democrats worried about appearing weak. They wanted to prove that they too could be bellicose and tough, and kill foreigners. But calling the war in Iraq wrong didn't necessarily mean that expanding the war in Afghanistan was right.

By September 2008 there were already about thirty-three thousand U.S. troops in Afghanistan and a total of sixty-five thousand troops in the international coalition. They were facing more resistance than ever, and by September 2008 the 2007 total of 111 dead troops had already been surpassed. Speaking at the National Defense University on September 9, President Bush announced a modest troop increase in Afghanistan, which he described as a "quiet surge" to help "stabilize Afghanistan's young democracy." He would not allow the Taliban to return to Afghanistan, he said, unaware that they already had, and that only negotiation with the Taliban could bring any hope of stabilizing Afghanistan. "Iraq, Afghanistan, and parts of Pakistan pose the same challenge to our country, and they are all theaters in the same struggle," he said, proclaiming his "faith in the power of freedom." But the Taliban had their own faith, and so far they were winning.

There was a glitch in the matrix when, on September 10, 2008, Adm. Mike Mullen, chairman of the Joint Chiefs of Staff, testified before the House Armed Services Committee. In his prepared testimony, which he submitted after it was approved by Defense Secretary Robert Gates and President Bush, Admiral Mullen stated, "I am convinced we can win the war in Afghanistan." His oral testimony was different. "I am not convinced we are winning it in Afghanistan," he said. In a war, if you are not winning, then you are usually losing.

BEFORE LEAVING KABUL I bought several pairs of kala, or *salwar kameez*, the traditional dress worn by Afghan men consisting of a long tunic-like shirt with buttons on the top and baggy pants. I had grown my beard longer than ever, and endured suspicious looks in New York City subways as a result. In New York I had also taken intensive Pashtu-language classes, to at least have some basic communication skills. Very few Western journalists knew Pashtu, but it is the language spoken by the ethnic group that dominates the Taliban, one of the biggest thorns in the side of the American military in Afghanistan. It is also the language of those people in Afghanistan and Pakistan who support or protect the Taliban, and what remains of the original senior Al Qaeda leadership. Regardless of who ended up winning the 2008 election, I knew America was certain to remain embroiled in conflicts with movements based in the lawless majority-Pashtun areas of South Asia. I didn't think conflicts could be understood by studying only one side; journalists needed to study Pashtu and not merely embed with the American military.

Pashtu was not exactly in high demand, and the book the language school gave me was pretty basic and clearly designed for the military. It had a list of ranks, such as "general of the Air Force" and "private first class." It also gave me a list of weapons such as land mines and bullets. It provided the Pashtu translation for important phrases like "You are a prisoner," "Show me your ID card," "Hands up," "Surrender," and "Let the vehicle pass." If I wanted to arrest an Afghan, I was now prepared. Interestingly, in the list of foods the book included hummus, which is eaten in the Arab world but not in Afghanistan (unless some fastidious Al Qaeda volunteer brought some with him). The book provided essential advice such as "Don't burp or fart in public," "Don't call everyone Hajji," "Don't trust everyone," "Don't use the same route every time," and "Don't offer pork to any Muslim." It also advised me not to whistle or make catcalls toward any woman and not to insult "a native" in public.

Ghazni fell to the Taliban in 1995, early in their campaign to seize Afghanistan from the warlords. I was told it fell without a fight, almost overnight, soon after Kandahar. There were many subcommanders allied with various mujahideen parties. Alliances shifted often, and it was easy for the Taliban to co-opt these commanders, who just put on turbans, flew the white flag of the Taliban, and said, "Okay, we're Taliban."

In the last few years of their reign the Taliban even succeeded in gaining the cooperation of Ghazni's Shiite Hazara community. So the area was fertile ground for the neo-Taliban, whose control was spreading once again. Tribal leaders were weak in Ghazni while religious leaders were strong, making it easier for the Taliban to embed themselves with the population. The neo-Taliban also seized upon the population's many grievances. Police would release prisoners in exchange for bribes, while Afghan soldiers looted people's homes and government officials took goods from shops without paying for them. In 2006 forty policemen quit, and some joined the Taliban, because their salaries were many months late. Police chiefs had to buy supplies with their own money, so they extorted from the population. More and more clerics started supporting the Taliban. In 2006 the former governor of Ghazni was assassinated after announcing he was taking over security in the Andar district so that he could defeat the Taliban there. By 2006, in Andar alone dozens of government officials and others viewed as collaborators had been killed by the Taliban; soon there was no government presence in most of Ghazni's countryside. When the Americans distributed cash to villagers, they would hand it over to the Taliban, and as soon as the Americans visited a village the Taliban would follow and seize anything that had been distributed. Former mujahideen commanders in Ghazni joined the Taliban. A 2006 military operation called Mountain Fury was said to have "dealt Taliban and foreign fighters a string of sharp defeats" in Andar. The U.S. Army claimed that "large swaths of southern and central Ghazni Province, described as ungovernable as recently as late August, embraced the allies and the reemerging provincial government." But things continued to worsen. Twenty-three South Korean missionaries were captured by the Taliban in Ghazni in 2007. That year eighteen Afghan de-miners were kidnapped from their base in Andar three weeks after a military operation attempted to remove the Taliban's "shadow government" there, and when President Karzai gave a speech in Andar, the Taliban fired fifteen rockets at the event. One month before I arrived, Afghan broadcasters showed clips of Taliban kidnapping and executing two Afghan women on charges of "immorality."

Before I left for Ghazni, I spoke to a senior UN official. "I don't think you should go," he said. "It's deteriorated. Many Taliban commanders were killed there, and the leadership is totally fragmented. There is a lot of criminality within. In the past there was a sense of protection for foreigners here, but being a foreigner there is a major risk. There are Taliban checkpoints in the middle of Ghazni at night. Much of Ghazni is under Taliban control." I put his admonitions out of my mind. Three months earlier an Afghan soldier returned to Andar to irrigate his land. He was wearing civilian clothes, but the Taliban arrested him and executed him near the district bazaar. "The Andar district compound near the bazaar has only fifteen police," said one local who now lived in Kabul and was afraid to return. "They can't even secure their compound, so how can they secure the district?" His cousin had once worked for the Parliament in Kabul, but the Taliban had threatened him with death if he returned to his work, so he stayed in Andar.

The Taliban governor for Ghazni issued ID cards and passports for the Taliban regime, the Islamic Emirate of Afghanistan. Farmers with land disputes went to the Taliban there to seek justice according to their interpretation of Islamic jurisprudence. Beginning in 2004 the roads in Ghazni started getting dangerous, but now the Taliban could stop you there in broad daylight and check your cellphone to determine from your calls if you were a worthwhile captive. The Taliban's former minister of education had been released in exchange for the Korean hostages in 2007. He returned to assume a position of importance among the Taliban of Ghazni. In order to gain control of one district, a senior UN official told me, the province's government-appointed governor had to move his troops and surrender control of another district. Before leaving I asked my friend if I should worry about my trip succeeding. "In Afghanistan you should always worry," he said.

Shafiq, another commander from Ghazni, drove us down as Mullah Abdillah sat in the front passenger seat. We were accompanied by Kamal, a twenty-eight-year-old Afghan who knew just enough English to confuse both of us. I had tried and failed to find a real translator; some were unavailable, and others refused when they were told what the trip entailed. With the Arabic I knew as well as my basic Farsi and Pashtu, I hoped I would manage.

Abdillah had been injured recently in clashes with a rival commander from the Taliban, though at first he told me the wound was from an American bullet. He paid one thousand dollars of his own money for two surgeries at a private Kabul hospital to repair nerve damage. The wound was now covered with a bandage. He bore older scars on his arm and leg, and had lost one of his legs in fighting in the civil war during the '90s. Abdillah was now a commander in the Dih Yak district of Ghazni. He told me he had five hundred men under his command. Abdillah was also a liaison with more senior Taliban leaders and regularly communicated with the Taliban's minister of defense. Shafiq had light skin with a short light-brown beard and wore a cap with embroidery and rhinestones. He had fought the Russians with the mujahideen. I asked him who was a more formidable foe: the Russians or the Americans. The Russians were stronger, he told me, more fierce. "We will put the Americans in graves," he said. Shafiq was a commander of fighters in Andar. He and Abdillah chatted and joked on the way to Ghazni. We were stopped at an Afghan army checkpoint, and the wary soldiers singled me out, growing more suspicious when they heard in my accent that I was a foreigner. One of the soldiers wore a brown T-shirt, and on his black vest he had a roll of plastic American flex-cuffs. My companions persuaded the soldiers that I was only a journalist. As we drove away, Abdillah and Shafiq laughed, explaining that the soldiers thought I was a suicide bomber.

We soon left Kabul province and entered Wardak. The road, lined with poplar trees and green fields, took us between arid sand-colored mountains with sharp peaks. Nomadic Kuchi women with colorful scarves draped over them ignored us, tending to camels as small boys herded sheep. On the hillsides were cemeteries with rough tombstones haphazardly pointing in various angles and multicolored flags flying above them. In Wardak the new road was torn apart by craters. We circled around them as if they were giant potholes, but most had been made by roadside bombs buried in culverts beneath the road. Without the culverts floods would wash away roads, but they were an ideal location to hide bombs targeting Afghan security forces, the U.S. military, and its allies, as well as the convoys of trucks that provided logistical support. We drove by a truck still smoldering from an attack the day before and a truck charred from an attack a month before. Three or four American armored vehicles drove by, as did Afghan National Army (ANA) pickup trucks.

By the time we reached the town of Salar in Wardak, we had passed about six trucks destroyed by Taliban bombs on the road. In Salar we approached a large group of cars with people standing on the side of the road by a gas station. Shafiq and Abdillah called Taliban friends on their mobile phones to see what was going on. "The Americans are fighting the Taliban," my companions explained. We could see smoke several hundred meters away and heard the chatter of machine-gun fire interrupted by the thuds of mortar fire and loud explosions—which clapped against my ears and got closer, shaking us. I flinched and ducked, gasping and cursing, as Shafiq and Abdillah laughed at me. *"Tawakkal ala Allah"* (depend on God), Shafiq lectured me, using a common expression to tell me not to be afraid. That same month in Salar the Taliban had tried to assassinate the governor of Ghazni, wounding two of his guards.

Two small green NATO armored personnel carriers zipped by driving away from the battle. Shafiq and Abdillah laughed. Bulgarians, they told me. As more cars stopped on the road, more men got out to watch the battle, point at what they could spot, and chat. At a small shop by the gas station, my companions bought a syrupy Taiwanese version of Red Bull called Energy. People went to urinate behind rusting shipping containers. Afghan men squat all the way down when they piss. I couldn't manage this feat of acrobatic skill, and a man standing as he relieved himself would have immediately attracted attention, so I waited until everybody had left before I went and pissed between shipping containers.

Several American vehicles drove by as well as two Polish and two ANA vehicles. A few minutes later three American vehicles sped in the direction of the fighting, shortly followed by three NATO vehicles. After an hour of waiting, everybody smiled and went back to their cars. Buses and cars drove toward us from the direction of the battle scene, honking to let us know the way was safe and the roadblocks had been opened. Trucks were ablaze on the side of the road, and large craters had torn through the asphalt, with chunks of the road tossed in our way. The trucks had been carrying drinks for the Americans, Abdillah told me. Sure enough, as we drove past them we could see hundreds of water bottles spilling out. We drove by the halted convoy. Dozens of trucks, some partially burned, crowded the road. The drivers stood outside the trucks, which had UKMOD (United Kingdom Ministry of Defense) stickers on their windshields. Armed escorts fanned around the road. Further down the road there were more craters and American armored vehicles blocked our path, with fire and smoke behind them. People told us to stop because the Americans were shooting at approaching cars. Shafiq slowly maneuvered the car to the front of the line and stopped. The Americans moved, and we all followed slowly like a nervous herd. We drove by yet more burning trucks down a stretch of road that had been smashed to bits. Abdillah pointed to three destroyed vehicles from an attack four days earlier.

We were on the "ring road," the most critical road in Afghanistan. It was the fastest, most direct and practical means of getting from hub to hub, if you ignored the increasing risk. Without the ring road, one was relegated to using small provincial roads—which greatly increased the length of the trip, since many were just gravel or dirt. The ring road was the only one that was close to being a highway in the country and was the only viable route for those wishing to move large convoys. The Kabul-Kandahar highway had been a showpiece for the American coalition, connecting the two main American bases—in Bagram and Kandahar—and linking two halves of the country together. Now it was destroyed, and traffic in support of the Afghan government or the coalition forces was becoming more difficult. On June 24, 2008, the Taliban attacked a convoy of fifty-four trucks passing through Salar: they destroyed fifty-one of them, seized two Toyota escort vehicles that belonged to the security guards, captured loot, and killed some of the drivers. More recently, on September 8, in Zurmat—which is between Gardez province and Ghazni—a convoy of thirty-five trucks was attacked, and twenty-nine of them were destroyed.

At a lonely desert checkpoint manned by the Afghan army, a few soldiers with AK-47s asked us what had happened on the road. Later we passed by a pickup truck full of more Afghan soldiers. "They are bad," Shafiq told me, explaining they were from Kandahar and were affiliated with President Karzai. "I fight them every day," he said. Night fell, and we passed a police station. "From now on it's all Taliban territory," they told me. "The Americans and police don't come here at night." We no longer had mobile phone reception. Shafiq and Abdillah explained that the Taliban ordered the local phone towers to be shut down every night so they could better conduct operations. We stopped at a gas station, and they pointed to an Afghan in an SUV who they knew worked with the Americans at the nearby base. In the darkness we slowly rolled into the village of Nughi. It was the holiday of Shab-e-Barat, when Muslims believe God determines the destinies of people for the coming year. It seemed as though all the young boys of the village had gathered in small groups to swing balls of fire connected to wires. Like orange stars, hundreds of fiery circles glowed far into the distance. Carefully Shafiq maneuvered the car on the bumpy dirt road between mud houses. A traditional house in these areas, called a *qala*, is made of an extremely durable mixture of mud and straw and built like a fort, with high walls surrounding large compounds that often include different quarters and even areas for agriculture. We pulled up in front of one house, and Shafiq banged on the metal door. A man led us by motorcycle to another house, where a group of young men emerged. In the darkness I could make out a couple of them carrying weapons. We greeted the traditional way, each man placing his right hand on the other's heart, leaning in but not fully embracing and inquiring about the other's health, home, and family.

Mullah Abdillah left us, returning to his house. We followed the Taliban on foot to another house with the moon lighting our path. We entered through a short door into a guest room with a red carpet and wooden beams on the ceiling. A dim bulb barely lit the room. I spotted a rocket-propelled grenade launcher with several rockets beside it and a PKM, or belt-fed machine gun, leaning against the wall. An old man named Haji Shir Muhamad was sitting in the room. Shafiq, Kamal, and I were joined by two Talibs: Mullah Yusuf, a commander from Andar, and a boy called Muhamad. Mullah Yusuf had dark reddish skin and a handsome face. He wore a black turban with thin gold stripes and carried an AK-47. A boy brought a pitcher and basin, and we rinsed our hands. We drank green tea and ate a soup of mushy bread called *shurwa* with our hands. Some chunks of meat were served to us, followed by grapes. Haji Shir Muhamad had lived in Saudi Arabia for five years, so we were able to communicate in Arabic a little.

Mullah Yusuf slept in different houses every night, he said. He went from village to village, as did other Talibs, to avoid the Americans. He was Mullah Abdillah's nephew and was originally from the Zarin village in Ghazni; although he was only thirty years old, he was an important commander in Andar. A year and a half before, Yusuf had been injured in battle by an American helicopter strike. The wound was in his thigh. He had been hospitalized but still had problems and walked with a pronounced limp. Yusuf's cellphone rang with a bells-and-cymbals version of the *Sorcerer's Apprentice* theme. Yusuf had been with the Taliban for five years. Before that he had studied at a famous religious school called Zia ul-Madaris al-Faruqia in Miranshah, center of Pakistan's North Waziristan, where many Afghan refugees lived. He joined the jihad because foreigners had come to Afghanistan, he told me, and were fighting Afghans and poor people in their villages. He had not received training but had learned from friends. He claimed that he did not receive assistance from foreigners, only from people in the villages, who provided weapons and money. Yusuf told me he used what money he had to buy weapons and ammunition before he bought food. Local villagers even helped when the Taliban attacked checkpoints, he said. "All of this village helps because they are Muslim," he said. "The Americans are not good. They go into houses. Some people from this area are in American jails. Fifteen days ago the Americans bombed here and killed a civilian." Foreigners did occasionally come to fight with them, he said, including Saudis and Uzbeks. It soon became clear that he referred to all foreign fighters who volunteered to fight with the Taliban as Arabs. "They are like my brothers," he said. Arabs and Chechens taught them how to use remotely detonated bombs.

"The Americans are blind in Afghanistan," Yusuf said. Afghanistan would be a graveyard for them. But when the foreigners left, the Taliban could negotiate with the Afghan army and police, instead of continuing to fight. "They are brothers, Muslims," he said. He fought with them now only because they were with the Americans. President Karzai would flee to America when the foreigners left, he said. When the foreigners left, girls could go to school and women could work, he added. I asked about the killing of aid workers. If foreigners didn't fight the Taliban, he said, he didn't fight them. The Afghans needed help, and it didn't matter if aid workers were Muslims or infidels, but "the UN is with the Americans, so I fight them."

A year before, in a big attack in Andar, the Americans killed a senior commander named Mullah Mu'min. Yusuf had been his deputy and assumed leadership after he was killed. Yusuf received his orders from his own commanders. The mujahideen always wanted to attack the Americans, he said, but their commanders told them when to attack. Mullah Yusuf operated only in Ghazni. Mullah Omar was the top commander, he told me, but only Yusuf's most senior commanders could communicate with the one-eyed former leader of Afghanistan, who called himself the "commander of the faithful."

Yusuf told me he would stop fighting when the foreigners left Afghanistan, but then he would go to other places like Chechnya, Palestine, Uzbekistan, Lebanon, and Somalia to fight. I doubted it was more than bravado; he knew little about the world outside Afghanistan and his refuge in Pakistan. Still, the pre–September 11 Taliban were much less connected to other struggles in the Muslim world. Globalized jihadism was penetrating even the remote Pashtun areas of Pakistan and Afghanistan. While most Afghan Taliban fought only for Afghanistan, the longer the Americans remained, the more links the Taliban might forge. Out of curiosity, I asked Yusuf what he thought about Hizballah. Throughout the Muslim world, tensions between Sunnis and Shiites were increasing. In Pakistan the Sunni groups backing the Taliban were bitterly anti-Shiite and often murdered innocent Shiites. At first my hosts were confused between Libya and Lebanon. Shafiq said they didn't like Shiites but they liked Hizballah because they fought America, though this was not exactly accurate. "Hizballah are mujahideen," Yusuf said. "It is no problem that they are Shiites.

They are our brothers. The Americans made problems between Sunnis and Shiites. All Muslims are one."

Muhamad, Yusuf's eighteen-year-old companion, was also from Ghazni but had gone to an Islamic school in the Pakistani city of Quetta, which borders Afghanistan and sheltered many Taliban leaders. The school was called Mahmadiya, and education was in Pashtu, the only language Muhamad knew. Room and board had been free. In Quetta he had joined the Taliban, he said, because they were Muslim and his whole village had joined, and because he didn't like the Americans entering his village. His parents did not know he had joined; they thought he was still studying in Pakistan. He had been a fighter for only fifteen days but had received two or three months of training in Ghazni. The training was not difficult, he said, but he had taken part in only one attack so far, against a police checkpoint in Ghazni. He had used an AK-47, and his friend had used an RPG. The Afghan police were not good fighters, he said. Shafiq added that the Afghan army was very good, and soldiers hit their targets when they shot. Referring to Muhamad, Shafiq proudly said, "All our boys are Mullah Omar and Osama."

After we finished eating we walked to a mud shed. Shafiq opened its wooden doors to reveal a white Toyota Corolla. The men loaded the RPG launcher and four rockets into the car, along with the PKM and the AK-47. We drove under the moonlit desert on dirt paths to the village of Kharkhasha, where Shafiq lived. Shafiq put a tape of Taliban chants on. They were in Pashtu and without music, which was officially forbidden by the Taliban. We walked over a short wooden footbridge, and Shafiq's older brother opened the door to greet us.

We entered the guest room in darkness and sat down on the thin mattresses that lined the walls. A small gas lamp was brought out as well as grapes and green tea. Shafiq belonged to the Jalalzai tribe, which was the biggest in Andar, he said. He fought the Soviets alongside Maulvi Muhamad Younes Khalis's hardline Hizb-e-Islami, a splinter group with the same name as the one led by Gulbuddin Hekmatyar. Shafiq was jailed for five years in the Communist era, and he bore tattoos on his wrist from that time. During the jihad against the Soviets, he worked with Arab doctors who volunteered to help the mujahideen. He picked up some Arabic from a Lebanese doctor called Sheikh Aqil, whom he described as a big, strong man. Following the Soviet withdrawal, as the mujahideen started to fight one another, Shafiq said he saw that the mujahideen had become robbers. He joined the Taliban in 1994 because they wanted peace and Islam.

When the American forces left, Shafiq said, he would be willing to negotiate with the Taliban's Afghan rivals—but not with President Karzai, who was not a Muslim but a Jew. "I cannot make a deal with Karzai because he is American," he said. Shafiq wanted a Sharia government, meaning one where Islamic law was imposed, and he hoped that Mullah Omar would return to rule the country. Girls could attend school, he said, and women could work, as long as they wore a *hijab* that covered them appropriately. Women could even serve as Parliament members and as governors, but not as the president, he said. Shafiq had a seven-month-old daughter; he said he would send his daughters to school, but only if the teachers were women. He was wary of giving too much freedom to women. They could go to cinemas only with their brothers or fathers, he said, not with other boys. There weren't many cinemas in Afghanistan, so I didn't know what he was so worried about. "If you give women freedom, they will go with boys and get HIV," he said. One of my favorite views in Kabul was of kites fluttering high above homes in Kabul. The Taliban regime had forbidden kite flying in the past, and I asked Shafiq what he thought. Kites are not good, he said; it was better to work or study, and flying a kite was not even a sport. Soccer was also bad, but exercise and martial arts were good. Even the boys we passed playing with fire were doing something that was *haram* (forbidden).

Shafiq wanted help from Saudi Arabia or Iran; he and his men needed money for ammunition. They received help from Saudi individuals, as well as Pakistanis, but he did not know of any state assistance. Iran did not help them, he said. "Whoever is fighting with America," he said, "he is my brother." Shafiq had a friend called Mullah Agha Jan, who was killed while fighting in Baghdad. They had benefited from the Iraq experience when remote-controlled bomb techniques were imported to Afghanistan. Shafiq had heard of Abu Musab al-Zarqawi, who had run a training camp in western Afghanistan before leading Al Qaeda in Iraq. "He is a big mujahid," Shafiq said, "famous in Afghanistan." Shafiq had met Osama bin Laden twice: once before the Taliban took over and once during its reign. He had been impressed by bin Laden's knowledge of Pashtu. (He must have had a better book than I did.) Shafiq had met Mullah Omar as well. He thought both Mullah Omar and bin Laden were very friendly. Arab, Pakistani, and Uzbek fighters had come through the Andar district, Shafiq said, mostly as suicide bombers but also as fighters. Some Afghans from Kandahar had also come to fight in Andar. The Kandaharis were the best fighters he had seen; they were not afraid. The Russians had fought fiercely, like dogs. He did not have a high opinion of his American foes. "Pakistan and Iran are not friends of Afghanistan," Shafiq said. "They want to take Afghanistan, they don't want peace." In this he was representative of most Afghan Taliban, who despite their extremely conservative views were fundamentally nationalists. Like most Afghans, he was against suicide bombings as well. "Suicide attacks are not good because they kill Muslims," he said.

I asked Shafiq what he thought of a recent attack that had killed the women and driver working for International Rescue Committee in Logar. It was not good to kill women, he said, even infidel women. The Taliban didn't know it was women, he said. The windows were tinted, and they couldn't see the passengers. On the other hand, UN staff were infidels. Human rights were American, so they were bad. The Koran gave all the rights. "People spent seven years in Guantánamo," he said. "Where are the human rights?" Shafiq told me he had recently purchased weapons in Kabul, where a man gave him two PKMs and an RPG for free. Shafiq bought two jeeps from the Afghan police, who later told the Interior Ministry that the vehicles were lost in an attack. "Some police work with us," he said. Shafiq told me that Taliban representatives visited different villages in the area to teach people about the Taliban and recruit on their behalf.

It was late, and the men washed themselves with a bucket of water for the final prayer of the day. We all lay down on the mattresses where we had been sitting and took the pillows that had been against the wall. Shafiq's older brother brought a thick flannel blanket and covered me. In the morning they took turns washing themselves again for the first prayer of the day. Shafiq's older brother brought tea and some dry bread for breakfast. I asked him if he was also with the Taliban. He was just a farmer, he said, pantomiming digging and pointing to the grapes. Shafiq had an eighteen-year-old brother at Ghazni University who was also a Taliban fighter. Another younger brother was in a local school. They owned a generator, which was their only source of occasional electricity, but fuel was expensive at five liters for four hundred Afghans, about eight dollars. I asked about a bathroom. Kamal told me there wasn't any, and instructed me to go outside in the yard.

Shafiq and Kamal went to the bazaar, leaving me with the young Taliban fighter Muhamad, but they said I could walk in the garden as I waited. It was untended and wild. Sunflowers towered over the large mud wall compound, bushes and dry trees grew in rows. There was a deep pit for a well and a crude pump to irrigate the field and draw water for personal use. As we sat waiting in the guest room Mullah Yusuf showed up with a companion called Qadim, who was missing his front teeth. Shafiq carried his AK-47, and the larger Qadim carried a heavier PKM. Mullah Yusuf played with a pair of binoculars he found on the floor. Yusuf wore a vest with pockets for magazines of ammunition, and he had several grenades stuffed in as well. Shafiq returned and spoke on the phone with a fellow Talib fighter from Meidan Shah in Wardak. They had conducted a successful attack, capturing four trucks and drivers.

We got back into the Corolla, loading the PKM, RPG launcher, and four rockets into the trunk. Shafiq and his PKM were in the front passenger seat. Yusuf drove, with his AK-47 beside him. I hoped we wouldn't hit too many bumps. Qadim rode his Honda motorcycle alongside us, an AK-47 strapped to his shoulder, a scarf around his face to protect from the sand and dust. As we drove I finally got to see the environment. It was flat and starkly arid. Everything was the color of sand, including the occasional man-made structure, the mud bleached by the sun. Yusuf pointed to a police checkpoint in the distance. The police knew him but did nothing, he said. "Every night I go on patrol and they don't fight me," he said. "They don't have guns, and they are afraid." I asked Shafiq and Yusuf what services or aid the Taliban provided people in Ghazni. They complained that they had no money to help.

Yusuf called a fellow commander and told him he was bringing over a journalist. The man on the other end of the call called me a devil and told him not to bring me. So we headed to another commander instead. Yusuf passed by a school called Ghams al-Ulum, which his predecessor, Mullah Mu'min, had built fourteen years earlier. There had once been three hundred boys studying at the school, but it had been closed since the Americans arrived. Three years earlier the Americans and Afghan army had used it as a base, he said, "but we fought them and they left."

We drove in the desert to the village of Khodzai and entered a mosque. Eight men and two boys sat on the floor drinking tea. An RPG and several AK-47s were on the floor or against the wall. In addition to Yusuf, another senior commander from Andar was present. The men talked about fighting the Afghan army two days earlier in the nearby Naniki village. The commander I spoke to told me they had ambushed a logistical convoy of trucks using machine guns and RPGs; they killed twenty Afghan soldiers, and one Talib was injured. The Americans didn't come here, and there was no Afghan government, he said. "We control this area. The Taliban is the government here." All the older men agreed that the Russians were more dangerous than the Americans. I asked to take a picture of some of the fighters. The commander wrapped his young son up with a scarf and showed him how to hold the AK. Everybody laughed as I took his picture with the others. The men got ready to go on a patrol, putting on their vests, checking magazines, slinging AK-47s on their shoulders, and wrapping scarves around their faces. We all went out, standing in a sunny courtyard. Small boys and girls emerged to watch the men ready themselves. They got on their Honda motorcycles and carried their RPGs. Suddenly a coalition military helicopter flew low overhead, nearly coming to a hover above us. I clenched my fists in terror waiting for the helicopter to fire a missile at us. I struggled to control the urge to flee. The other men ignored it and laughed at me. One told me that he had fired an RPG at a helicopter the day before, and that they would fire at this one if it attacked us. To my relief, the helicopter continued flying. The men took off on their motorcycles. We drove away in the Corolla. Shafiq told me he had killed more than two hundred alleged spies. After a trial, if the judge gave a verdict of guilty, he explained, they would cut the spy's head off. "First I warn people to stop, and if they continue I kill them," Shafiq said. He explained that they could only fight for about twenty minutes before the helicopters came: "I can't fight for two or three hours."

As we drove he played more Taliban chants about brave boys going to fight. We passed by another school that had been closed. The sun shown bright on old mud houses. Many were worn out and looked like sand castles after the first wave hit them. There was only one school open in the area, Shafiq told me as we drove through the village of Kamalkhel. He pointed to a new yellow school, explaining that it was a government school run by the Taliban. "There are no government people here," Shafiq said. One month earlier the Americans had arrested Mullah Faizani, the Taliban commander of Kamalkhel.

As we drove through villages a bearded man with his face partially concealed by a scarf stopped us on his motorcycle. He demanded to know who I was, and Shafiq told him I was a guest. He asked me if I was Pashtun. "*Pukhtu nayam,*" I said. "I am not Pashtun." He glared at me and drove off.

We entered an old adobe home built seventy years ago. Livestock brayed past the gate. A large group of Taliban were seated around the room. I met a seventeen-year-old called Isa. Like Muhamad, he had been a Talib for only two weeks. He had studied at a local Islamic school in Andar. I asked him why he had joined. "I like the mujahideen," he said, "and I want to do jihad." I asked him why. "Because the Americans are here," Yusuf said. Isa repeated Yusuf's answer. He hoped to continue studying religion when he was done fighting. Food was brought out. More *shurwa* and chunks of meat. They got most of their news from listening to BBC on the radio. They could not watch television because of lack of electricity, they said. In the past the Taliban had prohibited television. One of the Talibs told me he thought the Americans would leave in one year. "When the Americans leave I want to fight them, because why did they attack Afghanistan?" said one man. "America is at war with Islam," said Shafiq. "The war started with the Prophet Muhammad," said Yusuf.

I asked the men who they thought should lead Afghanistan. It didn't have to be Mullah Omar, they said, as long as Islamic law was imposed. I asked them if they would allow people like Osama bin Laden and other foreign fighters in once they controlled Afghanistan. "Islam has no borders," said Shafiq affirmatively. I asked why most Taliban were Pashtun. "Pashtun people have more principles and religious faith than others," said Shafiq. "It's also because Pashtuns are the majority." This is not exactly accurate: Pashtuns are the largest group in Afghanistan, but they are not the majority. "Life was better under the Taliban because it was an Islamic regime," said Yusuf. They asked me questions about the Americans: what they thought of their being in Afghanistan, and if they thought they would win. I struggled to find the right answer. One of the commanders told Shafiq that I was an American CIA agent. Shafiq told him I wasn't. I heard the words "*istikhbarat*" and "*jasus,*" which meant "army intelligence" and "spy," as we readied ourselves to leave.

We left to meet more fighters. Yusuf stopped the car at a house where an American strike had killed two Talibs a year earlier and asked me to photograph it. We crawled through rocky paths between mud homes, a vast labyrinth. Everything looked the same to me. We got stuck in the sand, and a dust storm hit us, blinding and suffocating us as we struggled to push the car. We stopped in front of a shop with the PKM in full view and Taliban music playing. The people in the shop greeted Yusuf warmly. Six men came out to greet us as we sat waiting in the car. Yusuf bought many shoulder straps for AK-47s and put them in the car.

We drove to another mosque and found twelve men inside. A large shoulder-fired missile was on the floor, an anti-armor weapon I had not seen before. Most of the men in this room were older. Shafiq told me we were waiting to meet the commander who would approve my trip. I thought it had all been approved already. One of the men was called Abu Tayyeb, an Arabic nom de guerre. He spoke Arabic, so we were able to talk to each other. He told me he commanded two thousand men in Wardak and was visiting. He had lived in Saudi Arabia for one year and spent three months in a Saudi prison for mujahideen-related activities. He had joined the mujahideen fourteen years ago, he said, and under the Taliban he was a commander in the northern Kunduz province. He told me the large shoulder-fired weapon on the floor was an RR82, or some kind of recoilless rifle. I continued to ask him questions, but then the angry man—the one who had asked me if I was a Pashtun—came in holding a walkie-talkie and barked at him to stop talking to me until the commander, called Dr. Khalil, showed up. I noticed that some other men had walkie-talkies too, and that Kamal was nervous. There was a problem, he told me; the judge would decide what would happen to us. Upon hearing the word qazi (judge), I started to panic inside. As Shafiq had told me, a meeting with a judge could end with your head getting cut off.

We got up to go, and when we were out I was told to get in the car with the angry man and other strangers, who would take me to the judge. Yusuf was praying and Shafiq said he would pray and catch up with us. I told him I was not leaving him, that I was his guest. A desperate feeling was beginning to take over me. Holding their rifles the commander's men shouted at me to get in their car. Yusuf came out, told me to get in our Corolla, and assured me he wouldn't leave us. He put Qadim in the car with us. A standoff ensued. I called and sent text messages to my contacts back in Kabul to let them know I was in trouble. Qadim sat menacingly with an AK-47, his face concealed by a scarf. His phone rang: its ring tones were machine-gun fire and a song about the Taliban being born for martyrdom. Lack of water, fear, and the dust had dried my mouth, and I felt as though I had lost my voice. My friend in Kabul who had helped arrange the trip called Shafiq and told him he should not leave me, that

I was Shafiq's responsibility and he would hold him personally responsible if anything happened to me.

After an hour Shafiq told us we could get out. Abu Tayyeb, the Arabic speaker, tried to reassure me and told me not to worry. The angry man and his companions departed, taking the rocket launcher with them. I thought it was over, and put my hand on my heart as they left, to indicate no ill will. Then Shafiq told us Dr. Khalil was coming to see us. Abu Tayyeb had tried and failed to get them to let us leave. I wondered if all the increased phone traffic and movement of Taliban commanders would attract the attention of whatever American intelligence agency might be spying on us, and if we would be attacked. Abu Tayyeb apologetically explained that there were many Taliban groups and that the one causing me problems was different. Then the order came for us to go see Dr. Khalil ourselves.

We left in a heavy dust storm. The car crawled forward slowly, rocking back and forth on the rocky paths, and I felt as though I were in a boat being tossed about by waves. Yusuf said not to worry, that if they came to take me he would fight them. We drove from village to village with Qadim ahead on the motorcycle. In my loneliness it occurred to me that we had driven through an entire district, through many villages, and there was no authority other than the Taliban, who seemed completely comfortable in their territory and not half as concerned about the Americans as I was. "We have problem," Kamal said, but he didn't elaborate when I asked what it was. On the road I struggled to find network reception for my phone, cursing as the bars appeared and disappeared. I reached another one of my contacts. "I spoke to Dr. Khalil," he said. "If they behave bad with you, don't worry. They just want to punish you, but everything is okay. I have only one more guy to call, who is bigger than Dr. Khalil." Shafiq also told me not to worry; he would get killed before he left me. We crawled at a snail's pace to our denouement in a dark empty desert, which only made me more tense. I could see nothing on the horizon; it was clear we had a long way to go. I asked Shafiq if Dr. Khalil was a nice guy, a good guy. "He's like you," Shafiq answered cryptically. "No Muslim is a bad man. Don't worry, the Doctor has a gun and I have a gun." Dr. Khalil, apparently, was a Tajik, not a Pashtun, which was very unusual for a senior Taliban commander like him, and he was from the Tajik village of Asfanda in Ghazni. He had recently been released from an Afghan prison in a prisoner exchange. Shafiq later said that as soon as Dr. Khalil heard I was a foreigner, he thought he would be rich. He called his superiors and told them he caught Shafiq with a foreign spy. He called Mansur Dadullah and told him, "I arrested a foreigner and an Afghan in Wardak and brought them to Ghazni." Mansur Dadullah was the brother of the slain Mullah Dadullah, who had commanded Taliban military operations after the 2001 American invasion until he was killed in May 2007. Mansur Dadullah was released with other Taliban prisoners in

March 2007 in exchange for the Taliban release of an Italian journalist. He then commanded Taliban operations in some of the most dangerous southern provinces and served as a spokesman until he was reportedly demoted by Mullah Omar.

Mullah Abdillah called to say that he had reached a Taliban leader in Quetta in Pakistan and somebody in the United Arab Emirates, and they had promised to call Dr. Khalil and tell him not to harm us. "The Doctor will fight with me, not with you," said Shafiq. My contact called again to tell me "they might slap you, but they won't hit you or kill you, just punish you for coming without permission. They might keep you overnight as a guest. You are lucky you called me." I felt some relief, but I was not convinced. Later he told me that Dr. Khalil had told him, "Don't worry, we won't do anything that isn't Sharia," but this was little consolation, since they considered Islamic law to permit beheading.

We drove through a Shiite village called Kara Barei on our way to the area between Gabari and Sher Kala village. "I'm a martyr, I'm a star," sang the Taliban chants on the tape. "I've reached my goal, I'm a martyr . . . I will testify on behalf of my mother on Judgment Day. When I was small my mother put me on her lap and spoke sweetly to me . . ." We finally arrived at the mosque where Dr. Khalil was waiting for us. Upon entering I inadvertently stepped on a pair of Prada sunglasses. Dr. Khalil walked in at that moment and picked them up to examine them somberly. He was a burly man with light skin and a dark brown beard. He had thick hands and was stern. He wore a cap on his head. After everybody prayed together, Dr. Khalil told everybody to leave the room except for Kamal, Yusuf, and me. We sat on the floor. He put his sunglasses on. "*Deir obekhi*," I said, apologizing for entering his territory without permission. He did not react but accused Kamal and me of being spies for the Afghan army. He asked how I got a visa to Afghanistan and why, and how I got visas to other countries. I told him I was there to write about the mujahideen and tell their story. If I liked them so much, he said, why didn't I join them? He asked about my contact. I said he was a former mujahid from Jamiat-i Islami. He scoffed dismissively, telling me they were not mujahideen. Suddenly he got up and said he would make phone calls to Pakistan and elsewhere to investigate us, so we had to spend the night in the mosque—he would come back for us in the morning. He got up and left in a hurry as I tried to protest.

I sat glumly on the floor in the guest room. A few minutes later Shafiq stuck his head in and said, "*Yallah*," Arabic for "come on." I stood up with alacrity, relieved to get out of there though confused about why. But the Talibs sitting with us insisted we drink the tea they had just made. I hurriedly gulped down the scalding tea. We stepped out into the darkness and heard helicopters in the distance. Soon we could spot their silhouettes; everybody ducked behind the car and motorcycle, so I did too, wondering if the men I was with had heard of night-vision goggles. After the sky was silent again, Yusuf apologized for having to leave me and go see his family. Shafiq told me we had to return to this mosque in the morning, and I was once again crestfallen. He drove the Corolla slowly, painstakingly winding through invisible paths. The moonlight was blocked by dust. I could see nothing out the window and wondered what was guiding Shafiq. The mobile phone network was shut down again, and I had no way of updating my contacts in Kabul.

At Shafiq's house I met his seventeen-year-old brother, who was studying at a nearby state school and knew some English. I was surprised that a Taliban commander would let his brother attend a government school. Shafiq's brother told me he wanted to study engineering and didn't want to fight. He had been with Mullah Abdillah all day, he said, and Abdillah had spent much of the day calling Taliban commanders to try to release me from Dr. Khalil. He had even called Mansur Dadullah in Kandahar.

Shafiq carried a television into the guest room and turned on the generator. He was able to read the English titles on the guide and found Al Jazeera, the Arabic satellite news channel. We watched coverage of attacks on the road from Kabul to Jalalabad and the ones we had driven by in Wardak. Boys were shown taking pieces of the trucks away. Shafiq got bored with Al Jazeera and put on Ariana, an Afghan channel, to watch an Indian soap opera dubbed in Dari. Women were shown in revealing Western attire. I was amazed that he would watch something so anathema to the Taliban. It was okay, he said. "It's a drama about a family." Later he put on a British Muslim channel called Islam and moved on to an Iranian American pop-music satellite channel. A portly singer with stubble and long hair imitated '80s rock in Farsi. The next video showed an Iranian pop singer dressed up in leather like Davy Crockett and wearing brand-name tank tops. It was terrible stuff, but Shafiq told me he had no problem with these things. Qadim and Shafiq's brother chatted. Shafiq read him something, and it became clear that Qadim was illiterate.

I finally managed to fall asleep, but at 11 p.m. there was shouting outside, and Kamal told me to wake up. "The Taliban are here for us," he said, and my heart started racing again. Three young men carrying AK-47s with scarves and blankets draped around their heads and shoulders walked in. My knees felt weak as I stood up to greet them. "They're a different group," Shafiq's brother said. They were not here for us at all. They hadn't even heard of us but were merely a night patrol passing by. One of them sat on the floor with his barrel pointing at Shafiq. I eyed him nervously as he played with the trigger absent-mindedly until Shafiq's brother told him that his safety was off and it was dangerous. They left and came back again, this time leaving with Shafiq.

In the morning, I woke up to the sound of military planes overhead. I stepped out of the *qala* and saw a convoy of American armored vehicles a mile away. I fought the strong urge to walk to them and be rescued, knowing they might shoot me themselves and that it would doom everybody who had helped me. I waited impatiently for the phone network to go back up. One of my contacts in Kabul told me that he had spoken to senior Taliban people everywhere and had told Dr. Khalil not to harm us, but Dr. Khalil insisted we were spies. My contact thought he was just trying to assert his independence and hoped to exchange us for a large ransom. Mullah Nasir, a one-armed Kandahari who served as Taliban governor for Ghazni, was also helping us. Zaibullah Mujahed, the Taliban spokesman, had promised to call Dr. Khalil as well. I tried to persuade Shafiq to drive us to Ghazni's capital, but he said that if he didn't return us to Dr. Khalil, then Khalil would arrest him.

Shafiq's nephew had been arrested the night before after a Taliban patrol spotted him walking with a girl. Shafiq left us to go release him. In the meantime I spoke to a contact in Kabul, who told me that we had gotten caught in a rivalry between Mullah Abdillah and Shafiq, on one side, and Dr. Khalil, on the other. Mullah Abdillah and his men had killed nearly a dozen Pakistanis and Arabs for trying to burn down a girls' school, but the foreigners were commanded by Dr. Khalil, so bad blood lingered. My contact told me he had been told by senior Taliban that we would be released in the afternoon but that once we were on the road we should take the batteries out of our phones. Shafiq had to deal with more headaches when other Talibs called to complain that they had heard music coming from his house when they called him the night before. Exasperated, Shafiq protested that it was only Al Jazeera.

Mullah Baradar, the Taliban minister of defense and Mullah Omar's deputy, called Dr. Khalil and demanded our release because he had given us permission to travel in Taliban territory. Another contact added pressure on Dr. Khalil by calling his former commander, who had arranged for his release in the prisoner exchange. Early in the afternoon Dr. Khalil finally showed up. He examined my passport and visas, and carefully went through my bags. He was most fascinated by my Gillette gel deodorant, opening it and smelling it. He took my toothbrush out of its container and carefully thumbed through the bristles, bringing it close to his eye to examine it. He leafed through my notebooks and was intrigued by my many medicines for diarrhea and dehydration. He asked me to show him the pictures I had taken. "Zaibullah Mujahed said I should hit you, but I will not," he told me. Dr. Khalil's attitude was markedly different, and he made me feel at ease. "What can I do for you?" he asked. I asked him a few questions. He was fighting for a government of Islamic law, he said, but Mullah Omar did not have to be the leader again. God willing, it would take up to twenty or thirty years until they got rid of the foreigners. If the foreigners left, he would still fight the Afghan army, and he refused to negotiate with President Karzai. Women could go to school and work, he conceded. Dr. Khalil had studied in the Hakim Sahib Sanai Islamic School in the Pakistani town of Jub and then studied internal medicine in Afghanistan. In

1992 he joined the Taliban, and he was a commander in the far northern Taluqan district.

I wasn't in the mood to ask too many questions, and we piled into the Corolla again, loading an RPG into the trunk just in case. Dr. Khalil got in the driver's seat with Shafiq beside him holding the PKM. Qadim held an AK-47 and squeezed in next to me. Dr. Khalil's escort followed on another motor-cycle, as did Shafiq's brother. We drove for about an hour through villages. The car got stuck, and I helped collect rocks to put beneath the tires. We drove through Dr. Khalil's village of Asfanda, and he pointed to its outer lim-its. "This is the border between the Taliban and the government," he said, proudly stressing his control. We drove undisturbed through the village. He asked me what I would write in my article. I told him that I would write about how much control the Taliban had in much of Afghanistan. He was now jocular and relaxed.

He pointed to a nearby American base with a spy blimp parked on the ground and told me to take a picture of it. At the edge of town close to the main road he got out, followed by Shafiq, who held his PKM. The locals ap-peared stunned. He stopped a pickup truck and ordered the driver to take us to the bazaar. We parted warmly and climbed on the back of the truck. Shafiq's younger brother followed us on a motorcycle to the bazaar, where we met Mullah Abdillah, who was very apologetic for what had happened to me. Abdillah was supposed to have been with me during my trip through Talibanistan, but he was tired from his surgery and had gone home to relax. "I paid for my mistake," he later said. "This Doctor, he is a very nasty guy," my contact told me on the phone. "He might send somebody to kidnap you on the way, and then I can do nothing for you." Abdillah was also worried that Dr. Khalil had set up an ambush for me on the road. Later I learned more. Shafiq had incorrectly told local Taliban that I worked for Al Jazeera. Dr. Khalil called the Al Jazeera bureau chief in Pakistan and asked him if he knew me. When the chief said no they decided I was a spy. By the time Mul-lah Baradar had made the call to Dr. Khalil, the leadership in Andar had al-ready decided to execute me.

We dodged craters in the road on the way back with Abdillah, and the sides of the road were strewn with burned-out and exploded cars. The trucks I had seen burning two days earlier were still smoldering, and chil-dren were playing with them, removing pieces. I teased Abdillah for his Tal-iban having destroyed the roads and made our drive more difficult and perilous, and was surprised when he seemed to agree. He later expressed disapproval of the Taliban for killing Afghan civilians, explaining that they were not acting like Afghans. We didn't stop fast enough at an army check-point, and the soldier raised his AK at us. It was a sunny day with clear skies, and I felt euphoric as we drove north to Kabul.

I RETURNED TO KABUL to find that the UN had been put on four days of restricted movement to coincide with Afghanistan's independence day and the anniversary of the 2003 attack on the UN in Baghdad. While I was there rockets were also fired at the airport in Kabul and at the ISAF base. I told a Western intelligence officer about the extent to which the Taliban were in charge of Ghazni. "Andar is a very bad place," he said, explaining that it had recently become one of the most dangerous areas in the country. "The Taliban showed a lot of confidence and freedom of movement," he said. "They pulled people off buses. That level of control is right on Kabul's front door. The writing was on the wall for the central region two years ago. The international effort was fixated with the south, but they didn't create conditions to act as a buttress against the insurgency. Environments regarded as extreme two years ago are still extreme but much worse. There has been a staggering intensification, and there are ominous signs elsewhere in country."

Between Ghazni and Kabul are the formerly peaceful provinces of Wardak and Logar. "Logar and Wardak were like canaries in a mine, and now they have gone," a senior development official told me. His NGO had divided Afghanistan into stable, unstable, and volatile areas. "Now unstable provinces have become volatile," he said. "Now it's too late." A former Taliban government official told me that Logar had become dangerous in the summer of 2007. "I was watching trends in Logar and Wardak because there was no movement from the government side to push them back," he said. "It was the weakness of the government and the strength of the Taliban." He explained that Logar was an important center for religious education in Afghanistan, with perhaps more Islamic schools than any other province. "In the south there are not many official Islamic schools, so you can deal with tribes," he said. But Logar was producing new Talibs in its schools. A waiter at my hotel in Kabul told me that he had been at a wedding in the town of Warajan in Logar on August 17 when suddenly about fourteen Talibs came in with AKs and RPGs. They didn't say anything but simply checked to see if there was music being played. Like most of the country, Kunduz province, in the far north, was also declining. "Kunduz was very safe last year," a senior humanitarian official told me. "I drove up there and spent Christmas there. Now there have been NGO staff killed, threats of kidnapping." The German contingent there was attacked every night and had recently accidentally killed Afghan civilians.

As I saw on the road to Ghazni, the Taliban were cutting off Kabul from the rest of the country. The road southwest to Kandahar was lethal. "The Kabul-to-Ghazni road is gone," the intelligence officer told me. "The Ghazni-to-Gardez road is exceedingly bad, the Wardak road is shitty, the Jalalabad road is sliding, and there is a sustainable deterioration in rural areas around the road—you run the risk of abduction. It's routine ambushes now, so they have a routine capability." In May and June 2007, the officer explained, there was a major shift in Wardak: "Within an eight-week period it went from nighttime ambushes to daylight roadblocks." He told me that warnings had been issued about the Sarobi district of Kabul and the Qarghai district in the province of Laghman, which borders Kabul to the east. There was also an IED cell in the Puli Khumri junction, which was a key road for anything going from the north to Kabul. Even Badakhshan at the extreme northeast of the country was beginning to have problems. In the last three months the northern Parwan province, which borders Kabul, had also become more dangerous. It was mostly Tajik, but the main road was under pressure there as well. "All of a sudden we see IEDs in Parwan on the main road, attacks on police checkpoints," he said. "It's the last remaining key arterial route connecting Kabul to the rest of the country." Hizb-e-Islami clerics were sent to Parwan to preach against the government, and an increase in violence soon followed. "Given the ethnicity of the area, it's not a permissive environment, but there are effective IED cells operating there," he said.

On August 13 the international community in Kabul and most Afghans were shocked when three Western female NGO workers from the International Rescue Committee (IRC) and their Afghan driver were ambushed on a road in Logar's Puli Alam district in the morning and shot to death. The initial Taliban statement claimed the targets were legitimate because they were ISAF soldiers. In the past the Taliban said they would not attack NGOs, including international NGOs, which were free to work throughout the country. At first the Taliban statement seemed to imply that they had relied on bad intelligence and that they thought the victims were military people using civilian vehicles. "The IRC attack was a big watershed," the intelligence officer told me, summarizing the final Taliban statement as "Yes, we killed them, and we're proud of it—screw you." He explained that the Taliban claimed they didn't believe the IRC's projects had merit or were in the interest of Afghanistan. In effect, the Taliban spokesman legitimized attacks on NGOs. On previous occasions the Taliban had admitted that similar attacks were mistakes, such as when they targeted organizations that disposed of land mines. "The IRC incident changed the whole rules of the game," a senior UN official told me. "In the past, when de-miners were taken hostage and killed, they have issued statements that it's Taliban policy not to attack de-miners," the intelligence officer said. "That's the story in Afghanistan with the Taliban, internal squabbling. They free de-miners in one place, and pick them up in another place." In June 2008 there were twenty-one security incidents against NGOs, and the IRC attack in August brought NGO deaths in 2008 to twenty-three. "In Darfur we had thirteen killed in one year, and the international community went ballistic," one senior Western NGO official told me. "Here there hasn't been much of an outrage."

Some NGO officials were not surprised. In 2006 Mullah Omar had issued a twenty-nine-article order that did not prohibit attacks against NGOs, which meant that in practice it allowed them. A former Taliban government official from Logar explained to me that if the Taliban abducted Afghans working for NGOs, then surely they would abduct internationals. Abductions were used to help finance their operations or for prisoner exchanges with jailed Taliban members. In the case of the IRC women, he said, "they were foreigners, that's reason enough." He explained that the Taliban had cars with armed men on standby. When they heard that a high-profile SUV with tinted windows was coming, they waited on the main road to ambush them and then simply returned to the villages. The same thing had recently happened in Logar's Muhammad Agha district, which was even closer to Kabul, on its southern border. The Taliban ambushed a police convoy and simply drove into their villages afterward, and the police didn't dare follow them "because everyone likes their life." The government remained in control of the main urban centers. But the Taliban had little need to take Kabul; it wasn't relevant, and it never fell even in the Soviet days. "But once you leave the city, how safe do you feel?" a senior UN official asked.

During this visit to Afghanistan I spoke with Western diplomats, security experts, former mujahideen commanders, former Taliban officials, NGO officials, and senior UN officials. All agreed that "things are not going well," that the situation was "incredibly bleak." Many told me that "what we've got to try and make happen is a fresh start" or "we have to start from zero again."

"I'm not optimistic," a longtime NGO official told me. "You can't help getting this increased uncomfortable feeling that you are waiting for something terrible to happen." Taliban confidence reminded him of the mujahideen he had known in the Soviet days. Another senior Western NGO official who had recently left Afghanistan with his family spoke of a "loss of hope" and told me that "Afghans with money want to move their families to Dubai or India—they're looking at an exit strategy. I'm increasingly unsure about the way forward except that we should start preparing our exit strategy. We're not up to the task of success in Afghanistan."

"At the center is an extremely weak president," said a European ambassador, "a corrupt and ineffective Ministry of Interior, an army that will fight but has no command or control, a dysfunctional international alliance." The "enlightened" Afghan elite who lead the government have little in common with the majority of rural Afghans, who are the sea where the Taliban swim. There had been small successes in health, education, rural development, roads, bridges, dams, and wells, but these were ephemeral, a senior development official told me, and it would be easy to blow them up. "From the beginning I've been very worried and negative," the European ambassador told me. "The analysis of our intelligence people is that things are getting worse. CIA analysts are extremely gloomy and worried. The administration in Washington is not fit for the purpose." But there was a divide between the analysts and the trigger pullers. The British army did not accept the negative prognosis provided by that country's intelligence and continued to insist that things were not getting worse.

"Last month was the worst ever and the month before that was the worst ever until then," a senior UN official told me in August 2008. "The UN has 50 or 55 percent access in this country—in some parts we have zero." UN maps divided the country into green areas for safety and red areas for danger. But the maps were misleading, he said: "Herat is green, but only essential staff are allowed there and only in the capital of the province. It's actually 97 percent off-limits. In Kandahar we have plenty of international staff, but they are all hiding behind the doors." The UN had declared Afghanistan to be in phase three out of its five phases of safety, with five being the worst. But in practice it was treated as phase four. "It's a political decision," he said. "They cannot say it's phase four because 'we are winning the war, we are controlling the situation.' We are thinking things will get much worse. There is a political interest in not acknowledging the situation. If they recognize that there are humanitarian issues, then they have failed."

Following the Taliban's speedy defeat by the Americans in 2001, there was a wholesale handover of government to the warlords and no institution building. NATO forces were restricted to Kabul, and the focus of the mission was counterterrorism. The Americans built up the warlords and let them become entrenched. They would find weapons caches and give them to the warlords. Those who had been responsible for atrocities in the past were given renewed legitimacy. The parliamentary elections of 2005 then legalized the legitimacy the Americans had bestowed upon the warlords. The Parliament was led by warlords; they served as governors and ministers. "The American intervention issued blank checks to these guys," one longtime NGO official told me. "They threw money, weapons, vehicles at them. Anyone willing to work with the Americans was welcome. The warlords haven't abandoned their bad habits. They're abusing people and filling their pockets." When President Karzai appointed governors and police chiefs, his options were limited. American-backed warlords were already in charge in many places, and Karzai had no choice but to appoint these same people—and he began to lose credibility.

"I thought the Americans and international community could succeed in 2001," a former mujahideen commander and Taliban government official told me. "I thought we would get rid of all these warlords, but in the first six months they supported the warlords and put them in power. Then there was hope for the elections, but warlords won. In 2002 the warlords were nervous about the justice process. Now they are in Parliament, ministers, deputy ministers. The main mistake was the agreement between the Northern Alliance and the U.S. before Bonn and the fall of the Taliban. In Kandahar drug gangs were appointed police chiefs and district administrators."

The UN, the U.S. embassy, and Karzai undermined justice and refused to take the warlords on because it would threaten stability. They ended up fundamentally undermining the process of creating a government that would be legitimate in the eyes of the population, who at best had an ambivalent view of a government that had done nothing to protect them. At the same time the American-led coalition dropped bombs on Afghans and shot them on the roads at greater and greater numbers.

"The amnesty bill gave all members of Parliament and warlords immunity from prosecution," the intelligence officer said. "Karzai was under pressure from the UN and international community to block it. I felt the ambience of Kabul change after the bill. There was increasing cockiness and a sense of impunity, corruption increased, there were more cash-in-transit robberies." But many of these warlords had violated the terms of the amnesty by maintaining their private militias. "The issue isn't who the combatants are," he said. "It's the elders and government members who have secret handshakes with local Taliban. That corruption is the absolute way of life here, from your smallest villager dealing with his melon crop to your minister." As the situation worsened, "there is desperation setting in among the government: 'Let's shove this into our pockets, because it won't last.' Government departments demand bribes."

The intelligence officer singled out the general who headed the Interior Ministry's Criminal Investigation and Terrorism department. The increased abuses coincided with the general's rise, he said. "He's a psychopath, that's the only way I can put it. He's a mafia don, a mini Al Capone, a nasty piece of work, the scum of the earth, a fucking hoodlum." Police harassment of foreigners also increased, he said. "The international community proved to be a paper tiger. The police will raid foreign companies, even security companies, and just steal everything: iPods, money, weapons, radios. They even tried arresting foreigners for not having passports on them, which is not illegal. Afghans connected to the government who have security companies wanted them out, they wanted their business. Afghan security teams were moonlighting as bank robbers. There is no respect for laws in this country whatsoever— it's meaningless. In my view this whole governance piece is the most critical part, but you have utterly disgusting people in power. People might hate the Taliban, but they hate the government just as much. At least the Taliban have rules. This government, they're parasites fucking with you on a deal. If you go through the legitimate process, you haven't got a chance."

A senior UN official agreed. "The police are highly corrupt," he said. "They are at the center of the collapse of the state and the Karzai government. They are involved in everything from corruption to harassment. Locals feel alienation from police, and they have been the best promoters of the Taliban. The police make them support the Taliban."

"The Afghan National Police are corrupt and parasitic on the population partly because they are not well paid or trained," according to Nathaniel Fick of the new Washington–based think tank the Center for a New American Security (CNAS). "It's corruption from need, not from greed. At three hundred dollars a month, a family with a couple of kids can live in rural Afghanistan. The average minimum monthly salary is three hundred a month; we pay them one hundred and twenty a month." Fick added that the salary was set to increase to a paltry two hundred a month, but one way or another, "the police always get paid." Logistics were also a problem. "We need paved roads," he said. "These guys get paid when the paymaster travels down a gravel road with an American escort with the money. So guys in rural outposts don't get paid, so they become parasitic, and the circle goes around."

Fick is a former Marine officer who served in Afghanistan in 2001 and 2002 and in Iraq in 2003. In 2007 he was an instructor at the counterinsurgency academy in Kabul. He was also portrayed in a positive light as the platoon leader in *Generation Kill*, a book based on a series in *Rolling Stone* that also became an HBO series. In August 2008 Fick returned from a visit to Afghanistan, where he and a colleague conducted research for CNAS's impending strategic assessment of U.S. policy in that country. "We met with tribal elders in Ghazni, and they told us they were slapped on one cheek by the Taliban and on the other by government," Fick told me. "There is bribery in every office, total lack of security, police corruption." Afghans didn't trust the coalition's commitment, he said. "They think we're going to leave, so they stay on the fence."

The Americans and their allies arrogantly presumed they could create a state out of nothing in a fissiparous country with barely any roads linking different regions to one another, and then tried to make it a strong centralized state at that. In the beginning, overcome with a sense of victory, they ignored the Taliban and Pakistan. The Taliban were not part of the peace process in Bonn because the Americans didn't want them there. Pakistan's role was neglected at the beginning of the power-sharing arrangement. Most of the members in Karzai's first cabinet had close to ties to India, archenemy of Pakistan, or to Iran, and there were too few Pashtuns. The Pakistanis felt alienated, and they invested in the Taliban to regain influence and power.

"The way people are treated in Afghanistan makes you feel disgusted about your own existence," a senior UN humanitarian official told me. "For almost thirty years, Afghans lived in extreme flux. They are the most resilient and courageous population. They are skilled survivors. I can see the return of symptoms I saw before the fall of the Taliban: uncertainty, you are with several sides at once. This is everywhere—Kabul too." A European ambassador added that even though Afghans don't want the Taliban to rule, they will back a winner. "They don't want to back the government, and in eighteen months' time, the Taliban will ride back into the village and behead anybody who has made a deal with the coalition," he said.

Living in a country with few resources and a legacy of thirty years of war has made Afghans the ultimate survivors. Pashtun elders have to negotiate competing claims and obligations as well as competition for resources and complex identities—their tribe, their region, the governor. (Is his tribe allied or at odds with ours? Was he with the Taliban before or opposed to them? Which party was he with in the '80s?) The elders can get resources from the government, the Americans, the Taliban, drug lords, and neighboring countries. If an elder meets with the Americans, he will have to answer to the Taliban that night. If he refuses to meet with the Americans, the Americans will perceive his village as hostile and might bomb it. There could be a blood feud with a neighboring town or tribe because somebody was killed as a result of competition over land or water resources.

Even the reform of the Afghan army, of which the Americans were so proud, was fraught with problems. The army was still predominantly Tajik, so when it went to the south it was confronted with serious linguistic problems that may cause ethnic tensions in the future. The Afghan army relies on the support of U.S. forces and airpower; it will always require an American presence. It cannot function on its own. The Americans decided to expand the Afghan army from eighty thousand to one hundred twenty thousand, but this would take another five years (time they don't have).

In August 2008 the American-led coalition, the UN, and the Karzai government were pinning their hopes on the 2009 presidential elections in Afghanistan. But a senior UN official told me, "You can't fix the insurgency with an election. It's a socio-economic phenomenon that goes well beyond the border of Afghanistan." A British intelligence officer told me, "The Taliban are only too happy to keep Karzai in power. He's impotent in every single way. He made a lot of deals to get in power and stay in power, he's all about his own political survival, he's a weak man who refused to stand up to the bullies. We need a clean individual who these other individuals can't nipple-tweak. We need a guy who can say, 'All the old deals are off.'"

Often very little distinguishes a tribe or village that decides to align itself with the government from one that decides to join the army or support the Taliban and send its sons to fight the Americans. It might be a contract, a personal dispute, a relative on one side or the other. "A lot of this is about power and local influence," the intelligence officer said. "Parts of society will be poor and powerless if they accept Karzai's order. They want to achieve status and influence. If they accept legitimate structures, they're accepting their doom. A lot can be explained in Darwinian terms. Across nature you see alternative strategies. Fighting is an alternative strategy: you can be Mr. Big in your community."

In 2006 the Taliban fought the Americans in conventional engagements. "The Taliban were being wiped out in huge numbers," the intelligence officer said. "They were going at it jihad-style. So the Taliban went for asymmetry." The Taliban were not experienced in insurgent warfare at the beginning of the occupation, but they showed themselves able to learn and adapt and even use technologies they had previously abhorred. They had a harder time accessing urban areas, so they made deals with criminal gangs. "The saving grace will be the winter," said one senior NGO official. "They can't move in the winter." But in January 2008 the Taliban attacked the five-star Serena Hotel in Kabul using shooters and suicide bombers. The attack was important because it showed an intention to kill foreigners regardless of who they were.

The Taliban were successfully bypassing traditional tribal mechanisms. Young men came into villages and ordered people around. Many did not care about Pashtunwali, the traditional code Pashtuns follow. Instead they were part of a new globalized jihadist identity. They established a harsh law and order, and didn't allow others to fight or carry weapons. They engaged in more car bombings and suicide attacks, using tactics imported from Iraq. These attacks persuaded people not to cooperate with the Americans and demonstrated that the Americans could not provide security. Local Taliban commanders could be pressured and influenced by the communities they came from, so the Taliban were replacing them with outsiders free from that pressure. The Taliban ran a very effective social terror campaign and could operate deep in civilian communities. "They're killing more and more tribal elders," the senior NGO official said. "We can't expect communities to show solidarity with the government when we can't provide for their security—it's ridiculous." The military was wrongly focused on what he called "symptomatic" factors, like how many bombs went off in an area. "The pulse of a community is what drives an insurgency, not symptomatic factors," he said. "Talk to Afghans, look at school burnings and assassinations. It's a qualitative assessment; you can't crunch it in quantitative terms. But the military can't do anything about it until it's symptomatic. The conflict is taking place at a lower and lower level. There are not enough foreign troops or local troops. We've disarmed warlords and traditional power structures, and the Taliban are destroying traditional power structures, so it's wiping out everything that stands in their way. Young Pashtuns are increasingly picking up arms against the government. We disarmed people and undermined traditional power structures, and we're now wondering why the Taliban are running riot."

My friend who had served as a commander for Gulbuddin Hekmatyar until 1992 and then as an official in the Taliban government was not sanguine when he drew comparisons. During the Soviet occupation the foreign army was larger and more powerful than the coalition today, at more than one hundred thousand, and the Afghan government was stronger than the current one as well, he told me. "The Russians never arrested women," he said. "The Americans arrest Afghan women and take them to bases. The end will be like with the Russians. The Americans will never succeed in containing the conflict. There will be more bleeding, evacuation of foreigners. It's coming to the same situation as the Communist forces, who were confined to the provincial capitals by 1985 or 1986. There were 465,000 military and civilian members of the puppet government, but the Russians were still confined to their bases."

"Two years ago you could build a road or a bridge in a village and say, 'Please don't let the Taliban come,'" a senior development official told me. "Now you've reached the stage where the hearts-and-minds business doesn't work. The countryside is caught between the coercive forces of state and coercive forces of antistate." He quipped that the Americans' continuous bombing of weddings wasn't helping either. The Americans tried to increase aid and development and improve the government's image only after it was too late. Afghans were already alienated, and the use of PRTs (Provincial Reconstruction Teams) delegitimized the aid, associating it with the military. American use of airpower convinced people that the coalition forces were not committed to fight and were cowardly, as I saw from my time with the Taliban.

After I left Afghanistan, I got regular e-mails from the U.S. military notifying me of how many Taliban coalition forces had killed, but all this showed me was how popular the Taliban continued to be and how many more of them there were than the U.S. claimed. Of course, many of those killed were civilians, and those casualties—along with the Americans' increasing reliance on warlords and militias, who had imposed a reign of terror on the population—meant that it was too late to win hearts and minds.

The former Taliban government official agreed. "It's too late to bring security by development." That phase, the development official told me, ended in 2004. The former Taliban official explained the problems facing Afghan villagers. "You have to decide to be with Taliban or be with government," he said. "In Logar, if you are with the government, you have to move to Kabul. If you are with Taliban you can stay, but you may have to give them your son."

IN MAY 2009 Defense Secretary Robert Gates—the only holdover from the Bush administration—announced that Gen. Stanley McChrystal would replace Gen. David McKiernan as the top commander in Afghanistan. The unceremonious defenestration of the respected McKiernan was meant to send a strong signal of a new approach to the war. McChrystal, known among colleagues as a "snake eater," had a background in special operations and counterterrorism. He ordered the fifth strategic review of the war since Obama's presidency.

McChrystal's promotion confirmed the ascendance of a new generation of officers epitomized by Gen. David Petraeus, now commander of Central

Command and charged with overseeing the wars in Iraq and Afghanistan. The wars had created a community of counterinsurgency proponents in the Defense Department and at Washington think tanks. Many were serious intellectuals and veterans of Iraq and Afghanistan who had spent years exhorting the military and government to embrace COIN in fighting the global war on terror. The 2007 surge in Iraq and its alleged success in reducing violence has led this new generation of officers to dominate strategic thinking.

In December 2008 General McKiernan asked for thirty thousand more troops and stressed that he needed them for a few years. It would not be a short surge, like the one in Iraq. In March 2009 President Obama unveiled his new strategy for Afghanistan and Pakistan. The goals were "to disrupt, dismantle, and defeat Al Qaeda and its safe havens in Pakistan and to prevent their return to Pakistan or Afghanistan." The tool would be COIN. The Americans gave themselves one year to "shift the momentum" in the war, meaning to stop losing. With thirty-six thousand American troops already in Afghanistan, Obama ordered an additional seventeen thousand combat troops and four thousand trainers. By mid-2010, troop numbers finally equaled the number stationed in Iraq, at nearly one hundred thousand.

Obama insisted that the war and extremism could not be solved through military means alone. He cautioned against focusing on the concept of "victory" when dealing with Al Qaeda, stressing that he wanted to deny the movement bases where they could train people or launch attacks. Obama's new strategy called for a civilian surge as well. But there were not many civilians available, and most of those duties would be filled by the military.

Despite admitting that there was no military solution, Obama was relying on the military. And he reproduced the pathologies of his predecessor, treating Muslims as if they were one entity and the world as if it was a battlefield. Under Obama the United States has expanded its operations in Pakistan, Yemen, and Somalia. In all cases violence has increased. In Al Qaeda's worldview, Muslims are under attack by Christians and Jews who want to take Muslims' resources and perhaps convert them too.

The Bush administration had to transform its response to the 9/11 attacks into a crusade because, in purely security terms, the most powerful nation the world has ever seen went to war against two hundred unsophisticated extremists. Looking at it like that diminishes to absurdity the enemy and the threat it poses, but many in the defense policy establishment were nostalgic for a real enemy, like fascism or communism, and so they made the conflict about culture. The United States adopted Al Qaeda's view of the world, and it too treated the entire world stage as a battlefield.

In July 2009 McChrystal issued new orders for soldiers not to pursue Taliban fighters if there was a chance of civilian casualties, and to drive slower and more respectfully on Afghanistan's roads. But his predecessor had issued similar orders, albeit with less media fanfare—the new ones were not more likely to be obeyed. Thousands of Afghan civilians had been killed by the Americans since the war began. Most were killed by U.S. airstrikes, but many others were shot at checkpoints or in raids. Usually the military denied the civilian deaths until the media showed videos of their corpses. Most American-caused civilian casualties happened when soldiers called for close air support in the midst of a battle, so there was no time to check for civilians in the target range. In one attack alone, in May, the Americans killed between 86 and 140 civilians in an airstrike in western Afghanistan.

In late June the U.S. military initiated the first big push of the Afghan surge. Four thousand Marines launched an offensive to take over Taliban-controlled villages in Helmand, the province with the most attacks and the most poppy production for the country's lucrative drug trade. But the plan called for an "Afghan face," in the form of the Afghan army and police, and the Americans were desperately short of those. Afghan police were essential because they knew the language and the people and could provide intelligence. Their presence was needed to convince Afghans that the Americans were fighting on behalf of Afghanistan, and that it wasn't a foreign occupation. If the Americans ever wanted to leave, they would have to train enough Afghan security forces so that they could hand the task of securing the country to them. There were only about 170,000 members of the Afghan army and police, although their expansion was being fast tracked. Afghan National Security Forces (ANSF) were supposed to hold an area after the Americans cleared it of insurgents, but there weren't enough of them. While the Americans were initially focused on creating an Afghan army, they neglected the important need for a police force.

In June 2009, in Helmand's provincial capital of Lashkar Gah, I met a group of Americans working with the Afghan police. The Americans shared a base with the Afghan National Civil Order Police (ANCOP) and the Provincial Reserve (PR), two special police units considered elite in comparison to local Afghan National Police (ANP). Authority in Helmand was divided between the British Army and the U.S. Marines. On my first day there I went to the ANCOP base and sat on the floor drinking green tea with the PR. One man asked me if I wanted to go sleep. He showed me where his bedroom was and offered to take me there. The next day he asked why I hadn't come there to sleep with him. Jawad, another member, had been with the PR for one year. He had lost between fifteen and twenty friends in attacks since then, he said. "I like this job," he told me when I asked if it wasn't too dangerous. "If something is in your destiny, it's coming, no one can save you. Every time we defeat them. It's hard to remove the Taliban roots because some of them live here." Many of the Americans had learned basic Farsi and Pashtu, the languages most commonly spoken in Afghanistan, and they bantered back and forth with the Afghans, teasing them with local expressions.

On my first night I had dinner with the Americans of Team Ironhorse and Colonel Saki, who headed the ANCOP in Helmand. Ironhorse was the U.S. squad training ANCOP. We found him watching Bollywood movies in his office. He brought out a pile of kabob and bread, and the Americans chatted with him through Bariyal, a thickly muscled translator the Americans called Shotgun. He was the 2002 weightlifting champion in Pakistan's North-West Frontier Province. Like most translators who spend enough time with the Americans, he adopted their argot as well. "ANCOP are fucking badass people," he told me. Colonel Saki and the Americans shared the same macho warrior culture, and the language divide proved easily surmountable. Ironhorse's captain was going on leave, and he asked Saki what he wanted from the United States. Saki said he just wanted him to come back.

The next morning the frustrated Americans on Team Prowler helped the PR unload a truck full of rifles and ammunition. The Afghans had just tossed them in a pile without conducting any inventory or organization. "I'm at my wits' end!" shouted Sgt. Ryan Kilaki. Captain Westby was exasperated because many of the cops were at home and not on the base. They are a quick reaction force, he told me, and they are supposed to live on base.

The British and Helmand police command had mismanaged a few hundred thousand dollars in back pay for the police, and the Americans had stepped in to cover the loss. "Jesus, fuck, they got a long way to go," said an exasperated Sergeant First Class Clark. The British army had taken sixty men from the Provincial Reserve with them on a recent operation in Babaji. The PR men didn't want to go with them, and the Americans were pissed off because the reserve was supposed to be one unit. Like many Afghans, the police believed that the British secretly supported the Taliban.

On the Fourth of July, Team Prowler set off with the PR to patrol Highway 601, the key road in the province. It connected to Highway 1, the main road in the country. All trade entering the province passed through Highway 601, and it was also the land route to supply British, American, and Afghan forces. The "skuff" hall in the British-run base was running out of food. Villages along the road were controlled by the Taliban. The British were supposed to control the route. Sergeant Dyer, a brawny former Navy SEAL with the stern gaze, square jaw, and low raspy voice of a real-life Marlboro man, complained to me about nightly reports that Highway 601 was mined but that the police didn't pursue the insurgents. Civilian vehicles avoided it because of IEDs. The police knew where the Taliban were but didn't pursue them, and they were growing too dependent on the Americans. "At one checkpoint they were still wearing their man-jammies, not uniforms," he said. "IEDs are placed two clicks from police checkpoints, they don't go on patrol, at the sound of the first shot they request air support. But they've cried wolf too many times, and then they say, 'If we don't get air support we're leaving.'"

Dyer was on his third combat deployment in Afghanistan. "There's too much talk of COIN and civil affairs," he said. "It requires security. You can't build a school if you can't protect the teacher." The rules of engagement had changed over the course of Dyer's three deployments. He worried that his men were more at risk because of limitations on when they could shoot. Like many American troops, he could barely hide his contempt for most of the other coalition members. Only the British, Australians, and Canadians were aggressive, he said. Americans joke that NATO's ISAF actually stands for "I see Americans fighting" or "I suck at fighting" or "I stay at the FOB." Some of the European allies, meanwhile, complained that the Americans were too aggressive.

Driving down Highway 601, an insurgent with an itchy trigger finger prematurely detonated his IED on the road in front of Team Prowler and the police. The police discovered the command wire for it and fanned around to look in vain for the trigger man. The blast slowed down the police. Captain Westby complained to me that the police were "squirrelly" and that he had to do a lot of "mentoring" to get them to go forward. They headed toward a village called Balochan. The National Directorate of Security men accompanying them—the NDS is the Afghan equivalent of the FBI—didn't know how to get there, and none of the police had ever been there, so they got lost. Westby worried that this would be a problem when the police ran their own operations. The Americans took the lead, but when they got to Balochan, Lieutenant Farid, the police commander, insisted it was the wrong town. In Balochan they were shot at from four hundred meters away. A British contingent was attacked with rocket-propelled grenades. The Americans, I was told, "lay devastating fire" on the tree line from where they received fire—then the insurgent fire subsided. The Americans couldn't confirm any dead insurgents. "Afghans suck at shooting," they said. The Americans thought they were up against foreign fighters because of the accurate shots. One policeman was shot in the head. The others thought he was dead; they laid him on the ground and covered his face. The Americans saw the man was still breathing and had a pulse, so they evacuated him by helicopter. The Americans searched the maze of compounds. One policeman was killed; his friend insisted on going out to save him, but the other Afghans were too scared. The police had no radios, so they couldn't communicate, and their fire was coming too close to the Americans. They also weren't wearing their armor. "They don't like it because it's heavy," one American explained. Another policeman was shot in the chest. The others backed off, abandoning their friend. An American tried to figure out where the fire was coming from and drag the man to safety, as the interpreter Mansur ran to help. They extracted the dead policeman, and Lieutenant Farid was wounded in his calf. He was wearing a black T-shirt without body armor. "You and I as leaders have to make the decisions to set examples for our men," Westby told him. Farid made excuses, and Westby felt like he was talking to a kid. Armor was hot and heavy and wouldn't have helped his leg, Farid argued. An American was wounded. Mansur picked up the American's rifle and started firing (all the interpreters were trained to fight as well). Sergeant Dyer was disappointed with the PR's performance. "They sucked," he said. "They folded," one of his soldiers agreed.

The next day Team Prowler and the PR trained at the shooting range. Sergeant Dyer was dejected. "The Provincial Reserve aren't ready," he said. "Their training is too short. They can't drive. They can't shoot. They're weak on tactics, lacking in motivation. In training the last few days, after two or three hours their performance drops even more. Squad leaders are terrible because in the Soviet system NCOs don't do anything." Mansur joined in, laughing. "They couldn't hit targets," he said. "Some hit the sand." Out of eight men in each group, three could aim at a target, Specialist Campos told me.

Police working in the south had a high rate of desertion. They often refused to work if Americans were not present, and they were afraid to go on operations. Their vehicles were more vulnerable to IEDs and attacks. They lacked ammunition, fuel, and other essential supplies, and they didn't have the logistical ability to provide it for themselves.

Bill Hix, an experienced Special Forces colonel with extensive COIN experience, led the Afghan Regional Security Integration Command in Kandahar, which was in charge of training and mentoring the Afghan police and army in southern Afghanistan, including Helmand. There were forty-one portraits on his wall of Americans from his organization who had died. All but two had been killed by IEDs. He would need a much bigger wall for the Afghans. From January 2007 to April 2009, he lost 2,096 Afghan police and 949 soldiers. Hix did not believe more American troops were needed, merely an "adequate" police force and army, whose numbers he hoped would double. "The police should be identifying clandestine networks," he said. But there weren't nearly enough of them: the ratio in southern Afghanistan was two police per thousand people. In the United States it was four per thousand; Afghanistan was at war, so more were needed. "We're driving this car as we're changing the engine," he said.

Should Afghanistan cease to be a protectorate of the West, it wouldn't be able to pay for its own security forces. It doesn't have the resources to fund such a large military. The result, instead, would be a heavily militarized society. With the end of American subsidies, the men with weapons and training would return to warlordism and militias, preying on the population. Pakistan's army, which had been subsidized by the Americans for years, became a state unto itself, independent of the civilian control it should have answered to.

An effective police requires an effective justice system, including judges, lawyers, court clerks, prisons, and an administrative system. Corruption among the police and other government officials was also a huge problem for the Soviet occupation of the 1980s. Afghan cops couldn't be expected to turn down bribes when they knew that everyone else in the system was taking them. And it was the cops who took the greatest risks in the country's most dangerous job. The high illiteracy rate also made it difficult to build a system of justice. How could records be kept? Training lasted only a couple of months. Creating and training security forces were difficult enough in peacetime, but they were even more challenging during war. After training the cops returned to the same conditions: corruption and lack of support. They were the only face of the Afghan government most people saw, and it was too often an ugly one.

Helmand is not only the worst province in Afghanistan; it is also the wealthiest. It has a sophisticated irrigation system and some paved roads. Its dam helps to pump out cheap, stable electricity. It is little wonder that Helmand, with some of the best agricultural land in the region, is the world's largest grower of poppy. With the best resources in the country, it has been a convenient place for an insurgency to sustain itself. Although taxing heroin sales is one source of the Taliban's finances, in fact the drug trade funds everybody and all sides in Afghanistan, and the Taliban get most of their funding from donors in the Arab Gulf and elsewhere. Heroin is Afghanistan's only real industry, but it has created a parallel shadow economy that undermines and corrupts the government. The drug trade is more of a consequence than a cause of Afghanistan's many problems.

In the 1980s and '90s the Alizais dominated Helmand at the expense of their rival tribe, the Ishaqzais. Nasim Akhundzada was the top mujahideen commander in the area and was responsible for creating the poppy industry in Helmand. He brutally forced farmers to grow opium and established a sharecropping system that trapped poor indebted farmers in an endless cycle of planting opium. His brother Muhamad was his army commander, and Muhamad's son Sher Muhamad Akhundzada, known as SMA, would go on to control Helmand. The Ishaqzais were dominant during the Taliban's reign, from 1994 until 2001. But when SMA became governor after the Taliban were removed in 2001, the Ishaqzais were once again marginalized and punished. The Taliban took advantage of this rivalry to increase their influence over both majority-Ishaqzai areas and also Alizai groups. Most of the governors appointed by Kabul in 2002 were warlords. Helmand had no effective administration after 2001. The provincial government did not provide anything to locals, and it abused them. Between 2001 to 2006, SMA and those around him labored to build a strong base of support in Helmand, and he placed his men throughout the province's police and government. Under his reign poppy growers affiliated with him were immune from eradication. SMA pressured farmers to grow poppy, leading to a 160 percent increase in the harvest. Meanwhile, the Taliban protected poppy farmers whose crops were targeted for eradication.

It took a while for Helmand to get really bad. In 2002 Afghan security locations in Helmand on the Pakistani border were attacked several times. In 2004 some clerics in the area urged their flocks to fight the Americans and Afghan government. Although militias allied with President Karzai helped ward off the Taliban, they also abused the population and took advantage of their power to punish rivals. They would also give false tips to the coalition or the Afghan security forces against their rivals. These fears drove many to seek protection with the Taliban. By 2004 it was clear that locals were being recruited in Helmand to join the new Taliban. Those who had suffered at the hands of Afghan security forces were especially susceptible to recruitment. In 2005 the Taliban began to set up strongholds in Helmand, and by 2006 they dominated most of Helmand. That year it became common for Taliban attacks in Helmand to involve hundreds of fighters.

Dad Muhamad Khan, the Helmand boss for the National Security Directorate under SMA's reign, was known for being abusive. But the American military backed him because of his loyal service. In 2006 the British and the UN insisted that SMA be removed, and Karzai finally relented. The British had just taken over control of Helmand and discovered ten tons of heroin in the governor's house. SMA's successor as governor was Engineer Daud. Though Daud had not had a militia in the past, he demanded that he be allowed to set one up for his own survival. The government allowed him to have up to five hundred men. SMA still had a good relationship with Karzai, though, and was made a senator. His loyalists plotted against Daud, and Karzai made sure SMA was still the real power by appointing his brother as the deputy governor. Daud was pressured to support poppy eradication, which cost him the support of the local population. In late 2006 Karzai fired Daud, who was trying to go after militias and the unruly police of Helmand. Daud's police chief was sent elsewhere. British Prime Minister Tony Blair tried to save Daud but failed. The British were angry and blamed the Americans for Daud's removal. Daud's successor was weak and too scared even to go to Lashkar Gah, the capital for Helmand, for the first few months. After SMA was removed his militias stopped fighting the Taliban, so security only worsened. The Americans got SMA to arm tribesmen to fight the Taliban, but many switched sides and joined the insurgency. Similar defections occurred when the Americans tried to set up tribal militias in other provinces. SMA kept his militia even after he was no longer in power; he and his men still worked with Afghan security forces and the British and abused the population.

Though the Taliban failed to set up a base in northern Helmand in 2004, two years later they succeeded—thanks to the increased popularity they enjoyed as a result of SMA's abusive attitude and arrogance. The rivalry between Alizais and Ishaqzais also led to fighting. When the government and the coalition began attempting to eradicate poppy in Helmand, the Taliban's popularity increased. Pro-Taliban songs and sermons could be purchased in Helmand markets. Villagers would act as informers and help the Taliban set up ambushes, and they would throw stones at coalition convoys. Soon districts began to fall under Taliban control. The Taliban recruited from the displaced people's camps in Helmand. During 2006 the area where poppy was harvested increased by 250 percent, and the next year it nearly doubled. By 2006 the Taliban had the support of the population in Helmand, and most of the fighters were locals. There were reports of the police collaborating with the Taliban against the coalition in Helmand, or even fighting against it. Helmand police would arrest people and demand ransoms for their release. Following six months of fighting in one district alone fifty-two Afghan police were dead. In another Helmand police unit of 350 men, seventy deserted in 2006. The British thought they would defeat the Taliban by the summer of 2006. Instead they realized they were besieged by up to two thousand of them in northern Helmand alone. Although the British had spent nearly ten million dollars on reconstruction projects in Helmand by the end of 2006, nobody seemed to notice. District governors and police chiefs in northern and southern Helmand were targeted. There were failed assassination attempts against Daud. Most districts were abandoned or unable to operate. The Taliban had a logistical base and a clinic for fighters close to the provincial capital that could handle nearly one thousand men. In May 2006 the British launched an operation to take control of Helmand, but in July the Taliban captured the Nawa and Garmsir districts. The British retook Garmsir, and then the Taliban re-retook it.

By the fall of 2006, the British were exhausted in Helmand and negotiated truces with the Taliban via village elders in two districts that allowed the elders to choose the governor, chief of police, and other officials in the district governments. The Afghan government and American military were opposed to this "surrender," but the UN backed the deal. A few months later the truces ended, with the British blaming the Americans for their demise. Daud had been crucial in negotiating the truces, but he was removed. Relations between the British and Afghan governments deteriorated. SMA maintained his pernicious control. In 2007 only four of the thirteen district police chiefs were appointed from Kabul, with the rest under the control of SMA, who remained close to Karzai. Karzai, meanwhile, complained that if it were not for pressure from British Prime Minister Gordon Brown, he would have reinstated SMA. Most police in Helmand were more like a militia, and mostly from the same tribe.

The year 2007 was the first in which the Taliban faced pressure in Helmand, but the situation continued to deteriorate. The Afghan army complained that police in Helmand were demanding road taxes from drivers and stealing private property. That year five hundred kilograms of opium were seized by security forces in the area and divided between the police and the army, with only fifteen kilograms given to coalition forces. The British were opposed to eradication, while Americans pushed for aerial eradication, which only further alienated the population. The British floundered, unable to hold territory or defeat an enemy that fought asymmetrically. On one occasion in 2007, the British responded to a single shot fired by the Taliban with mortars, heavy machine guns, and missiles, and they dropped a bomb for good measure.

In 2008 the deputy governor was assassinated by a suicide bomber while still inside a mosque. That year the U.S. Marines joined the eight thousand British troops. The Marines tried to take Garmsir and also failed. They spoke of implementing COIN, living among and protecting the people, holding the territory they cleared, and winning over the population. It seemed as though every year there was a new plan that was better than the previous one, and when the foreign troops moved on, the Afghans who had made the mistake of working with them would be killed. Although the stated goal of the Western coalition was to extend the reach of the Afghan government, in the past extending the reach of the very unpopular central government had only caused further instability. The Americans and the Taliban had a similar narrative: the Taliban promised to protect people from the Afghan government, and the Americans promised to protect them by extending the government's reach. By 2009 half of Afghanistan was controlled by Taliban, and Helmand was the province most surely in Taliban hands. "Control" might be overstating the strength of the Taliban in some areas, but at a minimum they could deny the government and international forces the ability to control. In some cases insurgents did not formally belong to the Taliban. They may have been locals who resented the American and British occupation just as they had resented the Soviet occupation. Increased foreign intervention had made the security situation only worse for locals.

In Helmand the security forces were dominated by the Nurzai tribe. Colonel Shirzad, from the Nurzai tribe, served in various security posts in Helmand before being appointed police chief. Abdul Rahman Jan, the first postwar police chief, was also a Nurzai, as was Lieutenant Colonel Ayub, who had served as deputy chief of police following the overthrow of the Taliban. Ayub was known as an uneducated illiterate warlord. Colonel Torjan, the logistics officer, was a Nurzai. The Helmand passport officer was a Nurzai. The Border Patrol chief for Helmand was a Nurzai. General Mirwais, the head of the police in southern Afghanistan, was a Nurzai. The Nurzais were a plurality in the province, especially in its important places. Marja, the district where the Taliban had its strongest hold, had a Nurzai plurality. In 2009 Marja had a bumper poppy crop thanks to Taliban protection. A few months later Marja was the first district targeted for a major U.S. offensive in 2010.

Every police chief in Helmand, including Shirzad, bought his post from officials at the Interior Ministry. Police in Helmand were known to release prisoners for bribes ranging from five hundred to twenty thousand dollars. Shirzad's predecessor arrested a Taliban commander and was offered fifty thousand dollars for his release, but the Americans caught wind of it, so he couldn't close the deal. To ease the pressure he was facing to release the prisoner, he asked for the prisoner to be flown to Kabul.

In 2007 a district police commander went to Colonel Torjan to receive his two mandated Ford Rangers, but Torjan demanded ten thousand dollars for each. The Americans took the commander's report, but two or three weeks later he was killed by an IED. Conducting routine affairs in the Education Department required a bribe. The Justice Ministry in Helmand was particularly notorious. In addition to the poor quality of the police in Helmand, there just weren't enough of them. Helmand was supposed to have an increase of five hundred police as part of the surge, but so far only 211 had been recruited.

Locals complained that the police charged taxes at checkpoints. "The police know we're here to watch them as much as fight the Taliban," said Sergeant Gustafson. "Shirzad is a wily adept politician," he told me. "He comes with a lot of baggage." Shirzad was tied to the warlords connected to the poppy trade. Following a large opium seizure in 2009, the drugs disappeared and the trail went cold at Shirzad's headquarters. It was not that Afghans were corrupt and the Americans would teach them how to govern. The Americans helped bring corruption to Afghanistan by funding warlords, paying off tribes, and creating parallel institutions and a network of foreign and Afghan contractors. They created an infrastructure of unaccountability.

July 2009 was the worst month since the war started for the Americans and their allies, with forty-two Americans and twenty-two British soldiers killed, and a total of seventy-five foreign troops killed. Most of the casualties that month occurred in Helmand, when the Americans launched an operation for the fourth time to secure the area. More than four thousand Marines descended on the Helmand River Valley in a mission that had been planned months earlier. It was the first major operation of Obama's presidency. Brig. Gen. Lawrence Nicholson, Marine commander for the operation, stressed that the focus was on getting the Afghan government back on its feet. He urged his men to get to know the people, to drink tea and eat goat with them. Six hundred and fifty Afghan soldiers also took part. Nicholson promised that "where we go we will stay, and where we stay, we will hold." The Marines hoped to win over the population. So too had the thousands of British soldiers who had been in the province since 2006. The British military was conducting a simultaneous operation in Helmand. Like the Marines, they hoped to provide enough security so that the August presidential elections could be held credibly.

About 750 Marines made it to an agricultural district called Nawa south of Lashkar Gah. Before they arrived there were only about forty British soldiers there, ensconced with some Afghan soldiers and police in the district center, unable to move outside a small secure zone one kilometer wide. Beyond that the Taliban manned checkpoints. "Everybody knew we were coming," a Marine colonel told me, "so we wanted to deceive the enemy about what that would mean." On June 19 three hundred Marines flew into Nawa and conducted patrols to lull the Taliban and give them ten days to think that was it, that they could handle the surge. The patrols had an average of one contact with their enemy every day. On July 2, the rest of the battalion came to block the Taliban escape and reinforcements. The Marines had expected their invasion to be more kinetic, meaning they had expected more shooting. They encountered a few days of stiff resistance and were impressed with their enemy's combat techniques. But then the Taliban wisely melted away, laying down their arms or fleeing to Marja, fifteen miles to the west. The Taliban left poorly hidden weapons caches and poorly placed IEDs, and the Marines caught some of them fleeing. The first two IEDs destroyed vehicles, but the Marines uncovered the next twenty before they detonated. The Taliban also set up antipersonnel mines, placing an IED in a tree with a kite string attached to it as a command wire, and another IED in a wall.

The Marines were led by Lieut. Col. William McCollough, who operated out of a partially constructed brick building covered with sandbags. Although they officially had 650 Afghan soldiers with them, in private the Marines complained that it was more like four hundred and that the lack of an "Afghan face" was their "Achilles' heel." For an operation months in the making, it was a huge and inexplicable shortage.

Team Ironhorse and the ANCOP were to go to Helmand at the same time to increase the Afghan veneer. "We will deliver stabilization and development," a Marine colonel in Helmand told me. "The Taliban filled the space. They took the governance high ground. The Taliban rule through intimidation and coercion. Harassment by the Taliban has become more intense, and the population is becoming more dissatisfied." There was now a civilian "stabilization adviser" in Nawa with the Marines, the colonel told me, who was "trying to coordinate with local Afghan leadership so that the district government and police chief can organize and take the governance high ground. We're going to deliver governance by demilitarizing it as soon as possible. The most important lesson from Iraq was the transition piece. You need to have Afghans involved at every phase and remind yourself it's about them and their country, and remind each other we have to get our Afghan partners involved at every level." The short-term goal was to provide security so they could deliver the upcoming August presidential elections in a meaningful way.

Major Contreras led Team Ironhorse and Prowler in mentoring the police. The ANCOP were a highly trained unit (by local standards) that took over temporarily for local police units while they were sent away for training. Contreras was excited about his role in the war. "This is in its infancy," he said. "We're beginning to see the military might that we as a nation can bring." A true believer, he explained that he was fighting to protect the American way of life and because his wife had been working in the Pentagon when it was hit on

September 11. Contreras was concerned about the "negative tone" of my previous article on Afghanistan for *Rolling Stone* and hoped I would write a more positive article this time. "We can win this," he told me. "We were doing it one year at a time before for seven years."

But first he would have to overcome Afghan bureaucracy. He couldn't go to Nawa to link up with the Marines because Colonel Saki had not received his official orders from the Interior Ministry. The order had been signed and sealed five days earlier, but it had to be delivered by courier to Saki. There was no e-mail or other way for Saki to receive his orders. This was minor compared with the problems Contreras usually had with the ministry, he joked. Colonel Saki had not received supplies like radios, ammunition, and fuel, so he did not even have the logistical ability to head down. Saki met Colonel Torjan, who was in charge of logistics, and asked him for a commitment to replenish the ANCOP's weapons and ammunition. Torjan took him to his depot to show him that he had nothing to spare. The following day Contreras went to meet Torjan in the police headquarters. He stuffed a pistol between his belt and the small of his back, just in case.

Torjan had not received the official document from the ministry ordering him to equip the ANCOP. All he had was a letter from the ANCOP. The ANCOP could have made it up themselves, Torjan said. There was fighting in many parts of Helmand, and many people were running out of ammunition, he said. He received about one-third of what he requested from the ministry in Kabul. Two British officers advising the police headquarters sat in on the meeting, as did a portly civilian contract police adviser. The provincial reserve requested eighty radios. Contreras and the British disputed how many they actually needed. Then they struggled to figure out which form they needed to fill out to get the Interior Ministry to ship supplies to Kandahar and then to Helmand, and how to make sure the staff at the Kandahar headquarters didn't keep most of the supplies for themselves. Contreras and Torjan discussed how the ANCOP would refuel in Nawa, with Torjan suggesting they find gas stations. Nobody knew if there were any gas stations in the area.

That evening Ironhorse sat waiting to be briefed by Contreras. They were all scouts, and some were snipers, chosen by their lieutenant because they were "rough" and "shooters." The major's original plan called for them to go to Nawa before the Marines got there. "We would have gotten eaten alive," one of them joked. The Marines in Nawa were attempting to provide a safe and secure environment for the Afghan government in order to facilitate the handover of the security mission to the ANSF, he explained. Ironhorse's mission was to conduct a movement to Nawa—traveling through the eastern desert to avoid the much faster main road, which had not been cleared of IEDs—in order to link up with Marines and support their operations.

Contreras said guys in police uniforms were harassing civilians in Nawa. The men seemed very skeptical about the whole thing. "Duration of mission and number of legitimate police in Nawa, and how will ANP get along with ANCOP, and who is mentoring the ANPs there?" Staff Sergeant McGuire tersely asked without moving or looking at the major. Staff Sergeant Verdorn complained that they would be doing the Marines' job of clearing. As the major concluded his brief, McGuire loudly muttered, "It's a cocksuck." Contreras left. "That was very well thought out," McGuire said. I asked him to elaborate. "Fuel will be the biggest issue," he said. "We don't know where we're gonna live, we're not taking tents." It was the worst operations order he had ever seen, he said, just telling them to go down there and the Marines would tell them what to do. "It's a 'fly by the seat of your pants' operation." There was no plan for what would happen after they got to the school where the Marines were based. McGuire wondered what the mission was. If it was to give an Afghan face, well then there were already hundreds of Afghan soldiers there. Staff Sergeant Thacker was also worried. There were "a lot of I don't knows" in the brief, he said, like the radio frequencies for the Marines. "A normal op order, even the lowliest private knows what everybody's going to do," McGuire told me.

The British warned against occupying a school, but Contreras dismissed the concern. "The point is to provide a safe and secure environment," he said. He told the men to plan for seven days before they returned to base. "The reason why we're going down is to put an Afghan face on the mission," he said. "There isn't enough ANSF there." Contreras explained to me later that the goal was to set the conditions to deploy the ANCOP to work with the Marines in that area. It was a clear-and-hold operation, a basic element of counterinsurgency. "The Afghans have to feel like we're there with them," he said. The Marines would clear the area of Taliban, and the police would hold it. "My Afghan counterparts say that loads of Taliban want to stop fighting and reform," Contreras told me. He believed the Taliban had seen the error of their ways. All evidence pointed to the contrary, though. The Taliban were more confident than ever.

"The Marines are trained to go off a ship, hit the ground and fucking charge," Contreras told me, worrying that they might not be suitable for COIN. "I've never been to the place where I'm going. I have no idea what it looks like," he admitted. Contreras drove to the ANCOP facility, and we walked to Saki's office. There was a marijuana plant in the garden. Saki was watching Bollywood movies. He had a picture of President Karzai on his wall, some plastic flowers next to it, a bare desk, and a coffee table in his office, along with a map of Helmand. Saki wore an ornate *salwar kameez*, cream-colored with shiny embroidery. He had thick eyebrows and a short, well-groomed beard. "Intelligence we received says that in two days all the Taliban will leave Nawa and go to Marja, because of the large number of Marines," he said. Saki warned that the Taliban planted at least one hundred IEDs in Nawa but added that most were of poor quality and would not explode. About twenty were properly planted and effective, he said, with remote control detonation. Saki showed the longer road through the desert we would take to avoid IEDs along the road to Nawa.

IEDs were the biggest threat, the perfect asymmetric weapon. In 2009 there were thousands of IED attacks on ANSF. Most of the American and British soldiers killed every month were victims of IEDs, not small-arms fire, but IEDs were not just effective when they exploded. The threat of them crippled foreign and Afghan security forces. It meant that their vehicles were not free to go to all areas, and that they had to proceed at a snail's pace with bomb detectors walking in front of convoys or their vehicles crawling ahead. IEDs were built from homemade explosives like fertilizer and fuel as well as old mortars from past wars. Some were detonated by remote control, by cable or a pressure plate. In Iraq paved roads made it harder to conceal them; in Afghanistan the prevalence of dirt roads made it easier.

The men of Ironhorse had lost their lieutenant and a sergeant, as well as an interpreter and a cop, in a February 2009 IED blast. Lieutenant Southworth and Staff Sergeant Burkholder had gone to examine an IED the ANCOP discovered. They asked for an explosive ordnance disposal team to destroy it because they needed the road open and they worried civilians would get blown up. The British told them to mark the location and move on. As the ANCOP tried to dismantle the IED, it blew up. Ironhorse and the police spent an hour picking up pieces of their friends from the road and even a tree. Ironhorse later got a good tip on the IED maker who had killed their two friends. They raided his house, arresting him and his son, but when the two prisoners were in police detention they paid $1,500 to two guards and escaped. Ironhorse had returned to the house three times looking for them.

Although the men were chosen by their lieutenant for being "meat eaters," the months of daily operations and shitting in bags had taken a toll on them. They hated being in Afghanistan and being sent on missions that weren't their own; they resented the neglect they felt and the lack of progress. One sergeant's parents owned a hardware store and sent the team four tow straps for their Humvees because their request through the military was going nowhere. One Humvee drove around with bad transmission for a month and a half because they couldn't get a mechanic. "That's the kind of shit that just wears on you," Sergeant McGuire told me. "We were doing repairs above our mechanical level because there wasn't anybody to look at it, and then we got an e-mail asking why we were doing it, a kick in the nuts." While stationed in southern Helmand, they had to find their own water supply because the Army wasn't providing them with any.

Southworth had been very passionate, his men told me; he believed he had come to give Afghan kids a better future, and he loved what he was doing. He paid Afghans $150 for pointing out IEDs. A rich aunt sent him the money. It was unusual but it worked, his men said. The men had been told they would be on a large base in a safe job. Southworth knew different. They were going into the shit. He spent over a year putting the team together, sending them to schools for sniper, scout, combat lifesaver, and mountain skills. He gave a speech to the men before their final leave back home, warning them that a couple of them wouldn't make it back. His death was a huge loss for the team.

Contreras agreed to go through the desert to avoid the main road. The Marines or police working with them would meet them on the other side of the Argandab River to guide them to the schoolhouse base. The Marines were in the desert between Marja and Nawa to prevent an exodus of Taliban to Marja and prevent reinforcements from Marja coming into Nawa. Saki thought the Marines couldn't distinguish between Taliban and civilians. He asked for gunpowder residue kits so that people's hands could be tested to see if they were handling weapons. None were available. Saki strongly believed most Taliban were local farmworkers who fired when they had a chance and then threw down their weapons and took up shovels. Contreras told Saki he wanted him to set up two checkpoints with thirty men each so there would be about thirty left for patrolling and other missions. "If there are Marines with us, we can man checkpoints," Saki said. "Otherwise we can't." It was too dangerous for his men to do it alone.

But Saki had still has not received his written orders from the Interior Ministry to go on the mission on Sunday, and it was already Friday. He joked that by the time he got the orders the Nawa operation would be over. He worried that his chain of command would make problems for him, especially if he lost somebody there. Saki asked Contreras to tell the American training headquarters in Kandahar to e-mail the deputy minister of interior and explain that they needed an order to move to Nawa. He still could not even confirm that he would go there. He needed orders or he would get in trouble, but he didn't have the authority to speak to the ANCOP commander in Kabul or the deputy minister of interior. He asked the Americans to do it for him and pressure his leadership to give him the mission orders. A key element in the year's largest operation was being held up by bureaucracy.

Saki was concerned about his informant in Nawa, who was traveling on foot. He asked Contreras for money to get him a motorcycle. It would cost $500 at the most, he said. He lost informants because of lack of resources, he said, and asked for more to help them. But Contreras was noncommittal. Saki had not heard from one of his informants for the past two days. He worried that the man had been captured by the Taliban. Saki had no food, fuel, or water for the mission. The Marines would help provide food, Contreras assured him, while Ironhorse would take care of the water. This left only the need for diesel fuel. The Marines had fifty heat casualties yesterday, Contreras told Saki: "They haven't learned to stop working in the middle of the day." Saki and his assistant laughed.

The next day Contreras met with Saki again. "The Marines are giving me a lot of problems because of the delay," he said. Contreras asked for an assurance that they could leave in two days. Saki was still waiting for supplies. A quick reaction force of forty men from Kandahar would also go along with Saki's sixty or so men from ANCOP, and he would equip them. "They will look like ANCOP, but will they act like ANCOP?" Contreras asked, worried that they might spoil the good name of Saki's ANCOP. "As long as you and I are in charge it will be okay," Saki said with a smile. He told Contreras he heard the Marines were trying to get close to the people but the local police were making problems and people were complaining that the police were thieves. "We will tie Taliban to trees and shoot them," Saki said. Contreras looked down and shook his head, laughing. "Enemy morale is low," said Saki. "The enemy is nothing." Saki didn't trust the local Nawa ANP. "They inform the Taliban," he said. He also didn't trust the police in Lashkar Gah and warned Contreras not to travel with them. "If they could, the ANP would hand me over to the Taliban," Saki said. The ANCOP liked to say about the ANP that "you can change the blanket on a donkey, but it's still a donkey."

Two days later they finally get the order to go. McGuire was in command of the first Humvee, and I joined him as a passenger. The gunner up top shot pen flares at cars that got too close. The pop sounded like a gunshot and served as a warning. We drove by a group of small kids fighting, punching one another in the face. The men cheered. McGuire opened the windows and shouted, urging them on. McGuire asked if I was sure I wanted to be in the first vehicle. It would be the first one to get blown up by IEDs.

The team linked up with the ANCOP and waited for them to get ready. Contreras met with Saki and assured him that he would also take part in all the meetings with the Marines. Saki suggested that the Americans' armored vehicles take the lead once they crossed the river because his vehicles were more vulnerable to IEDs, and recommended that the Americans stay in the lead in dangerous areas. Contreras agreed. He told Saki he still didn't know who would meet them on the other side.

As we drove south the ANCOP stopped in front of every culvert to search both sides of it. Progress was slow. Some of the police pickup trucks got stuck in the deep soft sand. The Americans grew frustrated with the way the AN-COP plodded through the desert. Our vehicle searched for a place to cross the hundred-meter Argandab River, avoiding the unexploded mortars on the sand. McGuire emerged to walk across it, making sure the vehicles could cross. The water reached his mid-thigh. Water seeped inside the Humvee, reaching up to my calves. The rest of the vehicles followed. One of the rangers got stuck in the water and had to be towed out. "ANCOP is better than the ANP in running checkpoints," McGuire said, "but little things like vehicle movement, and it all breaks down." "Instead of following each other they race around," Sergeant Sadler said, laughing at the ANCOPs crossing the river like they were at Nascar. Two of the police got into an argument about the driving, and one pointed his rifle menacingly at the other. This had happened before, Verdorn later told me. Once, on their base, two of the ANCOPs got pissed at each other and drew their pistols. "There was blood in their eyes," Verdorn said. The Americans were caught between them.

Two Marine Humvees met Ironhorse across the river. Thacker chatted with them about what kinds of IEDs they had encountered. We were in a thick vegetated area of farmland and trees. Cows grazed near flooded fields. We crossed narrow canals and arrived at the schoolhouse. Sandbags lined the top of it. Hundreds of Marines wandered around shirtless, wearing green shorts and kicking up dust as they walked. It looked like *Lord of the Flies*. They slept on the ground outside or in classrooms that smelled of sweaty feet.

A Marine captain thanked Contreras for his arrival. "Our weak spot" was the shortage of ANSF, he said, so the additional cops were helpful. Nawa had been quiet for the past five days, since July 2. "The Taliban left for Marja to lie low," the captain said, "but this is their breadbasket, so they're not likely to give it up." Ironhorse occupied two dirty arched rooms in the schoolhouse. The men hastily swept the broken glass, dust, and dirt and set up cots, unloading boxes of water bottles and food, making it home.

The Marine commander, Lieutenant Colonel McCollough, told Contreras that they had discovered "rogue" police who were abusing people in Aynak, to the north. In two communities people had complained about the police. When the Marines first encountered the local police in Aynak, the police were so startled that they fired warning shots and nearly got into a firefight. "They weren't disciplined and appeared to be on drugs," he said, addressing Saki. "They had no mentors and had no connection to a higher headquarters. It worries me that that's how those communities view the Afghan police, so I wanted the ANCOP to replace those police and show those communities what ANSF is about."

McCollough turned to Contreras and said, "I'm glad you're here. You couldn't have come at a better time." Nawa's chief of police, Nafaz Khan, sat in on the meeting. He had a long beard and a long, nervous face. The Marines described him as a local mafia boss. "The Taliban come to people's houses at night and demand collaboration," Khan said. "If people don't get away from the Taliban, the elections will fail." Although he had 250 men officially working under him, he said the real number for this large rural area of 180,000 people was only 138. "We had a lot of tough days here and we cannot handle those days anymore," he said. "There were times when we had no food and nobody came to ask us how we were doing." Sergeant Sadler suspected that Khan was keeping his men's salary for himself, forcing the police to steal for a living. Khan denied that the police in Aynak were under his authority and claimed he had never heard of them.

Saki didn't trust the Nawa commander and waited until he left to speak freely. McCollough told Saki that he should supplant the "rogue police" in Aynak. "Those are not police officers," he said. "They're criminals." He estimated there were about sixty of them. The Marines had to fight to get up to Aynak, and although it was only a few kilometers away, they planned our trip up there like a careful military operation.

The next day we waited. The men of Ironhorse played cards. The ANCOP sat in the shade of a tree.

The Marines promised that once in Aynak they would meet with locals in a *shura*, or council. But Thacker dismissed it. "These *shuras* are just a bitch session," he said. "They'll complain about cops shaking them down. The major will make promises, and the ANP will come back and go back to the same ways." After their additional training, when the ANP returned to one district where Ironhorse had taken over, they went back to setting up illegal checkpoints and demanding money from cars passing by. When Ironhorse and the ANCOP came in, towns that were formerly abandoned would slowly get repopulated with their residents, and when Ironhorse and the ANCOP prepared to leave and make way for the ANP again, people would flee and move back to Lashkar Gah. "We don't see what it's like after we leave," Thacker told me. One team of police who came back from training actually got into a firefight with the Afghan army and killed four men. In one district the ANP came back from their training with new body armor, boots, goggles, and rifles; later, when Ironhorse returned on a mission to support the British, whose base was in danger of being overrun, they found the same ANP wearing sandals but not their body armor or goggles. The problem with coming in for a short cycle as the local ANP were sent on training, Thacker told me, was that just when they got to know the area and the people, they had to leave.

The men prepared for a departure the following morning. The Marines gave them enough fuel for another day or so. McGuire worried about what they would do after that. "The homework wasn't done in advance," he said. At 5 a.m. Sergeant First Class Sadler showed the men the route. The military command for Helmand contradicted the Marines and Nafaz Khan, informing Contreras that the Aynak police were legitimate and that they belonged to the Nawa headquarters and Khan. We rumbled slowly along a green canal. Marine minesweepers walked ahead of us. At 9 a.m., nearly four hours after leaving, we had gone only four or five kilometers. It was a numbing pace and one that allowed the fleet-footed Taliban to flee well in advance. The Americans' enemy was elusive, normally engaging them from a few hundred meters away unburdened by the heavy body armor and gear the Americans had.

As we progressed, I watched children tending cows and sheep in dark green fields. It was almost idyllic. The men I was traveling with linked up with the Marines at 10:30 a.m. Dozens of their vehicles were parked off the dirt road on plowed fields, crushing corn plants. "This farmer is not gonna be happy," Corporal Chapman said. The Marines had paid damages to farmers in the past few days. They accidentally set one field on fire and ran around trying to put it out.

The *shura* meeting was canceled because we were so late. Instead, Marines lay about in the shade. Specialist Baker sat atop a Humvee. "We came, we parked, we relocated, then we parked," he said triumphantly.

Marine Captain Schoenmaker told Contreras that when they first arrived in Aynak and asked locals about the Taliban, they heard complaints about the police instead. He estimated that there were about 150 of them. They were stoned, he said, wearing beads and looking shady. "It was uncomfortable when we met them, they were all high," he explained. Aynak was mostly deserted, he said. The Marines didn't know what to expect up there, and Colonel Saki was frustrated with the lack of a plan.

We languished in the heat for hours, eating watermelons purchased from a local farmer. McCollough complained that he had been given only one hundred Afghan soldiers. The night before he had watched satellite footage of twenty-five guys dressed in black meeting the cops at the Aynak checkpoint, he told Contreras. I thought they might have just been other cops. Saki called his boss, Colonel Shirzad, who said he would send somebody down to Aynak. Shirzad said one station in Aynak belonged to Nawa district and the other one belonged to Lashkar Gah, and both would be instructed to hand over control of their stations to the ANCOP. Saki said all the Taliban had left the area. I asked him if the ANP improved after coming back from their additional training. "Only for the first five days," he joked, then they went back to their old ways. "The academy has good showers, free food—the result is these first five days. They need more training." He told me of an incident where police returned and then deserted to join the Taliban.

"Why are we driving into this town to remove the ANP?" Thacker asked. "Because the Marines want us to," Contreras told him. "These ANP up here sound like the ANP everywhere in this fucking country," Thacker said. "The ANP are crooked. This problem is everywhere in this country."

We wouldn't be leaving until 4:30 in the afternoon. Verdorn was concerned. "It seems like the Marines want to get in a firefight," he said. "5:30 PM is the beginning of fighting time." "I'm beginning to think these Marines are a bunch of cheese dicks," Thacker muttered. I asked the major why the operation was being delayed. "Because it's fucking hot," he said, and the Marines had to walk. Since the operation started they had lost dozens of casualties just to the heat.

A couple of Marines told Thacker that it seemed like there was going be a fight in Aynak. He dismissed them. "What, are there signs up?" he asked. "No briefing about what we're doing, how far it is, how the convoy will be spread out," McGuire complained. As the vehicles slowly lined up on the road, the Marines and soldiers had trouble communicating, which made McGuire even more impatient. "Unbelievable, there's no command and control. I'm awestruck. What a clusterfuck. A good leader puts together a plan, formulates an op order, and then briefs our men."

We finally began to plod along on the rocky road, the Marines walking in front of us. Kids stood motionless in front of homes and glared at the Americans, unlike the children in Lashkar Gah, who often waved (though sometimes they threw stones too). Men with black beards and black turbans stared at the Americans, expressionless, standing ramrod-straight. "That's a fucking Talib if I've ever seen one," McGuire said.

There were no paved roads in the villages we passed, only rocky paths. We drove around a large crater. "That's a pretty fucking good bomb there, hell yeah!" McGuire said. The wall next to it was destroyed, and a new one was being built of fresh mud. A boy emerged from behind a metal gate and mud walls to talk to the ANCOP, but none of them spoke Pashtu and he didn't know Farsi. The Americans' interpreter translated. There was an IED on the road up ahead, the boy said. His father came out wearing a green *salwar kameez*. He fingered red worry beads nervously. The IED was planted on the road on the side of their house. Several days before the Taliban were hiding in the house several hundred meters away, he said, pointing toward it. He worried locals would inform the Taliban that they had warned the Americans about the IED. McGuire walked five feet up to the IED and saw it partially buried and concealed by shrubs. "Plain as day," he announced. The minesweepers arrived but were dismissive. They didn't think a guy from the Army could find an IED or that they could miss one. They sent a robot to place plastic explosives on it. On the first attempt, the explosives blew up but not the IED. The second attempt worked, sending up a huge cloud of smoke and debris. Rocks rained down on us a few hundred meters away. The men speculated if it would have been a catastrophic kill. McGuire thought it would have just tossed us up a bit in our armored vehicle but would have obliterated the police.

We made it to Aynak after nightfall. It had taken an entire day to go twenty kilometers. Clouds hid the moon. It was pitch black, impossible to distinguish faces at the checkpoint. Dozens of local cops surrounded the five Americans, Saki, and some of his men. Many of the cops wore turbans and the *salwar kameez*. They looked like the Taliban. They were cooperative and friendly, unlike what the Marines described. They shook hands and moved out.

Thacker and McGuire were impressed with them; they seemed just like any other ANP, but their facility was cleaner than most. The Marines had never seen the ANP before and had nothing to compare them to.

We slept under the stars that night, the men taking turns on guard shift. Overnight we heard explosions and gunfire in the distance. The next morning we were able to explore the dusty abandoned schoolhouse. The police used an adjacent mud compound as a bathroom, and so did we. Shell casings from ANP battles with the Taliban littered the sand. There was nothing to do except wait. The men discussed the odds of getting into a firefight. The consensus was that there were too many Americans and the Taliban would not risk it. That morning an Afghan man approached the Marine captain. He poked him in the chest and said they were occupying his property. Then he slapped the Marines' interpreter.

Colonel Shirzad, the ANP commander for Helmand, showed up. I hitched a ride back to Lashkar Gah with him, sitting in one of the four Ford Rangers in his convoy. It took us thirty minutes to drive to Lashkar Gah. The trip from there to Aynak with the military had taken three days. Shirzad's men did not stop to check the road for IEDs, which could shred their vulnerable Rangers. I scanned the road desperately.

The next morning Ironhorse went out on patrol with the ANCOP and found five IEDs placed on the road I had just taken. That day a twenty-vehicle Marine convoy from a base in the desert to the west tried to go to Aynak to re-supply the Americans. Twenty kilometers away the Taliban attacked the convoy so fiercely that it turned back. Eight British soldiers had been killed in Helmand the previous night. On the afternoon of my return to Lashkar Gah, two mortars landed just outside the base.

The Afghan army refused to come to Helmand, the Americans said. Tens of thousands of Afghan soldiers had been trained at the cost of billions, and yet the Afghan army was a no-show in a major operation contingent on an "Afghan face" that wasn't there. What was the point of an army that didn't deploy?

EIGHT YEARS INTO THE WAR, the Americans and ISAF were making their big push. With more international troops and more combat would come more civilian casualties. The American focus on the south had allowed provinces like Logar and Wardak in Kabul's backyard to fall into Taliban hands. With only sixty thousand Afghan soldiers it would take too long to increase the size of the army and there would never be enough foreign troops to remain in villages and control them, a British counterinsurgency expert in Afghanistan told me, so the Americans would remain like firemen responding to crises but never achieving sufficient density to get to know the community.

Meanwhile, the Taliban were seamlessly embedded into communities. They *were* the locals. They did not need Kalashnikovs; a simple knock on the door could be as effective. The police were useless, timid during the day and terrified at night. Neither the Americans nor the Afghan security forces conducted night patrols. At night the Taliban controlled the communities, undoing whatever the Americans had tried to accomplish during the day. The Taliban took a step back in reaction to the American surge to measure their adversary. It did not matter if the Americans were effective here and there. "Emptying out the Titanic with a teacup has an effect, but it doesn't stop the ship from sinking," the Brit told me. The insurgents were learning, avoiding direct encounters. They could continue placing IEDs despite the increase in troops, which could make getting around close to impossible and easily neutralize police units.

The much-hailed operation in Helmand didn't fail, but there was little to show for the tremendous amount of effort that went into it—the operation merely advanced the stalemate longer. The Taliban weren't winning so much as the government was losing. Next the focus turned to nearby Kandahar, and there was talk of pouring troops in there. It was the same mistake. When the Americans were focused on the south, they let Logar and Wardak provinces slip under Taliban control; by the summer of 2009, it was clear that much of the formerly safe north, such as Kunduz, was falling to the Taliban as well.

Bill Hix, the commander of the American task force in charge of training Afghan security forces in southern Afghanistan, believed the Taliban had slid their Kalashnikovs under their beds and were waiting, observing their opponents, just as they did following a similar operation the Marines undertook in southern Helmand's Garmsir district in 2008. The Taliban melted away to other districts in Helmand. This year the Marines were back in Garmsir again. According to Hix, the lack of Taliban was not a sign of weakness but of strategy. "Their target is the Afghan people, not the British or the Americans," he said. "They are waiting and seeing." Hix spent twenty months working with the Afghan Regional Security Integration Command, and he enjoyed his job. In his view the Afghan army should have been pushing the enemy away from the population while the police should have been protecting and controlling the population.

Control is essential to a successful COIN campaign. According to Stathis Kalyvas, a Yale political scientist and expert on civil war whose book *The Logic of Violence in Civil War* was very influential among counterinsurgency theorists, "The higher the level of control exercised by the actor, the higher the rate of collaboration with this actor—and, inversely, the lower the rate of defection." Control leads to collaboration and allows the counterinsurgents to separate the insurgents from the community. But the Americans would never have enough troops in Afghanistan to achieve control. Unlike in Iraq, where the surge focused on Baghdad, a densely urban environment where a census could be conducted, neighborhoods closed off with Americans at the access points, in Afghanistan the war was rural. The Americans got lucky in Iraq, benefiting from sectarianism that changed the dynamics of the conflict from an anti-occupation struggle to a civil war. Millions were displaced, hundreds of thousands were killed. The Americans looked good in comparison, and they decided to focus on protecting the people. Then the Shiites defeated the Sunnis, and Sunni militias chose to ally themselves with the Americans. But a caricature of the surge dominated popular culture. Both Washington and the military came to believe that COIN just might be the magic formula in Afghanistan. While ignoring the right lessons from Iraq, such as the use of community outposts, there was much talk of bribing Afghan tribes, which misunderstood why Sunnis stopped resisting in Iraq and gave way too much importance to tribalism in Afghan society. The Americans were unable to grasp that material benefits were not the only thing that could motivate people. McChrystal called for a new focus on the urban population centers of the country and less on the rural areas. This was also the failed approach favored by the Soviet occupiers in the 1980s. Like the mujahideen, the Taliban are strong in the rural areas, in mountains and valleys.

McChrystal insisted that securing the people of Afghanistan was his goal. But why, then, were the Americans operating out of large bases and not in the communities? The community outposts that existed in Afghanistan were actually away from the population. In Iraq the Americans' best success came with their use of community outposts. If they set up similar outposts in Afghanistan, they would not have to "commute to work" on roads vulnerable to IEDs in mammoth vehicles that keep them removed from the people, staring at them like aliens in spaceships unable to breathe in their atmosphere. It was a paradox of population-centric COIN in Afghanistan that the areas where the population was most concentrated were not the insurgent strongholds; instead the insurgents were based in the rural areas, away from population centers. The surge in Iraq was urban-based, and much easier. In Baghdad the Americans figured out who lived where, what they did, and what they wanted. That lesson didn't make it over to Afghanistan.

THE AMERICANS' OBSESSION with Afghanistan's elections also resembled their Iraq approach, which erroneously focused on landmark events. Just as in Iraq, when elections helped enshrine sectarianism and pave the way to civil war, so too in Afghanistan the elections empowered warlords; enshrined a corrupt order; and, in the case of the August 2009 elections, completely discredited the government and its foreign backers. Strategy in Afghanistan was put on hold so that the elections could be held. Turnout in the south was less than 10 percent, and zero in some places. There was overwhelming evidence of systematic election fraud and ballot stuffing. The Taliban managed to reduce the turnout compared with previous years. There were seven thousand polling stations throughout the country, so the Taliban could not actually disrupt voting too much. It would have also been bad PR for them to kill too many civilians. Their lack of operations might have shown that even they knew the elections didn't matter and that nothing could better serve their ends than letting the elections take place and ending up with a deeply flawed result. Meanwhile, the Americans and their allies immediately hailed the elections as a success, merely because violence was low, thus further associating themselves with a corrupt government. How could Afghans take Americans seriously when they backed a corrupt government and were deeply implicated in corruption? The failed elections were a message to Afghans that there was no hope of improvement or change.

In September 2009 McChrystal's assessment of the war in Afghanistan was leaked to the media. He had been advised by a team of experts, many of them celebrity pundits from Washington think tanks. Only one of his advisers was an expert on Afghanistan. When Petraeus conducted his Iraq review, he called on people who really knew Iraq to join his "brain trust." McChrystal called in advisers from both sides of the political divide in Washington who already believed that population-centric COIN was the solution to everything. It was a savvy move, sure to help him gain support in Congress. There was a cult of celebrity in the D.C. policy set. Many of the same pseudo experts who were once convinced that the war in Iraq was the most important thing in the world, even at the expense of Afghanistan, were now convinced that Afghanistan was the most important thing in the world, and were organizing panels with other pseudo experts in Washington think tanks. They offered trendy solutions, like an industry giving managed and preplanned narratives about what was going on. COIN advocates from DC think tanks were connected to political appointees who came from DC think tanks. There was an explosion of commentary on Afghanistan coming from positions of ignorance, quoting generalities. McChrystal himself had been chosen because he could drum up bipartisan support. He was another hero general like Petraeus, with an aura of infallibility—he was there to save the day. Fawning articles praised his low percentage of body fat, his ascetic habit of eating one meal a day, his repetition of simple COIN aphorisms that had already become clichés in Iraq by 2007. He was another warrior scholar the media could write panegyrics about.

Just as Petraeus replaced a discredited General Casey in Iraq, and Abrams replaced a discredited General Westmorland in Vietnam, so too had McChrystal replaced a discredited McKiernan, and the media eagerly consumed the hype about the new general. The generals were manipulating public opinion, inviting celebrity pundits to take part in reviews and then write opinion pieces in newspapers in support of the conclusion that the pundits and generals proposed. The military was setting the agenda for the war, and in the end it came down to more troops. McChrystal and the military were playing Obama. They wanted billions of dollars and a war without end so they could experiment with COIN, the solution for all problems. McChrystal bluntly stated that if his strategy wasn't followed, then the mission in Afghanistan would fail. Neither he nor his backers explained what the qualitative difference would be. They were not doing COIN properly with the troops they had already, so why bring in more?

Even though McChrystal's assessment identified the biggest challenges the Americans faced as political, social, and economic, his solution was military. The generals were trying to make all of Afghanistan's problems look like a nail, and they kept wanting to apply the hammer. They were saying they could fight a war by not focusing on the enemy, but they were not actually taking the steps to protect people, either. Instead of relying on civilian experts, the government ended up using the military even to solve problems that weren't military. McChrystal advocated a war that was population-centric and not enemy-centric, and yet all the talk was over how many troops they would need, instead of what a successful COIN strategy would require. Despite all the talk of a civilian surge, the civilians—diplomats, advisers, trainers—to staff even the much lower requirements of the last seven years were not found. Nor were the civilians found to meet the requirements for the American mission in Iraq. Instead, McChrystal increased the number of special operators to kill Taliban instead of trainers for the police and army.

More than a specific code of action, COIN was a mentality. But it hadn't really trickled down. Once you got down to the rifle squad, COIN didn't make any sense. It was hard for the troops to keep the greater strategic picture in their minds. They were being asked to be Wyatt Earp and Mother Teresa at the same time. Most soldiers didn't care about the mission; they just wanted to live through the deployment. Lip service is paid to COIN, but the military isn't implementing its own plan very well. Officers speak of going into villages and "doing that COIN shit." COIN required the Americans in their bases to learn about and live with the people in the villages. They couldn't just go in for a few hours, call a *shura* with some elders, and then rush back to base before the chow hall closed. COIN was dangerous, and the military was risk-averse. In Iraq the American casualties peaked when the military got serious about protecting the people. The faces in charge of the war in Afghanistan had changed, but the strategy had not.

The American military and policy establishments were institutionally incapable of doing COIN. They lacked the curiosity to understand other cultures and the empathy to understand what motivated other people. In the military in particular, Afghans were still viewed as "hajjis." Alternative viewpoints were not considered. Many journalists failed to understand that when you're with the military you're changing your selection bias. By showing up with the white guys with guns, you are eliminating all the people who don't want to talk to the military, or talking to those who have an interest in engaging the foreign occupier. Regular people won't relate to you in a natural or honest way. For the U.S. military, seeing something from a reporter's or Afghan's perspective is an exception. Even the media were perceived as the enemy. Military officers had been talking for a long time about being good at complex operations, providing aid while engaging in military operations, but they still made it up as they went and hoped that the previous unit had learned something. Units were terrible at handing over the knowledge they had gained, and relationships formed with Afghans were lost. Even when officers got it right, the system wouldn't, because the military *Weltanschauung* could not account for complex social environments. The military's way of thinking was still very conventional. All the officers could do was to try to take COIN and graft it onto conventional doctrine, putting a COIN face on the same old army. The Pentagon cultivated engineers, but Afghanistan could not be approached from a systems engineering perspective. COIN was hard to translate into Power-Point, the military's favorite language. The greatest advantage the Taliban had may have been not relying on PowerPoint.

COIN inevitably required military action against a major segment of the Afghan population, and in doing so it undermined the project of state building and national consensus that the international community was simultaneously involved in. The new American mantra called not for targeting the insurgents but protecting the population. But the population was attacked by the Taliban only to the extent that it collaborated with the Americans and their puppet government. Does protecting the population mean protecting them from the Taliban or the police or the Americans? The Americans in Afghanistan were like firemen attracting pyromaniacs.

McChrystal did have an academic "red cell" formed under the auspices of Harvard, but they were never sent the strategy to review, so these bona fide experts were never really consulted. Instead McChrystal's team listened to urban Afghan expats, fluent in English, who "drank the Kool-Aid of the Kabulis," as one academic participant described it to me. The center of gravity in Afghanistan are the rural areas, where the Taliban has its greatest strength and where the war will be won or lost. But these expats prioritized the urban, had never been out in the hinterland, a strategy, ironically, out of the old Soviet playbook. They were giving McChrystal the advice Kabulis wanted to hear.

McChrystal had a list of goals with vague suggestions about how they might be achieved. His job was to answer the question of how Afghanistan could control its own territory. But President Obama was busy asking an entirely different question, about whether the strategy itself was correct. He was asking whether the goal was valid. First they had to agree on what the problem was. Was it global terrorism, as Obama said, or was it a unified, peaceful Afghanistan? For the narrow goal of preventing Al Qaeda from having bases in Afghanistan, the United States has prescribed for itself the creation of a new Afghanistan and a never-ending counterinsurgency. So defeating Al Qaeda became building Afghanistan. McChrystal was concerned less with Al Qaeda, the original cause of the mission in Afghanistan, and more with the problem of the expanding Taliban. If Obama's stated goal in Afghanistan was to disrupt, dismantle, and defeat Al Qaeda, then why was McChrystal determined to fight the Taliban? Perhaps he believed that if the Taliban took over, Al Qaeda might obtain bases in Afghanistan. But Al Qaeda was in Pakistan, it was on the Internet, it was in Europe (the 9/11 attacks were planned in Germany, after all).

There was an impossible disconnect between the assessment and McChrystal's plan. McChrystal provided an accurate assessment of the dismal situation in Afghanistan. But the plan he proposed failed to address the key problems he noted. He explained that building Afghan civilian government capacity was critical, but he devoted a single page in Annex C to what he thought would fix the government.

The assessment noted that the Americans needed a much larger Afghan army and proposed doubling it. Yet it did not address how to do that, given that after eight years the Americans still had not provided sufficient trainers to get the army to the earlier goal of 134,000.

The assessment noted that the Afghan police were a major problem. Yet it suggested no new ideas for how to eliminate police corruption. It never even mentioned the justice system. The proposed solution was to double the size of the police force, but it did not explain how doubling the corrupt and dysfunctional force could help with COIN. "If I take drug dealers and gang bangers from the streets of DC to an eight-week program and then put them back in the same environment, can we expect it to change their activities?" one skeptical COIN expert working on Afghanistan asked me. "This corrupt force is the problem, so why put twice as many corrupt police out there?"

The underlying assumptions were not addressed in the assessment. The most important assumptions were those dealing with the political situations in Afghanistan, the United States, and allied nations. One key assumption was that it is possible to create a centralized, functioning state in Afghanistan. The Americans wanted to extend the reach of the government, but in the past extending the reach of an unpopular central government in Afghanistan caused instability. And after almost eight years in power, the Karzai government was only one of several competing powers within the country.

Another assumption was that the Karzai government would be perceived as sufficiently legitimate to gain the loyalty of the population. Before the election, Karzai's legitimacy faced two major problems: many Afghans felt his government represented and was imposed by foreign interests, and it was permeated by widespread, systematic corruption that severely undercut the government's legitimacy even in those areas it controlled. After the 2009 elections it was clear that Karzai could never gain legitimacy. Associating themselves with an illegitimate government only discredits the Americans.

A third assumption was that ISAF (meaning, primarily, the United States) would provide the resources necessary to conduct a population-centric COIN campaign. But even with the infusion of seventeen thousand U.S. troops, ISAF had too few troops to meet the training program goal for the Afghan security forces and vastly too few to secure the population. The "civilian surge" simply did not occur, and there was no indication that it would.

The assessment also assumed that the voters of ISAF nations, including the United States, would support this effort for the decade that historical examples suggest would be necessary for population-centric COIN to work. But Canada reaffirmed its intention to withdraw its 2,500 soldiers in 2011. The Dutch also stated they would withdraw. British public opinion was strongly against the war, and the validity and cost of the war was becoming an issue in the United States. To last for ten more years, the support would have to survive five more Congressional and two presidential elections.

A final assumption was that failure to create a unified, centralized state in Afghanistan would result in it the country's reverting to a major base for Al Qaeda. But there was widespread disagreement about whether this would happen. Al Qaeda was already ensconced in Pakistan. Bases in Afghanistan could be bombed, and Afghans themselves might not be so welcoming to Al Qaeda.

If any of these five assumptions were not true or ceased to be true, then the Americans needed to rethink their strategy accordingly. This did not mean an immediate withdrawal, which could leave a vacuum that might make things even worse, but it required figuring out how to achieve the primary strategic ends in ways that could be supported by the means the Americans and their ISAF allies were willing to provide.

The underlying assumptions of the invasion of Iraq were that Iraqis would greet the Americans with flowers, that the Iraqi institutions would remain functioning with the leadership merely replaced, that the war would pay for itself, and that fewer troops would be needed to secure the country than were needed to invade it. All these assumptions proved wrong, and the result was a catastrophic setback for the United States—not to mention the further destruction of Iraq and the creation of Al Qaeda where it previously had not existed.

Assuming that Al Qaeda would set up bases in Afghanistan was like assuming Saddam would give his imaginary WMDs to Al Qaeda. It assumed that the Taliban were irrational and unaware of their interests. Their alliance with Al Qaeda was a result of common interests, but the Taliban were not interested in global jihad (though the longer the Americans are in Afghanistan, the stronger the alliance will become). Even Pashtuns who supported the Taliban were opposed to Al Qaeda attacks. And most Afghans disliked the Arab extremist volunteers.

For the first time in its history, the U.S. army had created a new category of warfare: "stability operations" were now given the same importance as offensive and defensive operations. Despite this the COIN community felt like insurgents in their own establishment, combating the forces of "Big Army." Many of the COIN pioneers in Iraq were very influential in Washington. But opponents feared that this focus on irregular warfare and low-intensity warfare was weakening the U.S. military. To bolster their case, the COIN critics pointed to the Israeli military, which after years of being bogged down as an occupying army was defeated by Hizballah in 2006.

Some see Iraq as a victory that vindicated COIN and showed just how much the U.S. military can do, while others saw Iraq as a catastrophe demonstrating the limits of U.S. military power. If the U.S. military had learned lessons from classic imperialist counterinsurgencies such as the French campaign in Algeria, did that make the COIN doctrine any less imperialist? Of course, the most important questions were, Should the United States be involved in any of this? Should it act as an imperial power? Should the U.S. Army be doing stability operations in the first place? But these were questions for the politicians, not the military.

In some ways COIN was a rejection of the neoconservative use of military power as the main tool of U.S. foreign policy, since COIN recognized that military force cannot solve conflicts alone. It was tempting to welcome the new doctrine, because tens of thousands of Iraqi and Afghan civilians had been killed as a result of the U.S. military not knowing how to operate in complex environments where "the terrain is the people." Just as the neoconservatives had taken over the Pentagon during the Bush administration, so it seemed that the proponents of counterinsurgency, former dissidents within the military, now held key positions and enjoyed a preponderance of influence over the Obama administration. Many were veterans of Iraq and Afghanistan. The lessons they learned from Iraq and Afghanistan were less about questions over strategy (such as whether to invade a country) and more about the practice. They criticized as counterproductive the overwhelming blunt force of the U.S. military, and maintained that repeated assassinations of senior insurgent leaders were not effective. They urged all the other civilian agencies of the U.S.

government to contribute to the effort to win the support of the population and separate them from the insurgents. The best way to do this was to learn what people's grievances were and respond to them. Chief among these needs was the provision of security. Another key element in winning a counterinsurgency war was the creation of an effective local security force. The COIN proponents urged a huge expansion of the Afghan security forces and the creation of many more military advisers to train the Afghan security forces.

COIN advocates fought such a determined and near fanatical battle to gain influence over a calcified military establishment that they started believing in themselves a bit too much. Even if you implement a perfect COIN campaign, you can still fail to achieve your goals. President Obama's new approach to Afghanistan was drafted by these counterinsurgency theorists. The idea was to get troops to where the population was, to deny the insurgents access to the population while increasing the number of aid workers and diplomats in the country who could improve governance. The focus would be on local leaders instead of the corrupt and incompetent central government in Kabul.

For liberals these COINdinistas, as they call themselves, might seem like kindred spirits. They emphasize nonlethal means, humanitarian aid, development work, making peace with enemies instead of just killing them, and protecting the civilian population. But the end result was still a foreign military occupation. Sometimes the very locals the Americans were promoting were the ones oppressing the population. Other times the Americans harmed the population even while trying to help. The neoconservatives also co-opted COIN. Neocons didn't care what it took; they just wanted an American combat presence on the ground. Though they preferred an enemy-centered presence, population-centric COIN was the best way to repackage and sell their goals. For liberal interventionists who think they can re-engineer societies—those who supported the U.S. interventions in the Balkans and elsewhere in the 1990s, some of whom supported the invasion of Iraq—COIN provides the perfect template, clearing and holding thousands of villages in the middle of nowhere, one at a time, on the road to civilization.

In 2005 the respected COIN theorist and practitioner Kalev Sepp—a former Special Forces officer and deputy assistant secretary of defense for special operations capabilities—wrote a seminal article, "Best Practices in Counterinsurgency," in *Military Review*. In the article Sepp claimed that a country's political leaders (and not the military) must direct the struggle to win the allegiance of the people, that the "security of the people must be assured along with food, water, shelter, health care, and a means of living. These are human rights, along with freedom of worship, access to education, and equal rights for women. The failure of counterinsurgencies and the root cause of the insurgencies themselves can often be traced to government disregard of these basic rights."

In addition, he noted, "Intelligence operations that help detect terrorist insurgents for arrest and prosecution are the single most important practice to protect a population from threats to its security. Honest, trained, robust police forces responsible for security can gather intelligence at the community level. Historically, robustness in wartime requires a ratio of 20 police and auxiliaries for each 1,000 civilians. In turn, an incorrupt, functioning judiciary must support the police."

On each of Sepp's criteria Afghanistan has been a study in abject failure. The civilian Afghan government is insignificant; it is the American military that is leading the war effort. The Afghan government does not provide any services or protect rights. Moreover, the U.S. military regularly kills civilians with impunity, arresting many more and holding them without trial. The Taliban have not been penetrated. There is no honest or well-trained police force, and the American-led coalition will never come near to the ratio that Sepp calls for.

In the article Sepp also called for population control measures, but there are too few troops to control the majority of the Afghan population, who live in remote rural areas. He called on counterinsurgents to "convince insurgents they can best meet their personal interests and avoid the risk of imprisonment or death by reintegrating themselves into the population through amnesty, rehabilitation, or by simply not fighting." This has been a total failure in Afghanistan. And why would the Taliban, who have all the momentum and are winning, contemplate an amnesty or rehabilitation program?

Ironically, what Sepp describes as the American experience in Vietnam and the Soviet one in Afghanistan, in which military staff rather than civil governments guided operations, resembles Afghanistan under American occupation today. "Indigenous regular armies, although fighting in their own country and more numerous than foreign forces, were subordinate to them. Conventional forces trained indigenous units in their image—with historically poor results. Special operations forces committed most of their units to raids and reconnaissance missions, with successful but narrow results. The Americans further marginalized their Special Forces by economy-of-force assignments to sparsely populated hinterlands. Later, Spetznaziki [Russian Special Forces] roamed the Afghan mountains at will but with little effect. . . . The Soviet command in Afghanistan was unified but wholly militarized, and the Afghan government they established was perfunctory."

COIN was a massive endeavor, I was told by retired Col. Pat Lang, who had conducted COIN operations in Vietnam, Latin America, and elsewhere. There were insufficient resources committed to doing it in Afghanistan, but if the Americans didn't plan on owning Afghanistan, he argued, why waste time on it? It was worth the expenditure of resources only if you were the local government seeking to establish authority, or an imperialist power that wanted to hang around for a while. There were thirty million people in Afghanistan, and they were widely dispersed in small towns. "You have to provide security for the whole country," he said, "because if you move around they just move in behind you and undo what you did. So you need to have effective security and a massive multifaceted development organization that covers the whole place. COIN advisers have to stay in place all the time; they can't commute to work. If you're going to do COIN, it really amounts to nation building, and troops are there to provide protection for the nation builders. Afghanistan doesn't matter. The Taliban is not part of the worldwide jihadi community at war with U.S. We need to disaggregate Taliban from Al Qaeda. The idea that Al Qaeda is an existential threat to the U.S., it's so absurd that you don't know how to deal with it."

Ariel David Adesnik, a defense analyst who works as a consultant for the U.S. government, has been critical of attempts to turn COIN into a science. "One of the hardest parts of COIN operations is measuring progress," he says. "There is a strong temptation to measure progress with statistics, since numerical data imply a measure of objectivity. The counterinsurgency manual says you need twenty pairs of boots on the ground for every thousand inhabitants in the area of operations. This ratio has become an article of faith across the political spectrum. Yet the twenty-per-thousand rule is little more than a plausible guess based on a handful of historical examples, such as the British operations in Malaya and Northern Ireland. No one is exactly sure how to count either soldiers or inhabitants. Does a logistics officer at headquarters count the same as an infantryman on patrol? Does a rookie Afghan cop count the same as a battle-hardened Marine? What about contractors?

"The population isn't much easier to count. The population of an Iraqi or Afghan district is often a matter of guesswork. Should peaceful districts be included in the area of operations, or only those with a certain amount of violence? If you change the rules for counting, the ratio of troops to inhabitants can go up or down by a factor of two, three, or more. Using historical data, my research team tried to figure out the actual ratios employed in around forty COIN operations over the past sixty-five years. We found a rough correlation between higher ratios and better outcomes, especially at ratios of thirty to fifty troops per thousand inhabitants. Other researchers found no correlation at all."

In theory, success to McChrystal would result in a handover to the Afghan security forces. But there weren't enough of them, they were hopelessly incompetent or corrupt, and the few good ones were too often killed. The Provincial Reserve police were not paid until they completed their training and took a urine test for drugs. Then they got their back pay. But out of the eighty men scheduled to take the test in July 2009, only fifty-three showed up, some refused to take it, and twenty tested positive. Meanwhile, of twenty-five new police recruits in Helmand, twenty tested positive for marijuana, opium, or both. An Air Force major conducting drug tests on police throughout the country told me that in some districts 60 percent of the police force tested positive. The south was the worst. Some police had tried to give him water instead of urine. Sergeant Kilaki thought the Provincial Reserve needed more training in tactics, techniques, and procedures as well as scenarios. "It sounded like they just dragged the eight-week curriculum to fourteen weeks," Captain Westby said.

The Taliban Is Everywhere

In July 2009 a police checkpoint on Highway 601 had observed the Taliban destroying the road and constructing a four-foot barrier on it. Team Prowler and the Provincial Reserve went back on the road and clashed with twelve to fifteen Taliban, killing at least one. The team had no engineer assets, so they couldn't take down the barrier. The Taliban cleverly diverted traffic through the village to shake people down and control who passed. Colonel Shirzad sent the Provincial Reserve, with Lieutenant Farid in command, without their American mentors to Highway 601.

Lieutenant Farid's Ford Ranger drove over an IED or was hit by an RPG and was blown to pieces. Farid was killed along with two other cops. Five PR men were killed and five wounded in action in seven days. "601 is the most insecure road in Afghanistan," said Sergeant First Class Clark. "There's nothing but Taliban out there. That road is the lifeline to Lashkar Gah. We're being asked to deal with it with fifty-five men, and we lost five last night and five in the last fight." Team Prowler was supposed to have eighty police with them, but the British had taken some for themselves. There weren't enough police to go around.

I had met Lieutenant Farid when I first arrived in Lashkar Gah. I had hoped to interview him at length. He was jovial and chubby and had a short beard, and he looked older than his twenty-eight years. Farid was Colonel Shirzad's cousin from Helmand. Before he set off on his mission, his kids came to see him at the base. He was good-humored and an advocate for his men, apparently. At first he had a hard time delegating responsibility. NCOs were weak in the Afghan security forces, so he was a dominant figure and his loss was even bigger. The Americans took Farid's loss heavily. "He was going to be a good commander," said Westby. "It's frustrating." Staff Sergeant Enriquez had worked with Farid for seven months. "He's one of the only noncorrupt officers there were," he said. "I was pissed. He worked his ass off for his men. It felt like losing one of our own."

"We're asking a lot from these men," Westby said worriedly about the police. Westby was also frustrated by the British army, who controlled security in the Helmand province and who he had to report to, as well as his American masters in Kandahar. "The British attitude is 'Go now, get your men out there and go.' These are cops, not soldiers, but we're treating them like soldiers." Clark sympathized with them too. "We come out here for a year and we're done. These ANP come out here until they get killed."

Despite the loss, the police were told to go on a mission the next night by the British to relieve four checkpoints of highway police. The highway police were supposed to have been disbanded because they were committing highway robbery, but they still existed. The police would set up three checkpoints while the highway patrolmen were sent to training. "These ANP are mentored by the British," I was told, "even the British say they're shit." One American added, "But all the cops mentored by the British are shit."

The British warned Team Prowler that Highway 601 was blown in three places and that there were IEDs all over, on and off the road. I wondered why eight thousand British soldiers in Helmand had such difficulty controlling one fifty-kilometer stretch of road. "601 is impassable," a British officer had admitted to Clark. Many officers I spoke to complained about how imperious the British were to them and the Afghans.

The British were commanded by Lieutenant Colonel Jasper de Quincy Adams, who worked closely with Colonel Shirzad. The mission was to clear Popalzai, a Taliban-dominated village along the highway. Prowler and the police would take one side, while the British and the Afghan army would take the other side and deny the Taliban an escape route. "There's nobody good left in Balochan and Popalzai," Dyer told me. "They sent all the women and children away. There's nobody good left. They're really bad." The police also said there was nobody good left in those towns. The Americans told me how odd it was that they never received a brief on the rules of engagement, which varied depending on what province they were in. It was as if there were no rules for Helmand. One American called it "an open-fire zone."

Clark was unhappy that Team Prowler was going in their more vulnerable Humvees and not in the Cougars, larger vehicles suspended higher above the ground. But the Humvees were necessary if they went off-road in villages. "We're not a fuckin' route clearance package," said Dyer. "Who are we gonna send out to blow 'em?" "We can say we're not going," Westby said with frustration. But even if he didn't go, his police would, and it was Prowler's job as the mentor team to go with them. "I'm pissed at [Lieutenant Colonel] Jasper too," he said. "I see people getting hurt or killed if we do route clearance with the police," Dyer said. "The police should be given assets. If you're not going to give us the assets, don't fucking ask us to do it."

A stout, bearded sergeant called Ahmadullah was placed in command until a replacement for Farid could be found. Ahmadullah, a former schoolteacher, had joined the police after he was threatened by the Taliban, the Americans told me. He and his senior men gathered around Westby and Dyer along with many of the police, who were on the verge of a mutiny after hearing that they had to go back to Highway 601. The mood was tense; the policemen had only hours earlier been collecting Farid's body parts off the road. "Today they lost their commander who they really respected," Westby texted to Jasper on the Blue Force Tracker (BFT), a computer in his vehicle that allowed him to communicate with other forces in the area.

The Afghans insisted they lacked ammunition, and the men of Prowler were confounded by the number of machine-gun and RPG rounds that were unaccounted for. The Afghans told them that twenty-seven RPG heads had been destroyed in Lieutenant Farid's vehicle as well thousands of rounds of machine-gun ammo. The Americans were skeptical that Farid had been carrying such a huge number of rounds; he was coming back to get more supplies, so his truck should have been empty. "They're claiming a suspicious amount of ammo is missing," Enriquez said. The police didn't want to go because it was a British operation, and they felt like the Americans didn't care about Farid's death. "To restore their confidence, they have to go wipe out some Taliban location," Sergeant Kilaki said.

The Americans weren't happy about going on the mission either. "This is a bullshit British mission," said Dyer. "It's obvious the Brits don't give a fuck about the men," Enriquez said. Westby persuaded the British to postpone the operation until the following day. "Sir, it's almost a mutiny right now," Westby told Jasper, who agreed to postpone. "He doesn't want a mutiny," said Westby. "They've lost nine guys in seven days, and they need to do weapons maintenance."

Because British clinics were full with their wounded, and the British media were focusing on the numerous British casualties, including a dead lieutenant colonel, the British decided to cancel their clearing operation in Popalzai. The Afghan army didn't feel like going on the mission anyway.

Instead, Westby focused on replacing the highway patrol checkpoints. He spread a blanket on the floor and split open a watermelon, sitting with four senior policemen to discuss the next day's mission. They thanked him for postponing until the morning and they discussed where they might set up their new checkpoint. The Afghans couldn't read the map even to tell that the blue undulating line was a river. One of the checkpoints on 601 had recently been attacked, with eleven Afghan policemen killed. Sergeant Abdulahad—an Afghan police officer from the Provincial Reserve—expected heavy Taliban attacks when we arrived. He worried that they wouldn't have enough supplies. Westby, meanwhile, tried to figure out how to get them money so they could buy food and fuel. Westby explained to the policemen that they had to depart at 7 a.m. so the highway policemen could be relieved in time to make it to their flight for training.

"When we get to the area where the diversion through the villages is, that's where we will definitely have contact with the Taliban," Abdulahad said. "It's all dirt roads there, and the Taliban put many IEDs on the roads, and it will be hard to see them." He was unenthusiastic about the mission and came up with numerous reasons not to do it. He suggested a different route through the desert along the river, which would take an entire day.

Westby was baffled but maintained his aplomb. "I think we are strong and we can attack them back," he said. "We have enough firepower with our trucks, and I can radio for helicopters."

Abdulahad explained that they were not scared of the Taliban but of IEDs. His men did not have armored vehicles like the Americans, and he worried that the sandy and rocky roads would be perfect cover for IEDs. Westby finally persuaded them to go, but then they raised more objections. There were many Taliban checkpoints, Abdulahad objected, and his men didn't have enough ammunition. There were only thirty-three Provincial Reserve men on the base that night, Westby said, so when the remaining twenty returned the following day they could solve the supply problems and join the rest of the team. The Afghans reluctantly agreed, having run out of objections. Westby painstakingly made sure each one of them knew his task and would do it.

BUT THE POLICE were not ready at 7 a.m. "New leadership and lack of motivation are making the PR slow this morning," Westby texted to his headquarters on the BFT. "I'm sure some of these dudes are scared shitless," one soldier from Team Prowler said as the PR slowly lined up. "Before Farid got killed, the men were usually on time," Enriquez told me. "I'm sick and fucking tired of waiting," Westby told his men, hiding his frustration from the Afghans. "Not getting paid, the high-op tempo, the casualties, are taking a huge toll on their morale," Westby texted to Jasper. Thirty-six Afghans from the PR finally got into seven Ford Rangers, and the fifteen men from Prowler along with their two interpreters joined the convoy in four Humvees.

We left, eventually, at 8:13 a.m. Highway 601 was a new road and the driving was smooth, with the PR hopping out every few minutes to look inside culverts for IEDs. At 8:40 Sergeant Gus radioed from the front of the convoy to announce that the Taliban had blown up a new part of the road. "There's pretty significant damage," he said of the culvert that had been blown up. "It's pretty fucked up here. It looks like we're gonna have to take a bypass." It took fifteen minutes to figure out how to bypass the road. Sergeant Dyer wanted to clear the compounds in the area to see if there was any sign of the Taliban and to look for command wires that could detonate an IED.

"I like Sergeant Dyer's enthusiasm, but we don't have time to clear every compound that's two hundred meters from the road," Westby said.

"Look for freshly dug ant trails" on the dirt road, Westby ordered. They would be signs of command wires leading to an IED. "That culvert was 1,100 meters from an ANP checkpoint, and they couldn't keep it protected," Westby said in wonder of the blown road, and there was another ANP checkpoint 1,500 meters after it. The diversion exposed traffic to the nearby compounds, he wrote in his BFT. "Textbook setup for pressure plate IED and command wire IED from those compounds."

Kilaki asked Westby if they should stop at a nearby ANP checkpoint. "I've got a feeling he'll say what he always says," said Westby. "There's Taliban all around us! They're all over!" We stopped at a schoolhouse that had been converted to a checkpoint. It was surrounded by concertina wire and sandbagged positions. The night before, it had been attacked by the Taliban. We reached another blown-up part of the road, and the vehicles rolled down into the desert, driving through a moonscape, passing sheep and their herdsmen and the mud compounds they shared.

We stopped at a checkpoint with mud walls. Outside were the charred carcasses of destroyed vehicles, including a police Ranger. It too had been attacked the previous night and early that morning by Taliban who shot machine-gun fire and RPGs from motorcycles and Toyota Corollas. "North of us the Taliban have a checkpoint," one of the highway patrolmen told me. Originally from the north, he had been in the police for a year and a half and had lost nearly a hundred comrades. "We have a graveyard for the police not far away," he said. Many police were not wearing uniforms or boots. They warned that if any of the checkpoints were abandoned, then the next day the road would be full of IEDs. The men left two Rangers and their occupants behind with only half a can of water and no food. "These motherfucking idiots, like Goddamn children," Westby complained, exasperated that their commanders gave them no supplies. Ahmadullah and many of his men were not wearing their body armor.

We passed another blown-up culvert only a few hundred meters away from the police checkpoint. Westby wondered how the police hadn't seen it happen. "They were sleeping," said Kilaki. Westby conceded that they didn't have night vision. The bypass took us over a canal. We leaned to the right and nearly tipped over. Locals struggling with their vehicles warned that the alternative bypass went through a Taliban-controlled area where they had their own checkpoint. "The village you go through just 800 meters away is Taliban territory," Westby wrote on the BFT. We passed another destroyed piece of road and then another IED crater. Westby decided to keep all the checkpoints open. Colonels Shirzad and Jasper had ordered one police commander to stay at a different checkpoint with the British army. He didn't trust the British, so he refused. He finally agreed but then went to town instead. "It wears on you, these guys," Westby sighed.

"The PR have no radios to communicate from checkpoint to checkpoint," Westby texted to Jasper. "Vehicle radios don't have enough range, food water fuel ammo resupply still an issue. PR not equipped to be self-sustaining here, no cooking equipment, only one CP has a well." Westby was still hoping the remaining PR would come that day, but he doubted it. "They'll come up with some excuse," he said. Westby gave the PR additional jugs of water so at least they wouldn't die in the heat. Most of the PR had not been paid for months, he told me. They didn't have radios, so they would have no way of notifying the Americans if they were attacked. He hoped their vehicle radios worked and tried to explain to the PR squad leader that communication was essential. Westby didn't expect his own position to be attacked because the Taliban probably saw that there were Americans there.

Lieut. Col. Jasper De Quincy Adams showed up. He was young, handsome, and full of energy. He complained about the highway police commander. "When locals interact with him, they think the Taliban are better," he said, worrying that the commander delegitimized the government. "We'll turn this around by aggressive patrolling," he told Westby. "Your mission is all about deterring and disrupting." He wanted Westby to lay ambushes and take the fight to the enemy. "I think that Popalzai needs to be patrolled very aggressively," he said. "Have large numbers of patrol and ambush." Jasper's men followed us and fixed the holes in the road, filling them with dirt. Jasper complained that about twenty of the twenty-five recruits had tested positive for opiates. "That's why the road is full of IEDs," Westby told me. "They're high all the time."

The men of Team Prowler broke the mud walls with sledgehammers so that they could fit their Humvees inside. Then they parked on all sides so that they could have 360 degrees of coverage. They broke the tops of walls so they could fire better. Garbage littered the compound, including sheeps' hooves and bones, the remnants of previous meals. The Americans tried to clean it all up and set it on fire. Westby told me he didn't think everybody in the villages around Highway 601 was Taliban; some were just normal civilians.

The commander of one of the checkpoints got on the radio to announce that his men had seen a Corolla full of Taliban with weapons. The commander met with local villagers by his checkpoint and explained that they were a different police unit replacing the old one to establish security. "It's good initiative," said Westby. That night the men drove up and down the road and found a suspected IED. It was too dark to do anything about it. They did a recon by fire, meaning they shot at the house where they suspected the trigger man might be hiding, but nothing happened. If anything detonated, they would have annihilated the suspected firing point.

The next morning the team drove to a compound they suspected had been used by the men who placed the IED. They dismounted with the PR, walking past green fields into the first mud compound. On one corner by the road was a spy hole and another hole at the bottom with two ant trails coming out of it. Inside was a cornfield, a marijuana field, and harvested poppy plants. Several of the police on patrol didn't wear their body armor and stood casually in fields of fire. Team Prowler kept pushing ahead. We passed by large poppy fields. The plants were dry and harvested. The police came across three small brothers who pointed to a narrow path between two mud walls and said five armed Taliban had just moved north of the compound. But Dyer didn't pursue the Taliban because he didn't want to be channeled through the narrow path.

The men found a mosque with mattresses and a room with corn kernels, bags of nitrogen, and a car battery. The nitrogen could have easily been used for fertilizer or explosives. While the Americans were poking around inside the mosque, the police sat in the shade beneath nearby trees. Some of them filmed the patrol with their camera phones. "I need those men from Lashkar Gah to get in some Rangers and drive their sorry asses out here," Westby complained, and asked Mansur, the translator, to radio them. Back at the mud checkpoint Westby briefed his men. Their mission was to "deter and disrupt enemy forces burying IEDs," and the "center of gravity is Popalzai."

That night Dyer led an ambush by the mosque, where the team suspected the Taliban were sleeping. They hoped that when the Taliban tried to leave, the ambush team blocking the narrow path between the mud walls would kill them. They drove without lights in blackout. Dyer told the men to make sure the ANP had no cigarettes, didn't play music, and didn't talk. "Enforce light and noise discipline," he said. "Throw some fucking grenades. We're not there to arrest people, just fucking kill people."

"The Hazara fighters are better than these lazy bones sleeping all day," said Westby, referring to the Pashtun police. "And they're better shots," Dyer added. Westby estimated there would be five to ten Taliban in the mosque. Somehow I doubted the Taliban would be there. They weren't stupid: they did not sleep in the same place every night, and they would know that the Americans had found their hideout.

At 3 a.m. they started getting ready. "I hope we catch these sons of bitches with their pants down," Kilaki said. "I'll be so pissed if there's nobody fucking there," said Campos. There were supposed to be only six police dismounts on the ambush, but twice as many got out of their vehicles to join the five Americans who went on the ambush. Westby got out of his Humvee to resolve the problem. "It just goes to show that no matter how many times you prep 'em . . ." said Kilaki. "They all thought they were going on patrol," Westby said with a laugh. "I just explained it to their commander, and they nodded north and south." An unmanned Predator drone was flying overhead, but Team Prowler had no way of talking to those controlling it.

As it happened, the mosque was empty. Several Afghans walking by on the way to their fields or morning prayers were taken down the alleyway. "They can fuckin' sit and shut up," Dyer said. "I wish I was the dismount watching the people come out all spooked," Campos said. "On the Fourth we had the women crying," said Kilaki. "Yeah, I know," said Campos. "I saw the women coming out, tears all down their faces. Shut the fuck up! We're doing you a favor."

When the rest of Team Prowler joined the ambush team, I found the Afghan men sitting and waiting to be let go. They were middle-aged and elderly. They asked to pray several times, and finally Dyer let them conduct their ablutions and pray on the grass. One of the old men told me that they were all very bothered by the Taliban. "They come here to shoot," he said. "They don't let us irrigate our fields. When the Taliban shoot from this area, the Americans and police come and we have to run away. Our neighbors were bothered by the Taliban, and they fled. We have to take our women and children away when the police respond to Taliban ambushes." Another old man chimed in. "Three months ago the Taliban set up an ambush on the road," he said. "The police entered our houses, they stole our sheep and everything from our houses. We complained to Lashkar Gah police headquarters, and they gave us back two motorcycles and one sheep but not the rest of our things. We had a shop, and they took all the merchandise from it."

"I'm very sorry to hear that. You can rest assured that this is a different police," said Westby. "Tell him we apologize for the disturbance, but we're adamant about keeping these people out."

"I am an old man," one of them said. "If we talk to them, the Taliban will slap us. The Taliban sometimes come here and demand money. If we refuse, they're going to kill us."

The old men asked if they could go take their vegetables to the market. The Americans agreed. Westby told them that if they gave information on the Taliban that led to arrests, they would receive money. "If the Taliban see us talking to you, they will slaughter us tonight," one of the men said. "The Taliban don't tell us when they are coming. We're sitting in our homes, and all of a sudden they come and we hear shots. The Taliban don't sleep here. They come here like thieves."

"Let them understand that we're not the bad guys," Westby told his translator. "We're trying to stop them from doing what they are doing. The best way to accomplish that is by a partnership. We can't keep coming here every day."

"We can't notify the police, but we'll send some small child to tell the police," one of the old men said.

The sun rose, golden over the shrubs, as we made our way back to the checkpoint. The police had mentioned seeing a Taliban car. "What was that about a Taliban car?" asked Kilaki. "The ANP think everything is Taliban,"

Westby replied. "I don't think they fuckin' know. They're so eager to impress that sometimes they call everything Taliban."

The police at the next checkpoint radioed to say there were Taliban around. "They're over there, and they're over there, and they're over there, but we can't go on that road because it's all IEDs, but the road is full of civilian traffic," Westby said, mocking the useless information he got from the cops.

A highway patrol commander called Torabas came by with his men. He and his men had just seen two Corollas full of Taliban in the distance. I asked him how he knew. He had been living here for two years, he said, and he recognized their faces. All the hills north of our position were said to be controlled by the Taliban, but the police were too scared to go there. I asked Torabas why the Taliban were so popular in Helmand. "The Taliban are supported by the British," he said, insisting that he had seen the British military drop fuel supplies to the Taliban. "Nobody likes the Taliban here," he said. "It's only out of fear. When the Taliban see people talking to the police, they kill them. They are here only by force, and many people dislike the police. Some police steal from houses. Before we recruited uneducated people who had no training." About fifty of his men had been killed by the Taliban since he took command.

He was from the Nurzai tribe, like Colonel Shirzad and most police in Helmand, he told me. His father and grandfather had fought the Soviets with Gulbuddin Hekmatyar's Hizb-e-Islami, the most radical faction of the mujahideen. When the Taliban seized Helmand and pushed out Hizb-e-Islami, Torabas's family fled to Pakistan. He said Taliban had seized their lands.

"I'm living in Lashkar Gah, but my fields are still in the hands of the Taliban," he said. "When the Taliban were defeated, they didn't have any power. Then we were living in our compound, but now the Taliban are back." It seemed his motive was to regain his land. "When the Russians attacked Afghanistan they were trying to destroy our country. The Taliban didn't like the mujahideen. When the Americans start oppressing or disrespecting our culture—touching our women, disrespecting our elders—then we will fight jihad against them."

That night Kilaki caught one of the police commanders smoking hashish in a car. "It looked like a Cheech and Chong movie," he said. Westby gave the PR money to buy cooking supplies. "Their logistics process doesn't work, and I can't have them going hungry," he said. Only one of the PR's senior men showed any initiative and wanted to set up his own ambushes. Colonel Shirzad didn't want to fight, Dyer told me, and without a charismatic leader like Farid the PR were content to just patrol Highway 601.

ONE AFTERNOON while I was marooned with Team Prowler and the PR in the small mud police outpost along Highway 601, languishing in the oppressive heat, surrounded by a moonscape of bleached rocks, hoping for some action to relieve my boredom, Sergeant Ahmadullah radioed to the young Afghan translator working with the Americans, called Mansur, and told him, "We found a Taliban, we have him here. What should we do, kill him or what?" Mansur told Ahmadullah he could not kill the prisoner, and instructed him to bring the man to the Americans.

The prisoner was a young man with a purple *salwar kameez*. He had long hair down to his neck and a cap atop his head. He looked bewildered. His eyes were wide with apprehension as he squatted on the dirt with his hands cuffed in front of him. He wore two different sandals. He had been a passenger in a taxi; the police had also brought the driver and the other passengers.

Ahmadullah said his prisoner's cellphone had a Taliban song on it. This was his evidence. Ahmadullah was by the roadside, while I was standing with his men, at the police outpost, out of his earshot. His men were privately angry about their commander's decision to arrest the man and wanted him released. Zahir, another translator working with the Americans, was outraged. "This is why people hate the fucking police and support the Taliban," he said. I asked Captain Westby, Team Prowler's commander, why the man was being held. "He had an anti-American ring tone," Westby said, "and he has some relatives that Ahmadullah says are in the Taliban."

Zahir explained to the Americans that the prisoner wanted to pray. The police were eager to uncuff him so he could, and the skeptical Americans relented. Zahir insisted the prisoner wouldn't attempt an escape.

Sergeant Gustafson took one of the passengers by the wall to enter his biometric data into a handheld device. He took the man's picture and another of his eyes, along with his fingerprints, name, father's name, and tribe's name. The man seemed amused. But he was now in the American system. Westby and a sergeant interrogated the prisoner, who was called Zeibullah Agha. He was a student in a famous religious school in the Pakistani city of Peshawar and was on his way back to Babaji, where the British were engaged in heavy combat with the Taliban, in order to help his family flee to safety because his father was an old man. The Americans asked him for the names of his brothers, father, and uncle, but they had trouble with the names and confused the Pakistani town he was studying in for another one, Quetta, more famous for being a Taliban safe haven. I told the Americans that the school in Pakistan he named practiced a moderate form of Islam anathema to the Taliban.

"People with a similar surname are known Taliban," Westby said.

"I am a poor man. I don't know why they arrested me," Zeibullah said.

The American sergeant asked him why he had this music on his cellphone. "One of my friends put it on my cellphone," Zeibullah said.

The sergeant smiled. "Bullshit," he said, looking at Zahir. "How do you say bullshit in Pashtu?"

Zahir looked at the prisoner and said, *"Kus eh shir,"* meaning "a pussy's poem."

Zahir and the police told me that Zeibullah's cellphone had some videos of battles and one of a graduation from a religious school to be a mullah. "Everybody has them on their phones—even I have them," Zahir said. Sergeant Ahmadullah told the Americans that he knew Zeibullah's father, who was a good man. "But I don't know him," he said, "and his uncle is Taliban."

Mansur the other translator scoffed: how could he know the man's father but not know him? "He's fucked up," Mansur said of Ahmadullah. "Maybe it's a personal vendetta. We also use Taliban songs," Mansur added. Other policemen complained Ahmadullah had killed many people in "personal hostility." One policeman told me that Ahmadullah told him he had killed seven or eight men in personal feuds in Babaji. Another policeman originally from Babaji also insisted the prisoner was innocent. But Zeibullah was taken away to be sent to the prison in Lashkar Gah. He might be released for money, the American sergeant told me. Or he might be in prison for years.

Westby and his men had been sent to patrol Highway 601 because the Taliban had blown up culverts along it, blocking traffic and forcing trucks to go through Taliban-controlled towns. It took Team Prowler about half a day to secure the road, while the British filled up broken culverts with earth so that vehicles could pass. Westby, a soft-spoken and taciturn soldier, was confronted with a Sisyphean task, but he never showed frustration in front of Afghans he worked with. On another afternoon, a few days later, while Westby and his men were recovering from an overnight mission, a soldier woke him up to tell him that two village elders were complaining that the British had blocked their water supply when they filled the craters with dirt. Westby was sleeping, groggy. "Well, I'm not here to solve all the world's fucking problems," he muttered.

He got up anyway and went to talk to the two old men. They wore white turbans and had long white beards and wrinkled leathery skin. They squatted, their tunics covering their bodies, and spoke in raspy voices. The British had blocked the water supply to thirty farming families when they filled in the craters on Highway 601, they said. The British ignored their complaints. They asked Westby to put a pipe through so they could water their crops. Westby promised to talk to local Afghan and American officials. They asked how long it would take. Westby guessed maybe a week. The two men seemed relieved. "We all have to work together to stop the Taliban," Westby told them. The two apologized for bothering him. To them he was probably just another in a long string of foreign officers and local warlords who had come and gone.

The next day we drove by the first compound they had searched. The sandbag they had stuffed into the spy hole was gone. Dyer wanted to destroy that part of the wall, but Jasper said the new orders issued by General McChrystal stated a compound could be destroyed only if the soldiers were in imminent danger. The men were baffled. With their tour in Afghanistan coming to an end, Westby was reluctant to let his men enter compounds. It was militarily useless, he said, and he didn't want any of his men killed a couple of weeks before they went home. When we got to town, one of the sergeants driving was ebullient. He started playing chicken with oncoming vehicles and laughing. As we left the ANCOP base to drive to the main base in Lashkar Gah, a kid picked up a rock to throw at the Humvee and a cop kicked him hard in the chest. The men of Iron-horse and Prowler returned to their lives in Illinois. Five men from Ironhorse went back to Afghanistan to work as private security contractors in Kandahar.

"That's why all the children are dying for you, Afghanistan."

Supporters of McChrystal said "he gets it," as if there was a magic COIN formula they discovered in 2009. But Afghans have a memory. They remember, for example, that the American-backed mujahideen killed thousands of Afghan teachers and bombed schools in the name of their anti-Soviet jihad. The Taliban atrocities had not arisen in a vacuum. Similarly, past American actions have consequences. Opinions were already formed. The Taliban were gaining power thanks to American actions and alliances. Warlords were empowered by the Americans. No justice was sought for victims. The government and police were corrupt. The president stole the elections. The message was that there was no justice, and a pervasive sense of lawlessness and impunity had set in. Afghans who had been humiliated or victimized by the Americans and their allies were unlikely to become smitten by them merely because of some aid they received. And the aid was relatively small compared with other international projects, like Bosnia, Haiti, Rwanda, and East Timor. The Americans thought that by building roads they could win over opinion. But roads are just as useful for insurgents as they are for occupiers. The Americans had failed to convince Afghans that they should like them or want them to stay, and they certainly had not been convinced that Karzai's government has legitimacy. You can't win hearts and minds with aid work when you are an occupying force.

The Taliban was the most obscurantist, backward, traditional, and despised government on earth. The fact that the Taliban was making a comeback was a testimony to the regime that the U.S. set up there, and to the atrocities that have been committed in Afghanistan by occupation troops and their Afghan allies. It was sheer arrogance to think that adding another thirty thousand or fifty thousand troops would change the situation so much that the occupation would become an attractive alternative.

There was little evidence that aid money in COIN had an impact. There was not a strong correlation between poverty and insecurity or between aid money and security. The more insecure you were, the more development money you got. The safer provinces felt as if they were being penalized for not having Taliban or poppy cultivation. The aid system raised expectations but didn't satisfy them. Life remained nasty, brutish, and short for most Afghans.

Aid and force do not go well together. The Americans assumed that material goods superseded all other values. This was not true in Iraq or Afghanistan. Positive as the aid was, it did not outweigh the civilian casualties or the offensive and humiliating behavior of the past eight years. In Iraq it took the trauma of the civil war to make the Americans look good. There might have been a new administration in Washington, but for Afghans it was the same America: the America of civilian casualties, night raids, foreign occupation, Guantánamo, Abu Ghraib—the America seemingly at war with Islam.

The Pentagon propaganda machine, for instance, turned Marja from a backwater to a key strategic city, and the American media accepted it. But in fact there were only a few thousand people living in Marja. It took months and thousands of troops for the Americans to seize Marja, only to learn that the Taliban were popular there. And there were up to twenty thousand similar Marjas throughout the country. In Marja the ANCOP too proved a failure, incompetent and dependent on the Americans. Fighting remained frequent. The Americans were not effective in evaluating Afghan police units. Although hailed as elite, the ANCOP annual attrition due to all causes ranged from seventy to one hundred and forty percent. Even by local standards they weren't elite.

The storming of Marja was meant to be the first sally in a larger campaign to expel the Taliban from their southern heartland, especially Kandahar. The Americans thought if they could wrest it from Taliban hands, then it would turn the tide against the Taliban. But Kandahar meant little to anybody who wasn't a Kandahari. It was part of the same focus on population centers that were overwhelmingly urban.

Violence was getting worse. How long would the Afghan people accept the presence of armed foreigners in their country? Even a message of help can be humiliating, more so when it is backed by a gun. The Americans underestimated the importance of dignity and the extent to which their very presence in Afghanistan was deeply offensive.

In May 2006 riots erupted in Kabul after a road accident with American forces, and the Americans shot at the crowd. The episode revealed an underlying anger that could explode at any moment. In September 2009 a British plane dropped a box of leaflets that failed to open, landing on a girl and killing her. Given that most Afghans are illiterate, it would not have been any more persuasive had it opened. Despite the lip service given to "protecting the population," in 2010 the American-led coalition killed far more civilians than previous years.

In February a night raid by American special forces killed two pregnant women; the Americans attempted to cover it up. "Son of an American" has become an insult among Pashtuns the way "Son of a Russian" once was.

Folk poetry throughout Pashtun areas of Afghanistan is now often anti-occupation. Below is one recent *ghazal* (poem), by a woman called Zerlakhta Hafeez:

> *Oh Afghanistan, you are my love*
> *You are my soul, you are my body*
> *They want peace while having guns in their hands*
> *That's why all the children are dying for you, Afghanistan*
> *Your children are dying for you because they want you*
> *To be sovereign, to be independent like they did before*
> *Pashtuns from both parts of the black line* [the border with Pakistan]
> *Call you their home, oh Afghanistan, so they fight for it.*

Americans lacked the political will for a long-term commitment, regardless of whether it was right or wrong. The Americans would bail on Afghanistan sooner or later. It would be tragic if it happened within Obama's eighteen-month deadline or after five years. There was no way to "fix" Afghanistan. According to Andrew Wilder, a longtime aid worker in the country, "It may be more realistic to look for ways to slow down the descent into anarchy." The Soviets never lost the war in Afghanistan. In fact, the puppet regime they installed had pretty much crushed the mujahideen until the Soviets withdrew support. The Soviets won their last battle in Afghanistan in Khost's Operation Magistral. But it made no difference. Only the rusting ruins of tanks and a few Russian-speaking Afghans remained in Afghanistan. The Americans too weren't losing, stressed a retired American military officer working on security in Afghanistan. "Every time our boys face them, they win," he said. "We're winning every day. Are we going to keep winning for twenty years?"

Postscript

I returned to Afghanistan in January 2010. In what was a routine incident, the Americans had just killed four Afghans in Ghazni's Qarabagh district: one of the men worked for the Basim phone company, one was a cobbler, and two were students. Locals took the bodies and protested on the highway between Kabul and Kandahar.

On the way to Maidan Shahr, the capital of Wardak province, I stopped to talk to bus drivers about the conditions on the road. "There are a lot of roadblocks because of the Americans," a bus driver called Mir Ali told me. "They oppress people a lot." A passenger chimed in. "Tell him the problem of the people," he said. "There are certainly attacks. The Americans attack and raid homes every night. They indiscriminately and continuously arrest people and take people out of their homes." Mir Ali told the man that we were only talking about security on the road. "Who cares about the road?" the man asked. "They are indiscriminately raiding and searching homes in places where there is no Taliban or enemy. People have personal conflicts, and the Americans come and arrest them and drag them and imprison them."

Gul Rahman was also a driver on the same route. "The road security is fine, but people are oppressed by the Americans," he told me. "They are raiding during the nights. Some people have hostility from the time of the factions [the 1990s], from the revolution in the past, some people have enmity with each other. Now some people report to the government or tribal militias, so the Americans continuously raid, arrest, and imprison people. They have done this in Andar and Badam. They have killed more innocent people than you can imagine." He told me to go see for myself. "You will see people tortured, arrested, and imprisoned for no reason," he said. Even at the bus station, he complained, the police beat people without reason.

Zainullah was a driver on the road between Kabul and Helmand. For the past two days the road past Qarabagh in Ghazni had been closed, he said. "The Americans have killed people there, women and children. That is why people are protesting, and they have blocked the highway. The Taliban do not harm us, but there is a danger of thieves, and people are bothered by Americans. When American forces come, then the road is blocked for hours, and then we have to wait for hours, sometimes the whole day. Sick passengers and women also have to wait. The road is 70 percent damaged and 30 percent built. There are no bridges, and most of the road is not paved."

The local travel agent at the bus stop agreed. "The situation was good before, but now it is worse," he said. "People cannot travel in these buses anymore because there is no security. About thirty or forty buses would leave from here before, but now the number is about ten to fifteen. During the evening and nighttime, it is not possible to leave." I asked if people were pleased with the work of the government or the Americans. "Nobody likes them," he said. "How can we be happy when travels are delayed by the national army, American troops, or the police? How can they be happy?"

Zainullah told me of a bus that was robbed by thieves in Ghazni and then in Khushkabad. "This bus was robbed two times in one night," he said. "The whole station knows this story. Taliban do not harm people. The Taliban deal with the people that they need to deal with. Taliban harms no one. The danger always comes from Americans and thieves. The danger from the Americans on the highway is that they check each and every bridge for their security, and we have to wait. Even if you have sick passengers or children, the Americans don't care at all. The road will be blocked by Americans. If something happens to them, then Americans indiscriminately shoot and arrest anyone. They don't care about anyone. The problems are because of American troops. This is certainly the job of government. They should stop it, and we don't have that power. My demand from the government is that the government should punish these people. If the government is not able to do so, then Afghans should be allowed to make a national movement. It is not going to work like this."

As we were speaking, several policemen showed up and made us leave, asking us to come to the police station because they hadn't been informed that we were in the area.

In Meidan Shah I attended a training session in basic science for several dozen village teachers from throughout Wardak (all of whom were men). When I showed up they were being taught the science behind basic hygiene.

The Taliban had a reputation for attacking state teachers, so I asked the men if they had been threatened. "There is no threat to education in this province," one man told me. "Education is neutral here," said another. "It neither supports the resistance nor the government." The Taliban did not harm schools and clinics, he said. "Most of the security problems are created by Americans. The Taliban do not make problems." I asked him what problems the Americans made. "Our hours start here at 8:00 or 8:30 a.m. We are not allowed to come here before American troops come to the provincial center. When we go to school, we experience the same problems. There is no alternative way. If we use another route, there is fear of thieves. There are many problems. This year somebody fired on the Americans, so the Americans entered the school and fired—which terrorized children so much that one boy wet himself. They were so scared that they did not come to school for five or six days, and finally the children were convinced and brought by their parents to school. The Americans first shot at the school, then they surrounded the school, then they entered and started firing inside it."

Outside the school the men pointed to villages only one kilometer away. Everything outside the provincial capital was in Taliban hands, they said. In the same town I attended a meeting of the National Solidarity Program, an Afghan-run, foreign-funded development program that gave grants to communities to develop local projects. I spoke to Muhamad Nasir Farida, the local government official in charge of the program in Wardak. "Many problems are created by the Americans," he said. "The Americans raid homes at nights, land helicopters, and whoever they see they kill them or arrest them."

Fazel Rabie Haqbeen was a former mujahid who worked as a senior official for the Asia Foundation, an American development NGO, in Kabul. He had twenty years of experience as an aid worker. He too wanted to talk about the deaths in Qarabagh. "Two hundred villagers are protesting with the dead bodies in Qarabagh," he said. "Villagers are crying and blocking the road for two days. Where are the hearts and minds of these villagers? The two hundred villagers are a casualty. It's not just the physical dead. Let me walk you through Kabul and ask a little child what he thinks of Americans. They are not winning hearts and minds."

Fazel was originally from the village of Miakhel in southern Kabul's Musahi district. In 2006 American Special Forces raided his village. "They killed a sleeping farmer," he said. "They dragged women and held them, they beat four villagers and detained four villagers. From that day Musahi district is not secure. The villagers don't care if the Taliban intrude into villages. After the raid the local Italian commander was killed, two district council members were killed. I am also a council member, but I don't go back much. The district police chief was killed, a local road construction company had its machines burned, and since then every day there is something."

The gap between the people and government was enormous, Fazel said. "Between the people and the international presence it's much more huge, and between the people and the Americans even more, and with the Special Forces much, much more."

When people compared the two evils of the Americans and the Taliban, they chose the lesser evil. "At least people can communicate with the Taliban," he said. "The elders can have influence; they are from the same culture. People are not progovernment or pro-Taliban, but they prefer the Taliban. The government isn't in a position to deliver any services."

The Americans relied on their own analysts, who didn't have in-depth knowledge of the Afghan context, he told me. "Our culture varies from village to village, tribe to tribe, region to region. As an Afghan I am not in a position to have in-depth knowledge; my knowledge will be superficial. Afghans don't trust you, so they won't tell you what's in their hearts and minds. They will say you are doing a great job."

He mocked the notion that the Americans could use Pashtunwali to their advantage. "The Americans are against Pashtunwali," he said. "They are carrying out house raids. Are you Pashtun so that you can do Pashtunwali with Pashtun? Before the war, if you were a foreigner or American, you could go everywhere safely. Today that is not the case. The whole situation is stirred into chaos, and everyone is provoking mistrust. The McChrystal plan is more troops, more casualties, more victims, more civilian dead. The wrong policies, the wrong approaches. If you come at 2 a.m. and kill my father, how will you expect me not to go mad?"

In late June a *Rolling Stone* magazine profile of General McChrystal revealed the contempt he and his men felt for their civilian counterparts and leadership. President Obama seized the opportunity to dismiss McChrystal and replace him with General Petraeus. McChrystal had opposed Obama's eighteen-month deadline. He had wanted "to win." Obama merely wanted to "halt the Taliban's momentum." COIN was a long-term strategy and a stable extremist-free Afghanistan was an open-ended commitment, but the president seemed determined to leave as soon as he could. McChrystal and Obama had always been mismatched. Afghanistan policy seemed subordinate to domestic political considerations. The Democrats did not want to appear weak and reinforce the belief that Republicans were stronger on defense, especially as the November elections approached. Petraeus promised to reconsider the restrictions placed on the military meant to reduce civilian casualties. He announced a plan for "local police forces" or local militias. Just before Petraeus made his announcement Afghan President Karzai met with leaders from Kandahar and promised them that he would never agree to the American plan to create more militias.

Local militias had been created before and given different names. Previous attempts to use militias led to cooptation by the Taliban and other abuses. The new militias would not receive any training. The plan risked further destabilizing Afghanistan for the sake of expedience. Unlike the Awakening groups that began in the Iraqi Anbar and spread throughout that country, the militias in Afghanistan are not the result of a strategic shift in the insurgency and are not composed of former insurgents. Afghanistan dose not have anything resembling the Sunni-Shiite divide and inter-Sunni conflict with al Qaeda that led insurgents in Iraq to temporarily ally with the Americans. In Afghanistan the creation of more militias can lead to a return to the chaos of the post-Soviet withdrawal. Decentralization is a good idea on the political level but not when it comes to security and the state's monopoly on violence. Creating militias means choosing sides in local tribal and inter-ethnic conflicts. According to one Afghan Army brigade commander in Helmand: "A militia empowers a man, an Army and Police force protect a people and empower a nation." Senior Afghan security officials worried that so-called local defense forces were the first step towards the return of the regionalism and warlordism that tore the country a part in the wake of the Soviet withdrawal. After 1989 small, local militias continued to fight against the central government. After the government was overthrown larger militias fought between themselves for control of Kabul. In a country torn by fighting, the Americans thought that more fighting was the solution. Meanwhile as Petraeus settled in the governor of Marja in Helmand was fired only months after the Americans helped install him.

With Petraeus, Obama had appointed the one general with the clout to ask for more troops and more time, but also the one sufficiently respected by all parties to be able to declare Afghanistan a lost cause. The Americans had won in Afghanistan when it was merely a punishment campaign. Once they lingered following the flight of bin Laden they began to flounder. And when they turned it into a war against the Taliban, an indigenous movement, they lost.

EPILOGUE

The New Iraq?

IT WAS IN THE SPRING OF 2009 THAT I BEGAN TO REALIZE THAT THINGS were changing in Iraq. The civil war was over. There was no group that could overthrow the government. The Iraqi Security Forces had monopolized power, even if it wasn't pretty. I felt this most intensely one day when I was driving down Baghdad's Saadun Street with Captain Salim from Washash and a couple of friends. Salim was dressed in civilian clothes, with a pistol tucked under his shirt. A man in a black sedan tried to cut us off, but my friend behind the wheel aggressively sped up and prevented him from doing so. A war of angry faces and waving hands ensued until we were stopped in traffic just before Tahrir circle, at a checkpoint manned by armed men. The driver of the sedan emerged and blocked our path. He was tall, with thick shoulders, a big belly, and a mustache—the Iraqi security look. He had a shaved head and a pistol on his waist. He demanded that we get out of the car. Salim told him to leave us alone, that he was an officer. Where was he an officer? the bald man insisted.

"I'm with a very dangerous ministry," warned Salim, "you don't want to know."

As armed guards looked on, they stood shouting at each other—each demanding to see the other's ID cards and each refusing, not knowing who was, in fact, more powerful. As I sat in the car, I was getting more and more nervous. But after ten tense minutes they embraced and kissed. It turned out they knew each other. This was fortunate, because the bald man was an officer with the puissant Office of the Prime Minister, and he trumped Salim, who was a mere army officer. A friend later commented that the standoff reminded him of Iraq under Saddam, when a plethora of security agencies competed with one another.

Six years after the fall of Baghdad, it felt as if the Iraqis were occupying Iraq. Roads were no longer blocked by aggressive American troops but by aggressive Iraqi Security Forces in military, police, or civilian attire, waving their weapons, shouting. They were just as intimidating as their U.S. counterparts.

They manned ubiquitous checkpoints throughout the city, stopping cars, searching them. They had brought a measure of security to the war-torn capital, but the price was a heavily militarized society. Even if the overt sectarianism of the security forces had been tempered—they no longer slaughtered Sunnis—their Shiite identity was apparent and made Sunnis who were stopped at checkpoints nervous.

On a different day I was driving with a friend in a car that belonged to a third friend of ours. We were stopped at an Iraqi National Police checkpoint. The policeman asked for the car's registration. When my friend told him that it was not in his name, the policeman became hostile. He demanded my friend's ID. He read his name out loud, "Hassanein," an obviously Shiite name, and his demeanor changed. He smiled and waved us on our way. When I visited government buildings and police stations, the walls were often festooned with posters of Hussein, a clear sign that they were dominated by Shiites. On the concrete barriers outside the National Assembly, there was a large mural of Shiite pilgrims marching to Karbala. These displays created a sense among Sunnis that the state and its security forces were Shiite, that they did not belong.

Not that the Americans had withdrawn. One friend working with the American military in Baghdad's Yarmuk and Qadisiya districts told me he knew of twenty or twenty-five innocent Iraqis who had been killed by U.S. Special Forces. One old man approached his door when he heard American soldiers coming so that he could open it for them. He was shot in the head. Shots to the head or shots to the chest were common at the slightest provocation, my friend complained.

According to the Baghdad morgue, every day there were ten to fifteen political murders in Baghdad alone, but this was far lower than the hundreds it received every day in 2006, when Iraqi women had to search through disfigured corpses to find their husbands and sons. But if the levels of violence had gone down, many still had not recovered. "During the last years we faced death many times," a doctor from Sadr City told me. "We became numb. We don't have feelings anymore."

But now it was possible to talk about post-American Iraq. And there were many worrying signs. "It will be like the Republican Guard," one American official told me. "[Maliki] has an extralegal counterterrorism force that answers to him." Maliki had empowered the Office of the Prime Minister and placed under its command thousands of elite soldiers capable of operating without American military or logistical support. Trained by American special operators, they were dominated by Shiites but loyal to Maliki, not the institution. Like their American trainers, they justified their above-the-law status with the mantra of counterterrorism; when they operated, the Iraqi Defense and Interior ministries were never informed. Sunnis and Kurds complained to the Americans that Maliki had become the new Saddam of the Shiites.

The random and indiscriminate violence had subsided. This was most evident in the conspicuous displays of wealth. Baghdad's roads were full of H3 Hummers and other expensive and large vehicles that cost tens of thousands of dollars in cash. New expensive restaurants catered to a new elite, or one that was in hiding. The girls in Baghdad's universities were dressing more fashionably than ever before, and young men were adopting the fashion trends of Lebanon. For years this would have been impossible to see. Anybody with any money would have been a target for kidnappers. Women immodestly dressed could have been killed. Men in clear Western fashions could have been beaten. Bars were back open, which was at least a sign that vigilante extremists had stopped blowing them up. Playgrounds were full of children, young men played soccer in new fields, people were no longer afraid to leave their houses. But none of it felt completely real.

One night I strolled along Abu Nawas Street with my friend Hussein. Couples walked by the river, children played. Nothing special there, no great achievement in returning normalcy and stability to a place that had both before America took them away, but still hard to get used to after the past few years of occupation, civil war, and terror. Hussein told me his children played games where they lay improvised explosive devices against each other, to blow each other up. He pointed to the security patrols that went by in the park. "All this is a lie," he gestured at the people. "If it was safe they wouldn't need a security patrol." Al Qaeda and other Sunni militias were just lying dormant, he said, as was the Mahdi Army. I expressed skepticism. He stopped a couple walking by. "Excuse me," he said. "My friend is a journalist. Do you feel safe now?" The young man did not hesitate: he said no and kept on walking.

The Americans rated the Iraqi National Police "the most improved security force," according to a U.S. diplomat in Baghdad. "It used to be a death squad," he said. "Now the worst officers have been fired or transferred to where they can do no harm." But even if the overt sectarianism had receded, it was still there. I met up with Captain Adil from the INPs in Dora. After Adil refused to arrest Sunnis without warrants, Brig. Gen. Abdel Karim had transferred him north to Mosul, a much more dangerous assignment. Adil was then accused of stealing cars and held in a secret prison on the second floor of the Interior Ministry's Internal Affairs Committee office. He told me he had been framed and that his accuser was a Mahdi Army commander in Abu Dshir.

Twenty-seven people were held in a small cell he described as three meters by two meters in size. They slept standing up. All the other men were Sunni. The torture started at midnight. "I was handcuffed and blindfolded and beaten like in movies," he told me. He was placed under a cold shower for many hours. A policeman named Gafar, who worked with the Mahdi Army in Dora and knew Adil, beat him so badly he urinated blood. "When Americans came they would make us shut up or threaten us," he said. "When they beat me they said, 'Why do you hate the Mahdi Army?' I said, 'Why are you asking me this? It's not about cars.' 'You are a collaborator,' they said. 'You worked with the Americans against the Mahdi Army, you know why you are here.'" Adil's fellow prisoners were there without their families' knowledge. They cried and wailed at night, he said, and the prisoners could hear Shiite religious songs on their jailers' cellphones. After twenty-two days, his captors demanded twenty thousand dollars for his release, but he negotiated it down to seven thousand, which his brother-in-law handed to a police captain outside a restaurant.

Adil resigned after he was released. "I served my country," he told me, but now he felt betrayed. He still supported Maliki, though. "He is a real nationalist," he told me. "Everybody likes him." He was very pleased with Maliki's moves to include former Baathists in the government. "Nuri al-Maliki is the best leader I saw in my life," he said. "He doesn't know about this prison. The Americans don't know."

Adil wasn't the only person I knew who was feeling punished by the new order. In late 2008, two weeks after the Americans handed authority over Dora's Awakening groups to the Iraqi National Police, Osama's comrade Abu Yasser was arrested by the INPs. Osama told me that Abu Yasser was taken to General Karim's headquarters, hung from his arms, and tortured. To end the torture he confessed to murders he hadn't committed but wisely confessed to killing people who were still alive. Then he was moved to the INP prison in Kadhimiya. He had already paid twenty thousand dollars, Osama told me. "They can't release him without money—everything costs money." Abu Yasser was worried that Al Qaeda men in prison with him would find out that he was an Awakening group member and kill him.

Soon after, Osama and Abu Yasser's fellow comrade Abu Salih arranged a lunch for Eid. He invited locals, including the local American unit. Abu Salih had become famous for helping many Shiite families come back and protecting them. The head of the Baghdad Operations Command, Abud Qanbar, came to shake his hand, and it was shown on Iraqi TV. But after lunch the Americans left, and a different American unit showed up and arrested him. He was taken to the major crimes unit of the Iraqi police and accused of terrorism. He too was tortured and hung by his arms, and had trouble walking afterward. Abu Salih also paid about twenty thousand dollars, Osama said, and his family expected him to be released when more money was paid.

"They torture and wait for them to confess; they don't use evidence," Osama said. At least eight other men I knew from Osama's group had been arrested since the INPs took over. His young deputy Hussein had managed to abscond safely. There was also a warrant out for Osama, and he could not return to Dora to visit his parents. Abu Yusef—Osama's former ally—had switched allegiances and joined with Muhammad Kashkul, Osama's old nemesis. But Kashkul was arrested by the Americans and taken to the prison at Camp Bucca. Abu Yusef fled before he could be arrested. Now a fat man called Abu Suleiman was in charge of Osama's old area. "He's not a good guy," Osama said. He felt betrayed. "The Americans were only with us when they needed us," he said. He called the Americans when Abu Yasser was first arrested, but they told him it was an Iraqi affair and that they couldn't do anything for him. "The SOI [Sons of Iraq] was never supposed to be an amnesty program," one American Embassy official in Baghdad told me defensively when I recounted this story to him.

The British special operators Osama and some of his men worked with also rotated units. "The new guys were assholes," he said. They warned Abu Yasser that the Americans would arrest him if he did not help them arrest Al Qaeda men. In his one year working with the British, Abu Yasser helped them arrest several senior Al Qaeda men, including an explosives expert called Abu Maryam. The British gave sources one hundred dollars per visit, but Osama refused to take their money. "I said I am not a source, I'm working for my country," he told me.

Dora had changed dramatically since Osama and I had toured its devastation in 2007. I got an introduction to the new Dora with Adil Adnan, a round man with a gray mustache, and his son Maher. For the past five years Adnan had been the Education Ministry's supervisor for seventy-six schools in southern Baghdad. Before that he had been a school principal for twenty-four years. He drove me down Dora's Masafi Street. "This street, you couldn't drive on it," he said. "It was empty. The concrete barriers helped a lot, even if it was annoying."

Adnan was originally from Arab Jubur. "I didn't visit for three years because it was unsafe," he said. "The Awakening saved the area." Adnan took me to his house in Dora's Jumhuriya area. He had a green yard and a small garden under a skylight in his living room, which he proudly told me was in a Spanish style. "In 2005 the resistance got strong here," Adnan said. "Then Americans brought random groups to run the government in 2006 and 2007." That's when sectarianism started in the Education Ministry. Adnan knew at least five Shiite and Sunni school principals who were killed and twenty or twenty-five teachers who were killed, including a Christian physical education teacher. Militias came into schools and ordered teachers to give certain students good grades. Many children whose parents were wealthy were kidnapped.

In 2006 Maher was kidnapped by the Mahdi Army. "They took me to the Kadhimein Husseiniya and beat me with pistols," Maher told me. The cleric interrogated him. They told him he had killed Imam Hussein. Maher protested that his father was Sunni but his mother was Shiite. They called him a *tali* (lamb), as the Mahdi Army refers to victims about to be executed. Maher asked for a glass of water. "What do you think this is?" they taunted. "The Sheraton?" They put him in the trunk of the car and drove him to be executed, but he kicked it open and managed to run away.

"There was no sectarianism before," Adnan recalled, but now "there are still bad people talking about sectarianism. Even in the worst times I had seven Shiite headmasters who stayed in Dora. Some were transferred so Shiites took salaries to Sunnis and Sunnis took salaries to Shiites. Sunni teachers from else-where would come, and I would give them jobs."

Adnan had a principal's impartiality and viewed all sides in the conflict as re-sponsible. "Who was killing if everybody says it wasn't me?" he asked dismis-sively. "The Awakening, the police, the Mahdi Army—all say it wasn't me." Then there was a change in the American behavior. "The Americans got bet-ter, they started to know the area, they spread out more, had more patrols." Unlike most Iraqis I met, Adnan wasn't worried about the impending Ameri-can withdrawal. "Let the Americans leave," he said. "It's the same thing."

Maher drove me around the neighborhood. He pointed to a young girl. "Al Qaeda killed her father and brother," he told me. Not far away some Shiites had returned and put up the religious flags traditional Shiites raise above their homes. Some people viewed it as a provocation and threw a concussion bomb at the house.

On a different day I met Maher again, and we drove to Arab Jubur, where his family originally hailed from. The banks of the Tigris, an idyllic rural area, had been the scene of some of the worst Al Qaeda violence of the war. We passed empty fields where Al Qaeda used to dump the bodies of Shiites they captured on the highway. "They would take whole Kia buses full of people," he said. "Ansar al-Sunna, the 1920 Revolution Brigade, the Army of the Mujahideen, Al Qaeda, were all here." There were numerous checkpoints manned by Iraqi sol-diers and Awakening men every few hundred meters. We drove past fields from where Al Qaeda had launched an attack on Abu Dshir. The road was scarred by IED craters that had been filled with dirt. On our left was the bank of the Tigris. Maher pointed to destroyed houses on the side of the road. "This one was Al Qaeda," he said. "This one was a slaughterer." Many homes had been destroyed by American airstrikes during the surge. The violence had destroyed the farms and roads. Most people in the area were farmers, and earning a living was much harder now. There were no services, no drinking water, no clinic.

In the schoolyard I found an eighteen-year-old boy watching younger chil-dren playing. In 2008 he lost his hand when an IED went off. His brother had lost a leg from an IED in a different incident. On the road I found a small boy on his way to school, leaning on a crutch. He was missing an arm and had a prosthetic leg. One day in 2008 he was tending his sheep when an IED went off. On the side of the road a man called Sami Adnan stood by his hardware.

Like many, he had fled the area when the situation was at its worst. "The Americans used to bomb randomly every day, and there were terrorists," he said. His house was burned and destroyed when he was away, but he didn't know who was responsible. He attributed the improved security to the Awakening men. "Even the Americans got better after the terrorists left," he said.

At a checkpoint I spoke with two Awakening men wearing blue uniforms. They had joined the Awakening a year and a half earlier to protect their area, they told me. Their salaries were two months late. "When the Americans were here, we got salaries every fifteen days," one of them said. Until now none of them had joined the ISF, though they had all applied. "It's only promises," they said. As we left Maher told me that both men were former members of the Army of the Mujahideen.

A local boy got in our car and directed us to the home of the Awakening boss, Amer Abdallah Khalal al-Rabia, of the Jubur tribe. "It became normal to see dead bodies here on the side of the road," the boy said as we drove. We turned off the road and drove several hundred meters through dense foliage and palm trees.

Amer was not home, but we met his twenty-five-year-old brother, Tahsin, who had joined the Awakening in 2007. He had been one of the first to join in all of southern Baghdad, he told me. In May 2007 he went to Mahmudiya to give the Americans information about Al Qaeda. His family had battled Al Qaeda even before the Awakening groups were formed, and Al Qaeda had killed three of his brothers. Another brother was killed after they established the Awakening group. In the early days of the occupation Islamist militants killed their tribe's sheikh, Khalid Dawud al-Rabia. "They accused him of collaborating and working with Chalabi," Tahsin told me, "but he was trying to open a police station here, and he wasn't working with Chalabi. A group of men belonging to Dr. Fatthi Yusuf Saleh al-Juburi, a local veterinarian, was responsible for the murder." Dr. Fatthi was the biggest terrorist in southern Baghdad, Tahsin said; his group distributed papers to schools saying girls can't attend.

Amer finally showed up wearing a loose-fitting suit, with a pistol tucked in his pants. A twenty-four-year veteran of the Iraqi army, he explained that he was responsible for the areas of Zunbaraniya, Uleimiya, and Beijia. Under the Americans he had commanded 629 men, but once authority for the Awakening shifted to the Iraqis, the Iraqi government fired fifty or sixty of his men every month. He now commanded only 490 men, not one of whom had joined the Iraqi Security Forces.

When two of Amer's men captured two Al Qaeda men, they turned them over to General Karim's national police in Dora. But General Karim had Amer's men arrested as well, and they had already spent three months in the serious crimes prison in Dora. "Our relationship with the Iraqi army is not good," Amer said. "They don't respect the Awakening. The Iraqi National Police don't like the Awakening." One month earlier Iraqi soldiers had beaten one of Amer's men because he did not salute them. Now that the Iraqi army paid them, many negative things were happening. Salaries had been reduced. Amer's salary was halved. Now he received the same amount as his men: about three hundred dollars. "The Americans used to come here to pay us," he said. "Now we have to go to the Iraqi army battalion and wait on long lines. Some people wait for two or three days. We are treated with disrespect. For the last two months, there is no salary. It was all false promises. We are targeted by Al Qaeda and we have no protection."

Amer spoke of a new trend: families of slain Al Qaeda men were filing charges against him and Tahsin. "They made fake death certificates," he said. "They said we killed people the Americans killed, and now there is a warrant for me in Baghdad."

Seven hundred and eighty-two families who had fled the area because of Al Qaeda had now returned. One factor limiting returns was the destruction of many homes. Sectarianism remained, but it was now more covert. The Americans were releasing terrorists from imprisonment in Camp Bucca, and there were rumors that the Awakening program would end in June. "Why did terrorism happen?" he asked me. "Because of the vacuum. If they don't put the Awakening men in the Iraqi army or Iraqi police, problems will happen."

"Metrics" to determine "progress" in Iraq have always been difficult to determine. The American surge was meant to give space for Iraq's politicians to achieve a modicum of reconciliation and progress. This had not happened, but it was an American-imposed standard. How did Iraqis feel about the situation? "The refugees are the best ones to determine the temperature on the ground, the best at keeping the pulse," UN Assistance Mission for Iraq (UNAMI) head Stefan de Mistura told me. "If they return, the situation is normalizing. If they don't, then there is a reason. They have returned but not in substantial numbers." This was a contrast to other crises where he had worked. "In Kosovo we had two million people return," he said. "We were delighted but overwhelmed." After the January 2009 elections the changes became apparent: "We saw that the city of Baghdad changed its color. There was a cleansing."

Back in Baghdad I went to the Jihad district's Mukhabarat area and met Ibrahim Saleh, also known as Abu Abdallah Hamdani. He was the local Awakening leader there; he was not pleased with Iraq's new course. His area was walled off and the entrance was guarded by INPs and a tense Awakening man who barked at all strangers entering. I drove by a large lake of sewage and garbage, on a dirt road to Ibrahim's large house, which was being built atop a hill. Hundreds of families had fled the area to the Anbar and elsewhere because mortars were falling on their homes. Ibrahim's wife was among the victims of these mortars. The displaced started to return after the Awakening was established.

Ibrahim took charge of 160 men in August 2008 after the INPs arrested his brother Taher, the previous leader. He and his brother joined the Awakening because there were no jobs and because they wanted to help protect the area. "Al Qaeda and the special groups were fighting each other, and the Friendly Forces [as he called the Americans] came to us and asked Taher to protect the area and give information. The Awakening was established here in July 2007." He claimed Taher had a good relationship with the INPs, but one day Taher invited them to lunch, and after they finished eating they arrested him. "He was taken to the Fifth Brigade of INPs. They accused him of murder and stealing. In the beginning they beat him badly. He passed out for two days." He was now in prison in the Shaab district. Both Taher and Ibrahim had been in the military before the war.

Ibrahim claimed that both Al Qaeda and Shiite militias had tried to assassinate him. Two weeks before I met him, one of his Awakening men was arrested and beaten until he confessed to murder. An Awakening commander in the nearby Furat district was arrested in October 2008. I told Ibrahim it seemed to me that the Awakening groups were used and disposed of. "This is the reality," he said. "I will be arrested, 100 percent. As soon as they finish with me, they will arrest me." He too felt betrayed. "We were with the government of Iraq and the Americans. The arrests can't happen without the permission of the Americans."

Jihad was a desperate area. Most young men had no jobs, Ibrahim said, and there were a lot of widows. There were many poor people and IDPs who didn't get any compensation. "You have to spend a lot of money to register," he told me. The Americans used to control the area firmly, he said, but since the Status of Forces Agreement took effect in January 2009, the Americans stopped coming around much, and whenever Ibrahim contacted them they told him he should talk to the Iraqi government. Although people started to return after security improved, once the arrests started again some fled anew. "People felt like it was a plan to make us come back and arrest us," he said. "It's only Sunnis being arrested." I met him alongside two members of the local council for Jihad and Furat, which had a total of twenty members. They all believed the Iraqi government was still sectarian and that when the Americans left the Iranians would occupy the country and fighting would resume. Only those loyal to Iran wanted the Americans to leave, they told me. Despite all this, Ibrahim had a positive view of Prime Minister Maliki.

Across Baghdad, I met other Awakening leaders who were experiencing the same frustrations that Ibrahim had. In Adhamiya I met Abu Omar, or Khalil Ibrahim, one of the Awakening leaders in the area. It was the birthday of the

Prophet Muhammad, the first time I had ever seen a festive mood and celebration in a Sunni part of the country, yet Abu Omar was not in a festive mood himself. I found him chatting with American soldiers across the street from the mosque. When he finished with them, he took me to sit with him on plastic chairs in the square by the mosque. Abu Omar had dark red skin, a bulbous nose, small eyes, and a large belly. As we sat and drank tea, small boys ran around us. One of them, whose father was a slain Awakening fighter, played with a plastic pistol, shooting at us. The main square was adorned with pictures of slain Awakening fighters, including two of Abu Omar's sons. I worried about suicide bombers, since several of Adhamiya's Awakening leaders had been killed by them. And it was a Yemeni suicide bomber who killed one of Abu Omar's sons.

Adhamiya was the last Sunni enclave in eastern Baghdad. "If the Awakening wasn't here, then in twenty years the Iraqi army and U.S. Army wouldn't be able to come in," Abu Omar said proudly, bragging that "this was the third-hottest area in Iraq." He was also proud that Saddam had made his last appearance in his neighborhood. Abu Omar fought the Americans on that day as well. "There were eleven Syrians [foreign fighters], God have mercy on them," he said. "They were martyred here." I asked him how he could collaborate with his former enemies. "The Americans are leaving, but the Iranians are staying," he told me.

In November 2007 Abu Omar joined the Awakening in his area with thirteen other family members. "Two previous groups tried but failed," he said. "They sat and would watch the killers." Most of the killers were from outside Adhamiya, he said. Abu Omar had been a noncommissioned officer in Iraqi army intelligence, with nineteen years of service. He claimed that after the war he was jobless and sold gasoline on the black market. "We saw the killing and kidnapping," he said, and wanted to put an end to it. The Americans approached them through the Sunni endowment. After an initial confrontation with Al Qaeda, Abu Omar and his men seized the Abu Hanifa Mosque. A comrade called Abu Muthana got on the mosque's loudspeakers and issued a statement to the people of Adhamiya, announcing the establishment of their Awakening group and their aim to rid the area of Al Qaeda. (Abu Muthana had since been arrested by the Iraqi authorities.) After Abu Muthana's statement, Al Qaeda men in nearby buildings opened fire on them, and one of Abu Omar's men was killed. Abu Omar says his men captured many Al Qaeda members and handed them over to the Americans.

Sheikh Ahmad al-Taha, the son-in-law of Ahmad Abdel Ghafur al-Samarai and the deputy of Harith al-Dhari from the Association of Muslim Scholars, was now the imam of the Abu Hanifa Mosque. "All bad things come from this mosque," he said, pointing to it. Al Qaeda used to keep prisoners inside it, he said, and one day five IEDs were placed next to the mosque on the street. He did not believe they could have been placed without the cognizance of people in the mosque. The mosque graveyard was an IED factory, he claimed, and his men had found RPGs and explosives in the mosque.

At first Abu Omar's men clashed with the Iraqi army, and he once waged a three-hour gun battle with them. "We don't accept the Iraqi police here," he told me. "They can only come with the army. We don't like them—they're all militias." He too was apprehensive about an American withdrawal, telling me that the civil war would resume. A friend of his called Abu Karar, who was a member of Iraqi intelligence, had joined us at the table. "I disagree with you, Abu Omar," he said. "Nothing would happen if the Americans left." I asked Abu Omar why he did not unite with other Awakening leaders to form a stronger front. "We tried in 2008," he told me. "Awakening leaders couldn't join together because they couldn't agree among themselves."

This failure to unite would become painfully obvious on March 28, 2009, when clashes erupted in Baghdad's Fadhil district after the Iraqi army arrested Adil al-Mashhadani, the head of the local Awakening group. Mashhadani's men staged a two-day uprising, and the U.S. Army ended up rescuing its Iraqi counterparts. The clashes provoked speculation that the surge in American troops, to which the dominant narrative attributed the drop in violence, was unraveling or that the civil war might restart. I had been hearing about Mashhadani from Shiites since 2007. Supporters of Muqtada al-Sadr, in particular, were upset that someone like Mashhadani—who, they believed, used to slaughter Shiite civilians—had been empowered by the Americans. One U.S. national security official told me that the Americans had held information on Mashhadani for years but considered him one of the first insurgents to see which way the wind was blowing. They had wanted him arrested at one point, but the Iraqi army was not ready yet. The official had been concerned that other Awakening groups would rise up; he was relieved to see that none did.

In fact, the ill-fated uprising in Fadhil was best seen as confirmation that the civil war between Sunnis and Shiites was over and could not begin again—not because of any reconciliation process or political settlement, neither of which had happened, but because the Shiite victory was definitive and the Sunni militias were crushed. The cleansing of Sunnis from much of Baghdad left Sunni insurgents with no sea of people to swim among. Shiites had numerical superiority and the growing strength of the state and its security forces, which they dominated, along with the support of the world's only superpower.

Following the clashes between the Supreme Council and the Mahdi Army, and then Prime Minister Maliki's assault on Shiite militias, there was no longer a unified Shiite bloc but instead a central government confident in its victory and eager to assert its full authority. One Iraq expert from the U.S. Army who worked closely with Gen. David Petraeus told me in 2008 that the civil war would end when Shiites realized they had won and Sunnis realized they had lost. Both sides had now come to those realizations. Advocates of the surge hoped that following the drop in violence a political settlement could be reached between Iraq's warring factions. But this wouldn't happen, and it wasn't necessary. The burgeoning Iraqi state, embodied by Maliki, could simply continue to expand its power. The more Maliki became a new Saddam, the more popular he became among Iraqis. But he actually had to earn support and provide services, because he answered to the Shiite majority. And his power was checked by other factions and by an energetic Parliament that controlled the purse strings.

In November 2008 the Americans handed authority over nearly one hundred thousand Awakening group fighters to the Iraqi government. But few were hired. Although in 2008 the Iraqi government agreed to integrate these men into the security forces or government ministries by the end of 2009, it had to push that back until mid-2010. But in April 2010 the U.S. special inspector general for Iraq reconstruction reported that only 37,041 had been integrated, even though the Iraqi government claimed the number was fifty thousand. But the Iraqi government declares an Awakening man integrated once he has been offered a job, regardless of whether he accepts it.

Senior Awakening leaders and many of their men were systematically arrested. Others were simply removed from their posts and told to go home. It was a quiet and slow process, but one that continued to emasculate the last groups that could compete with the state for authority. There was nothing the Awakening groups could do. As guerrillas and insurgents, they had been effective only when they operated covertly, underground, blending in with a Sunni population that was crushed in a brutal Shiite-led counterinsurgency campaign, which depopulated Sunni areas. Now the former resistance fighters were publicly known paid guards—their names, addresses, and biometric data possessed by the Americans and Iraqis. They could not return to an underground that had been cleared, so they were cornered. They had failed to unite, and many were on the run. Some had left the country, and others were being tried in court for killing the very Al Qaeda men the Americans had originally wanted them to kill.

The failed uprising in Fadhil was a symptom of the Sunni inability to unite. Although the Awakening groups were a formidable force when they were established, in retrospect it seemed that many of the former insurgent leaders had miscalculated. For the most part they had not been incorporated into the political system or the security forces. They were hated or mocked by members of the Iraqi Security Forces, who had their own nicknames for the men of the Awakening, or Sahwa, in Arabic: they called them Sakhla, meaning "sheep," or Shahwa, meaning "horniness."

"The Sahwa were always going to get screwed," Major Gottlieb told me. "In the fall of 2007, the Interior Ministry began demanding their names, addresses, family members, employment history, etc. from the Americans. To their credit, the units in our sector dragged their feet on providing the information. I suspect that the various, purposefully unsuccessful drives to vet Sahwa for Interior Ministry employment were designed to gather this information. Everyone turned in forms, but no one ever seemed to get hired."

In truth, the Awakening men were not the only ones who found it difficult to get jobs. Everybody in Iraq had this problem. Nobody could get a job with the security forces unless they were affiliated with a political party, which often also required a family connection. The alternative was to pay a bribe that amounted to several months' salary. But former Shiite militiamen had much less trouble integrating into the security forces than their Sunni counterparts.

A new, Shiite-dominated order was being established in Iraq. The cleansing of Sunnis had sufficiently weakened enemies of the Shiite state, and Sunni civilians needed not fear as long as they accepted the new order. Shiites had nearly succeeded in clearing Sunni areas from future threats. The occasional Al Qaeda–inspired suicide attack could kill masses of civilians, but it had no strategic impact. The drop in violence was complex and primarily a symptom of Iraqi dynamics, though the concrete walls built by the Americans and the increased American presence in neighborhoods at a time when the Americans were less aggressive and considered by Iraqis to be the least of all evils were also essential.

The surge strengthened Maliki and his security forces: it neutered the Sunni militias and allowed Maliki to weaken the Shiite militias. These Shiite militias were the initial storm troopers of the civil war, the ones who cleansed Sunnis from Baghdad and paved the way for the Shiite victory, but following that they only stood in the way of Maliki as he consolidated his control. There were still many battles left to be fought in Iraq, and when the Americans departed a new phase of violence and factional fighting would likely begin, but the war between Iraq's Sunnis and Shiites appeared to be over.

DESPITE THEIR MANY GRIEVANCES, the Sunni militias were holding their fire. I was curious to discover if the Sadrist militias were similarly conflicted, having been thrashed by Maliki, with American help, in the spring of 2008, during Operation Charge of the Knights. I met up with Muhamad, who worked in the Sadr Current's social affairs group in Shaab. Abul Hassan of the Mustafa Husseiniya, whom I had spent time with in previous years, had been arrested by the Americans with three other men one night in late 2008. Sayyid Jalil now worked in the main Sadrist office in Sadr City. The Shurufi Mosque had shut down after weapons were discovered inside it. Prayer was forbidden. Instead, about five hundred men sat on mats on the street beside it. Iraqi National Police were posted around the men, watching lazily. Sheikh Abdel Karim al-Saedi of the Suwaed tribe from Amara stood before them on a podium. Most of his audience was young. I spoke with Muhamad as the sheikh discussed religion. Muhamad's brother was killed by the Americans in May 2008. Many civilians were killed in Charge of the Knights, he said, and the Americans were still arresting people. Muhamad told me that Maliki was negotiating with Sadrists: if they joined his coalition he would release Mahdi Army prisoners.

Someone stood up and shouted a *hossa*. "We will keep the Friday prayers that Muhammad Sadr started regardless of what America and Israel or Britain say!" For Sadrists the Friday prayers had once been identified with defying oppression. Now the grievances were more mundane. Sheikh Abdel Karim's sermon was a litany of complaints about inflation, money laundering, immorality, homosexuality, alcohol, lack of food, lack of housing, and corruption. Now that security had improved, where were the service improvements? He complained. Where was the large budget people had been promised?

Although I paid little attention to his comment on homosexuality at the time, soon after, Sadrist militiamen began brutally slaughtering men suspected of homosexuality. One staff member in Sadr City's Chuwader hospital said he saw four corpses of suspected homosexuals brought in. One of the bodies was found in a garbage dump while the others were on the streets. Two of them were found with superglue clogging their anuses. This happened to many others. He said the victims were tortured to death in the area's garages. In some cases the victims' tribes were said to be complicit in the murders. Sadrist sermons were said to call for the "disciplining" of homosexuals. The Mahdi Army's militia activity was frowned upon, but in conservative areas like Sadr City nobody would condemn them for killing homosexuals. Women with "bad reputations" were also killed, their bodies thrown in garbage dumps.

After Friday prayers ended a man took me to his neighbor's home. The Americans had raided it the night before. The door had been blown up with plastic explosives. All the glass on the doors and windows was broken. All the furniture was overturned, closets were dumped, items seemed gratuitously broken. Five brothers were arrested. Their relatives complained that the Americans came with a Sudanese translator and an Iraqi informer who wore a mask. The Americans often searched homes in the area, they said, but they had never done this before. This time they ransacked the house and took the family's gold, forty thousand dollars (the brother had just sold his house), cellphones, and the computer's hard drive, and smashed the computer screen.

The next day I went to the Qiba Mosque in Shaab, which I had first visited in March 2004 after the twin Ashura bombings, when I encountered a nascent militia that nearly killed me (see Chapter Two). This time Iraqi soldiers stood guard outside and in the mosque's courtyard. There was a poster of Muqtada al-Sadr's father on the gate. Two brothers, Abu Ali and Abu Riyadh, took care of the mosque and cleaned it. They told me that Sheikh Walid had fled north to Salahaddin. His house was now occupied by IDPs from Diyala, who said they would leave when Sheikh Walid returned. Not far away men were fixing the Sunni Al Haq Mosque as well. Sayyid Nasr of the Sayyid Haidar Husseiniya, along with the head of the local Shiite Awakening group, had told them eight months earlier to open the Qiba Mosque. Now the Sunni endowment was helping to fix the mosque. The day before about sixty people had attended the Friday prayers, they told me. As I left with my friends I saw that many young men from the area had gathered around the mosque and were looking at us ominously.

The next week I attended Friday prayers in Sadr City. Driving to Martyrs' Square, I saw boys playing billiards and table soccer (Foosball) on the side of road. Men worked in their garages, traffic was heavy—it was not like Friday prayers of the past, when Sadr City's streets were deserted. We drove past a poster honoring Hizballah's slain hero Imad Mughniyeh. I was searched by young men from the Sadrist office who wore badges with the image of Lebanon's Imam Musa Sadr on them, something I had never seen before in Iraq. I walked past an animal market: chickens in cages, sheep being slaughtered, pools of blood collecting by the curb. A large mural of Muhammad Sadiq al-Sadr and Muhammad Baqir al-Sadr stood in the center of a large traffic circle. Thousands of mostly young men sat on mats or even cardboard. The cleric spoke from a podium next to the Sadrist headquarters. The sermon, on Shiite eschatology, had little to do with politics. The imam spoke about Muhammad Sadiq al-Sadr's twenty-five predictions about the arrival of the Mahdi. Infidels would gather against Muslims, the cleric warned. But then he turned to the Status of Forces Agreement. It was permissible to make peace with infidels, he said, but the SOFA took more from Iraq than it gave, and it was more about protecting the Americans than helping the Iraqis. At the end of the sermon he led the crowds in chants of "Go out, Americans," "Yes, Muqtada," and "Yes, hawza," but the chants seemed tepid, almost indifferent, lacking the passion of the past.

A local tribal sheikh called Karim al-Muhamadawi told me the thousands of men praying were inactive Mahdi Army members. After prayers we went to his house for a lunch of rotisserie chicken. He had a thick mustache and wore a black dishdasha. The Americans had put Sheikh Karim in charge of one sector of Sadr City and asked him to provide fifty men, who would each get three hundred dollars a month. "We don't call it Awakening here in the City," he said, referring to Sadr City in the abbreviated way its residents do. Instead they called the men night guards. Nine sectors of Sadr City were firmly under government control, with concrete walls surrounding them—together they were known as the Golden Square.

Sheikh Karim's family came to Baghdad from Amara in 1951. In 1961 Abdul Karim Qasim, the prime minister of Iraq, built this area for government

employees, Karim told me. He remembered when the fedayeen and different
state security bodies stormed into Sadr City in 1999 and killed demonstrators,
following the death of Muqtada's father. When the Mahdi Army took control
of Sadr City, the area became off-limits to other parties. The Sadrists destroyed the Communist Party headquarters and then the Supreme Council
headquarters, and because they didn't let other parties into the area, anything
bad that happened there was blamed on the Sadrists. After Charge of the
Knights, though, other parties such as Dawa had become active in Sadr City,
and the Sadrists lost popularity, Karim told me. But the Sadrists were still the
most popular movement in Sadr City.

"Muqtada was popular because of his father, and he was the only one opposed to the Americans," Karim said. "In the beginning the Sadr Current was
just and helped the poor," he continued. "Then gangs infiltrated and even
Muqtada didn't know. When they heard people were doing bad things in their
name, the Sadrists punished them. But the Mahdi Army was not organized; it
was a mess. The City is big, and Muqtada was in Najaf and couldn't control
it." The men who controlled gas stations and extorted from shops were far
from the Mahdi Army, he said. "They were gangs."

The Mahdi Army was still in Sadr City, but it was moribund. After the Iraqi
and American armies entered the area, services improved. The gangs were sidelined, and the prices of benzene and cooking gas went down. The Americans
built solar-powered street lights, increased electricity, and improved water and
sewage. Many people were hired to clear garbage. The Americans handed control of the services to the Iraqi government. "Even Sadrists here voted for Maliki," Karim told me. "People like going out at night without being bothered."

Washash, in western Baghdad, had also improved greatly in the year since I
had visited. The concrete walls were still up, but cars could now drive into the
market, and the Mahdi Army had been expelled. I met again with Abu Karar,
head of the Washash Tribal Council, who had helped lead the intifada against
the Mahdi Army. I asked him if the government was now active in Washash.
"We don't have a state," he said. "It was all autonomous, unilateral. We depend on ourselves and our sons." He proudly lifted up his arm and squeezed
his own bicep. "If we see anything, we call the army or police, because the
state can't enter every area. They protect the entrance and exits. The American army stopped entering Washash." Abu Karar told me that he expected the
militias to try to make a comeback. "We want the walls still up. The walls are
60 or 70 percent responsible for the success of the security. Why did we find
twenty-seven bodies in Washash? Because they couldn't go out? Now the market is good because there is security. This whole story in Washash is over. The
state didn't thank me. They never asked how I pay or feed those eighty young
men protecting the streets. Militias call me and threaten me."

Some of the fiercest battles in the civil war occurred in southwestern Baghdad, in areas like Seidiya and Bayaa. The area was now under the control of the local police and the national police. I drove down a road formerly known as the "Street of Death." An Al Qaeda sniper had targeted everyone on this road—women, children, even cats. The Omar Mosque on the main road was one of the only ones that had reopened. Its location made it relatively safe, but it was still guarded by police—and there was a police station next to it, just in case. Some Sunnis were praying there as we passed. Nearby was a destroyed house that had belonged to a Shiite family who were all killed when Al Qaeda blew it up. The Sunni Hamza Mosque in Turath had been converted into an INP station. In Maalif, I drove alongside garbage dumps and sewage canals. Maalif, possibly the poorest neighborhood in the area, had attracted many IDPs from Abu Ghraib, Haswa, Mahmudiya, Radwaniya, and Amriya. There were so many new students in the local elementary school that caravans were being used as classrooms. Many IDPs squatted in empty lots alongside vast piles of sewage and trash. Flies swarmed around my face when I stopped to talk to several young men. One of them, Safa Hussein Jumaa, was displaced from Haswa in April 2006 after Al Qaeda attacked his family, he explained. They chose Maalif because it was a cheap area and they had relatives there. They owned their house in Haswa but dared not go back, even to sell it. "We heard people go back and their house gets blown up," he said. Large groups of jobless young men loitered on the sides of Maalif's unpaved roads. Immense piles of garbage separated homes, with lakes and canals of sewage around them. The Neighborhood Advisory Council estimated that Maalif had grown from fifty thousand people in 2004 to one hundred and fifty thousand in 2009. The Sunni Ali Assajad and Mustafa mosques had both been converted into INP stations. I drove by a garbage dump where some enterprising IDPs had built a home entirely of disposed air-conditioning units. Dozens of them were piled atop one another and in rows to form walls covered by a tarp.

Amriya was harder than ever to get into. The Iraqi army had assumed more authority; the Awakening men were weaker and more obedient. After the army denied my request to enter, Um Omar—who had been my point person during my years in Iraq for the Sunni humanitarian situation—called a representative and persuaded him to relent. I found her in her office. Security had improved a lot, she said, attributing it to the Awakening men who had joined the Iraqi Security Forces. In Amriya the police were better than the army because of the presence of many Awakening men.

Abul Abed had caused problems for her. "He killed many people after he became head of the Awakening," she told me, and he had personally threatened her, forcing her to move from Amriya to Adil. "We found tens of dead bodies after Abul Abed left," she said. Her priority now was helping orphans.

Twenty percent of the displaced families registered in Amriya went back to their homes, and about 20 percent of the area's displaced Shiites had returned. But six months before I met her, the house of a Shiite family that had come back was blown up, she said, and an elderly Shiite man was killed in a different house. The problems in Amriya started with the displaced persons, she told me. Many were young men without work. "If they took your house, you have endured violence, you don't have a home, you will be violent and listen to anybody who gives you money," she said. "Young men stopped going to school, they are angry, they are promised stuff by a man who gives them a car, money, and weapons. They are still here, though the violence is over."

The army helped returnees a lot, she said, but there were problems with returnees who "returned with force," backed by the army. This was why some of them were killed. "If there was a balance with people returning to Amriya and people leaving Amriya, then there would be less problems," she said.

In July 2009 an internal memorandum written by Col. Timothy Reese, chief of the Baghdad Operations Command Advisory Team, was leaked. Reese urged the Americans to declare victory and go home: "Today the Iraqi Security Forces (ISF) are good enough to keep the Government of Iraq (GOI) from being overthrown by the actions of Al Qaeda in Iraq (AQI), the Baathists, and the Shia violent extremists that might have toppled it a year or two ago. Iraq may well collapse into chaos of other causes, but we have made the ISF strong enough for the internal security mission." Since the Status of Forces Agreement was signed with the Iraqis, and the June 30 handover of security to the Iraqis took effect, it was clear to Reese that the Americans were no longer wanted. "Prime Minister (PM) Maliki hailed June 30th as a 'great victory,' implying the victory was over the U.S.," Reese wrote. He worried that the longer the Americans remained, the more likely violence would break out between them and the Iraqi government that could "rupture the current partnership." Reese then detailed the "general lack of progress in essential services and good governance," including widespread corruption and the refusal to follow commitments to integrate Sunnis into the system.

"The GOI and the ISF will not be toppled by the violence as they might have been between 2006 and 2008," Reese wrote. Shiite violence could be controlled and Al Qaeda's influence was insignificant except "when they get lucky with a mass casualty attack." The Americans were now being targeted in order to send messages to Maliki. Violence was part of a political competition, but "there is no longer any coherent insurgency or serious threat to the stability of the GOI posed by violent groups." Reese called for an early withdrawal of all American troops by August 2010.

The memo was a strange epitaph for a failed occupation. The Americans were able to defeat Saddam's army in 2003, but they could not establish control. Militias took over instead. As the country descended into civil war, the

Americans devolved power to Iraqi security forces little better than death squads. It was only in 2007 that they finally conquered Iraq, with the help of stronger Iraqi Security Forces, but chiefly thanks to the Shiite defeat of the Sunnis in the civil war. The American surge of troops came at just the right time, and they proved flexible enough to take advantage of events on the ground. The subsequent relative decline in violence was meant to lead to political reconciliation, but it never happened. Instead, the Shiite-dominated government merely asserted its control and marginalized or co-opted its opponents. Iraq would hold, even if it remained corrupt and authoritarian. The puppets installed by the occupier were increasingly recalcitrant, and American officials complained about losing their "leverage" or being treated with hostility by the Iraqi government and its security forces. Just as they weren't welcomed with flowers and candies, as the advocates of the war predicted, so too will their departure be ignominious.

Iraq's New Order Evolves

One day in late February 2010, a few weeks before the March 7 elections in Iraq, I drove south from Baghdad to Iskandariya to see my friend Hazim, a jovial NGO worker, whom I had met on a trip to the town a year earlier. Iskandariya, a majority-Shiite town straddling the key road leading south to the Shiite holy city of Karbala, had been hammered especially hard by the violence of Iraq's civil war: pilgrims headed to Karbala were often ambushed on the road through town, and the area had seen fierce battles between Al Qaeda and the Mahdi Army.

Hazim recalled the worst phases of the civil war: "People couldn't go out of their houses. When Al Qaeda was strong, Shiites couldn't go out on the street. Then the Shiites got strong, and Sunnis couldn't go out on the street." But all that was now in the past. Iraqi and American forces had arrested members of armed groups in the town during Operation Fard al-Qanun (Rule of Law), the Iraqi name for what Americans called the surge. "The state is strong here now," Hazim told me. "The government is strong. You can't even fire a shot in the air now; the police will come in two minutes."

A year earlier Ali Zahawi, Iskandariya's chief of police, made an interesting observation to me. "Iskandariya is a small Iraq," he said. "It connects south to north. It went through very hard times: Al Qaeda was the first phase; then militias who did the same thing as Al Qaeda, killing and displacement; and the third stage was operation Imposing Law [The Surge]." Now he warned of a fourth stage in the battle. Al Qaeda and Mahdi Army men, he said, were falsely implicating their enemies to the courts and getting them arrested.

There were still active militias in Iraq, and the level of violence would be unacceptable almost anywhere else on earth. But the fears frequently voiced by foreign analysts and reporters—that the civil war was merely in abeyance, and that sectarian fury could break out again at any moment after a series of deadly attacks or an unfavorable election result—were overblown. The threat of civil war no longer seemed to loom; the country was decidedly not "unraveling," as many continued to suggest. Armed militias had not been eliminated, but they had been emasculated: they carried out assassinations with silenced pistols and magnetic car bombs, but they were no match for the Iraqi Security Forces, which had shed their reputation as sectarian death squads and appeared to have earned the support of much of the public. Apart from the occasional suicide bombing, Iraqi civilians were no longer targeted at random—and even the more spectacular attacks had little to no strategic impact.

As worldwide attention returned to Iraq in the run-up to the March 7 elections, a new chorus of concerns emerged. Many worried that the corrupt maneuvering of some Shiite parties—which banned prominent nationalist and secularist candidates under the thin pretense of de-Baathification—would lead to a Sunni boycott and then renewed sectarian violence and war. But just as the dismantling of the Sunni Awakening groups in 2009 failed to produce the disaster many analysts predicted, the results of the elections seemed unlikely to stoke the embers of a new insurgency.

The continued sectarian exhortations of Iraqi politicians were met with cynicism by the public, whose support for religious parties had diminished considerably. Iraqis were still "sectarian" to a degree: most Shiites preferred the company of Shiites and Sunnis the company of Sunnis. The vitriol and hatred of the war had faded, but a legacy of bitterness and suspicion remained. Gone was the fear of the other—and it was this fear that led to the rise of the militias and sectarian religious parties.

A year later, during my travels in Iraq that February—in the capital and, more important, in the surrounding provinces of Diyala, Babil, and Salahuddin—I found Sunnis and Shiites alike talking of the civil war as if it were a painful memory from the distant past. Just as the residents of Northern Ireland refer obliquely to "the Troubles," Iraqis spoke of "the Events" or "the Sectarianism"—as in, "My brother was killed in the Sectarianism." Uneducated Iraqis might even say, "When the Sunni and Shiite happened."

The looming election—signposted in the foreign media as a critical "turning point" liable to wreck the fragile gains of the previous two years—seemed to be of little interest to most Iraqis, who were disenchanted with the pitiful performance of their political leaders and the tired rhetoric of sectarian religious parties.

In Shuwafa, a Shiite village alongside a canal west of Iskandariya, I met a schoolteacher named Akil, who had led a Shiite Awakening group that battled Al Qaeda after the ethnic cleansing of the village in 2006. He and his men had laid down their weapons the year before—after a portion of their salaries had been siphoned off by official corruption—but he said the security situation had improved dramatically. "The Awakening is over," he told me. "The Iraqi army is here, with two Hummers, so we feel safe. And nearby there is an army base." Akil had returned to teaching biology to children.

Like many Iraqis, Akil seemed indifferent to the approaching elections. "People don't like the religious parties anymore," he said. Many believed Prime Minister Nuri al-Maliki, head of the religious Shiite Dawa Party, had transcended his sectarian affiliation. "He is not considered to be from a religious party anymore," Akil said.

Reconstruction proceeded haltingly in Shuwafa: fifty families of the hundreds who had fled to Karbala to escape Al Qaeda had returned, but few had the funds to rebuild their homes or repair their farms. In the nearby village of Malha, where well-fed sheep were grazing on dark green grass around the rubble of destroyed houses, the situation was much the same. Only two homes were being rebuilt, and the majority of the village's residents had not yet returned. Those who came back survived by working in a local Shiite Awakening group—earning only two hundred dollars a month, barely enough to replace a single one of the hundreds of sheep that had been killed or stolen by Sunni insurgents when they fled. The lives of Iraq's millions of internal refugees remained bleak, and the country's humanitarian crisis was grave. But the restoration of some semblance of security had bolstered the authority of the state and the prime minister. "The Awakening, the Americans, the Iraqi army, and the tribes made it safer here," one man in Malha told me. "Everybody here is with Maliki."

In the town of Shat al-Taji, northwest of Baghdad, I drove past orange groves, palm trees, and boys in school uniforms walking home on the side of the road alongside schoolgirls wearing pink backpacks and holding hands. The majority-Sunni town, which stretches along the Tigris River, had been the site of brutal conflict in the civil war. I walked along the banks with Abu Taisir, a small man with a pistol tucked into the side of his trousers who was the deputy head of the local Awakening group. "Al Qaeda used to behead people and dump them in the river right there," he said, pointing over the tall reeds to a spot on the shore.

Abu Taisir took me to meet Abdulrahman Ismail, a Shiite neighbor who was displaced from Shat al-Taji in October 2006 but had since returned home. After a series of death threats—and the murder of four of his cousins, who were beheaded and tossed in the river—"we feared for our children and went to Kut," Ismail said. But after security improved in the town, he continued, the Awakening men contacted the displaced Shiite families to tell them it was safe to return. Ismail found that his home had been taken over by an Al Qaeda man who was later killed; his family's belongings and livestock had been stolen. "We feel safe now," he said, "but we still feel a little scared."

Abu Taisir's outfit had arrested eighty-five Al Qaeda suspects, he told me; ten of his men had been killed in the fighting. Abu Taisir himself had been shot twice, most recently in November. Some of the Al Qaeda men were still in town, he said, but they hadn't been arrested because nobody would testify against them. "They have roots here like us," Abu Taisir said. Both men agreed that there was a new balance of power in the town—the remnants of the insurgency were overwhelmed by the Awakening men and the Iraqi Security Forces. "Now if we call the police, they come," Abu Taisir said.

He had commanded 360 men, but only eighty-two were offered jobs in the government, and low-ranking ones at that. Many felt betrayed. "We're fighters," he said. "We brought peace to this area, we fought Al Qaeda. Now we are janitors?"

The failure to integrate the Awakening men into government security forces had been widespread, and many feared the consequences of the continuing disenfranchisement of Iraq's Sunnis. But they had been disenfranchised since 2003, in part thanks to their own miscalculations. Iraq's new order was dominated by Shiites, and that was not easily undone: the government was soundly in Shiite hands; the only question with regard to the upcoming elections, then, was whether it would remain in Maliki's comparatively reliable hands or pass into those of his more divisive and inflammatory Shiite rivals. At the time of my visit to Shat al-Taji, the de-Baathification committee had just banned the leading Sunni politician, Saleh al-Mutlaq, from the elections. Outside observers worried that excluding him could agitate Sunnis, but his removal was met with barely a whimper; even other Sunni politicians failed to unite to support him. "People here are upset about Saleh al-Mutlaq," Abu Taisir said, "but they saw from the last elections that the people they voted for weren't sincere, so they don't care for politics." The other Awakening men we met had been impressed by Maliki; he was an effective strongman. "We want secular people, nationalist, not religious parties," Abu Taisir averred.

In Baghdad a few days later, I saw Omar al-Juburi, a leading Sunni member of Parliament and a former adviser to Vice President Tariq al-Hashimi. He was now living in a gaudy mansion in the Yarmuk district. I first met Juburi in 2006, when he presented me with detailed files demonstrating that Sunnis had been killed by Shiite death squads and Iraqi police. Since then, he said, "the minister of interior has expelled sixty thousand bad policemen; today the police is better than the army." The Sunni presence in Iraq was now stable. "The storm has passed," he said. But there were 2.4 million unemployed Iraqis, he warned, and no job opportunities.

Compared with their actions during the early years of the occupation, Iraq's Sunnis seemed downright docile. A little angry, yes, and bitter and wistful, but there was no fuel for a return to the fighting, and the Sunni community lacked even a single charismatic political figure with real appeal. In

Baghdad I went to the Ghazaliya neighborhood to visit the Um Al Qura Mosque. This was once the most significant "proresistance" mosque in the city; the neo-Baathist Association of Muslim Scholars used to broadcast calls to jihad against the Americans from its loudspeakers. Now it was a massive construction site, with housing complexes, hotels, and party halls being built. Plastic trees with lights lined the stone path leading to the mosque. Sunnis who had been killed by Shiite death squads used to be brought there; now a senior sheikh was showing me the numerous certificates of appreciation that American forces had bestowed on him. He did continue to insist, however, that Sunnis were really the majority in Iraq, while two of his bodyguards complained loudly that Saddam was a better leader than Maliki. I thought, It's no surprise that some Shiites still think all Sunnis are Baathists.

I had been hoping to meet Abu Omar, the Awakening leader in Adhamiya. Just a year earlier, he and I had been drinking tea together in the main square, but he was now keeping a low profile, and he sent his son to meet me at the tea house. His son and I walked down the main street for a few minutes, then turned left into an alley with short, bullet-ridden buildings that had shops on the bottom floors. Abu Omar was standing at the bottom of a stairwell, still wearing the same brown tracksuit as last year, with a pistol holster strapped around his shoulder. We sat on a nearby bench and had sweet Iraqi tea. Abu Omar lamented the loss of his American patron, who had been protective of him. He now lived anxiously, looking over his shoulder, worried about revenge attacks from Al Qaeda or arrest from the Iraqi Security Forces. His Awakening men had been granted the most menial and demeaning jobs—they were the cleaning staff in government offices—so many had quit.

Three days before my visit to Adhamiya, Saleh al Mutlaq's local office had been bombed. "This is because the Awakening is less," Abu Omar told me; it was not able to control the street. He recommended I visit Adhamiya's Kam neighborhood but explained it was too dangerous for him to go there with me. In Kam I found an entire building taken over by squatters. The displaced families had been assigned apartments by members of the resistance and Awakening.

One woman, called Kifah Hadi Majid, had been expelled from Haifa Street by the Mahdi Army after they killed her son three years earlier. Her son Mutlab, who wore an Iraqi army uniform, was in the local Awakening group. A gang had killed his wife for jewelry. "The Awakening were given jobs with the Baghdad sanitation, and we fought the terrorists," he said. "It was better before. We controlled the street. Nobody could talk to us—not the army, nobody. We communicated directly with the Americans. Now nobody respects us, and payment is a problem." They hadn't been paid in fifty-eight days.

I told an Iraqi army intelligence officer that Awakening men were complaining about the lousy jobs they were given. "What education do the Awakening men have?" he asked. "If you don't have an education, of course you will be a cleaner." He had arrested three Awakening men whom the army had warrants against for working with Al Qaeda. He didn't think Abu Omar was a bad man, he told me, just corrupt.

In Washash Abu Karar was still in charge of the tribal council. But one of its members, Sheikh Amer Asaedi, had fled the area after someone blew up his car. I met up again with Abu Karar's cousins Hassan and Fadhil Abdel Karim, who helped lead the intifada against the Mahdi Army in Washash. They told me their nemesis, Ihab al-Tawil, had recently been released from prison. A few months before I met them, their brother Ali was shot and killed in his home nearby, his wife wounded. Ali's killers came around 7 p.m. and announced, "We are the Mahdi Army!" The children, who saw their parents shot in front of them, were still in shock.

"We became victims," Hassan told me. "We get threatening calls warning us we will be killed." I asked him why he didn't leave. "If we leave, then the whole neighborhood will leave," he said. "We cleaned the mosques that militias used, we made Sunnis pray together with Shiites. Now I can't go out. I stay home in my brother's house in the back room."

Friday prayers were less important, no longer a symbol of defiance. How could Sadrists defy the state when they were represented so well in ministries and Parliament? How could they be anti-establishment when they were part of the establishment? Friday prayers at the main Sadrist office in Sadr City were tamer than I had ever seen; the only hint of politics was a prayer for the release of prisoners. In Ur I visited the Mustafa Husseiniya, once a Mahdi Army hub. "People don't come here anymore," said the young man who guarded it. "They are scared since all the arrests." Abul Hassan, the Mustafa Husseiniya's former caretaker, who had been my guide in the area, was still in prison, and his assistant Haidar had absconded. Sheikh Safaa, its former Imam, was still safe in Qom, Iran.

In Amriya I visited Um Omar's NGO again. Several days earlier Sheikh Muhamad, of the nearby Hassanein Mosque—with whom Lieut. Col. Gian Gentile claimed he had worked closely—had been killed. "He was our friend," she told me. "The killers were teenagers." Sheikh Hussein of the Maluki Mosque and his old friend Sheikh Walid of the Tikriti Mosque had absconded, fearing both the government and Al Qaeda. Thirty-five Sunni sheikhs had been killed in Baghdad in the past month. "Al Qaeda is killing all the sheikhs who stood against them," she said. Meanwhile, Sheikh Khalid of the Amriya Council—who was seen by both Gentile and his successor, Lieut. Col. Dale Kuehl, as a decisive figure in defeating Al Qaeda in the area—had been jailed in October of 2009. He was accused of terrorism, a deliberately vague charge, but he was said to have had a role in bombings against Shiite areas in 2006. He was also alleged to have belonged to the Islamic Army of Iraq.

Most local Awakening leaders were either dead or arrested, Um Omar said, and the Awakening was now very weak. Abul Abed's successor, Muhamad, had survived several assassination attempts. "The Awakening project was a lie, an American lie," she said. "They said, 'Come in, throw your weapons, join the Awakening, fight Al Qaeda,' to discover the identity of the resistance." The Americans came around now only when there was an arrest to be made.

Six days before my visit, all of Amriya had been closed off as American and Iraqi Special Forces raided the area. Three local children were kidnapped for ransom. There were also assassinations with silencers. Um Omar's brother-in-law had been killed in 2009; he had been head of the Amriya Neighborhood Advisory Council.

Sheikh Khalid was a bad man, Um Omar insisted; he used to provide the *fatwas* for Abul Abed to kill people, and he had his own court for killing people. Sheikh Walid was like Sheikh Khalid too. But Sheikh Hussein was good, she said; he never killed people.

"In the time of displacement," as she called it, five thousand families fled to Amriya, while 1,800 families fled from Amriya. Since violence had subsided, 559 families had returned. But ten months earlier the returning Iraqis had stopped coming because of intimidation. In January a bomb was placed under one Shiite returnee's car. Most returnees were Shiites, but only about one-third of them returned to stay. The rest sold their homes.

Al Qaeda men in Abu Ghraib had recently threatened Um Omar's local office there, accusing it of being a "Jewish organization." Um Omar was forced to close her local school as well as her vocational training for women in tailoring. A year earlier she had gone to Abu Ghraib with her husband and some engineers. She called the resistance and told them she was coming, but as soon as she arrived armed men with masks put guns to their heads. She started shouting at them angrily, "I'm Um Omar!" and her husband told her to relax. They were taken to a destroyed house in a remote area, separated, and interrogated. She was accused of being Shiite. The men from the resistance made phone calls and then released the couple once they established their identity and apologized to the mayor.

Um Omar still had 225 needy children in her school, and she also ran a successful program finding husbands for the many widows while continuing to assist IDPs. Amriya was now so crowded that displaced families would share houses. Government schools had more than sixty children in each class. I met Um Ala, who was displaced from the Jihad district. Um Omar had found a widow to marry one of Um Ala's sons. Her family fled to Amriya with three others, and now they shared a house. Um Ala's husband was "killed in the sectarianism," she told me, and her sister was also a widow. They had owned their house in Jihad but were too scared to go back. Now a Shiite family lived in it and paid a nominal rent. In Amriya one of her sons and a nephew had been killed by Al Qaeda. "Things can't go back to how they were before," her son said about Iraq. "There was blood, vengeance." They heard a Sunni from the Mashhadani tribe was killed after he tried to return to Hurriya. "Every Sunni who returns to a Shiite area and gets killed," her son said, "they say he was a terrorist or Baathist." I asked if the relations between Sunnis and Shiites could ever go back to the way they were. "Impossible," they all said. "Every displaced person says it's impossible," Um Omar said with disapproval. "I don't think it's impossible."

After listening to thousands of traumatized Iraqis, I had become inured to the stories of heartbreak that I had heard. But when Um Omar took me to Amriya's squatter settlement, on a sandy lot on the outskirts of the neighborhood, it was as if I was twenty-five years old again and taking my first footsteps in Iraq.

Behind the squatter settlement, a large wall divided Amriya from an American military base. Guard posts with tinted windows and rotating sensors towered above the shacks. Most of the squatter families here were from Amil, and as we explored the settlement Um Omar was visibly uncomfortable and warned me not to speak English. She worried about Al Qaeda supporters among the displaced who came in, she said, and tricked poor people who wanted to be mujahideen. Sixty-eight families lived in makeshift shacks, and in one of them I found a middle-aged woman sitting alone in a cold room, bare except for a mattress Um Omar had provided. She had rented a home with her daughters in the Amil district. "When the Sunni and Shiite started," she said, Shiite militiamen told her to leave or they would take her daughters. She started crying as she told me this, and I was suddenly reminded of my mother, whom she resembled, and I got tearful. As I left, I tried to fix the corrugated iron shield that was protecting her hovel from the cold, howling wind, but the wind kept knocking it down.

"THE SITUATION CANNOT go back to how it was," said Captain Salim, the Iraqi army intelligence officer I had known in Washash. "We have a strong government; you can use the law." I had joined him and his Sunni lieutenant for lunch at their base in Baghdad—a Saddam-era palace in Adhamiya. Both men insisted that the era of sectarian division within the armed forces and the police was over. "The army was not built on a sectarian basis," the captain said. "It was built by the Americans to serve Iraqis, and it was strong in the fight against Al Qaeda and against the Mahdi Army."

The Mahdi Army was finished now, Salim continued, though it was still killing Iraqi army officers in a campaign of targeted assassinations; more than five officers who had taken part in the operation to crush the Mahdi Army in Sadr City had been killed in Baghdad in the past two months. In the past, they said, armed groups could easily attack police and army checkpoints; they had the firepower and the quiet support of the civilian population. "Before people would say that they didn't see anything after an attack," the Sunni lieutenant said. "Now they call us before anything happens." Anonymous tips, he added, were leading to numerous arrests. "We can't work without the people's help, and the calls help a lot."

Salim told me that he had detained "bad" Awakening leaders and that he was waiting until after the elections to arrest even more, in order to avoid any destabilizing effects. His main challenge was obtaining arrest warrants. "The judge asks for more evidence," he said. "The prisons are full of innocent people, so they want more evidence. They don't want random arrests like in the past." Though Salim had once feared his police counterparts for their associations with Shiite militias, now, he said, the police were good, and Iraqi Security Forces were continuing to arrest Mahdi Army men.

Neither man thought it possible that the civil war could resume. "The people understand now," Salim said. "Before Shiites loved the Mahdi Army, but the Mahdi Army worked for its own interests, for the interests of Iran. The Sunnis supported Al Qaeda because they didn't trust the government, but then the Awakenings were established." In the army, they said, most officers supported Maliki or the secular former Baathist Ayad Allawi—and Salim said he worried only about the Shiite Alliance leader, former Prime Minister Ibrahim al-Jaafari, whom many blamed for the intensification of the civil war that occurred under his watch. "Only he can bring sectarianism back," Salim said.

Salim was confident the Americans would not leave Iraq because of their conflict with Iran and because of their continued support and training of the Iraqi army. Although the Americans had saved the Iraqi Security Forces from humiliation during the battles with Shiite militias in 2008, "Now we have engineers, intelligence, armor, 120-millimeter mortars, helicopters, good logistics," he boasted.

I asked if the army was stronger now than it was before the overthrow of Saddam. As a fighting force it was, he said, "but before, when you fought, you had trust that the government had your back. Now, you don't know. If Sadrists win the elections, they will find a way to fire us. The army has no relation with the government. We weren't Saddam's army either."

Ironically, for all Salim's talk about the improving security situation and the strength of the state, like many of his colleagues, he had moved his family to Suleimaniya, a Kurdish city in the north, for safekeeping. The Iraqi Security Forces were more confident and less sectarian, it seemed, but still vulnerable. Having their wives up north also freed the men to attend parties with liquor and prostitutes, called *gaada*.

After lunch Salim invited me to join him for shooting practice—which I did. He also invited me to join him and other officers for a *gaada*—which I did not.

We descended to their shooting range by the river. Saddam's initials were etched in the tiles on the walls. Some of his men were shooting fish in the river with shotguns. I observed that Salim had lost weight since I had last seen him. He smiled and told me that he had stopped eating rice and started running. Salim gave me his American M4, which had a laser scope. I went through several magazines firing it.

In Diyala, a majority-Sunni province northeast of Baghdad, I met with Dhari Muhamad Abed, head of the government's Returnee Assistance Center. "Now sectarianism is completely over," he said. "Security is good." Indeed, as we drove through villages in Diyala where numerous atrocities had taken place, we found that Iraqi police and soldiers were pervasive, as was the case almost everywhere I traveled in Iraq, no matter how rural or remote. The security forces were no longer hiding their identities to avoid being killed by Al Qaeda, and they were no longer acting as death squads, though arbitrary detention of suspects remains the norm. Human rights abuses persist in Iraq, but they can no longer be described as sectarian; the state has achieved security in part by returning to its authoritarian roots.

More than thirty-seven thousand families had been displaced in Diyala— about 25 percent of the province's total population—and eighty-five villages were destroyed during the civil war. Only one-third of the refugees have returned. With the end of the civil war and the establishment of a security infrastructure, the refugee crisis remains Iraq's most serious issue. Hundreds of thousands of Iraqis are homeless and landless, squatting on government property. A senior United Nations official put the figure at half a million, calling it "an acute humanitarian crisis."

In Baquba, the provincial capital, seven hundred Sunni families are squatting at Saad camp, on the grounds of an army base on the outskirts of the city. They were driven from their homes shortly after the American invasion in 2003 by Kurdish militias eager to seize territory in the chaos that followed the fall of Saddam.

I asked one man if he would like to return to his home. "Who will protect us if we go back?" he asked. The police regularly raided their camp, arresting men and telling the people they would have to leave. "Where will we go?" one old man asked me.

Similar scenes can be found across the country. In the Abu Dshir district of Baghdad, an immense and sprawling squatter camp houses thousands of Shiites who fled rural areas around the capital; they live in tents and makeshift shelters built from scrap metal and mud. The enormous Sadrein camp, in Baghdad's Sadr City, contains more than 1,500 families, who live on a rubbish dump with the choking stench of sewage clotting the air. Most of the men I met were unemployed. Children played in mountains of rubbish. Like most poor Iraqis, the squatters depended on the state rations, known as the Public Distribution

System, for survival. "If they decide to remove the squatters, there will be an uprising and chaos," said the leader of one compound in Hurriya where hundreds of families were living. "No one can remove the squatters," Captain Salim told me. "We have to solve the problem first, give them land. The government only builds housing for its workers, not the poor citizens."

SUNNIS LARGELY did not take part in the January 2005 parliamentary elections. They voted in the October 2005 constitutional referendum but resoundingly opposed the majority's support for the Constitution. The December 2005 parliamentary elections enshrined the new sectarian order and empowered a Shiite-dominated government, leading to the civil war.

But the January 2009 provincial election results showed that Iraqis were tiring of the overtly sectarian parties: they repudiated incumbents throughout the country, punishing them for their failure to perform. The results signaled that the civil war was over. People felt secure enough to look for new representatives and to begin to demand the provision of services and proper governance. The January 2009 votes by Arab and other non-Kurdish Iraqis were in favor of a strong centralized government that was not openly sectarian. In 2009 explicitly sectarian and religious parties were rejected, but Shiites still voted for Shiite parties and Sunnis voted for Sunni parties, and it seemed Iraq's elections had crystallized internal differences, entrenching sectarianism.

Between August 2009 and January 2010 Baghdad suffered four major coordinated terrorist attacks. The August 2009 bombings were spectacular and devastating. At the foreign ministry three hundred people were killed or wounded from a local staff of five hundred. Maliki blamed Syria and created a diplomatic scandal. Iran offered to intervene and act as intermediary, but Iraq chose Turkey as the intermediary instead. The Iraqi government failed to convince anybody that Syria had played a role, but the effort was seen as an example of the government strategy of deliberately picking fights with neighbors. Despite these violent attacks, the political arena was the main front for disputes. And despite the sectarian competition for power, there were other divides and cross-sectarian alliances, especially in Parliament.

Maliki, for instance, had a particularly acrimonious relationship with the Parliament, which was the strongest one in Iraqi history, able to check the power of the executive. In 2009 Parliament charged Abdul Falah al-Sudani, the trade minister, who came from Maliki's Dawa Party, with corruption. The Integrity Committee subjected him to fierce questioning, which was broadcast on television. Interestingly, the head of the Integrity Committee was from the Shiite Fadhila Party, which showed that politics in Iraq didn't necessarily rotate on a Shiite-Sunni axis. Parliament also cut funding for Maliki's Tribal Support Councils.

Maliki's Dawa was still an elitist party without grassroots support and with no ability to mobilize the street. Despite relative improvements in security, Maliki had failed to deliver notable improvements in services. In both the 2009 and 2010 elections, Iran tried and failed to unite Maliki with the Sadrists and the Supreme Council, but Maliki spurned them because with them he had no guarantee of occupying the prime minister's position. Maliki tried and failed to reach a nonsectarian alliance with Allawi and Mutlaq in the months leading up to the 2010 elections.

The Supreme Council included more women on its list, even unveiled ones. The parties were forced to mature; even the sectarian ones turned to technocrats as candidates. They were responding to pressure from the 2009 elections, when sect and religion were discredited as sufficient to win elections.

In 2008 a new de-Baathification law was passed—this time by the Iraqis—and a new commission was supposed to be established, with new staff and new rules. But this never happened, and the same people who were appointed by Paul Bremer's CPA in 2003 remained in control—including the director, Ali al-Lami (whose origins were exposed in Chapter Two), and the postwar Sadrists from Ur, who allied with the ubiquitous chairman of the committee, Ahmad Chalabi.

The de-Baathification Committee, now renamed the Accountability and Justice Commission, announced in January 2010 that it was banning 511 candidates from the elections for being former Baathists. The Independent High Electoral Commission approved the decision, as did Maliki. Curiously, Accountability and Justice Commission leaders such as Lami and Chalabi were candidates in the March elections as well. The timing made it clear that the committee was politicized, as did the massive list of candidates who were banned.

While many of the banned candidates were secular Shiites, the best known were Sunnis, and it was the nonsectarian parties that suffered the most from the decision. Candidates with a Sunni base were especially targeted, regardless of whether they were Sunni or Shiite. In Iraq secular Arab nationalism is often wrongly identified by sectarian Shiites to be Sunni and Baathist. The ban was also a great way for the weakened religious Shiite parties to eliminate their rivals. Mutlaq was the most prominent victim, but even Abdel Qader al-Obeidi, the defense minister and an ally of Maliki who was running on his list, was targeted.

Gen. Ray Odierno, the American commander in Iraq, as well as Christopher Hill, the American ambassador, played on Iraqi fears by accusing Lami and Chalabi of working on behalf of Iran, hoping to ruin Chalabi's long ambition of becoming prime minister. As the Americans' former anointed one, Chalabi had better access to them than any other Iraqi in 2003 and 2004, and he benefited from them more than any other politician. According to a CIA source, he certainly would have had secrets to sell. But even Chalabi was not a proxy or tool; it was possible to be a sectarian Shiite actor in Iraq without being controlled by the Iranians. Iran had pawns in Iraq but not proxies. It had groups who were poor and desperate but did not willingly do Iran's bidding. Even then the Supreme Council hated Iran. Its members remembered the humiliation of being looked down upon by Iranians for being Arabs. When they were in Iran all the Supreme Council men wanted was to get out of Iran. If the so-called pro-Iranian groups took power they would not need Iranian support. They would have access to their own resources and power. As long as the Americans were in Iraq then Iran had an existential interest in undermining American efforts. The rise of Turkey as a regional actor with influence and popularity among Arabs counterbalanced both Iran and Saudi Arabia, creating a third pole. The Turks wanted to turn the Kurdish regional government in the north into a Turkish vassal state. Meanwhile the Turkish ambassador in Baghdad was so active internally that he was called in to the foreign ministry twice for them to issue formal complaints about his meddling.

Prime Minister Maliki had cultivated an image as a nationalist with a petrostate agenda: a powerful leader spreading Iraq's oil wealth. He had even flirted with ex-Baathist Sunni candidates in the past. The de-Baathification moves by Chalabi and his allies were designed to force Maliki back into the sectarian camp. If he supported the decision, he would lose support among Sunnis and nonsectarian Shiites. But if he opposed it, he would lose support among many Shiites.

Maliki's candidate in Diyala, Muhammad Salman, explained that Maliki still had his base of Shiite voters and that he could not reach out to or defend ex-Baathists like Mutlaq at their expense, lest he lose Shiite voters. Because of this Maliki quickly backed the de-Baathification move, even though his ally Defense Minister Obeidi was on the list. With false rumors of a Baathist coup and the recent bombings, the environment was ripe for targeting opponents under the pretext of anti-Baathism. The campaign took a sectarian turn thanks to the de-Baathification crisis. Anti-Sunnism masqueraded as anti-Baathism, with gruesome posters of mass graves and different Iraqi TV stations, each controlled by a political party, showing videos of Baathist torture and executions. Former Prime Minister Jaafari warned on his posters that he would not give space for the return of the Baathists.

President Jalal Talabani condemned the ban and questioned the committee's legal existence. U.S. Vice President Joe Biden rushed to Baghdad to try to pressure the Iraqi government to resolve the crisis, with the support of the European Union and the United Nations. But the Americans had lost their leverage, as they often said starting in 2009, when Maliki grew more confident of his ability to survive without them. The appeals committee decided that there wasn't enough time before the election to review the appeals, so it postponed decisions about them until after the elections—meaning candidates who won could still be banned after the fact.

Then Maliki made the appeals committee overturn its decision to delay matters and review some of the candidates immediately. Two dozen decisions were reversed, including the one banning Obeidi but importantly not the one banning Mutlaq. The election commission then approved all this maneuvering. Allawi, in turn, threatened to boycott the elections, and Mutlaq initially called for one (though he later changed his mind, probably because he would have been ignored anyway). Meanwhile, beyond the Green Zone, candidates throughout Iraq were being intimidated and blown up, including allies of Maliki, who may have been targeted by the Mahdi Army.

Since the beginning of the Iraq War, American planners and observers had been preoccupied with the consequences of decisive singular events—from the arrest of Saddam Hussein to the battle for Falluja and the previous rounds of national and provincial elections. At each easily identifiable juncture, exaggerated claims were advanced by those in search of a turning point, whether for the better or for the worse.

The elections of March 7 were the first to be held in a formally sovereign Iraq, and they *did* represent a milestone in the country's political evolution. Maliki remained a popular candidate, supported by Iraqis for having crushed both Sunni and Shiite armed groups, but his list came a close second to Allawi's Iraqiya list, which was a surprise after his dismal performance in 2005. Even though Allawi is a Shiite, he was a secular candidate par excellence, capturing the Sunni vote and a sizable Shiite vote, signaling that many Iraqi voters were craving the secular nationalism of old. But it also signaled that the Saudi-Iranian competition in the region dominated Iraqi politics just as it did in Lebanon and even Palestine. Allawi could not have achieved his victory without the tremendous backing of Saudis, financially and in the media.

But regardless of the outcome—Maliki contested but could not overturn the vote count—the elections would not precipitate a return to the civil war. The state was too strong, and there was no longer a security vacuum. The security forces took their work seriously—perhaps too seriously. The sectarian militias had been beaten and marginalized, and the Sunnis had accepted their loss in the civil war. But in the United States, there was considerable trepidation about the election result, and suspicions of Iranian influence still clung to Maliki—an echo of the tendentious Sunni notion that an Arab cannot have a strong Shiite identity without being pro-Iranian. In the elections Maliki was the most popular individual candidate, with Allawi a distant second. Maliki wanted a coup but it would not succeed. Most Shiite parties and candidates did not want Maliki to be prime minister. The debate in Baghdad political circles is how to get rid of Maliki. But Allawi could not form a coalition. Regardless of who became prime minister, Iraq would become increasingly authoritarian. Oil revenues will not kick in for several years so there will not be an immediate improvement in services. Even when revenues reach Iraqi coffers, they will have to initially go to cover the infrastructure costs. The fact that the government cannot provide better services means it will have to become more authoritarian. It will use democratic methods and a façade to seem less authoritarian.

Maliki and his allies, after all, like many other Iraqis, were extremely nationalistic and chauvinistic. They believed Iraq was the only democracy in the region, better than its neighbors, and they zealously wanted to secure their control over a sovereign and increasingly powerful nation. Those who warned of Iranian interference in Iraq ignored Saudi, American, and other foreign involvement. And they too often assumed that Iran was a negative actor in the region that had to be countered, and that only Sunni dictatorships could do that. Indeed, having overcome its fear of Iraqi Shiites, Egypt signed a strategic agreement with Iraq. Egypt could see the shifting alliances in the region and was hedging its bets, an American intelligence official told me: "Iraq is a major opportunity. Iraq will be the number-one or -two oil producer in the world."

Some pundits, including several leading neoconservatives, had begun to argue that the United States should keep a larger number of troops in Iraq than was previously agreed—but this risked undermining America's partnership with the Iraqi government. "You want Iraq to be pro-Western and to invite you in," an American intelligence official told me. "So you build that relationship by strictly adhering to the agreement you signed."

By 2011 the Americans are expected to reduce their provincial presence to Basra, Erbil, Mosul, Diyala, and Kirkuk, with an eye on the restive fault line between Arabs and Kurds that runs from Iran to Syria. Were it not for the American presence along the so-called disputed territories between Kurdistan and the rest of Iraq, it is possible that war would have broken out already. Kirkuk has long been described as a powder keg, but of late, Nineveh province has become equally dangerous. Its governor, Atheel al-Nujaifi, campaigned in the 2009 election on a rabidly anti-Kurdish platform. Whenever he traveled into areas that the Kurds claimed were theirs, even if they were outside the jurisdiction of the Kurdish Regional Government, Kurdish security forces harassed him, even drawing their guns. As a result he traveled with a U.S. Army escort, since he was the governor and had the right to go wherever he wanted in the province, even if he was merely being provocative. In February 2010 Kurdish security forces drew guns on him and the Americans, even firing at their convoy. With American backing, the Iraqi Security Forces arrested three Kurdish men; the next day the Kurds arrested five ISF members.

The Kurds were getting jittery, realizing the Americans really were leaving. But even if the Kurdish star was fading, the Kurds were more than likely to play the kingmaker in the long process of assembling a government after the elections, and anyone forming a government would have to make concessions to them if they wanted to avoid dependence on Shiite rivals. The lack of a unified sectarian bloc in Iraq was a positive development, militating against future conflict between Sunnis and Shiites. "U.S. strategic interests are best served when Shiites of Iraq are divided," an experienced American intelligence officer explained to me.

FROM THE BEGINNING of the occupation, the U.S. government and media focused too much on elite-level politics and on events in the Green Zone, neglecting the Iraqi people, the atmosphere of the "street," neighborhoods, villages, mosques. They were too slow to recognize the growing resistance to the occupation, too slow to recognize that there was a civil war—and now, perhaps for the same reason, many were worried that there was a "new" sectarianism or a new threat of civil war. But the U.S. military was no longer on the streets and could not accurately perceive Iraq, and journalists were busy covering the elections and the de-Baathification controversy but not reporting enough from outside or even inside Baghdad. Just as they didn't understand the power of militias in the past, now they did not understand the power of the Iraqi Security Forces. Iraqis were no longer so scared of rival militias or being exterminated, and they no longer supported the religious parties so vehemently. Another thing people would have noticed, had they cared to look, was that the militias were weaker than ever. The Awakening groups were finished, so violence was very limited in scope and impact. Politicians might have been talking the sectarian talk, but Iraqis had grown very cynical.

But even though Iraq's elections may have been transparent, Iraq remained colonized by tens of thousands of American soldiers. The Status of Forces Agreement deprived Iraq of its full sovereignty. Part of it was "legally" confiscated by the continuing UN mandate, and the rest was denied by the United States. Throughout the occupation major decisions concerning the shape of Iraq had been made by the occupiers with no input or say by the Iraqis: the economic system, the political regime, the army and its loyalties, all the way to the control over airspace and the formation of all kinds of militias and tribal military groups. The effects of all this will likely linger for decades. While the Americans have mostly, if not totally, withdrawn from the population centers, no occupying army ever wants to be present in the daily lives of citizens if it can have local clients do the job. In the early twentieth century, the British had no presence in the daily lives of Iraqis until Iraqis misbehaved and had to face the wrath of the Royal Air Force. Britain colonized Iraq with fewer than four brigades, most of which were based behind the walls of Habbaniya. But in 1941 they defeated the Iraqi army and occupied the whole country with two brigades.

The presence of the U.S. Army forecloses many options for Iraqis, drawing the parameters within which they can act. There are varieties of colonialism and occupation, and they depend more on the financial interests and strategic aims of the colonizers than their wish to grant independence to their vassals. The continued American military presence in Iraq was still a constant implied threat. The Americans could stay on their bases if the Iraqis behaved, or they could emerge and kill whomever they wanted, as they once had. Moreover, Iraq was still burdened by several UN sanctions dating back to the Saddam era. It was forced to pay 5 percent of its oil revenues in reparations, mostly to the Kuwaitis. The Chapter VII resolutions denied Iraq full sovereignty and isolated it from the international financial community. In addition, with Saudi and Iranian interference and money in post-Saddam Iraq, as in Lebanon, it is impossible to have true democracy or sovereignty.

The Bush administration had tried to implement an "80 percent solution," based on the notion that if Kurds and Shiites could reach agreement, then Sunnis could be ignored. But Sunni frustration can still lead to destabilization. Sunnis might not be able to overthrow the new Shiite sectarian order, but they can still mount a limited challenge to it. According to Iraqi political scientist Ghassan Atiyyah, the Kurds, with only the mountains as their friends (to paraphrase a Kurdish proverb), were able to destabilize Iraq for eighty years. Sunni Arabs are present in much more of the country and have allies throughout the Arab world who can supply them well enough to destabilize Iraq more than the Kurds ever could. It is not only Baathists and Al Qaeda supporters who oppose the new order. There are Sunnis who see themselves as Iraqi nationalists and worry that Iraq is falling under Iranian control. They see signs of this when much of the Iraqi Kurdish and Shiite leadership goes to Iran to negotiate political deals and work out the postelection order. But Shiites and Kurds cannot reach agreement without the Sunnis. It is Sunnis who dominate the border area between Kurdistan and the rest of Iraq. And as long as the Iraqi state insists on its Shiite identity, there will be Sunnis willing to undermine it.

While violence was down even in Baghdad's worst-hit neighborhoods, and many Sunnis and Shiites strived to rebuild old friendships, Iraqi social relations were deeply wounded. I visited my friend Maher in Dora once again. He took me to the home of his old schoolmate Ra'fat Abid Alwan, a young Shiite man. Ra'fat had once owned a successful local curtain shop. In 2005 his family received a threatening letter. Then his brother was shot in the head and killed in the Dora market. Another brother was kidnapped later that year by an Interior Ministry vehicle. He was released three weeks later for a ransom of eighty thousand dollars, and the family fled to Syria. But they didn't like Syria. They'd had a nice life in Iraq and didn't want to end up working as bakers in Syria. So in August 2006 they returned to Baghdad's I'ilam neighborhood, buying a new shop for curtains.

They lived in I'ilam for a year. "Sectarianism started," Ra'fat told me. "We saw bodies on the street," so they returned to Syria again. In their absence Dr. Nabil, the local Al Qaeda boss, had taken over their home and given it to a Sunni family. The Americans discovered IEDs in the house and took it over, and then handed it over to the Iraqi army. While they were away four Shiite neighbors in Dora were beheaded. Ra'fat paid twenty-three thousand dollars to be smuggled from Syria to Turkey to Greece to Sweden in late 2007. After a year the Swedes told him Iraq was safe again and sent him home. His family returned to Iraq from Syria, and he joined them in December 2008.

In April 2009 nine houses in Dora belonging to Shiites were blown up. One belonged to Ra'fat's brother. "It's wrong to stay here, they blew up his house," he told me. "We are not comfortable emotionally," Ra'fat's mother told me. Now they were trying to sell their house and move back to I'ilam. "Most of the neighborhood is gone," Ra'fat said. "People only come back to sell homes." I asked if relations could go back to the way they were. "Impossible!" they said. Ra'fat and Maher laughed at the notion. "This was the prettiest area of Dora, people knew each other," Maher said. "We could enter each other's homes like family." I asked them how people could turn on one another like that. They blamed the Al Qaeda men who were mostly from the rural areas adjacent to Dora. "They wanted Dora for themselves," they said. "It was criminally motivated." Both Ra'fat and Maher agreed that there was still a lot of hatred.

A NEWSWEEK ISSUE in March 2010 declared U.S. victory in Iraq. But for Iraqis there was no victory. Since the occupation began in 2003, hundreds of thousands of Iraqis had been killed. Many more had been injured. There were millions of widows and orphans. Millions had fled their homes. Tens of thousands of Iraqi men had spent years in American prisons. The new Iraqi state was among the most corrupt in the world. It was often brutal. It failed to provide adequate services to its people, millions of whom were barely able to survive. Iraqis were traumatized. This upheaval did not spare Iraq's neighbors, either. Hundreds of thousands of Iraqi refugees languished in exile. Sectarianism increased in the region. Weapons, tactics, and veterans of the jihad made their way into neighboring countries. And now the American "victory" in Iraq was being imposed on the people of Afghanistan.

Seven years after the disastrous American invasion, the cruelest irony in Iraq is that, in a perverse way, the neoconservative dream of creating a moderate, democratic ally in the region to counterbalance Iran and Saudi Arabia had come to fruition. But even if violence in Iraq continues to decline and the government becomes a model of democracy, Iraq will never be a model to be emulated by its neighbors. People in the region remember, even if those in the

West have forgotten, the seven years of chaos, violence, and terror, and to them this is what Iraq symbolizes. Thanks to the wars in Iraq and Afghanistan and other failed U.S. policies in the Middle East, the U.S. had lost most of its influence on Arab people, if not the Muslim world—even if it could still exert pressure on Arab regimes. At first some Arab elites thought they could benefit from Bush and the neoconservatives, but now reformists and the elite want nothing to do with the U.S., which can only harm their credibility. Every day there are assassinations with silenced pistols and the small magnetic car bombs known as sticky bombs; every day men still disappear and secret prisons are still discovered. In Sunni villages Awakening men are being found beheaded. And although some militiamen have been absorbed into the security forces, others have turned to a life of crime, and brazen daylight robberies are common. But despite this, the worst might be over for Iraqis. On my trips to Iraq in years past, I had made a habit of scanning the walls of Baghdad neighborhoods for bits of sectarian graffiti, spray-painted slogans that were pro–Mahdi Army, pro-Saddam, anti-Shiite, or pro-insurgency. This time, however, there were almost none to be found. The exhortations to sectarian struggle had been replaced with the enthusiasms of youthful football fans: now the walls say, "Long Live Barcelona."

ACKNOWLEDGMENTS

This book would not be possible without the strong support of the New York University Center on Law and Security. I am very grateful to its generous director, Karen Greenberg, as well as Steve Holmes and David, Nicole, Jeff, Fransesca, Sarvenaz, and the rest of the family I have made there. They have given me a place to feel at home, the freedom to do my work, and the confidence of knowing I have their backing. My editor at Nation Books, Carl Bromley, was supernaturally patient with me and believed in my vision. Without him it would not have come to reality. Thanks to Mark Sorkin for his excellent copy editing and suggestions. I am also very grateful to my agent, Denise Shannon, for her enthusiasm and support.

I also acknowledge the Investigative Fund of The Nation Institute—particularly Joe Conason and Esther Kaplan—who have supported my work.

Many Iraqis welcomed me as a brother into their families. Meitham, Ali, Osama, Abbas, Hassanein, Aws, Wisam, the Hamdi family, Omar Salih, Omer Awchi, Rana al-Aiouby, and others made this book possible, and took great risks to care for me and share their lives with me. In Lebanon my close friends Mohamad Ali Nayel, Naim Assaker, Bissane el Cheikh, Amer Mohsen, Michel Samaha, and Patrick Haenni taught me all I needed to know. Thanks also to Ambassador Imad Moustapha, Toufic Alloush, Mirvat Abu Khalil, Seyid Nawaf al-Musawi, Haj Osama Hamdan, Wisam, Hamelkart Ataya, Mansour Aziz, Walid Abou Khashbee, Abdo Saad, Omar Nashabi, the brave members of Samidoun, Rami Kanan, Sharif Bibi, and Najat Sharafeddine.

Jon Sawyer and Nathalie Applewhite of the Pulitzer Center on Crisis Reporting supported my work in Afghanistan. Deb Chasman and Josh Cohen at the *Boston Review* gave me the opportunity and the space to write important chapter-length articles. Likewise, Monika Bauerlein of *Mother Jones*. Betsy Reed gave this manuscript a vigorous read, which I thank her for. I owe a big debt to Jonathan Shainin, my good friend who runs the best weekend review section in the English language at the *National* in Abu Dhabi.

Ghaith Abdul Ahad, Hannah Allam, Tom Bigley, Leila Fadel, Seymour Hersh, Bob Bateman, and Andrew Exum are friends and colleagues who helped, advised, challenged, and inspired me. In Afghanistan, Shahir and

Melek gave me friendship, help, and also saved my life. Thanks to Qais for helping out with that too. Thanks to Aziz Hakimi, Aners Fange, Andrew Wilder and Peter Jouvenal, Fazel Rabie Haqbeen, Mullah Tariq Osman, Josh Foust, Professor Tom Johnson, Tom Stanworth, John Moore, Matt Bruggmann, Steve Clemons, As'ad Abu Khalil, Kristele Younes, Peter Bergen, Elizabeth Campbell, Joel Charney, Scott Armstrong, the Theros family, Ahmad, Marika, Nick, the Zivkovic family, the Lombardi family, and my editor at *Rolling Stone*, Eric Bates.

Numerous Iraqis, Lebanese, Egyptians, Syrians, Palestinians and Jordanians, as well as American soldiers, officers, and officials, trusted me with their knowledge and experience anonymously—I thank them all.

Lastly, to my parents, my brothers, my wife, Tiffany, and Dakota (for not totally destroying my laptop while I wrote this book), I love you and I thank you.

A NOTE ON SOURCES

In writing this book I relied on very few secondary sources; the bulk of it is based on the seven years I have spent reporting in the Muslim world, from Somalia to Afghanistan. I cannot thank the many hundreds of people who welcomed me, helped me, educated me, and shared pieces of their lives with me, but it is thanks to their trust and generosity that this book is possible. I tried to avoid senior officials on any side to avoid propaganda and simplistic generalizations, and instead I tried to find out what was really transpiring myself. I was helped by local and international academics, journalists, historians, soldiers, policemen, militiamen, and aid workers. My colleagues at the Warlord Loop listserv were very helpful and stimulating. When it comes to secondary sources, I did, however, learn a lot from *Military Review* and the *Small Wars Journal,* which informed my thinking for the chapters on the surge in Iraq and Afghanistan. Articles in McClatchy's, the *Washington Post,* and even some in the *New York Times* were also important. The reports of the International Crisis Group are essential for background, as are the articles in the *Middle East Research and Information Project* (merip.org) and the *Middle East Journal.*

INDEX

Abbas Mosque, 292

Abbas (son of Ali), tomb of, 9

Abdel Mahdi, Adil, 97, 99

Abdillah, Mullah, 439, 445, 446, 447, 448, 457, 459, 460

Abdul-Ahad, Ghaith, 311–312, 325, 326

Abdullah, King (of Jordan), 112, 126, 129, 145, 148, 188, 383, 384

Abed, Abul, 281, 296–297, 303–304, 305, 306–308, 309–310, 311–314, 315, 321–329, 352, 537, 545

Abed, Dhari Muhamad, 548

Abizaid, John, 222, 223, 291, 294

Ablawi, Salih (Abu Jaafar), 194

al-Absi, Shaker, 196, 197, 198, 200, 201, 202, 203, 204, 205, 206, 208, 209, 213, 432, 434

Abu Abdallah. See bin Laden, Osama

Abu Anas, 191–192, 194–196

Abu Bakr, 177

Abu Bilal, 307–308

Abu Dira, 103–104

Abu Dshir, 244, 245, 251, 252, 255, 266, 273, 274, 275, 277–278, 523, 526, 548

Abu Ghraib prison, 3–4, 24, 59, 70, 93, 105, 107, 316, 419

Abu Hanifa, 33

Abu Hanifa Mosque, 33, 34, 37, 70, 95–96, 97, 102, 530

Abu Hatem (Karim Mahud al-Muhammadawi), 66, 67

Abu Hudheifa (Marwarn Yassin), 424–425

Abu Hureira, 201, 209, 432

Abu Jaafar (Salih Ablawi), 194

Abu Jaafar (Sheikh Ali), 258, 261, 267, 273, 286

Abu Jaber, 203, 205–206

Abu Karar, 368–369, 536, 544

Abu Khalel family, 48

Abu Khalid, 202

Abu Khalil, As'ad, 391, 393

Abu Lahab, 145

Abu Laith, 201

Abu Midyan, 197, 201

Abu Muhamad / Abu Shahid (Mustafa Ramadan), 418–419, 420

Abu Muhamad (in Jordan), 138–139

Abu Muhammad, Sheikh, 252

Abu Musa, 197, 202

Abu Muthana, 530

Abu Nidal Organization, 209, 210

Abu Obeida (Abdallah Khalaq), 425

Abu Omar (Firas Yamin), 425

Abu Omar (Khalil Ibrahim), 529–530, 531, 543, 544

Abu Qutaiba, 131

Abu Risha, Ahmad, 250, 286–287

Abu Risha, Sheikh Sattar, 234, 250, 261, 286, 313, 322, 372

Abu Rumman, Mohammad, 147–148

Abu Teiba, 324

Abu Yasser, 197, 198, 199, 201, 202–203, 204, 206, 207

Accountability and Justice Commission, 550

Adesnik, Ariel David, 501

al-Adhami, Sheikh Muayad, 36

Adhamiya, 62, 70, 75, 76, 84, 95–96, 111, 174, 326, 339, 530, 543

al-Adib, Ali, 99

Adnan, Adil, 523

Afghan Ministry of Interior, 463, 465, 478, 481, 484

Afghan Ministry of Justice, 479

Afghan National Army (ANA), 446, 467, 482, 490

Afghan National Civil Order Police (ANCOP), 471–472, 480–489, 490, 514

Afghan National Directorate of Security (NDS), 473, 476

Afghan National Police (ANP), 465–466, 471, 488, 489–490, 502, 503, 509

Afghan National Security Forces (ANSF), 471, 481, 482, 483

Afghan Regional Security Integration Command, 474, 491

Afghanistan, 25, 105, 128, 140, 190, 193
  assumptions about, 498
  attacks on NGOs in, 462–463
  civilian death toll, 471
  civilian surge in, call for, 494, 497
  COIN theorists' failure to question the U.S. invasion of, 227
  context of, in-depth knowledge of, lack of, 518
  and defensive jihad, 131, 133, 140
  drug trade in, 471, 475, 476, 478, 479
  failure of U.S. COIN operations in, 513–514
  fighting picking up in, 218
  jihadis in, 131, 134, 136, 137, 139
  loss of U.S. influence due to war in, 556
  new U.S. strategy for, 470
  oppression in,
    continuation of, by U.S. military, 515–516, 517–518

  population of,
    characteristics of, 466, 467
  prisons in, 456–457, 512
  Rumsfeld's view of U.S. troops in, 19
  situation in, and the resurgence of U.S. troops, aspects of, 439–518
  Soviet invasion and occupation of, 124, 125, 131, 146, 440, 468, 469, 474, 492, 500, 510, 515
  and the surge in Iraq, 225
  U.S. initial invasion of, 143
  withdrawal of Soviets from, American neglect following, 441

Aflaq, Michel, 90

Ahad, Ghaith Abdul, 151

al-Ahdab, Musbah, 406, 411, 413, 433–434

Ahmadinejad, Mahmoud, 436

al-Ajami, Mukhtar Shaaban, 388–389

Akef, Mahdi, 169

Akhundzada, Sher Muhamad (SMA), 475, 476, 477

Akkawi, Khalil, 386, 416

Al Akhbar newspaper, 393

Al Aqsa Mosque, 213

Al Arab al-Yawm newspaper, 176

Al Arabiya television, 95

Al Ashur al-Hurm period, 116

Al Azhar University, 131

Al Basa'ir newspaper, 95

Al Furat television, 70, 72, 338

Al Hawza newspaper, 51, 90

Al Hayat newspaper, 322

Al Iraqiya television, 70

Al I'tisam newspaper, 95

Al Jazeera television, 42, 177, 403, 412, 458, 460

Al Manar television, 191, 404

Al Mustafa Mosque, 81

Al Mutaibeen alliance, 111

Al Qaeda, 30, 35, 57, 58, 71, 98, 108, 109, 131, 156, 174, 177, 178, 190, 199, 255, 384, 391, 423, 436, 501
  accusation of Syria helping, 207, 208
  and Afghanistan, 143, 441, 497, 498
  and Fatah al-Islam, 201, 204, 211, 383–384
  groups/people inspired by, 23, 25, 57, 110, 414–415, 533
  and Lebanon, 187, 200, 389, 391, 394, 416, 417, 422, 426, 434
  major reason for the growth of, 218
  new U.S. strategy for targeting, 470, 496
  sources of funding, 196
  worldview of, 470
  Zarqawi's rejection of, 139, 143
  See also Tawhid and Jihad group

Al Qaeda in Iraq (AQI), 27, 57, 80, 103, 112, 116, 125, 128–129, 144, 170, 172, 190, 194, 207, 221, 231, 238, 256, 285, 292, 301, 309, 323, 353, 354, 355, 415, 523, 535, 543, 544, 553
  in Amriya, 294, 302, 303, 309, 312, 313, 315, 322, 323
  and the Awakening groups, 258, 261, 287, 288, 292–293, 303, 322,

328, 528, 529, 530, 532, 543

and the banks of the Tigris River, 526, 541

believed to be lying dormant, 525

creation of, 498

and implementation of COIN, 242, 243, 244, 248

initial Sunni support for, 390, 547

jihad conditions breached by, 323–324

and Lebanon, 181, 198, 202, 433

local resistance against, 225–226, 232, 233–234, 237, 291, 304, 305, 321–322, 324–325, 527

and the Mahdi Army, 231, 239, 240, 245, 247, 249, 250, 259, 260, 276, 294–295, 342, 350, 351, 539

remnants of, targeting, 273, 542

Sunni opponents of, 170, 171, 368

and the surge, 241, 251, 263, 266, 267, 277, 285, 295, 333, 334, 357, 358

and tribal leaders, 279, 544

Al Qaeda paradigm, 182

Al Qaqa Battalions, 58

Al Rai newspaper, 172

Al Rusufa prison, 9

Al Sabah newspaper, 343

Al Sahwa (the Awakening), 226

See also Awakening program/groups; Sons of Iraq (SOI)

Al Sajjad Mosque, 70–71

Al Tanf refugee camp, 153, 156, 157, 158

Al Wathba (The Leap) movement, 374

Al Zawra TV, 167, 175, 176, 177, 178

Alawites, 20, 102, 105, 182, 202, 385, 388, 411, 413, 415, 416, 431, 432

Algeria, 227

Ali (cousin and son-in-law of the Prophet Muhammad), 8, 9, 42, 46, 88, 89, 102, 103, 153, 437

Ali, Jamal Jaafir Mohammed (Abu Mahdi al-Muhandes), 60

Allawi, Ayad, 31, 64, 66, 97, 110, 119, 547, 550, 552

Allush, Mustafa, 205

al-Alousi, Mithal, 22

Amal Movement, 379, 380–381, 390, 396, 397, 398, 401, 402–403, 404, 407

Amawi, Mohammad Zaki, 123

America/Americans. *See* United States

American Enterprise Institute, 17

American proxies, 435

Amir, General Abdul, 260

al-Amiri, Hadi, 59, 62

al-Amli, Abu Khalid, 197, 199

Amman, 105, 108, 123, 125, 130, 131, 136, 138, 146, 169, 170, 223

Amriya, 45–49, 64, 72, 88, 232, 233, 235, 246, 289–335, 352, 355, 356, 537–538, 544, 545–546

Amriya Freedom Fighters (AFF). *See* Fursan (Amriya Freedom Fighters/Thurwar)

Anbar Awakening, 226, 234, 289, 293, 313, 356

Anbar province, 16, 23, 32, 47, 63–64, 66, 73, 80, 105, 107, 108, 109, 118,

153, 154, 169, 170, 171, 190, 225, 233, 295, 419

See also Falluja

Annadawi, Muhamad Fawad Latufi, 96

Ansar al-Islam group, 110, 143, 144

Ansar al-Sunna group, 109, 110, 111, 138, 144, 280, 526

Ansar al-Tawhid wa al-Sunna group, 111

al-Ansari, Sheikh Haitham, 57, 65, 66–67, 68, 77, 82

Anti-Saddam militias, Iranian-sponsored, 9

See also Shiite militias

Aoun, Michel, 187, 217, 438

Arab Current, 398

Arab League, 94, 435

Arab University of Beirut, 381

Arabiya television, 412

Arabsat network, 176

Arafat, Yasser, 190, 206

al-Araji, Baha, 236, 361

al-Araji, Hazim, 68

Arbaeen ceremonies, 41–42

al-Aridi, Ghazi, 216

Armed Forces Journal, 332, 333, 334

Army of Muhammad, 58

Army of the Mujahideen, 58, 248, 261, 287, 526

Ash Sharq radio, 403

Ashura holiday, 41, 42, 48, 151, 153, 361, 362, 534

Asia Foundation, 517

al-Askari, Sami, 29

Askari Shrine, 70, 72

See also Samarra shrine attack

al-Assad, Bashar, 52, 388

al-Assad, Hafiz, 184, 394

Association of Free Prisoners, 5–6

Association of Muslim
Scholars, 37, 38, 41, 42,
52, 57, 58, 62, 64, 72,
86, 87, 95, 102, 112,
133, 163, 169, 390, 530,
543
Assumptions, underlying,
about Iraq and
Afghanistan, 497–498
al-Aswad, Muhamad, 413
Atiyyah, Ghassan, 554
Australia, 473
Awakening Council, 250,
261, 286
Awakening phenomenon,
226, 289, 292, 293
Awakening
program/groups, 226,
228, 230, 234, 237, 242,
243, 247, 250, 252, 254,
257, 258–259, 260, 261,
266, 268, 271, 275, 279,
280, 281, 283, 284, 285–
286, 288, 303, 307, 308,
315, 317, 318, 319, 322,
325, 326–327, 328, 340,
344, 352, 364, 368, 369,
372, 524, 527, 528–531,
537, 540, 540–541, 541–
542, 543, 545, 547, 552,
556
See also Iraqi Security
Volunteers (ISVs); Sons
of Iraq (SOI)
al-Awamli family, 145
al-Awar, Hossam, 353
Ayn al-Hilweh refugee camp,
190–196, 197, 200, 201,
204, 211, 420, 432–433
Azzam, Abdallah, 130–131,
133, 136, 139, 140, 145
Azzam, Hudheifa, 131–134,
140, 143, 145

Baath Party/Baathists, 7, 15,
17, 18–19, 28, 30, 40,
55–56, 61, 66, 76, 110,

133, 162, 163, 169, 172,
173, 258, 265, 289, 410,
543, 550, 551
See also Hussein, Saddam
Bab al-Tabbaneh area, 384–
387, 392, 411, 412–413,
416, 430–431
Badr Brigade, 22, 32, 36, 41,
48, 59, 60, 62, 63, 65,
69, 108, 157, 166, 250,
257, 262, 266, 267, 342,
354, 370
Badr Organization (formerly
the Badr Brigade), 90,
95, 363
Baghdad, 18, 30, 35, 41, 42,
49, 72, 109–110, 111,
159–160, 165
American devolving their
authority in, 109
battle for, 12, 228, 231, 367
as a city of decay, 5, 9–15
concentration of attacks
against the coalition in,
80
continued escalation of
violence in, 101–102
economic center of, 113
improved security in,
reason for, 335
main no-go zone of, 86
major coordinated
terrorist attacks in, 549
media coverage of inside
and outside of, issue
with, 554
number of refugees from,
162
sectarian cleansing in, 32,
63, 65, 159, 164, 528
and the shifts in
sectarianism, 27, 28
six years after the fall of,
changes that were
apparent, 525–556

surge efforts in and
around, aspects of the,
221–288
*See also specific districts,
neighborhoods, and sites*
Baghdad Brigade, 275
Baghdad International
Airport, 291
Baghdad Operation Center
(BOC), 228, 366, 524
Baghdad Security Plan, 227
Baghdad TV station, 70
al-Baghdadi, Abu Omar, 321
al-Baghdadi, Ayatollah Ali,
92
Baghdadiya television, 375
Bahrain, 105, 436, 437
Bakri, Nada, 401
Balkans, 30
al-Banna, Hassan, 125, 130
Baquba, 546
Barack, Obama, 25, 469, 470,
479, 496
Baradar, Mullah, 439, 459
Baram, Amatzia, 178
al-Barrak, Abdul Rahman
bin Nasser, 112
Barudi, Sheikh Bilal, 199,
382, 391, 432, 434
Barzani, Massoud, 97, 175,
176
Basair (The Mind's Eye)
newspaper, 52
Basra, 27, 35, 166, 364–365,
370–371, 372–373, 553
Batal al-Tahrir (Heroes of
Liberation) section, 7
al-Bawi, Ghassan Adnan, 69–
70
Bayat al-Imam (Oath of
Loyalty to the Leader),
140, 141, 146
Bazzaz, Hassan, 174–175
Bedawi refugee camp, 194,
196, 197, 200, 211, 214,
216

Beirut, 159, 188, 195, 196, 197, 209, 373–374, 384–387, 395, 396–397, 401–405, 415, 429, 433, 434–435
See also specific districts and neighborhoods
Beirut International Airport, 400
al-Beit, Ahl, 125
Beri, Nabih, 402
al-Berjawi, Shaqer, 398
"Best Practices in Counterinsurgency" (Sepp), 499
Biden, Joe, 551
bin Aqil, Muslim, 90
bin Jabrin, Sheikh Abdallah, 437
bin Laden, Osama, 35, 45, 57, 126, 131, 134, 138, 139, 143, 144, 146, 147, 163, 198, 381, 422, 433, 436, 451, 454
See also Al Qaeda
bin Sultan, Bandar, 395
Bishara, Azmi, 22
Black September (Palestinian uprising), 125, 130–131, 213
Blair, Tony, 139, 476
Bodine, Barbara, 18
al-Bolani, Jawad, 66, 67, 227, 364
Bonn conference, 441, 464, 466
Bosnia, 19, 131, 132, 193, 513
Bremer, Paul, 15, 17, 18–19, 20, 30, 31, 38, 173, 175, 225, 240, 249, 550
Britain, 97, 106, 109, 125, 139, 175, 227, 247, 361, 364, 372, 374, 501, 525, 554
and Afghanistan, 463–464, 472, 473, 476, 477–478,

479, 497, 502–503, 504, 506, 512, 514
and Basra, 370–371, 373
British colonizers, 20
British Mandate authority, 28
Brookings Institution, 17
Brown, Gordon, 477
Buratha Mosque, 94–95
Burj al-Barajneh refugee camps, 196, 197, 200, 216
al-Burqawi, Isam Taher al-Oteibbi, 140
Bush administration, 18, 25, 64–65, 103, 143, 184, 238, 394, 406, 435, 436, 442, 469, 470, 498, 555
Bush, George W., 15, 19, 85, 119, 123, 132, 177, 222, 223, 224, 230, 232, 234, 275, 348, 362, 365, 373–374, 375, 376, 442, 557

Cairo, 159, 164–169
Campbell, John, 228, 229
Canada, 473, 497
Carter, Phil, 69–70
Casey, George, 100, 222, 223, 226–227, 228, 229, 230, 290, 294, 493
Celebrity pundits, 17
Center for New American Security (CNAS), 217, 229, 466
Center for Strategic International Studies, 17
Central Command, 469
Chadarchi, Naseer, 52
Chalabi, Ahmad, 22, 42, 61–62, 66, 67, 345, 527, 550
Chamberlin, Robert, 225
Charge of the Knights campaign, 364, 368, 369, 371, 372, 533, 534, 536
Chechnya, 131, 132, 193, 449

Chesney, Ed, 344–345
Chiarelli, General, 291
Children
art from Palestinan, 216
fear in, 164, 317, 319, 517–518
fights between Sunni and Shiite, 169
and IEDs, 524
as orphans, 315, 316
view of Americans, 278
Christian Lebanese Forces, 403
Christian militias, 185, 199, 215, 216–217
Christians, 115, 144, 194
in Baghdad areas, 110, 165
in Lebanon, 183, 186, 189, 195, 373–374, 380, 381, 387, 390, 391, 398, 403, 409, 419, 426, 438
relocation of, 159, 162, 164
as the third target of AQI, 323
City of Mosques, 16
See also Falluja
City of Peace cemetery, 4, 88
Civilian Police Assistance Training Team (CPATT), 60
Clerics, rise of, 32–38
CNN, 442
Coalition Press Information Center, 80
Coalition Provisional Authority (CPA). *See* Office of the Coalition Provisional Authority (OCPA)
Cockburn, Patrick, 370
COIN Academy, 289, 293, 294, 466
COIN warfare. *See* Counterinsurgency (COIN)

College of Technology, 160, 161

Colombia, 32

Colonial case, labeling Iraq as a, effort to avoid, 21

Combat outposts (COPs), 225, 232, 329, 331

Commanders of the Jihad (chanting), 194

Communists, 5, 17, 18, 28, 39, 65, 285, 370, 371, 391, 469, 536

Confederation of Iraqi Tribes, 170

Conference of Iraqi Sunnis, 115

Council of Ministers, 400

Council of Notables, 335

Counterinsurgency (COIN), 25, 231, 291, 292, 344, 359, 518
  in Afghanistan, 466, 478, 482, 491–492, 493, 494–495, 496, 497, 498, 500–501, 513–514
  average time period of, 80
  manual on, 224, 225, 227, 331, 332
  paradox involving, 492
  population-centric, 222, 492, 493, 494, 497
  proponents of, influence of, 224, 227, 470, 498–499
  soldiers' perspectives on, 241–242, 246–247, 329, 330, 331, 332, 334, 472
  as still violence, 376
  training in, 289, 293, 466

Counterinsurgency Warfare: Theory and Practice (Galula), 241

Crane, Conrad, 224

Crider, Jim, 240, 241–242, 243, 250, 258

Criminal Medicine Department, 13

Critical Infrastructure Security guards, 237

Crocker, Ryan, 364–365, 374, 375

The Da Vinci Code (book/movie), 147

Dadullah, Mansur, 456–457, 458, 473, 474, 508, 511, 512

Dadullah, Mullah, 456

al-Damalouji, Meisoon, 110

Damascus, 59, 99, 151–153, 159–164, 169–171, 173, 176, 197, 419, 438

Damascus International Airport, 207, 208

Danish cartoons, 103, 195, 380, 386, 428

Dar al-Ifta. *See* Sunni Endowment

al-Daraji, Abdul Hadi, 84

Darfur, 462

Darwinian approach, 467–468

Daud, Engineer, 476, 477

Dawa Party, 5, 6, 29, 30, 31, 39, 54, 63, 75, 78, 79, 90, 97, 98–99, 100, 116, 117, 162, 240, 248, 363, 536, 541, 549, 550

de Mistura, Stefan, 526

de Quincy Adams, Jasper, 503, 506, 507, 512

De-Arabization idea, 22

Death squads, 59, 67, 68, 69, 82, 101, 109–110, 111, 156, 222, 539, 540

De-Baathification policy, 19, 31, 67, 78, 225, 540, 542, 550, 551, 554

Defensive jihad, 131, 133, 140

Democracy, 130, 141, 148, 171, 175, 373–374, 391, 556

Democrats and Republicans, 442

Denmark, 153, 497

Department for the Protection of Professors, 111

Dermer, P. J., 279, 280–281, 365, 366, 367–368

Dhaher, Khaled, 406, 408, 410, 413, 426–428, 432

al-Dhari, Dhamer, 42

al-Dhari, Harith, 37–38, 58, 62, 64, 102, 108, 112, 163, 169, 174, 390, 530
  See also Association of Muslim Scholars

Di Rita, Larry, 19

Diab, Salim, 379

al-Din Albani, Muhamad Nasir, 124

Dinniyeh group, 195, 391, 419

District Advisory Councils (DACs), 243, 252

Diwaniya, 17, 271

Diyala province, 69–70, 548, 551, 553

Dora, 53–54, 95, 164, 165, 238–261, 246, 326, 345, 352, 354, 368, 524, 525, 527, 555

Druze revival, 182

Dulaimi, Adnan, 95, 104, 115–116, 174, 297, 299, 343

al-Dulaimi, Asma, 110

al-Dulaimi, Saadoun, 62

Dulaimi tribe, 106, 107

East Timor, 513

"Eating Soup With a Spoon" (Gentile), 332

Economic sanctions, impact of, 20–21, 73, 554

Egypt, 103, 116, 126, 130, 131, 136, 140, 153, 164–169, 167, 178, 186,

188, 389, 392, 395, 436, 437

Eid al-Adha holiday, Saddam's execution during, 116–117

"80 percent solution" attempt, 555

Elections, 52, 130, 175, 287, 391

in Afghanistan, 464, 467, 492–493

based on proportional representation, effect of the, 31–32

exaggerated claims made about, 552

groups banned from, 542, 550

media coverage of, 554

public indifference to, 540, 541

that enshrined sectarianism, 64–65, 549–550

that signaled the civil war was over, 549

threatening those participating in, 47, 170

waiting to be told who to vote for in, 372–373

See also Political participation

El-Hindi, Marwan Othman, 123

Erbil, 553

Ethar Association, 314, 316, 320

Euphrates River, 15

European Union, 551

Everyday Jihad (Rougier), 192–193

Exiles, 31, 98, 369

in Iran, 39, 41, 51

in Jordan, 115

living as, aspects of, 151–179

number of, 73, 556–557

return of, 38

See also Iraqi refugees

Experts, self-styled, 17

Exum, Andrew, 217

Facility Protection Service (FPS), 338

Fadhil, Abu Ahmad, 432–433

Fadhil area, 271, 326, 531, 532

Fadhila movement, 39, 67, 111

Fadhila Party, 549

Fadlallah, Ayatollah Muhammad Hussein, 177

al-Faidih, Muhammad Bashar, 58

Faisal, Ali (Ali al-Lami), 66, 67

al-Faisal, Saud, 148

Faith Campaign, 30, 40

Faizani, Mullah, 454

Falah, Haji, 65

Falcon Brigade, 104

Falluja, 23, 49, 118, 144, 192, 194, 224, 304, 352, 363, 366, 426, 552

destruction of, shift following, 36–37

status of, in 2004, 15–17

al-Faqih, Sheikh Jawad, 134, 139, 140

Fard al-Qanun (Imposing the Law), 227, 228

Fares, Walid, 185

al-Fartusi, Sheikh Muhammad, 41

Fatah, 190, 191, 192, 193, 199, 205, 206, 209, 398, 432, 435, 436

Fatah al-Intifada, 196–199, 201, 202, 203, 204, 383

Fatah al-Islam, 196–217, 383–384, 389, 391, 392, 393, 395, 396, 414, 415, 416, 432, 433, 438

Fatah Revolutionary Council, 209

Fatfat, Ahmad, 195, 394

Fedayeen militia, 82

Federalism, 51

Feith, Doug, 19

Females. *See* Women

Fick, Nathaniel, 466

Fil, Joseph, 60, 221, 229, 231

Force Strategic Engagement Cell (FSEC), 279–280, 281

Foreign fighters, 18, 37, 40, 61, 80, 112, 192, 193–194, 419, 530

Foreign military occupation, meaning of, 23, 284, 499

Forward Operating Bases (FOBs), 222, 290, 296, 329, 330, 356

France, 163, 183, 227, 388

Franjieh, Suleiman, 216

Frank, Pat, 281–283

Franks, Tommy, 15

Free Patriotic Movement, 426

Freedom fighting vs. terrorism, difficulty distinguishing, 148

Free-market economy, 21, 225

Friedman, Thomas, 376

Front for Fighting the Jews and Crusaders, 143

Fursan (Amriya Freedom Fighters/Thurwar), 304–308, 310–311, 312, 319, 322, 325

Future Current, 379, 421

Future Movement, 184, 185, 199, 204, 205, 206, 207, 209, 210, 211, 379, 380, 381, 382, 383, 384, 385, 386–387, 388, 389, 391, 393, 394, 396, 397–398, 400, 402, 403, 404–405,

Future Movement (*continued*)
406, 407–411, 413, 416,
419, 422, 426, 429, 430,
431, 432, 433, 434–435

Future newspaper, 184

Future TV station, 387, 402,
403, 405, 406, 412

Gallagher, Brendan, 301–302,
307, 309, 310–311, 314,
330

Galula, D., 241

Garner, Jay, 15

Gates, Robert, 330–331, 442,
469

Gaza, 188, 197, 314, 436, 437

Geagea, Samir, 195, 403, 419

Gellhorn, Martha, 24

Gemayel, Bashir, 216

General Federation of Labor
Unions, 400

Generation Kill (book/HBO
series), 466

Geneva Convention, 161

Gentile, Gian, 289–293, 329,
330, 331–332, 332–333,
333–334, 344, 544

Ghazaliya, 37, 40, 49, 86, 87,
222, 232, 233, 235, 246,
290, 293, 334, 368

Ghazni, 439, 443–445, 446,
449, 459, 461, 515

Gheit, Ahmed Abul, 437

Ghorayeb, Amal Saad, 182–
183

"Ghost police" problem, 262

Globalized jihadism, 449, 468

Godfather, The (book/movie),
19

Gottlieb, Jeffrey, 259, 262,
263, 268, 532

Graffiti, sectarian, shift away
from, 557

Grand Mosque in Mecca,
124, 134, 392, 438

Green, Toby, 229

Green Zone, 22, 24, 59, 222,
251, 255, 284, 295, 297,
364, 552, 554

Guantánamo, 70, 105

Guardian article, 311, 325,
326

Gulf War, 11, 29, 33, 37, 38,
125, 135, 137, 155, 171

Hadley, Stephen, 222, 229,
375

Haenni, Patrick, 392

al-Haeri, Ayatollah Kadhim,
39, 41, 50, 51, 104, 152

Hafeez, Zerlakhta, 515

Haiti, 513

al-Haj, Muhammad, 208, 209

al-Hajj, Francois, 396

al-Hakim, Abdul Aziz, 36,
41, 51, 97, 98, 113, 173,
174

See also Supreme Council
for the Islamic
Revolution in Iraq
(SCIRI)

Hakim family, 39

al-Hakim, Muhammad Bakr,
41, 44, 47, 419

Halba attack, 406–410

Halliday, Dennis, 20

Hamas, 130, 191, 197, 207,
208, 382, 394, 398, 431–
432, 435, 436, 437

al-Hamdani, Raed, 173–174

Hammond, General, 366

Hammoudah, Mohamad,
410

Hammoudah, Nasr, 410

Hamza Mosque, 537

Haqbeen, Fazel Rabie, 517–
518

Haqqani, Jalaluddin, 440

Harakat al-Tawhid al-Islami
(The Islamic Unity
Movement), 195, 196,
199, 391

al-Hardan, Sheikh Saad
Mushhan Naif, 105–109

al-Hareth, Abu, 201–202

al-Hariri, Bahiya, 204, 205

Hariri family, 205, 208, 381,
391, 395, 413

Hariri Foundation, 204

al-Hariri, Rafiq, 183–184,
185, 188, 199, 202, 212,
214, 379–380, 382, 385,
386, 388, 389, 390, 391,
393, 394, 395, 398, 403,
407

al-Hariri, Saad, 184, 204, 209,
385, 386, 387, 388, 392,
396, 399, 400–401, 404,
405, 406, 411, 412, 413,
428, 431, 434–435, 438

See also Future Movement

Hasan, Monaem Ibrahim,
124

Hashaika, Abdallah, 142

Hashem, Albu, 125

Hashem, Hassan, 364

Hashemites, 123, 125, 144

Hashim, Haji, 243, 250, 251

al-Hashimi, Saad, 108

al-Hashimi, Tariq, 100, 110,
322, 343, 542

Hassan Mosque, 40, 47, 79–
80

Hassan (son of Ali), 46

Hassanein Mosque, 292, 544

al-Hassani, Sayyid Jalil
Sarkhi, 268–269, 268–
270

Haswa, 341

al-Hawali, Sifr, 112

Hayaniya, 371–373

Hekmatyar, Gulbuddin, 440,
450, 468, 510

Helmand province, surge in,
471–490, 491, 502, 503,
510

Helweh camp, 197

Hill, Christopher, 550

Hitler, Adolf, 18

Hix, Bill, 474, 491

Hizballah, 64, 91, 103, 177, 182, 183, 185, 186, 187–188, 189, 190, 191, 192, 194, 195, 197, 202, 203, 204, 206, 207, 208, 210, 213, 362, 380–381, 382, 384, 386, 387, 389, 390, 392, 393–394, 395, 396, 399, 400, 401, 402, 403–404, 405–406, 407, 412, 414, 415, 418, 421, 422, 426, 427, 430, 431–432, 433–434, 435, 436, 437, 438, 449–550, 498, 535

Hizb-e-Islami faction, 440, 450, 462, 510

Homosexuals, targeting, 534

Honorable resistance, defined, 108

Hospitals, issues facing, 14–15, 109, 159–160, 161, 315

Hot Bird (broadcast company), 176

al-Huda, Bint, 90

Human Rights Watch, 116

Huquq political party, 174

Hurra television, 95

Hurriya, 118, 157, 235, 246, 272–273, 294, 299, 320, 321, 328, 342, 343, 549

Hussein, King (of Jordan), 125, 126

Hussein, Qusay, death of, 117

Hussein, Saddam, 9, 15, 16, 17, 18, 18–19, 20, 22, 28, 30, 31, 32–38, 37, 39, 40, 82, 89, 90, 97, 105, 107, 125, 130, 133, 137, 143–144, 155, 169, 172, 177–178, 256, 389, 412, 525, 538, 547, 548, 552

comparing America to, 85, 93, 361

comparing Bush to, 275

comparing Maliki with, 100, 530, 543

comparing the SCIRI to, 271

coup attempts on, 174, 175, 178, 179

failed uprising against, 5, 29, 173, 372

honoring/praise for, 175, 176, 191, 200, 212, 213, 373, 428

Lebanese views of, 386, 423

regime of, collapse of, 3, 9

and sectarianism, 173, 265

treatment of prisoners under, 3–4, 5, 6–7, 9

trial and execution of, impact of, 116–119, 436

Hussein, Sheikh, 45, 46–47, 64

Hussein (son of Ali), 29, 41–42, 46, 47, 89, 90, 99, 105, 151, 152, 153, 361, 363, 525

Hussein, Uday, 65–66, 117, 179

Ibn al-Alqami, 36

Ibn Taimiya, 35–36, 96, 139, 144

Ibrahim al-Khalil convent, 163

Ibrahim, Khalil (Abu Omar), 529–530, 531, 543, 544

Identity politics, 27, 182, 183

Idu, Walid, 393

IED attacks and ambushes, 70, 71, 236, 241, 242, 243, 253, 255, 256, 274, 292, 293–294, 299, 301, 303, 310, 355, 357, 367, 441, 462, 473, 480, 483, 489, 503, 526

Imam Ali. *See* Ali (cousin and son-in-law of the Prophet Muhammad)

Imam Hussein. *See* Hussein (son of Ali)

Imam Ridha shrine, 72

Implementation and Follow-up Committee for National Reconciliation (IFCNR), 242, 280

Independent High Electoral Commission, 550

Independent Islamic Gathering, 199, 382, 391–392, 427, 434

India, 466

Institute for the Study of Diplomacy, 148

Integrity Committee, 549

Interim government, 31, 38

Internal displacement, 28, 32, 153, 548

See also Iraqi refugees; *specific areas with displaced population groups*

International Crisis Group, 392

International Islamic University, 132

International Rescue Committee, 451, 462

International Security Assistance Force (ISAF), 441, 497

Iran, 31, 51, 52, 67, 97, 102–103, 105, 143, 161, 271, 272, 363, 372, 382, 435, 436, 550, 552

accusations against, 87, 103, 109, 169, 174, 194, 383, 437

and Afghanistan, 451, 466

and the Badr Brigade, 60, 363

and Chalabi, 550–551

Iran (*continued*)
  exiles in, 39, 41
  fear of, 176
  holy city of, 41
  illegals from, paranoia
    about, 52, 53
  interference and money
    from, effect of, 555
  and the July War, 186
  and Lebanon, 188, 381,
    389, 425
  and the Mahdi Army, 365,
    547
  and the March 8 coalition,
    186
  nuclear intransigence of,
    American response to,
    436
  perceived gain from Iraqi
    civil war, 148
  possible intervention by,
    105, 549
  regional rivalry between
    Saudi Arabia and, 181,
    188
  role of, 98
  seen as gaining more
    power, 248, 326, 335
  Shah of, 182, 361, 374
  as Syria's ally, 163
  talk in Washington about,
    25
Iranian pilgrims, 89
Iranian proxy, 112, 177
Iranian Revolution, 124, 182,
  361, 390
Iranian Revolutionary
  Guards, 95
Iranian-sponsored militias, 9,
  22, 226, 547
  See also Badr Brigade
Iran-Iraq war, 21, 28–29, 63,
  133, 178, 316
Iraq Study Group report, 230
Iraqi Accord, 110, 297
Iraqi army

  critique of the, during the
    Battle for Baghdad,
    367–368
  disbanding of the, 19, 21,
    30, 223, 225, 249, 265
  former colonel of, 168–
    169
  and the impact of
    cooperation with U.S.
    troops, 355
  including leaders of the,
    in planning sessions,
    356
  national embrace of the,
    30
  vs. the police, 346
  previous support for the,
    21, 265
  viewed as the most
    competent of the
    security forces, 296
  views of the, 347–348,
    349, 531
  See also Iraqi Security
    Forces (ISF)
Iraqi Civil Defense Corp.,
  349
Iraqi civil war
  burn out of the, 25
  civilian casualties during
    the surge vs., 227
  and the cleansing of
    Amriya, 45–49
  context behind the, 27–32
  continuing civilian deaths
    due to, and the surge,
    285
  elections that signaled the
    end of, 549
  end of the, and the
    changes that were
    apparent, aspects of,
    521–557
  escalation of the, 64–65
  fiercest battles of the, sites
    of the, 537
  first outbreaks of, 53–54

  and how it made the U.S.
    occupation good, 514
  Lebanese blaming
    Americans for, 383
  and the Mahdi Army
    cease-fire, 235
  and Muqtada's influence,
    49–53
  names for the, 24
  power during the, 538–
    540
  restart of the, speculation
    over, 529, 539–540
  and the rise of the
    mosques, 32–38
  road to the, aspects of,
    27–73
  and the Sadr Current, 38–
    45
  signal indicating ending
    of, 363
  Sunni and Shiites
    reflecting back on, 540
  Sunnis accepting their loss
    in the, 552
  U.S. acknowledging the,
    290
  vital battleground during
    the, 256
  warning about regional
    destabilization from,
    148–149
  winner of the, 238, 285
  See also Sectarian
    cleansing; Shiite
    militias; Sunni militias
Iraqi Constitution, 31, 51–52,
  116, 549
Iraqi death toll, 24, 227, 285,
  556
Iraqi Governing Council
  (IGC), 18, 31, 36, 38,
  51, 67, 107
Iraqi government
  integration, failure to
    achieve, 532, 538, 539,
    543

See also specific governmental agencies, institutions, and people

Iraqi Homeland Party, 175

Iraqi Islamic Party. *See* Islamic Party of Iraq

Iraqi military. *See* Iraqi army

Iraqi Ministry of Defense, 60, 96, 241, 280, 524–525

Iraqi Ministry of Education, 525–526

Iraqi Ministry of Health, 13, 70, 71–72, 160, 312, 318

Iraqi Ministry of Higher Education, 111

Iraqi Ministry of Information, 34

Iraqi Ministry of Interior, 32, 59, 60, 61, 62, 63, 64, 67, 69, 73, 95, 96, 98, 104, 111, 156, 160, 167, 223, 241, 266, 268, 316, 337, 338, 524–525, 532

Iraqi Ministry of Justice, 255

Iraqi Ministry of Migration, 318

Iraqi Ministry of Oil, 338

Iraqi Ministry of Transportation, 72

Iraqi National Alliance, 67

Iraqi National Congress (INC), 66

Iraqi National Guard (ING), 88, 95, 96, 156–157, 167, 249, 316, 325, 339

Iraqi nationalism, 22

Iraqi National Police (INP), 222, 248, 251, 254–255, 257, 258, 260, 262, 263, 266, 274, 287, 295–296, 348, 349, 350, 356, 524, 525, 526, 528

See also Iraqi Security Forces (ISF)

Iraqi Office of the Prime Minister, 524

Iraqi Parliament, 94

Iraqi police. *See* Iraqi National Police (INP)

Iraqi Rabita website, 115

Iraqi refugees

composition of, 162

crisis of displaced, 153–154, 548–549

and Fatah al-Islam, 201

following the 2005 elections and violence, 32

in Jordan, 66, 149, 171, 173

number of, 73, 556–557

in Saudi Arabia, 39

in Syria, 151–153, 154, 159

See also Exiles; Internal displacement

Iraqi resistance. *See specific organizations and groups*

Iraqi Security Forces (ISF), 8, 45, 58, 61, 66, 80, 85, 94, 95, 96, 98, 100, 102, 109, 114, 156, 223, 226, 228, 236, 255, 260, 291–292, 293, 313, 356, 364, 365, 370, 372, 533, 540, 553

and the Awakening groups, 285, 527, 532, 542, 543

composition of the, 60

confidence expressed in the, 367, 538

linked to Shiite militias, 105, 289, 290

and the Mahdi Army, 63, 272, 274, 339

monopolized power of the, 523–524

obstacles to ISV/Awakening integration into, 256, 258–259, 266, 532

power of, not understanding, 554

professionalism and nonsectarianism exhibited by some

members of, 291–292, 296, 298–299, 302

rebuilding of the, 59

responsibility for training, 224–225

sectarianism of the, 245, 251

smuggled weapons originally from, 423

stronger, 539, 547

transitioning authority to, 221, 289, 290, 294, 298

Zarqawi pushing the, effect of, 222

See also Iraqi army; Iraqi National Police (INP)

Iraqi Security Volunteers (ISVs), 237, 246, 248, 249, 250, 252, 256, 258–259, 260, 266, 268, 285, 286, 287

See also Awakening program/groups

Iraqi Special Operations Forces, 75, 81, 82–83, 85, 545

Iraqiya Party, 110

Iraq-U.S. relationship, previous, 21

Iskandariya, 537

Islam Memo website, 118

Islam, radical, spread of, 130, 440

Islamic Army of Iraq, 58, 233, 280, 321, 324, 325

Islamic Emirate of Afghanistan, 445

Islamic Group of Egypt, 136, 140

Islamic Party of Afghanistan. *See* Hizb-e-Islami faction

Islamic Party of Iraq, 70, 102, 110, 144, 256, 311, 315, 321, 322, 328, 343, 371

Islamic State of Iraq, 112, 194, 238, 251, 263, 312, 321, 323

Islamists, power used against, effect of, 414

Israel, 97, 129, 130, 139, 155, 187, 207, 211, 361, 498
  Al Qaeda and, 190
  defiance of UN rulings, 137
  difficulty of going to fight, 192, 194, 203, 436
  future security of, 53
  and the July War, 161, 184, 185, 186, 187–189, 196, 380, 436, 437
  and the Lebanese army, 195
  seen as the common enemy, 390, 421

Israeli peace process, 125

Italian Ministry of Foreign Affairs, 148

Jaafar Al Tayar shrine, 66

al-Jaafari, Ibrahim, 60, 61, 75, 78–79, 97, 98, 99, 100, 173, 176, 240, 547, 551

Jabril, Ahmed, 209

al-Jadri, Bassima, 240–241, 256, 280–281, 352

Jaish al-Mahdi (JAM), 293
  Black, 358–361
  Golden, 236, 271–272, 273, 276
  meaning of, 236
  White, 358
  See also Mahdi Army

Jalalabad, 458

Jalil, Sayyid, 269, 362–363, 533

Jalul, Nabil, 418–421, 423, 424, 425

JAM. *See* Jaish al-Mahdi (JAM)

Jamaa Islamiya movement, 392

Jamia, 345, 355, 358, 368

Jamiyat al-Turath al-Islami (The Society of Islamic Heritage), 140

Jan, Abdul Rahman, 478

Jarrah, Ziad, 388

Jassim, Abdul Qader Muhammad, 227

al-Jayusi, Azmi, 124, 146

Jeish al-Fatihin group, 111

Jeish Muhammad group, 135, 137, 146

Jeish Nasr Salahedin (The Army of Salahedin's Victory), 171

Jewish militias, 158

Jews, 53, 214
  See also Israel

Jihad and Reform Front, 233, 280

Jihad fighters/jihadis
  being among, aspects of, 123–149
  following Zarqawi, 36–37, 61, 173
  Iraq considered a loss for, 217–218
  of Muqtada, 85
  Sunnis as, 18, 62
  See also specific jihadist leaders/people and organizations

Jihad, four conditions of, breached by AQI, 323–324

Jihadism, globalized, 449, 468

Jisr, Samir, 382–383

Johnson, Lyndon, 374

Johnston, Rob, 278

Joint security stations (JSS), 232, 257–258, 262, 345, 355, 356, 359

Jolles, Lorens, 161, 162

Jordan, 101, 103, 112, 115, 123–127, 124, 188, 190, 203, 328–329

attitude towards Palestinians, 156, 158, 159

civil war in, 130–131

closed borders of, 161, 172, 192

and the Geneva Convention, 161

and the impact of jihadis, 130, 131–149

Iraqi refugees in, 66, 162, 163, 171, 173, 175

July 7 attack in, 139, 145

monarchy of, Zarqawi's hatred of, 144–145

as part of Iraq, 52–53

poll on attitudes in, 146–147

population of, 171

possible intervention by, 105, 381

Saudi Arabia aligning with, 148–149

and sectarianism, 173, 437

Sunnis being trained in, 185, 186

and a U.S.-backed military alliance, 395

Jordanian General Intelligence Directorate, 171

Jordanian Ministry of Education, 125

Journalism/journalists. *See* Media

al-Jubauri, Mishan, 175–176, 177–178, 179

al-Juburi, Fatthi Yusuf Saleh, 527

al-Juburi, Omar, 542

July War, 161, 184, 185, 186, 187–189, 196, 198, 380, 436, 437

Juma, Saad, 319–320

Jumblatt, Walid, 216, 398, 399–400, 405

Jumhuriya newspaper, 179

Jund Allah militia, 199, 200, 392, 413
Jund al-Sahaba group, 111
Jund al-Sham (Soldiers of Sham/Levant), 140, 190, 191, 192, 193, 201, 204, 207, 211, 433
Jund al-Sitt (The Army of the Lady), 205
Juzu, Sheikh Muhamad Ali, 389–390

Kabul, 440, 441, 451, 452, 458, 461, 464, 465, 466, 468, 469, 475, 514, 518
Kabul-Kandahar highway, 447
Kadhim, Imam, 33, 151
Kadhim Mosque, 49
Kadhimayn Mosque, 266, 273, 274, 275
al-Kadhimi, Adnan, 99
al-Kadhimi, Sheikh Raed, 152–153
Kadhimiya, 62, 84, 153, 161, 345
Kadhimiya prison, 255, 284, 524
Kagan, Fred, 229, 230
Kahl, Colin, 229
Kalyvas, Stathis, 491
Kandahar, 440, 451, 464, 474, 481, 491, 514, 519
al-Kanj, Basim, 194, 419
Karameh, Omar, 413
Karar Brigade, 61
Karbala, 36, 40, 41, 84, 153, 365
Karkh cemetery, 3, 4
Karzai, Hamid, 441, 442, 444, 447, 449, 450, 459, 464, 465, 466, 467, 476, 477, 482, 497, 513, 519
Kaywan, Raed Ahmed, 124
Keane, Jack, 229, 230
Kentucky Fried Chicken, 414, 415

Khadra, 49, 290, 293, 295, 301, 302, 326, 334
Khalaq, Abdallah (Abu Obeida), 425
al-Khalaylah, Ahmad Fadhil Nazal, 139
See also al-Zarqawi, Abu Musab
Khaldan Camp, 131
al-Khaleq, Abdel Rahman, 140
Khalid, Sheikh, 292–293, 297, 303, 308, 309, 544, 545
Khalil, Dr., 455, 456, 457, 458, 459–460
Khalilzad, Zalmay, 75, 97, 171
Khalis, Maulvi Muhamad Younes, 450
Khamenei, Ayatollah, 44
Khan, Dad Muhamad, 476
Khan, Nafez, 486–487
Khatib, Ismail, 419, 420
al-Khatib, Sahar, 405
al-Khattab, Omar ibn, 177
al-Khazraji, Sheikh Muayad, 57
al-Kheiqani, Abu Haidar, 65, 66
al-Khirbit, Sattam, 170
al-Khirbit, Sheikh Mudhir, 170
Khomeini, Ayatollah, 39, 44, 50, 51, 89, 90, 182, 361, 374, 381, 390
Khreis, Samih, 146
Khudeir, Sheikh Ahmed, 342
Khudeir, Walid, 342
Kidnappings, 32, 62, 82, 102, 104, 113–115, 152, 156, 157, 173, 247, 267, 293, 444, 525
al-Kinani, Sheikh Hussein Karim, 282
Kirkuk, 175, 553
Kites, issue of, 451
Kitson, Frank, 241n

Koran, the, 8, 16, 37, 49, 412, 425
Korean War, 293
Kosovo, 19, 528
al-Kubaisi, Sheikh Abdul Ghafar, 33, 34–35, 36
Kubeisi, Ahmad, 33
al-Kubeisi, Sheikh Abdul Salam, 112
Kuehl, Dale, 293–297, 301, 302–303, 306, 308–309, 310, 311–312, 313, 315, 321, 322, 326, 329, 330, 331, 332–333, 333–334, 356, 544
Kufa Mosque, 89, 89–90, 91, 92
al-Kufi, Abbas, 271
Kunduz province, 461
Kurdish militias, 548
"Kurdish north" label, 17
Kurdish *pesh merga*, 90, 144
Kurdish revival, 182
Kurdistan, 73, 143, 153, 175, 553, 555
Kurdistan Democratic Party (KDP), 90
Kurds, 40, 51, 52, 97, 100, 156, 162, 173, 525, 553
and the "80 percent solution," 555
empowerment of the, 18
and the execution of Saddam, 116, 118–119
following American invasion, 179
internally displacing, 28
periphery vs. center, 73
and secession, 101, 105
and sectarian cleansing, 175
and the shifts in sectarianism, 30, 31
status of, 9
Kuwait, 21, 115, 125, 137, 140, 155, 159, 171, 316, 436–437, 555

Lahoud, Emile, 189

Lake Habbaniya, 15

Lamb, Graeme, 281

al-Lami, Ali (Ali Faisal), 66, 67, 550

The Lancet, 24

Lang, Pat, 500–501

Langan, Sean, 439

Latifya, battles in, 61–62

LBC television, 387, 405

Learning to Eat Soup With a Knife: Counterinsurgency Lessons from Malaya and Vietnam (Nagl), 293, 332

Lebanese army
  agreement made with militias by, 408
  standing by, 407, 410
  strength of the, 404
  treatment of Palestinians, 214, 215–216, 438

Lebanese Civil Defense, 216

Lebanese Interior Ministry, 201, 212, 394–395, 399, 416, 420

Lebanese Internal Security Forces, 170, 205, 209, 399, 401, 406, 407, 410

Lebanese Red Cross, 410

Lebanese refugees, 161

Lebanese University, 185

Lebanon, 20, 25, 52, 64, 101, 103, 136, 153, 159, 162, 177, 218
  aftermath of the war in Iraq on, aspects of, 379–438
  civil war in, 164
  conditions of the population in, 429
  and the Geneva Convention, 161
  identity politics in, 27
  Israel's invasion of, 361
  and the July War, 161, 184, 185, 186, 187–189, 196, 198, 380, 436, 437
  political tensions in, pushed to armed conflict, America's role in and goal of, 435–436
  and sectarianism, 105, 183, 184, 185
  war in Iraq spilling over into, aspects of, 181–218

Libya, 153

Lieberman, Joseph, 207

Little Triangle, 155

Loftis, Robert, 374

Logar province, 461, 462, 469, 490, 491

The Logic of Violence in Civil War (Kalyvas), 491

Looting, 5, 10, 13, 34, 159, 268

Lynch, Rick, 80

Maalif, 537

Maan, Hikmat Hussein (Hakami), 352–353, 358, 361

Madain, battles in, 61

Maghawir al-Dakhiliya (special police force), 114

Mahad al-Ansar (Supporters' Institute), 131

Mahdi Army, 33, 59, 60, 61, 62, 63, 64, 65, 68, 73, 75–76, 78, 79, 82, 83, 84, 86, 89, 92, 95, 103, 104, 108, 113, 116, 194, 221, 223, 224, 244, 248, 249, 266, 270, 284, 287, 299, 300, 313, 318, 319, 320, 326, 338, 367, 524, 525–526, 531, 534, 535, 536, 543, 545, 547, 551
  and Al Qaeda in Iraq, 231, 239, 240, 245, 247, 249, 250, 259, 260, 294–295, 539
  ascension of, 98
  believed to be lying dormant, 523
  cease-fire of, 235, 236, 239, 259, 266, 269, 271, 272, 273, 274, 275, 326, 338, 339, 363, 364, 365
  classification of the, question of, Muqtada's response to, 90–91
  eclipse of the, aspects of the, 337–375
  following Samarra Shrine bombings, 70–71
  full-scale war declared on, 360
  and the INP, 254, 257
  legend involving, 104
  mosques and, 40, 70–71, 109, 256, 544
  regional differences in the, 58
  and the surge, 234–237, 239–240, 253, 255, 265, 266, 267, 268, 269, 281, 285
  war inside the, 271–278
  See also Shiites

Mahdi, Sheikh Jihad, 128, 129, 129–130

al-Majali, Sheikh Abdel Majid, 131

Majd al-Anjar area, 388, 403, 417–418, 419, 420–421, 422, 425, 433, 438

Majid, Ali Hassan (Chemical Ali), 119, 257

Makiya, Kanan, 22

al-Maksusi, Adnan, 352

Maktab al-Khidmat al-Mujahideen (Office of Mujahideen Services), 131, 139

Malaya, 227, 501

Maliki government, 309, 312

al-Maliki, Nuri, 75, 99–101, 102, 109–110, 111, 162, 176, 223–224, 227, 228, 230, 234, 235, 240, 241, 248, 260, 279, 280, 288, 352, 360, 363, 364–367, 371, 372, 374, 375, 524, 526, 529, 531, 532, 533, 534, 538, 541, 542, 543, 547, 549, 550, 551, 552, 553

Maliki, Walid Abdel, 173–174

Maluki Mosque, 46, 64, 292, 303, 324, 335, 544

Mansour, 87, 293, 334, 342, 356, 358, 360

Mao Zedong, 293

al-Maqdisi, Abu Muhammad, 125, 140–141, 142, 143, 433

March 8 coalition, 186–187, 187–188, 381, 387, 407

March 14 coalition, 184, 186, 187, 188, 207, 379, 381, 382, 387, 389, 391, 392, 396, 398, 403, 405, 406, 435, 438

Marginalization, issue of, 335

Marka military court trials, 123–124, 126–127

Maronites, 20, 183, 189, 216, 387, 390

Marshall, George C., 225

al-Mashhadani, Adil, 271, 531

al-Mashhadani, Taysir Najah, 102

al-Masihi, Amar, 266

al-Masri, Hussein, 408

al-Masri, Khalid, 413

al-Masri, Muhamad, 410

Massoud, Ahmad Shah, 131, 132

Mattis, James, 224

Mayha, Rauf Aballah Abu, 124

Mazloum, Wassim I., 123

McCain, John, 442

McChrystal, Stanley, 469–470, 470–471, 492, 493–494, 495–496, 512–513, 518–519

McCollough, William, 480, 486, 487, 488

McDonalds, 415

McFarland, Sean, 225, 226

McGurk, Brett, 222–223, 223–224, 229, 367, 374, 375

McKiernan, David, 469, 470, 493

McMullen, Chris, 19

Mecca, 37, 112, 116, 124, 129, 134, 269, 381, 392, 438

Media
in Afghanistan, 439
Arab, resentment toward, 5
and the battle of Nahr al-Barid camp, 214, 215
and the COIN manual, 227
conduct of the, 10, 12, 18, 23, 24, 63, 70, 238, 326, 400, 429, 441, 442, 493–494, 540
embedding with the American military, criticism of, 443
freedom of the, issue of, 94
holed up in Lebanon, 403
importance of the, realizing the, 366
kidnapping involving the, 62
killing of a member of the, 343
Lebanese, blaming the, 387
local Lebanese attitude towards, 412
perceived as the enemy, 495

Saudis use of the, 394
and selection bias, 495
and the surge, 222
U.S., focus of the, since the beginning of the occupation, issue with, 553–555

Media blackout, 176

Medical City, 14

Medina, 112, 129, 381

al-Meis, Khalil, 389

Meshal, Khalid, 436

Mesopotamia, capture of, 27–28

Mexico, 32

Middle East
euphemism for American-backed militias in the, 379
failed U.S. policies in, effect of, 556–557
identity politics in the, resurgence of, 182
impact on the, 25, 105, 181
largest refugee crisis in the, 153
perceived Jewish and Zionist strategy in the, 53
perception of Al Qaeda and Americans in the, 177
Shiite vs. Sunni revival in the, 181–182
youth in the, recruitment of, 147
See also specific countries

Midhat, Kamal, 432

Mikati, Najib, 390–391, 413

Milat Ibrahim (Maqdisi), 140

Milestones on the Road (Qutb), 130

Military Review, 225, 226, 241, 499

Military Transition Team (MTT), 69

Militia power, original and shifting, U.S. not understanding, 553–554

Militias. *See specific militia groups*

Minority power, 20

Miska, Steve, 228, 232, 236, 237, 255

Mohsen, Amer, 181–182, 380

Mongols, occupation by, 35

Morgado, Andy, 228, 230, 231

Morocco, 437

Mosques, 40, 50, 109, 124, 137, 147
  rise of, 32–38
  See also specific mosques

Mossad, 146

Mosul, 29, 73, 170, 175, 179, 553

Moussa, Ammar, 410

Moustapha, Imad, 208

Muawiya, 46, 47

Mubarak, Hosni, 103, 139, 188, 389

Mufti of Lebanon (Grand Mufti), 207

Mufti of Tripoli, 208

Mughniyeh, Imad, 437, 535

al-Muhamadawi, Sheikh Karim, 535–536

Muhammad, Prophet, 8, 16, 42, 44, 46, 62, 77, 85, 92, 94, 96, 111, 118, 125, 136, 145, 151, 178, 195, 206, 212, 328, 371, 380, 437, 454, 529–530

al-Muhammadawi, Karim Mahud (Abu Hatem), 66, 67

al-Muhandes, Abu Mahdi (Jamal Jaafir Mohammed Ali), 60

Mujahed, Zaibullah, 459

Mujahideen Advisory Council, 233

Mujahideen, first generation of, 193

Mujahideen Shura Council, 111, 392

Mullah Omar (Taliban group), 132

Mullen, Mike, 442–443

Multi-National Corps-Iraq (MNC-I), 228, 229

Multi-National Division-Baghdad (MND-B), 221, 228, 230, 231

Multi-National Division-Central (MND-C), 228, 230

Multi-National Forces-Iraq (MNF-I), 80, 226, 228

Multinational Security Transition Command-Iraq (MNSTCI), 59, 60

Murabitun militia, 385, 398, 399

Murr, Elias, 380

al-Musawi, Nawaf, 394–395, 434

al-Musawi, Sadeq, 177–178

al-Musawi, Sayyid Hassan Naji, 33, 64, 104

Muslim Brotherhood, 124, 125, 130, 131, 147–148, 169, 187, 388, 392, 428, 429, 430, 431–432

Muslims
  call to all, to defeat the occupying forces, 38
  liberal, imposing strict interpretation of Islam on, 50
  original split between, 47
  percentage of Sunnis comprising, 102

Mustafa Husseiniya (worship place), 67, 68, 75, 76–80, 81–86, 93, 268, 270, 339, 533, 537, 544

Mustansiriya University, 110

Muthana Brigade, 257

al-Mutlaq, Saleh, 96, 321, 542, 543, 550, 551–552

Muwahidun group, 134

Nagl, John, 224, 237, 293

Nahr al-Barid refugee camps, 181, 196, 197–217, 199, 380, 383, 385, 390, 394, 396, 414, 420, 422, 430, 432, 433, 438

Najaf, 40, 88, 89, 224, 234, 366

Naji, Hamudi, 343, 344, 345, 349, 350, 351, 352, 355, 358–359, 360, 361

Naji, Kanan, 199, 200, 392, 413, 416

Nashabe, Omar, 393

Nasir, Mullah, 459

Nasr, Sayyid, 44, 45, 535

Nasrallah, Sayyid Hassan, 91, 103, 185, 202, 210, 213, 214, 362, 380, 389, 394, 400, 402, 405, 407, 414, 434, 436
  See also Hizballah

Nasser, Gamal Abdel, 28, 382

National Accord Front, 73

National Assembly, 51, 52

National Defense University, 442

National Police Training Team (NPTT), 262

National Solidarity Program, 517

NATO forces, 225, 441, 446, 464, 473

Nazi Party, 18–19, 20

Neighborhood Advisory Councils (NACs), 251–252, 261, 309, 537

Neoconservatives, 229, 435, 498, 499, 553, 557

New TV channel, 412

New York Times, 175, 375–376, 401, 439

Newsweek, 112, 556

Nicaragua, 196

Nicholson, Lawrence, 479

Nilesat network, 176, 178

9/11 attacks. *See* September 11 attacks

1920 Revolution Battalions, 248, 261, 280, 287, 526

Nineveh, 553

Nongovernmental organizations (NGOs), situation of, in Afghanistan, 461, 462–463, 517

See also specific organizations

North African community, 163

Northern Alliance, 132, 137, 464

Northern Ireland, 24, 501, 540

al-Nujaifi, Atheel, 553

Nur Muhammad (Light of Muhammad) group, 107

Nuri, Riyadh, 92

Obaid, Nawaf, 112, 381

Obama administration, 498

Obama, Barack, 25, 229, 373, 442, 499, 518–519

al-Obeidi, Abdel Qader, 550, 551–552

al-Obeidi, Sheikh Khalid, 335

Odierno, Raymond, 228, 229, 230–231, 550

Office of Mujahideen Services, 131, 139

Office of Reconstruction and Humanitarian Assistance (ORHA), 15, 19

Office of the Coalition Provisional Authority (OCPA), 15, 18, 19, 22, 49, 173

Oil reserves, in Iraq, 11, 364

Oil revenue, sanctions imposed on, 555

Oil-for-food program, 20

Ollivant, Douglas, 228, 229, 231

Omar Mosque, 56, 535

Omar, Mullah, 449, 451, 454, 457, 459, 462

"Omar" name, targeting Sunnis based on, 71, 154, 158, 160, 166, 239, 320–321

al-Omar, Sheikh Nasser bin Suleiman, 112

Operation Arrowhead Strike 9, 294

Operation Close Encounters, 241

Operation Fard al-Qanun (Rule of Law), 539

Operation Iraqi Freedom deployment, 344

Operation Mountain Fury, 443, 444

Operation Sawlat al-Fursan. *See* Charge of the Knights campaign

Operation Seventh Veil, 273

Operation Together Forward I, 294

Operation Together Forward II, 342

Operation Valhalla, 82–83

Organization of the Islamic Conference, 94

Organized Movement of Islamic Call and Jihad, 137

Orphans, number of, 315, 316, 556

Osama bin Laden. *See* bin Laden, Osama

Oslo accords, 193, 206

O'Sullivan, Meghan, 97, 222–223, 229

Ottomans, 20, 28, 102, 388

"Our COIN Doctrine Removes the Enemy from the Essence of War" (Gentile), 334

Pakistan, 25, 32, 105, 115, 128, 131, 136, 140, 143, 440, 474

and Afghanistan, 451, 457, 466

double game played by, 441

new U.S. strategy for, 470

religious schools in, 440, 448, 450, 459, 511

Palestine, 105, 130, 131, 135, 136, 158, 192, 194, 214, 426, 435–436

Palestinian Liberation Organization (PLO), 190, 193, 196, 203

Palestinian refugee crisis, 171

See also specific refugee camps

Palestinians and Palestinian refugees, 130, 135, 192, 214, 217, 385, 386, 387, 398, 436

fleeing Nahr al-Barid refugee camp, 211–212, 214–216

granting citizenship to, issue of, 434

as jihadists, 126, 129, 192, 193–194

marooned, 155, 156–157, 159, 189–196

numbers of, in Iraq, 155

opposition to early coalition of in Lebanon, 183

relocation of, 125, 136, 140, 155, 158–159, 164, 171

shift in treatment of, in Iraq, 155–156, 157–158

status of, 438

Palestinians and Palestinian refugees (*continued*)
staying out of internal Lebanese conflict, 431, 432, 433
as the Sunni army, 387, 394–395
in Syria, 161, 415
uprising of, in Jordan, 125, 130–131, 213
See also specific leaders/people and organizations
Parwan province, 462
Pashtun ethnic group, size of, 441, 454
Pashtunwali, 440, 441, 468, 518
Patriotic Union of Kurdistan (PUK), 90, 162
Petraeus, David, 59, 60, 224–225, 226, 228, 231, 232, 237, 279, 281, 294, 330, 352, 359, 364–365, 366, 372, 469, 493, 518–519, 531
Pew poll, 146–147
Philippines, 227
Political participation, 108, 115, 170, 177, 248
See also Elections
Popular Front for the Liberation of Palestine (PFLP), 203, 205–206, 209, 216
Prisoners
files kept on, 5–7, 7–9
treatment of, 3–4, 5, 6–7, 9, 93, 137, 142, 146, 255, 270, 281–283, 284, 300–301, 523–524
Prisons
in Afghanistan, 456–457, 512
in Lebanon, 415, 425

men detained in, on scant evidence, 281, 300, 345, 524
number of men who spent years in, 376, 556
during peak of the surge, number of Iraqis held in, 284–285
in Saudi Arabia, 455
secret, 9, 59, 93, 160, 521, 557
in Syria, 424–425
See also specific prisons
Progressive Socialist Party, 399
Provincial Reconstruction Teams (PRTs), 469
Provincial Reserve (PR), 471, 472, 474, 501, 502, 505, 507, 510
Provisional auxiliary police, 226
Public Distribution Service, 20, 339, 341, 548–549

Qabbani, Mufti, 402, 422
Qanbar, Abud, 228, 280, 365, 366, 367, 368, 524
Qaqa'a Mosque, 126, 127, 128
Qartarneh, Yasar, 148
Qasim, Abdul Karim, 28, 270, 535
Qasim, Sheikh Naim, 400
Qatar, 382, 435
al-Qeisi, Sheikh Dhafer, 55–56
Qiba Mosque, 42–43, 44, 45, 534, 535
al-Qiblawi, Abu Jaafar, 420
Qutb, Sayyid, 130

Racism, 27, 30, 190, 379
Radical Islam, spread of, 130, 440
Radio Sawa, 116
Rafidein Brigade, 251

Rahman, Omar Abdel, 136, 140
Rahman, Sheikh Muhamad Abdel, 421
Ramadan, Mustafa (Abu Muhamad/Abu Shahid), 418–419, 420
Ramadi, 133, 170, 225, 286, 368
al-Ramah, Basil Muhamad, 124
Ramah, Muhamad Qasim Sulaiman, 124
al-Rantisi, Abdel Aziz, 207
Rashas women's prison, 9
Rashid, Sheikh Khalid, 433
Reconciliation efforts, 240, 242, 277, 279–286, 327
Reconstruction, 469, 477, 541
Red Cross, Lebanese, 410
Reese, Timothy, 538
Refugee camps. *See specific camps*
Refugees. *See* Exiles; Iraqi refugees; Palestinians and Palestinian refugees
Refugees International, 153, 156
Republican Guard, 12, 20, 30, 173, 524
Republicans and Democrats, 442
Resistance fighters. *See specific resistance groups and leaders*
Resistance, honorable, defined, 108
Rice, Condoleeza, 98, 187, 222, 264, 375, 395, 435
Ricks, Tom, 291
Rifai, Osama, 406, 427, 432
Riffi, Ashraf, 416
Rite of passage for young jihadis, 145
Rogers, Chris, 333–334

Rohde, David, 439
Rolling Stone, 466, 481, 518
Rougier, Bernard, 192–193, 202, 217
al-Rubaei, Muafaq, 29
Rumsfeld, Donald, 19, 59, 101, 222, 224
Russia, 124, 125, 131, 132, 146, 440, 453, 468, 469, 474, 492, 500, 510, 515
Russian embasssy attack, 195
Rwanda, 22, 30, 513

Saadeh, Antoine, 407
Sabean minorities, 159
Sada Camp, 131, 134, 136
Sadat, Anwar, 116, 126, 207
Sadda dam, 104
Saddam City, 5, 65, 89
    See also Sadr City
Saddam City security prison, 5
Saddam University, 29
Sadr City, 40, 50, 65, 68, 84, 89, 102, 104, 160, 340, 364, 366, 367, 532, 533–534, 542, 546
Sadr Current, 38–45, 79, 271, 353, 372, 536
Sadr, Imam Musa, 390, 533
al-Sadr, Muhammad Baqir, 39, 42, 90, 117, 535
al-Sadr, Muhammad Sadiq, 6, 39, 42, 44, 57, 77, 78, 84, 85, 89, 90, 151, 152, 268, 362, 532, 533
al-Sadr, Muqtada, 33, 39–40, 41, 49–53, 57, 58, 60, 63, 65, 66, 67, 68, 72, 76, 78, 85, 89, 90–91, 92–94, 98, 101, 102, 103, 104, 108, 112–113, 117, 152, 153, 163, 194, 234, 235, 236, 240, 268, 269, 272, 275, 278, 312, 338, 342, 345, 360, 362,

363, 364, 367, 370, 372, 373, 531, 536
    See also Mahdi Army
Sadrein camp, 546–547
Sadrists, 17, 31, 39, 52, 65, 67, 97, 110, 117, 160, 166, 168, 234, 235–236, 240, 262, 266, 269, 271, 275, 312, 338, 339, 358, 361, 362, 363, 372, 534, 536, 550
    See also Mahdi Army; Sadr Current
al-Saedi, Sheikh Abdel Karim, 533–534
Safavids, 112, 118, 175–176
"Safawis" epithet, 175–176
al-Saghir, Jalaluddin, 62, 95, 277
as-Said, Nuri, 38
Salafi chanting, 194
Salafi Current, 417
Salafi Mujahideen movement, 144
Salafis, 16, 33, 35, 49, 61, 62, 68, 102, 124, 130, 134, 136, 140, 143, 144, 146, 177, 186, 189–190, 196, 199, 202, 206, 210, 383, 390, 391, 392, 395, 411, 412–413, 414, 415, 416, 430, 434, 437
Salafism, 147–148, 195, 388
Salahedin Camp, 136
Salahuddin Brigades, 58
Salam Mosque, 382, 434
al-Samarai, Sheikh Ahmad Abdel Ghafur, 42, 58, 62–63, 64, 530
Samarra shrine attack, 27, 29, 70, 71, 75, 78, 84, 92, 93, 96, 101, 289, 290, 349
Sanctions, impact of, 20–21, 73, 555
Sattar, Sheikh. *See* Abu Risha, Sheikh Sattar

Satterfield, David, 375
Saudi Arabia, 28, 39, 52–53, 101, 102, 103, 105, 115, 125, 130, 134, 163, 207, 395, 412, 415, 455
    and Afghanistan, 440, 449
    and Al Qaeda, 112, 391
    aligning with Jordan, 148–149
    apprehension of, 112, 382
    and Fatah al-Islam, 201, 205, 207, 211
    ignoring involvement of, 553
    interference and money from, effect of, 381–382, 388, 391, 392, 393–394, 399, 554
    and Lebanon, 183, 186, 188, 381, 422, 435
    and the March 14 coalition, 184
    regional rivalry between Iran and, 181, 188
    sectarianism in, 437–438
Saudi proxies, 435
Sayyaf, Abdul Rasul, 137
al-Sayyid, Ridwan, 185–186
Schools
    ban on attending, 109–110
    religious, in Pakistan, 440, 448, 450, 459, 511
    teaching jihad ideas in, 137
Schwarzenegger, Arnold, 15
Secret prisons, 9, 59, 93, 160
Sectarian cleansing, 32, 45–49, 63, 64, 65, 68, 71, 88, 101, 159, 164, 175, 235, 237, 238, 290, 302, 342, 528, 533
    See also Iraqi civil war
Sectarianism
    artificial, in Lebanon, 379
    and Basra, 370–371
    blaming Americans for, 109

Sectarianism (*continued*)
continued slaughter due to, aspects of the, 75–119
degree of, diminished, 540
descent into, 24
dividing the militias, effect of, 363
in the Education Ministry, 525, 526
in Egypt, 169
elections that enshrined, 64–65, 549–550
frustration over, potential for continued, 552–553
in the government, 354
history of, 27–28
and identity politics, 27
of the Iraqi Security Forces, 245, 251
and Jordan, 173
and Lebanon, 183, 184, 185, 396–399
as more covert, 528
overt, receding of, 523
perceptions based on, 21–22
in the police force, 69
provoking in the regional, possibility of, 105
regional, rise in, 28–29, 435–438, 556
rise in, 27–32
and Saddam, 173, 265
sign of shift away from, 557
during the surge, 294
Syria and, 152, 162, 185
in universities towards students, 320–321
U.S. occupation promoting, 16, 18, 179
See also specific geographical areas
Sects, religious. *See specific sects*

Secure Plus security company, 399, 404, 411, 430
Seidiya Guard, 257
Selection bias, 495
Sepp, Kalev, 499–500
September 11 attacks, 3, 125, 130, 133, 145, 388, 423, 441, 449, 470, 481, 496
Sermons, impact of, 32–33, 35, 58, 62, 84–85, 92–93, 96–97, 128–129, 269, 274, 434, 534, 535
Shaab, 65, 75–76, 79, 83, 84, 86, 246, 367
Shab-e-Barat holiday, 447
Shah of Iran, 182, 361, 374
al-Shahal, Sheikh Dai al-Islam, 195, 199, 204, 208, 209–210, 383–384, 416, 417, 420, 430, 431, 432, 434, 438
Shallaq, Fadil, 184–185
Sham, 136, 138, 425
See also Jund al-Sham (Soldiers of Sham/Levant)
al-Shami, Abu Anas, 125
Shanshal, Falah Hassan, 67
Shaqis, recruitment of, 10
Sharikat al-Sadr (Rays of Sadr) newspaper, 90
al-Sharman, Muhamad Mahmud, 124
Sharon, Ariel, 407
Sharqiya television, 72
Shatila refugee camp, 196
Shawish, Zuheir, 388
Shawkat, Asef, 204
Shehab, Fouad, 216
al-Sheikh, Fattah, 84
"Shiite crescent," 148, 183, 188, 212, 383
Shiite Hizballah-Iranian model, 182
Shiite House, 67

Shiite militias, 9, 23, 32, 70, 102, 108, 110–111, 183, 188, 194, 237, 364, 525, 529, 533
accusations against, 36, 95, 174
in Amriya, 47, 289, 291, 319, 320, 546
cease-fire of, 25
depending on Al Qaeda for protection from, 238
and ease of integration into the ISF, 533
Hizballah training, media accusation of, 400
linked to Iraqi Security Forces, 105, 289, 290
other targets of, 72, 168–169, 174
and the road to civil war, 54–59
treatment of Palestinians, 155–156, 157, 158
See also specific militia groups and leaders
Shiite mosques, 36, 37, 40, 42, 251
See also specific mosques
Shiite pilgrims, 62, 63, 84, 88, 89, 151, 524
Shiite Political Council, 67
Shiite revival, 181–182
Shiite shrines, 9, 66
See also specific shrines
"Shiite south" label, 17
Shiites, 47–49, 102, 116, 145, 194, 363
actual representation of Sunnis and, 19–20
American perception of, 16, 17, 18, 19, 20, 21–22
beliefs held by, 8
common epithet involving, 175–176
divided, and U.S. strategic interests, 553

empowerment of, 18
failed uprising against
Saddam by, 5, 6, 29,
173, 372
in the first outbreaks of
civil war, 53–54
as the first target of AQI,
323
important holidays of, 41–
42
moderate, losing, 98
and mosque attendance,
91–92
new Saddam of the, 523
periphery vs. center, 73
preferred burial site for, 4
reported missing on the
Internet, 115
Salafi view of, 139
secular, 101
as the winners, 238, 285,
531
Zarqawi's warning to, 144
*See also specific Shiite
leaders/people and
organizations*
Shiite-Sunni
conflict/violence. *See*
Iraqi civil war;
Sectarian cleansing;
Sectarianism; Shiite
militias; Sunni militias
"Shock and awe" doctrine,
19, 229
"Shock therapy" techniques,
21
Shoter, Faris Sayid Hassan,
124
Shrine of Ali, 89
Shuhada Mosque, 191, 193
Shuqair, Wafiq, 400
Shurufi Mosque, 65, 66, 268,
269, 361–362, 533
Shuwafa, 540–541
Siniora, Fouad, 185–186, 189,
381, 389, 393, 406, 416,
423

al-Sistani, Grand Ayatollah
Ali, 38, 42, 44, 50, 77,
89, 91, 97, 98, 102, 118,
144, 173
Slocombe, Walter, 19
Smugglers, 419, 420, 423
Soccer, views of, 113, 451,
557
Social engineering, 28
Solagh, Bayan Jabr, 59
Somalia, 25, 151, 164, 188,
218, 449, 470
Sons of Iraq (SOI), 226, 231,
232, 233, 243, 244, 291,
296, 312, 313, 329, 330,
331, 356, 357, 358, 360,
525
See also Awakening
program/groups
Soviets/Soviet Union. *See*
Russia
Special Republican Guard, 20
Stalin, Joseph, 19
Status of Forces Agreement,
374, 375, 529, 535, 538,
554
Straw, Jack, 98
Sudan, 151, 164, 167
al-Sudani, Abdul Falah, 547
Sufis, 16, 33
Suicide bombings, 18, 95,
118, 125, 138, 144, 148,
172, 194, 425, 451, 468,
478, 540
Suleiman, Michel, 216
Suleiman, Muhamad Haidar,
110
Sunna, the, Salafis view of, 16
"Sunni Arab" label, 17
Sunni Endowment, 58, 115,
195, 207, 386–387, 407,
421, 530
Sunni militias, 24, 49, 73, 86,
111, 185, 238, 287, 291,
339, 525, 533
believed to be lying
dormant, 523

building, in Lebanon, 395,
399
cease-fire of, 25
escalation between Mahdi
Army and, 65, 71, 295
funding for, significant
source of, 112
new, creation of, 284
other targets of, 72, 165
paid by the U.S. military,
237, 289
*See also specific militia
groups and leaders*
Sunni mosques, 33, 34, 37,
40, 42–43, 70, 72, 75,
256
See also specific mosques
Sunni newspapers, 95
Sunni revival, 181–182
"Sunni Triangle" label, 17
Sunnis, 45–49, 102, 103, 382
American perception of,
16–17, 18, 19, 20, 21–
22, 30, 31, 57
changing attitude of, 542–
543
coup attempts by, 174
global *fatwa* calling on all,
112
lack of alternatives facing,
23
loss accepted by, 552
and mosque attendance,
91
overrepresentation of, 19–
20
percentage of, comprising
the Muslim world, 102
periphery vs. center, 73
reported missing on the
Internet, 115
Salafi belief about Shiites
view of, 139
as the second target of
AQI, 323
secular, 101

Sunni-Shiite
conflict/violence. *See*
Iraqi civil war;
Sectarian cleansing;
Sectarianism; Shiite
militias; Sunni militias
Supreme Council for the
Islamic Revolution in
Iraq (SCIRI), 22, 29, 31,
32, 36, 39, 41, 42, 47,
51, 52, 59, 60, 62, 63,
69, 70, 72, 90, 95, 97,
98, 99, 111, 113, 117,
173, 235, 236, 271, 277,
363, 370, 372, 419, 531,
536, 550
Supreme Iraqi Islamic
Council, 363
Suyuf Allah group, 392
Swindell, Sean, 82–83
Syria, 20, 52, 99, 100, 101,
102, 105, 126, 130, 156,
159, 161, 163, 186, 190,
316, 382, 390, 410, 419,
424–425, 435, 555
accused of helping Al
Qaeda, 207, 208
blamed for major terrorist
attack in Baghdad, 549
closed borders of, 192, 194
exiles in, 151–153, 154,
159, 161, 162, 175, 369
Fatah al-Intifada in, 197,
202
and Fatah al-Islam, 201,
203, 204, 207, 415
foreign fighters from, 381,
530
and the March 8 coalition,
186, 187
patrolling the borders,
193–194
political and military
domination of
Lebanon, 183, 184, 189,
385, 388, 395, 412

population of, 161
and sectarianism, 152,
162, 185
and starting jihad in
Sham, 136, 138, 425
U.S. threat toward, 146,
166
Syrian Social Nationalist
Party (SSNP), 403, 406,
407–411, 427

Taamir, 200, 201, 204
Tactical Humintelligence
Team, 244
Taha, Abu Salim, 205, 207,
211
al-Taha, Sheikh Ahmad, 530–
531
Tahash, Muhamad
Mahmud, 408, 410
Taif Accords, 183
Tajik-dominated
government, 441
Tal Afar, 223, 225
Talabani, Jalal, 100, 115, 119,
162, 258, 551
Taliban, 132, 134, 137, 143,
178, 502
origins of the, 440, 441
and the resurgence of U.S.
troops in Afghanistan,
aspects of, 439–518
speedy defeat of the, in
2001, 464
symptoms before the fall
of the, 466
al-Tamimi, Abu Azzam, 281
al-Tamimi, Sheikh Safaa, 68,
75, 76, 78–79, 80, 82
Tariq al-Jadida area, 213, 384,
397, 398, 399, 401, 404,
412, 414, 430, 431
Tawhid and Jihad group, 36–
37, 61, 66, 125, 144,
173, 381
See also Al Qaeda

Tawhid Brigade, 341
Tawhid (Harakat al-Tawhid
al-Islami) group, 195,
196, 199, 391
Tawhid movement, 144, 386,
391, 392, 416
Tawhid (Unity) association,
66, 76
Team Ironhorse, 472, 480–
481, 483, 485–487, 490,
513
Team Prowler, 472–474,
502–503, 505, 507, 508,
509, 510–511, 512–513
Tel al-Zaatar refugee camp,
215
Terror in the Hands of Justice
(television show), 57, 61
Terrorism vs. freedom
fighting, difficulty
distinguishing, 148
Thar Allah group, 370, 371,
372
Thuwar. *See* Fursan (Amriya
Freedom
Fighters/Thurwar)
Tigris River, banks of the,
526, 541
Tikrit, 29, 118, 170, 171
Tikriti Mosque (Fardos
Mosque), 292, 303,
321–322, 544
Time magazine, 10
al-Titi, Muhamad Jamil, 124
Together Forward I and II,
222
Torture device, popular, 69,
71, 157, 222
Townsend, Steve, 230
Treaty of Portsmouth, 374
Tribal elders in Afghanistan,
466, 467, 468
Tribal leaders, shift in
treatment of, 233–234,
279, 327
See also specific leaders

Tribal militias, 226, 234
  See also specific groups
Trinquier, Roger, 241n
Tripoli, 195, 196, 197, 199,
  206, 207, 210, 214, 382–
  384, 390–391, 392–393,
  434
  *See also specific districts and
  neighborhoods*
Tripoli Brigades, 396, 411
Turkey/Turks, 18, 52, 105,
  153, 175, 549
Turki, Prince, 381–382
al-Tuweijiri, Sheikh
  Abdullah, 112

Um Al Qura Mosque (Um al
  Maarik), 37, 40–41, 58,
  62, 86–87, 543
Um Omar, 314–318, 320,
  322, 328, 537–538, 544–
  546
Um Qasr, fall of, 12
Um Qasr prison, 93, 107
al-Umama, Sheikh Adnan,
  388, 421–422, 423
Umayyad dynasty, 42
UN Assistance Mission for
  Iraq (UNAMI), 528
UN Security Council, 400
United Arab Emirates, 33,
  35, 88, 105, 166, 199,
  457
United Iraqi Alliance, 52, 58,
  97, 98, 101
United Nations, 15, 20–21,
  73, 94, 137, 143, 143–
  144, 155, 173, 190, 374,
  392, 452, 460–461, 464,
  465, 467, 476, 551, 554–
  555
United Nations High
  Commission for
  Refugees (UNHCR),
  154, 155, 156, 161–162,

163, 164, 166, 167, 168,
  172, 255
United Nations Interim
  Force in Lebanon
  (UNIFL), 204
United States, 97, 100, 207,
  208, 361
  as adopting Al Qaeda's
  worldview, 470
  Afghani view of, 453, 454,
  513, 514, 518
  comparing Saddam to
  the, 85, 93, 361
  continuing involvement
  of, in spiraling
  violence, 218
  and control over
  Saddam's execution,
  issue of, 117
  demanding compensation
  from, 165
  failure of the, to question
  the invasion, 227, 281
  focus of the, from the
  beginning of the
  occupation, issue with,
  554–555
  ignoring involvement of,
  553
  influence of, loss of, due
  to wars in Iraq and
  Afghanistan, 556–557
  international community
  waiting for leadership
  from, on the refugee
  crisis, 154
  and Iraq, previous
  relationship between,
  21
  Iraqi views of the, 15, 18,
  78, 79–80, 132, 177,
  238, 278, 345, 348
  Jordanian jihadis view of,
  146
  Lebanese views of the,
  383, 389

and Lebanon, 188–189
  military alliance backed
  by, 395
  perceptions/views held
  by the, 11, 16–17, 18,
  19, 20, 21–22, 23, 30,
  31, 57, 192
  planners and observers,
  exaggerated claims of,
  551–552
  presidential campaign in
  the, 442
  push by, in Palestine and
  Lebanon, 435–436
  response to Iran's nuclear
  intransigence, 436
  sermon blaming the, 84–
  85, 93, 274
  and shifting support
  between sects, 72
  and the Soviet invasion of
  Afghanistan, 440
  and the Taliban, previous
  relationship between,
  440–441
  trepidation in, over the
  Iraqi elections, 552
  victory for, magazine
  declaring, 556
  *See also specific U.S.
  government agencies,
  institutions, and people*
Unity, calls for, 34–35, 36, 38,
  42, 44, 47, 133, 171
Universities
  sectarianism in the, 320–
  321
  as targets, 109–110, 111
  See also specific schools
University of Baghdad, 110,
  172, 174
University of Haifa, 178
University of Jordan, 147
University of Technology,
  111
University of Zarqa, 115

U.S. Army, manual for, 224
  See also U.S. troops
U.S. Central Intelligence
  Agency (CIA), 39–40,
  66, 69, 146, 223, 224,
  281, 463, 548–549
U.S. Combined Arms Center
  (USACAC), 224
U.S. Defense Department,
  470
U.S. Defense Intelligence
  Agency (DIA), 66
U.S. embassy, Afghanistan,
  465
U.S. Government
  Accountability Office,
  193
U.S. House Armed Services
  Committee, 442
U.S. Marine Corps.
  in Afghanistan, 478, 479–
  480, 481, 482, 484, 487,
  488, 489
  manual for, 224
  See also U.S. troops
U.S. National Security
  Agency, 224
U.S. National Security
  Council (NSC), 97, 100,
  222, 229, 231, 367
U.S. occupation
  actions during, giving a
  bad name to
  democracy, 148, 171
  based on a vision, 22
  COIN theorists' failure to
  question the U.S.
  invasion and, 227
  demographic changes
  brought by, article
  warning of, 52–53
  failed, strange epitaph for
  a, 538–539
  focus of the U.S.
  administration from
  the beginning of the,
  issue with the, 553–555

impact of, aspects of the,
  3–25
incompetency of the, 68–
  70
and making major
  decisions without Iraqi
  input, 555
new security plan for, 174
opposition to, from the
  beginning, 285
role shift during the, 25
stated goal of the, 21
suffering brought on by,
  9–15, 16–23, 24, 32,
  375–376, 556–557
as a systemic imposition
  of violence, 23, 284
*See also specific aspects
  related to the occupation
  of Iraq and Afghanistan*
U.S. Senate, 230
U.S. Special Forces, 352–353,
  441, 500, 517–518, 524,
  545
U.S. State Department, 18,
  156, 281
U.S. troops
  in Afghanistan, number
  of, 442
  cease-fire with, 287
  change in behavior of, for
  the better, 526, 527
  changing role of the, 25
  COIN manual for, 224
  continuing presence of, as
  a constant implied
  threat, 555
  decline in casualties of,
  227
  films of the resistance
  against, 132
  Iraqi views of, 347–348
  leaving more, than
  previously agreed, talk
  of, 553
  legitimizing withdrawal
  of, need for, 442

onerous presence of, 15,
  23–24
power dynamic between
  the street and, 24–25
provincial presence of,
  expected reduction of,
  554
questioning the approach
  of, 108, 109, 154, 155
recruiting by, 360
withdrawal of, timetable
  for, issue of, 51, 93, 94,
  375, 538
U.S. troop surge
  in Afghanistan, 442, 470,
  471, 479, 480, 491, 492
  airstrikes during, 526
  alleged success of,
  problem with the, 441–
  442
  and the battle over
  Amriya, aspects of,
  289–335
  costly toll of the, 376
  and the eclipse of the
  Mahdi Army, aspects
  of, 337–376
  initiating the, and the
  move toward Iraqi-
  based solutions, aspects
  of, 221–288
  Maliki benefiting from,
  533
  overview of the, and its
  influence, 24–25
  purpose of the, 528, 532,
  539
  reduction in violence
  falsely attributed to,
  442, 531
  timing of the, 539
Usbat al-Ansar (The League
  of Supporters), 190,
  191, 192, 193, 195, 201,
  204, 206, 211, 432, 433
al-Utaibi, Juhayman, 134, 392
al-Uzri, Abdel Karim, 29

Vietnam, 177, 227, 493, 500

Violence
  decline in levels of, 442,
    524, 533, 539, 554–557
  extreme and
    indiscriminate, 154
  future, and the Bush
    administration legacy,
    25
  increase in, in areas of
    U.S. expanded
    operations, 470
  purpose of the, 285
  self-sustaining cycle of, 98
  shift in the source of, 9,
    13–14
  spiraling, continuing U.S.
    involvement in, 218
  systemic imposition of,
    23, 284, 375–376
  triggers of, 30
Volcano Brigade, 63

Wahhabi Mosque (Abdel
  Rahman Auf Mosque),
  421
Wahhabis, 40, 43, 44, 57, 63,
  65, 67, 77, 102, 112,
  144, 163, 340
  See also Sunnis
Wardak province, 446, 458,
  461–462, 490, 491, 517
Warlords, U.S. backing of,
  and reliance on, 441,
  464, 469, 475, 479, 513
Wasfi, Muhamad Abu
  Muntasar, 136–138,
  141–142, 143

Washash, 342–348, 349–354,
  358–361, 364, 368, 369,
  536, 544
Washington Post, 112, 224,
  381
Weapons of mass
  destruction (WMDs),
  issue of, 15, 35
West Point, 231, 329
Widows, number of, 317,
  556
Wilder, Andrew, 515
al-Windawi, Mouayad, 172–
  173
Winds of Victory (video), 71
Wolf Brigade, 61, 251, 257
Wolfowitz, Paul, 19
Women
  in Afghanistan, 451, 458,
    468
  attending markets, issue
    of, 113
  with "bad" reputations,
    targeting, 534
  clothing covering, in
    Jordan, 135–136
  held as hostages by
    Americans, 106
  imposing strict
    interpretation of Islam
    on, 50
  militias and, 56
  in prison, treatment of,
    284
  using, in anti-regime
    operations, 65
World Trade Center
  bombing, 136

Yakan, Fathi, 187

Yamin, Firas (Abu Omar),
  425
al-Yaqoubi, Muhammad, 39,
  66, 67, 102, 110–111
Yaqubi Camp, 131
Yarmuk, 111, 297, 315, 356,
  524
Yarmuk refugee camp, 197,
  415
Yazid (son of Muawiya), 46,
  47, 99, 361, 362
Yemen, 18, 25, 134, 153, 196,
  201, 218, 437, 470
Younes, Kristele, 153–154,
  156–157

Zafraniya, 104, 111
al-Zarqawi, Abu Musab, 36–
  37, 44, 57–58, 61, 64,
  80, 103, 115, 124, 125,
  126, 129, 133, 137, 138,
  139–145, 146, 147, 148,
  172, 173, 177, 182, 190,
  192, 194, 197, 203, 204,
  222, 233, 312, 386, 415,
  420, 426, 433, 451
  See also Al Qaeda in Iraq
    (AQI)
al-Zawahiri, Ayman, 35, 126,
  131, 144, 190, 392, 422,
  433, 436
al-Zeidi, Muntadhar, 375,
  376
Zeinab (daughter of Ali),
  151, 153
Zia ul-Madaris al-Faruqia
  religious school, 448
Zionists, perceived strategy
  of, 53